The State and its Critics
Volume I

Schools of Thought in Politics

Series Editor: *Brian Barry*
> Professor of Political Science, London
> School of Economics and
> Political Science

Future titles will include:

The State and its Critics
Volume I

Edited by

Andrew Levine
Professor of Philosophy
University of Wisconsin-Madison

An Elgar Reference Collection

Published by
Edward Elgar Publishing Limited
Gower House
Croft Road
Aldershot
Hants GU11 3HR
England

Edward Elgar Publishing Limited
Distributed in the United States by
Ashgate Publishing Company
Old Post Road
Brookfield
Vermont 05036
USA

A CIP catalogue record for this book is available from the British Library

Library of Congress Cataloguing in Publication Data
The State and its critics/edited by Andrew Levine.
    p.   cm. – (Schools of thought in politics; no. 3) (An Elgar reference collection)
  1. State, The. I. Levine, Andrew, 1944–   . II. Series.
III. Series: An Elgar reference collection.
JC325.S73515 1992
320.1–dc20   91–37845
                                                        CIP

ISBN 1 85278 413 X (2 volume set)

Printed in Great Britain at the University Press, Cambridge

Contents

Acknowledgements

The editor and publishers wish to thank the following who have kindly given permission for the use of copyright material.

American Political Science Association for articles: G. Miller and T. Moe (1983), 'Bureaucrats, Legislators and the Size of Government', *American Political Science Review*, **77**, 297–322; K. A. Shepsle and B. R. Weingast (1984), 'Political Solutions to Market Problems', *American Political Science Review*, **78**, 417–34.

Basic Books, Inc., a division of Harper Collins Publishers for excerpt: Robert Nozick (1974), *Anarchy State and Utopia*, chapters 1, 2, 5, 3–25, 88–119.

Basil Blackwell Ltd. for article: Jeffrey D. Goldsworthy (1987), 'Nozick's Libertarianism and the Justification of the State', *Ratio*, **XXIX**, 180–89.

Cambridge University Press for excerpt: Michael Taylor (1982), *Community, Anarchy and Liberty*, chapter 2, 39–94.

Elsevier Science Publishers B.V. for article: Richard A. Musgrave (1985), 'Excess Bias and the Nature of Budget Growth', *Journal of Public Economics*, **28**, 287–308.

Helbing & Lichtenhahn Verlag AG, Basle and Frankfurt/M for article: R. D. Tollison (1982), 'Rent Seeking: A Survey', *Kyklos*, **35**, 575–602.

New York University Press for articles: James M. Buchanan (1978), 'A Contractarian Perspective on Anarchy', *Nomos*, J. Roland Pennock and John W. Chapman (eds), **XIX**, 29–42; Richard A. Falk (1978), 'Anarchism and World Order', *Nomos*, J. Roland Pennock and John W. Chapman (eds), **XIX**, 63–87.

Routledge for excerpt: F. A. Hayek (1979), *Law, Legislation and Liberty*, **3**, *The Political Order of a Free People*, chapters 12 and 13, 1–40.

University of California Press and Basil Blackwell Ltd. for excerpt: John Burnheim (1985), *Is Democracy Possible?*, chapters 1 and 3, 19–50 and 106–24.

University of Chicago Press for articles and excerpt: C. Wolf, Jr. (1979), 'A Theory of Non-Market Failure: Framework for Implementation Analysis', *Journal of Law and Economics*, **XXII**, 107–39; Sam Peltzman (1980), 'The Growth of Government', *Journal of Law and Economics*, **XXIII**, 209–87; James Buchanan (1975), *The Limits of Liberty: Between Anarchy and Leviathan*, chapters 9 and 10, 147–80.

Every effort has been made to trace all the copyright holders but if any have been inadvertently overlooked the publishers will be pleased to make the necessary arrangement at the first opportunity.

In addition the publishers wish to thank the library of the London School of Economics and Political Science and The Alfred Marshall Library, Cambridge University for their assistance in obtaining these articles.

Introduction

The political philosophers of the 17th and 18th centuries whose writings we still read today were concerned, above all, to account for *sovereignty*, supreme authority over a particular territory or population. At issue was the right of some individual(s) or, more generally, of the occupants of some institutionally constituted offices to compel compliance on the part of other individuals, if need be through the use or threat of force. To this problem was joined another closely related one: the question of the individual's obligation to obey political authorities. Because these themes were central to the thought of Hobbes, Locke and Rousseau, among others, they continue to command the attention of anyone concerned with the history of Western political thought. They also resonate throughout contemporary discussions, both celebratory and critical, of state institutions. But the core concerns of the political philosophy of the early modern period have virtually ceased to matter for political theorists today. Except when they focus on figures in political philosophy's past, philosophers and theoretically-minded political scientists now pay scant attention to the questions that engaged their predecessors several centuries ago. Recent philosophical treatments of the state have therefore taken on a more peripheral aspect than readers immersed in the tradition of Western political theory might expect. Accounts of sovereignty and political obligation have largely given way to disputes about the proper role of the state in the economy and society, and about the nature of state institutions. The essays collected here reflect this focus.

This is not the place to try to explain the directions political theory has taken. But it is plain that the shift away from the core themes of earlier political philosophy cannot be ascribed to a successful theoretical resolution of the old disputes. Despite the best efforts of so many for so long, it is far from clear even now that sovereignty can be justified satisfactorily or that individuals are ever obligated to obey political authorities. These questions were settled *politically*, not philosophically. In the early modern period, state building and consolidation challenged received ways of thinking about political life, eliciting a philosophical response. By the mid-19th century, the nation state had become an established fact. Then the concentration of political authority into a single institutional nexus no longer generated the puzzlement it formerly did. The legitimacy of the state form of political organization, once so contentious, became so deeply entrenched in the popular imagination and in its theoretical expressions that it effectively ceased to be an issue. Political philosophers and political scientists continue to be educated, in part, through the study of a canon focused squarely on the old, core themes. But the perplexity earlier political philosophy addressed has effectively dissipated. In consequence, even when the state is still an object of philosophical inquiry, basic questions about its normative status are seldom broached.

If it is fair to say that real world political transformations brought the state into philosophical consciousness several centuries ago, it is likely that changes in the world order may soon do so again. Formerly, the diffusion of political power characteristic of medieval and early modern Europe was an obstacle in the way of the development of (relatively) independent national economies organized, for the most part, through capitalist market arrangements. A national economy required a nation state to superintend it. If any of the explanations proffered by the founders of modern social theory – by Marx most famously, but also by Weber and Durkheim and even by de Tocqueville – are generally on track, this functional exigency led eventually to the demise of feudal institutions and to the consolidation of the nation state. But the nation state is not likely to dominate political life forever, even if, *pace* Marx and most other modern social theorists, capitalist market arrangements should somehow survive indefinitely. In all likelihood, real world economic forces will eventually outgrow national economies and the states that govern them, generating pressures for the establishment and consolidation of inter- and supra-national forms of administration. To some degree, these processes are already evident. Thus we can expect puzzlement about the state to arise again, and the state to become once more a fundamental philosophical concern.

Needless to say, the old questions are unlikely to revive in the form familiar from the political philosophy of earlier times. Previously, the state was conceived as a means for coordinating the behaviours of distinct individuals who, if left to their own devices in a 'state of nature', would find themselves in an inexorable and devastating 'war of all against all' – to the detriment of their most fundamental concerns. The state was therefore a solution to a problem confronted by individuals conceived atomistically; a problem generated in the main by individuals' discrete and antagonistic interests. The solution was to concentrate all authority into a single 'repressive apparatus' as Marxists are wont to say; to create, in Weber's celebrated expression, 'a monopoly of the means of (legitimate) violence'. From this perspective, relations between states were, at most, incidental to the central issues of political life. However, now and in the future, it would seem that *inter*-state relations, and once again the state itself – not, this time, as an alternative to a state of nature, but in contrast with less integrated forms of political association – are bound to appear increasingly problematic. If so, and if philosophers rise to the challenge, we can expect that, before long, defenders of the state and critics of it will address very different questions from those theorists nowadays engage. The old issues, tied as they were to atomic individualist assumptions and to a world order consisting of discrete national economies, are not likely to regain their former preeminence. But questions about authority and obligation – in a form consonant with the social and economic life that is emerging – probably will supersede the more peripheral inquiries that predominate today.

However, as the work collected here attests, this situation is not yet widely appreciated, at least not by philosophers and political scientists. Despite a rapidly changing political order, and despite the tradition in which political theorists are schooled, recent work on the state, with very few exceptions, evades the principal philosophical questions the state now raises. At the same time, because of this tradition, when fundamental questions are broached, it is from the perspective of political philosophies several centuries old. It will become clear from the selections that follow that these old perspectives, however anachronistic they have become, still provide a framework for subtle and ingenious theorizing. But this framework is far less apt than it used to be for comprehending the state philosophically.

This situation partly explains the very disparate concerns of contemporary writers on the state. Thus, in assembling this collection, it was unclear even what topics to represent in a volume devoted to recent work on the state and its critics. Most of the pieces included here in some way address the legitimacy or wisdom of state activities that affect the economy and society. In arranging topics for presentation, I have been guided *faute de mieux* by this consideration. At one extreme are the anarchists, then proponents of the minimal state, then less ardent critics of the welfare state, then proponents of it, and finally defenders of states capable of radically transforming the economies and societies they govern. However, it will become clear to anyone who reads the essays collected under these rubrics, that this attempt at connecting the topics assembled here is, at best, strained. It will also become clear that there is important recent work on the state, some of it represented in this volume, that cannot be arrayed along this continuum at all. This collection is therefore something of a hodgepodge. A representative sample of recent work on the state could not be otherwise.

It is also worth noting that, in recent years, there has been a dearth of journal literature on all but the most peripheral topics concerning the state. The welfare state excites a certain amount of attention in journals, and there is a large literature on state imperfections. But the more central philosophical issues, insofar as they remain current, are more likely to be treated in books. This fact suggests, I think, the absence of an active 'research agenda' at the core of the subject, a situation that is not surprising when the dominant paradigm is increasingly inappropriate for the tasks at hand.

In what remains of this Introduction, I shall not attempt to guide the reader through the essays that follow, but only to provide some very general indications of their principal concerns.

As a political current, anarchism's fortunes have varied widely. But anarchism has seldom escaped marginality – in part for reasons internal to anarchist movements, in part thanks to the unrelenting hostility of their opponents, including socialists and communists. Nevertheless, it is anarchism, more than any other political tendency, that has kept the question of the state alive throughout the past century. If I am right in thinking that real history will again force this problem onto philosophical consciousness, it is the anarchists who will then seem the harbingers of future developments. But the anarchists, above all, have remained immersed in the problematic of the early modern period and in traditional convictions about what statelessness entails. The readings that follow, from James Buchanan, Richard Falk and Michael Taylor, exemplify this situation perspicuously. For each of them, the fundamental problem of political life remains the coordination of individuals' behaviours. In each case, the authors claim that the requisite degree of coordination can be achieved, at least in principle, without the state. Thus philosophical anarchists advance a *stateless* solution to the problem most writers think only the state can solve. It is for the reader to judge how successful anarchist solutions may be. The fact that they can still be reasonably proposed, centuries after the question of the state was settled *politically*, suggests how fragile the *philosophical* settlement has been.

Depending on how the term is understood, the institutional arrangements John

Burnheim envisions may or may not suffice to place him in the anarchist camp. Virtually alone among political theorists now writing, Burnheim addresses questions about institutional arrangements with some sensitivity to the real world processes that, before our eyes, are rendering the state increasingly inappropriate to contemporary conditions. In Burnheim's contribution to this volume, excerpted from his book *Is Democracy Possible?*,[1] the principal normative value with respect to which the state is faulted is *democracy*. His objective is to imagine ways in which democratic values might be better implemented, not by eliminating political structures altogether, as traditional anarchists propose, but by exploding the idea, definitive of the state form of political organization, that political authority is best concentrated into a single institutional nexus, a sovereign power. The nation state, in Burnheim's view, is, at once, too large and too small; too large to implement democratic values at the real interstices of social life; too small to address economic, social and ecological problems with increasingly global dimensions. His suggestions for the radical decentralization of authority relations along functional lines represents a step towards the kind of speculative theorizing about institutional arrangements that political theorists must undertake if political theory is to remain relevant at all to political life.

However, to date, very little reflection on feasible, post-state institutional arrangements has taken place. Indeed, in recent years, expressly rearguard departures in political theory have been far more common than attempts to move beyond traditional concerns. Thus one important strain of work on the state has self-consciously revived the Lockean idea of the minimal state. The principal impetus for this current has been Robert Nozick's seminal *Anarchy, State and Utopia*,[2] sections of which are included in this volume. Nozick's book attracted considerable attention throughout the 1970s, and continues to generate a stream of commentaries. Two representative pieces, by Geoffrey Hunt and Jeffrey Goldsworthy, are included here.

Partisans of the minimal state are not anarchists; they acknowledge a need for state institutions as a condition for the feasibility of organizing social life through market arrangements. However the state they endorse is limited in the range of things it may legitimately do. Above all, for Nozick and his co-thinkers, in a proper political regime, market allocations would be immune from coerced redistributions and therefore from state interventions that have a redistributive effect.

A political philosophy is *liberal* if it acknowledges principled limitations on the use of public coercive force, and therefore on the sovereign's authority.[3] Thus the minimal state is a type of liberal state. In this sense, Locke was a liberal, while Hobbes and Rousseau, since they regarded the sovereign's power as absolute in principle, were not. What distinguishes the minimal state from liberal states generally is its respect for the inviolability of property rights and, more fundamentally, its role as a guarantor, not an originator, of these rights. Defenders of the minimal state are defenders of economic freedoms, indeed of economic policies bordering on *laissez-faire* – not for (putative) efficiency reasons, but as a matter of right. For them as for Locke, these rights do not derive from a social contract or from any prior moral principle. Instead, they are the foundations upon which normative political philosophy is built; they go 'all the way back'. Political institutions are legitimate, on this view, to the extent that they respect antecedently specified property rights. Most defenders of the minimal state in its contemporary incarnations assume this stance as a point of departure. They suppose, in effect, that private property and market transactions are justified, and then go on to reflect on what states that respect these institutions must be like. Obviously, philosophers who are wary of rights ascriptions that go all the way back – and also those who are not, but whose intuitions about ownership and markets differ from defenders of the minimal state – will find the questions Nozick and his co-thinkers raise beside the point. It is worth noting that, in contrast to his contemporary continuators, Locke felt obliged to try to justify the property rights he considered inviolable.[4]

A different kind of challenge to the kind of state that now exists in modern liberal democracies focuses on so-called state imperfections. The problem is not, as for contemporary neo-Lockeans, the violation of fundamental property rights, but *inefficiencies* that arise in consequence of state operations. However, this kind of argument too has its roots in the political and economic theory of the early modern period: it traces back to Adam Smith's strictures against mercantilism and for *laissez-faire*. Smith argued for limitations on governmental operations in part to limit the power of merchants and manufacturers who, Smith thought, would deploy a larger state to protect themselves from market discipline, thereby impeding economic growth at the national level. Contemporary public choice theorists and critics of the 'rent-seeking' society advance essentially the same complaint against legislators and state functionaries in liberal democracies. They argue that as long as the state is able to confer benefits on groups selectively (while dispersing the costs of procuring these benefits throughout the general population), those with power will secure popular support by responding to group pressures – with resulting efficiency losses. Whenever institutional arrangements are such that opportunities for 'rent-seeking' exist, rational agents will seize these opportunities, and society will suffer in consequence. Of course, markets too are flawed: among other things, they give rise to externalities that detract from overall efficiency, and there are desirable social ends, like the provision of public goods, that markets cannot supply. In general, however, public choice theorists deem state incompetences worse than market incompetences. Like Smith, they therefore conclude that the state should intervene sparingly, if at all, in the workings of capitalist economies.

The villain, for writers in this genre, is the domination of government by coalitions of organized interests. In principle, therefore, there are two remedies that could be deployed singly or in combination: the state could prevent group formation by limiting associational freedoms or state institutions could be restructured to eliminate interventions that create incentives for rent-seeking groups to form. The former option is, of course, manifestly illiberal; public choice theorists therefore favour the latter strategy. Thus they seek to limit the state by restricting its power to provide benefits that encourage interest-group formation. The consequence, they believe, will be a state that functions in greater harmony with free market arrangements – with resulting efficiency gains.

F.A. Hayek and James Buchanan have provided intellectual foundations for contemporary work of this kind. Excerpts from seminal books of theirs – *The Political Order of a Free People* and *The Limits of Liberty*, respectively – are included in this collection. The critique of rent-seeking has been pursued mainly by political scientists and economists interested in formal modelling. In consequence, work in this area often takes on a technical aspect that some readers may find forbidding. Others may conclude that the formalisms only mask a poverty of theory. A survey article by Robert Tollison, included here, reviews the recent literature. The essays that follow – by G. Miller and T.M. Moe, K.A. Shepsle and B.R. Weingast, Sam Peltzman and C. Wolf – pursue some of the issues involved in assessing the comparative competence of markets and states. A rebuttal by Richard Musgrave to some key contentions of the rent-seeking critics is also included.

By most accounts, both popular and theoretical, the welfare state is the obverse of the minimal state. Very generally, welfare state institutions *correct* some of the consequences of capitalist market allocations, particularly those that render individuals who fare poorly as markets work their course unusually dependent or vulnerable. For defenders of the minimal state and critics of the rent-seeking society, the state is a necessary evil, necessary for protecting antecedently given rights or superintending market arrangements, but otherwise serving only to restrict individuals' liberties coercively. Partisans of the welfare state, on the other hand, view the state affirmatively, as an instrument for pursuing a (potentially) beneficent social policy. They would concede that sovereign power, because it compels compliance through the use or threat of force, is inimical to freedom. In this sense, they too want as small a state as necessary for the purposes they consider legitimate. But welfare state theorists countenance many more legitimate state functions than do defenders of the minimal state or critics of state imperfections. Within this much expanded range, they envision a state that intervenes actively to address pressing social problems.

Welfare state institutions – from state organized public assistance programmes to social insurance against a range of misfortunes (like unemployment and ill health), to public provision for education, child rearing and the care of the elderly – were instituted, in varying degrees and in different ways, throughout the advanced capitalist world between, roughly, the 1880s and 1930s. In Northern Europe particularly, these institutions developed prodigiously after the Second World War. In the past decade and a half, however, the welfare state has been under attack from ideologues of the New Right and, more recently, by some of its erstwhile defenders. If it has not yet been undone, its growth has been halted nearly everywhere. Most of the authors represented here, though hardly of one mind about the merits of welfare state institutions, seek to counter this tendency of contemporary political life by defending the welfare state against some of the criticisms that have been recently levelled against it.

It is with this end in view that Christopher Morris, Michael Davis, James Sterba and Robert Goodin, in their contributions to this volume, develop what are, in effect, *ad hominem* arguments against the New Right assault on the welfare state. By adducing very different sorts of considerations, they each maintain that the various claims that critics of the welfare state advance in order to argue for a more minimalist conception of legitimate state functions actually support welfare state arrangements. This kind of argument may, at first, seem paradoxical. However it makes eminently good sense. So long as the welfare state violates no morally primary rights, it can only be faulted for its effects. But if the welfare state genuinely is a corrective for institutional arrangements structured in the main by private property and market transactions, whatever supports private property and markets should also support the welfare state. The welfare state would then be justified precisely because it allows these other institutions to function properly. Defenders of private property and market arrangements *should* therefore also defend the welfare state.

This kind of brief for the welfare state differs from arguments to the effect that welfare state institutions are instrumental for realizing worthwhile objectives that defenders of capitalist market arrangements could in principle fail to uphold. Claims of this sort – or, more commonly, undeveloped intimations of them – are more prevalent in traditional political interventions on behalf of the welfare state than in sustained philosophical justifications. An exception is Sheldon Wolin's contribution to this collection which explores, critically but sympathetically, some important connections between the welfare state and democratic values.

It is widely believed that, however the welfare state might be defended, there is at least some conflict between the ends it serves and other worthwhile social objectives. In his contribution to this volume, Julian Le Grand examines the very common view that, in social policy concerns, there is a 'trade-off' that must be struck between efficiency and equity. Inasmuch as the welfare state is generally thought to promote equity, *any* case for it would have to be balanced off against efficiency considerations. Le Grand argues that this understanding, though widespread, is impossible to sustain under scrutiny. In his view, the putative trade-off with efficiency that even partisans of the welfare state assume they must make is more nearly a conceptual confusion than a genuine exigency.

Anyone who engages in contemporary debates about the welfare state cannot fail to realize that, to the detriment of clear thinking on the subject, considerable confusion clouds understandings of what the welfare state is. A number of the pieces collected here, particularly Brian Barry's but also the two contributions by Robert Goodin, help to clarify this issue. Paradoxically, the debate on the welfare state may actually be more importantly advanced by focusing on such ostensibly pre-philosophical issues than by more direct normative assessments. In reflecting theoretically on real world welfare state institutions, it becomes evident that the welfare state incorporates very traditional understandings of human beings' needs and of the kinds of expectations individuals can reasonably demand that states fulfil. These understandings may be deeply flawed. In addition, they are likely to come into tension with changing perceptions and norms. Some of the complexities of this issue are addressed from a feminist perspective by Nancy Fraser in her essay in this volume.

The relation between state power and the class structure of societies has been a central theme of Marxist political theory since its inception. In the past two decades, considerable attention has been paid to this issue by writers who draw in various ways on the conceptual resources the Marxist tradition provides. As a result, some of the theoretical intuitions implicit in traditional Marxist writings have been clarified, developed and, in some cases, modified or abandoned. The pieces included here by Claus Offe, Bob Jessop, David Easton and Ralph Miliband illustrate this line of research, drawing the issues in contention into focus. Finally, despite the recent (arguably temporary) eclipse of socialist politics throughout the world, questions about the state under socialism – and about the relation between socialism and democracy – continue to attract attention. These issues are addressed in the pieces included in this volume by Roger Harris and myself.

As remarked, a representative collection of recent work on the state and its critics is bound to be a hodgepodge, anchored precariously by the philosophical concerns of an era in which pressing political issues differed considerably from those of our world today. Partly in consequence, recent work on the state is much less central to contemporary political philosophy and political science – and to real world politics – than was formerly the case. In a world changing as rapidly as ours now is, it is unlikely that this situation can long endure. However much political philosophy may lag behind political realities, the vicissitudes or real world states can be counted on, sooner or later, to make the state *and its (possible) future(s)*, a fundamental concern, once again, of anyone who reflects on politics philosophically.

Notes

1. John Burnheim, *Is Democracy Possible?* (Berkeley and Los Angeles: University of California Press, 1985).
2. Robert Nozick, *Anarchy, State, and Utopia* (New York: Basic Books, 1974).
3. Some recent definitions of liberalism emphasize a different aspect of the same idea: neutrality on the part of public institutions with respect to competing (controversial) conceptions of the good. This formulation has become prominent thanks, in large part, to the influence of John Rawls' *A Theory of Justice* (Cambridge, Mass.: Belknap Press, 1971). For an exemplary statement, see Ronald Dworkin, 'Liberalism', in *Public and Private Morality* (Stuart Hampshire, ed.) (Princeton: Princeton University Press, 1978).
4. cf. John Locke, *Second Treatise of Government*, section 5.

Part I
Anarchism

[1]

Excerpt from *Nomos*, 29–42

2

A CONTRACTARIAN PERSPECTIVE
ON ANARCHY

JAMES M. BUCHANAN

I. TWO-STAGE UTOPIA

I have often described myself as a philosophical anarchist. In my conceptualized ideal society individuals with well defined and mutually respected rights coexist and cooperate as they desire without formal political structure. My practical ideal, however, moves one stage down from this and is based on the presumption that individuals could not attain the behavioral standards required for such an anarchy to function acceptably. In general recognition of this frailty in human nature, persons would agree to enact laws, and to provide means of enforcement, so as to achieve the closest approximation that is possible to the ideally free society. At this second level of norms, therefore, I am a constitutionalist and a contractarian: constitutionalist in the sense of recognizing that the rules of order are, and must be, selected at a different level and via a different process from the decisions made within those rules; contractarian in the sense that conceptual agreement among individuals provides the only benchmark against which to evaluate observed rules and actions taken within those rules.

This avowedly normative construction enables me to imagine the existence of an ideal social order inhabited by real persons, by men and women that I can potentially observe. In moving from stage one, where the persons are themselves imaginary beings, to stage two, the persons become real, or potentially so, while the rules and institutions of order become imaginary. But I must ask myself why I consider the second stage to be an appropriate subject for analysis and discussion whereas the first stage seems methodologically out of bounds, or at least beyond my interest. Presumably, the distinction here must rest on the notion that the basic structure of order, "the law," is itself chosen, is subject to ultimate human control, and may be changed as a result of deliberative human action. By contrast, the fundamental character traits of human beings either cannot be, or should not be, manipulated deliberately. In other terms, attempts to move toward an idealized first-stage order may require some modification of human character, an objective that seems contrary to the individualistic value judgments that I make quite explicit. On the other hand, attempts to move toward an idealized second-stage ideal require only that institutions be modified, an objective that seems ethically acceptable.

As a preliminary step, I have called for the adoption of a "constitutional attitude," a willingness to accept the necessity of rules and an acknowledgment that choices among rules for living together must be categorically separated from the choices among alternative courses of action permitted under whatever rules may be chosen. But what happens if I should be forced, however reluctantly, to the presumption that individual human beings, as they exist, are not and may not be capable of taking on such requisite constitutional attitudes. In this case, my treatment of an idealized constitutionalist-contractarian social order becomes neither more nor less defensible than the discourse of those who go all the way and treat genuine anarchy as an ideal. Yet, somehow, I feel that my discussion of idealized social order is more legitimate, more productive, and less escapist, than the comparable discussion of the libertarian anarchists, perhaps best exemplified here by Murray Rothbard.[1] I shall return to this proposition below, and I shall attempt an argument in defense.

II. THE LOGIC OF AUTHORITY?

Before doing so, however, I want to examine one possible consequence of abandoning the constitutionalist-contractarian perspective. If we say that persons are simply incapable of adopting the requisite set of constitutionalist attitudes, which is another way of saying that they are incapable of evaluating their own long-term interests, we are led, almost inexorably, to imposed authority as the only escape from the genuine Hobbesian jungle. Anyone who takes such a position, however, must acknowledge that a "free society," in the meaningful sense of process stability, is not possible. The analysis turns to alternative criteria for authority, both in terms of the basic objectives to be sought and in terms of the efficiency properties of structures designed to accomplish whatever objectives might be chosen. But whose values are to be counted in deriving such criteria? We have, in this setting, already rejected the individualistic base, at least in its universalized sense, from which such criteria might be derived. But if only some persons are to be counted, how do we discriminate? Of necessity, the treatment of the idealized limits to authority must be informed by the explicit or implicit value norms of some subset of the community's member-ship. In the extreme, the value norms become those of the person who offers the argument and his alone.

Most discussion of social reform proceeds on precisely this fragile philosophical structure, whether or not the participants are aware of it. When an economist proposes that a particular policy measure be taken, for example, that the ICC be abolished, he is arguing that his own authority, backed presumably by some of the technical analysis of his professional discipline which has its own implicit or built-in value norms (in economics, Pareto efficiency), is self-justificatory. But since different persons, and groups, possess different norms, there is no observed consensual basis for discriminating between one authority and another. The linkage between the consent of indi-viduals and the policy outcomes is severed, even at the purely conceptual level and even if attention is shifted back to basic rules of order.

The implication of all this is that the authority which emerges from such a babel of voices, and from the power struggle that these voices inform and motivate, carries with it no legitimacy, even in some putative sense of this term. The authoritarian paradigm for the emergence and support of the state lacks even so much as the utilitarian claims made for the basic Hobbesian contract between the individual and the sovereign, whomever this might be. There can be no moral legitimacy of government in this paradigm, no grounds for obligation to obey law, no reasons for the mutual respect of individuals' boundaries or rights.

If most persons, including most intellectuals-academicians, view

government in this perspective, and more importantly, if those who
act on behalf of government view themselves in this manner, both
the libertarian anarchist and the constitutional-contractarian exert
didactic influence in their attempts to expose the absence of moral
underpinnings. But does not such activity, in and of itself, reduce to
nihilism under the presupposition that universalized individual
values are not acceptable bases for moral authority? If individuals
are not capable of acting in their own interest in the formulation of
social institutions, both the anarchist and the contractarian may be
deemed genuinely subversive in their "as if" modeling of society, in
their establishment of normative standards for improvement that
are empirically nonsupportable. The activity in question weakens
the natural subservience to the existing authority, whomever this
might be, and may disrupt social order without offering redeeming
elements that might be located in some constructive alternative.

III. INDIVIDUALISTIC NORMS

The libertarian anarchist and the contractarian must ask these
questions and somehow answer them to their own satisfaction. I
pose these questions here in part for their own intrinsic interest and
importance but also in part because they place the libertarian
anarchist and the constitutionalist-contractarian squarely on the
same side of the central debate in political philosophy, the debate
that has gone on for several centuries and which promises to go on
for several more. Both the libertarian anarchist and the constitutionalist-contractarian work within the *individualistic* rather than the
nonindividualistic framework or setting.[2] I use the term "nonindividualistic" rather than "collectivist" explicitly here because I
want to include in this category the transcendent or truth-judgment
paradigm of politics, a paradigm that may produce either collectivist or noncollectivist outcomes at a practical level.

I want to argue first that it is normatively legitimate to adopt the
individualistic model, regardless of empirical presuppositions, and
secondly, that within this model broadly defined the constitutionalist-contractarian variant is superior to the libertarian-anarchist
variant. It is morally justifiable, and indeed morally necessary, to
proceed on the "as if" presumption that individuals, by their
membership in the human species, are capable of acting in their

own interest, which they alone can ultimately define. Empirical observation of human error, evaluated *ex post,* can never provide a basis for supplanting this "as if" presumption; for no acceptable alternative exists. If persons are considered to be incapable of defining and furthering their own interests, who is to define such interests and promote them? If God did, in fact, exist as a suprahuman entity, an alternative source of authority might be acknowledged. But failing this, the only conceivable alternative authority must be some selected individual or group of individuals, some man who presumes to be God, or some group that claims godlike qualities. Those who act in such capacities and who make such claims behave immorally in a fundamental sense; they deny the moral autonomy of other members of the species and relegate them to a value status little different from that of animals.

The primary value premise of individualism is the philosophical equality of men, as men, despite all evidence concerning inequalities in particular characteristics or components. In thinking about men, we are morally obligated to proceed as if they are equals, as if no man counts for more than another. Acceptance of these precepts sharply distinguishes the individualist from the nonindividualist. But we must go one step further to inquire as to the implications of these precepts for social order. It is at this point that the libertarian anarchist and the constitutionalist-contractarian part company, but, philosophically, they have come a long way together, a simple statement but one that is worthy of emphasis.

IV. ANARCHY AND CONTRACTUAL ORDER

The issue that divides the anarchist and the contractarian is "conjecturally empirical." It concerns the conceptually observable structure of social order that would emerge if men could, in fact, start from scratch. Would they choose to live in the idealized anarchy, or would they contractually agree to a set of laws, along with enforcement mechanisms, that would constrain individual and group behavior? This question cannot actually be answered empirically because, of course, societies do not start from scratch. They exist in and through history. And those elements of order that may be observed at any point in time may or may not have emerged contractually.

It is at this point that the constitutionalist-contractarian paradigm is most vulnerable to the criticisms of the anarchist. How are we to distinguish between those elements of social order, those laws and institutions which can be "explained" or "interpreted" (and by inference "justified") as having emerged, actually or conceptually, on contractual precepts and those which have been imposed noncontractually (and hence by inference "illegitimately")? If the contractual paradigm is sufficiently flexible to "explain" all observable institutions it remains empty of discriminant content, quite apart from its possible aesthetic appeal.

Careful usage of the model can, however, produce a classification that will differentiate between these two sets of potentially observable institutions. For example, the existence of unrestricted political authority in the hands of a political majority could never be brought within contractarian principles. Persons who could not, at a time of contract, predict their own positions, would never agree to grant unrestricted political authority to any group, whether this be a duly elected majority of a parliament, a judicial elite, or a military despot. Recognition of this simple point is, of course, the source of the necessary tie-in between the contractarian paradigm and constitutionalism.[3] But what are the constitutional limits here? What actions by governments, within broad constitutional authority, may be thrown out on contractarian precepts?

Arbitrary restrictions or prohibitions on voluntary contractual agreements among persons and groups, in the absence of demonstrable spillover effects on third parties, cannot be parts of any plausible "social contract." For example, minimum-wage legislation, most restrictions on entry into professions, occupations, types of investment, or geographical locations could be rejected, as could all discrimination on racial, ethnic, religious, grounds.

This is not to suggest that the appropriate line is easy to draw and that borderline cases requiring judgment are absent. More importantly, however, the classification step alone does not "justify" the institutions that remain in the potentially allowable set. To conclude that an observed institution may have emerged, conceptually, on generalized contractarian grounds, is not at all equivalent to saying that such an institution did, in fact, emerge in this way. Many, and perhaps most, of the governmental regulations and restrictions that we observe and which remain within possible contractarian limits, may, in fact, represent arbitrary political impositions which could never have reflected generalized agreement.

Consider a single example, that of the imposition of the fifty-five-mile speed limit in 1974. We observe this restriction on personal liberties. Where can we classify this in terms of the contractarian paradigm? Because of the acknowledged interdependencies among individual motorists, in terms of safety as well as fuel usage, it seems clearly possible that general agreement on the imposition of some limits might well have emerged, and fifty-five miles per hour might have been within reasonable boundaries. But whether or not the fifty-five-mile limit, as we observe it, would have, in fact, reflected a widely supported and essentially consensual outcome of some referendum process cannot be determined directly. The observed results could just as well reflect the preferences of members of the governmental bureaucracy who were able to exert sufficient influence on the legislators who took the policy action.

V. CONSTITUTIONAL CONTRACT

If we look too closely at particular policy measures in this way, however, we tend to overlook the necessary differentiation between the constitutional and the postconstitutional stage of political action. Should we think of applying contractarian criteria at the postconstitutional level at all? Or should we confine this procedure to the constitutional level? In reference to the fifty-five-mile limit, so long as the legislature acted within its authorized constitutional powers, which are themselves generally acceptable on contractarian grounds, the observed results in only one instance need not be required to meet conceptual contractarian tests.

At this juncture, the contractarian position again becomes highly vulnerable to the taunts of the libertarian anarchist. If specific political actions cannot be evaluated per se, but must instead be judged only in terms of their adherence to acceptable constitutional process, the basic paradigm seems lacking in teeth. Improperly applied, it may become an apology for almost any conceivable action by legislative majorities or by bureaucrats acting under the authorization of such majorities, and even strict application finds discrimination difficult. This criticism is effective, and the contrast-

ing stance of the uncompromising libertarian anarchist is surely
attractive in its superior ability to classify. Since, to the anarchist,
all political action is illegitimate, the set of admissible claims begins
and remains empty.

The constitutionalist-contractarian can, and must, retreat to the
procedural stage of evaluation. If his hypotheses suggest that
particular political actions, and especially over a sequence of
isolated events, fail to reflect consensus, he must look again at the
constitutional authorizations for such actions. Is it contractually
legitimate that the Congress and the state legislatures be empowered by the constitution to impose speed limits? What about the
activities of the environmental agencies, acting as directed by the
Congress? What about the many regulatory agencies? Such questions as these suggest that the constitutionalist-contractarian must
devote more time and effort into attempts to derive appropriate
constitutional limits, and notably with respect to the powers of
political bodies to restrict economic liberties. Furthermore, the
many interdependencies among the separate political actions, each
of which might be plausibly within political limits, must be
evaluated.[4] Admittedly, those of us who share the constitutionalist-
contractarian approach have been neglectful here. We have not
done our homework well, and the research agenda facing us is large
indeed.

Meanwhile, we can, as philosophical fellow travelers, welcome
the arguments put forth by the libertarian anarchists in condemning the political suppressions of many individual liberties. We can
go part of the way on genuine contractarian principles, and we can
leave open many other cases that the anarchists can directly
condemn. As I have noted elsewhere,[5] the limited-government
ideals of the constitutionalist-contractarian may not excite the
minds of modern man, and given the demonstrable overextension of
political powers, the no-government ideals propounded by the
libertarian anarchists may help to tilt the balance toward the
individualistic and away from the nonindividualistic pole.

I have acknowledged above that the anarchist critique of existing
political institutions is probably intellectually more satisfying than
that which may be advanced by the contractarian. But where the
anarchist critique falters, and where the contractarian paradigm is
at its strongest, is at the bridge between negative criticism and

constructive proposals for change. To the libertarian anarchist, all political action is unjustified. He cannot, therefore, proceed to advocate a politically orchestrated dismantling of existing structure. He has no test save his own values, and he has no means of introducing these values short of revolution. The contractarian, by contrast, has a continuing test which he applies to observed political structure. Do these basic laws and institutions reflect consensus of the citizenry? If they do not, and if his arguments to this effect are convincing, it becomes conceptually possible to secure agreement on modification. The rules of the game may be modified while the game continues to be played, so long as we all agree on the changes. But why not eliminate the game?

This returns us to the initial distinction made between the ideal society of the philosophical anarchist and that of the contractarian. To eliminate all rules and require that play in the social game take place within self-imposed and self-policed ethical standards places too much faith in human nature. Why do we observe rules in ordinary games, along with referees and umpires? Empirical examination of such voluntary games among persons offers us perhaps the most direct evidence for the central contractarian hypothesis that rules, laws, are generally necessary.

VI. DEFINITION OF INDIVIDUAL RIGHTS

I could end this paper here and remain within the limits of most discussion by economists. Traditionally, economists have been content to treat exchange and contract, in all possible complexities, on the assumption that individual participants are well-defined entities, capable of making choices among alternatives, and in mutual agreement concerning legal titles or rights to things that are subject to exchange. The distribution of basic endowments, human and nonhuman, among persons has been taken as a given for most economic analysis, both positive and normative. The libertarian anarchist has gone further; in order to develop his argument that any and all political structure is illegitimate, he finds it necessary to presume that there are definitive and well-understood "natural boundaries" to individuals' rights. These boundaries on rights are held sacrosanct, subject to no justifiable "crossings" without consent.[6]

The problem of defining individual boundaries, individual rights, or, indeed, defining "individuals" must arise in any discussion of social order that commences with individuals as the basic units. Who is a person? How are rights defined? What is the benchmark or starting point from which voluntary contractual arrangements may be made?

I stated earlier that the primary value premise of individualism is the moral equality of men as men, that no man counts for more than another. This remains, and must remain, the fundamental normative framework even when we recognize inequalities among persons in other respects. The libertarian anarchist accepts this framework, but in a much more restricted application than others who also fall within the individualistic set. The libertarian anarchist applies the moral equality norm in holding that each and every man is *equally* entitled to have the natural boundaries of his rights respected, regardless of the fact that, among persons, these boundaries may vary widely.[7] *If* such natural boundaries exist, the contractarian may also use the individual units defined by such limits as the starting point for the complex contractual arrangements that emerge finally in observed, or conceptually observed, political structures.[8] Within the presupposition that natural boundaries exist, the differences between the constitutionalist-contractarian and the libertarian anarchist reduce to the variant hypotheses concerning the interdependencies among persons, as defined, interdependencies that could be, as noted above, subjected to testing at a conjecturally empirical level.

But do such natural limits or boundaries exist? Once we move beyond the simple rights to persons in the strictly physical sense, what are the distinguishing characteristics of boundary lines? In all cases where separate individual claims may come into conflict, or potential conflict, what is the natural boundary? Robin Hood and Little John meet squarely in the center of the footbridge. Who has the right of first passage? [9]

Robert Nozick makes a bold attempt to answer such questions by referring to the process of acquisition. In his formulation, the legitimacy of the boundary limits among persons depends upon the process through which rights are acquired and not on the absolute or relative size of the bundle that may be in the possession or nominal ownership of a person or group. A person who has acquired assets by voluntary transfer holds the rights to these assets within admissible natural boundary limits. A person who holds assets that have been acquired, by him or by others in the past, by nonvoluntary methods has little claim to include these assets within the natural limits.

What is the ultimate test for the existence of natural boundaries? This must lie in the observed attitudes of individuals themselves. Do we observe persons to act as if there were natural boundaries on the rights of others, beyond those formally defined in legal restrictions? The evidence is not all on one side. In rejecting the extreme claims of the libertarian anarchists, we should not overlook the important fact that a great deal of social interaction does proceed without formalized rules. For large areas of human intercourse, anarchy prevails and it works. We need no rules for directing pedestrian traffic on busy city sidewalks; no rules for ordinary conversation in groups of up to, say, ten persons; no rules for behavior in elevators.

In the larger context, however, the evidence seems to indicate that persons do not mutually and simultaneously agree on dividing lines among separate rights. There is surely a contractual logic for at least some of the activity of the state in defining and enforcing the limits on the activities of persons. To accept this, however, does not imply that the legally defined rights of individuals, and the distribution of these rights, are arbitrarily determined by the political authorities. If we reject the empirical existence of natural boundaries, however, we return to the initial question. How do we define "individuals" for the purpose of deriving the contractual basis for political authority?

VII. THE HOBBESIAN SETTING

The only alternative seems to be found in the distribution of limits on individuals' spheres of action that would be found in the total absence of formalized rules, that is, in genuine Hobbesian anarchy. In this setting, some "equilibrium," some sustainable distribution of allowable activities would emerge. This distribution would depend on the relative strengths and abilities of persons to acquire and to maintain desirable goods and assets. The "law of the jungle" would be controlling, and no serious effort could be made to attribute moral legitimacy to the relative holdings of persons. But this construction does have the major advantage of allowing us to define, in a conjecturally positive sense, a starting point, an "original position" from which any contractual process might commence.[10] Individuals need not be "natural equals" in this Hobbesian equilibrium, but they would still find it mutually advantageous to enter into contractual agreements which impose limits on their own activities, which set up ideally neutral governmental units to enforce these limits.

The perspective changes dramatically when this, essentially Hobbesian, vision is substituted for the natural boundaries or Lockean vision, when the existence of natural boundaries to the rights of persons that would be generally agreed upon and respected is denied. In the Nozick variant of the Lockean vision, anarchy, the absence of formalized rules, the absence of law along with means of enforcement, offers a highly attractive prospect. By contrast, in the basic Hobbesian vision, or in any paradigm that is derivative from this, anarchy is not a state to be desired at all. Life for the individual in genuine anarchy is indeed predicted to be "poor, nasty, brutish, and short." The Hobbesian jungle is something to be avoided, and something that rational self-interested persons will seek to avoid through general agreement on law, along with requisite enforcement institutions, even if, in the extreme, the contract may be irreversible and Hobbes's Leviathan may threaten.[11]

VIII. CONCLUSIONS

We have here a paradox of sorts. The libertarian anarchist and the contractarian share the individualistic value premise. In addition, their diagnoses of current social malaise is likely to be similar in condemning overextended governmental authority. Further, the items on both agenda for policy reform may be identical over a rather wide range. In their descriptions of the "good society," however, these two sets of political philosophers are likely to differ widely. The constitutionalist-contractarian, who looks to his stage two set of ideals, and who adopts at least some variant of the Hobbesian assumption about human nature, views anarchy, as an institution, with horror. To remove all laws, all institutions of order, in a world peopled by Hobbesian men would produce chaos. The contractarian must hold fast to a normative vision that is not nearly so simplistic as that which is possible either for the libertarian anarchist or for the collectivist. The contractarian seeks "ordered anarchy," that is, a situation described as one that offers maximal freedom for individuals within a minimal set of formalized rules and constraints on behavior. He takes from classical economics the important idea that the independent actions of many persons can be spontaneously coordinated through marketlike institutions so as to produce mutually desirable outcomes without detailed and direct interferences of the state. But he insists, with Adam Smith, that this coordination can be effective only if individual actions are limited by laws that cannot themselves spontaneously emerge.

The contractarian position requires sophisticated discrimination between those areas of potential human activity where "law" is required and those areas that had best be left alone. The "efficient" dividing line must be based on empirical reality. Formal law may be severely limited in a society characterized by widespread agreement on the structure of rights and embodying agreed-on ethical standards of mutual respect. The scope for law becomes much more extensive in a society populated by hedonists who neither agree upon reciprocal rights nor upon desired standards of personal conduct. Between the libertarian anarchist, who sees no cause for any laws, and who trusts to individuals' own respect for each others' reciprocal natural boundaries, and the collectivist-socialist, who sees chaos as the result of any human activities that are not politically controlled, the constitutionalist-contractarian necessarily occupies the middle ground. Regardless of his empirical presuppositions, his ideal world falls "between anarchy and Leviathan," both of which are to be avoided.

NOTES

1. Murray Rothbard, *For a New Liberty* (New York: Macmillan, 1973). See also David Friedman, *The Machinery of Freedom* (New York: Harper and Row, 1973). I shall not discuss those putative anarchists who fail to see the internal contradiction between anarchy and socialism. The absurdity of such juxtaposition should be apparent without serious argument.
2. This is recognized by Plattner when he places John Rawls, an avowed contractarian, and Robert Nozick, almost a libertarian-anarchist, in

the same category "on the deepest level." Against both, Plattner advances the transcendentalist view of politics as supraindividualistic. See Marc F. Plattner, "The New Political Theory," *The Public Interest,* 40 (Summer 1975), 119-28, notably p. 127.

3. For an elaboration of the underlying theory, see James M. Buchanan and Gordon Tullock, *The Calculus of Consent* (Ann Arbor: University of Michigan Press, 1962).

4. For a general discussion of this sort of interdependence, see James M. Buchanan and Alberto di Pierro, "Pragmatic Reform and Constitutional Revolution," *Ethics,* 79 (January 1969), 95-104.

5. See my review of David Friedman's book, *The Machinery of Freedom,* in *Journal of Economic Literature,* XII (September 1974), 914-15.

6. One merit of Robert Nozick's analysis is his explicit discussion of the underlying presumptions of the "natural-boundaries" model. See Robert Nozick, *Anarchy, State, and Utopia* (New York: Basic Books, 1974).

7. For purposes of discussion here, I am including Robert Nozick as being among the libertarian anarchists. Although he defends the emergence of the minimal protective state from anarchy, and specifically refutes the strict anarchist model in this respect, he does provide the most sophisticated argument for the presumption of inherent natural boundaries on individuals' rights, which is the focus of my attention here. Cf. Robert Nozick, *Anarchy, State, and Utopia,* op. cit.

8. John Locke provides a good example.

9. I use this example in several places to discuss this set of problems in my recent book, *The Limits of Liberty: Between Anarchy and Leviathan* (Chicago: University of Chicago Press, 1975).

10. In his much-acclaimed book, *A Theory of Justice* (Cambridge: Harvard University Press, 1971), John Rawls attempts to derive principles of justice from conceptual contractual agreement among persons who place themselves in an "original position" behind a "veil of ignorance." Rawls does not, however, fully describe the characteristics of the "original position." I have interpreted this position in essentially Hobbesian terms, with interesting implications. See my "A Hobbesian Interpretation of the Rawlsian Difference Principle," Working Paper CE 75-2-3, Center for Study of Public Choice, Virginia Polytechnic Institute and State University, 1975.

11. The argument of the few preceding paragraphs is developed much more fully in my book, *The Limits of Liberty,* op. cit. Also see *Explorations in the Theory of Anarchy,* edited by Gordon Tullock (Blacksburg: Center for Study of Public Choice, 1972).

[2]

Excerpt from *Nomos*, 63–87

4

ANARCHISM AND WORLD ORDER

RICHARD A. FALK

Mere anarchy is loosed upon the world.
—W. B. Yeats, "The Second Coming"

We do not fear anarchy, we invoke it.
Mikhail Bakunin, *The Program of the International Brotherhood*

I. AN INTRODUCTORY PERSPECTIVE

Anarchism has largely directed its thought and actions against the sovereign state, seeking primarily to bring about the radical reconstruction of economic, political, and social life within individual domestic arenas. In addition, however, like any radical movement that challenges fundamental organizing norms and structures, anarchism has wider implications. These wider implications extend the critique of the state as domestic institutional nexus to a critique of statism or the state system as a global framework for political organization. Nevertheless, surprisingly little attention has been given to anarchism as a perspective relevant to global reform.[1] This neglect is somewhat surprising because anarchists generally appreciate the extent to which their goals can be realized only by the transformation of the world scene as a whole.

This lack of attention can, however, be explained by several factors. First, it reflects the previously noted domestic focus of anarchism—indeed, of all modern revolutionary theory. Second, it probably reflects the popular association of anarchy with disorder, while by almost everyone's definition disorder is precisely the opposite of the primary desideratum of global reform, namely, a quantum leap in the capacities to maintain order. Even an antistatist, progressive thinker such as Doris Lessing seems to associate anarchist potentialities of our present civilization, and the declining capacities of governments to sustain elementary order and reliability even within national boundaries, with still further disintegration.[2] This identification of anarchism with disarray is juxtaposed against a generally accepted conviction that global reform will entail the globalization of governmental structures rather than the destructuring of national governments. The League of Nations and the United Nations are generally viewed as positive experiments to the extent that they have constituted tentative steps toward world government, as failures because they have represented too little by way of bureaucratic centralism.[3] Alternatively, an anarchist might hold that the League and the United Nations present suitable pretexts for partially dismantling bureaucratic structures at the state level *without* building up a superstate to compensate at the global level. In other words, it is the weakness of global institutions as bureaucratic presence that would appeal to anarchists. (Of course, in actuality, these global institutions, in both their mode of creation and their mode of operations, have proven to be elitist in the extreme and therefore antithetical to the anarchist ethos.) [4]

Third, there is a lingering tendency, given plausibility by the pervasiveness of nongovernmental terror in contemporary life, to dismiss anarchism on moral grounds as a more or less explicit avowal of terrorism, and on political grounds as an absurdly romantic gesture of nihilistic sentiment whose only consequence is to strengthen the case for governmental repression. The belief that anarchists glorify terror has historical roots in the nineteenth century, especially in Russia, and was given widespread currency in Dostoevski's great novel *The Devils* which re-created in fictional form the actual nihilism of Nechayev, an extremist follower of Bakunin.

Jean-Paul Sartre has for this reason, until very recently, avoided acknowledging his own anarchist affinity: "then, by way of philosophy, I discovered the anarchist being in me. But when I discovered it I did not call it that, because today's anarchy no longer has anything to do with the anarchy of 1890." [5]

True, one form of individual resistance to state power is the use of random violence by self-styled anarchist revolutionaries for the avowed purpose of exposing the vulnerability of individuals or of the community as a whole. It is no accident when antibureaucratic radicals identify with anarchism as a means of registering their dissent from the prevailing forms of state socialism; typical in this regard was the unfurling of black flags from Sorbonne buildings liberated during the student uprisings of May 1968. [6] However, terrorism bears no inherent relationship to anarchist thinking; many pacifists, including Tolstoy, Gandhi, and Paul Goodman, have been associated with anarchist traditions of thought. [7]

Conversely, the mere adoption of terrorist tactics does not necessarily imply a disavowal of statist goals, as witness the manifold examples of terrorism by contemporary "liberation groups." The Palestinian Liberation Organization, consumed by statist objectives, has embraced indiscriminate terror for apparently expediential reasons: to get a hearing for its grievances, and to give its claims a potency allegedly unattainable through less extreme forms of persuasion or even through conventional warfare. Terrorism is a desperate strategy of a powerless (or unimaginative) claimant, but it is not a necessary component of the anarchist perspective. [8]

In this essay I regard the anarchist position as characterized mainly by its opposition to bureaucratic centralism of all forms and by its advocacy of libertarian socialism. This attempt to delineate the anarchist position is less drastic than the dictionary definition of anarchism as entailing the absence of government. My understanding of anarchist thought, admittedly a personal interpretation, suggests that the basic anarchist impulse is toward something positive, namely, toward a minimalist governing structure in a setting that encourages the full realization of human potentialities for cooperation and happiness. As such, the quest is for humane

government, with a corresponding rejection of large-scale impersonal institutions that accord priority to efficiency and rely upon
force and intimidation rather than upon voluntary patterns of
cooperation to sustain order. This quest puts the anarchist into a
posture of opposition to the modern state, especially the most
successful and powerful states, but it is only the most extreme
examples of anarchist thought that devote their main energy to
negation rather than to their affirmative case for radical reform on
all levels of social, economic, and political organization.

On this basis, I believe that the anarchist tradition has something
important to contribute to the emergent dialogue on the tactics and
shape of global reform. This contribution must be predicated on a
response to each of the three issues just considered. In effect, (1) an
anarchist concept of global reform needs to be fully worked out; (2)
anarchist ideas on "security" and "organization" must be set forth;
(3) anarchist thinking on the relevance of violence must be clarified
in relation to its practical and moral consequences. This paper seeks
to take tentative constructive steps in these directions, after first
considering two additional preliminary issues:

· What kind of "a vision" do anarchists propose for the future?

· Why is anarchism an attractive antidote (or complement) to
mainstream thinking on global reform?

In a perceptive essay on the full sweep of anarchist thought,
Irving Louis Horowitz observed that "it scarcely requires any feats
of mind to show that modern industrial life is incompatible with the
anarchist demand for the liquidation of State authority. Anarchism
can be no more than a posture. It cannot be a viable political
position." [9] The validity of such an assertion depends on what is
meant by "modern industrial life" and by "the anarchist demand
for the liquidation of State authority." For example, representatives
from many and diverse disciplines now contend, independent of any
concern with statist organization, that the modern industrial ethos
as we have known it is not sustainable on ecological grounds. [10] The
revival of interest in "benign" or "gentle" technology, and of life-
styles outside the money economy, provide further evidence that the
momentum of industrial civilization may possibly be reversible. [11]

Indeed, one could reverse Horowitz's assertion and contend that
any political perspective that does not propose doing away with
modern industrial life is doomed to failure and futility, and is an

exercise in bad faith. Furthermore, the anarchist demand is not directed at eliminating all forms of authority in human existence, but at their destructive embodiment in exploitative institutions associated with the modern bureaucratic state. Contrary to general impressions, nothing in anarchist thought precludes a minimum institutional presence at all levels of social organization, provided only that this presence emanates from *populist* rather than *elitist* impulses, and that its structure is deliberately designed fully to protect the liberty of all participants, starting with and centering on the individual. Indeed Bakunin, with his admiration of American federalism of the nineteenth century [12] and his tentative advocacy of a universal confederation of peoples, lent anarchist support to the globalist approach to world order challenges. As Bakunin put it in 1866: "it is absolutely necessary for any country wishing to join the free federations of peoples to replace its centralized, bureaucratic, and military organizations by a federalist organization based on the absolute liberty and autonomy of regions, provinces, communes, associations, and individuals." [13] In essence, the anarchist proposes dismantling the bureaucratic state and reconstituting a world society from the bottom up (what Bakunin calls a "universal world federation" and "directed from the bottom up, from the circumference to the center"), with constant accountability to the bottom. Paul Goodman has expressed in a modern idiom this anarchist view of creative reordering: "My own bias is to decentralize and localize wherever it is feasible, because this makes for alternatives and more vivid and intimate life.... On this basis of weakening of the Powers, and of the substitution of function for power, it would be possible also to organize the world community, as by the functional agencies of the United Nations, UNICEF, WHO, somewhat UNESCO; and to provide *ad hoc* cooperation like the Geo-physical Year, exploring space, or feeding the Chinese." [14] Furthermore, anarchist thinking has a notable antiterritorial bias which tends to deride national frontiers as artificial and dangerously inconsistent with the wholeness of its humanist affirmations. [15]

But reverting to Horowitz's characterization once again, doesn't such an anarchist approach to global reform lie far beyond the horizon of attainability? And hence, how can anarchism reasonably be regarded as a viable possibility that could materialize in our lifetimes? One could answer these questions in several ways. To quote Bakunin once more, as he is discounting the failures of the revolutionary uprisings of 1848 in Europe, "Must we ... doubt the future itself, and the present strength of socialism? Christianity, which had set as its goal the creation of the kingdom of justice in heaven, needed several centuries to triumph in Europe. Is there any cause for surprise if socialism, which has set for itself a more difficult problem, that of creating the kingdom of justice on earth, has not triumphed in a few years?" [16] In this view, the anarchist position is no less coherent or relevant merely because its prospects of realization are not proximate. Bureaucratic socialists, those who seek to seize state power rather than to decompose it, contemptuously dismiss anarchist or libertarian socialists as utopians, or worse, as reactionaries.[17] But the anarchist response is more credible than the challenge here presented. The anarchist quite properly contends that merely to seize power is to default upon the humanist content of socialism and to create a new form of despotism. The real revolution cannot be rushed, but neither can it be dispensed with. I think, in this regard, that Herbert Read is wrong when he says of anarchism that "... if the conception of society which it thus arrives at seems utopian and even chimerical, it does not matter, for what is established by right reasoning cannot be surrendered to expediency." [18] I think it does matter, and anarchists generally act as if it matters, both by their arguments about the cooperative capacities of human society (which, incidentally, Read strongly endorses) and by their belief in the revolutionary possibility lying dormant within mass consciousness. Of course, Read correctly stresses the principled character of anarchist thinking, its unwillingness to corrupt its values merely for the sake of power. This high-mindedness distinguishes anarchism from bureaucratic socialism in theory and vindicates its ethical purism in practice. The contrast seems particularly great in view of the consistent betrayal of socialist ideals at each new opportunity—not only in the Soviet Union but even in China and Cuba.[19] In this regard, the anarchist refuses both the facile radicalism of the conventional Marxist (who would merely replace one form of exploitation and repression with another) and the facile gradualism of the liberal (who would acquiesce in the structure of exploitation and repression, provided its cruelest manifestations can be gradually diminished).

A further anarchist response to the counsel of patience claims that the revolutionary possibility is hidden from view in the evolving currents of popular consciousness. According to Bakunin, revolutions "make themselves; they are produced by the force of circumstance, the movement of facts and events. They receive a long preparation of the masses, then they burst forth, often seemingly triggered by trivial causes." [20] Thus, the revolutionary moment may be closer than we think; it may be building toward eruption; and it may enter the field of history with unexpected haste and fury. The Paris Commune of 1871 is a favorite illustration of this possibility.[21] A time of crisis enhances revolutionary prospects; it creates receptivity to new ideas, however radical; it exposes existing injustice; and it generates a willingness to take risks. Naturally, however, there is no available calculus for determining the most propitious moment for actually instituting an anarchist program of destructuring the state and replacing international statism with global confederation.

Finally, the anarchist is not obliged to wait for the days of triumph. Although his concept of the future is visionary and vital to his position, it is not detached in time from present possibilities for actualization.[22] As Howard Zinn writes, "The anarchist sees revolutionary change as something immediate, something we must do now, where we are, where we live, where we work. It means starting this moment to do away with authoritarian, cruel relationships—between men and women, between children and parents, between one kind of worker and another kind. Such revolutionary action cannot be crushed like an armed uprising." [23] Paul Goodman vividly makes the same point through his characterization of a well-known peace activist: "Best of all, in principle, is the policy that Dave Dellinger espouses and tries to live by, to live communally and without authority, to work usefully and feel friendly, and so positively to replace an area of power with peaceful functioning." [24] By conducting his life in this way, the anarchist can initiate a process of change that is virtually invulnerable to external pressures, criticisms, and threats. The anarchist posture is thus deepened through experience and engenders credibility for the seriousness of its claims about the future. Unlike the utopian who tends to dichotomize present and future, regarding one mode as suitable given present practicalities and another as desirable given future wishes, the anarchist integrates his present behavior with his future hopes. The anarchist correctly perceives that the future is the eventual culmination of the present and that liberty is an existential condition enabling degrees of immediate realization.

The anarchist thus joins immediate action with his program for drastic societal reform. Herbert Read expresses this dual commitment as follows: "Our practical activity may be a gradual approximation towards the ideal, or it may be a sudden revolutionary realization of that ideal, but it must never be a compromise." [25]

Of course, despite this attempt at refutation, there is still a measure of common sense in Horowitz's observation. Surely, anarchism may serve as no more than a posture, and its immediate impact may consist primarily in leavening the more deeply rooted political traditions of Marxism and liberalism. However, even in this ancillary capacity, anarchism can perform the highly positive function of providing a corrective for the bureaucratic and repressive tendencies of Marxist politics, and for the apologetics and rationalizations of liberal politics.[26] Therefore, I would argue that anarchist thought, correctly understood, is both a position *and* a posture.

Let us consider now our second preliminary question: Why is anarchism an attractive antidote (or complement) to mainstream thinking on global reform? Most proposals for global reform have uncritically affirmed the ordering contributions of the state to domestic life and have, in one or another form, sought to make those contributions available to the world as a whole. Indeed, the argument for global reform, at least since World War I, has assumed the strident tones of necessity. Since Hiroshima these claims of necessity have been pitched on an apocalyptic level and have been extended to embrace biosocial survival in light of the allegedly deepening ecological crisis—the crowding, poisoning, and straining of planetary facilities. The unexamined premise in world-order thinking has been that *only* governmental solutions can organize planetary life, that only existing governmental structures and their leaders can command the authority required for this essential undertaking, and that only argument and persuasion can release the political energy needed to overcome the inertia that sustains the state system in the face of the most unmistakable writing on the wall. A major variant to this line of reformist thinking is that persuasion must be supplemented by tragedy before enough political energy is released to achieve a world-order solution.

Generally, such advocacy of bureaucratic centralism is coupled with confidence in the moderating capacities of law and institutionalism. The ideal world order would still consist of a realm of states, but with the venom drawn by substituting "law" for "force." Conflict would remain, but war would disappear. Peaceful methods of resolving conflicts would be accepted since all states would be unanimously committed to upholding the federalist edifice.

This kind of mainstream "idealism" often coexists with "realism." Until the existing world system is reconstructed according to the principles of legalist architecture, one is thrown back into the state system with its logic of power and its reliance on force to achieve "security" and to "manage" change. The world-order idealist of tomorrow can easily justify being Machiavellian today. Hence, the issue of "transition" emerges as critical, and it is a fascinating indictment of mainstream thinking that no sustained attention has been given to the central challenge of transition—namely, access to, and transformation of, state power.

The anarchist comes forward with a quite different set of ideas, easily adapted to the world-order debate: first of all, a skeptical regard for the state and an unwillingness to accept it as "a model" for achieving a just order on any level of social organization; second, a positive belief in the capacities of various other collectivities—communes, cities, provinces, regions, associations—to provide the creative impetus for reorganizing the human enterprise; third, a bias toward decentralization of wisdom, authority, and capability, coupled with an insistence upon the autonomy of smaller units and the absolute status of individual liberty; fourth, a structural critique of the present organization of power, wealth, and prestige coupled with a revolutionary set of demands that existing leaders of society would never voluntarily meet; fifth, a processive view of the future, based on embodying the vision of a new order in immediate personal and political activities; sixth, a substitution of "justice" for "order" as the primary test of the adequacy of a given arrangement of power in world society; seventh, a refusal to blueprint the future in a manner that precludes creativity within the eventual setting that will give rise to the revolutionary possibility itself.[27]

These seven elements of anarchist thinking can be positively adapted to movement for global reform. What is most impressive about anarchist thought, taken from a world-order perspective, is its blending of critique, vision, and transition strategy. In the words of George Woodstock, a close student of anarchism:

> Historically, anarchism is a doctrine which poses a criticism of existing society; a view of a desirable future society; and a means of passing from one to the other.[28]

Often, proposals for global reform have been sterile because they lacked one or more of these three essential elements (most typically, the transition strategy), or else presented one of them in unacceptable form (e.g., the vision as a blueprint). Despite this general attractiveness of anarchism as a world order perspective, the anarchist position also poses several difficulties that must be considered in the course of evaluating its possible relevance to a beneficial movement of global reform.[29]

II. THREE HARD QUESTIONS FOR ANARCHISTS

1. *Are not the preconditions for anarchist success insurmountable?* The great anarchist success stories have been episodic, short-lived (e.g., the Paris Commune of 1871, the anarchist collectives in parts of Spain during the 1930s, the May uprising in Paris in 1968). Nowhere have anarchists enjoyed a period of sustained success. Generally, anarchist success has generated an overpowering reaction of repression, as when the mercenary soldiery of Versailles crushed and massacred the Paris Communards in May 1871 only weeks after their extraordinary triumph. Anarchists view such failures as inevitable "first attempts"; Kropotkin calls "the Commune of Paris, the child of a period of transition ... doomed to perish" but "the forerunner of social revolution." [30] Murry Bookchin and Daniel Guérin make a similar assessment of the Paris uprising of 1968, regarding its occurrence as proof of the anarchist critique, its collapse as evidence that "the molecular movement below that prepares the condition for revolution" had not yet carried far enough.[31]

On a deeper level, anarchists understand that the prerequisite for anarchist success *anywhere* is its success *everywhere*. It is this vital precondition that is at once so convincing and so formidable as to call into question whether the anarchist position can in fact be taken seriously as a progressive alternative to state socialism.

Bakunin expressed the anarchist demand and rationale with clarity: "A federalist in the internal affairs of the country, he desires an international confederation, first of all in the spirit of justice, and second because he is convinced that the economic and social revolution, transcending all the artificial and pernicious barriers between states, can only be brought about, in part at least, by the solidarity in action, if not of all, then at least of the majority of the nations constituting the civilized world today, so that sooner or later all nations must join together." [32] Or, as Daniel Guérin expressed it: "An isolated national revolution cannot succeed. The social revolution inevitably becomes a world revolution." [33]

In essence, not only is it difficult for anarchists to attain power, but once they manage to do so their "organic institutions" seem incapable of holding it. Their movements will be liquidated ruthlessly by statists of "the left" or "the right." [34] Given such vulnerability, it may even be a betrayal of one's followers to expose them to slaughter by mounting a challenge against the entrenched forces of statism in the absence of either the will or the capabilities to protect the challengers.[35]

There is a report of a fascinating conversation between Lenin and Kropotkin in May 1919 in which Lenin mounts such an argument in two ways. First, he makes his familiar point that "You can't make a revolution wearing white gloves. We know perfectly well that we have made and will make a great many mistakes. . . . But it is impossible not to make mistakes during a revolution. Not to make them means to renounce life entirely and do nothing at all. But we have preferred to make errors and thus to act. . . . We want to act and we will, despite all the mistakes, and will bring our socialist revolution to the final and inevitably victorious end." [36] Lenin here in effect acknowledges the errors that flow from using state power to secure the revolutionary victory from external and internal enemies, and he rebuffs the anarchist view that state power can be dissolved. Lenin's second rebuff of the anarchist position is his condescending view of its revolutionary power: "Do you really think that the capitalist world will submit to the path of the cooperative movement? . . . You will pardon me, but this is all nonsense! We need direct action of the masses, revolutionary action of the masses, that activity which seizes the capitalist world by the throat and brings it down." [37] Of anarchist concepts of "social revolution," Lenin says "these are children's playthings, idle chatter, having no realist soil underneath, no force, no means, and almost nothing approaching our socialist goals. . . . We don't need the struggle and violent acts of separate persons. It is high time that the anarchists understood this and stopped scattering their revolutionary energy on utterly useless affairs." [38] In sum, Lenin is arguing that the ends of anarchists must be pursued by mass violent revolution and secured through state power. The anarchist response is, of course, that the choice of such means perverts and dooms the ends. The antagonism of anarchists toward the Bolshevik Revolution has been vindicated many times over.[39] On the level of their discussion, it seems that both Lenin and Kropotkin are correct,[40]—Lenin in saying that there is no other way to succeed, the anarchists by contending that such success is as bad as, if not worse than, defeat.

But, in my view, the strongest case for the feasibility of the anarchist position still remains to be argued. It is implicit, perhaps, in Kropotkin's own work on the origins of the modern state and on its feudal antecedents in the European cities of the eleventh and twelfth centuries.[41] Kropotkin's argument rests on the historical claim that a vital society of communes and free cities created by brotherhoods, guilds, and individual initiative existed earlier: ". . . it is shown by an immense documentation from many sources, that never, either before or since, has mankind known a period of relative well-being for all as in the cities of the Middle Ages. The poverty, insecurity, and physical exploitation of labor that exist in our times were then unknown." [42] Drawing on non-Western experience as well, Kropotkin argues in effect that societal well-being and security based on anarchist conceptions of organic institutions (of a cooperative character) were immensely successful over a wide geographical and cultural expanse until crushed by the emergent states of the fifteenth and sixteenth centuries. Thus, there is a kind of *prima facie* case for plausibility of the anarchist model, although in a prestatal context.

But evidence of the anarchist potential for "success" does not end with medieval Europe. The direction of contemporary China, especially its antiparty, populist phase that culminated in the

Cultural Revolution, contains strong anarchist elements.[43] Indeed, it was precisely on these grounds of repudiating "organization" and "bureaucracy" as a basis for communist discipline that China made itself so offensive to communist ideologues in the Kremlin.[44] China is, of course, a mixed case. In its foreign policy it places great stress on statist prerogatives. Nevertheless, in its domestic patterns the Chinese example lends some credibility to Bakunin's and Kropotkin's claim that there are nonbureaucratic roads to socialism, and gives the anarchist orientation renewed plausibility as a serious political alternative.[45]

Such plausibility can, it seems to me, be extrapolated in a poststatal context. Here, my argument, sustained by sources as dissimilar as Saul Mendlovitz and Henry Kissinger, is that we are undergoing a profound historical transformation that is destroying the organizational matrix of a global system based on territorial states.[46] That is, we are entering a poststatal period, although its character remains highly conjectural. Whatever the outcome, however, the anarchist stress on nonterritorial associations and communal consciousness seems highly relevant because of its basic compatibility with the inevitable shift in the relation of forces.

In sum, the anarchist case for radical reform (i.e., for social revolution) was *chimerical within* the confines of the state system. However, the state system is now being superseded. In this context, one set of plausible possibilities is the globalization of societal life in a way that allows cooperative organizational forms to flourish. That is, the anarchist vision (as epitomized in Bakunin's writings) of a fusion between a universal confederation and organic societal forms of a communal character lies at the very center of the *only* hopeful prospect for the future of world order.[47] Needless to say, such a prospect has slim chances for success, but at least the possibility is no longer chimerical, given the change of objective circumstances. The state system is not an implacable foe, for many economic, political, technological, and sociological forces are everywhere undermining its bases of potency, if unevenly and at an uncertain rate. Therefore, although the political precondition of scale imposed by anarchism still remains formidable, it may yet prove historically surmountable. It may be surmountable because the preparatory processes going on throughout the world during this historical period are creating more favorable global conditions for the

anarchist cause than have hitherto existed for several centuries. This
assessment arises from several distinct developments. Perhaps the
most significant is the growing disenchantment with the values,
goals, and methods of industrial society. This sense of disenchantment is coming to be shared by increasing numbers of citizens,
particularly in the developed nations of the West, and is finding
various forms of expression that reflect revised notions of necessity
based on "limits to growth," notions of well-being based on
intermediate technology and small-scale institutions, and notions of
personal transcendence based on a new spiritual energy that
repudiates both conventional religion and secular humanism. In
this setting, the quest for an appropriate politics coverges rather
dramatically with the central tenets of anarchist belief. This modern
sensibility realizes, at last, that the state is simultaneously *too large* to
satisfy human needs and *too small* to cope with the requirements of
guidance for an increasingly interdependent planet. This realization
is temporarly offset by a rising tide of statism in many other parts of
the world, where political independence is a forbidden fruit only
recently tasted, but where the fruit will be poisoned, as everywhere
else, by a world of nuclear weapons, ecological decay, and mass
economic privation. The main *problematique* of our age is whether an
appropriate politics of global reform, combining a centralized form
of functional guidance with decentralized economic, social, and
political structures, can be shaped by voluntary action, or whether
it must be formed in a crucible of tragedy and catastrophe.
Attentiveness to the anarchist tradition can be one part of an effort
to achieve an appropriate politics *this* side of catastrophe. Obviously, the objective conditions which require such a reassessment
of political forms are not by themselves sufficient to effect a
transformation. Indeed, the very relevance of these ideas may lead
their powerful opponents to regard them as even more dangerous
now than in the past. Prudence and patience are essential in these
circumstances. The crisis of the state system may yet require several
decades to develop to the point where eruptions of spontaneous
anarchistic energies would not unleash a variety of devastating
backlashes.

2. *Given the urgency of global reform, isn't the anarchist prospect too remote
in time?* Even accepting the optimistic assessment of the preceding
section, namely, that the hour of anarchism may coincide with the

collapse of statism, restructuring of the world system would still appear to be developed for an unnecessarily and dangerously long period of several decades or more. Just as the emergence of the state system was a matter of centuries, so might the consolidation of a new system of political order require hundreds of years.[48] Two sets of questions call for judgment based on imponderables. First, how serious and pressing is the crisis? Is the fire close at hand, or still barely visible on a distant horizon? How can we know? Second, are any alternative means available through which the principal goals of global reform could be attained more reliably and rapidly than through anarchism? Do we have any responsible basis for selecting or rejecting these alternatives? In part, we are forced here to confront the most fundamental issues of politics, knowledge, and action. In the abstract, we do not know enough to choose or to act. Of course this same limitation bears on every school of political thought, including those that defend the status quo or incline toward gradualism. But it has even greater bearing on a political position that proposes radical tactics and goals, especially if large-scale violence is likely to ensue. On the other hand, this line of reasoning may be deceptive. In a moment of crisis, to do nothing may be the most risky of all postures toward the future. It is generally better to jump from a sinking ship than it is to stay on board, even if one knows nothing about the prospects of rescue from the waters below. The collective situation of human society cannot be cast in such deceptive simplicity. The veil of ignorance is thick indeed when it comes to assessing policy alternatives for the future of world society.

But the argument from ignorance cuts the other way as well. We have no real way to assess the degrees of progress along the transition path. Perhaps the collapse of statism is closer than we think. As Paul Goodman wrote:

It will be said that there is no time. Yes, probably. But let me cite a remark of Tocqueville. In his last work, *L'Ancien Régime*, he notes "with terror," as he says, how throughout the eighteenth century writer after writer and expert after expert pointed out that this and that detail of the Old Regime was unviable and could not possibly survive; added up, they proved that the entire Old Regime was doomed and must soon collapse; and yet *there was not a single man who foretold that there would be a mighty revolution.*[49]

In the face of such uncertainty, compounded by the many evidences of pressure on the state system, it makes political as well as moral sense to pursue a *principled set of conclusions* even if their realization cannot be immediately foreseen. In one sense Herbert Read is correct in saying that "the task of the anarchist philosopher is not to prove the imminence of a Golden Age, but to justify the value of believing in its possibility." [50]

Such a value depends on some degree of plausibility, but also on whether or not there are any preferable alternatives. Given the established bankruptcy of statist solutions on the right and left, given the vulnerability of the state system as a whole to catastrophic and, quite possibly, irreversible damage, and given the insufficiency of gradualist strategies of amelioration, the case for some variant of radical anarchism seems strong despite the inability of the anarchist to provide skeptics with a credible timetable.

In essence, the issue of urgency reinforces the anarchist case. The primary world order need is to find an alternative to statism. Anarchism, despite its limited political success during the statist era, provides the most coherent, widespread, and persistent tradition of antistatist thought. It is also a tradition that has generally been inclined toward world-order values: peace, economic equity, civil liberties, ecological defense. As such, it represents the most normatively acceptable sequel to the state system. Other sequels include imperial consolidation; world state; regional federation; intergovernmental functionalism.[51]

To affirm the relevance of the anarchist tradition is not to accept the adequacy of its current formulations but only of its general orientation. Advocates of an anarchist approach need to formulate the globalist implications of anarchism in a manner responsive to the current world-order crisis. As far as I know, this has not yet been done. Indeed, anarchism suffers from the tendency of other traditions of philosophical speculation generated during the statist era, namely, to concentrate upon the national question and to assume that the global question will disappear when all nations have correctly resolved their own domestic problems. As I have suggested, anarchists are more dependent than other reformers on supportive transnational developments; but their analysis of international events is usually identical to that of Marxists, on the level of critique, and highly impressionistic when it comes to making specific proposals. Thus, the claims of anarchism are not weakened by the urgency of the world crisis, but the need for a more historically sensitive interpretation and for a globally oriented formulation of anarchist response is essential.

3. *Does the receptivity of anarchism to violence undermine the moral basis of its claim to provide an ideology for global reform?* I am not discussing here the anarchist as "bomb-thrower," but neither do I identify anarchism with pacifist ethics. As a philosophical position anarchism adopts an equivocal view of violence as an agent of change. Although anarchists tend to rely on spontaneous militancy of a nonviolent character—most typically, the general strike or other forms of unarmed struggle and resistance—there is no prevailing anarchist view on the role of violence.

I think Howard Zinn has sympathetically, but reliably, presented the anarchist position on violence in this assessment:

Some anarchists—like other revolutionaries throughout history ... have emphasized violent uprising. Some have advocated, and tried, assassination and terror. ... What makes anarchists unique among revolutionaries, however, is that most of them see revolution as a cultural, ideological, creative process, in which violence would be as incidental as the outcries of mother and baby in childbirth. It might be unavoidable—given the natural resistance to change—but something to be kept at a minimum while more important things happen.[52]

The question is whether, given the technology of destruction and the ruthlessness of statist leadership, this view of violence is adequate. It can be attacked from either side, as underestimating the role of violence for any serious revolutionary position, or as too willing to accept the moral Trojan Horse of political violence.

Mainstream Marxists and neo-Marxists generally contend that revolution depends upon mass-based armed struggle. A recent formulation is "the political statement of the Weather Underground" released under the title *Prairie Fire:*

It's an illusion that imperialism will decay peacefully. Imperialism has meant constant war. Imperialists defend their control

of the means of life with terrible force. There is no reason to
believe they will become humane or relinquish power. . . . To
not prepare the people for this struggle is to disarm them
ideologically and physically and to perpetrate a cruel hoax.[53]

The cruel hoax is, of course, the illusion that revolution can occur
without armed struggle, that a revolution can be made with white
gloves. But as Kropotkin soon perceived, once the white gloves have
been thrown away, it becomes all too easy to adopt terror and
torture.[54] In my view, the abuse of state power by socialism has
reversed the presumption that violence is a necessary concomitant
of revolution. On the contrary, it now seems a cruel hoax to promise
humane outcomes from any revolutionary process that embraces
violence with anything other than the utmost reluctance. Any
genuinely radical position that purports moral (as well as political)
credibility must, above all else, reject a cult of violence, and justify
the use of specific forms of violence in the most careful and
conditional manner.

But what, then, of the revolutionary triumphs of China, Vietnam,
and Cuba? Was not violence essential to their success, and did they
not achieve a net gain by prevailing on the level of armed struggle?
I would answer that first of all, in each of these domestic contexts
there were no options other than extremist ones. Second, reliance on
violent tactics may yet doom these revolutionary societies to
Stalinist or other repressive patterns of governance. Third, the
struggle for global reform should not be confused with the struggle
for reform within an individual nation, although the two undertak-
ings are closely related.

In other words, it is not enough to acknowledge that the
imperialists are also violent, nor even that anarchists are prepared
to accept violence only reluctantly and as incidental to their
purposes. Something more considered, more explicit, is needed, even
though specific choices cannot always be anticipated or determined
in the abstract.

At the same time, an unequivocal renunciation of violence is
probably "a cruel hoax," given the realities of power. There may be
no way, in particular situations, to remain aloof from armed
struggle without acquiescing, oneself, in violence of at least equal
proportions.

If anarchism is to qualify as a morally suitable ideology for global reform, it requires a considered analysis of the role of violence, with emphasis on:

- Necessity of recourse, as an instrument of last resort (the futility of nonviolent militancy having already been demonstrated beyond reasonable doubt);
- Discrimination in application (with no intentional subjection of innocent people to foreseeable risks of harm);
- Limitation of the form and degree of application (absolute prohibition on torture and cruelty).

Such a middle position is no guarantee against revolutionary excess, but this doctrinal stance may at least exert some influence when it comes to choosing tactics, strategies, and policies. Also, it provides a defense against both Leninist and pacifist critiques. Finally, it acknowledges what has been so agonizingly confirmed in recent decades, namely, that revolutionaries must protect their own programs from their own propensities to embrace "evil."

Violence in the context of global reform is even more problematic. If national struggles are waged successfully in critical countries, then violence will not be necessary on a global level. On the other hand, if such struggles end inconclusively or are defeated, then no degree of global violence will help. Given both the preponderance of military power possessed by state institutions, and the objectives of global reform, it is possible to renounce violence for the exclusive purpose of reform but to retain militant nonviolence as a tactic. Indeed, in the years ahead it will be vital for the forces of global reform to confront statist institutions, in order that the latter be forced to expose their destructive patterns of behavior to a wider public.

III. SOME CONCLUSIONS

Several broad lines of conclusion emerge from the preceding discussion:

(1) There are no serious obstacles to the adoption of an anarchist perspective toward global reform; there are, to be sure, unacceptable variants of the anarchist position, but they do not invalidate

the main lines of anarchist thought as represented by Proudhon, Bakunin, and Kropotkin, and more recently exemplified by Guérin, Herbert Read, and Paul Goodman.

(2) Anarchism impressively links its goals for revolutionary change within national societies with a vision of a transförmed global society; the linkage is integral and progressive in terms of world order values commonly affirmed; as a consequence, anarchism deals with entrenched power and avoids the political sterility associated with legalistic and moralistic blueprints of "a new world order," as well as the static images of the future characteristic of utopography.

(3) Anarchist thought is alive to the twin dangers of socialism and capitalism if pursued within the structure of statism; its espousal of populist strategies of change gains some historical credibility from its affinity with Mao Tse-tung's efforts to avoid the decay of revolutionary momentum in contemporary China.[55]

(4) Anarchist thought on organic institutions of cooperation is creatively freed from either territorial or statist constraints and draws inspiration from both prestatist (Kropotkin) and poststatist possibilities of moving dialectically toward decentralizing bureaucratic power while centralizing human function (Goodman); in this regard, images of global functionalism and political confederation of nations merge with the deconcentration of power and role of national governments; the state is understood to be both inhumanly large in its bureaucratic dimension, and inhumanly small in its territorial and exclusionary dimensions; this dualism implicit in anarchism is excellently adapted to the purposes of global reform.

(5) Anarchist thought, although often perceived as oscillating between extremes of terrorism and pacificism, is capable of evolving from within its framework of values an intermediate interpretation of violence. Such an interpretation would bias action in the direction of militant nonviolence, without depending on either the "white gloves" of utopians or the torture chambers of state socialists and cultist advocates of violence.

(6) As yet, there is no comprehensive and satisfactory formulation of an anarchist position on global reform, only fragments here and there; a well-integrated statement could help crystallize enthusiasm for global reform of a drastic, yet constructive kind in many parts of the world where the internal strains of an obsolescent and moribund

statism are being rapidly translated into repression, militarism, imperialism, and interventionary diplomacy; for weak states, even genuine national autonomy requires a radical program of global reform.

For those who view our era as one of transition between the state system and some globalist sequel, the anarchist perspective becomes increasingly relevant and attractive. Of course, it remains to be tested as an ideology for hope and action, as well as a basis for social, economic, and political reconstruction. Maoism, as embodied in the China of the 1960s and 1970s, is a peculiar mixture of statism and populism that should be generally, although not fully, encouraging. As Franz Schurmann notes: "... the very word 'Maoism' came to mean a kind of anarchist, ultraleft troublemaking-for-troublemaking's sake. And when the New Left began to clash with older communist parties, as in France, China was invoked as a new Marxist Rome sanctioning this path to revolution." [56]

NOTES

1. For one notable exception see Thomas G. Weiss, "The Tradition of Philosophic Anarchism and Future Directions in World Policy" (mimeographed); I have treated the anarchist briefly and analytically in *A Study of Future Worlds* (New York: Free Press, 1975), pp. 214-19.

2. "We believed we were living in a peculiarly anarchist community." Doris Lessing, *Memoirs of a Survivor* (New York: Knopf, 1975), p. 81.

3. See depiction of Franklin Roosevelt's vision of a new world order based on the primacy of the United Nations in Franz Schurmann, *The Logic of World Power* (New York: Pantheon, 1974), pp. 13-17, esp. 67-76.

4. Sir Herbert Read expresses the anarchist attitude toward order and efficiency in social relations as follows: "... anarchism implies a universal decentralization of authority, and a universal simplification of life. Inhuman entities like the modern city will disappear. But anarchism does not necessarily imply a reversion to handicraft and outdoor sanitation. There is no contradiction between anarchism and air transport, anarchism and the division of labour, anarchism and industrial efficiency." Sir Herbert Read, *Anarchy and Order* (Boston: Beacon, 1971), p. 134. In other words, anarchist images involve reconstituting order in the world rather than eliminating it.

5. "Sartre at Seventy: An Interview," *New York Review of Books*, August 7, 1975, pp. 10-17, at p. 14. Because anarchists are viewed as extremists there is a temptation to avoid the label. Consider, for instance, this

passage by E. M. Cioran: ". . . from the moment your actions and your thoughts serve a form of real or imagined city you are its idolators and its captives. The timidest employee and the wildest anarchist, if they take a different interest here, live as its function: they are both citizens internally though one prefers his slippers and the other his bomb." *A Short History of Decay* (New York: Viking, 1975), pp. 75-76.

6. See interpretation by French anarchist Daniel Guérin in *Anarchism: From Theory to Practice* (New York: Monthly Review Press, 1970), pp. 155-59.

7. For consideration of pacifist ethos in relation to an anarchist orientation see Karl Shapiro, "On the Revival of Anarchism," in Irving Louis Horowitz, ed., *The Anarchists* (New York: Dell, 1964), pp. 572-81; also Howard Zinn's Introductory essay in Read, note 4, pp. ix-xxii.

8. The PLO's adoption of terror as a tactic can also be condemned as a consequence of its failure to initiate a mass movement of nonviolent struggle. Such a movement would not necessarily succeed, but its failure is far from assured.

9. Introduction, Horowitz, ed., *The Anarchists,* pp. 15-64, at p. 26.

10. E.g., Barry Commoner, *The Closing Circle* (New York: Knopf, 1971); Edward Goldsmith and others, *Blueprint for Survival* (Boston: Houghton Mifflin, 1972); Donella Meadows and others, *The Limits to Growth* (Washington, D.C.: Potomac Associates, 1972); R. A. Falk, *This Endangered Planet: Prospects and Proposals for Human Survival* (New York: Random House), 1971.

11. Among those who have discerned and charted this new direction of human energy, perhaps Theodore Roszak is most notable. See *The Making of a Counter Culture* (New York: Anchor, 1969); *Where the Wasteland Ends* (New York: Anchor, 1973).

12. Sam Dolgoff, ed., *Bakunin on Anarchy* (New York: Knopf, 1972), p. 107: Bakunin characterized the American system as "the finest political organization that ever existed in history." [Hereafter cited as *Bakunin.*]

13. *Bakunin,* p. 98; see also p. 152.

14. Goodman, "The Ambiguities of Pacifist Politics," in Leonard I. Krimerman and Lewis Perry, eds., *Patterns of Anarchy* (New York: Anchor, 1966), pp. 125-36, at 127.

15. E.g., Bakunin's conceptions are based on federations of many different, overlapping units, including "regions, provinces, communes, associations, and individuals," p. 98.

16. *Bakunin,* pp. 121-22.

17. On dismissal see George Plekanov, "Anarchist Tactics: A Pageant of Futility, Obstruction, and Decadence?" in Krimerman and Perry, note 15, pp. 495-99; for an anarchist response to these kinds of allegations

see Guérin, *Anarchism*, pp. 41-69; Read, note 4, pp. 22-23 usefully distinguishes between positive and negative roles for utopian projections of the future.

18. Read, *Anarchy and Order*, p. 129.
19. In general see Nadezhda Mandelstam, *Hope Against Hope* (New York: Atheneum, 1970); also on repression at Kronstadt by Soviet government see Guérin, *Anarchism*, pp. 102-5; Alexander Berkman, "Kronstadt: The Final Act in Russian Anarchism," in Horowitz, *The Anarchists*, pp. 495-506.
20. *Bakunin*, p. 155.
21. See Kropotkin's essay "The Commune of Paris," in Martin A. Miller, ed., *Selected Writings on Anarchism and Revolution by P. A. Kropotkin* (Cambridge, Mass.: MIT Press, 1970), pp. 119-32 [hereafter cited as *Kropotkin*] for a comparable anarchist appreciation of the spontaneous character of the Paris risings of 1968 and their relationship to the experience of the Paris Commune a century earlier see Murray Bookchin, *Post-Scarcity Anarchism* (Berkeley, Calif.: Ramparts Press, 1971), pp. 249-70.
22. See Kropotkin's essay "Must We Occupy Ourselves with an Examination of the Ideal of a Future System?" in *Kropotkin*, pp. 47-116.
23. Howard Zinn, Introduction, Read, *Anarchy and Order*, p. xviii.
24. Goodman, "Ambiguities of Pacifist Politics," at p. 136.
25. Read, *Anarchy and Order*, p. 129.
26. Sartre ascribed a similar role to existentialism in relation to Marxism. Sartre, *Search for a Method*, tr. Hazel E. Barnes (New York: Vintage, 1968), pp. 3-34.
27. See Bookchin's discussion of spontaneous features of the Paris 1968 events, in Bookchin, *Post-Scarcity Anarchism*, pp. 250-52; Herbert Read, *Anarchy and Order*, p. 23, argues that blueprints of the future pervert the genuine utopian impulse to transcend present societal arrangements. Such blueprints are condemned as "an advance on the spontaneous sources of life itself. They presume to plan what can only germinate . . . such scientific utopias will certainly fail, for the sources of life when threatened are driven underground to emerge in some new wilderness."
28. George Woodstock, *Anarchism* (New York: World Publishing Co., 1962), p. 9.
29. By "beneficial" I mean a movement that realizes world-order values associated with peace, economic well-being, social and political justice, and ecological balance. For an elaboration of why these values have been preferred and of the interplay between them see Falk, *Future Worlds*, pp. 7-55.

86   RICHARD A. FALK

30. *Kropotkin,* p. 127.
31. Bookchin, *Post-Scarcity Anarchism,* p. 258.
32. *Bakanin,* p. 118.
33. Guérin, *Anarchism,* p. 69.
34. See references in note 19; Woodstock, *Anarchism,* pp. 275-424.
35. Such allegations have been made with respect to Salvador Allende's efforts in the early 1970s to transform the societal base of Chile without dismantling the state apparatus with its strong links to the vested interests of the old order.
36. *Kropotkin,* p. 328.
37. *Kropotkin,* pp. 329-30.
38. *Kropotkin,* p. 330.
39. One of the earliest and most eloquent anarchist critics of the Soviet experience was Emma Goldmann. See her *My Disillusionment with Russia* (Garden City, New York: Doubleday, 1923).
40. Kropotkin's position can be extrapolated from his general anarchist writings; he did not state the anarchist case in his conversations with Lenin.
41. See Kropotkin's excellent essay, "The State: Its Historic Role," in *Kropotkin,* pp. 211-64.
42. *Kropotkin,* p. 231.
43. See perceptive discussion, in Schurmann, *Logic of World Power,* pp. 369-80.
44. Schurmann, *Logic of World Power,* p. 380.
45. For a skeptical interpretation of China's domestic experience see Donald Zagoria, "China by Daylight," *Dissent* (Spring 1975), pp. 135-47.
46. For opposing interpretations on the durability of the state and the state system see Saul H. Mendlovitz, Introduction, in Saul H. Mendlovitz, ed., *On the Creation of a Just World Order* (New York: Free Press, 1975), pp. vii-xvii, and Stanley Hoffmann, "Obstinate or Obsolete? The Fate of the Nation-State and the Case of Western Europe," *Daedalus* (Summer 1966), pp. 862-915.
47. A general interpretation can be found in Robert Heilbroner, *An Inquiry into the Human Prospect* (New York: Norton, 1974); see also Falk, *Future Worlds,* pp. 417-37; Richard A. Falk, "A New Paradigm for International Legal Studies: Prospects and Proposals," *Yale Law Journal* 84: 969-1021 (1975).
48. See Joseph R. Strayer, *On the Medieval Origins of the Modern State* (Princeton University Press, 1970).
49. Goodman, "Ambiguities of Pacifist Politics," p. 136; see also *Kropotkin,* pp. 121-24.

50. Read, *Anarchy and Order,* p. 14.
51. For consideration of world order option see Falk, *Future Worlds,* pp. 150-276; Falk, "A New Paradigm . . ." pp. 999-1017.
52. Zinn, Introduction, Read, *Anarchy and Order,* p. xvii.
53. *Prairie Fire,* Political Statement of the Weather Underground, 1974, p. 3.
54. See Kropotkin letter to Lenin date 21 December 1920, in *Kropotkin,* pp. 338-39.
55. See Schurmann, *Logic of World Power,* p. 369; generally, pp. 268-80.
56. Schurmann, *Logic of World Power,* p. 369.

[3]

Excerpt from *Community, Anarchy and Liberty*, 39–94

2

Social order without the state

My point of departure for the main argument to be developed in this book is that, in *any sort of society*, social order is generally found desirable, but its maintenance is nevertheless problematical and the chief immediate sources of the problem are to do with social order being an example of what economists call a *public* or *collective* good and with individual preferences having certain characteristics. I shall explain and provide a partial defence of this starting point in the following section.

When I say that the maintenance of social order is a problem, I mean roughly that it is not ensured merely by socialisation reinforced by ritual and the gestures and signs of everyday conversation and other social intercourse (important though these are), but requires in addition the use of controls which involve the use of threats. In this sense, the maintenance of social order is a problem which is not peculiar to possessive market societies; it is also a problem (though perhaps a less acute one) for primitive societies without markets and with individual possession of only the barest 'non-strategic' goods; and even in the sort of society envisaged by certain utopian socialist and communitarian anarchist writers it would not be solved as effortlessly as they generally suppose.

2.1 Social order and public goods

Before embarking on the argument about the maintenance of social order, a brief account of the concept of a public good is required.

A good is said to be *public* if it is characterised by some degree of *indivisibility* or *jointness of supply* (with respect to a given public), that is, if consumption of any unit of the good by any member of the public in question does not prevent any other member of the public consuming the same unit, or if, equivalently, any unit of the good, once produced, can be made available to every member of the public.[1] Clearly, there are degrees of indivisibility. The good may be only partially available to some individuals and in varying degrees; and actual consumption of the good may vary between individuals. If every individual's actual consumption of any given unit is the same, then the good is said to be *perfectly* indivisible. This does not imply that every individual's *utility* in consuming the good is the same. An example of a good which approximates fairly closely to perfect indivisibility is clean air (for publics in areas in which the air is uniformly clean). National defence is a standard example of a jointly supplied good, but it is perhaps less than perfectly indivisible (and possibly not viewed as a good at all by every member of the nation). A perfectly *divisible* good, on the other hand, is one which can be divided between individuals, and once any part of it has been appropriated by an individual, the same part cannot simultaneously be made available to others. Such a good is called a *private good*. A private good is thus a polar case, and any good which is not a pure private good is in some degree public. It is clear, then, that a great many goods have *some* element of publicness.

Private goods and public goods are often inseparable; it is not possible to provide the public good without also providing a private good, and conversely. I have cited the standard example of national defence as an imperfect public good: in fact it can be decomposed (analytically at least) into deterrence, which is a pure public good, and protection from attack, which is an

[1] On public goods, see my *Anarchy and Cooperation* (London and New York: Wiley, 1976), ch. 2, and the works cited there.

SOCIAL ORDER WITHOUT THE STATE   41

impure public good (i.e. is imperfectly indivisible), and of
course the expenditures necessary to create national defence
also produce private goods for the shareholders and employees
of business firms.[2]

A good may exhibit indivisibility or jointness of supply and
yet be such that it is possible to prevent particular individuals
from consuming it. A road or bridge or park is such a good.
Once supplied to one individual, it *can* be made available to
others but it need not be, for particular individuals can be
excluded. If this is not possible, the good is said to exhibit *nonexcludability*. Clearly, if a good is non-excludable it is not
possible to make an individual pay for consuming or using it, as
it is in the case of roads, bridges and parks, for which tolls and
admission charges can be imposed on users. Some indivisible
goods are necessarily non-excludable; it is simply not possible
to exclude particular individuals from consuming them. This is
more or less true of clean air and many other environmental
public goods. But many indivisible goods can be supplied in
either the excludable mode or the non-excludable.

For some goods which have been cited in the past as instances
of non-excludable goods, it has been claimed that a closer
inspection would show that they *can* be provided in the
excludable mode (though often at an 'uneconomic' cost) or
that they can be decomposed into several component goods
some of which are divisible or, though indivisible, are excludable.
Generally speaking in these cases, if excludable provision of
the good is to be brought about, there has to be a redefinition
of existing property rights or creation of individual property
rights where none existed before, as well as technological
innovation.[3] This argument has been made in connection with

---

[2] Cf. William Loehr and Todd Sandler, eds., *Public Goods and Public Policy*
(Beverley Hills: Sage, 1978), p. 23 and ch. 6.
[3] For some illustrations see David Friedman, *The Machinery of Freedom: Guide to a
Radical Capitalism* (New York: Harper and Row, 1973), for example in ch. 15
('Sell the streets').

social order and I shall have more to say about it later in this section and in Section 2.3 which examines the claim that social order can be satisfactorily provided by private firms competing in the open market. It is true that it is usually taken for granted that social order is a non-excludable public good,[4] and it does indeed turn out that some of the component goods which make up 'social order' are very imperfectly indivisible and can be provided in the excludable mode. Nevertheless, as I shall argue below, there remains an important element of publicness.

If a good is both indivisible and non-excludable, it is possible for an individual to be a 'free rider', that is, to consume or benefit from the good without contribution to its production costs. More precisely, if some of the good is already in supply, then an individual may be a free rider only if the good exhibits some degree of indivisibility *and* the individual in question is not in fact excluded from consumption, whether he contributes or not; and if the good is not yet provided in any amount, then an individual can *expect* to be able to take a free ride only if the good will be jointly supplied *and* he expects that he will not be excluded. If exclusion is actually impossible, this second condition obviously obtains; but it may also obtain even when the good is to be excludable.

Under certain conditions (to be discussed below) an individual may decide to attempt to be a free rider, making no contribution to the cost of providing a public good in the hope of benefiting from others' contributions. If every member of the public so decides, the public good will not be provided at all. Non-contribution would be the rational course of action for an egoist (one who considers only his own costs and benefits) if the costs to him of making any contribution exceed the benefits *to him* of the additional amount of the public good which could be provided out of his contribution.

[4] As I did in *Anarchy and Cooperation*.

Relatively straightforward and important instances of public goods and the free rider problem are to be found in connection with problems of resources and the environment. Consider for example a polluted lake, a receptacle for sewage and industrial wastes. Let us assume that an improvement in the quality of the water in the lake is considered to be a good by all the owners of houses and factories on its shore, who like to swim in it, sail on it, use it in their industrial processes, and so on, if it is sufficiently clean. If the water is well-circulated around the lake, such an improvement would be a public good for this group of people; it would be both indivisible (tending to perfect indivisibility with increasingly thorough circulation) and non-excludable (assuming that particular individuals cannot be or are not in fact excluded from using the lake). A lakeshore dweller or factory-owner could contribute to an improvement in water quality by taking his wastes elsewhere, treating them before discharging them into the lake or modifying his product. Making such a contribution to the public good is costly, and each member of the public good would most prefer everyone else to make a contribution while he has a free ride; but he would prefer everyone to contribute, including himself, to nobody doing anything about the polluted lake. Despite everyone having a common interest in a cleaner lake, nobody would voluntarily contribute to improving it if the costs of his doing so would exceed the benefits *to him* of the improvement in the water's quality which would result from *his* contribution.

Most, if not all, jointly supplied goods are characterised by a certain degree of *rivalness*. A good is said to be *rival* to the extent that the *consumption* of a unit of the good by one individual affects the benefits to others who *consume* the same unit. In the polar case of a private good, the consumption of a particular unit prevents any other individual from consuming it at all, and it is said to be *perfectly rival*. Such public facilities as parks, beaches, roads and 'wilderness' areas are examples of goods with some degree of rivalness: beyond a certain level of use, an individual's utility from consumption is lowered as a result of consumption by others.

Related to, but distinct from publicness is the phenomenon of *externality* or external effect. On the widest definition, an externality is said to be present whenever an individual's utility is affected by an activity of some other individual. On this account, most activities exert some sort of externality. A more restrictive definition stipulates that the interdependence between the two individuals must be 'untraded', that is to say, the individual affected by the externality is not compensated for the harm done him in the case of a negative externality and does not pay for the benefit accruing to him in the case of a positive externality. On either the wider or the more restrictive account of 'externality', the production of a non-excludable indivisible good produces external effects, but externalities are involved in interactions other than those associated with the production or consumption of public goods.

I asserted at the outset that social order is a public good. This assertion must now be amplified and defended.

In the most restrictive of its common usages, 'social order' refers to an absence, more or less complete, of violence, a state of affairs in which people are relatively safe from physical attack.

On a somewhat broader view, 'social order' is security of property (against theft and damage at the hands of other individuals) as well as of persons. This is the order Hobbes was concerned with and he called it Peace. 'Property' is here a shorthand for a variety of entitlements or use-rights. These range from property in the narrow modern sense of lawful, exclusive, individual ownership backed ultimately by the force of the state to the more conditional and non-exclusive usufructs sanctioned by the community in primitive societies. The point in both cases is that the individual or household has an entitlement, sanctioned by the community at large or by the state, to control and use the resources in question. In primitive societies ownership of important resources, especially land, is formally vested in chiefs, clans, lineages, bands or a kin-based collective core of the living group, but the households have access to the resources and day to day control over their use – conditional entitlements which in tribal societies can be over-ridden by the chief or the lineage of which they are a part.[5]

It is widely assumed that social order, viewed as security of persons and their property, is a good and furthermore that it is a public good. That it is a *good* (i.e. is desired) is widely taken for granted because life *without* it is acknowledged to be undesirable. For a strong statement there is the famous passage in Chapter 13 of *Leviathan* where the state of nature, 'wherein men live without other security, than what their own strength, and their own invention shall furnish them withall', is described by Hobbes as a condition in which

> there is no place for Industry; because the fruit thereof is uncertain: and consequently no Culture of the Earth; no Navigation, nor use of the commodities that may be imported by Sea; no commodious Building; no Instruments of moving, and removing such things as require much force; no Knowledge of the face of the Earth; no account of Time; no Arts; no Letters; no Society; and which is worst of all, continuall feare, and danger of violent death; And the life of man, solitary, poore, nasty, brutish, and short.

Without necessarily agreeing with the details of this picture, we can agree that, because it is a precondition of the pursuit and attainment of a variety of desired ends, security of person and property is generally found attractive (to put it no more strongly). But this conclusion needs to be qualified and tightened

[5] See Sahlins, *Stone Age Economics*, especially pp. 92–3. For a detailed hunting–gathering example, see Richard Borshay Lee, *The !Kung San: Men, Women, and Work in a Foraging Society* (Cambridge: Cambridge University Press, 1979), especially pp. 118–19, 334–9, 360–1.

up. There seems little doubt that almost everyone prefers more security of person and property to less, at least if everything else remains the same, that is to say, if he can enjoy without cost greater security without others doing so. In this sense, security is clearly a good. Of course, an individual can enjoy greater security without others doing so only if security can be provided as a *private* good – as indeed it can, to some extent, in the form of bodyguards and other forms of individual protection having no or negligible side effects on the security of others. But it cannot be inferred from an individual's preference for security for himself that he has a preference for greater security for everyone. This applies to any individual *ceteris paribus* preferences. An individual may want to be the owner of a car, other things being equal; but this does not imply that he prefers everyone owning a car to nobody owning one, since universal ownership brings with it costs to the individual (in the form of danger, pollution, and so on) as well as the assumed benefits of his owning a car, and these must be set against the benefits of safety, health, peace and quiet of universal non-ownership (as well as the costs of his not owning a car). Similarly, a preference for greater wealth rather than less, other things being equal, does not imply a desire for greater wealth if others are to have greater wealth as well. Again, this is so, even if we disregard envy and other ways in which the individual's utility depends on comparisons between others' wealth and his own, because there may (in the view of the individual) be costs associated with living in a generally wealthier society which are absent in a poorer one.[6]

Security of person and property can, as I have said, be provided as a private good and so enjoyed exclusively by a single individual. But there are a wider range of ways in which it can be provided as an indivisible and non-excludable good, for

[6] Cf. Brian Barry, *The Liberal Theory of Justice* (Oxford: Clarendon Press, 1973), ch. 11.

SOCIAL ORDER WITHOUT THE STATE   47

example in the form of police, law courts, and so on, operating
so as to enhance the security of every individual's person and
property. In this case (and in the case of any non-excludable
indivisible good), an individual's *ceteris paribus* preference for
more rather than less is of a hypothetical nature; he cannot
have more security (or cleaner water in his lake or cleaner air
over his city) without others having more also. He may or may
not prefer an increased provision of security in these circumstances. He may *not* desire such security because, say, he is a
member of a society with unequally distributed property who
has little property to protect and who expects to benefit from a
free-for-all and to be able to defend his gains, and because the
security in question – which in any case would generally be far
from perfectly indivisible – affords him much less protection
than many others enjoy. ('The empirical data . . . make it
abundantly clear that the poor do not receive the same
treatment at the hands of the agents of law-enforcement as the
well-to-do or middle class. This differential treatment is systematic and complete.')[7] For such a person, who would want
security for himself *only if* it were denied (some) others, it is not
clear that non-excludable, indivisible security is to be reckoned
a good at all. We might say that when he can get it privately, it is
a good; but when it can only be had publicly, it is for him a bad.
If it is indeed the case that, while some people have the
Hobbesian preference for security of person and property over
the 'state of nature', there are others who, for whatever reason,
have the opposite preference, then it could be (and has been)
argued that the likely upshot is that security is maintained and
enforced unilaterally by those who benefit from it. It could also
be argued that this asymmetric social order is just the sort of
order which is in fact maintained by modern states; and some

---

[7] William J. Chambliss and Robert B. Seidman, *Law, Order and Power* (Reading,
Mass.: Addison-Wesley, 1971), p. 475.

(Marxist) writers would argue that this is necessarily so, that this is a central part of what the state *is*.

Whatever the truth of these arguments, it is surely the case that a sufficiently symmetric security would be preferred by everyone to insecurity; that there is a security of person and property which is desired by all. Thus, that part of social order (viewed as security of person and property) which cannot be provided in the form of private goods – and I shall argue in Section 2.3 that there is such a part – is a public *good*. This is true *a fortiori* of the more restricted conception of social order as safety from physical attack, or security of persons.

There are two other, much broader, common conceptions of social order. According to the first of these, social order lies in the day-to-day *predictability* of social life. There is social order, on this account, to the extent that most of the time people do not have their expectations upset – they do not venture unwarned onto the (English) road one morning to discover that everyone is driving on the right-hand side, for example. For most of the people most of the time the existence of this kind of order is convenient or comforting. But it is not itself a public good; only parts of it are public goods, or rather, the production of certain public goods contributes to it. Security of person and property, for example, would presumably be a part of social order in this broader sense, and as we have seen this is typically a public good. Consider, however, the almost universal practice of driving on the left in Great Britain. This too contributes to social order in the broad sense, but no public good is involved. It is a *convention*, a solution to a coordination problem, and once a convention is established there is no incentive for any participant to deviate from conformity to it.[8] An individual

---

[8] See David Lewis, *Convention: A Philosophical Study* (Cambridge, Mass.: Harvard University Press, 1969).

benefits from the provision of a public good *whether or not* he contributes, but this is plainly not so in the case of a convention; there is little satisfaction to be had in driving on the right when others are driving on the left. A second reason why social order in the sense of predictability is not a public good is that while much of this order depends on general conformity to established norms, customs, conventions and other regularities, some of a particular individual's day-to-day expectations may be based on established relations with specific others which may be neither customary, conventional or normal in the wider society nor productive of a public good even for the individuals involved.

According to the second broad conception of social order, it consists of a general conformity to social norms. Social order on this account is not a public good, though again the production of certain public goods contributes to it. And this is so, whether we think of norms as regularities in behaviour or action, or as prescriptions or standards, or as a combination of these. I prefer the last of these approaches, according to which a social norm is a prescription or standard with which most people actually comply. Plainly, this account of social order as general conformity with norms has much in common with the preceding account, for a degree of conformity to norms conduces to, indeed is a condition of, the day-to-day predictability of social life, and it encompasses the two narrow accounts of social order, provided that the norms to which there is to be conformity include prescriptions against assaults on persons and their property. Conformity to these two norms, and to many others which would presumably be included in those to which conformity is required for social order, contributes to the production of a public good (with the qualifications noted earlier). But there are many norms, conformity to which does not contribute to the production of a public good. These include conventions, which if they are solutions to pure coordination problems, emerge 'spontaneously' and do not need to be maintained by any sort of controls, because there is no incentive for any participant to deviate from them (as there is for a rational egoist to deviate from agreement to contribute to the provision of public goods – that is, to be a free rider).[9]

My concern here is with social order of a kind which is thought desirable by most people in any society but which at the same time is not maintained without controls of one sort or another. This is true of any form of social order which is a public good. It is thus true, with certain qualifications, of the narrow conceptions of social order as security of persons and their property. It is social order in these senses which I shall have chiefly in mind in the following discussion of social control.[10] But, as we have seen, there are public goods elements in social order viewed either as predictability or as conformity to norms, and most of what I shall have to say about social control applies to the production of these public goods. It applies also to the production of public goods not involved in social order.

Now insofar as social order is a (non-excludable) public good, there is a problem, as we have seen, about its provision. Because an individual benefits when a public good is provided whether or not he has made any contribution to its provision, he would most prefer everyone *else* to provide it. Under certain conditions, the result is that the public good is not provided at all or a less than optimal amount is provided (that is, everyone would prefer a larger amount to be provided). This, as Mancur Olson has argued in his well-known study of *The Logic of Collective Action*,[11] is more likely to happen in larger publics than

[9] See Lewis, *Convention*.
[10] I shall use the term 'social control' in the correspondingly narrow sense according to which it refers only to the production of behaviour which contributes to this sort of social order.

in smaller ones. The chief reason for this is that the larger the public, the smaller the benefit which accrues to any individual member from the additional amount of the public good provided out of his contribution, so that in a relatively large group this benefit is likely to be exceeded by the cost to him of making the contribution, whereas in a relatively small group this is less likely to be the case. A further reason is that the difficulty and costs of organising the provision of the public good are likely to increase with the size of the group. The large group will provide itself with the public good only if there is a *selective* incentive for an individual to contribute, a private benefit which the individual can enjoy *only if* he contributes. Thus, a trade union is primarily formed in order to provide for its members certain public goods, such as higher wages and better working conditions. But no individual, though he desires such things, would pay his dues; he would hope to be a 'free rider'. Hence the 'closed shop' is operated (employment is conditional upon membership), members enjoy sickness benefits, and so on. These things are selective benefits. The respect and approval of one's community for contributing to a public good by refraining from violence, for example, is also a selective incentive.

Olson's conclusion is broadly correct, but partly for reasons which do not appear in his argument. In the first place, the relation between the size of the public and the amount of the public good its members will provide for themselves in the absence of selective incentives is somewhat more complicated than Olson supposed. In particular, the extent of an individual's contribution to the provision of a public good depends not only on the size of the public but also on the individual's utility function (which tells us how much of a *numéraire* private good he is willing to sacrifice for a given increase in the supply of the public good) and on the transformation function (which

---

[11] Cambridge, Mass.: Harvard University Press, 1965.

specifies the quantity of the public good which can be produced with a given input of the private good) and on the degrees of divisibility and of rivalness of the public good.[12]

The second problem with Olson's analysis of public goods provision is that it is entirely static. Its conclusions about public goods provision are derived from assumptions about individual preferences at one point in time. Individuals are supposed, in effect, to make only one choice, once and for all, about how much to contribute to the provision of the public good. Time plays no part in the analysis. Plainly, with respect to most public goods, the choice of whether or not to contribute and how much to contribute is a recurring choice and in some cases it is a choice which is permanently before the individual. This is certainly true of the individual's choice of whether or not to act peaceably, to refrain from violence, robbery and fraud, and so on. However, although a more realistic, dynamic analysis of public goods provision would be vastly more complex and has yet to be developed, recent preliminary work in this direction suggests that there is greater scope for rational cooperation to provide public goods than the static model allows, but that it nevertheless remains true that voluntary cooperation to provide optimal amounts of public goods is less likely in relatively large groups than in smaller ones.[13]

The introduction of time in a more dynamic analysis of the process of public goods provision allows for the possibility of *conditional* cooperation. An individual can make his or her contribution to the provision of a public good conditional on others making contributions. He can, for example, refrain

[12] See, for example, John Chamberlin, 'Provision of collective goods as a function of group size', *American Political Science Review*, 68 (1974), 707–16; Taylor, *Anarchy and Cooperation*, ch. 2; and Russell Hardin, *Collective Action* (Baltimore: Johns Hopkins University Press for Resources for the Future, 1982), ch. 3.

[13] This was a conclusion of a grossly simplified dynamic analysis carried out in *Anarchy and Cooperation*, ch. 3.

from theft or from discharging wastes into a lake or from
hunting whales, or he can make contributions to an organisation
which seeks to get a public good provided, just as long as a
sufficient number of others do. Such conditional cooperation
can under certain conditions be rational, and if enough people
cooperate conditionally, then the public good – some amount
of it at any rate – gets provided.[14] Much voluntary cooperation
in the provision of public goods is no doubt of this conditional
kind. Unfortunately, it too is less likely to occur in large groups
than in small ones, since a conditional cooperator must be able
to monitor the behaviour of others in the group so as to
reassure himself that they are doing their parts and not taking
advantage of him. Clearly, as the size of the group increases,
this mutual monitoring becomes increasingly difficult and the
'tacit contract' of conditional cooperation becomes increasingly
fragile. In a relatively small group, on the other hand, especially
one with an unchanging or only very slowly changing membership, people come into contact with and can observe the
behaviour of most of their fellows, so that conditional cooperation is more likely to be workable. But even here, unless the
group is *very* small, the arrangement is obviously a precarious
one if it has no other supports. The nature of those supports
will be discussed in Section 2.4.

2.2 Social order and the state

This argument – that people will not voluntarily cooperate to
provide themselves with certain public goods if they are
members of a large public – provides the foundation for an
appealing justification of the state. The state, according to this
liberal theory, is necessary because it alone can maintain

---

[14] For the details of one such analysis (which are too messy to be usefully
summarised here) see *Anarchy and Cooperation*, ch. 3.

conditions in which contribution to the provision of public goods *is* rational, essentially by altering the structure of incentives facing potential free riders. The first full, explicit statement of this argument was set forth by Hobbes. He was the first to give a clear account of the free rider problem and to understand its importance for social and political life. The heart of his justification of the state has been accepted by many political theorists, though they all professed to reject his theory; and modern economists who have written about public goods generally take for granted the Hobbesian inference about the necessity or desirability of the state. The public goods Hobbes was concerned with were above all domestic order (in the sense of security of persons and their property) and also defence against foreign aggression. More recently, essentially the same argument has been made by a number of writers concerned with environmental problems. According to them, such public goods as cleaner air, rivers and lakes, control of population growth, protection of wilderness and maintenance of ecological diversity must be provided by the state or the state must ensure that people will cooperate to provide them. The persuasiveness of this justification of the state – and it has always been a popular one – lies in the fact that the state, on this view, exists to further *common* interests, to do what everybody wants done. Other arguments for the state, for example that income redistribution is desirable and can be achieved only through the intervention of the state, do not appeal to common interests – not, at any rate, in an obvious or uncontroversial way.[15]

As a justification of the state the liberal theory rests on shaky foundations and is fundamentally flawed. I have made this critical case in detail elsewhere (in *Anarchy and Cooperation*), but I

---

[15] The claim that redistribution is a public good is discussed in Section 3.2 below.

should like to summarise very briefly three of the arguments
made in the earlier work because they are relevant to the
argument of the rest of the present book. The first point is to
do with the assumptions on which the entire liberal theory is
founded. It is an essential feature of the theory that it takes
individual preferences as given and fixed. In particular, it is
effectively assumed that every individual is an egoist, in the
sense that he is concerned solely with his own costs and
benefits. He chooses not to contribute to the provision of a
public good because the cost *to him* of making a contribution
exceeds the benefit *to him* of the additional amount of the public
good which could be provided out of his contribution. (In
Hume's version of this justification of the state, individuals are
assumed to be both egoistic and altruistic, but the altruism – in
the form of 'private' and extensive benevolence – is effectively
assumed to be sufficiently outweighed by the egoism for the
resulting individual preference structures, when these also
incorporate a discounting of future benefits, to make non-
contribution to the provision of public goods the rational
course of action. Interestingly, Hume anticipates the 'size'
argument of Olson's *Logic of Collective Action* and makes it clear
in the *Treatise* that his argument applies only to *large* societies,
several times proclaiming his belief that the members of small
societies may live without government – though the belief
seems to be based in large part on his view that small societies
tend to be 'uncultivated', that is, lacking very many possessions
to quarrel about.)[16] Clearly, if an individual is sufficiently
altruistic (in the sense of attaching some weight to others'
benefits as well as his own), the total benefit (to himself and
others) of contributing will exceed his costs, and therefore he
will contribute. In other words, Olson's argument and the

---

[16] I have discussed this, and Hume's justification of government generally, in
Anarchy and Cooperation, ch. 6.

liberal theory of the state critically depend on the assumption
that individuals are pure egoists or at least are 'insufficiently'
altruistic; with enough altruism, this rationale for the state
evaporates. It might be thought that this observation is
irrelevant or of theoretical interest only, for we have only to
look around us (at the amount of violence and robbery, or at
environmental pollution and resource depletion, for example)
to see that people are *not* sufficiently altruistic because they do
not in fact cooperate in the provision of public goods. It may be
the case, however, that this lack of altruism (at least in public
goods interaction) is in part the product of state intervention –
that it characterises people who have for a long time lived
under states. In *Anarchy and Cooperation* I argued that this is in
fact the case; and that preferences change over time as a result
of the activities of the state. Now if the state is in part the cause
of changes in individual preferences, then clearly it cannot be
deduced from the structure of preferences in the absence of the
state that the state is desirable (as is done in the liberal theory);
for the state modifies, one might say, the assumptions from
which its desirability has been deduced. If individual preferences
change over time, the question of the desirability (or 'preferability') of the state becomes much more complex than it is in
the static liberal theory; and if preferences change as a result of
the state itself, then it is not even clear what is *meant* by the
desirability of the state.[17] Any theory which attempts to justify
or recommend or prescribe an institution, practice, rule, new
technology or whatever, by reference to fixed, given preferences
(for example, by arguing that the institution, or whatever, is, in
terms of the given preferences, unanimously preferred to the

[17] An analogous point has been made about methods of social choice by
Kenneth Arrow, who nevertheless bases his work on the assumption that
individual preferences are not affected by the decision process itself. See his
Social Choice and Individual Values, 2nd edition (New York: Wiley, 1963),
pp. 7–8.

status quo or one which ensures Pareto-optimal outcomes) falls foul of the same fundamental objection, if the object to be justified has some effect over time on the individual preferences. Much of neo-classical welfare economics is vitiated by this objection.[18] I am not objecting here to the use of the assumption of pure egoism in *explanatory* theories, at least not those which are narrowly circumscribed (especially temporally) in the scope of their application. Without this assumption, or one close to it, it would indeed be hard to understand why, amongst other things, so many public goods are under-supplied. I am objecting to its use in 'normative' theories – theories which seek to justify or prescribe.

It seems to me that this general argument clearly applies to the liberal (or perhaps we should say 'neo-classical') theory of the state, for it would be hard to deny that individual preferences are affected, at least in the long run, by the state.

The second argument against the liberal justification of the state also concerns a dynamic effect and it is that the state tends to undermine the conditions which make the alternative to it workable, and in this way makes itself more desirable. It does this by weakening or destroying *community*, which is, as I shall argue, a necessary condition for the maintenance of social order without the state. Of course states were not alone in contributing to the decline of community. In particular, in the modern period it is difficult to disentangle the contributions of the growth of the state and the expansion of capitalism. But certainly the state, almost by definition, undermined communities by displacing many of the local activities once accomplished through reciprocity (one of the three core characteristics of community: see Section 1.4) by various forms of central

---

[18] Herbert Gintis argues something like this in 'A radical analysis of welfare economics and individual development', *Quarterly Journal of Economics*, 86 (1972), 572–99, and in 'Welfare criteria with endogenous preferences: the economics of education', *International Economic Review*, 15 (1974), 415–30.

58   COMMUNITY, ANARCHY AND LIBERTY

mediation, including centralised redistributive, welfare and
insurance activities and the provision of a range of public goods
(local as well as national).[19] As part of this process, the
formation – in the face of centuries of 'tenacious and widespread
resistance' – of the modern national states in Europe involved
'co-opting, subordinating or destroying' village councils and
other deliberative assemblies and 'abridging, destroying or
absorbing' a variety of rights previously lodged in less inclusive
political units, including the right of households to pasture
animals on the village common and the right of the head of the
household to punish its members.[20] We shall see in Section 3.3
that at the very origin of the state the normal process of fission,
which characterises all stateless societies and ensures that they
remain small communities, is halted because it has become
impossible or unattractive for part of the community to split
off and establish a replicate community elsewhere. This contain-
ment of the normal centrifugal forces, which results in a
community growing in size or being absorbed into another
community and losing its autonomy, is a central part of the
process of state formation and growth; and although the
constituent communities are eventually assimilated to each
other culturally (through increasing communication, trade and
so on, and through the efforts usually taken by the state to
institute a common language, religion, legal system, educational
curriculum, etc.), the resulting society becomes too large to be
a community in anything except a very weak sense: direct and
many-sided relations and the practice of reciprocity are not
possible on a large scale.

The third criticism of the liberal justification of the state

[19] Reciprocity, it should be remembered, is not the same thing as altruism
(though it involves short-term altruism) or charity or benevolence.
[20] Charles Tilly, 'Reflections on the history of European state-making', in Tilly,
ed., *The Formation of National States in Western Europe* (Princeton, NJ: Princeton
University Press, 1975), especially at pp. 21–4, 37 and 71.

which is relevant to the argument of this book concerns the concluding step in the justification. Even if the premises of the theory are accepted and even if we accept too the argument that the members of large publics will not voluntarily provide themselves with public goods – including the fundamental public good of social order – it does not follow that the state is the *only* means of ensuring the supply of such goods or that other means would not suffice and must be supplemented by the state. All that can be inferred is that, if public goods are to be provided, *some* means must be found of getting people to do their part in providing them.

Broadly speaking, three 'methods' have been proposed for ensuring the provision of the public good of social order. In practice the methods are found in various combinations. To characterise them briefly, they are: the state, the market and the community. The claim that social order can be satisfactorily provided by private firms competing in the marketplace is the subject of the next section. I then turn to the third, communitarian anarchist, method which is my main concern.

2.3 *Social order on the market*

The last two sections of this chapter will give an account of how social order is maintained in stateless societies and argue that social order without the state can be maintained only in community. I shall not take very seriously the claim that the *market* is an alternative to the state as a sole means of ensuring the provision of social order. The less radical claim, made by many laissez-faire liberals, that *some* of the goods whose provision constitutes social order can be put on the market, has, I think, some validity. But the full claim, made especially in the United States by people calling themselves 'anarcho-capitalists' or 'libertarians', that *all* the components of social order could be satisfactorily put on the market is in my view indefensible. In market societies, social order is maintained by a combination of 'state', 'community' and 'market'; and whereas order was once well-maintained in societies lacking states and markets, and in certain contemporary societies is imperfectly maintained principally (though never quite wholly) by the state, I doubt that it could be very successfully maintained in any societies by markets alone.

The argument which I shall make about social order and community shares with the liberal argument about social order and the state a common starting point, namely that there are significant externalities associated with the provision of social order and hence there is potentially a free rider problem. Libertarians generally minimise the importance of these externalities or even deny their existence altogether. They do not deny the existence of *all* externalities or that *some* goods are public. It is, for example, admitted by some libertarians that there would be a problem in an anarcho-capitalist society about national defence because it provides, amongst other things, a public good. The solutions they give to this particular public goods problem are unconvincing, though they have offered more plausible solutions to the problems of providing certain other public goods. It is suggested, for example, that an entrepreneur would get each member of the relevant public to sign a contract committing him to contributing to the provision of the public good on condition that every other member participates.[21] The trouble with this and other proposals is that they are likely to work only in very small publics (smaller even than the communities discussed below).[22]

But so far as social order and many other public goods are

---

[21] David Friedman, *The Machinery of Freedom*, ch. 34.

[22] In part for the same reasons (mentioned earlier) that conditional cooperation in the provision of public goods is less likely as the size of the public increases. Friedman admits (in *The Machinery of Freedom*) that all his proposals suffer from this size difficulty.

concerned, the libertarian view is that, if private property rights are greatly extended, rigorously defined and strictly defended, there would be no externalities or there would be a great reduction in activities with external costs.[23] Thus, if streets were in private hands, their owners would (it is assumed) have an interest in keeping them safe. If they were owned jointly by the landlords of rented property on them, it would pay the landlords to have order maintained on them because this would increase demand for their property and increase their incomes from rents. Similarly, traders who owned the street they operated on would pay to keep order on it. Or, if streets but not the properties on them were owned by 'street companies', the companies would charge the property owners for maintaining the streets and their safety, and the profits and stock values of these companies would depend on their providing a good service.[24]

In these libertarian proposals the protection of person and property is to be provided of course by private firms – 'protection agencies' – and a central claim of most libertarian accounts is that in the absence of the state a market in protection services would arise which would be and would remain *competitive*. The market would therefore be efficient. The competing firms would provide people with just the amounts and types of security they wanted. The inefficiency, corruption and brutality found in the state police forces would be bad for business (whereas state police forces continue to get

---

[23] If, for example, lakes, rivers and seas were privately owned, then according to this argument potential polluters would be deterred by the high costs they would have to pay (by prior agreement or in court). If every individual's property rights in his or her own body were rigorously defined and defended, there would be far less air pollution. And so on. 'Only private property rights will ensure an end to pollution-invasion of resources' – Murray Rothbard, *For a New Liberty; the Libertarian Manifesto*, revised edition (New York: Collier, 1978), p. 203.

[24] Cf. Rothbard, *For a New Liberty*, ch. 11, and Friedman, *The Machinery of Freedom*, ch. 15.

paid no matter what sort of service they provide). And when two protection agencies come into conflict in defence of their respective clients' grievances, it would not pay them to shoot it out; they would take their problem to arbitration (there would be a market in firms specialising in arbitration, and even, in some libertarian schemes, a market in systems of law). And so on.

This is the competitive scenario favoured by libertarians who are also anarcho-capitalists. Other libertarians are less sanguine about the likely outcome of competition between protection agencies, and admit that the prospect of violence between them (and other problems peculiar to the provision of order and defence) make necessary a minimal state whose sole function is the provision of internal and external security; or they argue, as Robert Nozick has done in *Anarchy, State and Utopia*, that the upshot of competition between protection agencies would be the emergence in each area of a single dominant protection agency (a proto-state, in effect, but not a state), since every individual, if he wanted to buy protection at all, would gravitate towards the largest firm, for this would tend to come out on top in disputes with smaller firms. According to another monopolistic scenario, which in Brian Barry's view is more plausible than Nozick's and in fact 'corresponds closely to a commonly found reality', an agency declares that it will 'represent the collective interests of Aryans against Jews, settlers against aboriginal inhabitants, whites against blacks, Protestants against Catholics, or any other against others', always supporting a member of the privileged group in a dispute against a member of an excluded group and perhaps even preventing excluded groups from forming their own protection agencies.[25]

[25] Brian Barry, review of Robert Nozick, *Anarchy, State and Utopia, Political Theory*, 3 (1975), 331–6.

Is the market in protection of persons and their property, in the absence of a state, likely to be competitive or monopolistic or oligopolistic? If one of the last two, what sort of restrictive business practices, if any, are firms likely to engage in? Will the protection agencies be as well-behaved as the anarcho-capitalists suppose? I don't think that any of these questions can be answered with confidence. The right sort of evidence just isn't there. Oligopoly is in fact the commonest market form in the industrial West and near-monopoly is common, but the libertarians would argue (with some justice in many cases) that these market structures survive only with the help of the state. There are, furthermore, already extensive markets in security services in some countries,[26] with firms contracting to protect individuals, factories, art galleries, office-blocks, department stores and other premises, to collect debts and pursue adulterous spouses, to transport cash, bullion and other valuables, and so on. But the nature of these markets and the behaviour of the firms operating in them cannot provide reliable evidence of the kind required to judge the libertarians' claim, since the markets are not free: they are subject to government regulation and operate only in areas neglected by the state's police forces or as a supplement to them. In England, at any rate, this (regulated and truncated) market in security seems to be fairly competitive, but the personnel and methods of many firms are apparently such as to cast doubt on the optimistic scenarios of the anarcho-capitalists. A recent survey of private police in the United Kingdom[27] quotes from an article in the *Police Review* of March 1972 by Chief Inspector Sydney Pleece, who writes that, in the estimation of the Metropolitan Crime Prevention Branch, 'of about 150–200 medium to very small companies offering

---

[26] There are currently about as many private policemen in England as there are in the regular police force. See Hilary Draper, *Private Police* (Harmondsworth: Penguin, 1978), p. 23.

[27] Draper, *Private Police*, p. 117.

various security services in the Metropolis, some 30–40 *per cent*
are to be regarded as dubious, either because the principals
have criminal records or employ men with such records or
because of limited ability, equipment or unsatisfactory selling
methods'.

Whether the market in security is competitive or not, its
ability to supply the security people want will be seriously
hampered by the presence of externalities. As I have said,
libertarians generally minimise the importance of externalities
in this area or deny their existence altogether. It is true that
much of what goes to make up social order can be decomposed
into particular *private* goods and that this fact is ignored by
those who treat social order as a public good *tout court*. When I
hire a firm to protect my person or house or factory, the firm's
service benefits mainly myself. But even if the firm's agents
decline to intervene when they see property being stolen from
the house of my neighbour (who is not one of their clients),
there is nevertheless *some* external benefit to others arising
from my purchase of protection. For a protection agency, like
the state, would have to provide security mainly by *deterring*
theft and violence with threats that it would track down the
offender and exact retribution (and of course it would have to
try, at least some of the time, to carry out these threats when
deterrence failed, so that the threats remained credible). Thus
everyone in the area covered by the protection agency benefits
from any individual's purchase of protection – *unless* the
agencies all publish (or aspiring violators can otherwise obtain)
a list of those persons who have bought no protection.
Deterrence, then, is a non-excludable public good.[28] With or
without this proviso about knowledge of the non-contributors,
it is hard to see how, for example, a group of traders, who

---

[28] If a public good can be provided in an *excludable* mode and exclusion is not too
costly, then competitive private production can be efficient. See Harold
Demsetz, 'The private production of public goods', *Journal of Law and
Economics*, 13 (1970), 293–306.

SOCIAL ORDER WITHOUT THE STATE   65

engage a firm to keep their street safe for customers, do not provide *some* benefit to others, including fellow-traders on their street who decline to contribute. In other words, there is, as I have already argued in other ways in Section 2.1, a non-excludable public good element in the provision of security; and therefore in general the market will not produce a Pareto-optimal outcome: individuals will not get all the security they want.

If the market in security is *not* competitive – if it consists mainly of a monopoly firm or of colluding oligopolists – then it will in any case resemble a state, being a repository of concentrated force and political specialisation. Finally, whether the market is competitive or not, it must be remembered that the product is a peculiar one: when we buy cars or shoes or telephone services we do not give the firm power based on force, but armed protection agencies, like the state, make customers (their own and others') vulnerable, and having given them power we cannot be sure that they will use it only for our protection.

2.4 Social order in stateless societies

I asserted earlier that, broadly speaking, there are three ways of ensuring the provision of the public good of social order, which can be summarily characterised as the state, the market and the community. Having rejected the market, I shall argue that the other alternative to the state, community, is in fact a necessary condition for the maintenance of stateless social order. I begin the argument in this section by looking at the range of means by which social order was in fact maintained in the stateless primitive societies and other quasi-anarchic societies introduced in Section 1.5. Most of these means of maintaining order are still to be found in modern societies with well-developed states, but in atrophied and attenuated forms.

The means of maintaining social order in primitive societies fall (though not very neatly) into three categories. In the first place there are of course the social controls proper, by which I mean the use of threats and offers (and throffers) of negative and positive sanctions. In the second category are the various processes of socialisation, which can be thought of as setting the stage for the use of the social controls by moulding the preferences which the threats and offers go to work on, as well as helping reduce a community's need to rely on them. And finally, certain basic structural characteristics of these societies contribute to or play a role in the maintenance of social order; they are not *specifically* mechanisms of social control and cannot be separated from what is controlled, but provide a framework in which the social controls can be used and establish conditions for their effectiveness. Let us consider these first.

The spirit of Marcel Mauss's celebrated essay on *The Gift* is that in primitive society peace and order is secured by reciprocal giving. For Marshall Sahlins, in his essays on Mauss and primitive exchange, this reciprocity apparently alone suffices to maintain social order. He writes, 'the gift is the primitive way of achieving peace that in civil society is secured by the State',[29] and he argues that Mauss's thinking bore a close resemblance to a central part of Hobbes's argument in *Leviathan*. Without the state, in the Hobbesian 'state of nature', there is a rough equality of vulnerability amongst individuals and they live without security of person and property, not necessarily fighting amongst themselves but with this potentiality ever present. So too, in primitive society, without gift-giving, Mauss saw a rough equality of force, though among groups rather than individuals, and an ever present predisposition to open fighting between them. Mauss wrote that 'To refuse to give, or to fail to invite is – like refusing to accept – the equivalent of a declaration of war; it is a refusal of friendship and intercourse',

[29] Marshall Sahlins, *Stone Age Economics*, p. 169.

and such refusals are made on pain of 'private or open warfare'. To get out and to stay out of this primitive 'state of nature', men 'learnt to renounce what was theirs and made contracts to give and repay', and, 'opposing reason to emotion', they succeeded in 'substituting alliance, gift and commerce for war, isolation and stagnation'.[30]

The reciprocity which Mauss and Sahlins believe to play a vital role in maintaining order refers presumably to a range of types of reciprocity corresponding to the generalised–balanced segment of Sahlins' spectrum – most often towards the general-ised end.[31]

There is a strong correlation between the form of reciprocity and kinship distance: as the kinship distance separating two individuals increases, the more do relations between them incline towards the unsociable negative end of the spectrum. Kinship groups – and simultaneously residential groups, since kinsmen generally live near by and neighbours are kin – can be thought of as a series of nested sectors. Generalised reciprocity is confined to the household and local lineage sectors, balanced reciprocity mainly to the village and tribal sectors, and negative reciprocity to the intertribal sector. (The strength of this correlation between reciprocity and kinship will of course vary, and in particular the negative reciprocity usually characteristic of intertribal relations may be replaced by a more balanced reciprocity in cases where there is trading or other intertribal symbiosis.) Certainly, generalised reciprocity predominates in the acephalous hunting–gathering bands and in the household and local lineage sectors of those tribal societies which are stateless.[32]

---

[30] Marcel Mauss, *The Gift: Forms and Functions of Exchange in Archaic Societies* (London: Routledge and Kegan Paul, 1969), pp. 11, 13, 79–80. (French first edition, 1925.)

[31] See Section 1.4 above.

[32] See the appendices to ch. 5 of *Stone Age Economics* for examples, and for an especially interesting discussion of a hunting–gathering case see Lorna Marshall, 'Sharing, talking and giving: relief of social tensions among !Kung Bushmen', *Africa*, 31 (1961), 231–49.

How close in fact is the Maussian argument to Hobbes? What Sahlins has in mind in pointing to the resemblance between the two is Hobbes's argument that conditional cooperation (to produce the public good of social order) is rational in the state of nature. Hobbes's first or fundamental Law of Nature is *'That every man, ought to endeavour Peace, as farre forth as he has hope of obtaining it; and when he cannot obtain it, that he may seek, and use, all helps, and advantages of Warre'*, and from it is derived the second, *'That a man be willing, when others are so too, as farre-forth, as for Peace, and defence of himselfe, he shall think it necessary, to lay down his right to all things.'* Sahlins is right to see in this second law, and in the third (covenant-keeping) and fifth (mutual accommodation), an analogy with Mauss's reciprocity, though the congruence is far from precise, as we shall see. But the fourth law of nature, as he says, *is* very close to 'the gift'. This is the law of gratitude:

That a man which receiveth Benefit from another of meer Grace, Endeavour that he which giveth it, have no reasonable cause to repent him of his good will. For no man giveth, but with the intention of Good to himselfe; because Gift is Voluntary; and of all Voluntary Acts, the Object is to every man his own Good; of which if men see they shall be frustrated, there will be no beginning of benevolence, or trust; nor consequently of mutual help; nor of reconciliation of one man to another; and therefore they are to remain still in the condition of War . . .

Nevertheless, despite the obvious resemblance between the spirit of *The Gift* and a central (and often misunderstood) part of Hobbes's argument in *Leviathan*, there are important differences. In the first place, of course, Mauss and Sahlins certainly part company with Hobbes here if, as seems to be the case, they believe that 'the gift' is a *substitute* for the state, that by itself it can secure Peace. Conditional cooperation is rational for everyone, says Hobbes, but only if it is made safe by the state; so it is not a substitute for the state. But then Mauss and Sahlins are talking mainly about primitive society (although even in primitive society, reciprocity does not stand alone as a surrogate for the state). More importantly, generalised reciprocity (of which food sharing is perhaps the most widespread and frequently occurring instance) is not the same thing as the conditional cooperation central to Hobbes's argument – the mutual laying aside of the 'right of nature' ('the Liberty each man hath, to use his own power, as he will himselfe, for the preservation of his own Nature; that is to say, of his own Life; and consequently, of doing anything, which in his own Judgement, and Reason, hee shall conceive to be the aptest means thereunto'), which in practice means refraining from violence, theft, etc., or in more recent versions of the Hobbesian argument, refraining from such things as having 'too many' children, discharging untreated wastes into rivers and lakes, hunting whales and other species threatened with extinction, and so on. This is not to say that the reciprocity of which Mauss and Sahlins speak does not help to secure order (which it does in part by initiating and maintaining certain kinds of social relations); only that this is not exactly what Hobbes had in mind (except in the fourth law, 'gratitude', which, like the fourteen laws following it, stands in an unsatis-factorily loose relation to the crucial first three laws).

Within the household, the local lineage and the village, the most important kind of reciprocity is probably food sharing. Between local communities, lineages, clans and moieties, it is the *exchange of women in marriage*. In its simplest form (as practised, for example, by the Shoshone and Eskimo, who lived in families which temporarily united in bands for cooperative hunts or for winter settlement), the men of two families exchange sisters, so that a man's sister marries his wife's brother. The same form of exchange, continued over generations, serves also to unite patrilocal bands, as well as tribal lineages, clans and moieties. In some cases, bands are grouped into two moieties, a band of one moiety exchanging women with one or perhaps several bands of the opposite moiety. This type of exchange corresponds to bilateral cross-cousin marriage: a man marries his father's sister's daughter who is at the same time his mother's brother's daughter – though it is the exchange between groups which is important, marriage partners usually being only classificatory cross-cousins. In another form of exchange, corresponding to patrilateral cross-cousin marriage, a woman marries into the group from which her *mother* came; thus there is delayed exchange, in the sense that reciprocation is made in the following generation. All these exchange systems are direct or symmetrical: a woman is received from the group to which one was given. There are also indirect or asymmetrical systems, such as that corresponding to matrilateral cross-cousin marriage, in which a man receives a wife from one group or set of groups but gives wives to a different group or set of groups. Thus, in these systems, there are chains of wife-giving, which must be cyclical (for example: A → B → C → A, or A → B → C → D → A *and* C → A), otherwise there would be wifeless wife-givers at one end of the chain and the system could not be perpetuated. Women are thus circulated rather than exchanged, but the whole set of groups involved is bound together nevertheless.[33]

The exchange of women in marriage creates and cements bonds between individuals and groups. 'Among tribes of low culture', wrote Edward B. Tylor, 'there is but one means known of keeping up permanent alliance, and that means is inter-marriage ... Again and again in the world's history, savage tribes must have had plainly before their minds the simple practical alternative between marrying-out and being killed

---

[33] For an excellent introduction to marital alliance theory, see Robin Fox, *Kinship and Marriage* (Harmondsworth: Penguin, 1967), chs. 7 and 8.

out.'[34] But it is not just as a form of reciprocity that exchange of women contributes to peace and order; it does so as well because it helps to create the conflicting loyalties which result from the *crosscutting* of marital and other ties. In a dispute between two individuals from groups which exchange women in marriage, each man's primary loyalty may be to his own group but the zeal with which he and co-members of his group pursue his claim will be diminished because of their affinal ties with the other group. Of course, clan exogamy or local group exogamy or any other form of exogamy practised by groups will create crosscutting ties, but in the absence of a positive marriage rule (an 'elementary' marriage system) these ties presumably are weaker, as they bear on disputes between any two particular groups, though they link a group to a greater number of other groups. In elementary marriage systems (of the kinds mentioned above, for example), groups are perpetually allied and are bound together by more links than in the case of 'complex' marriage systems having rules of exogamy but otherwise no positive rules specifying marriage partners.

Two other important sources of conflicting loyalties are clans and age-groups. Clans, especially in segmentary tribes, are very often geographically dispersed, with members of several clans in each local community, which is an amalgam of lineage branches of different clans. Division into clans is thus a cleavage which crosscuts division into local communities, and in a dispute between members of different communities a man's loyalties may be divided between loyalty to his local community and loyalty to his clan brothers.

In very many tribes, age-sets and age-grades, into which males are recruited on the basis of age or generation, serve to unite males irrespective of descent or residence or both. Thus,

[34] Edward B. Tylor, 'On a method of investigating the development of institutions: applied to laws of marriage and descent', *Journal of the Royal Anthropological Institute*, 18 (1888), 245–67.

72   COMMUNITY, ANARCHY AND LIBERTY

loyalties to age-mates conflict in these cases with loyalties to
kin or the local community. If, unusually, members of an age-
set form a separate local community (as with the so-called age-
villages of the Nyakyusa),[35] then kin are dispersed, so that there
is crosscutting between kinship on the one hand and the
mutually reinforcing age and residence cleavages on the other.
The rites of initiation from boyhood into manhood, which in
many cases mark the creation of the age-sets, may have special
significance as part of another means of social control which
will be discussed below.

In a society characterised by patrilineal descent but matrilocal
post-marital residence, descent and residence give rise to
crosscutting cleavages. The same of course is true of matrilineal,
patrilocal societies and indeed there will be some degree of
crosscutting in any society where residential groups do not
correspond to or are not closely based upon descent groups – as
they cannot be where there are, for example, cognatic (or
bilateral) descent groups, unless these are of the restricted
type, or where there are double (or dual) descent groups.[36] But
there is a crucial difference, where the maintenance of order is
concerned, between matrilocal and patrilocal systems. It is
always a group of closely related men which is responsible for
coming to the defence of an aggrieved person and which in
particular must exact vengeance if one of its members is killed.
This group has been referred to as a 'fraternal interest group'
and as the 'vengeance group'. In a patrilocal system it is

---

[35] Monica Wilson, *Good Company: A Study of Nyakyusa Age-Villages* (London:
Oxford University Press, 1951).
[36] Fox, *Kinship and Marriage*, chs. 5 and 6. Note that crosscutting between
residence groups and descent groups is not the same thing as that referred to
earlier in connection with marital exchange systems. In a patrilineal,
patrilocal society where local communities are based on descent groups,
there is no crosscutting of residence and descent groups, but there are of
course affinal links between the local communities. The effect on peace and
order of this latter type of crosscutting (if it deserves the name), and the
conflict of loyalties it engenders, is presumably weaker than the effect of the
crosscutting of residential and descent groups.

SOCIAL ORDER WITHOUT THE STATE   73

localised, hence able to spring into action and more likely to act
than in a matrilocal system where its members are dispersed.
Thus, matrilocality contributes to the maintenance of peace
and order. So too, though presumably not to the same degree,
do neo-local, ambilocal and other residence rules which disperse
the vengeance group.[37]

Once mutual hostilities are under way, crosscutting cleavages
often serve to temper or terminate them. Indeed it is doubtful
that a society could long survive under a system of self-help
retaliation and vengeance if it were not for extensive crosscutting of important cleavages. Crosscutting becomes particularly important whenever, as is often the case, the individual
parties to a dispute are supported by *groups* (usually comprising
their close kinsmen). In this case, the dispute is enlarged and is
therefore potentially more disruptive, but this has the effect of
making it more likely that a disputant will have ties of loyalty to
the other side as well as to his own group, and hence there will
be more individuals with a desire to end the dispute.

A special case of this massing of groups behind individuals in
conflict is the 'complementary opposition' characteristic of
'segmentary lineage societies'. 'The segmentary lineage system
consists of this: the focal lines of primary segments can be
placed on a single agnatic genealogy that accounts for much
(all, in the Tiv case) of the tribe. The closer the genealogical
relation between focal lines, the closer their respective segments

---

[37] A clear correlation between matrilocality and peacefulness was found in a
cross-cultural test by H. U. E. Thoden van Velzen and W. van Wetering:
'Residence, power groups and intra-societal aggression', *International Archives
of Ethnology*, 49 (1960), 169–200. See also K. F. and C. S. Otterbein, 'An eye
for an eye, a tooth for a tooth: a cross-cultural study of feuding', *American
Anthropologist*, 67 (1965), 1470–82, and G. E. Kang, 'Conflicting loyalties
theory: a cross-cultural test', *Ethnology*, 15 (1976), 201–10. Unfortunately,
these last two studies of crosscutting substitute 'feuding' (defined as blood-
revenge following a homicide) for violence. On crosscutting and social order,
see generally Max Gluckman, *Custom and Conflict in Africa* (Oxford: Blackwell,
1955), ch. 1, and Elizabeth Colson, 'Social control and vengeance in Plateau
Tonga society', *Africa*, 23 (1953), 199–212.

are on the ground.'[38] The idea of complementary opposition is, very roughly speaking, that of a society divided into sections, each subdivided into subsections, and each of these divided into primary segments (the Nuer villages or Tiv minimal *tar*, for example), such that in a dispute between two men from different 'villages' each man is supported by all the men of his respective village (and nobody else is involved), but if a man from one of these villages is in dispute with a man from any village of a different tribal subsection, then each man's subsection will drop any internal quarrels and unite behind him in opposition to the other subsection. Similarly for disputes involving men of different sections. This principle of complementary opposition operates in different forms in all societies,[39] but is not important in many of them as far as the maintenance of order is concerned; and though a wide variety of societies were once thought to be of the segmentary lineage type (and some writers seemed almost to equate 'segmentary lineage society' with 'stateless society'), it is now realised that the only fairly pure examples are the Tiv and the Nuer.

It is an exaggeration to claim, as Southall does, that 'the order, balance and equilibrium that obtain throughout a society as perceived by its members depend largely on the complementary opposition of groups and categories of varying permanence'.[40] It seems to me that what the complementary opposition mechanism (with its correlative 'segmentary soli-

---

[38] Marshall Sahlins, 'The segmentary lineage: an organization of predatory expansion', *American Anthropologist*, 63 (1961), 332–45. This article gives an excellent brief exposition of the segmentary lineage system. See also Laura Bohannan, 'Political aspects of Tiv social organization', in J. Middleton and D. Tait, eds., *Tribes Without Rulers* (London: Routledge and Kegan Paul, 1958).

[39] As M. G. Smith has emphasised: 'On segmentary lineage systems', *Journal of the Royal Anthropological Institute*, 86 (1956), 39–80.

[40] Adrian Southall, 'Stateless society', *International Encyclopedia of the Social Sciences* (1968), vol. 15, pp. 157–68. Even if crosscutting is to be included with complementary opposition proper (as Southall seems to assume) this is still, I think, an exaggeration.

darity') does perhaps contribute to order is to ensure that whenever there is a dispute between individuals it will always be escalated to a dispute between groups and, furthermore, these groups will always be of approximately equal strength. The results of this balanced massing of opposing groups are, first, to make a dispute more serious, the consequences of actual fighting much nastier, and hence to introduce a more powerful deterrent to causing disputes; second, by calling forth two approximately equal groups, to ensure that the deterrence is mutual; and third, to increase the amount of interrelatedness between the two sides, hence to introduce or intensify a conflict of loyalties, which increases the pressures brought to bear to terminate the dispute. Complementary opposition calls to mind certain features of contemporary international relations. When it fails to act as a deterrent, it serves to escalate the conflict, which presumably does not in itself promote peace and order.

The means of maintaining social order so far discussed are in effect aspects of the social structure. They are not *specifically* mechanisms of social control and cannot be separated from what is controlled. In this fundamental respect they differ from such characteristic instruments of social control in societies with a well-developed state as police and prisons. Malinowski brought this out well in his studies of the Trobriand Islanders when he wrote that 'law' and 'legal phenomena' (by which he meant, in effect, the means by which social order is maintained) 'do not consist in any independent institutions'. They represent 'rather an aspect of their tribal life, one side of their structure, than any independent, self-contained social arrangements' and are 'the specific result of the configuration of obligations, which makes it impossible for the native to shirk his responsibility without suffering for it in the future'.[41] And in an

---

[41] Bronislaw Malinowski, *Crime and Custom in Savage Society* (London: Routledge and Kegan Paul, 1926), pp. 58–9.

acephalous primitive society his sufferings will often be considerable and prolonged – because his deviant behaviour
ramifies, disrupting normal social life all around him. This in
turn is the result of what Nadel has called the 'multivalence' of
social activities and of what Southall calls the 'multiplexity' of
social relations.[42] The multivalence of a social activity is its
capacity 'to serve also ends or interests other than the one for
which it is explicitly or primarily designed', so that deviation
from it has the effect of frustrating this whole range of
interests, and the prospect of this serves to inhibit deviation.
The multiplexity of social relations results from the lack of
specialised roles characteristic of these stateless societies.
Activities are not compartmentalised; relations between people
are multifaceted; the individual does not interact with distinct
groups of people for different purposes. In such societies there
are, in particular, no specialised political or economic roles,
and there are no activities which are *only* economic or political.
Activities which are 'primarily' economic (if indeed one can
talk of the economic at all), for example exchange characterised
by generalised reciprocity, serve other ends as well, as we have
seen; they are multivalent. It follows that 'neither economic
nor political ends can be exclusively pursued by anyone to the
detriment of society'.[43]

On the role played by socialisation and education in the
maintenance of social order, I can be brief. Evidently there is a
simple sense in which education and socialisation are fundamental to social order, since the values they inculcate (some of
them at least) are presupposed by other means of control and
there must obviously be a large measure of agreement on some

---

[42] S. F. Nadel, 'Social control and self-regulation', *Social Forces*, 3 (1953), 265–
73; Southall, 'Stateless society'.
[43] Southall, 'Stateless society'.

matters if controls are to be effective in the absence of
concentrated force and a division of political labour. Ridicule
and shaming devices, for example, could not have their effect
(to be, discussed below) unless people had the appropriate
values and emotions. But in my view it does not make much
sense to single out socialisation for the central role in the
maintenance of social order, to claim, as Morton Fried does,
that 'in all societies the single most significant complex of
social-control apparatuses is to be found in the system of
education, including both formal and informal means'.[44] The
use of the devices of ridiculing and shaming – and the practice
of all the other methods of control considered here – itself
contributes to the socialisation of individuals. But there are of
course negative sanctions associated with these devices and the
use of the tacit threats to implement them is manifestly
necessary in the maintenance of order. The same goes for the
positive and negative sanctions associated with other controls.
In other words, although the way in which children are brought
up obviously can make an important difference to their
behaviour as adults,[45] socialisation is not enough.

It has been suggested that age-grading initiation ceremonies
or 'puberty rites' are a phase of the process of socialisation
which plays a particularly important part in the maintenance of
social order, since by associating great physical pain with
lectures on the standards expected of an adult member of the
community, it is ensured that these standards will never be
forgotten and hence will be conformed to. Ronald Berndt
relates that among the people (Kamano, Fore, Usurufa and
Jaté) he studied in the eastern Highlands of New Guinea, the

---

[44] Morton H. Fried, *The Evolution of Political Society* (New York: Random House,
    1967), p. 9.
[45] For some interesting examples of this from primitive peoples (especially
    hunters and gatherers), see Ashley Montagu, ed., *Learning Non-Aggression*
    (New York: Oxford University Press, 1978).

following operations are performed serially on the novice during the initiation ceremonies: his nasal septum is pierced with a salt-smeared bamboo sliver which is then twirled around in the hole; his tongue is cut; some of his fingers are pierced under the nail; his nose is bled by forcing several salt-smeared leaves of pipit cane up his nostrils and twirling them about; later his penis is bled by having forced into it first 'spear' grass, then a twig, then leaves bunched together; and finally the apex of his penis is cut with a bamboo knife and a sharpened bone from a pig's leg is inserted into the penis, then replaced by bundles of leaves which are forced up and twirled around.[46] During these rites the novices are subjected also to harangues on what is expected of them as adults. The Aranda bands of Australia subjected their initiates to subincision – the final stage of several weeks of ordeals. A long thin bone was inserted into the urethra and the penis split open by hacking down to the bone with a piece of flint. The aboriginal Luiseño bands of Southern California required their novices 'to lie motionless while being bitten repeatedly by hordes of angry ants', amongst other things, and 'as ordeal passed to new ordeal throughout the ceremony, the candidate received long lectures on proper conduct, on how to become a man of value, and on the religious practices of his band'.[47]

There may be something in this argument about the importance of these rites and their accompanying lectures in the maintenance of social order, but there are a number of problems with it. First, there is the awkward fact that the lectures delivered during the initiation ceremonies may in some societies (those studied by Berndt, for example) place great emphasis on competitive, aggressive, fighting and other

---

[46] Ronald M. Berndt, *Excess and Restraint: Social Control Among a New Guinea People* (Chicago: University of Chicago Press, 1962).
[47] Peter Farb, *Man's Rise to Civilisation as Shown by the Indians of North America from Primeval Times to the Coming of the Industrial State* (London: Paladin, 1971), p. 72.

qualities hardly conducive to the maintenance of order. Second, though it is indeed plausible that the lessons (whether cooperative and pacific, or otherwise) learned in association with such memorable ordeals will not be quickly forgotten, it does not follow that the norms enjoined by them will be adhered to. If, however, socialisation also results in a well-developed sense of guilt and sensitivity to ridicule and shaming, then well-remembered norms would indeed be effective in the maintenance of order (provided the norms are of an appropriate sort). Third, even if comparisons are limited to stateless societies, there is great variation – which needs to be explained – in the severity of the initiation ordeals, in the proportion of youths who have to submit to them, in the nature and amount of the accompanying indoctrination (in some societies there is none at all) and in the extent of initiation of girls. The Kuma of the New Guinea Highlands, for example, have much in common with the nearby communities studied by Berndt but their male initiation ceremonies are much less prolonged and harsh and do not affect all youths uniformly, for they are held at long intervals and there is great variation in the youths' ages at initiation and in the extent of participation in the various rites and lectures (some youths, chiefly because of their age, do not participate at all). The ethnographer offers no evidence to suggest (and appears not to believe) that it is those who escape the ordeals and the lectures who grow up to be the non-conformists, though she does claim that the result of this uneven socialisation at the time of initiation is more diversity and less conformity in adult behaviour.[48] In Nuer society, to take another example, the rites of initiation to manhood undergone by all males include 'a very severe operation' in which their brows are cut to the bone several times from ear to ear, but, says Evans-Pritchard, 'there is no purposive education or moral training in the procedure of initiation'.[49]

Even if in many societies the ceremonies and rituals associated with the passage to adulthood do not contribute much to the process of socialisation by joining great physical pain to explicit lectures on the social behaviour of an adult, they may nevertheless play a part in socialisation simply by emphasising – sometimes, as we have seen, rather dramatically – the initiate's accession to a new status, which of course makes him a full member of the community with well-defined obligations and responsibilities. And in general there is little doubt that the rituals and ceremonies of primitive societies – marking seasonal changes, life crises and the installation of chiefs and headmen – reinforce socialisation by symbolising the social structure and reaffirming the norms and beliefs of the society, and cooperation in their performance requires people to be at peace with one another.[50] This 'ritual superintegration' extends beyond the limits of the political unit, uniting bands, lineages, clans or other groups recognising no common authority.

I come now to the social controls proper. Before considering each of them in turn, a general point should be noted. Recall that in a pure anarchy there is no concentration of force and no

---

[48] Marie Reay, *The Kuma: Freedom and Conformity in the New Guinea Highlands* (Melbourne: University Press, 1959). Farb (*Man's Rise to Civilisation*, p. 73) cites with approval the argument that the severity of initiation rites varies with the harshness of the environment, the rites being most severe where a particularly harsh environment makes a precarious survival dependent upon minimising anti-social behaviour. The argument appears to be based on a comparison of the subincising Aranda with other Australian aborigines who live in better circumstances on the coast and who merely do such things as pound out one of the initiate's teeth; it looks less secure when, for example, some of the relatively well-placed New Guinea Highlands societies are brought in to the comparison. Besides, it is not clear that survival *is* precarious for the hunter-gatherers of harsh environments. For a discussion of the evidence, see Sahlins, 'The original affluent society', in *Stone Age Economics*.

[49] E. E. Evans-Pritchard, *The Nuer* (Oxford: Clarendon Press, 1940), pp. 249 and 253.

[50] See Max Gluckman, *Politics, Law and Ritual in Tribal Society* (Oxford: Blackwell, 1977), ch. 11; Victor W. Turner, *The Ritual Process* (Chicago: Aldine, 1969).

political specialisation. Thus, in a *pure* anarchy nobody is denied participation in whatever means are used to maintain social order, and in particular no individual or group is denied the use of force, or of threats to use force, in seeking to redress a grievance, retaliate wrongs or deter others from committing them. In the primitive anarchies which are the closest historical or prehistorical approximations to this theoretical ideal of pure anarchy, there is some concentration of the use of force (in the hands of adult males) and there is a minimal division of political labour, though the specialists are not backed by organised force, so cannot enforce their decisions throughout the community. In the primitive anarchies, then, we should find wide participation in the processes of social control and in the use of force or of threats to use force, wherever these are used. This is indeed the case.

Unsurprisingly, then, a basic social control in primitive stateless societies is the threat of retaliation – 'self-help justice' carried out against the offender (and perhaps also his close kinsmen) by his victim or the victim assisted by his close kinsmen or, if the victim is dead or incapacitated, by his kinsmen alone. One form of this is the feud – a relation governed by recognised rules between groups of kinsmen, continuing through generations and in some cases interminable, and consisting eventually if not immediately in exchanges of homicide. The growth of the state (see Section 3.3 below) must by definition entail the removal of the right to pursue feuds and other forms of violent retaliation by offended individuals and groups, so that 'with rare exceptions . . . the practice of feud . . . is confined to societies in which there is little or no instituted "civil government"'.[51]

Clearly the practice of the feud itself does little to enhance

---

[51] Jacob Black-Michaud, *Cohesive Force: Feud in the Mediterranean and the Middle East* (Oxford: Blackwell, 1975), p. 146.

the security of persons and their property; but the *fear* of incurring violent retaliation and perhaps precipitating a feud is itself a potent deterrent from violence and theft. Among the Nuer, in Evans-Pritchard's view, 'fear of incurring a blood-feud is, in fact, the most important legal sanction within a tribe and the main guarantee of an individual's life and property'.[52] There is of course some similarity between this mechanism of social control and the state, inasmuch as control is afforded in both cases by the threat of retaliation by force; but there are fundamental differences, most notably that the 'self-help' system, as it is practised in stateless societies, is much more egalitarian.

I have already written on the role which reciprocal giving plays in maintaining social order by initiating and sustaining friendly social intercourse. I want now to emphasise briefly that the system of reciprocity is also an important source of social control. Food sharing and the pooling and exchange of labour, especially in certain hunting, fishing, horticultural and agricultural operations, are highly valued forms of aid which are given conditionally. Without them the individual would generally be materially much worse off and in some cases unable to subsist. So he is faced with a throffer, a threat and offer combined: if he does his part and if he refrains from anti-social behaviour, he will continue to receive reciprocal aid; otherwise it will be withdrawn. Malinowski in his studies of the Trobriand Islands was the first to give a central place to the role of this throffer in the maintenance of social order.[53] Some would say that he attached too great an importance to it, to the neglect of other means of maintaining order, but there is no doubt that this ever present throffer is one very potent form of social control.

[52] Evans-Pritchard, *The Nuer*, p. 150.
[53] Malinowski, *Crime and Custom in Savage Society*, especially Part I, chs. 3–5.

Less serious sanctions than the withdrawal of reciprocal aid but ones which nevertheless play a part in maintaining social order in stateless primitive societies are the various forms and degrees of ostracism and excommunication. By ostracism I mean only the exclusion of an individual from everyday social intercourse and withdrawal of courtesy and company, and by excommunication the exclusion from participation in rituals.[54] An individual can be subjected to either or both of these without at the same time being denied the benefits of reciprocity, or all three forms of sanction may be applied together.

Ostracism and excommunication and the withdrawal of reciprocity between them cover a range of sanctions which consist in the denial of benefits of different aspects of social interaction. An extreme sanction of this kind is expulsion from the community, a sanction which is rarely used in most primitive societies and not found at all in some. Its severity depends of course on the expelled individual's prospects of being received into another community and his likely standing in it. In some societies expulsion is a virtual death sentence; in others, there are a small number of other communities which might accept him, but he will suffer there from being stigmatised as one who has been expelled (or has had to flee) from his home community.

The positive and negative sanctions associated with the giving and withdrawal of reciprocal aid, with 'self-help' violent retaliation, and with ostracism, excommunication and expulsion, all of course *result* from and give expression to approval and disapproval; but they are to be distinguished from approval and disapproval, which are themselves sources of satisfaction and suffering and so can be sanctions in their own right. Offers and

[54] For examples of excommunication, see Christoph von Fürer-Haimendorf, *Morals and Merit: A Study of Values and Social Controls in South Asian Societies* (London: Weidenfeld and Nicolson, 1967), e.g. at pp. 49–50 and 123–6.

threats to give and withhold approval, esteem, respect, and so on, can have a deterrent effect independently of threats and offers using these other sanctions, and approval and disapproval need not give rise to them. Disapproval may give rise to shame and a sense of guilt – the rough distinction between these being that a person can feel *guilt* privately, without others knowing of its cause, whereas *shame* is felt as a result of disapprobation, so presupposes consciousness of public exposure. Some writers (but not including anthropologists) appear to believe that in primitive societies the sanctions of disapproval, guilt and shame are alone responsible for maintaining social order – or what little of it that is not already explained (by them) as an automatic outcome of dire poverty. It is true that these sanctions, which make a contribution to order in every society, are much more important in those small, face-to-face communities in which the individual is well-known to most others, typically expects to spend his entire life, and is usually dependent on the goodwill of others for vital economic cooperation; and it is reported of the members of most stateless societies that they are highly sensitive to the opinions of those around them and have an easily excited sense of shame. But, as the whole of this section makes plain, this set of sanctions is only one of the means by which order is maintained in primitive anarchies and there is no basis for arguing that it is in some sense the most important or most potent.

In addition to gossip and casual criticism, these societies have a great variety of practices – usually institutionalised, standardised and hedged about with conventions so as to prevent them getting out of hand – whose aim is to criticise, shame or ridicule persons suspected of committing delicts or in some cases to publicise the delict and to discover its perpetrator. An example of both is given by the Hopi's use of a sort of public crier, who chants grievances in a standardised manner from a rooftop, expressing regret that such things should be done (thereby underlining Hopi norms) and reprimanding the offender or

SOCIAL ORDER WITHOUT THE STATE   85

calling on the pueblo for help in identifying him.[55] The use of
ridicule among the Eskimo, especially in the form of the 'song
duel', is well known. Among those of the Canadian Northwest
Territories, for example, derision is used '(a) constantly in daily
intercourse; (b) in spontaneously sung lampoons during common
gatherings in the large winter festival house; and (c) in formal
"song-duels" in the same situation'.[56] In these duels, contestants
'sing' before an amused and applauding audience which acts as
arbitrator, and with sarcasm, irony and wit accuse one another
of 'incest, bestiality, murder, avarice, adultery, failure at
hunting, being henpecked, lack of manly strength'. These
duels serve to keep the whole community informed about its
members' behaviour (and indeed good performance in song
duels *requires* that a man keep himself well-informed about
others) as well as reiterating and underlining social norms.

An elaborate example of institutionalised public shaming is
the system of competitive food exchanges on Goodenough
Island (off Papua) described by Michael Young in his *Fighting
with Food*.[57] Sorcery accusations (to be discussed below) are a
potent instrument of social control in this Melanesian society;
harangues delivered from a house-top on a dark night publicise
delicts to most of the village with the intention of shaming an
unknown offender and may result in the exile of a named
offender; and the clans (between which there is imperfect
exogamy) are crosscut by ties of kinship, by 'eating companion-
ships' (food is very important to these people), and by traditional
food-giving partnerships (*fofofo*). But according to Young the
most important instrument of order in this acephalous society
is the *abutu* or 'food-giving-to-shame'. An *abutu* is triggered by a

[55] R. A. Black, 'Hopi grievance chants: a mechanism of social control', in D.
Hymes and W. E. Brittle, eds., *Studies in Southwestern Ethnolinguistics* (The
Hague: Mouton, 1967).
[56] Gluckman, *Politics, Law and Ritual*, p. 304.
[57] Michael W. Young, *Fighting with Food* (Cambridge: Cambridge University
Press, 1971).

delict and takes place about once a year between hostile
factions of the village, less frequently between villages. Each
side attempts to shame the other by giving it more and better
food (domestic pigs, taro, bananas and especially yams) than it
is able to pay back simultaneously. The principals, who initiate
the *abutu*, do not retain this food; it must be redistributed
among their respective *fofofo*, who also make speeches at the
abutu on behalf of the principals. Young concludes that,
although this practice may in a limited sense be redressive and
that it may sometimes compound problems of social control
rather than solve them, the threat of *abutu* is nevertheless seen
by the natives as a very real sanction and it evidently serves
effectively to shame offenders by publicising delicts (and
shame is a well-developed emotion in this society) as well as
bringing about a *détente* through the temporary mutual exhaus-
tion of resources by the village's political factions.

The final group of social controls which I shall consider consists
of threats of sorcery and accusations of witchcraft and of
supernatural sanctions. Witchcraft beliefs are not found universally (and where accusations are made they are not a sanction of
first resort). It appears that witchcraft beliefs are less likely to
be found where social relations are well-defined, where social
interaction is not intensive and especially where people can
move away from each other easily. Such beliefs are not, for
example, found among the Mbuti pygmies of the Congo and
are unimportant among the Nuer.[58] Where beliefs in witchcraft
do exist, a person who suffers some misfortune may accuse

[58] See Mary Douglas, ed., *Witchcraft Accusations and Confessions* (London: Tavistock,
1970), editor's Introduction, p. xxxiii, and ch. 13 by Godfrey Lienhardt on
'The situation of death: an aspect of Anuak philosophy'; and Paul Baxter,
'Absence makes the heart grow fonder; some suggestions why witchcraft
accusations are rare among East African pastoralists', in Max Gluckman, ed.,
The Allocation of Responsibility (Manchester: Manchester University Press,
1972).

another individual of working witchcraft against him or consult a diviner or oracle to discover the witch, and the individual accused is invariably a personal enemy and one already known for his anti-social conduct. (In acephalous societies – always egalitarian – accusations may be made against anyone who acquires much more than others or who becomes eminent. I return to this in Chapter 3.) The punishment meted out varies from the accused's identity being publicised by gossip to ostracism or death. This deters the individual from anti-social behaviour and encourages cooperativeness and generosity and the performance of obligations by creating both a fear of being accused of working witchcraft and a fear of being bewitched by someone he would displease.[59]

Fear of the misfortune and adversity meted out as punishment by a variety of spirits and deities is an important and widespread instrument of social control. In many societies, certain spirits are thought to be angered by hostile relations between kinsmen or between members of the same local community. In parts of Africa, for example, the earth is venerated and the greatest sacrilege against it is to spill blood in fighting.[60] Often, actions are religiously sanctioned which, though they do not contribute directly to social order (in the narrow senses discussed above), may contribute indirectly by helping to maintain other practices or structures which play a role in the maintenance of order (and generally they contribute to social order in the wider senses). Thus, ancestral spirits punish people for defaulting on their obligations to kinsmen (as well as for failing to worship the ancestral spirits themselves); and *kwoth*, the central deity of the Nuer, is offended by, amongst other things, incest.

[59] See generally Gluckman, *Politics, Law and Ritual*, ch. 6; and Guy E. Swanson, *The Birth of the Gods* (Ann Arbor: Michigan University Press, 1960), ch. 8.
[60] See for example M. Fortes, 'The political system of the Tallensi of the Northern Territories of the Gold Coast', in M. Fortes and E. E. Evans-Pritchard, eds., *African Political Systems* (London: Oxford University Press, 1940).

88   COMMUNITY, ANARCHY AND LIBERTY

Finally, it is worth noting that although the authorities and
leaders of stateless societies lack power, the positions they
occupy often have a religious and mythical warrant; they are to
some degree sanctified. In view of the role these authorities
play in preventing and settling disputes directly and in upholding
other institutions and practices which I have already discussed,
such sanctity doubtless enhances the contribution they make
to the maintenance of order.[61]

When we turn from primitive stateless societies to peasant
societies, we find essentially that, with certain qualifications
and a redistribution of emphasis, the means by which social
order is maintained are the same. Having described these in
some detail for the primitive societies, I shall simply summarise
here very briefly the qualifications that have to be made in the
case of peasant communities, which, as I noted in Section 1.5,
are internally only quasi-anarchic and vary considerably in the
degree to which they possess the three core attributes of
community.

Reciprocity and the threat of the withdrawal of reciprocal aid
(and of ostracism and expulsion) are of great importance in
peasant communities of the closed corporate kind, as they are
in primitive anarchies. Their importance is diminished in the
'open' peasant communities, because there is less economic
interdependence between members of the community and
greater dependence of its members on outsiders. The threat of
'self-help' retaliation, including feuding, is found in peasant
communities, but much less commonly than in primitive
societies, precisely because the peasant community is an
integral part of a society with a state, and is subject to some

[61] Roy A. Rapoport has claimed (a little exaggeratedly, I think) that sanctity is a
functional equivalent of political power and steadily diminishes with the
growth of centralised power. 'The sacred in human evolution', *Annual Review
of Ecology and Systematics*, 2 (1971), 23–44.

SOCIAL ORDER WITHOUT THE STATE 89

extent to the laws and the power of lord and state. It is this feature of social control which the state (in part by definition) first displaces. 'The pressure of public opinion' – shaming, ridiculing, gossiping, and so on – seems to play a central role in maintaining order in every peasant community. Threats of witchcraft accusations and of supernatural sanctions are important in many peasant societies, but in some communities (including some closed corporate communities) supernatural sanctions do not seem to be very much feared and witchcraft is unimportant.

Intentional communities are, like peasant communities, in general quasi-anarchic internally but embedded in a society with a state. As in peasant communities, the social controls they use are therefore supplementary to those exercised by the state, though the state may have little penetration in these communities and recourse to its sanctions is often avoided where possible. Partly because they are subject to a state and partly because in almost every case their members are opposed to the use of violence, the threat of 'self-help' retaliation is rarely encountered, at least in the American and English intentional communities of the nineteenth and twentieth centuries. In the religious communities, supernatural sanctions, ceremonial and ritual played a part in maintaining order, though in most cases a small one; and witchcraft was not practised. Controls based on the sanctions of approval and disapproval played the most important role in all these communities. These controls are explicitly recognised and used in institutionalised public criticism, shaming and ridiculing devices in the 'utopian' communities. In the modern secular communes, however, such devices are rare, and in most cases their members would not approve of them; nevertheless informal and unorganised gossip and signs of approval and disapproval conveyed in everyday interaction play an important part, and it is hard to see how it could be otherwise among people living, eating and often working together in small groups. Ostracism and expulsion are of course practised, but the threat of them, especially expulsion, cannot have the powerful deterrent effect which they have in primitive communities, for if a person becomes unpopular and chooses to leave or if he or she is expelled, it is a less serious matter. Finally, in nearly all intentional communities, of both utopian and secular types, the threat of withdrawal of reciprocal aid is not an important means of social control. The chief reason for this is that in most of these communities there is approximately equal access to communal property and equal availability of collectively produced goods (especially food) and services, usually subject to everyone's needs first being satisfied, and, crucially, free access and availability are not denied those who do not exchange their labour reciprocally with the rest of the community and do not do their part in producing these goods and services. This principle of distribution creates its own free rider problem and failure to solve it is a main cause of the collapse of these communities; I shall have more to say about it in the next chapter.

I have given here only a very brief summary of the similarities and differences between the social controls of the primitive anarchies and those found (in addition to such controls as the state exercises) in peasant and intentional communities. This summary will be filled out with some illustrations in Section 3.2 where I shall discuss the use of these same controls to contain the development of inequality.

2.5 Community and stateless social order

There are, then, four principal groups of social controls which are used to maintain social order in the primitive stateless societies and to a lesser extent also in quasi-anarchic peasant and intentional communities where they are supplemented by controls associated with the state. The principal types of social controls are (i) the threat of 'self-help' retaliation, (ii) the offer of reciprocity and the threat of its withdrawal, (iii) the use of the sanctions of approval and disapproval, the latter especially *via* gossip, ridicule and shaming, and (iv) the threat of witchcraft accusations and of supernatural sanctions. Controls based on supernatural sanctions obviously differ from the rest since, although they are a product of a community's beliefs, the sanctions are not entirely at the disposal of the community's members. With the exception of the use of supernatural sanctions, all four types of social control characteristic of anarchies can be effective only in groups which are relatively small and have little turnover in their memberships. The practice of reciprocity is unlikely to flourish (and therefore the threat of its withdrawal cannot be an important social control) where people do not have *stable* relations with *known* individuals – individuals who are expected to remain in the group and to be able therefore to reciprocate aid. Like reciprocity, 'self-help' retaliation *can* be practised in large and mobile societies but is clearly more difficult to pursue in such societies than in smaller and more stable ones. The same is evidently true of the use of gossip and of ridiculing and shaming devices. These operate more effectively on an individual if he is known to all or most of the community, if his delicts or his defaulting on reciprocal giving become known to virtually everyone in his world, if he cannot escape into anonymity and must continue to live for the rest of his life with the same small set of people (or with a breakaway subset of them in the case of fission: see below). Finally, the threat of witchcraft accusations can also contribute more effectively to the maintenance of social order in small, stable groups since, like ridiculing and shaming, their use depends critically both on people being well-informed about each other's behaviour and on the prospect of having to live (if allowed to live) among the same group of familiar people with the reputation resulting from a successful witchcraft accusation.

The primitive stateless communities discussed in the preceding section are of course small and very stable. Even where there is population growth, a community remains small by breaking up whenever it has grown too large for its members to work local land: a part of the community splits off and establishes itself on new land. This process of *fissioning* (which I shall have more to say about in Section 3.3 on the origins of the state) is a normal part of the life of stateless societies. Merely by helping to ensure that communities remain small, it contributes indirectly to the maintenance of social order. But fissioning may also occur when there is persistent internal conflict, especially where population densities are low and unused productive land is available, and even more readily among gatherers and hunters and shifting cultivators who have negligible property and minimal sunk investments in whatever land they are using. In this case, the people who move away may be able to join kinsmen elsewhere and thus gain support and protection.[62]

Now if community is characterised (as it was in Section 1.4) by shared values and beliefs, direct and many-sided relations, and the practice of reciprocity, then communities must be small and stable, for in a large group with changing membership few relations between individuals can be direct and many-sided and reciprocity cannot flourish on a wide scale. But smallness and stability do not entail community. A small set of individuals with fairly stable membership *need* not have many values and beliefs in common, or deal with each other directly and as rounded individuals rather than as specialists, or practise reciprocity amongst themselves. I have argued that smallness and stability are necessary conditions for the social controls

[62] For an example of fission of this kind, see Jack Stauder, 'Anarchy and ecology: political society among the Majangir', *Southwestern Journal of Anthropology*, 28 (1972), 153–68.

SOCIAL ORDER WITHOUT THE STATE

characteristic of anarchies to be effective. But they are clearly not sufficient, since, in the first place, one of the attributes of community, reciprocity, must be practised if the threat of its withdrawal is to be an effective control. Furthermore, the effectiveness of gossip, ridicule and shaming in maintaining social order depends not only on smallness and stability but on the other two features of community – shared beliefs and values and direct many-sided relations; for a person who does not deal directly with those around him or has only one-sided or specialised relations with some of them, and has few values and beliefs in common with them, is unlikely to be very sensitive to their criticism. Thus the two most important means of maintaining social order in stateless societies – those based on reciprocity and on approval and disapproval – together depend on community for their effectiveness.

Let us recall the argument about public goods and group size which was summarised in the first section of this chapter. It is that public goods are more likely to be provided, or provided in optimal amounts, by the members of *small* publics than by those of large ones. In the static analysis given by Olson, this is chiefly because the larger the public, the smaller the benefit which accrues to any individual member from the additional amount of the public good provided out of his contribution, so that in a relatively large group this benefit is likely to be exceeded by the cost to him of making the contribution, whereas in a relatively small group this is less likely to be the case. But a more realistic dynamic analysis leads to a similar conclusion, for it shows (what is intuitively nearly obvious) that the only rational cooperation is *conditional* cooperation whereby an individual contributes if and only if enough others contribute, and such conditional cooperation is possible only in a relatively small public in which people have contact with and can observe the behaviour of many of their fellows and which has a fairly stable membership. Now we have just seen that these same conditions – smallness and stability – are also necessary conditions for the methods of social control characteristic of anarchies to be effective. However, the size at which it would be rational for the members of a group to provide themselves with a public good like social order would generally be smaller than the range of sizes necessary for these methods to function. In other words, in *very* small publics, no 'selective incentives' or controls are needed: it is rational to cooperate voluntarily in the production of the public good of social order; but in larger publics, controls of some kind – *some* means of getting people to do things they otherwise would not do – are necessary if social order is to be maintained. The methods which are used by societies without a state are effective only in small and stable communities.

Part II
Alternatives to the State

[4]

Excerpt from *Is Democracy Possible?* 19–50

1

Democracy and the state

I THE STATE IS UNNECESSARY

Must there be some single organization in a given territory
that has a monopoly of legitimate force to deal with issues of
common interest and assert the common interest over all
more particular interests? Anarchists apart, all political
thinkers in modern times have thought so. Marxists have seen
the necessity of the state as historically provisional. Under
socialism it will wither away. Other historically minded
theorists have stressed that abstract conceptions of the state
neglect the radical differences between political organizations
in different epochs and circumstances. But most agree that
there are sound arguments that show that in any large society
a supreme authority is indispensable for the foreseeable
future.

In spite of all efforts to sanctify or justify it the state remains
a paradox, the great Leviathan that is meant to suppress
violence by monopolizing it, the supreme constraint on our
liberties that is meant to guarantee liberty, the provider of
goods with an inexhaustible appetite for taxation. In its central function as the monopolist in the provision of peace and
order the state is quite literally a protection racket. It insists
that we buy its protection whether we want it or not. If we try
to deal with another firm we are punished as rebels or
traitors. Moreover, the need for the sort of protection the
state supplies takes the particular form that it does as a direct

20   *Democracy and the state*

result of the system of states. It is because of the concentra-
tions of power that states make possible that nothing less
than the power of a state can protect us. We are so afraid of
what states can do to people that we must have our own. Of
course states provide many other public services besides
defence and policing, and many of these are less spurious.
But that it has fallen to the state to provide them is due
almost wholly to the fact that the state has a monopoly on
legitimate violence. There are alternatives. There can be
legitimate authorities quite independently of the state, and it
is possible for them to have adequate sanctions to ensure that
they are obeyed.

Community

Even many anarchists agree that the only alternative to the
state is community control,[1] which is only possible in groups
small enough for their members to share many common
beliefs, and to have direct and many-sided relations among
themselves, including many involving reciprocity, particularly mutual assistance but also retaliation. All societies need
to enforce a variety of actions and abstentions from action.
They must be able to do this by social pressure if they are to
escape the need for a police force and a state. In a large
anonymous community it is too easy to evade social pressure.

The argument is by no means decisive. I shall argue that the
crucial problem is that of controlling not individuals but
organizations. A multiplicity of authorities with specialized
competences and activities could be co-ordinated without being subordinate to any single overarching authority. Basically
they would co-ordinate their activities by negotiation among
themselves. Of course such specialized authorities could come
into conflict between themselves and there would need to be
some body with authority to settle their differences authori-
tatively. But it is at least conceivable that such a body might
have only an arbitrating function, with no right to dictate

Democracy and the state 21

policy. Its only sanction might be that most individuals and organizations would accept its verdicts and enforce them against recalcitrants by peaceable means, boycotts, disobedience and moral pressures. Such a state of affairs would presuppose that the society did not generate organizations with interests that were so wide ranging, self-contained and strong as to enable them to defy community sanctions. I shall argue that specialization of function could ensure that no large body of people had so strong an identification with any one organization as to regard it as representing uniquely their supreme interests. People would see themselves as belonging to a large number of overlapping communities, not to any single total community at any level. It will be part of my task to show how such a decentralization of power might be possible in societies of a very high degree of complexity.

In effect I shall argue that specialized organizations can themselves form communities of organizations, highly analogous to communities of individuals. Just as mutual interaction and interdependence against the background of shared beliefs and practices can produce a stable order among individuals and families, the same factors can discipline organizations, under certain conditions. Among those conditions are that no organization is self-sufficient, none is in a position to dictate to the others, and that each organization has a strong incentive to co-operate with others even where there is no immediate pay-off in doing so. Satisfying these conditions presupposes that there are effective barriers to individuals and groups getting control of enough organizations to subvert the patterns of mutual interdependence and turn them into largely one-way relations of power. I shall show how this is possible. Meanwhile let us take stock of the other arguments for the necessity of the state.

Violence

The first of these arguments is essentially Hobbesian. There is a tendency among human beings to settle their arguments by

22   *Democracy and the state*

violence. The tendency for the use of violence to lead to further violence in a self-reinforcing process can be halted only by an authority powerful enough to suppress the use of violence by all others. The argument applies not only to individuals but to organizations, and so to states themselves. It need not rest on any claim that we have an innate disposition to violence. It is sufficient that from time to time we do use it, and that violence breeds violence. Ultimately world peace demands a world state, a supreme monopoly of effective legitimate violence.

In order to answer this argument we need to distinguish three main areas in which violence must be controlled. The first is that of violent crime, where individuals or small groups use violence for gain or personal satisfaction against other individuals and groups whose recognized rights they violate. This, I shall argue, can be handled in well-established ways, and the agencies needed for controlling it can themselves be controlled by demarchic institutions, especially if these agencies are relatively specialized or local. There will always be problems in this area, though some of the worst of them would be reduced if societies did not persist in attempting to control so much of people's behaviour.

The second area is that of the use of violence for political ends against an established order. This kind of violence is rare and relatively easily controlled where the order is commonly accepted and just and its normal institutions function well. It should not be a problem in a demarchy, particularly because there would be no powerful state apparatus that the insurgents could hope to control or subvert.

The third is that of states themselves, or of groups acting with a state's connivance, where there is no commonly recognized and enforced basis of justice between the contending parties. In 'state of nature' situations of the kind envisaged by Hobbes even very small groups may be involved in violent conflict of this sort, and it may even be that the state was an historical necessity for humankind to get beyond cer-

tain historical situations. In its more primitive forms, however, radical conflict depended for its attractiveness not only
on the absence of a law-enforcing state, but also on the
simplicity of the productive relations and technology of
hunter-gatherer and largely agricultural societies. One could
simply kill, expel or enslave the conquered population and
immediately set up in production on their territory. Under
modern conditions effective conquest is a very much more
complex and difficult business to carry through effectively
and profitably. Keeping large subject populations in order is
an expensive and not particularly cost-effective enterprise.
Only the resources and organization of the state make it
possible. Only 'reasons of state', and state aggrandizement
and paranoia, make it attractive. Economically it is almost
always cheaper to buy coal than to 'mine it with bayonets'.
The key to extirpating state violence is the abolition of the
state as we know it.

There is no way of abolishing particular states without
abolishing the system of states. As long as one national community confronts others that are organized as nation-states, it
too must take the form of a nation-state. In particular, it
must be prepared for war. There is at the present time no adequate guarantee of the security of any nation-state that is
not prepared to defend itself by force. It has often been
argued that, short of a world state, there cannot be. But that
is false. What is required is not some higher body more
powerful than any of its subordinates but the removal of
causes of war and disarmament. Short of that, a nation with
a well-entrenched pattern of decentralized government might
well be able to make the cost to a foreign power of attempting
to take it over too high to be worth the effort. In the absence
of any centralized chain of command there would be no point
in attempting to use the existing machinery of government.
An aggressor might, of course, succeed in taking control of
some key facilities that were particularly significant to it but it
is unlikely that it could secure the sort of co-operation in their

24   *Democracy and the state*

own suppression that conquered states commonly extend to
their conquerors.

At the same time other functions of states could be inter-
nationalized. There already are some international agencies
that exercise considerable authority in specific areas.[2] If we
restrict ourselves to questions of abstract possibility there is
little doubt that many functions of nation states could be
transferred to such bodies, to the advantage of practically
everybody affected. There is no compelling reason why all
the functions of the nation state should not be dispersed to
more limited agencies from the point of view of functional
necessities, or even advantages.

Obviously, in practice the difficulties are insurmountable
in the present state of the world. There is no adequate common political culture that could provide the basis for the
authority of such bodies, except perhaps in those areas where
such bodies as the international scientific community would
be the main relevant constituency. The tendency of nation
states is to stress and promote ideological differences between
national groups. Even more importantly, the vast disparities
of economic power between nations, the trap of underdevelop-
ment and exploitation, have largely destroyed Marx's vision
of a genuinely and effectively international movement of the
economically oppressed. Even where they do not actively support national chauvinism or imperialism, workers in advanced
countries are desperately afraid of the effect of immigration
and competition from their poorer counterparts in underdeveloped countries. They are determined not to abrogate
any of the collective goods that the relatively high wealth of
their communities guarantees to them. On the other hand,
the poor nations fear that international agencies would work
in favour of the rich and cling desperately to their mostly
illusory political independence.

Nevertheless, if we are to take the measure of the problems
that face human beings in general and the oppressed in particular, it is vital that we do not deny the existence of prob-

lems simply because they are at present intractable. At the worst it may be that only a global catastrophe, most probably a full-scale nuclear war, could change the situation and people's perceptions of it so as to make a radical movement towards the abolition of states possible. At best, there might be a series of fairly specific crises that would lead to the formation of more international authorities leading up to the crucial step of disarmament and the gradual abandonment of the traditional conception of sovereignty. In either case progress is unlikely to be made unless there is a widespread conviction that the only satisfactory solutions are those that constitute advances towards whittling away the state.

It has not always been obvious to everybody that the recourse to violence to settle disputes is a bad thing. Willingness to risk one's life to affirm what one believes in has often been seen as the supreme test for 'manhood', or even of spiritual worth. Wars have been seen as the indispensable solvents of rigid and anachronistic forms of life, the means of social change. They have been compared to the great storms that, as the metaphor would have it, purify the seas and lakes by destroying the polluted stagnation of peace. Only in ultimate conflict, it is alleged, can a whole people rise above its petty particular interests and assert a common and transcendent interest that is both nobler and more truly rational than any lesser good.

Such arguments are utterly specious. Wars are always waged for particular, and usually illusory, interests. It is a much greater and more difficult thing to work consistently and constructively for a common good than to risk one's life for it. There is nothing inherently noble about risking death. People risk their lives every day for transient thrills. The element of truth in this romantic view of war is that one ought not to allow oneself to be coerced by the threat of force into abandoning something worth defending. But it is infinitely more desirable to find ways in which the threat of force can be eliminated. There may indeed be good reasons for using

26   *Democracy and the state*

violence to overthrow oppressive regimes. But that necessity
arises from the monopoly of power enjoyed by particular
groups, not from the desirability of violence as such. The
danger of rigidity and stagnation is a function of entrenched
power, not of peace. There is no reason to believe that a
decentralized society would not be one of rapid and healthy
non-violent change.

Integration of the common good

The second argument for the necessity of the state questions
this last assertion. It sees the common good as an integrated
whole that can be achieved only by concerted and authoritative
action planned and sanctioned by a very powerful central
authority. This view is usually associated with 'communism'
or state socialism, but it clearly has conservative proponents
as well. It emphasizes not so much the danger of particularist
violence, as traditional liberals did, but the constructive task
of building a genuinely common good. That good not only
comprises an integrated set of material conditions in which
individuals and groups can flourish but encourages and enforces specific social relationships and a subordination of the
individual to the common good. This argument is not incompatible with many versions of the argument regarding violence
but insists that violence is only a secondary aspect of the
problem.

   All that can come out of a decentralized polity, it insists, is
a series of limited, *ad hoc* compromises between existing
interests that leave the broader and deeper problems of social
structure and relationships untouched. The historic roles of
nations or classes cannot be reduced to piecemeal changes.
The will of the people cannot be reduced to some simple
function of particular interests or wills. It must be articulated
and expressed in common action, leadership and organization,
through which people can recognize and respond to a vision
and a reality that eludes more myopic views.[3]

Democracy and the state   27

It is possible, and, I believe, correct, to concede a good deal of force to the premisses of this argument. The common good is in many of its components something that can only be possessed collectively. It is like a game in which an individual participates but cannot play on her own. But common goods in this sense can exist without there being a single authority that is charged with producing them. Even where some specific common good needs an authority to organize it, or a variety of common goods must be co-ordinated, there is no compelling reason for such a task to fall to a state. Many of our most important cultural goods, our languages, arts and sciences, have been produced without the state playing any substantial constructive role in their production. Decentralized societies do not have to be individualistic or lacking in communal organizations and recognized authorities.

What is at issue is not the production of common goods but control over that production. That democratic control over the production of common goods is seen in terms of democratic control of the state is simply a result of the role that the state has made for itself. The state dominates the units that we call 'peoples', forcing homogeneity on its population through educational, legal and economic policies, integrating diverse goods into a single package. So 'the people' come to be defined as the citizens of a nation state, and their interests as the totality of interests that the state can encompass. Granted this situation, realistic democrats recognize that a mass electorate can articulate an opinion only about the major direction of administration and legislation. So, if the people are to have a say through the electoral process on the major questions of government, they must exercise their power through a central authority that attempts to give specific expression to the will of the people through a host of co-ordinated decisions. The more control is centralized the more likely it is that a genuinely common interest transcending particular entrenched interests will prevail.

28   *Democracy and the state*

Some of the arguments against this view have become very
familiar. A highly centralized administration can control a
vast number of particular operations only through a bureaucracy that inserts many levels of decision-making between
broad policy decisions at the top and final implementation
at the bottom level. Bureaucracies tend to be rigid and have a
high degree of inertia. They function on the basis of rules that
are designed with more attention to ease of administration
than to the substantive interests they are meant to serve.
Diversity, experimentation, flexibility are sacrificed to uniformity, the avoidance of risk and predictability. The bureaucracy puts very tight limits on what its master can do. It
controls the formulation of specific proposals. It controls the
flow and form of information. It monopolizes expertise. The
better it is at its tasks the more difficult it is to control, to
change, to challenge.

These costs might be bearable if the bureaucracy did in fact
achieve some desirable kind of rational co-ordination of
public policy over a wide domain. But in fact the bureaucracies of various departments of government are often more
concerned to prevent incursions of other departments into
their domain than to co-operate with them. At the most particular level, a road being resurfaced seems to ensure that
some other authority will dig it up next week to lay new cables
or pipes. At the highest levels bureaucrats soon establish a
symbiotic relationship with the particular interests they are
supposed to control and devote themselves to the defence and
advancement of those interests at the expense of conflicting
interests.

No doubt a strong and determined government can bring a
bureaucracy to heel, reorganize and redirect it. Revolution
from above is possible at the cost of a great deal of authoritarian administration. But ultimately the effect of such
methods is to transform the old bureaucracy into a new one
that is vastly more powerful and rigid than its predecessor.
Gentler and more gradualist uses of bureaucracy as a means

of social transformation tend to produce precisely that piece-meal accommodation to particular interests that centralized power is supposed to avert. In a relatively free society it evokes a proliferation of organized interest groups that demand and get all sorts of concessions, subsidies and exceptions, often institutionalized in special agencies, that effectively nullify the sweep of general policy, especially where those groups have specific bases of economic, ideological or electoral power.

These counter-arguments to the centralization of power are, I believe, decisive if one sets a high value on democratically controlled social change. However, even the conservatives, valuing stability and continuity above innovation and experiment have reason to be disenchanted with bureaucracy. Its mechanical and instrumental rationality is hardly conducive to the flexibile, consensual ways of dealing with social problems that they wish to promote.[4] They do not know how such an ideal is to be given concrete form in a very complex and unstable society. So they have proved very vulnerable to the so-called neo-conservatives who preach a fundamentalist version of classical liberalism.

Dividing the cake

The more fundamental counter to the argument that strong central authority is necessary to produce a coherent common good is to question its basic premisses and presuppositions.

The idea that an unified social policy is desirable can rest on a variety of bases. One is that there is some good that is of such over-riding importance that it must be promoted or protected above every other and that only a supremely powerful organization can do this. At times this may be the case, but the assumption that there is such a good and that the state can protect it, or is the only way of protecting it, must always be subject to intense scrutiny. The state usually devours what it is supposed to protect. A slightly weaker form of this view

30   *Democracy and the state*

is that there is a firm list of priorities that must be imposed on
recalcitrant institutions, groups and individuals, and that a
supreme authority is necessary to do so. Against such assumptions I shall argue that there are ways of so governing specific
functional institutions that they work directly for the common
good without being subject to any higher government.

The common good is an interrelated set of more specific
goods that are not to be identified simply as the goods of particular individuals or groups. Rather they are the good functioning of a variety of institutions, practices and resources that
interest many different individuals and groups in a variety of
ways and degrees. What is important for each of these instru-
mentalities in terms of social co-ordination is that the other
related institutions, practices and resources that it does not
control function in ways that provide favourable conditions
for its own functioning. The best way of achieving this is by
direct negotiation between various specialized authorities
directed to producing arrangements that are mutually advantageous. Failing that, some form of arbitration between them
should produce a more satisfactory solution than any persistent intervention from a higher level. If each of these bodies
for producing some public good does its job *qua* producer of
public goods in the light of the interests of those involved with
that good, the result should be that the complex that is the
common good will be better served than by any attempt to
articulate it from above.

The crucial questions are, How can those who make the
decisions in these specific agencies be in touch with the needs
they are supposed to serve, and the relevant expertise about
what is possible? How can they be encouraged adequately or,
if need be, constrained to act in the interests of the public
good? How can they be chosen and prevented from becoming
entrenched? These are central questions that I believe I can
answer. For the moment I ask that it be granted for the sake
of argument that my answers are satisfactory. One crucial
question remains, however, namely that of adjudicating be-

Democracy and the state   31

tween conflicting claims to scarce resources. Let us ignore for a moment the question, Where do the resources come from? Still, dividing up the resources involves a very important degree of policy decision and control. Are we not left with something suspiciously like a state? Who pays the piper calls the tune. The allocation of resources is, in the short run at least, a zero-sum game. That does not mean that it must be run by a single authority. There could be a variety of bodies that allocate finance to various institutions and projects, each making its grants conditional on the receipt or non-receipt of grants from other sources. Such a system might be quite flexible and efficient if the membership of various granting bodies were competent and reliable. It could, I shall argue, even be democratic if the granting bodies were representative of the whole spectrum of interests in the community.[5]

Law

Even if it is the case that there is no compelling reason for material public goods to be produced or supervised by a central authority, the common good includes at least one vital element that appears necessarily to involve a central authority, namely law. Decentralized powers must be defined and machinery of arbitration set up. Bodies such as those we have been suggesting can only be stable and legitimate if constituted and supported by law. In very complex and artificial societies there are no 'natural' authorities of the sort that there may be in simple or traditional societies. The scope, functions, entitlements and limits of specific authorities need constantly to be redefined in the light of changed circumstances. The scope and limits of entitlements, rights and duties must be spelled out so that people can know what they can and cannot do. The law must not only articulate what is valid or invalid, it must punish wrongs and protect those who are not able to protect themselves. Above all it must express a common conception of justice and seek to promote it.

32   *Democracy and the state*

Some kinds of dispute may be settled by recognized arbi-
trators without any explicit legislative or juridical system, but
clearly many could not in any complex society. This is a point
that I do not propose to deny. What I do deny is that it entails
the sort of power that is given to modern states. There might
be a plurality of law-making bodies for specific functional
rather than geographical areas, a sort of federalism of function. In such a polity the role of any supreme legislature and
supreme court might be quite limited, consisting for the most
part of reviews of and appeals from laws and decisions of
more specialized authorities, and readjustments to their jurisdictions and procedures, without any power to initiate judgement on substantive 'first order' questions. Such executive
functions as were necessary to carry out legal decisions might
be exercised directly by the courts without any independent
executive arm being necessary. Such an authority would rely
on invoking community sanctions against recalcitrant authorities rather than exercising specific penal powers such as
fines or imprisonment. It would rest its authority on the common recognition of its right to make these decisions and the
importance and general acceptability of the decisions themselves.

No doubt a widely shared democratic political culture
would be an indispensable condition of the operation of an
institution such as I have sketched. Institutions and practices
do not function automatically and without preconditions.
Even in present states the effect of such a culture on the functioning of political institutions is not achieved primarily by
force or the sanctions of electoral success and failure. It is to
a very great extent a matter of what people are prepared to
accept as right or at least reasonable. Even those who do not
accept the substance of that culture are forced to give at least
an hypocritical endorsement to its externals. I assume that the
present aspirations for rational, just and responsive decision-
making in public affairs are capable of substantial development and that increasing the variety and specificity of the

Democracy and the state

institutions in which public affairs are conducteᴏ
duce greater participation in and awareness of
political culture and in turn enrich that culture. I sha.
show in detail how this might be brought about.

II WHY WE SHOULD GET RID OF THE STATE

In the preceding paragraphs I have been assuming that it is
desirable to get rid of the state for two obvious reasons. The
state is the means of war and of repression. Whether one
adopts the view that human beings are naturally territorial
and bellicose or naturally peaceable and reasonable the conclusion is the same. If they are bellicose it is folly to let
modern weapons of destruction fall into their hands. If they
are peaceable there is no good reason for running the risk of
mistakes and accidents. In any case whatever innate disposi-
tions people, or significant proportions of them, may have,
these are heavily overlaid by training, repression and social
organization. No matter how one attempts to romanticize
violence, it is supreme folly to put ourselves in the hands of
the few who, at the touch of a button, can unleash in-
calculable and irreversible destruction upon humankind.

Even apart from war and the threat of war, the repressive
potential of the state is enormous and largely uncontrollable.
This potential may not be apparent where the society is not
under great strain or overt conflict. The capacity to escape
such strains, however, is much more the exceptional case than
the norm.

I shall return to this point later when various other
economic and social theses have been argued.

Functions of the state

Meanwhile, let us look more closely at the functions of the
modern state. The state exists to express and promote the unity
of a given territorial community. Its monopoly of legitimate

violence has been used to attempt to safeguard and promote a great variety of things that have been regarded as important to the community: its military power relative to other states, its religious and other culturally important beliefs, its internal law and order, its economic well-being and its prestige. It has an ideological function, a military one and an economic one. The history of the modern state system is a history of struggles about the exercise of these functions, various forces striving to maximize or minimize each or all of them or to produce decisive shifts in policy in each or all of them.

The net effect of these struggles has been a vast increase in the scope and efficacy of state operations and a marked change in their characteristic forms and modes. Even those who have been hostile to the state and to the particular socio-economic order that it buttresses have by and large succeeded only in extending the range or changing the mode of its operations. Some of the disabilities of the oppressed have been alleviated by social services of many kinds, at the cost of making the recipients clients of the state. Abuses have been controlled at the cost of proliferating agencies of state regulation. Greater economic stability has been achieved at the price of massive intervention by state agencies in the economy. In electoral regimes parties compete for votes by offering to use state power to the pretended advantage of various groups. Even the advocates of the minimal state succeed only in transferring the emphasis on welfare to an emphasis on armaments and 'law and order', strengthening one branch of the state at the expense of others and one segment of the community at the expense of others.

This enormously complicated organization is the site of a host of conflicts between fragmented interest groups. In Robert Dahl's phrase, what we have is not majority rule or minority rule but *minorities* rule, according to the ever-changing opportunities for diverse particular interests to gain some partial ascendancy over policy-making and its implementation in some specific areas. Within a limited perspective

Democracy and the state   35

this sort of polyarchy, as Dahl aptly calls it, is on balance desirable. It mitigates the formal concentration of power and breaks down the tendency to bureaucratic inflexibility. Most groups get some relief from their most pressing problems. No group is in a decisive position on every issue. A certain sort of stability is achieved together with a significant degree of adaptability.

Such a view seems a far cry from Marx's view expressed in the aphorism that 'the executive of the modern state is the committee for handling the common affairs of the bourgeoisie'. Marx, of course, spoke only of the executive. He was aware that the state, even in his day, was much more than that. Contemporary Marxists have tried to cope with the problem of understanding the enormous qualitative and quantitative changes in the role of the state over the past hundred years or more.[6] At a very high level of generality it is easy enough to keep the substance of Marx's thesis intact. Modern states in the Western world, even when their governments profess some 'socialist' ideology, all maintain the capitalist system, and at least to that extent the central common interests of the bourgeoisie. Moreover in economic matters they are tightly constrained to safeguard the central motor of capitalism, the accumulation of capital, and their policies in other areas are closely governed by this central requirement.

In most countries the central electoral issues are issues of 'economic management'. Governments are made and unmade by perceptions of their success in administering the existing economic order. Attempts at even relatively modest change are rarely successful and produce great apprehension. The state is not a capitalist conspiracy, but it serves capital well. The commonly perceived alternative is state socialism and the evidence that that would be worse is generally regarded as overwhelming. Radical theorists may talk of various possibilities of socialism without the state, but there are no practical political programmes for achieving it, and its very possibility remains highly debatable. The capitalist state is

36   *Democracy and the state*

generally accepted. It is no doubt a site of class struggle, but
that struggle has rarely taken any radical orientation. It is not
a struggle for a decisive socio-economic change but for small
readjustments of policy that leave the system intact.

In the middle of the nineteenth century both conservatives
and radicals thought that the advent of full adult suffrage
would herald a decisive political class confrontation. The
have-nots would dispossess the haves, the repressive apparatus of the state would be destroyed, and the dictatorship of
the proletariat would inaugurate either a new tyranny or a
new freedom in democracy. Five generations later these
hopes and fears have been decisively disappointed. By and
large the state is not perceived by the workers as the prime
instrument of class oppression. For it is not, for the most
part, overtly repressive.

The mode of state control has changed, as Foucault has
emphasized, from overt show of force on sporadic occasions
to a pervasive surveillance and regulation of vast areas of
social life.[7] As long as one goes about one's ordinary occupations in the normal way one is hardly conscious of the state's
omnipresent regulation. Very often it appears as a protective
shield, a big brother much more benign and permissive than
Orwell's fiction. In 1984 one cannot take *1984* very seriously
most of the time, at least as it affects most people in most
democratic countries. The purported demonstration that the
state is deeply oppressive seems excessively metaphysical.
Protest pays. Even the most entrenched bureaucrats want to
appear fair and compassionate. The police are brutal and
arbitrary only with those who are marginal to the community
and deviant from its broad consensus. That consensus
changes to incorporate and domesticate even more of the
rebellious.

Strains in the system

Nevertheless, the state system is under very strong internal
strains. In the first place, in advanced countries the state has

Democracy and the state   37

to appropriate rarely less than a third and sometimes more than half of the gross national product to meet its commitments. Taxation is inherently arbitrary in its incidence. Even those who accept a given scheme of taxation almost always feel entitled to avoid its imposts. When large sums are involved evasion becomes an industry and every economic and political activity is affected by it. It stifles, corrupts and constrains what people can do. Even where taxation is formally redistributive from rich to poor it normally ends up being redistributive in the other direction, if only because the rich have so many more ways of evasion open to them and can afford the best advice on how to use them. The self-employed gain at the expense of the wage and salary earner, the unproductive speculator at the expense of the regular producer. Conversely, those who receive benefits from the state are placed under strong temptations to fake the bases of entitlement. Both tendencies can be countered only by even more detailed regulation and surveillance. Is there no better way of providing for public goods and for those in need of assistance?

In the second place, there is an insidious tyranny of numbers. The state homogenizes and atomizes social relationships. The horizons and expectations of people contract to the limits of those variations that the system constitutes as practical possibilities. Even where people are vaguely aware that things could be otherwise they often cling to the devil they know and find virtue in doing so. They settle for quiet passivity, shunning risk, experiment, confrontation and uncertainty. As the neo-conservatives have emphasized, they lose their resilience and initiative. Lacking something significant and constructive to do in public life they shrink into a private life that is increasingly trivial and boring. At worst they take to drugs, crime, charlatan religions and cynicism. The political culture on which the system depends is profoundly threatened.

Thirdly, nation states under internal strains have always tended to seek to overcome these strains by uniting the nation

38   *Democracy and the state*

to respond to some real or contrived external threat. Threats lead to counter-threats and eventually to war, as the Falkland–Malvinas episode so recently reminded us.

Short of war, 'security' systems consistently increase the role of military and police power in society. Almost everywhere the military establishment is closely integrated with those forces in society that seek to maintain existing stratification and privileges, restrict information and debate and weaken the power of popular organizations of all sorts, especially trade unions and radical political groups. Most countries live under some degree of threat that the response to any significant shift of power away from the existing establishment will be military intervention, often direct military dictatorship. In any unstable situation the military are vastly better organized and better equipped to take the initiative effectively than any insurgent group can hope to be. Conversely, the greater the likelihood of confrontation with the military, the more any realistic radical group is likely to see itself forced to organize itself on military lines. The result is that even if it attains power it is likely to be as authoritarian and ultimately as reactionary in many respects as its opponents.

Fourthly, the military in most countries depend to some very significant degree on one or other of the superpowers for 'aid' in hardware, training and other support. They become pawns in the cold war, guardians of various forms of neo-colonialism. Poor nations devote scarce resources to armaments and economically and socially destructive organizations. Rich nations devote the little aid they are prepared to give to the poor mostly to military or para-military projects.

No doubt in a more fundamental analysis of the role of the state, the military would appear as secondary to basic economic and ideological forces. Nevertheless those forces could not operate or maintain themselves without the military and the state apparatus which in a crisis is always prepared to

Democracy and the state   39

submit to military directions. The practical salience of military power is all but complete. A democratic state is a dialectical contradiction. The more powerful the state the less are people able to control it. The weaker the state the more power non-state elites enjoy. A state may, of course, in certain respects and under certain conditions, be more or less democratic, but only in conflict with its own inherent tendencies. The democratic state is an exceptional and unstable compromise. It is time to explore more deeply why this must be so.

III   DEMOCRACY VERSUS THE STATE

In the liberal tradition there has always been a tension between a specific democratic ideal, the rule of the majority, and the view that the role of the state should be minimized in the interests of individual freedom. The freedom that was uppermost in the minds of the classical Anglo-American liberals was the freedom of the property-owning classes to dispose of their property as they saw fit. They feared that an envious propertyless majority would use their power to dispossess the rich and so ruin all classes. But there were other aspects as well.[8] Freedom of thought and expression, freedom of religion and freedom of association and movement were also important. A populist majority might be as intolerant as any absolute monarch.

The constitutional state

Their perceived solution to the problem was the constitutional state which had only those limited powers assigned to it in the constitution, or was expressly forbidden by the constitution from using its powers in certain specific ways. The guarantee of the constitution was the separation of powers, designed in such a way that each of the major functions of government kept a check on the others. Let us leave aside for the moment

40   *Democracy and the state*

the inadequacies and dangers of this system and concentrate
on the conception of democracy that came to be associated
with it. The dominant theme was that a democratic government was a minimal government. The liberal property-owner's
state could correspond to the interests of the overwhelming
majority of the people precisely because the people wanted to
be governed as little as possible. Their greatest interest was to
maximize their freedom. This in turn presupposed a society in
which the provision of goods by the state was unnecessary
because people were in a position to provide for themselves,
apart from the basic goods of law, defence and a minimal
infrastructure of facilities such as lighthouses. People would
see any unnecessary increase in state power as a threat to their
freedom. The will of the people was not to rule for fear of being ruled. An inherent contradiction between the state and
democracy was tacitly acknowledged, but in a limited and
unsatisfactory form.

The transition from the classical liberal to the liberal
democratic state rested on a change in its view of who constituted the people. As C. B. Macpherson has emphasized,
for the liberals it did not originally mean the whole population of the territory of the state, but rather the responsible
members of society, in practice owners of substantial property,
generally excluding not only women, slaves, foreigners and
criminals, but the vast majority whose only property was
their own labour power. Sometimes these, as servants, were
deemed to be represented by their masters. In any case they
were seen as lacking experience, education, good judgement
and a stake in the economic system. Not being free in their
daily occupations they were in no position to understand and
defend freedom.

It is easy to dismiss this conception of the people, as a self-
serving ideology promoted in the name of freedom by the
rising bourgeoisie, deriving its emotive force from its rejection of feudal privilege, but consecrating a new set of forms
of exploitation. In many respects, however, it was both more

honest and more realistic than the populist democracy to which it succumbed. It recognized that the state in fact functions to defend the existing social order, and that only those who have good reasons to support that order can be expected to make sound decisions about state policy. It aspired towards a rational administration of an actually functioning society rather than towards some illusory ideal. It realized clearly that the rule of the majority of inhabitants was not, at least in class societies, compatible with the stability of the state. Not just anything the majority may choose is politically possible. There can be a stable state only when there is basic harmony between the requirements of social and economic stability and the political power structure. Otherwise the state must either stand as a superior power above society and inevitably slide into tyranny or become the instrument of conflicting social forces. The normal result of the latter is a state of political chaos that also ends in tyranny.

Constricting the political agenda

The crucial way in which the system is safeguarded from fickle majorities is by narrowing the political agenda. If this has the happy result of preventing the state being used for some purposes in which its use is dangerous, it certainly does not prevent all such uses. More importantly for our present purpose, the fact that many urgent problems are distorted or not recognized as open to constructive solution is not just an effect of reactionary political tactics. It is endemic in the constitutional solution to the problem of tyranny. In the first place, the constitutional state remains a state. It cannot be an effective means of calling in question the consequences of the system of states. While nearly everybody would place the abolition of the arms race very high on their list of desiderata, the popular will for peace is almost wholly ineffectual. The state system cannot articulate such basic and pervasive needs realistically. It is nonsense to talk of rule by the people when

42 *Democracy and the state*

such questions cannot even get on to the political agenda. Narrowly constricting the political agenda is an inevitable effect of constitutional government designed both to maintain and restrict the power of the state. One cannot exclude political tyranny without firmly entrenching institutions and practices that have a narrowly circumscribed scope and efficacy and a political culture that confines the tactics and issues of politics in the spirit of the constitution. It must become accepted that what is politically possible is limited and that it is right that these limits be observed.

The fact that constitutional politics cannot deal with those issues that bring into question the state system itself is not the only result. A host of other issues of vital importance are either effectively excluded from the horizon of practical politics or posed in a form that excludes awareness of appropriate solutions.

Fission suppressed

The most obvious rigidity is that states do not tolerate secession of any substantial part of their population. The very arbitrariness and precariousness of the boundaries of most states is the most powerful reason for their *not* being open to legitimate challenge. Once they are changed there is no particular natural limit to change. Conversely, states through a host of legal and 'educational' activities strive to suppress the cultural and economic bases of the distinct identity of lesser communities in an attempt to preserve the state's unity. The processes of free formation of communities are deliberately and effectively curtailed. The results are particularly damaging in places such as Africa where tribal and other community forms of development are still alive. As Michael Taylor emphasizes, fission has always been the normal means of evading internal conflict in communities. Deprived of this normal recourse communities that wish to resist absorption into the dominant state culture are repressed.

Democracy and the state 43

Paradoxically this repression is often hailed as a liberation. The old particular cultures are seen as outmoded and constricting, and their replacement by modern cultures is progress. Formally, of course, this is a liberation. The power of communities other than the state to exercise authority over their members is destroyed. It remains a very complex question whether freedom in one respect is not bought at the price of worse enslavement in another. Obviously many people affected by such changes feel that it is. The balance sheet for every community and every individual will be different. What is of more concern to us at present is whether or not non-state communities could tackle the sort of problems that arise when the material and technological bases of life are transformed to exploit modern scientific knowledge. The argument of this book is that they can, provided they are not total communities but overlap with a variety of other specialized communities in an open pattern.

If that is correct then the rigidity of the state system must be measured not only against all the destruction of minorities and their cultures for which it has been responsible but against the possibilities of a much more fluid and diverse political order that it excludes.

Collective property

The state is the supreme property-owner, enjoying the right of overriding all private property rights within its territory by resumption for public use, taxation, or punitive confiscation. It is only the law of the state that fixes determinate titles to property and what those titles entail in the enforceable exclusions of others. The state excludes itself from interfering with property only for reasons of prudence. One reason it cannot brook secession is that those seceding take with them part of its property.

Even more severely than any historical form of private property, state rights to property are sources of absolute

44   *Democracy and the state*

exclusion of any responsibility to others. So the only ways in which other communities can obtain what they want from a state are by force, trade or appeals to pity. The poor communities remain poor because they lack resources with which to trade and force with which to threaten. The pity of the rich nations is miniscule.

If certain activities are to take place on a piece of land others must be excluded, at least temporarily. The farmer must exclude animals from grazing on the growing crop. But there can be a multiplicity of kinds of right to the exclusive use of land in particular ways under specific safeguards and for legitimate purposes. Various kinds of rights can belong to specific sorts of individuals and organizations. Assigning those rights need not rest on any overriding right, but simply on the authority to adjudicate conflicting claims.

What the state's supreme property rights express is an incoherent recognition that there is no natural claimant to the earth other than the whole community. Humankind, however, has no political existence. So each state acts in effect as if it were itself the whole, thus denying the rights of humankind as a whole. Once again it is easy to conclude that the problem can be solved only by the emergence of a world state that does represent all humankind. I am maintaining the contrary. Every all-embracing claim must be abolished and the system of entitlements changed to represent the real interest of the various overlapping communities that constitute the whole. Some of the *initial* moves in this reconstruction of property rights will involve the use of state power, but I hope to show how it need not depend on state power once it is launched.

Migration and population

One of the boasts of the liberal state is that, unlike most other states, it does not try to stop individuals and small groups leaving it. It does, however, impose severe restrictions on

Democracy and the state   45

people joining it. Unquestionably, whom to exclude from group membership is one of the most difficult problems that any group has to solve. No group can absorb more members indefinitely without losing its original character, and having very different effects on its own members and on other groups. No group can fall below a certain size and still be viable. Nevertheless, where voluntary groups are concerned, we commonly uphold the freedom of people to leave them, much as we may regret the demise of the group. But joining is another matter. It is difficult to see precisely why this should be so. Clearly a group is entitled to set a fair price on the benefits that it provides for new entrants from the accumulated efforts of past members. Indeed, where the benefits are wholly the product of the members and impose no costs on others there is no compelling reason why the group may not exclude whom it likes and impose what price it likes on membership.

However, the most significant voluntary organizations do affect non-members' opportunities quite substantially. In some cases they have an effective monopoly of certain opportunities. A sporting club may for a variety of reasons have a monopoly on facilities for a particular sport in an area, a cultural club may have exclusive use of the facilities necessary for staging plays and concerts and so on. Where such monopolies exist it seems reasonable that clubs be required to admit appropriate applicants, at least up to the number at which it might reasonably be split into two viable clubs. But who is to lay down such requirements, on what authority and on what criteria?

There is a series of dilemmas that arise in any attempt to make such judgements. On the one hand, the group of voluntary associates ought to be able to determine their own way of doing things, the size of their membership and the rhythm of change in response to changing circumstances. Not only the liberty of the individuals but the diversity and spontaneity of social relations is at stake. From these points of view control

46   *Democracy and the state*

is counterproductive. On the other hand, the strategic or monopoly power of voluntary organizations can be used to discriminate against people arbitrarily, and to enforce restrictive practices to the detriment not only of excluded individuals but of a range of social relationships. So we have various forms of anti-discrimination legislation. As we expand the scope and importance of the associations the problem becomes more acute.

In general, as I have suggested, and will argue more fully later, monopolies of material resources necessary for a particular activity should not be allowed to become a source of power for those who control or use them. The use of such resources should be subject to conditions that preserve the community interest. If one carries through that principle to the international situation then it seems that no nation should be permitted to have exclusive power over its own territory, but should enjoy it only subject to conditions that preserve the interests of other nations and their members. The nation itself should not have unqualified rights to exclude immigrants any more than to impose just any restrictions it likes on the sort of communities that are formed within its borders.

On the one hand, it is utterly unreasonable to expect any community or association or nation to maintain the sort of open door policy that can lead to its being destroyed in the way that the American Indian and Australian aboriginal communities were. Quite apart from the killing, plunder and treachery so conspicuous in those cases, the mere fact of overwhelming numbers of people, given to utterly new ways of social interaction, entering the territory in which a community lives can make it impossible to continue in the old ways or even to adapt constructively to the new circumstances. Communities of all sorts need time and elbow room if they are to preserve anything worthwhile through cultural and social change. It is not only in their interests but in the common interest that they be given the chance of dealing with external forces rather than being simply overwhelmed by

Democracy and the state   47

them. On the other hand, the rigid demarcations that allow
privilege to entrench itself are not in the long term interests of
anybody or any community, at least once one discounts all
claims to religious or cultural absolutes.

The state system, however, is just such a rigidly entrenched
way of preventing free interchange of members between communities. The interests of a certain established community
and power structure are preserved without regard to the needs
of outsiders or the desirability of change within the nation.

Nations, states and community

A pure market system of relationships and a purely organizational system both put a premium on efficiency over other
values. 'Instrumental rationality' is destructive of community.
Flexible reciprocity, giving in the hope that one may get a
similar service back from somebody else when one needs it,
does not stand up in the context of strict contracts. Where
each person looks after only his or her own interests and purposes, community norms and values wither. Where cash
payments for specified tasks are the only basis of exchange
the many-sided relationships that constitute communities
wither. The nuclear family may succeed in insulating itself
from these pressures because of the enormous internal
pressures in favour of reciprocity that it generates. Small
groups of families may extend some familial relations into
areas of obvious mutual interest. Areas of civility may survive
in more casual personal relationships, but community does
not.

In these circumstances the crumbling identity of the nation
finds expression only in the state and in a nostalgia that is
wrongly called tradition. The nation not only attempts to use
the state to assert its own reality and importance but strives to
preserve itself by suppressing the very sources of internal
variety and initiative that might give it life. The nation and
non-formal communities more generally can maintain their

48   *Democracy and the state*

identity through change only by adapting to meet the problems that threaten them. In general, in a complex world of increasingly specialized and differentiated activities no such
open and flexible community can be a total community or be
identified with a formal organization. It will destroy itself in
the attempt, as so many nations have done.

At first sight the state represents the supreme example of
reciprocity. It calls on its members to risk their lives for the
nation, it preaches and (selectively) enforces a public morality
of duty, service and altruism. But voluntary service is replaced
by conscription, moral sanctions by law, and public service
by professional careerism. The flexible, evolving common
good of the nation is replaced by the goods that the state is
designed to produce and regulate. Nationalism becoming
statism ensures the death of those relationships that constituted the nation as a community and not just as an
organization. The state, of course, has to keep alive the myth
of the nation to justify its pretensions. People need to believe
the myth because they have no other earthly hope of significant common achievement. But this myth is not the anticipation of an ideal. It is a mystification, a tragic illusion.

The need for an alternative

The most common complaint against contemporary liberal
democracies is the remoteness of the decision-makers from
those affected by decisions. Those affected have little say in
those decisions unless they happen to be in a position to bring
organized pressure on the decision-makers, and the ability to
bring such pressure is very unequally distributed, usually in
favour of groups that are already highly advantaged in their
socio-economic power. But the present complaint is more
fundamental. It concerns not only the existence of great inequalities in the distribution of power, but the incapacity of
most people to do anything towards righting them. The result
is a disillusionment with liberal politics among substantial

groups in the community that threatens the political culture itself. A democracy that renders people impotent is no democracy.

It is not surprising, therefore, that realistic radicals have generally seen reformism as the enemy of any desirable attack on the problems generated by existing power relationships. If the people are to exercise power to change the system all constitutional limits on the exercise of power must be overthrown. But these very realists become utterly unrealistic when they are called on to answer how a popular or proletarian dictatorship is to be prevented from turning into the dictatorship of a small political elite. Even if we grant that the people can articulate what it finds objectionable in present practices and policies and the general direction in which they must be changed, it cannot articulate the concrete means by which changes are to be implemented. It is the particular things that are in fact done that have effects. The more these things are done through the exercise of state power by a small executive the more dangerous they are likely to be.

It is not just a question of the opportunity offered to the power hungry to pay lip-service to popular demands while entrenching repression, important though that is. It is not only that radical change must involve conflicts to which there is no right answer or that all specific conflicts become conflated with the basic conflict of 'the people' against its enemies. In practice the executive has to demand and enforce on the people the sort of discipline that a general must demand of an army once battle is joined. Since this demand itself creates new enemies the battle is never over, and the people have no more control over their leaders than privates have over generals.

The attempt to give more power to the people ends in tyranny over the people just as the attempt to exclude tyranny keeps the people from exercising power in the things that matter most. Neither the constitutional state nor the unlimited state can be controlled effectively by the people. Neither can do

50   *Democracy and the state*

very much to improve the provision of public goods without
increasing either the scope and rigidity of the state apparatus,
or its arbitrariness and lack of accountability. Neither can be
a means of calling into question the state system itself.
Neither can offer satisfactory ways of dealing with the most
pervasive social and economic problems. The question, Is
democracy possible? is at least partially reducible to the question, Is it possible to provide for public and common needs
by other institutions and practices than those of the state? If
we are serious about answering this question it is not sufficient to point out the abstract possibility of alternatives to
the state. We must give solid grounds for thinking that they
could function effectively under realistic conditions.

[5]

Excerpt from *Is Democracy Possible?* 106–24

III THE ALTERNATIVE TO
ELECTORAL DEMOCRACY

Negotiation and size

I have already argued that most issues of any complexity need to be settled by negotiation in a co-operative framework. The most advantageous feasible solution for each party is often possible only if it is prepared to make concessions to other parties who are in a position to block many of the possible outcomes. In any case there are almost always long-term advantages in encouraging reciprocity by striving to achieve solutions that are at least seen as fair by all involved. Negotiation involves attempts to construct comprehensive packages through a process of exploration of possibilities, expanding or contracting the scope of the packages, trying to get clear about what is important and what is negotiable for each party.

Such work must be done in committee. The point of the small committee, the reason why large assemblies often refer problems to them, is that the members of the committee can spare the time to familiarize themselves with all the details of a matter in a way that is not possible to most members of the assembly, granted the range of other problems demanding their attention. Moreover, in informal debate in a committee, the members can explore and construct a wide variety of possible solutions to a problem and attempt to find ways of conciliating divergent interests. The larger assembly, by contrast, is usually capable only of accepting or rejecting a given proposal, perhaps with some minor amendments.

Committees, precisely because they cannot claim to be fully representative of all the interests involved may come under strong pressure to demonstrate that they have made every effort to take them all into account. Committees strive to achieve as much unanimity as possible in their final proposals because unanimity enhances the force of their decision. Committees tend to accommodation, large assemblies to confrontation. In the large assembly there is neither the time nor the capacity for detailed negotiation, and partly because of this each agent is usually reduced to representing a single interest. Each member of a large body can have some impact on the outcome only by making some single clear and telling point. By and large in such situations it is easier to be effective in stopping proposals than in proposing constructive alternatives.

The large assembly is usually forced to bring the question to a vote whether or not it has been discussed adequately. In modern parliamentary situations party discipline ensures that government sponsored legislation goes through with the minimum of amendment. The committees in which the real work of negotiation is done conduct their meetings in secret, sometimes because they are in fact clandestine, sometimes behind a veil of officially sanctioned 'confidentiality'. Clearly it is desirable that negotiations on public policy decisions should be conducted publicly. At the same time, however, the negotiators should be free to consider alternatives without being called to heel by those whose interests they represent. The process of exploration of possibilities cannot proceed if pressure groups are in a position to lay down in advance what is negotiable and what is not.

Representation and function

Two main reasons why one ought to entrust the furtherance of one's interests to somebody else are the opportunity costs of pursuing them oneself and one's lack of the appropriate knowledge and skill. My representative should have at least as strong an interest in advancing my interests as I have,

108   *Democracy and representation*

should be in a position to devote more time and effort to the task and bring to it superior knowledge and skill. It is very unlikely that anybody can meet these requirements in regard to my interests generally, or even my interest in public goods. But once one specifies a particular interest, the local library, for example, it is quite likely that there are people who share my interests, have a stronger motivation to work for them than I do, and are better equipped to do so.

If the range of interests that I have, many of them conflicting interests, are to be properly represented, it is most unlikely that any one person will be appropriate.[9] What I need is a host of specialized representatives each of whom has the same interest as I in the relevant respect, and the appropriate motivation, knowledge and skill. How is it possible for me to have such representation?

In most democratic countries a large number of common goods are provided at local level by municipal councils, which are elected by the residents (or property-holders) in a certain area and draw the bulk of their revenue from taxes, especially on landed property, that they levy on residents or property-holders in that area. Among the functions of these bodies the salient ones are usually to lay down and enforce rules about and provide services in areas such as town planning and building regulations, public health, garbage disposal, parks and recreational facilities, local roads and drainage, libraries and some educational facilities, environmental protection and the promotion of local industry. The basic reasons why these different functions are vested in the same body are: (1) that it is the source of finance for them, and (2) that it is the means by which the exercise of those functions is controlled in some degree by the governed. There is no particularly strong relation between the functions themselves. Many of them have stronger practical links with similar functions in neighbouring municipalities or in higher levels of government than with other functions at the local level. It is not always the case that the geographical area of a municipality is the most suitable unit from the point of view of efficiency of operations. It is not very likely that a library authority and a garbage disposal authority for example would break up into the same geographical units, particularly in the large conurbations in which most people in Western countries now live. The city, the town, the suburb no longer exist as communities in the way that they did when the structure of our patterns of local government was formed. People's activities take place in a variety of localities and they belong to many overlapping communities, most of which have no precise location or boundaries or membership.

Of the two reasons given above why these various functions are united in the same body, the first, that it provides the bulk of the finance for them is historically important but not very cogent, since there is no particular reason why each of these functions should draw its revenue from the same source. Even if they did, the function of the fundraising body might simply be that of apportioning funds to a variety of agencies, leaving the responsibilities for deciding on what use is to be made of those funds to the agencies themselves, provided there is appropriate control of those agencies by some other means. So the decisive reason for making a single body responsible for a variety of functions is that it is a way of keeping some degree of democratic control over their operations. What this form of organization does is to add an administrative level to the levels that are required to perform the specific functions and attempt to achieve democratic control of all of them through this level. The obvious alternative would be to have specific elections for the controlling bodies in each function. The advantages would be numerous. Representatives with particular interest in one or other of the bodies would nominate for it. The number of opportunities for people to take an active role in public life would be increased enormously, and many people who would not be willing to set themselves the whole range of problems of a municipal council would probably be willing to take a strong

110   *Democracy and representation*

interest in a particular function, especially if in doing so they had a fairly free hand.

The central difficulty, of course, is that there would be too many elections. Each voter would belong to many different electorates, and most would lack the time, information and motivation to make any informed personal judgement about most of them. In practice most people, if they bothered to vote, would tend to vote for party lists or 'tickets'. The net result might well be simply to strengthen the party apparatuses. The game of power-trading and building a power base would tend to take precedence over the specific issues involved. The value of functional representation would be lost.

Representation and sampling

The most reliable way of getting a group that is representative of a particular population is to take a statistical sample of the population. The theory and practice of sampling is now highly developed. Such a representative group could be trusted to act as representatives if they had some stronger than average motive for devoting themselves to the interests they represent and acquiring adequate knowledge and skill for the task. If they were compensated for the time and effort involved the mere fact of their being chosen to be representatives might be sufficient motivation for many. For others it would, like jury service today, be an unwelcome imposition.

It seems preferable, therefore, that representatives should be volunteers. Once a statistical characterization of the various interests to be represented is established there should be no problem in selecting from those who are willing to serve a group that is representative in the statistical sense.[10] Granted that they volunteer to work in this particular area rather than some other or none, it is likely that they feel more strongly than most people about the issues involved and that they have or are prepared to acquire superior knowledge of the problems. So it would be reasonable for the group that

Democracy and representation   111

these people represent statistically to accept them as representatives in decision-making. One could envisage a well-based
convention granting authority to such bodies and appropriate
procedures for selecting them.

The first thing that would need to be clearly defined is the
function to be supervised and a reasonably comprehensive
analysis of the various interests that people might have in the
supervision of that function. In general the main groups
affected would be those who work at providing the good in
question, those who are consumers of it and those who are affected by its side-effects. But within these groups there might
well be very substantial conflicts of interest and differences of
opinion.

So the question immediately arises whether it is interest or
opinions that are to form the basis of selection. There is no
insuperable difficulty in either case. One could take a broad
opinion survey, classify groups of opinions and choose representatives on the basis of their own answers to the survey
questions so as to match the strength of the various opinions
in the population. There would be some incentive for those
with unpopular opinions to disguise them in the hope of being
chosen. It is statistically unlikely, however, that this would
affect the result substantially unless a very large proportion
of those who volunteer to serve entered into a conspiracy to
manipulate the sampling process. There could be safeguards
against this possibility. Candidates might be required to
declare publicly their beliefs and the interests they claim to
represent and even be liable to legal actions for gross misrepresentation or fraud.

Such a system would still leave representatives a great deal
of room for negotiation, and even for changing their
opinions whenever they had defensible ground for doing so.
It would approximate more closely than any other system to a
fully participatory democracy. The main objection to it is
that if people are not very well informed about a matter and
express opinions about it in relative isolation those opinions

are not well-grounded. There is no good reason for taking them seriously as the basis for structuring the body that is to make the decisions.

The objection could be met by making the survey not a matter of 'off the cuff' answers to a questionnaire but an educative and exploratory exercise. A demographically representative sample could be chosen and the people in the sample could be given special information and opportunities for discussions about the issues before giving their answers. Perhaps they might even be paid to take the time to study the problems. Such measures might be expected to improve the quality of the basis for choosing representatives, the quality of the representatives and the general quality of on-going debate in the community about such matters. They would not abolish conflicts of interest or differences of opinion, but they would create an atmosphere of rational open and constructive discussion in which optimal solutions would be most likely to emerge and gain acceptance.

In most situations, however, such an elaborate method of choosing representatives might not be warranted. It would be simpler to choose them on the basis of an analysis of the interests involved. Interests are more important and even more cogent in the long-run than opinions. Rationally I should prefer my interests to be safeguarded rather than have my more or less shaky opinions prevail. In practice, of course, I may often set a higher priority on getting my own way than on securing my long-term interests because of pride, spite, impatience, stupidity or other human failings. But most of us in most matters that affect us do not have such a definite will. Even when we know what we would like to happen we are well aware that if we knew all the relevant facts our practical choice could well be different.

Moreover, in many cases there is no 'right' decision. Our long-term interests are not fixed. Different and largely incommensurable possibilities exist. Choosing one or other of those possibilities means entering a different situation in which some of our tastes, hopes and relationships will change. There is no unchanging point of reference, no fixed set of needs or preferences, against which such possibilities can be so measured and evaluated as to produce a right answer. There are indeed many wrong answers. It is not the case that we are infinitely malleable. We need to be assured that clearly wrong choices are not made. But the quest for a way of finding *the* right answer is radically pointless.

In general it is more in our interests that a variety of possibilities be explored than that attempts should be made to discover and impose what purports to be the best way of dealing with a problem. The great strength of the case for the superiority of the market over planning is just such a point. However, allowing great opportunities for diverse solutions to problems, diverse projections of needs, and differing opinions to be tried is not an exclusive property of the market. If representatives in charge of various functional enterprises had a free hand to try whatever solutions they thought best there is little doubt that a great variety of ways of doing things would be tried. I shall argue that this would be an advantage and that it need not carry with it any serious disadvantages.

Representation and responsibility

In some circumstances we may sensibly consent to be represented by a person over whom we have no control. In some circumstances we may reasonably be presumed to consent to being represented by somebody without even knowing what is going on. But the relationship of representation is undoubtedly stronger in proportion to the degree of willingness of the person represented to accept the representative. In political contexts it has commonly been assumed that the degree in which a polity is democratic is proportional to the degree of control that the citizens have over their representatives. Clearly acceptance is not enough or any legitimate regime would be democratic. Some authoritarian regimes may have enjoyed as high a degree of acceptance as many a democracy.

What control involves is not as simple as it might at first seem. If one is in a position to decide quite determinately what one wants the degree of control one has over a representative is just a matter of one's capacity to ensure that the representative acts as effectively as possible to implement one's decision. Corporate bodies, especially large bodies of people with diverse interests in relation to a type of activity, are not in a position to have a fully determinate will about the practical matters to be decided. They may, of course, have many areas of agreement and share a number of aspirations, but a host of issues remain to be resolved. There is in general no correct resolution of these issues and no correct procedure of arriving at a resolution of them. In other words, there cannot be anything like Rousseau's *general will*, as he himself recognized, except in the very simplest societies. There can only be conventions to accept certain results or decision procedures for the sake of getting things done, So, for example, there is no right system of voting. As long as the results are not too disastrous we agree to abide by the results of the system we have simply because it is accepted. It is the convention.

But do we, in order to have democracy, have to find a way in which the *demos* first makes up its mind what is to be done and then controls its representatives in the process of carrying it out? What I want to suggest is a different conception. Let the convention for deciding what is our common will be that we will accept the decision of a group of people who are well informed about the question, well-motivated to find as good a solution as possible and representative of our range of interests simply because they are statistically representative of us as a group. If this group is then responsible for carrying out what it decides, the problem of control of the *execution* process largely vanishes. Those directing the execution process are carrying out their own decisions. They may need a little prodding to keep them up to the mark, but there is no institutional basis for a conflict of interest between bodies responsible for making decisions and those responsible for execution. They have an overriding interest in showing that their decisions were practical and well-grounded.

Granted that this process may be expected to generate effective social decisions and actions the question comes down to the sense in which the people control the decision-making process. It is useful to look at this question first statistically and then in terms of the dynamics of representation. If the group making a decision is statistically representative of the group on whose behalf it is made then it is very likely that the decision will be in accord with the result of some reasonable decision procedure for that group. The statistical selection procedure controls the distribution of the interests represented and so controls the decisions that are likely to emerge by rational negotiations among those representatives. Granted a sound statistical procedure the people automatically control the broad outlines of the result simply by being what they are. The mapping ensures a correspondence between the character of the representatives and the represented. Again, the group of representatives are all themselves members of the people. Nobody is selected because of professional knowledge or skill or prestige or privilege or institutional position. What the representatives are expected to bring to the decision process is that sensitivity to the interests involved that comes from having those interests. They are supposed to be typical of those affected by the decisions to be made. The decisions that the representatives will arrive at will differ from the actual wishes of those they represent because better information and the results of negotiations will make a difference. However, this is precisely the divergence from one's actual views that a rational person is normally willing to accept in the actions of a delegate.

Naturally, the mere fact that representatives come from a certain social group does not guarantee that they will cherish the interests of that group. They may be quite deluded about what those interests are. They may put some other interest they have ahead of the interests they are supposed to represent. They may be bribed or bought off. What safeguards are there against these things? One safeguard against delinquency is to suppress the causes that tend to produce temptations. Most of these fall within a wider context of property arrangements and social rewards that we shall look at later on. The crucial question, however, is that of public scrutiny. Everything that these committees do must be open to inspection. It is not difficult to ensure this if there are enough people around who follow closely what is done and have a strong motivation for making public anything that others would like to conceal.

If political office is attained by lot there are no professional political careers. Nobody has to acquire debts to party organizations or patrons in order to gain office or to hang on to it. The usual pressures to keep quiet are absent. On the other hand, the greatest reward that a person is likely to get from public service is recognition of his or her ability and integrity. In any committee, granted that there will be a diversity of interests and loyalties there are almost certainly going to be people who will expose any attempts to suborn members of the committee. Moreover, since membership would change in a regular pattern there would rapidly grow up a body of experienced, informed people who would have an interest in the doings of their successors and try to expose their errors or delinquencies, if only to enhance their own record.

More positively, it seems very likely that high standards of presentation of proposals for public discussion and responsiveness to the results of such discussion would emerge. Since the representatives would not be up for re-election they could afford to look at the various objections and suggestions raised on their merits. In some cases they might do things that were quite unpopular with a majority in the interests of a disadvantaged minority. In others they might assert a majority interest in spite of the objections of a powerful minority. The cheap rhetoric of political discourse would lose in representative committees. Ultimately their motivation would be to be recognized as having done a good job. Whether or not to be held in high regard is the strongest of motivations for people generally, there can be little doubt that it is always a strong motivation for the sort of people who are attracted to public office.

In a large and complex society very few people can be well known to the general public. Very many people, however, can be well known in some specialized activity. If that activity becomes the focus for a partial community, fame within it can be a significant reward, especially if the activity is in turn seen as important to the wider community or complex of partial communities.

Representation and co-ordination

It is not too difficult to envisage the solution I have proposed to the problem of democratic control of functional units producing specific public goods and services. The problems of co-ordination between these units are in many respects much easier than is often imagined. For the most part they can be left to negotiation between the bodies concerned, once the obstacles that bureaucratic structures place in the way of co-operation are removed. To a large extent the common good consists in the good functioning of a number of services that conjointly meet our various needs. The substantive criteria of good functioning are derived not from some higher-order set of concepts but from the specific tasks and the social realities in which they are embedded.

The point of democracy is to govern society from within the specific groupings that constitute the relevant population for each of the different public activities. The whole grows by the growth of the parts. The whole is integrated by each part adjusting itself continuously to the others with which it interacts. The illusion that democracy can be assured by so-called

118   *Democracy and representation*

democratic control of the state is disastrous. The state cannot
be controlled democratically. It must be abolished.

Of course, it is desirable that general movements of social
thought and aspiration in the community should find expression in the overall direction of public policy. There is no
reason, however, why these emphases and preferences should
not be developed through their influence on the decisions of
the representatives who share them. In this way they are likely
to find more appropriate, diverse and direct expression than
if that expression were mediated by electoral and bureaucratic
processes. The spirit of public policy should in these circumstances reflect the spirit of the most articulate and
responsible members of the community.

Higher-level bodies

Nevertheless there remain important problems in setting up
the various functional bodies, hearing appeals about their
structure, restructuring them to meet changed circumstances,
adjudicating their disagreements and dividing up resources
between them. Determining these matters would be the task
of higher-order bodies which would seek to adjudicate conflicting claims in the light of generally accepted criteria. Such
bodies, on the view I am advocating, would not be empowered to initiate policy, much less to dictate to various
functional bodies, but to provide a legal framework within
which productive bodies operate. There are important questions about how such bodies are to be prevented from exceeding their legal role and becoming administrative authorities.
For the moment, however, I am concerned about the sense in
which they ought to be representative.

Very roughly, what I want to argue is that it would be appropriate for them to be representative neither of interest nor
opinions but of the social experience of the community. The
people chosen to staff such bodies should have substantial
firsthand experience of the problems and practices of first-

order functional bodies. They should be able and trusted. The best way to meet these requirements would be to choose them by lot from a pool of candidates nominated by their colleagues on first-order bodies as having shown the special skill, knowledge and dedication that would fit them for a judicial role. They would constitute a sample of those judged most suited to the task by those in the best position to know.[11]

In their decision-making such bodies would work by a case-based rather than rule-based procedure, arguing by analogy for the relevance of various considerations and moderating precedent in the light of new circumstances. Since they, too, would have only a limited term of office, there would be plenty of opportunity for variation within a reasonable continuity. No professional class would emerge but a body of interested, informed critics would be formed who would be at liberty to criticize judgements. There would not be any need, I believe, for protection of these legal processes by the permanent threat of sanctions. I assume that responsible public functional bodies would not be nearly as likely as private citizens or corporations to reject a reasonably constituted judicial body's authority. In most cases they would be brought to heel by sanctions from other bodies if they did.

In extreme cases, however, it might be possible to defy such judgements with impunity. Their being open to this threat would, I believe, operate as salutary restraint on any tendency of judicial bodies to step beyond their proper role. The society would cohere only as long as the conventions on which it was based were respected. Ultimately, of course, that is almost trivially true of any society. However, in a society where there is a centralized and overwhelmingly powerful police and military force, control of a sort can be maintained as long as the conventions that ensure control over that force hold. In the society I am envisaging the cohesion of the whole is dependent on a much more dispersed and varied set of conventions holding, simply because of the variety of social pressures that tend to maintain them.

120   *Democracy and representation*

Anarchy and community

In *Community, Anarchy and Liberty* Michael Taylor argued
that anarchy in the strict sense, a social order without a state
apparatus, is possible only if there is community. The three 'core
characteristics' of community in Taylor's sense are: (1) The
set of persons who compose a community have beliefs and
values in common; (2) Relations between members should be
direct and many sided; (3) There should be a high level of
reciprocity, covering such things as exchanges, mutual aid,
co-operation and sharing, as well as mutual enforcement of
these arrangements. [12]

What I am suggesting, in effect, is that we can envisage a
community of organizations rather than a community of individuals as constituting a modern society. It seems to me
very doubtful whether the variety and capacity for change
that are characteristic of modern mass technologically advanced societies can be preserved in small communities based
on individuals. In modern societies individuals belong to a
multiplicity of partial communities and organizations that are
continually changing. Within various specific contexts they
may have relations with other individuals that are communal,
but their relations with the society as a whole are much more
formal, legal, inflexible and impersonal. Taylor and many
other anarchists want to restore small, face-to-face, relatively
comprehensive communities. I am very doubtful whether this
is either possible or desirable, though I cannot argue the
matter in any detail here. The point I am trying to make is, in
any case, independent of the possibility or desirability of
community among individuals under modern conditions.
Rather it is that there can, even on the modern scale, be community among certain kinds of organizations and partial
communities, without their being a total community at any
level.

Obviously a set of organizations devoted to producing a
variety of public goods governed by representative members

Democracy and representation   121

of the communities affected is likely to have many shared
values and beliefs, particularly values and beliefs concerning
the standards and procedures by which the organizations
should operate. They will deal directly with each other and
since each is highly specialized it will in practice have relations
of interdependence with a number of other bodies. Finally,
the pattern of exchanges between these bodies will be a matter
of mutual trust and co-operation backed by sanctions of
withdrawal of co-operation. The individual men and women
responsible for carrying out the various functions that constitute these organizations would find themselves constrained to
act in accordance with a communal pattern. Everything in
their social relations, all the pressures on them, would con-
spire to make them conform to their roles.

Although that would not necessarily produce an atmosphere of community among those agents in matters outside
their roles, it might well do so. It would be possible, pleasant
and usually advantageous that there be an atmosphere of
politeness, kindness, consideration, respect and friendliness
among people. Such an atmosphere sustains a great deal of
communal life even between strangers. It may not be strong
enough to ensure the enforcement of social order. For that
you need the tighter controls of the small community, as
Taylor argues. But granted that the substance of social order
is guaranteed on a non-repressive and co-operative basis a
generalized sense of social co-operation can flourish fairly
easily. In turn, such an atmosphere makes the task of ensuring social order very much less difficult in the residual areas
where there are temptations to crime.

In other words, a sense of community, interdependence
and reciprocity is not restricted to small communities or to
relatively self-contained communities. If there is a sufficiently
strong sense, diffused through a network of partial but overlapping communities, that doing favours for strangers one
will never meet again, acting considerately towards everybody or being open to other people's points of view is itself

122   *Democracy and representation*

pleasant and likely to be reciprocated, then the conduct of public affairs on a basis of reciprocity will appear natural. The principal condition for achieving such an atmosphere is to eliminate zero-sum conflicts from the structures of personal and social relationships as far as possible. In that way co-operative behaviour can become more than a veneer of morality and courtesy imposed on relations that constantly tend to confrontation. The ways in which entitlements to resources and rewards are generated and appropriated are crucial in this respect.

Protection of person and property
In a society in which people are free to change their jobs, their residence, their friends and their activities very easily, it is not difficult to kill, steal of injure without it being known who committed the crime. If it is known only in a small group it is easy to evade the sanctions that group can bring to bear. It is to be expected that many people will have strong motives for crime, and need to be deterred. In a complex and large society there seems no substitute for police forces. It is by no means clear, however, that there needs to be a single agency with global power to enforce the law in all areas, much less that such an agency should be the custodian of public morals. From the point of view of detention and investigation there can be a number of specialized agencies, as there are in effect within modern police forces. These agencies could co-operate rather than be under a single control.

The type of policing that seems to require an open brief is that of 'the cop on the beat', whose presence is supposed to deter criminals and ensure public order. That role went out with the motor car and the changes in the pattern of urban living. In any case, it was in its heyday primarily a means of controlling the poor, and especially the young, preventing the emergence of street gangs and the like. In so far as these or analogous functions remain in contemporary societies, there are better ways of dealing with them by provision of specific

Democracy and representation   123

services and opportunities for those who have nothing better
to do than fight or 'disturb the peace'.

Once again, the point is that a local authority is likely to be
too total and too repressive, a wider-based authority too
powerful and too subject to corruption. Specific law enforcement agencies dealing with specific kinds of problems are
much more likely to be effective provided the problems of
controlling them can be dealt with, and the structure can be
changed to meet changing circumstances. Once these problems are clearly distinguished, they can be met at different
levels by different kinds of bodies. The problems of supervision of specialized agencies can be handled by representative
committees with managerial and policy-making powers. The
problems of restructuring must be dealt with in a way that
avoids giving to the body that decides on restructuring proposals any overall executive power. In no area is it more important to avoid centralization of power. The decisions must
take the form of arbitration between conflicting proposals to
extend the jurisdiction of existing agencies or create new
agencies. The arbitrating body must have no power to engage
in police work of any kind. It must not direct the policy of
bodies that do so except by way of settlement of disputes.

It seems likely that, given reasonably active organs of public
opinion, there would be little difficulty in holding higher-order
bodies to their adjudicative role. The lower-order bodies
would be jealous of their autonomy, and to some extent
jealous of each other. It is not quite so clear, however, that in
some other contexts, such as police work, a particular agency
might not come to occupy such a strategic position in the complex of agencies that it would effectively dictate to the rest in
crucial matters. It could be, for example, that an agency set up
to guard against computer crime might, in a highly computer-
ized society, gain the power to control any information transaction and thus any formal social action in that society. Its
operations, moreover, might be extremely difficult to monitor,
and virtually impossible for a lay person to understand.

124   *Democracy and representation*

There is no doubt that this kind of development would be controlled only by constant vigilance by people involved in the ordinary running of the dangerous agency.[13] These people would need to be given every incentive to keep the operations of the agency fully public, to discuss their problems and dangers and make proposals for change. There is, of course, an inherent tension between the need for a certain amount of guile in criminal investigation and the need for public accountability of the investigation. But the major deterrent to crime must always be the difficulty of concealing it in the first place. Publicity about the kinds of actions being taken to prevent crime is a sound deterrent if the actions are well conceived. If they are not well conceived the criminals are likely to be aware of it before the public in any case. Public scrutiny may detect problems if there is adequate discussion and it is certainly likely to encourage critical thinking within agencies. Such publicity about policy is quite compatible with discretion within the context of particular investigations.

In the day-to-day running of police agencies, as with other agencies, a balance will have to be struck between reasonable autonomy for the full-time professionals and adequate access to information for the lay supervisory bodies. There is no recipe for such a balance, and it cannot be denied that statistically representative bodies may from time to time be dominated by people who are so intrusive that they make sound professional work impossible, or so complacent that they do not exercise proper supervision. Nevertheless, compared to the present arrangements in most countries, it is hard to believe that such citizen committees would not on the whole constitute an enormous improvement. The links that at present exist between the people who control policing and the rest of the government powers, both constitutionally and informally through the party system, constitute a standing invitation to the abuse of police power for oppressive ends.

Part III
The Minimal State

[6]

Excerpt from *Anarchy, State, and Utopia*, 3–9

CHAPTER

1

Why State-of-Nature Theory?

IF the state did not exist would it be necessary to invent it? Would one be *needed*, and would it have to be *invented?* These questions arise for political philosophy and for a theory explaining political phenomena and are answered by investigating the "state of nature," to use the terminology of traditional political theory. The justification for resuscitating this archaic notion would have to be the fruitfulness, interest, and far-reaching implications of the theory that results. For the (less trusting) readers who desire some assurance in advance, this chapter discusses reasons why it is important to pursue state-of-nature theory, reasons for thinking that theory would be a fruitful one. These reasons necessarily are somewhat abstract and metatheoretical. The best reason is the developed theory itself.

4   *State-of-Nature Theory*

POLITICAL PHILOSOPHY

The fundamental question of political philosophy, one that pre-
cedes questions about how the state should be organized, is
whether there should be any state at all. Why not have anarchy?
Since anarchist theory, if tenable, undercuts the whole subject of
political philosophy, it is appropriate to begin political philosophy
with an examination of its major theoretical alternative. Those
who consider anarchism not an unattractive doctrine will think it
possible that political philosophy *ends* here as well. Others impa-
tiently will await what is to come afterwards. Yet, as we shall see,
archists and anarchists alike, those who spring gingerly from the
starting point as well as those reluctantly argued away from it, can
agree that beginning the subject of political philosophy with state-
of-nature theory has an *explanatory* purpose. (Such a purpose is absent when epistemology is begun with an attempt to refute the
skeptic.)

Which anarchic situation should we investigate to answer the
question of why not anarchy? Perhaps the one that would exist if
the actual political situation didn't, while no other possible political one did. But apart from the gratuitous assumption that everyone everywhere would be in the same nonstate boat and the enormous unmanageability of pursuing that counterfactual to arrive at
a particular situation, that situation would lack fundamental theoretical interest. To be sure, if that nonstate situation were sufficiently awful, there would be a reason to refrain from dismantling or destroying a particular state and replacing it with none,
now.

It would be more promising to focus upon a fundamental abstract description that would encompass all situations of interest,
including "where we would now be if." Were this description
awful enough, the state would come out as a preferred alternative,
viewed as affectionately as a trip to the dentist. Such awful descriptions rarely convince, and not merely because they fail to
cheer. The subjects of psychology and sociology are far too feeble
to support generalizing so pessimistically across all societies and
persons, especially since the argument depends upon *not* making
such pessimistic assumptions about how the *state* operates. Of

Why State-of-Nature Theory?   5

course, people know something of how actual states have operated, and they differ in their views. Given the enormous importance of the choice between the state and anarchy, caution might suggest one use the "minimax" criterion, and focus upon a pessimistic estimate of the nonstate situation: the state would be compared with the most pessimistically described Hobbesian state of nature. But in using the minimax criterion, this Hobbesian situation should be compared with the most pessimistically described possible state, including *future* ones. Such a comparison, surely, the worst state of nature would win. Those who view the state as an abomination will not find minimax very compelling, especially since it seems one could always bring back the state if that came to seem desirable. The "maximax" criterion, on the other hand, would proceed on the most optimistic assumptions about how things would work out—Godwin, if you like that sort of thing. But imprudent optimism also lacks conviction. Indeed, no proposed decision criterion for choice under uncertainty carries conviction here, nor does maximizing expected utility on the basis of such frail probabilities.

More to the point, especially for deciding what goals one should try to achieve, would be to focus upon a nonstate situation in which people generally satisfy moral constraints and generally act as they ought. Such an assumption is not wildly optimistic; it does not assume that all people act exactly as they should. Yet this state-of-nature situation is the best anarchic situation one reasonably could hope for. Hence investigating its nature and defects is of crucial importance to deciding whether there should be a state rather than anarchy. If one could show that the state would be superior even to this most favored situation of anarchy, the best that realistically can be hoped for, or would arise by a process involving no morally impermissible steps, or would be an improvement if it arose, this would provide a rationale for the state's existence; it would justify the state.*

This investigation will raise the question of whether all the ac-

----

* This contrasts with a theory that presents a state's arising from a state of nature by a natural and inevitable process of *deterioration*, rather as medical theory presents aging or dying. Such a theory would not "justify" the state, though it might resign us to its existence.

tions persons must do to set up and operate a state are themselves morally permissible. Some anarchists have claimed not merely that we would be better off without a state, but that any state necessarily violates people's moral rights and hence is intrinsically immoral. Our starting point then, though nonpolitical, is by intention far from nonmoral. Moral philosophy sets the background for, and boundaries of, political philosophy. What persons may and may not do to one another limits what they may do through the apparatus of a state, or do to establish such an apparatus. The moral prohibitions it is permissible to enforce are the source of whatever legitimacy the state's fundamental coercive power has. (Fundamental coercive power is power not resting upon any consent of the person to whom it is applied.) This provides a primary arena of state activity, perhaps the only legitimate arena. Furthermore, to the extent moral philosophy is unclear and gives rise to disagreements in people's moral judgments, it also sets problems which one might think could be appropriately handled in the political arena.

EXPLANATORY POLITICAL THEORY

In addition to its importance for political philosophy, the investigation of this state of nature also will serve explanatory purposes. The possible ways of understanding the political realm are as follows: (1) to fully explain it in terms of the nonpolitical; (2) to view it as emerging from the nonpolitical but irreducible to it, a mode of organization of nonpolitical factors understandable only in terms of novel political principles; or (3) to view it as a completely autonomous realm. Since only the first promises full understanding of the whole political realm,[1] it stands as the most desirable theoretical alternative, to be abandoned only if known to be impossible. Let us call this most desirable and complete kind of explanation of a realm a *fundamental* explanation of the realm.

To explain fundamentally the political in terms of the nonpolitical, one might start either with a nonpolitical situation, showing how and why a political one later would arise out of it, or with a

Why State-of-Nature Theory?   7

political situation that is described nonpolitically, deriving its political features from its nonpolitical description. This latter derivation either will identify the political features with those features
nonpolitically described, or will use scientific laws to connect distinct features. Except perhaps for this last mode, the illumination
of the explanation will vary directly with the independent glow of
the nonpolitical starting point (be it situation or description) and
with the distance, real or apparent, of the starting point from its
political result. The more fundamental the starting point (the
more it picks out basic, important, and inescapable features of the
human situation) and the less close it is or seems to its result (the
less political or statelike it looks), the better. It would not increase
understanding to reach the state from an arbitrary and otherwise
unimportant starting point, obviously adjacent to it from the
start. Whereas discovering that political features and relations
were reducible to, or identical with, ostensibly very different nonpolitical ones would be an exciting result. Were these features fundamental, the political realm would be firmly and deeply based.
So far are we from such a major theoretical advance that prudence
alone would recommend that we pursue the alternative of showing
how a political situation would arise out of a nonpolitical one; that
is, that we begin a fundamental *explanatory* account with what is
familiar within political philosophy as state-of-nature theory.

A theory of a state of nature that begins with fundamental general descriptions of morally permissible and impermissible actions,
and of deeply based reasons why some persons in any society would
violate these moral constraints, and goes on to describe how a state
would arise from that state of nature will serve our explanatory
purposes, *even if no actual state ever arose that way.* Hempel has discussed the notion of a potential explanation, which intuitively
(and roughly) is what would be the correct explanation if everything mentioned in it were true and operated.[2] Let us say that a
law-defective potential explanation is a potential explanation with a
false lawlike statement and that a *fact-defective* potential explanation is a potential explanation with a false antecedent condition. A
potential explanation that explains a phenomenon as the result of a
process P will be defective (even though it is neither law-defective
nor fact-defective) if some process Q other than P produced the

8   *State-of-Nature Theory*

phenomenon, though *P* was capable of doing it. Had this other
process *Q* not produced it, then *P* would have.* Let us call a potential explanation that fails in this way actually to explain the
phenomenon a *process-defective* potential explanation.

A *fundamental* potential explanation (an explanation that would
explain the whole realm under consideration were it the actual explanation) carries important explanatory illumination even if it is
not the correct explanation. To see how, in principle, a *whole realm*
could fundamentally be explained greatly increases our understanding of the realm.† It is difficult to say more without examining types of cases; indeed, without examining particular cases, but
this we cannot do here. Fact-defective fundamental potential explanations, if their false initial conditions "could have béen true,"
will carry great illumination; even wildly false initial conditions
will illuminate, sometimes very greatly. Law-defective fundamental potential explanations may illuminate the nature of a realm almost as well as the correct explanations, especially if the "laws"
together form an interesting and integrated theory. And process-
defective fundamental potential explanations (which are neither
law-defective nor fact-defective) fit our explanatory bill and purposes almost perfectly. These things could not be said as strongly,
if at all, about nonfundamental explanation.

State-of-nature explanations of the political realm *are* fundamental potential explanations of this realm and pack explanatory

---

* Or, perhaps yet *another* process *R* would have if *Q* hadn't, though had *R*
not produced the phenomenon, then *P* would have, or. . . . So the footnoted
sentence should read: *P* would have produced the phenomenon had no member
of [*Q, R, . . .*] done so. We ignore here the complication that what would
prevent *Q* from producing the phenomenon might also prevent *P* from doing
so.

† This claim needs to be qualified. It will not increase our understanding of
a realm to be told as a potential explanation what we know to be false: that by
doing a certain dance, ghosts or witches or goblins made the realm that way. It
is plausible to think that an explanation of a realm must present an underlying
mechanism yielding the realm. (Or do something else equally productive of understanding.) But to say this is not to state precisely the deep conditions an underlying mechanism must satisfy to explain a realm. The precise qualification of
the claim in the text awaits advances in the theory of explanation. Yet other difficulties call for such advances; see Jaegwon Kim, "Causation, Nomic Subsump-
tion, and the Concept of Event," *The Journal of Philosophy*, 70, no. 8 (April 26,
1973), 217–236.

punch and illumination, even if incorrect. We learn much by seeing how the state could have arisen, even if it didn't arise that way. If it didn't arise that way, we also would learn much by determining why it didn't; by trying to explain why the particular bit of the real world that diverges from the state-of-nature model is as it is.

Since considerations both of political philosophy and of explanatory political theory converge upon Locke's state of nature, we shall begin with that. More accurately, we shall begin with individuals in something sufficiently similar to Locke's state of nature so that many of the otherwise important differences may be ignored here. Only when some divergence between our conception and Locke's is relevant to *political* philosophy, to our argument about the state, will it be mentioned. The completely accurate statement of the moral background, including the precise statement of the moral theory and its underlying basis, would require a full-scale presentation and is a task for another time. (A lifetime?) That task is so crucial, the gap left without its accomplishment so yawning, that it is only a minor comfort to note that we here are following the respectable tradition of Locke, who does not provide anything remotely resembling a satisfactory explanation of the status and basis of the law of nature in his *Second Treatise*.

[7]

Excerpt from *Anarchy, State, and Utopia*, 10–25

CHAPTER

2

The State of Nature

INDIVIDUALS in Locke's state of nature are in "a state of perfect freedom to order their actions and dispose of their possessions and persons as they think fit, within the bounds of the law of nature, without asking leave or dependency upon the will of any other man" (sect. 4).[1] The bounds of the law of nature require that "no one ought to harm another in his life, health, liberty, or possessions" (sect. 6). Some persons transgress these bounds, "invading others' rights and . . . doing hurt to one another," and in response people may defend themselves or others against such invaders of rights (chap. 3). The injured party and his agents may recover from the offender "so much as may make satisfaction for the harm he has suffered" (sect. 10); "everyone has a right to punish the transgressors of that law to such a degree as may hinder its violation" (sect. 7); each person may, and may only "retribute to [a criminal] so far as calm reason and conscience dictate, what is proportionate to his transgression, which is so much as may serve for reparation and restraint" (sect. 8).

There are "inconveniences of the state of nature" for which, says Locke, "I easily grant that civil government is the proper remedy" (sect. 13). To understand precisely what civil government remedies, we must do more than repeat Locke's list of the inconveniences of the state of nature. We also must consider what arrangements might be made within a state of nature to deal with

The State of Nature   11

these inconveniences—to avoid them or to make them less likely
to arise or to make them less serious on the occasions when they do
arise. Only after the full resources of the state of nature are
brought into play, namely all those voluntary arrangements and
agreements persons might reach acting within their rights, and
only after the effects of these are estimated, will we be in a position to see how serious are the inconveniences that yet remain to
be remedied by the state, and to estimate whether the remedy is
worse than the disease.*

In a state of nature, the understood natural law may not provide
for every contingency in a proper fashion (see sections 159 and 160
where Locke makes this point about legal systems, but contrast
section 124), and men who judge in their own case will always
give themselves the benefit of the doubt and assume that they are
in the right. They will overestimate the amount of harm or damage they have suffered, and passions will lead them to attempt to
punish others more than proportionately and to exact excessive
compensation (sects. 13, 124, 125). Thus private and personal enforcement of one's rights (including those rights that are violated
when one is excessively punished) leads to feuds, to an endless
series of acts of retaliation and exactions of compensation. And
there is no firm way to *settle* such a dispute, to *end* it and to have
both parties know it is ended. Even if one party *says* he'll stop his

---

* Proudhon has given us a description of the *state's* domestic "inconveniences." "To be GOVERNED is to be watched, inspected, spied upon, directed, law-driven, numbered, regulated, enrolled, indoctrinated, preached at,
controlled, checked, estimated, valued, censured, commanded, by creatures
who have neither the right nor the wisdom nor the virtue to do so. To be GOV-
ERNED is to be at every operation, at every transaction noted, registered,
counted, taxed, stamped, measured, numbered, assessed, licensed, authorized,
admonished, prevented, forbidden, reformed, corrected, punished. It is, under
pretext of public utility, and in the name of the general interest, to be placed
under contribution, drilled, fleeced, exploited, monopolized, extorted from,
squeezed, hoaxed, robbed; then, at the slightest resistance, the first word of
complaint, to be repressed, fined, vilified, harrassed, hunted down, abused,
clubbed, disarmed, bound, choked, imprisoned, judged, condemned, shot,
deported, sacrificed, sold, betrayed; and to crown all, mocked, ridiculed, de-
rided, outraged, dishonored. That is government; that is its justice; that is
its morality." P. J. Proudhon, *General Idea of the Revolution in the Nineteenth
Century,* trans. John Beverly Robinson (London: Freedom Press, 1923), pp.
293–294, with some alterations from Benjamin Tucker's translation in *Instead of
a Book* (New York, 1893), p. 26.

acts of retaliation, the other can rest secure only if he knows the
first still does not feel entitled to gain recompense or to exact retribution, and therefore entitled to try when a promising occasion
presents itself. Any method a single individual might use in an attempt irrevocably to bind himself into ending his part in a feud
would offer insufficient assurance to the other party; tacit agreements to stop also would be unstable.[2] Such feelings of being mutually wronged can occur even with the clearest right and with
joint agreement on the facts of each person's conduct; all the more
is there opportunity for such retaliatory battle when the facts or
the rights are to some extent unclear. Also, in a state of nature a
person may lack the power to enforce his rights; he may be unable
to punish or exact compensation from a stronger adversary who has
violated them (sects. 123, 126).

PROTECTIVE ASSOCIATIONS

How might one deal with these troubles within a state of nature?
Let us begin with the last. In a state of nature an individual may
himself enforce his rights, defend himself, exact compensation,
and punish (or at least try his best to do so). Others may join with
him in his defense, at his call.[3] They may join with him to repulse
an attacker or to go after an aggressor because they are public spir-
ited, or because they are his friends, or because he has helped them
in the past, or because they wish him to help them in the future,
or in exchange for something. Groups of individuals may form
mutual-protection associations: all will answer the call of any
member for defense or for the enforcement of his rights. In union
there is strength. Two inconveniences attend such simple mutual-
protection associations: (1) everyone is always on call to serve a
protective function (and how shall it be decided who shall answer
the call for those protective functions that do not require the services of all members?); and (2) any member may call out his associates by saying his rights are being, or have been, violated. Protective associations will not want to be at the beck and call of their
cantankerous or paranoid members, not to mention those of their
members who might attempt, under the guise of self-defense, to

The State of Nature   13

use the association to violate the rights of others. Difficulties will also arise if two different members of the same association are in dispute, each calling upon his fellow members to come to his aid.

A mutual-protection association might attempt to deal with conflict among its own members by a policy of nonintervention. But this policy would bring discord within the association and might lead to the formation of subgroups who might fight among themselves and thus cause the breakup of the association. This policy would also encourage potential aggressors to join as many mutual-protection associations as possible in order to gain immunity from retaliatory or defensive action, thus placing a great burden on the adequacy of the initial screening procedure of the association. Thus protective associations (almost all of those that will survive which people will join) will not follow a policy of nonintervention; they will use some procedure to determine how to act when some members claim that other members have violated their rights. Many arbitrary procedures can be imagined (for example, act on the side of that member who complains first), but most persons will want to join associations that follow some procedure to find out which claimant is correct. When a member of the association is in conflict with nonmembers, the association also will want to determine in some fashion who is in the right, if only to avoid constant and costly involvement in each member's quarrels, whether just or unjust. The inconvenience of everyone's being on call, whatever their activity at the moment or inclinations or comparative advantage, can be handled in the usual manner by division of labor and exchange. Some people will be *hired* to perform protective functions, and some entrepreneurs will go into the business of selling protective services. Different sorts of protective policies would be offered, at different prices, for those who may desire more extensive or elaborate protection.[4]

An individual might make more particular arrangements or commitments short of turning over to a private protective agency all functions of detection, apprehension, judicial determination of guilt, punishment, and exaction of compensation. Mindful of the dangers of being the judge in his own case, he might turn the decision as to whether he has indeed been wronged, and to what extent, to some other neutral or less involved party. In order for the occurrence of the social effect of justice's being seen to be done, such a party would have to be generally respected and thought to be neutral and upright. Both parties to a dispute may so attempt to safeguard themselves against the appearance of partiality, and both might even agree upon the *same* person as the judge between them, and agree to abide by his decision. (Or there might be a specified process through which one of the parties dissatisfied with the decision could appeal it.) But, for obvious reasons, there will be strong tendencies for the above-mentioned functions to converge in the same agent or agency.

People sometimes now do take their disputes outside of the state's legal system to other judges or courts they have chosen, for example, to religious courts.[5] If all parties to a dispute find some activities of the state or its legal system so repellent that they want nothing to do with it, they might agree to forms of arbitration or judgment outside the apparatus of the state. People tend to forget the possibilities of acting independently of the state. (Similarly, persons who want to be paternalistically regulated forget the possibilities of contracting into particular limitations on their own behavior or appointing a given paternalistic supervisory board over themselves. Instead, they swallow the exact pattern of restrictions a legislature happens to pass. Is there really someone who, searching for a group of wise and sensitive persons to regulate him for his own good, would choose that group of people who constitute the membership of both houses of Congress?) Diverse forms of judicial adjudication, differing from the particular package the state provides, certainly could be developed. Nor do the costs of developing and choosing these account for people's use of the state form. For it would be easy to have a large number of preset packages which parties could select. Presumably what drives people to use the state's system of justice is the issue of ultimate enforcement. Only the state can enforce a judgment against the will of one of the parties. For the state does not *allow* anyone else to enforce another system's judgment. So in any dispute in which both parties cannot agree upon a method of settlement, or in any dispute in which one party does not trust another to abide by the decision (if the other contracts to forfeit something of enormous value if he doesn't abide by the decision, by what agency is *that* contract to be enforced?), the parties who wish their claims put into effect will have no recourse permitted by the state's legal sys-

The State of Nature   15

tem other than to use that very legal system. This may present persons greatly opposed to a given state system with particularly poignant and painful choices. (If the state's legal system enforces the results of certain arbitration procedures, people may come to agree—supposing they abide by this agreement—without any actual direct contact with what they perceive to be officers or institutions of the state. But this holds as well if they sign a contract that is enforced only by the state.)

Will protective agencies *require* that their clients renounce exercising their right of private retaliation if they have been wronged by nonclients of the agency? Such retaliation may well lead to counterretaliation by another agency or individual, and a protective agency would not wish *at that late stage* to get drawn into the messy affair by having to defend its client against the counter-retaliation. Protective agencies would refuse to protect against counterretaliation unless they had first given permission for the retaliation. (Though might they not merely charge much more for the more extensive protection policy that provides such coverage?) The protective agencies need not even require that as part of his agreement with the agency, a client renounce, by contract, his right of private enforcement of justice against its *other clients*. The agency need only refuse a client C, who privately enforces his rights against other clients, any protection against counterretaliation upon him by these other clients. This is similar to what occurs if C acts against a nonclient. The additional fact that C acts upon a client of the agency means that the agency will act toward C as it would toward any nonclient who privately enforced his rights upon any one of its clients (see Chapter 5). This reduces intra-agency private enforcement of rights to minuscule levels.

THE DOMINANT PROTECTIVE ASSOCIATION

Initially, several different protective associations or companies will offer their services in the same geographical area. What will occur when there is a conflict between clients of different agencies? Things are relatively simple if the agencies reach the same decision about the disposition of the case. (Though each might want to

exact the penalty.) But what happens if they reach different decisions as to the merits of the case, and one agency attempts to
protect its client while the other is attempting to punish him or
make him pay compensation? Only three possibilities are worth
considering:

1. In such situations the forces of the two agencies do battle. One of
    the agencies always wins such battles. Since the clients of the losing
    agency are ill protected in conflicts with clients of the winning
    agency, they leave their agency to do business with the winner.[6]
2. One agency has its power centered in one geographical area, the
    other in another. Each wins the battles fought close to its center of
    power, with some gradient being established.[7] People who deal
    with one agency but live under the power of the other either move
    closer to their own agency's home headquarters or shift their pa-
    tronage to the other protective agency. (The border is about as
    conflictful as one between states.)

In neither of these two cases does there remain very much geographical interspersal. Only one protective agency operates over a
given geographical area.

3. The two agencies fight evenly and often. They win and lose about
    equally, and their interspersed members have frequent dealings and
    disputes with each other. Or perhaps without fighting or after only
    a few skirmishes the agencies realize that such battling will occur
    continually in the absence of preventive measures. In any case, to
    avoid frequent, costly, and wasteful battles the two agencies, per-
    haps through their executives, agree to resolve peacefully those
    cases about which they reach differing judgments. They agree to set
    up, and abide by the decisions of, some third judge or court to
    which they can turn when their respective judgments differ. (Or
    they might establish rules determining which agency has jurisdic-
    tion under which circumstances.)[8] Thus emerges a system of ap-
    peals courts and agreed upon rules about jurisdiction and the con-
    flict of laws. Though different agencies operate, there is one unified
    federal judicial system of which they all are components.

In each of these cases, almost all the persons in a geographical
area are under some common system that judges between their
competing claims and *enforces* their rights. Out of anarchy, pressed
by spontaneous groupings, mutual-protection associations, division of labor, market pressures, economies of scale, and rational

The State of Nature   17

self-interest there arises something very much resembling a minimal state or a group of geographically distinct minimal states. Why is this market different from all other markets? Why would a virtual monopoly arise in this market without the government intervention that elsewhere creates and maintains it? [9] The worth of the product purchased, protection against others, is *relative:* it depends upon how strong the others are. Yet unlike other goods that are comparatively evaluated, maximal competing protective services cannot coexist; the nature of the service brings different agencies not only into competition for customers' patronage, but also into violent conflict with each other. Also, since the worth of the less than maximal product declines disproportionately with the number who purchase the maximal product, customers will not stably settle for the lesser good, and competing companies are caught in a declining spiral. Hence the three possibilities we have listed.

Our story above assumes that each of the agencies attempts in good faith to act within the limits of Locke's law of nature. [10] But one "protective association" might aggress against other persons. Relative to Locke's law of nature, it would be an outlaw agency. What actual counterweights would there be to its power? (What actual counterweights are there to the power of a state?) Other agencies might unite to act against it. People might refuse to deal with the outlaw agency's clients, boycotting them to reduce the probability of the agency's intervening in their own affairs. This might make it more difficult for the outlaw agency to get clients; but this boycott will seem an effective tool only on very optimistic assumptions about what cannot be kept secret, and about the costs to an individual of partial boycott as compared to the benefits of receiving the more extensive coverage offered by an "outlaw" agency. If the "outlaw" agency simply is an *open* aggressor, pillaging, plundering, and extorting under no plausible claim of justice, it will have a harder time than states. For the state's claim to legitimacy induces its citizens to believe they have some duty to obey its edicts, pay its taxes, fight its battles, and so on; and so some persons cooperate with it voluntarily. An openly aggressive agency could not depend upon, and would not receive, any such voluntary cooperation, since persons would view themselves simply as its victims rather than as its citizens. [11]

INVISIBLE-HAND EXPLANATIONS

How, if at all, does a dominant protective association differ from the state? Was Locke wrong in imagining a compact necessary to establish civil society? As he was wrong in thinking (sects. 46, 47, 50) that an "agreement," or "mutual consent," was needed to establish the "invention of money." Within a barter system, there is great inconvenience and cost to searching for someone who has what you want and wants what you have, even at a marketplace, which, we should note, needn't become a marketplace by everyone's expressly agreeing to deal there. People will exchange their goods for something they know to be more generally wanted than what they have. For it will be more likely that they can exchange this for what they want. For the same reasons others will be more willing to take in exchange this more generally desired thing. Thus persons will converge in exchanges on the more marketable goods, being willing to exchange their goods for them; the more willing, the more they know others who are also willing to do so, in a mutually reinforcing process. (This process will be reinforced and hastened by middlemen seeking to profit in facilitating exchanges, who themselves will often find it most expedient to offer more marketable goods in exchange.) For obvious reasons, the goods they converge on, via their individual decisions, will have certain properties: initial independent value (else they wouldn't begin as more marketable), physically enduring, nonperishable, divisible, portable, and so forth. No express agreement and no social contract fixing a medium of exchange is necessary.[12]

There is a certain lovely quality to explanations of this sort. They show how some overall pattern or design, which one would have thought had to be produced by an individual's or group's successful attempt to realize the pattern, instead was produced and maintained by a process that in no way had the overall pattern or design "in mind." After Adam Smith, we shall call such explanations *invisible-hand explanations*. ("Every individual intends only his own gain, and he is in this, as in so many other cases, led by an invisible hand to promote an end which was no part of his intention.") The specially satisfying quality of invisible-hand explanations (a quality I hope is possessed by this book's account of the

The State of Nature   19

state) is partially explained by its connection with the notion of fundamental explanation adumbrated in Chapter 1. Fundamental explanations of a realm are explanations of the realm in other terms; they make no use of any of the notions of the realm. Only via such explanations can we explain and hence understand everything about a realm; the less our explanations use notions constituting what is to be explained, the more (*ceteris paribus*) we understand. Consider now complicated patterns which one would have thought could arise only through intelligent design, only through some attempt to realize the pattern. One might attempt straightforwardly to explain such patterns in terms of the desires, wants, beliefs, and so on, of individuals, directed toward realizing the pattern. But within such explanations will appear descriptions of the pattern, *at least within quotation marks*, as objects of belief and desire. The explanation itself will say that some individuals desire to bring about something with (some of) the pattern-features, that some individuals believe that the only (or the best, or the . . . ,) way to bring about the realization of the pattern features is to . . . , and so on. Invisible-hand explanations minimize the use of notions constituting the phenomena to be explained; in contrast to the straightforward explanations, they don't explain complicated patterns by including the full-blown pattern-notions as objects of people's desires or beliefs. Invisible-hand explanations of phenomena thus yield greater understanding than do explanations of them as brought about by design as the object of people's intentions. It therefore is no surprise that they are more satisfying.

An invisible-hand explanation explains what looks to be the product of someone's intentional design, as not being brought about by anyone's intentions. We might call the *opposite* sort of explanation a "hidden-hand explanation." A hidden-hand explanation explains what looks to be merely a disconnected set of facts that (certainly) is not the product of intentional design, as the product of an individual's or group's intentional design(s). Some persons also find such explanations satisfying, as is evidenced by the popularity of conspiracy theories.

Someone might so prize each type of explanation, invisible hand and hidden hand, that he might attempt the Sisyphean task of explaining each purported nondesigned or coincidental set of isolated facts as the product of intentional design, *and* each purported product of design as a nondesigned set of facts! It would be quite lovely to continue this iteration for a bit, even through only one complete cycle.

Since I offer no explicit account of invisible-hand explanations,[13] and since the notion plays a role in what follows, I mention some examples to give the reader a clearer idea of what we have in mind when speaking of this type of explanation. (Examples given to illustrate the type of explanation need not be *correct* explanations.)

1. Explanations within evolutionary theory (via random mutation, natural selection, genetic drift, and so on) of traits of organisms and populations. (James Crow and Motoo Kimura survey mathematical formulations in *An Introduction to Population Genetics Theory* (New York: Harper & Row, 1970).

2. Explanations within ecology of the regulation of animal populations. (See Lawrence Slobodkin, *Growth and Regulation of Animal Populations* [New York: Holt, Rinehart & Winston, 1966] for a survey.)

3. Thomas Schelling's explanatory model (*American Economic Review*, May 1969, pp. 488–493) showing how extreme residential segregation patterns are producible by individuals who do not desire this but want, for example, to live in neighborhoods 55 percent of whose population is in their own group, and who switch their place of residence to achieve their goal.

4. Certain operant-conditioning explanations of various complicated patterns of behavior.

5. Richard Herrnstein's discussion of the genetic factors in a society's pattern of class stratification (*I.Q. in the Meritocracy*, Atlantic Monthly Press, 1973).

6. Discussions of how economic calculation is accomplished in markets. (See Ludwig von Mises, *Socialism*, Part II, *Human Action*, Chapters 4, 7–9.)

7. Microeconomic explanations of the effects of outside intervention in a market, and of the establishment and nature of the new equilibria.

8. Jane Jacobs' explanation of what makes some parts of cities safe in *The Death and Life of Great American Cities* (New York: Random House, 1961).

9. The Austrian theory of the trade cycle.

10. Karl Deutsch and William Madow's observation that in an organization with a large number of important decisions (which can later be evaluated for correctness) to be made among few alternatives, if large numbers of people have a chance to say which way the

The State of Nature   21

decision should be made, a number of persons will gain reputations as sage advisers, even if all randomly decide what advice to offer. ("Note on the Appearance of Wisdom in Large Bureaucratic Organizations," *Behavioral Science,* January 1961, pp. 72–78.)

11. The patterns arising through the operation of a modification of Frederick Frey's modification of the Peter Principle: people have risen three levels beyond their level of incompetence by the time their incompetence is detected.

12. Roberta Wohlstetter's explanation (*Pearl Harbor: Warning and Decision* [Stanford: Stanford University Press, 1962]), contra the "conspiracy" theorists, of why the United States didn't act on the evidence it possessed indicating a Japanese attack forthcoming on Pearl Harbor.

13. That explanation of "the intellectual preeminence of the Jews" that focuses on the great number of the most intelligent male Catholics who, for centuries, had no children, in contrast to the encouragement given rabbis to marry and reproduce.

14. The theory of how public goods aren't supplied solely by individual action.

15. Armen Alchian's pointing to a different invisible hand (in our later terminology, a filter) than does Adam Smith ("Uncertainty, Evolution, and Economic Theory," *Journal of Political Economy,* 1950, pp. 211–221).

16. F. A. Hayek's explanation of how social cooperation utilizes more knowledge than any individual possesses, through people adjusting their activities on the basis of how other people's similarly adjusted activities affect their local situations and through following examples they are presented with, and thereby creates new institutional forms, general modes of behavior, and so on (*The Constitution of Liberty,* chap. 2).

A rewarding research activity would be to catalog the different modes (and combinations) of invisible-hand explanations, specifying which types of invisible-hand explanations can explain which types of patterns. We can mention here two types of invisible-hand processes by which a pattern P can be produced: filtering processes and equilibrium processes. Through filtering processes can pass only things fitting P, because processes or structures filter out all non-P's; in equilibrium processes each component part responds or adjusts to "local" conditions, with each adjustment changing the local environment of others close by, so that the sum of the ripples of the local adjustments constitutes or realizes P. (Some processes of such rippling local adjustments don't come to an equilibrium pattern, not even a moving one.) There are different ways an equilibrium process can help maintain a pattern, and there also might be a filter that eliminates deviations from the pattern that are too great to be brought back by the internal equilibrating mechanisms. Perhaps the most elegant form of explanation of this sort involves two equilibrium processes, each internally maintaining its pattern in the face of small deviations, and each being a filter to eliminate the large deviations occurring in the other.

We might note in passing that the notion of filtering processes enables us to understand one way in which the position in the philosophy of the social sciences known as methodological individualism might go wrong. If there is a filter that filters out (destroys) all non-P Q's, then the explanation of why all Q's are P's (fit the pattern P) will refer to this filter. For each particular Q, there may be a particular explanation of why *it* is P, how it came to be P, what maintains it as P. But the explanation of why all Q's are P will not be the conjunction of these individual explanations, even though these are all the Q's there are, for that is part of what is to be explained. The explanation will refer to the filter. To make this clear, we might imagine that we have *no* explanation of why the individual Q's are P's. It just is an ultimate statistical law (so far as we can tell at any rate) that some Q's are P; we even might be unable to discover any stable statistical regularity at all. In this case we would know why all Q's are P's (and know there are Q's, and perhaps even know why there are Q's) without knowing of any Q, why it is $P!$ The methodological individualist position requires that there be no basic (unreduced) social filtering processes.

IS THE DOMINANT PROTECTIVE
ASSOCIATION A STATE?

Have we provided an invisible-hand explanation of the state? There are at least two ways in which the scheme of private protective associations might be thought to differ from a minimal state, might fail to satisfy a minimal conception of a state: (1) it appears

The State of Nature 23

to allow some people to enforce their own rights, and (2) it appears not to protect all individuals within its domain. Writers in the tradition of Max Weber [14] treat having a monopoly on the use of force in a geographical area, a monopoly incompatible with private enforcement of rights, as crucial to the existence of a state. As Marshall Cohen points out in an unpublished essay, a state may exist without *actually* monopolizing the use of force it has not authorized others to use; within the boundaries of a state there may exist groups such as the Mafia, the KKK, White Citizens Councils, striking unionists, and Weathermen that also use force. *Claiming* such a monopoly is not sufficient (if *you* claimed it you would not become the state), nor is being its sole claimant a necessary condition. Nor need everyone grant the legitimacy of the state's claim to such monopoly, either because as pacifists they think no one has the right to use force, or because as revolutionaries they believe that a given state lacks this right, or because they believe they are entitled to join in and help out no matter what the state says. Formulating sufficient conditions for the existence of the state thus turns out to be a difficult and messy task. [15]

For our purposes here we need focus only upon a necessary condition that the system of private protective agencies (or any component agency within it) apparently does not satisfy. A state claims a monopoly on deciding who may use force when; it says that only it may decide who may use force and under what conditions; it reserves to itself the sole right to pass on the legitimacy and permissibility of any use of force within its boundaries; furthermore it claims the right to punish all those who violate its claimed monopoly. The monopoly may be violated in two ways: (1) a person may use force though unauthorized by the state to do so, or (2) though not themselves using force a group or person may set themselves up as an alternative authority (and perhaps even claim to be the sole legitimate one) to decide when and by whom the use of force is proper and legitimate. It is unclear whether a state must claim the right to punish the second sort of violator, and doubtful whether any state actually would refrain from punishing a significant group of them within its boundaries. I glide over the issue of what sort of "may," "legitimacy," and "permissibility" is in question. Moral permissibility isn't a matter of decision, and the state need not be so egomaniacal as to claim the sole right to decide moral questions. To speak of legal permissibility would require, to avoid circularity, that an account of a legal system be offered that doesn't use the notion of the state.

We may proceed, for our purposes, by saying that a necessary condition for the existence of a state is that it (some person or organization) announce that, to the best of its ability (taking into account costs of doing so, the feasibility, the more important alternative things it should be doing, and so forth), it will punish everyone whom it discovers to have used force without its express permission. (This permission may be a particular permission or may be granted via some general regulation or authorization.) This still won't quite do: the state may reserve the right to forgive someone, *ex post facto;* in order to punish they may have not only to discover the "unauthorized" use of force but also prove via a certain specified procedure of proof that it occurred, and so forth. But it enables us to proceed. The protective agencies, it seems, do not make such an announcement, either individually or collectively. *Nor does it seem morally legitimate for them to do so.* So the system of private protective associations, if they perform no morally illegitimate action, appears to lack any monopoly element and so appears not to constitute or contain a state. To examine the question of the monopoly element, we shall have to consider the situation of some group of persons (or some one person) living within a system of private protective agencies who refuse to join any protective society; who insist on judging for themselves whether their rights have been violated, and (if they so judge) on personally enforcing their rights by punishing and/or exacting compensation from those who infringed them.

The second reason for thinking the system described is not a state is that, under it (apart from spillover effects) only those paying for protection get protected; furthermore, differing degrees of protection may be purchased. External economies again to the side, no one pays for the protection of others except as they choose to; no one is required to purchase or contribute to the purchasing of protection for others. Protection and enforcement of people's rights is treated as an economic good to be provided by the market, as are other important goods such as food and clothing. However, under the usual conception of a state, each person living

The State of Nature 25

within (or even sometimes traveling outside) its geographical boundaries gets (or at least, is entitled to get) its protection. Unless some private party donated sufficient funds to cover the costs of such protection (to pay for detectives, police to bring criminals into custody, courts, and prisons), or unless the state found some service it could charge for that would cover these costs,* one would expect that a state which offered protection so broadly would be redistributive. It would be a state in which some persons paid more so that others could be protected. And indeed the most minimal state seriously discussed by the mainstream of political theorists, the night-watchman state of classical liberal theory, appears to be redistributive in this fashion. Yet how can a protection agency, a business, charge some to provide its product to others? [16] (We ignore things like some partially paying for others because it is too costly for the agency to refine its classification of, and charges to, customers to mirror the costs of the services to them.)

Thus it appears that the dominant protective agency in a territory not only lacks the requisite monopoly over the use of force, but also fails to provide protection for all in its territory; and so the dominant agency appears to fall short of being a state. But these appearances are deceptive.

---

* I have heard it suggested that the state could finance itself by running a lottery. But since it would have no right to forbid private entrepreneurs from doing the same, why think the state will have any more success in attracting customers in this than in any other competitive business?

Excerpt from *Anarchy, State, and Utopia*, 88–119

[8]

CHAPTER

5

The State

PROHIBITING PRIVATE ENFORCEMENT
OF JUSTICE

AN independent might be prohibited from privately exacting justice because his procedure is known to be too risky and dangerous—that is, it involves a higher risk (than another procedure) of punishing an innocent person or overpunishing a guilty one—or because his procedure isn't known not to be risky. (His procedure would exhibit another mode of unreliability if its chances were much greater of not punishing a guilty person, but this would not be a reason for prohibiting his private enforcement.)

Let us consider these in turn. If the independent's procedure is very unreliable and imposes high risk on others (perhaps he consults tea leaves), then if he does it frequently, he may make all fearful, even those not his victims. Anyone, acting in self-defense, may stop him from engaging in his high-risk activity. But surely the independent may be stopped from using a very unreliable procedure, even if he is not a constant menace. If it is known that the independent will enforce his own rights by his very unreliable procedure only once every ten years, this will *not* create general fear and apprehension in the society. The ground for prohibiting his widely intermittent use of his procedure is not, therefore, to avoid any widespread uncompensated apprehension and fear which otherwise would exist.

If there were many independents who were all liable to punish wrongly, the probabilities *would* add up to create a dangerous situation for all. Then, others would be entitled to group together and prohibit the *totality* of such activities. But how would this prohibition work? Would they prohibit *each* of the individually non-fear-creating activities? Within a state of nature by what procedure can they pick and choose which of the totality is to continue, and what would give them the right to do this? No protective association, however dominant, would have this right. For the legitimate powers of a protective association are merely the *sum* of the individual rights that its members or clients transfer to the association. No new rights and powers arise; each right of the association is decomposable without residue into those individual rights held by distinct individuals acting alone in a state of nature. A combination of individuals may have the right to do some action C, which no individual alone had the right to do, if C is identical to D and E, and persons who individually have the right to do D and the right to do E combine. If some rights of individuals were of the form "You have the right to do A provided 51 percent or 85 percent or whatever of the others agree you may," then a combination of individuals would have the right to do A, even though none separately had this right. But no individual's rights are of this form. No person or group is entitled to pick who in the totality will be allowed to continue. *All* the independents might group together and decide this. They might, for example, use some random procedure to allocate a number of (sellable?) rights to continue private enforcement so as to reduce the total danger to a point below the threshold. The difficulty is that, if a large number of independents do this, it will be in the interests of an individual to abstain from this arrangement. It will be in his interests to continue his risky activities as he chooses, while the others mutually limit theirs so as to bring the totality of acts including his to below the danger level. For the others probably would limit themselves some distance away from the danger boundary, leaving him room to squeeze in. Even were the others to rest adjacent to the line of danger so that his activities would bring the totality across it, on which grounds could *his* activities be picked out as the ones to prohibit? Similarly, it will be in the interests of any individual to refrain from otherwise unanimous agreements in the state of nature: for example, the agreement to set up a state. Anything an individual can gain by such a unanimous agreement he can gain through separate bilateral agreements. Any contract which really needs almost unanimity, any contract which is essentially joint, will serve its purpose whether or not a given individual participates; so it will be in his interests not to bind himself to participate.

"THE PRINCIPLE OF FAIRNESS"

A principle suggested by Herbert Hart, which (following John Rawls) we shall call the *principle of fairness,* would be of service here if it were adequate. This principle holds that when a number of persons engage in a just, mutually advantageous, cooperative venture according to rules and thus restrain their liberty in ways necessary to yield advantages for all, those who have submitted to these restrictions have a right to similar acquiescence on the part of those who have benefited from their submission.[1] Acceptance of benefits (even when this is not a giving of express or tacit undertaking to cooperate) is enough, according to this principle, to bind one. If one adds to the principle of fairness the claim that the others to whom the obligations are owed or their agents may *enforce* the obligations arising under this principle (including the obligation to limit one's actions), then groups of people in a state of nature who agree to a procedure to pick those to engage in certain acts will have legitimate rights to prohibit "free riders." Such a right may be crucial to the viability of such agreements. We should scrutinize such a powerful right very carefully, especially as it seems to make *unanimous* consent to coercive government in a state of nature *unnecessary!* Yet a further reason to examine it is its plausibility as a counterexample to my claim that no new rights "emerge" at the group level, that individuals in combination cannot create new rights which are not the sum of preexisting ones. A right to enforce others' obligation to limit their conduct in specified ways might stem from some special feature of the obligation or might be thought to follow from some general principle that all obligations owed to others may be enforced. In the absence of argument for the special enforcement-justifying nature of the obligation supposedly arising under the principle of fairness, I shall consider first the principle of the enforceability of all obligations and then turn to the adequacy of the principle of fairness itself. If either of these principles is rejected, the right to enforce the cooperation of others in these situations totters. I shall argue that *both* of these principles must be rejected.

Herbert Hart's argument for the existence of a natural right [2] depends upon particularizing the principle of the enforceability of all obligations: someone's being under a special obligation to you to do A (which might have arisen, for example, by their promising to you that they would do A) gives you, not only the right that they do A, but also the right to force them to do A. Only against a background in which people may not force you to do A or other actions you may promise to do can we understand, says Hart, the *point* and purpose of special obligations. Since special obligations do have a point and purpose, Hart continues, there is a natural right not to be forced to do something unless certain specified conditions pertain; this natural right is built into the background against which special obligations exist.

This well-known argument of Hart's is puzzling. I may release someone from an obligation not to force me to do A. ("I now release you from the obligation not to force me to do A. You now are free to force me to do A.") Yet so releasing them does *not* create in me an obligation to them to do A. Since Hart supposes that my being under an obligation to someone to do A gives him (entails that he has) the right to force me to do A, and since we have seen the converse does not hold, we may consider that component of being under an obligation to someone to do something over and above his having the right to force you to do it. (May we suppose there is this distinguishable component without facing the charge of "logical atomism"?) An alternative view which rejects Hart's inclusion of the right to force in the notion of being owed an obligation might hold that this additional component is the *whole* of the content of being obligated to someone to do something. If I don't do it, then (all things being equal) I'm doing something wrong; control over the situation is in his hands; he has the power to release me from the obligation unless he's promised to someone else that he won't, and so on. Perhaps all this looks too *ephemeral* without the additional presence of rights of enforcement. Yet rights of enforcement are themselves merely *rights;* that is, permissions to do something and obligations on others not to interfere. True, one has the right to enforce these further obligations, but it is not clear that including *rights* of enforcing really shores up the whole structure if one assumes it to be insubstantial to begin with. Perhaps one must merely take the moral realm seriously and think one component amounts to something even without a connection to enforcement. (Of course, this is not to say that this component *never* is connected with enforcement!) On this view, we can explain the point of obligations without bringing in rights of enforcement and hence without supposing a general background of obligation not to force from which this stands out. (Of course, even though Hart's argument does not demonstrate the existence of such an obligation not to force, it may exist nevertheless.)

Apart from these general considerations against the principle of the enforceability of all special obligations, puzzle cases can be produced. For example, if I promise to you that I will not murder someone, this does not *give* you the right to force me not to, for you already have this right, though it does create a particular obligation *to you*. Or, if I cautiously insist that you first promise to me that you won't force me to do A before I will make my promise to you to do A, and I do receive this promise from you first, it would be implausible to say that in promising I give you the right to force me to do A. (Though consider the situation which results if I am so foolish as to release you unilaterally from your promise to me.)

If there were cogency to Hart's claim that only against a background of required nonforcing can we understand the point of special rights, then there would seem to be equal cogency to the claim that only against a background of *permitted* forcing can we understand the point of *general* rights. For according to Hart, a person has a general right to do A if and only if for all persons P and Q, Q may not interfere with P's doing A or force him not to do A, unless P has acted to give Q a special right to do this. But not every act can be substituted for "A"; people have general rights to do only particular types of action. So, one might argue,

The State   93

if there is to be a point to having general rights, to having rights
to do a particular type of act A, to other's being under an obligation not to force you not to do A, then it must be against a contrasting background, in which there is *no* obligation on people to
refrain from forcing you to do, or not to do, things, that is,
against a background in which, for actions generally, people do *not*
have a general right to do them. If Hart can argue to a presumption against forcing from there being a point to particular rights,
then it seems he can equally well argue to the absence of such a
presumption from there being a point to general rights.[3]

An argument for an enforceable obligation has two stages: the
first leads to the existence of the obligation, and the second, to its
enforceability. Having disposed of the second stage (at least insofar
as it is supposed generally to follow from the first), let us turn to
the supposed obligation to cooperate in the joint decisions of
others to limit their activities. The principle of fairness, as we
stated it following Hart and Rawls, is objectionable and unacceptable. Suppose some of the people in your neighborhood (there are
364 other adults) have found a public address system and decide to
institute a system of public entertainment. They post a list of
names, one for each day, yours among them. On his assigned day
(one can easily switch days) a person is to run the public address
system, play records over it, give news bulletins, tell amusing
stories he has heard, and so on. After 138 days on which each person has done his part, your day arrives. Are you obligated to take
your turn? You *have* benefited from it, occasionally opening your
window to listen, enjoying some music or chuckling at someone's
funny story. The other people *have* put themselves out. But must
you answer the call when it is your turn to do so? As it stands,
surely not. Though you benefit from the arrangement, you may
know all along that 364 days of entertainment supplied by others
will not be worth your giving up *one* day. You would rather not
have any of it and not give up a day than have it all and spend one
of your days at it. Given these preferences, how can it be that you
are required to participate when your scheduled time comes? It
would be nice to have philosophy readings on the radio to which
one could tune in at any time, perhaps late at night when tired.
But it may not be nice enough for you to want to give up one
whole day of your own as a reader on the program. Whatever you

want, can others create an obligation for you to do so by going ahead and starting the program themselves? In this case you can choose to forgo the benefit by not turning on the radio; in other cases the benefits may be unavoidable. If each day a different person on your street sweeps the entire street, must you do so when your time comes? Even if you don't care that much about a clean street? Must you imagine dirt as you traverse the street, so as not to benefit as a free rider? Must you refrain from turning on the radio to hear the philosophy readings? Must you mow your front lawn as often as your neighbors mow theirs?

At the very least one wants to build into the principle of fairness the condition that the benefits to a person from the actions of the others are greater than the costs to him of doing his share. How are we to imagine this? Is the condition satisfied if you do enjoy the daily broadcasts over the PA system in your neighborhood but would prefer a day off hiking, rather than hearing these broadcasts all year? For you to be obligated to give up your day to broadcast mustn't it be true, at least, that there is nothing you could do with a day (with that day, with the increment in any other day by shifting some activities to that day) which you would prefer to hearing broadcasts for the year? If the only way to get the broadcasts was to spend the day participating in the arrangement, in order for the condition that the benefits outweigh the costs to be satisfied, you would have to be willing to spend it on the broadcasts rather than to gain *any* other available thing.

If the principle of fairness were modified so as to contain this very strong condition, it still would be objectionable. The benefits might only barely be worth the costs to you of doing your share, yet others might benefit from *this* institution much more than you do; they all treasure listening to the public broadcasts. As the person least benefited by the practice, are you obligated to do an equal amount for it? Or perhaps you would prefer that all cooperated in *another* venture, limiting their conduct and making sacrifices for *it*. It is true, *given* that they are not following your plan (and thus limiting what other options are available to you), that the benefits of their venture *are* worth to you the costs of your cooperation. However, you do not wish to cooperate, as part of your plan to focus their attention on your alternative proposal which they have ignored or not given, in your view at least, its proper

The State 95

due. (You want them, for example, to read the Talmud on the radio instead of the philosophy they are reading.) By lending the institution (their institution) the support of your cooperating in it, you will only make it harder to change or alter.[4]

On the face of it, enforcing the principle of fairness is objectionable. You may not decide to give me something, for example a book, and then grab money from me to pay for it, even if I have nothing better to spend the money on. You have, if anything, even less reason to demand payment if your activity that gives me the book also benefits you; suppose that your best way of getting exercise is by throwing books into people's houses, or that some other activity of yours thrusts books into people's houses as an unavoidable side effect. Nor are things changed if your inability to collect money or payments for the books which unavoidably spill over into others' houses makes it inadvisable or too expensive for you to carry on the activity with this side effect. One cannot, whatever one's purposes, just act so as to give people benefits and then demand (or seize) payment. Nor can a group of persons do this. If you may not charge and collect for benefits you bestow without prior agreement, you certainly may not do so for benefits whose bestowal costs you nothing, and most certainly people need not repay you for costless-to-provide benefits which yet *others* provided them. So the fact that we partially are "social products" in that we benefit from current patterns and forms created by the multitudinous actions of a long string of long-forgotten people, forms which include institutions, ways of doing things, and language (whose social nature may involve our current use depending upon Wittgensteinian matching of the speech of others), does not create in us a general floating debt which the current society can collect and use as it will.

Perhaps a modified principle of fairness can be stated which would be free from these and similar difficulties. What seems certain is that any such principle, if possible, would be so complex and involuted that one could not combine it with a special principle legitimating *enforcement* within a state of nature of the obligations that have arisen under it. Hence, even if the principle could be formulated so that it was no longer open to objection, it would not serve to obviate the need for other persons' *consenting* to cooperate and limit their own activities.

PROCEDURAL RIGHTS

Let us return to our independent. Apart from other nonindependents' fear (perhaps they will not be so worried), may not the person about to be punished defend himself? Must he allow the punishment to take place, collecting compensation afterwards if he can show that it was unjust? But show to whom? If he knows he's innocent, may he demand compensation immediately and enforce *his* rights to collect it? And so on. The notions of procedural rights, public demonstration of guilt, and the like, have a very unclear status within state-of-nature theory.

It might be said that each person has a right to have his guilt determined by the least dangerous of the known procedures for ascertaining guilt, that is, by the one having the lowest probability of finding an innocent person guilty. There are well-known maxims of the following form: better m guilty persons go free than n innocent persons be punished. For each n, each maxim will countenance an upper limit to the ratio m/n. It will say: better m, but not better $m + 1$. (A system may pick differing upper limits for different crimes.) On the greatly implausible assumption that we know each system of procedures' precise probability of finding an innocent person guilty,[5] and a guilty person innocent, we will opt for those procedures whose long-run ratio of the two kinds of errors comes closest, from below, to the highest ratio we find acceptable. It is far from obvious where to set the ratio. To say it is better that any number of guilty go free rather than that one innocent person be punished presumably would require *not* having any system of punishment at all. For any system we can devise which sometimes does actually punish someone will involve some appreciable risk of punishing an innocent person, and it almost certainly will do so as it operates on large numbers of people. And any system S can be transformed into one having a lower probability of punishing an innocent person, for example, by conjoining to it a roulette procedure whereby the probability is only .1 that anyone found guilty by S actually gets punished. (This procedure is iterative.)

If a person objects that the independent's procedure yields too high a probability of an innocent person's being punished, how can it be determined what probabilities are too high? We can imagine that each individual goes through the following reasoning: The greater the procedural safeguards, the less my chances of getting unjustly convicted, and also the greater the chances that a guilty person goes free; hence the less effectively the system deters crime and so the greater my chances of being a victim of a crime. That system is most effective which minimizes the expected value of unearned harm to me, either through my being unjustly punished or through my being a victim of a crime. If we simplify *greatly* by assuming that penalties and victimization costs balance out, one would want the safeguards at that most stringent point where any lowering of them would increase one's probability of being unjustly punished more than it would lower (through added deterrence) one's vulnerability to being victimized by a crime; and where any increasing of the safeguards would increase one's probability of being victimized by a crime (through lessened deterrence) more than it would lessen one's probability of being punished though innocent. Since utilities differ among persons, there is no reason to expect individuals who make such an expected value calculation to converge upon the identical set of procedures. Furthermore, some persons may think it important in itself that guilty people be punished and may be willing to run some increased risks of being punished themselves in order to accomplish this. These people will consider it more of a drawback, the greater the probability a procedure gives guilty people of going unpunished, and they will incorporate this in their calculations, apart from its effects on deterrence. It is, to say the least, very doubtful that any provision of the law of nature will (and will be known to) settle the question of how much weight is to be given to such considerations, or will reconcile people's different assessments of the seriousness of being punished when innocent as compared to being victimized by a crime (even if both involve the same physical thing happening to them). With the best will in the world, individuals will favor differing procedures yielding differing probabilities of an innocent person's being punished.

One could not, it seems, permissibly prohibit someone from using a procedure solely because it yields a marginally higher probability of punishing an innocent person than does the procedure you deem optimal. After all, your favorite procedure also will

98   *State-of-Nature Theory*</>

stand in this relation to that of someone else. Nor are matters changed by the fact that many other persons use your procedure. It seems that persons in a state of nature must tolerate (that is, not forbid) the use of procedures in the "neighborhood" of their own; but it seems they may forbid the use of far more risky procedures. An acute problem is presented if two groups each believe their own procedures to be reliable while believing that of the other group to be very dangerous. No *procedure* to resolve their disagreement seems likely to work; and presenting the nonprocedural principle that the group which is right should triumph (and the other should give in to it) seems unlikely to produce peace when each group, firmly believing itself to be the one that is right, acts on the principle.

When sincere and good persons differ, we are prone to think they must accept some procedure to decide their differences, some procedure they both agree to be reliable or fair. Here we see the possibility that this disagreement may extend all the way up the ladder of procedures. Also, one sometimes will refuse to let issues stay settled by the adverse decision of such a procedure, specifically when the wrong decision is worse even than the disruption and costs (including fighting) of refusing to accept it, when the wrong decision is worse than conflict with those on the other side. It is dismaying to contemplate situations where both of the opposed parties feel that conflict is preferable to an adverse decision by any procedure. Each views the situation as one in which he who is right must act, and the other should give in. It will be of little avail for a neutral party to say to both, "Look, you both *think* you're right, so on that principle, as you will apply it, you'll fight. Therefore you must agree to some procedure to decide the matter." For they each believe that conflict *is* better than losing the issue.* And one of them may be right in this. *Shouldn't* he engage

---

* Must their calculation about which is better include their chances of success? There is some temptation to define this area of conflict as one where such chances of wrong are for certain purposes thought to be as bad as the wrong for sure. A theory of how probability interacts with the moral weight of wrongs is sorely needed.

In treating the question as one of whether the benefits of conflict outweigh its costs, the text seriously oversimplifies the issue. Instead of a simple cost-benefit principle, the correct principle requires for an act to be morally permis-

in the conflict? Shouldn't *he* engage in the conflict? (True, both of them will think the one is themselves.) One might try to avoid these painful issues by a commitment to procedures, come what may. (May one possible result of applying the procedures be that they themselves are rejected?) Some view the state as such a device for shifting the ultimate burden of moral decision, so that there never comes to be that sort of conflict among individuals. But what sort of individual could so abdicate? Who could turn *every* decision over to an external procedure, accepting whatever results come? The possibility of such conflict is part of the human condition. Though this problem in the state of nature is an unavoidable one, given suitable institutional elaboration it need be no more pressing in the state of nature than under a state, where it also exists.[6]

The issue of which decisions can be left to an external binding procedure connects with the interesting question of what moral obligations someone is under who is being punished for a crime of which he knows himself to be innocent. The judicial system (containing no procedural unfairness, let us suppose) has sentenced him to life imprisonment, or death. May he escape? May he harm another in order to escape? These questions differ from the one of

---

sible, not merely that its moral benefits outweigh its moral costs, but that there is no other alternative action available with less moral cost, such that the additional moral cost of the contemplated action over the alternative outweighs its additional moral benefit. (For a detailed discussion of these issues see my "Moral Complications and Moral Structures," *Natural Law Forum,* 1968, pp. 1–50, especially the discussion of Principle VII.) One would be in a position to advance the discussion of many issues if one combined such a principle with a theory of the moral weight of harms or wrongs with certain specified probabilities, to get an explicitly probabilified version of this principle. I mention only one application here that might not spring to mind. It is often assumed that the only pacifist position which is a moral position absolutely forbids violent action. Any pacifist position that considers the effectiveness of pacifist techniques is labeled tactical rather than moral. But if a pacifist holds that because certain techniques of significant effectiveness are available (civilian resistance, nonviolent defense, satyagraha, and so on) it is *morally* wrong to wage or prepare for war, he is putting forth a comprehensible position that is a *moral* one, and which does require appeal to facts about the effectiveness of pacifist techniques. Given the lack of certainty about the effects of various actions (wars, pacifist techniques) the principle to govern the moral discussion of whether nonpacifist actions are morally permitted is a probabilified version of the principle (Principle VII) described briefly above.

whether someone wrongfully attacking (or participating in the attack of) another may claim self-defense as justifying his killing the other when the other, in self-defense, acts so as to endanger his own attacker's life. Here the answer is, "No." The attacker should not be attacking in the first place, nor does someone else's threatening him with death unless he does attack make it permissible for him to do so. His job is to get out of that situation; if he fails to do so he *is* at a moral disadvantage. Soldiers who know their country is waging an aggressive war and who are manning anti-aircraft guns in defense of a military emplacement may *not* in self-defense fire upon the planes of the attacked nation which is acting in self-defense, even though the planes are over their heads and are about to bomb *them*. It is a soldier's responsibility to determine if his side's cause is just; if he finds the issue tangled, unclear, or confusing, he may not shift the responsibility to his leaders, who will certainly tell him their cause is just. The selective conscientious objector may be right in his claim that he has a moral duty not to fight; and if he is, may not another acquiescent soldier be punished for doing what it was his moral duty not to do? Thus we return to the point that some bucks stop with each of us; and we reject the morally elitist view that some soldiers cannot be expected to think for themselves. (They are certainly not encouraged to think for themselves by the practice of absolving them of all responsibility for their actions within the rules of war.) Nor do we see why the political realm is special. Why, precisely, is one specially absolved of responsibility for actions when these are performed jointly with others from political motives under the direction or orders of political leaders? [7]

We thus far have supposed that you know that another's procedure of justice differs from your own for the worse. Suppose now that you have no reliable knowledge about another's procedure of justice. May you stop him in self-defense and may your protective agency act for you, solely because you or it does not know whether his procedure is reliable? Do you have the right to have your guilt or innocence, and punishment, determined by a system known to be reliable and fair? Known to whom? Those wielding it may know it to be reliable and fair. Do you have a right to have your guilt or innocence, and punishment, determined by a system *you* know to be reliable and fair? Are someone's rights violated if he thinks that only the use of tea leaves is reliable or if he is incapable of concentrating on the description of the system others use so that he doesn't know whether it's reliable, and so on? One may think of the state as the authoritative settler of doubts about reliability and fairness. But of course there is no guarantee that it *will* settle them (the president of Yale didn't think Black Panthers could get a fair trial), and there is no reason to suppose it will manage to do so more effectively than another scheme. The natural-rights tradition offers little guidance on precisely what one's procedural rights are in a state of nature, on how principles specifying how one is to act have knowledge built into their various clauses, and so on. Yet persons within this tradition do not hold that there are *no* procedural rights; that is, that one may not defend oneself against being handled by unreliable or unfair procedures.

HOW MAY THE DOMINANT AGENCY ACT?

What then may a dominant protective association forbid other individuals to do? The dominant protective association may reserve for itself the right to judge any procedure of justice to be applied to its clients. It may announce, and act on the announcement, that it will punish anyone who uses on one of its clients a procedure that it finds to be unreliable or unfair. It will punish anyone who uses on one of its clients a procedure that it already knows to be unreliable or unfair, and it will defend its clients against the application of such a procedure. May it announce that it will punish anyone who uses on one of its clients a procedure that it has not, at the time of punishment, already approved as reliable and fair? May it set itself up as having to pass, in advance, on any procedure to be used on one of its clients, so that anyone using on one of its clients any procedure that has not already received the protective association's seal of approval will be punished? Clearly, individuals themselves do not have this right. To say that an individual may punish anyone who applies to him a procedure of justice that has not met his approval would be to say that a criminal who refuses to approve anyone's procedure of justice could legitimately punish anyone who attempted to punish him. It might be thought that a protective association legitimately can do this, for it would not be partial to its clients in this manner. But there is no guarantee of this impartiality. Nor have we seen any way that such a new right might arise from the combining of individuals' preexisting rights. We must conclude that protective associations do not have this right, including the sole dominant one.

Every individual does have the right that information sufficient to show that a procedure of justice about to be applied to him is reliable and fair (or no less so than other procedures in use) be made publicly available or made available to him. He has the right to be shown that he is being handled by some reliable and fair system. In the absence of such a showing he may defend himself and resist the imposition of the relatively unknown system. When the information is made publicly available or made available to him, he is in a position to know about the reliability and fairness of the procedure.[8] He examines this information, and if he finds the system within the bounds of reliability and fairness he must submit to it; finding it unreliable and unfair he may resist. His submission means that he refrains from punishing another for using this system. He may resist the imposition of its particular decision though, on the grounds that he is innocent. If he chooses not to, he need not participate in the process whereby the system determines his guilt or innocence. Since it has not yet been established that he is guilty, he may not be aggressed against and forced to participate. However, prudence might suggest to him that his chances of being found innocent are increased if he cooperates in the offering of some defense.

The principle is that a person may resist, in self-defense, if others try to apply to him an unreliable or unfair procedure of justice. In applying this principle, an individual will resist those systems which after all conscientious consideration he finds to be unfair or unreliable. An individual may empower his protective agency to exercise for him his rights to resist the imposition of any procedure which has not made its reliability and fairness known, and to resist any procedure that is unfair or unreliable. In Chapter 2 we described briefly the processes that would lead to the dominance of one protective association in a given area, or to a dominant federation of protective associations using rules to peacefully adjudicate disputes among themselves. This dominant protective association will prohibit anyone from applying to its members any procedure about which insufficient information is available as to its reliability and fairness. It also will prohibit anyone from applying to its members an unreliable or unfair procedure; which means, since *they* are applying the principle and have the muscle to do so, that others are prohibited from applying to the protective association's members any procedure the protective association deems unfair or unreliable. Leaving aside the chances of evading the system's operation, anyone violating this prohibition will be punished. The protective association will publish a list of those procedures it deems fair and reliable (and perhaps of those it deems otherwise); and it would take a brave soul indeed to proceed to apply a known procedure not yet on its approved list. Since an association's clients will expect it to do all it can to discourage unreliable procedures, the protective association will keep its list up-to-date, covering all publicly known procedures.

It might be claimed that our assumption that procedural rights exist makes our argument too easy. Does a person who *did* violate another's rights himself have a right that this fact be determined by a fair and reliable procedure? It is true that an unreliable procedure will too often find an innocent person guilty. But does applying such an unreliable procedure to a *guilty* person violate any right of his? May he, in self-defense, resist the imposition of such a procedure upon himself? But what would he be defending himself against? Too high a probability of a punishment he deserves? These questions are important ones for our argument. If a guilty person may not defend himself against such procedures and also may not punish someone else for using them upon him, then may his protective agency defend him against the procedures or punish someone afterwards for having used them upon him, independently of whether or not (and therefore even if) he turns out to be guilty? One would have thought the agency's only rights of action are those its clients transfer to it. But if a guilty client has no such right, he cannot transfer it to the agency.

The agency does not, of course, *know* that its client is guilty, whereas the client himself does know (let us suppose) of his own guilt. But does this difference in knowledge make the requisite difference? Isn't the ignorant agency required to investigate the question of its client's guilt, instead of proceeding on the assumption of his innocence? The difference in epistemic situation between agency and client *can* make the following difference. The agency may under some circumstances defend its client against the imposition of a penalty while promptly proceeding to investigate the question of his guilt. If the agency knows that the punishing party has used a reliable procedure, it accepts its verdict of guilty, and it cannot intervene on the assumption that its client is, or well might be, innocent. If the agency deems the procedure unreliable or doesn't know how reliable it is, it need not presume its client guilty, and it may investigate the matter itself. If upon investigation it determines that its client is guilty, it allows him to be punished. This protection of its client against the actual imposition of the penalty is relatively straightforward, except for the question of whether the agency must compensate the prospective punishers for any costs imposed upon them by having to delay while the protective agency determines to its satisfaction its own client's guilt. It would seem that the protective agency does have to pay compensation to users of relatively unreliable procedures for any disadvantages caused by the enforced delay; and to the users of procedures of unknown reliability it must pay full compensation if the procedures are reliable, otherwise compensation for disadvantages. (Who bears the burden of proof in the question of the reliability of the procedures?) Since the agency may recover this amount (forcibly) from its client who asserted his innocence, this will be something of a deterrent to false pleas of innocence.*

The agency's temporary protection and defense against the infliction of the penalty is relatively straightforward. Less straightforward is the protective agency's appropriate action after a penalty has been inflicted. If the punisher's procedure was a reliable one, the agency does not act against the punisher. But may the agency punish someone who punishes its client, acting on the basis of an

---

* Clients no doubt would empower their agency to proceed as described in the text, if the client himself is unable to say whether he is guilty or innocent, perhaps because he is unconscious, agreeing to replace any compensating amount the agency must pay to the prospective punisher.

This deterrent to false pleas of innocence might act also to deter some innocent people against whom the evidence is overwhelming from protesting their innocence. There will be few such cases, but it may be to avoid this undesirable deterrence that a person who is found guilty beyond a reasonable doubt after having pleaded innocent is not also penalized for perjury.

unreliable procedure? May it punish that person independently of whether or not its client *is* guilty? Or must it investigate, using its own reliable procedure, to determine his guilt or innocence, punishing his punishers *only* if it determines its client innocent? (Or is it: if it fails to find him guilty?) By what right could the protective agency announce that it will punish anyone using an unreliable procedure who punishes its clients, independently of the guilt or innocence of the clients?

The person who uses an unreliable procedure, acting upon its result, imposes risks upon others, whether or not his procedure misfires in a particular case. Someone playing Russian roulette upon another does the same thing if when he pulls the trigger the gun does not fire. The protective agency may treat the unreliable enforcer of justice as it treats any performer of a risky action. We distinguished in Chapter 4 a range of possible responses to a risky action, which were appropriate in different sorts of circumstances: prohibition, compensation to those whose boundaries are crossed, and compensation to all those who undergo a risk of a boundary crossing. The unreliable enforcer of justice might either perform actions others are fearful of, or not; and either might be done to obtain compensation for some previous wrong, or to exact retribution.[9] A person who uses an unreliable procedure of enforcing justice and is led to perform some *unfeared* action will not be punished afterwards. If it turns out that the person on whom he acted was guilty and that the compensation taken was appropriate, the situation will be left as is. If the person on whom he acted turns out to be innocent, the unreliable enforcer of justice may be forced fully to compensate him for the action.

On the other hand, the unreliable enforcer of justice may be forbidden to impose those consequences that would be feared if expected. Why? If done frequently enough so as to create general fear, such unreliable enforcement may be forbidden in order to avoid the general uncompensated-for fear. Even if done rarely, the unreliable enforcer may be punished for imposing this feared consequence upon an innocent person. But if the unreliable enforcer acts rarely and creates no general fear, why may he be punished for imposing a feared consequence *upon a person who is guilty?* A system of punishing unreliable punishers for their punishment of guilty persons would help deter them from using their unreliable system upon anyone and therefore from using it upon innocent people. But not everything that would aid in such deterrence may be inflicted. The question is whether it would be legitimate in this case to punish after the fact the unreliable punisher of someone who turned out to be guilty.

No one has a right to use a relatively unreliable procedure in order to decide whether to punish another. Using such a system, he is in no position to know that the other deserves punishment; hence he has no right to punish him. But how can we say this? If the other has committed a crime, doesn't *everyone* in a state of nature have a right to punish him? And therefore doesn't someone who doesn't know that this other person has committed the crime? Here, it seems to me, we face a terminological issue about how to merge epistemic considerations with rights. Shall we say that someone doesn't have a right to do certain things unless he knows certain facts, or shall we say that he does have a right but he does wrong in exercising it unless he knows certain facts? It may be neater to decide it one way, but we can still say all we wish in the other mode; there is a simple translation between the two modes of discourse.[10] We shall pick the latter mode of speech; if anything, this makes our argument look *less* compelling. If we assume that anyone has a right to take something that a thief has stolen, then under this latter terminology someone who takes a stolen object from a thief, without knowing it had been stolen, had a right to take the object; but since he didn't know he had this right, *his* taking the object was wrong and impermissible. Even though no right of the first thief is violated, the second didn't know this and so acted wrongly and impermissibly.

Having taken this terminological fork, we might propose an epistemic principle of border crossing: If doing act A would violate Q's rights unless condition C obtained, then someone who does not know that C obtains may not do A. Since we may assume that all know that inflicting a punishment upon someone violates his rights unless he is guilty of an offense, we may make do with the weaker principle: If someone *knows* that doing act A would violate Q's rights unless condition C obtained, he may not do A if he does not know that C obtains. Weaker still, but sufficient for our purposes, is: If someone knows that doing act A would violate Q's rights unless condition C obtained, he may not do A if he has not ascertained that C obtains through being in the best feasible position for ascertaining this. (This weakening of the consequent also avoids various problems connected with epistemological skepticism.) Anyone may punish a violator of this prohibition. More precisely, anyone has the right so to punish a violator; people may do so only if they themselves don't run afoul of the prohibition, that is, only if they themselves have ascertained that another violated the prohibition, being in the best position to have ascertained this.

On this view, what a person may do is *not* limited only by the rights of others. An unreliable punisher violates no right of the guilty person; but still he may not punish him. This extra space is created by epistemic considerations. (It would be a fertile area for investigation, if one could avoid drowning in the morass of considerations about "subjective-ought" and "objective-ought.") Note that on this construal, a person does not have a right that he be punished only by use of a relatively reliable procedure. (Even though he may, if he so chooses, give another permission to use a less reliable procedure on him.) On this view, many procedural rights stem not from rights of the person acted upon, but rather from moral considerations about the person or persons doing the acting.

It is not clear to me that this is the proper focus. Perhaps the person acted upon does have such procedural rights against the user of an unreliable procedure. ·(But what is a *guilty* person's complaint against an unreliable procedure. That it is too likely to mispunish him? Would we have the user of an unreliable procedure compensate the guilty person he punished, for violating his right?) We have seen that our argument for a protective agency's punishing the wielder of the unreliable procedure for inflicting a penalty upon its client would go much more smoothly were this so. The client merely would authorize his agency to act to enforce his procedural right. For the purposes of our subargument here, we have shown that our conclusion stands, even without the facilitating assumption of procedural rights. (We do not mean to imply that there aren't such rights.) In either case, a protective agency may punish a wielder of an unreliable or unfair procedure who (against the client's will) has punished one of its clients, independently of whether or not its client actually is guilty and therefore even if its client is guilty.

THE DE FACTO MONOPOLY

The tradition of theorizing about the state we discussed briefly in Chapter 2 has a state claiming a monopoly on the use of force. Has any monopoly element yet entered our account of the dominant protective agency? *Everyone* may defend himself against unknown or unreliable procedures and may punish those who use or attempt to use such procedures against him. As its client's agent, the protective association has the right to do this for its clients. It grants that every individual, including those *not* affiliated with the association, has this right. So far, no monopoly is claimed. To be sure, there is a universal element in the content of the claim: the right to pass on *anyone's* procedure. But it does not claim to be the sole possessor of this right; everyone has it. Since no claim is made that there is some right which it and only it has, no monopoly is claimed. With regard to its own clients, however, it applies and enforces these rights which it grants that everyone has. It deems its own procedures reliable and fair. There will be a strong tendency for it to deem all other procedures, or even the "same" procedures run by others, either unreliable or unfair. But we need not suppose it excludes *every* other procedure. Everyone has the right to defend against procedures that are in fact not, or not known to be, both reliable and fair. Since the dominant protective association judges its own procedures to be both reliable and fair, and believes this to be generally known, it will not allow anyone to defend against *them;* that is, it will punish anyone who does so. The dominant protective association will act freely on its own understanding of the situation, whereas no one else will be able to do so with impunity. Although no monopoly is claimed, the dominant agency does occupy a unique position by virtue of its power. It, and it alone, enforces prohibitions on others' procedures of justice, as it sees fit. It does not claim the right to prohibit others arbitrarily; it claims only the right to prohibit anyone's using actu-

The State   109

ally defective procedures on its clients. But when it sees itself as acting against actually defective procedures, others may see it as acting against what it thinks are defective procedures. It alone will act freely against what it thinks are defective procedures, whatever anyone else thinks. As the most powerful applier of principles which it grants everyone the right to apply *correctly,* it enforces its will, which, from the inside, it thinks *is* correct. From its strength stems its actual position as the ultimate enforcer and the ultimate judge with regard to its own clients. Claiming only the universal right to act correctly, it acts correctly by its own lights. It alone is in a position to act solely by its own lights.

Does this unique position constitute a monopoly? There is no right the dominant protective association claims uniquely to possess. But its strength leads it to be the unique agent acting across the board to enforce a particular right. It is not merely that it *happens* to be the only exerciser of a right it grants that all possess; the nature of the right is such that once a dominant power emerges, it alone will actually exercise that right. For the right includes the right to stop others from wrongfully exercising the right, and only the dominant power will be able to exercise this right against all others. Here, if anywhere, is the place for applying some notion of a *de facto* monopoly: a monopoly that is not *de jure* because it is not the result of some unique grant of exclusive right while others are excluded from exercising a similar privilege. Other protective agencies, to be sure, can enter the market and attempt to wean customers away from the dominant protective agency. They can attempt to replace it as the dominant one. But being the already dominant protective agency gives an agency a significant market advantage in the competition for clients. The dominant agency can offer its customers a guarantee that no other agencies can match: "Only those procedures *we* deem appropriate will be used on our customers."

The dominant protective agency's domain does *not* extend to quarrels of nonclients *among themselves.* If one independent is about to use his procedure of justice upon another independent, then presumably the protective association would have no right to intervene. It would have the right we all do to intervene to aid an unwilling victim whose rights are threatened. But since it may not intervene on paternalistic grounds, the protective association would have no proper business interfering if both independents were satisfied with *their* procedure of justice. This does not show that the dominant protective association is not a state. A state, too, could abstain from disputes where all concerned parties chose to opt out of the state's apparatus. (Though it is more difficult for people to opt out of the state in a limited way, by choosing some other procedure for settling a particular quarrel of theirs. For that procedure's settlement, and their reactions to it, might involve areas that not all parties concerned have removed voluntarily from the state's concern.) And shouldn't (and mustn't) each state allow that option to its citizens?

PROTECTING OTHERS

If the protective agency deems the independents' procedures for enforcing their own rights insufficiently reliable or fair when applied to its clients, it will prohibit the independents from such self-help enforcement. The grounds for this prohibition are that the self-help enforcement imposes risks of danger on its clients. Since the prohibition makes it impossible for the independents credibly to threaten to punish clients who violate their rights, it makes them unable to protect themselves from harm and seriously disadvantages the independents in their daily activities and life. Yet it is perfectly possible that the independents' activities including self-help enforcement could proceed without anyone's rights being violated (leaving aside the question of procedural rights). According to our principle of compensation given in Chapter 4, in these circumstances those persons promulgating and benefiting from the prohibition must compensate those disadvantaged by it. The clients of the protective agency, then, must compensate the independents for the disadvantages imposed upon them by being prohibited self-help enforcement of their own rights against the agency's clients. Undoubtedly, the least expensive way to compensate the independents would be to *supply* them with protective services to cover those situations of conflict with the paying customers of the protective agency. This will be less expensive than leaving them unprotected against violations of their rights (by not

The State III

punishing any client who does so) and then attempting to pay them afterwards to cover their losses through having (and being in a position in which they were exposed to having) their rights violated. If it were *not* less expensive, then instead of buying protective services, people would save their money and use it to cover their losses, perhaps by jointly pooling their money in an insurance scheme.

Must the members of the protective agency *pay* for protective services (vis-à-vis its clients) for the independents? Can they insist that the independents purchase the services themselves? After all, using self-help procedures would not have been without costs for the independent. The principle of compensation does not require those who prohibit an epileptic from driving to pay his full cost of taxis, chauffeurs, and so on. If the epileptic were allowed to run his own automobile, this too would have its costs: money for the car, insurance, gasoline, repair bills, and aggravation. In compensating for disadvantages imposed, the prohibitors need pay only an amount sufficient to compensate for the disadvantages of the prohibition *minus* an amount representing the costs the prohibited party would have borne were it not for the prohibition. The prohibitors needn't pay the complete costs of taxis; they must pay only the amount which when combined with the costs to the prohibited party of running his own private automobile is sufficient for taxis. They may find it less expensive to compensate in kind for the disadvantages they impose than to supply monetary compensation; they may engage in some activity that removes or partially lessens the disadvantages, compensating in money only for the net disadvantages remaining.

If the prohibitor pays to the person prohibited monetary compensation equal to an amount that covers the disadvantages imposed *minus* the costs of the activity where it permitted, this amount may be insufficient to enable the prohibited party to overcome the disadvantages. If his costs in performing the prohibited action would have been monetary, he can combine the compensation payment with this money unspent and purchase the equivalent service. But if his costs would not have been directly monetary but involve energy, time, and the like, as in the case of the independent's self-help enforcement of rights, then this monetary payment of the difference will not by itself enable the prohibited party to overcome the disadvantage by purchasing the equivalent of what he is prohibited. If the independent has other financial resources he can use without disadvantaging himself, then this payment of the difference will suffice to leave the prohibited party undisadvantaged. But *if* the independent has no such other financial resources, a protective agency may *not* pay him an amount *less* than the cost of its least expensive protective policy, and so leave him only the alternatives of being defenseless against the wrongs of its clients or having to work in the cash market to earn sufficient funds to total the premium on a policy. For this financially pressed prohibited individual, the agency must make up the difference between the *monetary* costs to him of the unprohibited activity and the amount necessary to purchase an overcoming or counterbalancing of the disadvantage imposed. The prohibitor must completely supply enough, in money or in kind, to overcome the disadvantages. No compensation need be provided to someone who would not be disadvantaged by buying protection for himself. For those of scanter resources, to whom the unprohibited activity had no monetary costs, the agency must provide the difference between the resources they can spare without disadvantage and the cost of protection. For someone for whom it had some monetary costs, the prohibitor must supply the additional monetary amount (over and above what they can spare without disadvantage) necessary to overcome the disadvantages. If the prohibitors compensate in kind, they may *charge* the financially pressed prohibited party for this, up to the monetary costs to him of his unprohibited activity provided this amount is not greater than the price of the good.[11] As the only effective supplier, the dominant protective agency must offer in compensation the difference between its own fee and monetary costs to this prohibited party of self-help enforcement. It almost always will receive this amount back in partial payment for the purchase of a protection policy. It goes without saying that these dealings and prohibitions apply only to those using unreliable or unfair enforcement procedures.

Thus the dominant protective agency must supply the independents—that is, everyone it prohibits from self-help enforcement against its clients on the grounds that their procedures of enforcement are unreliable or unfair—with protective services against its clients; it may have to provide some persons services for a fee that

The State   113

is less than the price of these services. These persons may, of course, choose to refuse to pay the fee and so do without these compensatory services. If the dominant protective agency provides protective services in this way for independents, won't this lead people to leave the agency in order to receive its services without paying? Not to any great extent, since compensation is paid only to those who would be disadvantaged by purchasing protection for themselves, and only in the amount that will equal the cost of an unfancy policy when added to the sum of the monetary costs of self-help protection plus whatever amount the person comfortably could pay. Furthermore, the agency protects these independents it compensates only against its own paying clients on whom the independents are forbidden to use self-help enforcement. The more free riders there are, the more desirable it is to be a client always protected by the agency. This factor, along with the others, acts to reduce the number of free riders and to move the equilibrium toward almost universal participation.

THE STATE

We set ourselves the task, in Chapter 3, of showing that the dominant protective association within a territory satisfied two crucial necessary conditions for being a state: that it had the requisite sort of monopoly over the use of force in the territory, and that it protected the rights of everyone in the territory, even if this universal protection could be provided only in a "redistributive" fashion. These very crucial facets of the state constituted the subject of the individualist anarchists' condemnation of the state as immoral. We also set ourselves the task of showing that these monopoly and redistributive elements were themselves morally legitimate, of showing that the transition from a state of nature to an ultraminimal state (the monopoly element) was morally legitimate and violated no one's rights and that the transition from an ultraminimal to a minimal state (the "redistributive" element) also was morally legitimate and violated no one's rights.

A protective agency dominant in a territory does satisfy the two crucial necessary conditions for being a state. It is the only generally effective enforcer of a prohibition on others' using unreliable enforcement procedures (calling them as it sees them), and it oversees these procedures. And the agency protects those nonclients in its territory whom it prohibits from using self-help enforcement procedures on its clients, in their dealings with its clients, even if such protection must be financed (in apparent redistributive fashion) by its clients. It is morally required to do this by the principle of compensation, which requires those who act in self-protection in order to increase their own security to compensate those they prohibit from doing risky acts which might actually have turned out to be harmless [12] for the disadvantages imposed upon them.

We noted in beginning Chapter 3 that whether the provision of protective services for some by others was "redistributive" would depend upon the reasons for it. We now see that such provision need not be redistributive since it can be justified on other than redistributive grounds, namely, those provided in the principle of compensation. (Recall that "redistributive" applies to reasons for a practice or institution, and only elliptically and derivatively to the institution itself.) To sharpen this point, we can imagine that protective agencies offer two types of protection policies: those protecting clients against risky private enforcement of justice and those not doing so but protecting only against theft, assault, and so forth (provided these are not done in the course of private enforcement of justice). Since it is only with regard to those with the first type of policy that others are prohibited from privately enforcing justice, only they will be required to compensate the persons prohibited private enforcement for the disadvantages imposed upon them. The holders of only the second type of policy will not have to pay for the protection of others, there being nothing they have to compensate these others for. Since the reasons for wanting to be protected against private enforcement of justice are compelling, almost all who purchase protection will purchase this type of protection, despite its extra costs, and therefore will be involved in providing protection for the independents.

We have discharged our task of explaining how a state would arise from a state of nature without anyone's rights being violated. The moral objections of the individualist anarchist to the minimal state are overcome. It is not an unjust imposition of a monopoly;

the *de facto* monopoly grows by an invisible-hand process and *by morally permissible means*, without anyone's rights being violated and without any claims being made to a special right that others do not possess. And requiring the clients of the *de facto* monopoly to pay for the protection of those they prohibit from self-help enforcement against them, far from being immoral, is morally required by the principle of compensation adumbrated in Chapter 4.

We canvassed, in Chapter 4, the possibility of forbidding people to perform acts if they lack the means to compensate others for possible harmful consequences of these acts or if they lack liability insurance to cover these consequences. Were such prohibition legitimate, according to the principle of compensation the persons prohibited would have to be compensated for the disadvantages imposed upon them, and they could use the compensatory payments to purchase the liability insurance! Only those disadvantaged by the prohibition would be compensated: namely, those who lack other resources they can shift (without disadvantaging sacrifice) to purchase the liability insurance. When these people spend their compensatory payments for liability insurance, we have what amounts to public provision of special liability insurance. It is provided to those unable to afford it and covers only those risky actions which fall under the principle of compensation—those actions which are legitimately prohibited when uncovered (provided disadvantages are compensated for), actions whose prohibition would seriously disadvantage persons. Providing such insurance almost certainly would be the least expensive way to compensate people who present only normal danger to others for the disadvantages of the prohibition. Since they then would be insured against the eventuation of certain of their risks to others, these actions then would not be prohibited to them. Thus we see how, if it were legitimate to prohibit some actions to those uncovered by liability insurance, and were this done, another *apparent* redistributive aspect of the state would enter by solid libertarian moral principles! (The exclamation point stands for *my* surprise.)

Does the dominant protective agency in a given geographical territory constitute the *state* of that territory? We have seen in Chapter 2 how the notion of a monopoly on the use of force is difficult to state precisely so that it does not fall before obvious counterexamples. This notion, as usually explained, cannot be used with any confidence to answer our question. We should accept a decision yielded by the precise wording of a definition in some text only if that definition had been devised for application to cases as complicated as ours and had stood up to tests against a range of such cases. No classification, in passing, by accident can answer our question in any useful manner.

Consider the following discursive description by an anthropologist:

The concentration of all physical force in the hands of the central authority is the primary function of the state and is its decisive characteristic. In order to make this clear, consider what may not be done under the state form of rule: no one in the society governed by the state may take another's life, do him physical harm, touch his property, or damage his reputation save by permission of the state. The officers of the state have powers to take life, inflict corporal punishment, seize property as fine or by expropriation, and affect the standing and reputation of a member of the society.

This is not to say that in societies without the state one may take life with impunity. But in such societies (e.g., among Bushmen, Eskimo, and the tribes of central Australia) the central authority that protects the household against wrongdoers is nonexistent, weak, or sporadic, and it was applied among the Crow and other Indians of the western Plains only as situations arose. The household or the individual is protected in societies without the state by nonexplicit means, by total group participation in suppression of the wrongdoer, by temporarily or sporadically applied force that is no longer needed (and so no longer used) when the cause for its application is past. The state has means for the suppression of what the society considers to be wrongs or crimes: police, courts of law, prisons, institutions which explicitly and specifically function in this area of activity. Moreover, these institutions are stable within the frame of reference of the society, and permanent.

When the state was formed in ancient Russia, the ruling prince asserted the power to impose fines and to wreak physical pain and death, but allowed no one else to act thus. He asserted once again the monopolistic nature of the state power by withholding its power from any other person or body. If harm was done by one subject to another without the prince's express permission, this was a wrong, and the wrongdoer was punished. Moreover, the prince's power could only be explicitly delegated. The class of subject thus protected was thereby carefully defined, of course; by no means were all those within his realm so protected.

No one person or group can stand in place of the state; the state's acts can only be performed directly or by express delegation. The state in delegating its power makes its delegate an agent (organ) of the state. Policemen, judges, jail guards derive their power to coerce, according to the rules of the society, directly from the central authority; so do the tax-collectors, the military, frontier guards, and the like. The authoritative function of the state rests on its command of these forces as its agents.[13]

The writer does not claim that the features he lists all are necessary features of the state; divergence in one feature would not serve to show that the dominant protective agency of a territory was not a state. Clearly the dominant agency has almost all of the features specified; and its enduring administrative structures, with full-time specialized personnel, make it diverge greatly—in the direction of a state—from what anthropologists call a stateless society. On the basis of the many writings like that quoted, one would call it a state.

It is plausible to conclude that the dominant protective association in a territory is its state, only for a territory of some size containing more than a few people. We do not claim that each person who, under anarchy, retains a monopoly on the use of force on his quarter acre of property is its state; nor are the only three inhabitants of an island one square block in size. It would be futile, and would serve no useful purpose, to attempt to specify conditions on the size of population and territory necessary for a state to exist. Also, we speak of cases where almost all of the people in the territory are clients of the dominant agency and where independents are in a subordinate power position in conflicts with the agency and its clients. (We have argued that this will occur.) Precisely what percentage must be clients and how subordinate the power position of the independents must be are more interesting questions, but concerning these I have nothing especially interesting to say.

One additional necessary condition for a state was extracted from the Weberian tradition by our discussion in Chapter 2: namely, that it claim to be the sole authorizer of violence. The dominant protective association makes no such claim. Having described the position of the dominant protective association, and having seen how closely it fits anthropologists' notions, should we weaken·the Weberian necessary condition so that it includes a *de facto* monopoly which is the territory's sole effective judge over the permissibility of violence, having a right (to be sure, one had by all) to make judgments on the matter and to act on correct ones? The case is very strong for doing so, and it is wholly desirable and appropriate. We therefore conclude that the protective association dominant in a territory, as described, *is* a state. However, to remind the reader of our slight weakening of the Weberian condition, we occasionally shall refer to the dominant protective agency as "a statelike entity," instead of simply as "a state."

Have we provided an invisible-hand explanation (see Chapter 2) of the state's arising within a state of nature; have we given an invisible-hand explanation of the state? The *rights* possessed by the state are already possessed by each individual in a state of nature. These rights, since they are already contained whole in the explanatory parts, are *not* provided an invisible-hand explanation. Nor have we provided an invisible-hand explanation of how the state acquires rights unique to it. This is fortunate; for since the state has no special rights, there is nothing of that sort to be explained.

We have explained how, without anyone having this in mind, the self-interested and rational actions of persons in a Lockean state of nature will lead to single protective agencies dominant over geographical territories; each territory will have either one dominant agency or a number of agencies federally affiliated so as to constitute, in essence, one. And we have explained how, without claiming to possess any rights uniquely, a protective agency dominant in a territory will occupy a unique position. Though each person has a right to act correctly to prohibit others from violating rights (including the right not to be punished unless shown to deserve it), only the dominant protective association will be able, without sanction, to enforce correctness as it sees it. Its power makes it the arbiter of correctness; *it* determines what, for purposes of punishment, counts as a breach of correctness. Our explanation does not assume or claim that might makes right. But might does make enforced prohibitions, even if no one thinks the mighty have a *special* entitlement to have realized in the world their own view of which prohibitions are correctly enforced.

Our explanation of this *de facto* monopoly is an invisible-hand explanation. If the state is an institution (1) that has the right to enforce rights, prohibit dangerous private enforcement of justice, pass upon such private procedures, and so forth, and (2) that effectively is the *sole wielder* within a geographical territory of the right in (1), then by offering an invisible-hand explanation of (2), though not of (1), we have partially explained in invisible-hand fashion the existence of the state. More precisely, we have partially explained in invisible-hand fashion the existence of the *ultraminimal* state. What is the explanation of how a *minimal* state arises? The dominant protective association with the monopoly element is morally required to compensate for the disadvantages it imposes upon those it prohibits from self-help activities against its clients. However, it actually might fail to provide this compensation. Those operating an ultraminimal state are morally required to transform it into a minimal state, but they might choose not to do so. We have assumed that generally people will do what they are morally required to do. Explaining how a state could arise from a state of nature without violating anyone's rights refutes the principled objections of the anarchist. But one would feel more confidence if an explanation of how a state *would* arise from a state of nature also specified reasons why an ultraminimal state would be transformed into a minimal one, in addition to moral reasons, if it specified incentives for providing the compensation or the causes of its being provided in addition to people's desire to do what they ought. We should note that even in the event that no nonmoral incentives or causes are found to be sufficient for the transition from an ultraminimal to a minimal state, and the explanation continues to lean heavily upon people's moral motivations, it does not specify people's objective as that of establishing a state. Instead, persons view themselves as providing particular other persons with compensation for particular prohibitions they have imposed upon them. The explanation remains an invisible-hand one.

[9]

Irish Philosophical Journal 5 (1988), pp. 22-30

THE PARADOX OF THE MINIMAL STATE

GEOFFREY HUNT
(University College of Swansea)

At the heart of liberalism is the idea of individual freedom. On this basic idea is elaborated the minimalist liberal conception of the minimal state; one which allows any individual action except that which curtails or impedes the free action of another individual.[1] I will show that the conception of the minimal state, in conjunction with a view of politics which cannot be reasonably disputed, leads to a paradox.

A recent article by Gordon Graham is typical and most convenient for my purposes as it unwittingly sets out the path into this paradox in the process of arguing that 'political association' cannot be grounded on religion.[2] The arguments he puts forward for this view are convincing, given his assumptions. The very same kind of arguments, however, can be employed to show that 'political association' as minimalist liberals understand it cannot be founded on politics. The existence of politics, it will transpire, is both the ground of the necessity of 'political association' and of its impossibility. This has a further paradoxical corollary which can only be resolved, I shall argue, by rejecting the concept of 'political association' (and that of the 'minimal state') as incoherent.

I

Graham follows the minimalist liberal tradition in treating 'political association' (or 'civil association') as a framework in which individuals can pursue their purposes whatever they may be: 'its terms cannot presuppose some particular purpose but must facilitate the pursuit of any and every purpose...'.[3] This means that the only feature the framework requires is a negative one, namely rules against the pursuit of purposes which obstruct other individuals' purposes (purposes which, in turn, are to be non-obstructive). The use of violence or threat of violence to attain one's purpose is, I suppose, an uncontroversial example of what would be ruled out. The reciting of prayers is, I suppose, an uncontroversial example of what the framework would be silent on and therefore allow.

Religion, however, requires the active pursuit of particular purposes (e.g. the regular saying of prayers) and, sometimes, the abstinence from certain activities (e.g. abstinence from the consumption of pork). Thus a religious state might require that all citizens pursue certain purposes (e.g. the saying of prayers) even for those who do not wish to pursue them and might require abstinence from certain pursuits (e.g. eating of pork) even if those pursuits do not obstruct anyone else's. Religion, then, cannot be the foundation of 'political association'.

Politics, I think, is not at all different from religion in the respect which Graham finds religion incompatible with 'political association'. A political doctrine or viewpoint (and, as Graham recognizes, we cannot but have one[4]) enjoins the positive pursuit of particular purposes (e.g. support for an increase, or a decrease, in state expenditure on welfare programmes) and sometimes the forbearance from certain activities (e.g. forbearance from support for labour strikes). Thus a political state might 'legitimately' require all citizens to pursue certain purposes (e.g. pay direct taxes) even for those who do not wish to pursue them, and might require forbearance from certain pursuits (e.g. supporting labour strikes). Politics then cannot be the foundation of 'political association'.

The liberal will immediately point out, no doubt, that the two cases are not strictly parallel insofar as the religious state may demand abstinence even from those pursuits (e.g. eating pork) which do **not** obstruct anyone else's pursuits, whereas the political demand for forbearance from a certain pursuit (e.g. supporting labour strikes) cannot be directed to the non-obstructive in this way. But the difference is misidentified by Graham in such a way as to lend false support to his position. Religious people who demand abstinence from x on religious grounds do in all important cases maintain that the pursuit of x

is obstructive to the pursuits of others. Thus for Moslems
one pork-eater in their midst threatens the whole community
with pollution. To tolerate the eating of pork is to
tolerate pollution as well as to tolerate disrespect for
that which demands the highest respect, and to tolerate
such disrespect is to be implicated. I should add that
whether or not pork-eating 'in fact' poses such a threat to
the community depends on one's ontology, and liberalism,
after all, usually demands tolerance of alternative
ontologies and ways of seeing the world.[5]

The real difference, and this is a difference which does
not undermine my argument, is that the religious demand is
a demand for conformity to a certain fundamental cosmological and ontological conception concerning humanity's
place in a morally ordered universe (which has political
implications) while the political demand is the narrower
demand for conformity to a certain fundamental conception
of social organization. Religious difference is not
settled except by the acceptance by some party of change in
its fundamental cosmological conception and thus in its
practice, while political difference is not settled except
by the acceptance of some party of a change in its
fundamental social conception and thus in its practice. In
politics as in religious disputes there are different
conceptions of what is to the advantage of all.

The liberal might reply: quite so, the point of 'political association' is precisely to avoid the imposition of
particular political beliefs and practices on others.
'Political association' is thus seen as a framework in
which everyone can follow any **political** purpose which
does not obstruct the political purposes of others. But it
is plain that this is an incoherent idea. Political
purposes are not the kind of purposes which can be pursued
without obstruction and conflict. Here they are similar to
religious ones. While religious differences are differences about the very meaning of life itself, political
differences are precisely differences about political
association itself. The man who does not believe in direct
taxes (for anyone at all) cannot be left alone by any state
which demands taxes, for the simple reason that in the view
of the state and of the willing taxpayers he cannot help
benefitting from the direct taxes as anyone does who pays
taxes. Those in favour of direct taxes and those against
have fundamentally different views about how society should
be organized. The same kind of point goes for any particular political purpose one cares to mention. Indeed, if
this were not the case with a given purpose then it would
not be a **political** purpose.

The Paradox of the Minimal State   25

II

We cannot but reject the notion of 'political association' as Graham and the minimalist liberals understand it once we grasp the dilemma they put themselves in. The very existence of fundamental disagreement about the particular or specific nature of political association (this disagreement **is** politics) rules out the possibility of 'political association' in general. 'Political association' in general is only possible where there is no disagreement about the particular nature of political association, that is, no politics at all, and in such a situation 'political association' would not be necessary. Where it is necessary it is impossible and where it is possible it is unnecessary.

This has an important implication which leads directly to the paradox of the minimal state. The requirements of 'political association' in general may be convincingly claimed to be met even though some group within that association is, in its own political terms, disadvantaged or oppressed. That is, in practice the purely formal nature of 'political association' may be made compatible with any actual political state of affairs, including those regarded as oppressive by a large minority.

This is most readily grasped by examining the liberal notion of 'the dividing line between legitimate and illegitimate activities', as Graham puts it.[6] Graham does give us an account of how this line should be drawn so as to meet the liberal requirement of 'political association'. He says that, in contrast to drawing the line for religious reasons,

> we may set reasons like the protection of life and the preservation of peace. If the dividing line between illegitimate and legitimate is drawn where it is for reasons of this sort, then the law can be defended in terms of reasons which are **reasons for us all, whatever our purposes,** since without the protection of life and the existence of peace we cannot pursue any purpose at all.[7] (emphasis mine)

But I maintain that politics is such that there are never 'reasons for us all, whatever our purposes' which can function as Graham thinks. If it is true that politics is always conflict about the actual and specific terms of political association then it is clear that any drawing of 'the dividing line' whatsoever, including a universal and negative one, will favour one party to a conflict and

disfavour another. Consider Graham's example of protection
of life and preservation of peace, which on the face of it
appears quite uncontroversial.[8] It is often overlooked
by liberals that these principles in any actual political
situation must be instruments of disadvantage, and even
oppression, to someone or some group. If politics is about
conflict any principle which rules out non-peaceful action
as illegitimate favours the *status quo* (i.e. favours the
existing political state in any conflict) by ruling out
certain kinds of resolution of conflict.

Thus if group B in a society is a group which rejects the
actual terms of existing association favoured by group A
then group A's legislation based on 'protection of life'
and 'preservation of peace' discriminates against any
attempt by B to resolve the conflict by means which may be
regarded as threatening life or undermining the peace. One
should keep in mind that 'non-peaceful' is not synonymous
with 'violent' which is an extreme case of the non-
peaceful. One need not bring to mind here extreme cases
such as 'terrorism' although it may be argued that even
these are justifiable.[9] It may be countered that group B
would only have to resort to such means where A is already
transgressing the liberal framework and its minimal state.
That is, it may be said that a truly liberal state is one
which allows the possibility of resolving all conflicts
peacefully. Non-peaceful opposition is only necessary
where a state is not truly liberal. Indeed the necessity
of non-peaceful opposition, on the liberal conception, is
the very mark of an authoritarian state. The authoritarian
state is one which tries to universalize a **particular**
purpose. If the state is truly liberal then non-peaceful
opposition is unnecessary, claims the liberal.

I do not argue that the existence of non-peaceful
opposition in itself shows the incoherence of the conception of 'political association'. What has to be shown
is that a potential for non-peaceful opposition is
necessary wherever there is politics, even under conditions
in which the requirements of 'political association' are
formally met. Non-peaceful action is necessary in some
cases because it follows from the existence of structural
conflict, conflict about the very terms of political
association. The most liberal state is only liberal in
form. In content there will always be elements which for
some will justify non-peaceful action. This is so because
the law, whatever it is, is **itself** a form of non-peaceful
action. On this last point Graham, at least, does not
disagree as he writes, 'The essence of political rule is
compulsion'.

The Paradox of the Minimal State   27

It is important to keep in mind that by saying that
political conflict is irresolvable within a system I mean
it is conflict about the system itself. The terms by which
conflicts are resolved must be terms embedded in the
foundations of the system itself (indeed, are part of the
system) and as such cannot resolve conflict about those
terms themselves.

It may be said that true liberalism does allow such
actions or purposes as support for labour strikes, for
conscientious objection to taxation, for communism, for
anti-war protests, and the like. States which do not are
not truly liberal whatever they may claim to be. This is
another version of the objection we have already considered. Let us approach it another way. The fact is that
the individualistic terms of liberalism allow such political positions as those mentioned only insofar as they are
so restricted that the **political** nature of the positions
is frustrated. Thus if I wish to stand on a soapbox and
proclaim the merits of communism I am regarded as acting
within the bounds of my 'right to freedom of speech' and
other liberal rights, and I am not imposing my wishes on
anyone. But if I take my commitment to communism to
require belonging to a movement which is prepared to
overthrow the existing economic and political order in the
belief that the guardians of that order will defend it
non-peacefully (i.e. by means of the law, itself based on
appeals to the 'security' and 'peace' of all) then I am
regarded as a 'subversive' or 'terrorist', i.e. one who
threatens peace and security and property. If as a
'private' individual I refuse to fight in a national war
then I am a 'conscientious objector', but if I physically
destroy draft files or damage weapons of war or if I
distribute anti-war pamphlets to troops then I am a
'traitor' or 'conspirator', i.e. one who threatens peace
and security and property.[11]

The point is that in each case the more individual (or
personal or 'private') the action is the less does it
conflict with the principle of non-obstruction and so tends
to the legitimate. The price I pay for legitimacy is that
my action is almost certainly ineffective, in fact is
hardly political at all. As soon as my action is clearly a
social and political one, and directly and publicly
influences or tries to influence others, then it contra-
venes the principle of non-obstruction and is illegitimate.

III

I shall now deal with some other possible objections from defenders of the minimalist liberal conception of 'political association' and the minimal state.

It might be said that precisely because there is irresolvable, structural conflict the minimalist framework is the only one which is workable because it is the only one acceptable to **all.** There could be disagreements without any conflict about the minimalist framework ('political association'). I have already touched on this, but let us approach it from another angle. It should be recalled that this is a result of the way 'political association' has been defined. It is, by definition, one in which **particular** purposes, the very bases of conflict, have been excluded. This is done by making 'political association' an empty form. Where the form is so general as to please everyone all dispute is then transferred to the **content.** That is, if we agree on the form then we shall soon discover that we disagree on how to interpret it.

It may be said that some people would regard the very notion of 'structural politics' objectionable here because it is itself a particular political idea. In other words, it may be said that it is an idea which belongs to or is associated with socialism or Marxism, which are particular political doctrines. One can understand how those who are dissatisfied with the *status quo* will tend to believe that political conflict is at least partly structural, requiring a fundamental change of system. It would be easy--too easy--to dismiss my argument in this paper from this standpoint.

To begin with, one can equally understand how those who are satisfied with the *status quo* will tend to believe that the only political conflict which is irresolvable is that in which at least one party involved is being 'unreasonable' or 'irrational' (fanatical, dogmatic, intolerant, shortsighted, inhumane, prejudiced, intransigent, etc.). In such situations, it is said, one can only hope for enlightenment.

Thus the question of 'structural politics' may become part and parcel of the very terms of political disagreement. Asserting the existence of structural politics is no more 'political' than denying this existence. The fact is that liberals and radicals see the social world differently. They have different conceptions of the social structure. For the liberal, society is an aggregate of individuals ('perfect strangers' says Graham[12]) pursuing various purposes of their own. For the radical, society is a structure of supremacy and subordination which the individual finds, together with his or her position in it, as a **given**.

Resort to the 'facts' about society will not resolve the matter, because part of the dispute is precisely over what the facts are. I do not resort to 'facts' in this paper. I make use of the existence of differences in conception, in interpretation. This is a fact of another order: the fact that different fundamental conceptions of society exist. By 'structural politics' I do not refer to the 'fact that Western capitalist society is fundamentally exploitative', etc. This would transfer the debate from the philosophical to the political level. The only fact that I expect general acceptance of is the existence of 'structural politics' in the sense of fundamental differences in the conception of political association as it is and should be. This is a ratiocinative strategy which liberals should find acceptable. It is, after all, their own strategy in a new guise. The point, then, is that as long as there are such fundamental differences (i.e. politics) a 'minimal state' is paradoxical. This paradox can now be simply stated.

On the assumption that politics is the interplay of mutually obstructive views about the terms of social organization, any application by a state of a framework by which any action is allowed except that which is obstructive to others will be obstructive to others. Any 'minimal state' will not be a minimal state. Thus the concept of 'minimal state' is paradoxical and should be rejected.

To conclude I should add that this springs from the formal nature of the rule (or principle or framework) and not from the nature of its application, which is contingently coercive but almost certain to be so in reality.[13]

Notes

1. By 'minimalist liberal' I refer to the classical *laissez-faire* school with its concept of the 'nightwatchman state' and the libertarian-liberal school. The most recent libertarian account of the minimal state is, of course, Robert Nozick, *Anarchy, State, and Utopia* (Oxford: Blackwell, 1974). Nozick's minimal state is founded on the argument that any extension of the state beyond the minimal functions of protection against force, theft, fraud and enforcement of contracts must involve infringement of individual rights. To be completely effective against Nozick my

30   Irish Philosophical Journal

arguments would have to be extended to a critique of
his concept of 'rights'.

2. Gordon Graham, 'Religion and Politics', *Philosophy*
    58 (1983), pp. 203-213.

3. Ibid., p. 205.

4. Ibid., p. 204.

5. Cardinal Robert Bellarmine (1542-1621) was arguing in
    perfect accord with the logic and ontology of his
    religion when he said that the persecution and killing
    of heretics was not only a Christian right but a duty,
    and that it was even good for the heretics themselves
    since it saved them from a worse fate in Hell. Of
    course, there is a great deal which can be said in
    favour of criteria to distinguish truly other-regarding
    actions from those which are not, but in my view none
    can overcome the difficulties created by the way in
    which actions are differently defined by different
    ontologies.

6. Op. cit., p. 208.

7. Op. cit., p. 208.

8. Graham does not forget property (p. 206). In fact just
    like Nozick he does not seem to attach any more
    functions to the state than protection of life,
    property and the contract form.

9. See John Harris, 'The Morality of Terrorism', *Radical
    Philosophy* **33** (1983), pp. 1-5.

10. Op. cit., p. 210.

11. Consider the debates surrounding the anti-war actions
    of Father Philip Berrigan in the U.S.A. See P.
    Berrigan, *Prison Journals of a Priest Revolutionary*
    (New York: Ballantine, 1971) and *A Punishment for
    Peace* (New York: Ballantine, 1971).

12. Op. cit., p. 205.

13. I am indebted to Professor William McBride of Purdue
    University and to an anonymous *IPJ* reader for their
    comments and criticisms.

[10]

Ratio XXIX 2 December 1987
0034–0066 $2.00

NOZICK'S LIBERTARIANISM AND THE JUSTIFICATION OF THE STATE

Jeffrey D. Goldsworthy

In his controversial 'Anarchy, State and Utopia',[1] Robert Nozick defends a libertarian political philosophy grounded in a strongly rights-based moral theory. That moral theory combines extreme forms of individualism and deontology: it prohibits the compelling of a person (other than a wrongdoer) to act either for his own sake or for the sake of others, and does so absolutely – that is, regardless of the consequences, even if they include a greater number of violations of this very prohibition than would otherwise occur (that is, it rejects what Nozick calls 'utilitarianism of rights') [28–30]. In conjunction with a Lockean theory of property rights, including rights of acquisition, transfer and rectification of rights-violations, this moral theory generates what he calls 'the entitlement theory of justice' [150–82]. On the strength of this theory of justice, Nozick launches an unremitting attack on alternative theories of social justice, and especially that of Rawls, which require the compulsory redistribution of income or wealth [183–275]. Nozick argues that morality strictly confines the legitimate sphere of governmental activity to the protection of rights to life, liberty and property; in other words, only the minimal or 'night-watchman' state can be justified.

Most of the ensuing debate has concerned these aspects of Nozick's book. But a large part of the book deals with another issue. Given his moral theory, Nozick finds it difficult to justify even minimal government. His problem is to justify the two primary characteristics of government: its monopoly of the authorisation of force within its territory (its monopoly of force); and its attempt to protect the rights of everyone within its territory (universal protection) [23–25, 115–19]. He finds both characteristics problematic. As for the monopoly of force, the state forbids all private rights enforcement, apparently for reasons such as preserving public order, preventing feuds, and so on. But among the Lockean rights endorsed by his moral theory is the right to defend (i.e., to enforce) one's rights [10]: how may this be suppressed in

---

[1] Robert Nozick, *Anarchy, State and Utopia* (New York: Basic Books 1974). All references in square brackets are to this book.

NOZICK'S LIBERTARIANISM   181

the cause of some overall 'social good' without violating the
fundamental prohibition of the theory? [24, 52]² As for universal
protection, when a state attempts to protect the rights of everyone
within its territory, some will be unable to afford their share of the
overall cost. The attempt would therefore appear to involve a
redistribution of resources from wealthier to poorer individuals
[25–27]. But of course his moral theory condemns any redistribution
of wealth which is not freely consented to by all contributors
[167–73] (which would almost certainly be the case here).

Nozick's attempt to solve the second problem will be the subject
of this paper. I will argue that the attempt fails, and that therefore
Nozick fails to justify the state. This conclusion is significant
because of its relevance to the plausibility of a libertarian political
philosophy distinct from anarchism. If the moral theory underlying
libertarianism is an insurmountable obstacle to the justification of
even minimal government, libertarianism collapses into anarchism.
Conversely, the repudiation of anarchism may presuppose a moral
theory which necessarily justifies not just a minimal but a
redistributive state. Nozick himself explicitly recognises this
possibility, when he asks in relation to the problem of universal
protection: 'If some redistribution is legitimate in order to protect
everyone, why is redistribution not legitimate for other attractive
and desirable purposes as well? [27]'

Nozick purports to solve the problem of universal protection by
arguing that it is morally required by a 'principle of compensation',
and is therefore not wrongfully redistributive [26–27, 114]. This is
because the state itself, in (quite justifiably) exercising its monopoly of force, reduces the ability of certain individuals to protect
their rights and consequently is morally obligated to compensate
them. It is unnecessary to fully explain Nozick's justification of the
monopoly of force, which rests on a sometimes obscure discussion
of principles governing the moral status of risky acts (acts which
only *might* violate other people's rights) [73–78]. In brief, rights
enforcement is subject to principles which, in Nozick's moral
theory, sometimes permit risky acts to be prohibited. Individuals
who do not voluntarily subscribe to the state's protective services
(thereby assigning to it their right to enforce their rights) may be
prohibited from enforcing their own rights because of the risk that
they might punish an innocent person or punish a guilty person

---

² It is irrelevant that this social good might also benefit those who would prefer to be able
to engage in their own private rights-enforcement, because Nozick's theory is equally hostile
to paternalism [34, 58 and 109].

excessively [88–90]. It is the enforcement of this prohibition which constitutes the monopoly of force [108–10, 118–19]. But the state must comply with the following principle:

> [T]hose who are disadvantaged by being forbidden to do actions that only might harm others must be compensated for those disadvantages foisted upon them in order to provide security for the others [82–83].

In this context, the principle requires compensation for the disadvantage suffered by individuals who may no longer enforce their own rights. The most efficient form of compensation is the extension to them of the state's own protective services [110–13]. Thus is the state morally bound to provide universal protection.

Two objections to Nozick's reliance on this principle to justify universal protection will be discussed here; the first, put forward by Gerald Postema and others,[3] is that Nozick's use of the principle makes his argument internally inconsistent; the second is that the principle cannot bear the weight put on it. I will argue that Nozick can meet the first objection, but not the second. It follows that his attempt to justify the state fails.

I. The Internal Consistency of the Argument

The principle of compensation requires that when a risky act (such as the use of inaccurate enforcement procedures) is forbidden, those who forbid it in order to enjoy added security must compensate the person whose act is restrained. But the compensation need only extend to 'disadvantages' suffered by that person, to be calculated by a comparison with the 'normal situation' of others in the community. Nozick explicitly denies that 'full' compensation is required – that is, the person restrained need not be returned to the indifference curve he would have occupied before the prohibition [82–83, 86–87]. A person may be made worse off by a prohibition without being 'disadvantaged' relative to the normal activities of others – for example, someone prevented from playing Russian roulette with other people's lives (who is made worse off by being denied a source of enjoyment) [79, 82]. Full compensation is not required because the prohibition is not itself a violation of a

---

[3] G. Postema, 'Nozick on Liberty, Compensation, and the Individual's Right to Punish', *Social Theory and Practice*, 6 (1980) 311, 317–18; R. Holmes, 'Nozick on Anarchism' in J. Paul, ed., *Reading Nozick* (Oxford: Basil Blackwell 1982) 57, 60–61; J. Paul, 'The Withering of Nozick's Minimal State', in *Reading Nozick* 68, 70.

NOZICK'S LIBERTARIANISM   183

right (to act) on the part of the person restrained, like rights
violations (assault, theft, etc) which do require the payment of full
compensation. The requirement of compensation for disadvantage
does not stem from the prohibition being wrongful in that, or any
other, sense. Indeed, if the first part of Nozick's strategy (justifying
the monopoly of force) is to succeed, the prohibition must itself be
fully justified. It is here that objections are raised: if the prohibition
is justified, why is compensation required?

Nozick offers two alternative justifications for the prohibition of
unreliable enforcement procedures. The first is that there may be a
natural right, held by everyone, to be tried only by procedures
known to be reliable and fair [101–3]. Gerald Postema and others[4]
argue that if there is such a right, then there can be no requirement
that persons prohibited from using unreliable procedures be
compensated: by using such procedures, they would be violating
someone else's right not to be subjected to them. Postema asks why
anyone should be compensated for being prohibited from violating
another's rights: '[a]m I due compensation for being forbidden to
murder my brother-in-law?'[5].

Nozick proposes an alternative to this natural right because it is
questionable when the person subjected to an enforcement procedure (of whatever degree of reliability) is, in fact, guilty.[6] This, in
turn, raises doubts about the propriety of the state prohibiting the
use of particular procedures in such cases, even though it does not
know whether or not such a person *is* guilty [103–5]. The
alternative is the 'epistemic principle of border crossing', which
condemns the imposition of an unreliable procedure even upon a
person who is actually guilty. The wrongfulness does not stem from
any right of the guilty person not to be subjected to the procedure,
but from moral considerations applying directly to the person
seeking to impose it [107]. The principle is:

> If someone knows that doing act A would violate Q's rights
> unless condition C obtained, he may not do A if he has not
> ascertained that C obtains through being in the best feasible
> position for ascertaining it [106–7].

[4] Ibid.

[5] Postema, 318.

[6] 'It is true that an unreliable procedure will too often find an innocent person guilty. But
does applying such an unreliable procedure to a guilty person violate any right of his? May
he, in self-defense, resist the imposition of such a procedure upon himself? But what would he
be defending himself against? Too high a probability of a punishment he deserves?' [103]

But perhaps the guilty person can defend himself against the risk of excessive punishment to
which a risky procedure might subject him. This risk is relevant: see [88].

Postema argues that his objection still applies even if the prohibition of unreliable procedures is justified by this principle (rather than by the natural rights of those subjected to them). There should still be no requirement of compensation: violating the 'epistemic principle' would be wrong, and why must someone be compensated for being prevented from doing wrong?

This objection amounts to the charge that Nozick's attempt to justify the monopoly of force and universal protection is internally inconsistent. As to the monopoly of force Nozick argues that the prohibition of unreliable enforcement procedures is morally justified. But the state's protection of all its citizens is then said to be required because the state must compensate for the prohibition previously held to be justified. Postema's objection is that Nozick cannot have both – the two are inconsistent.[7]

Postema fails to acknowledge that Nozick has anticipated precisely this objection, when he refers to the view that 'either you have a right to forbid it so you needn't compensate, or you don't have a right to forbid it so you should stop'. Nozick replies that this is 'too short'. 'It may be that you have a right to forbid an action but only provided you compensate those to whom it is forbidden [83]'. Later in the book, when Nozick applies the principle of compensation to the different but related problem of 'preventive restraint', he returns to this question. He denies that permitting prohibition only if compensation is paid is an indecisive compromise between two alternative positions. Rather, it is 'the correct position that fits the (moral) vector resultant of the opposing weighty considerations, each of which must be taken into account somehow' [146].

[7] More exactly, Postema argues that Nozick can extricate himself from the dilemma by what he calls the 'risk argument': Postema, 320. He goes on to argue that this too is unsatisfactory: ibid., 329ff. But what he calls the 'risk argument' is used by Nozick to support the two alternative justifications of the principle of compensation I have just referred to: see [101–3] and [106–7]. It has no independent import in the context of unreliable procedures. Postema misses this partly for the reasons I am about to give, which reasons also entirely undermine his rebuttal of the 'risk argument' at ibid., 329–30. Because Nozick uses the risk factor to support the existence of individual rights, or alternatively, duties (the epistemic principle), he does *not* treat protection against risk as a 'public good', thereby violating his own individualist premises. Postema's suggestion that Nozick treats the use of unreliable enforcement procedures 'as a kind of fear-causing risk activity' (ibid., 329) is explicitly denied by Nozick [88–89] (although fear is relevant: [105–6]). It must be conceded that Nozick's use of the argument from general, uncompensable fear in the earlier section dealing with the prohibition not of risky acts, but of acts certain to violate rights [65–71] does open itself up to Postema's objection (but see Nozick's implicit recognition of this at [69]). But the relationship between this earlier section, and both the subsequent discussions of risky acts generally [73ff.] and unreliable enforcement procedures [88ff.], while certainly obscure in several respects is not as Postema conceives it, in part for the reasons just given.

In the case of unreliable enforcement procedures, the 'opposing weighty considerations' are set out in a single paragraph [78–79]. Perhaps they are not sufficient to establish Nozick's conclusions: nevertheless, it is not enough for Postema to simply allege inconsistency, by assuming that rights are necessarily of an 'all or nothing' sort – he must either show that a right cannot have this alternative structure suggested by Nozick, or that such a right in this case is not supported by the reasons adduced. This will be difficult, because there is at least one other right whose structure is similar (but not identical) to the 'principle of compensation', and which is relatively uncontroversial. Elsewhere, Nozick discusses cases where an action would violate a person's rights unless performed with his consent, but it is impossible or too costly to negotiate with him in order to purchase his consent although it seems likely that consent would be given. For instance, it might be impossible to locate the right-holder, or it may be impossible to speak to him without 'first performing a brain operation on him, or finding him in an African jungle . . . and so on [72]'. In some cases of this sort (but not those in which the proposed action is one normally feared) it may be permissible to go ahead and act without the right-holder's prior consent – but only if compensation is subsequently paid if it is claimed by the right-holder or his estate. Here too, the objection that 'either there is a right to act (so no compensation is due), or there is not (so the act should not be done)', fails. Once again, 'opposing weighty considerations' give rise to a 'moral vector' in which there is a right to act, but only if compensation is paid. But the similarity with the 'principle of compensation' is not complete, since in this case 'full' compensation, and not compensation only for disadvantage, is required.

II. The Inadequacy of the Principle of Compensation

There is a much more serious objection to the principle of compensation or rather, to its adequacy as the justification for universal protection. The principle requires the state to ensure that no one is disadvantaged by being prevented from using unreliable fact-finding procedures in attempting to enforce his or her own rights. The compensation required cannot exceed the sum of these disadvantages: the state cannot provide any person with *more* protection than he would have enjoyed in the absence of its interference (unless it is simply impossible to provide adequate compensation without doing so). But the extent to which many

186   JEFFREY D. GOLDSWORTHY

people could protect themselves without the assistance of the state might be very limited. Indeed, those lacking the physical ability to personally exact compensation or inflict punishment, and economic resources to hire the assistance of others (such as protection agencies), and sufficiently appealing qualities to attract the gratuitous assistance of others, would be largely defenceless in the state of nature. By threatening to use unreliable fact-finding procedures, such people would be able (due to the principle of compensation) to obtain access to the state's judicial procedures. But after those procedures establish guilt and fix the appropriate penalties these individuals could be left again to their own devices. What claim would they have to further assistance in physically carrying out the determinations of the judicial procedure? The state's duties end once compensation is made for what has been prohibited – the use of inaccurate fact-finding or penalty-fixing procedures. Any further assistance would actually be wrong – an impermissible redistribution of resources from the wealthier individuals who pay for the upkeep of the state's enforcement apparatus, to their poorer fellows.

Nozick never distinguishes the different stages involved in the full enforcement of a right, but there are at least three (assuming that the right in question has already been established): the fact-finding, guilt-determining process; the determination of the precise amount of compensation or punishment due; and the physical execution of the determination. Nozick speaks vaguely of 'protection', 'enforcement', and 'exacting justice' without acknowledging that different processes are involved. At one early point he mentions the diverse agencies which may be needed – he refers to 'detectives, police to bring criminals into custody, courts, and prisons' – but he fails to see any significance in this diversity [25]. Yet the 'unreliable procedures' which the state is entitled to prohibit (with compensation) are those of fact-finding and penalty-fixing. Nozick says that the risk to be prevented is two-fold: that of punishing the innocent, and that of over-punishing the guilty [88]. Throughout the ensuing discussion [88–89, 96–110], the former has his exclusive attention. Finally, in summarizing his argument, he explains that the rationale for the prohibition of unreliable procedures '. . . rests on the ignorance, uncertainty, and lack of knowledge of people. In some situations, it is not known whether a particular person performed a certain action, and procedures for finding out differ in reliability or fairness [140–41]'.

It might be argued that physical execution, too, can be

'unreliable' and hence risky. But if the state's own reliable judicial procedures have been used to fix the precise amount of compensation or punishment that is due, where is the risk? There are two possibilities here.

First, if physical execution is not resisted by the guilty party, there is surely very little risk: the procedure will (subject to an exception dealt with below) be a straight-forward, even mechanical one. True, a person executing a judgment in his favour against an enemy who has temporarily lowered his defences might be tempted to take or inflict more than the judgment authorizes. But within Nozick's theory *this risk cannot be relevant*, because it would eventuate only if the person concerned should decide to act wrongly, which (generally) cannot be known in advance. The principle established in Nozick's discussion of 'pre-emptive attack' [126–29] and 'preventive restraint' [142–43] applies, and this principle forbids interference with freedom of action on the grounds of such a risk. In that discussion, he draws a distinction between a pre-emptive strike on an enemy which is known to have decided to launch an (unjustified) attack, and a pre-emptive strike against a merely potential enemy which is arming itself but whose intentions are not known to be aggressive. He accepts the orthodox view that the first strike is justified but the second is not [126]. He suggests as a rationale the principle that

> *only* wrong decisions and actions on them (or dangerous actions requiring no further wrong decisions) [may be prohibited]. One may *not* prohibit actions which are not based on decisions that are wrong, merely on the grounds that they facilitate or make more likely the agent himself later making wrong decisions and doing the wrong actions which follow from them. [128]

This principle is later applied to the question of preventive restraint, subject to a qualification which is not relevant here [143]. It follows that although the use of unreliable fact-finding and penalty-fixing procedures may be prohibited (because it is dangerous without further wrong decisions having to be made), the private physical execution of a properly determined judgment against a non-resisting adversary may not.

The second possibility is that execution is resisted by the guilty party. If so, there may be a risk of excessive punishment due to the uncertainties and hazards of battle. Actually this is unlikely in the particular cases with which we are concerned, where the parties attempting to exact justice are so weak that they are unlikely to inflict significant damage on their adversaries. But putting this aside, wrongful resistance would surely justify the imposition of such a risk; indeed, the resister himself would be responsible for it.

It might be objected that, whether or not it is resisted, the execution of *some* judgments will not be straight-forward and mechanical because it will require the resolution of further uncertainties. For example, the state's judicial procedures might decide that John Smith must pay a certain amount in compensation for a wrong done, but in attempting to enforce this it may be difficult to establish whether a particular person *is* John Smith or whether property in his possession (which could be seized to realise his debt) belongs to him. But just as the state can provide judicial procedures to minimize the risks inherent in initially determining the liabilities of wrong-doers, so it can provide further, ancillary assistance to minimize the risk that such outstanding questions will be resolved inaccurately. It could, if necessary, prohibit enforcement of a judgment until those questions should have been resolved to its satisfaction, while still leaving subsequent enforcement to the injured party. This problem, like that posed by risky guilt-finding and penalty-fixing procedures, can be resolved without the state providing full universal protection, which Nozick's own theory therefore forbids.

Thus, the state may prohibit the use of unreliable procedures to determine liability, fix penalties, and find other facts relevant to enforcement, because of the risks they create, provided that those thereby prevented from enforcing their rights are given access to its own procedures. But Nozick's moral theory requires that once guilt and penalty are determined, and any further, outstanding uncertainties are resolved, the state may – indeed, must – leave such persons to their own devices, unless someone pays for further assistance. Further assistance cannot be justified by the principle of compensation; since private physical execution of judgments complying with the directions of the state's judicial procedures may not be prohibited, the relevance of that principle has been exhausted. If the guilty party resists execution of the penalty, the state can do nothing unless its taxpayers agree to the provision of further assistance, at their expense. Without such agreement further assistance would be a compulsory and therefore wrongful redistribution of resources. But without such further assistance the weak and poor would be helpless against powerful predators.

The principle of compensation does not require the provision of full, or in many cases even adequate, protection of the defenceless.

It is therefore nonsense to say that what until now we have called a state really is a state. It is what Nozick calls an 'ultraminimal state' [26], exercising a monopoly of force but not providing universal protection. Nozick's attempt to justify the state fails. Moreover, it appears that universal protection does, after all, involve a redistribution of wealth, and libertarians who seek to justify it are therefore confronted by Nozick's question: 'If some redistribution is legitimate in order to protect everyone, why is redistribution not legitimate for other attractive and desirable purposes as well? [27]'.

Faculty of Law
Monash University
Clayton
Victoria 3168
Australia

Part IV
State Imperfections

[11]

Excerpt from *Law, Legislation and Liberty*, 1–19

TWELVE

MAJORITY OPINION AND CONTEMPORARY DEMOCRACY

> But the great number [of the Athenian Assembly] cried out that it was monstrous if the people were to be prevented from doing whatever they wished. . . . Then the Prytanes, stricken with fear, agreed to put the question—all of them except Socrates, the son of Sophroniscus; and he said that in no case would he act except in accordance with the law.
>
> Xenophon*

The progressive disillusionment about democracy

When the activities of modern government produce aggregate results that few people have either wanted or foreseen this is commonly regarded as an inevitable feature of democracy. It can hardly be claimed, however, that such developments usually correspond to the desires of any identifiable group of men. It appears that the particular process which we have chosen to ascertain what we call the will of the people brings about results which have little to do with anything deserving the name of the 'common will' of any substantial part of the population.

We have in fact become so used to regard as democratic only the particular set of institutions which today prevails in all Western democracies, and in which a majority of a representative body lays down the law *and* directs government, that we regard this as the only possible form of democracy. As a consequence we do not care to dwell on the fact that this system not only has produced many results which nobody likes, even in those countries in which on the whole it has worked well, but also has proved unworkable in most countries where these democratic institutions were not restrained by strong traditions about the appropriate tasks of the representative assemblies. Because we rightly believe in the basic ideal of democracy we feel usually bound to defend the particular institutions

1

MAJORITY OPINION AND CONTEMPORARY DEMOCRACY

which have long been accepted as its embodiment, and hesitate to criticize them because this might weaken the respect for an ideal we wish to preserve.

It is no longer possible, however, to overlook the fact that in recent times in spite of continued lip-service and even demands for its further extension, there has arisen among thoughtful persons an increasing disquiet and serious alarm about the results it often produces.[1] This does not everywhere take the form of that cynical realism which is characteristic of some contemporary political scientists who regard democracy merely as just another form of an inevitable struggle in which it is decided 'who gets what, when, and how'.[2] Yet that there prevails deep disillusionment and doubt about the future of democracy, caused by a belief that those developments of it which hardly anybody approves are inevitable, can scarcely be denied. It found its expression many years ago in Joseph Schumpeter's well known contention that, although a system based on the free market would be better for most, it is doomed beyond hope, while socialism, though it cannot fulfil its promises, is bound to come.[3]

It seems to be the regular course of the development of democracy that after a glorious first period in which it is understood as and actually operates as a safeguard of personal freedom because it accepts the limitations of a higher nomos, sooner or later it comes to claim the right to settle any particular question in whatever manner a majority agrees upon. This is what happened to the Athenian democracy at the end of the fifth century, as shown by the famous occurrence to which the quotation at the head of this chapter refers; and in the next century Demosthenes (and others) were to complain that 'our laws are no better than so many decrees; nay, you will find that the laws which have to be observed in drafting the decrees are later than the decrees themselves.'[4]

In modern times a similar development started when the British Parliament claimed sovereign, that is unlimited, powers and in 1766 explicitly rejected the idea that in its particular decisions it was bound to observe any general rules not of its own making. Though for a time a strong tradition of the rule of law prevented serious abuse of the power that Parliament had arrogated to itself, it proved in the long run the great calamity of modern development that soon after representative government was achieved all those restraints upon the supreme power that had been painfully built up during the evolution of constitutional monarchy were successively dismantled

2

MAJORITY OPINION AND CONTEMPORARY DEMOCRACY

as no longer necessary. That this in effect meant the abandonment of constitutionalism which consists in a limitation of all power by permanent principles of government was already seen by Aristotle when he maintained that 'where the laws are not sovereign . . . since the many are sovereign not as individuals but collectively . . . such a democracy is not a constitution at all';[5] and it was recently pointed out again by a modern author who speaks of 'constitutions which are so democratic that they are properly speaking no longer constitutions'.[6] Indeed, we are now told that the 'modern conception of democracy is a form of government in which no restriction is placed on the governing body'[7] and, as we have seen, some have already drawn the conclusion that constitutions are an antiquated survival which have no place in the modern conception of government.[8]

Unlimited power the fatal defect of the prevailing form of democracy

The tragic illusion was that the adoption of democratic procedures made it possible to dispense with all other limitations on governmental power. It also promoted the belief that the 'control of government' by the democratically elected legislation would adequately replace the traditional limitations,[9] while in fact the necessity of forming organized majorities for supporting a programme of particular actions in favour of special groups introduced a new source of arbitrariness and partiality and produced results inconsistent with the moral principles of the majority. As we shall see, the paradoxical result of the possession of unlimited power makes it impossible for a representative body to make the general principles prevail on which it agrees, because under such a system the majority of the representative assembly, in order to remain a majority, *must* do what it can to buy the support of the several interests by granting them special benefits.

So it came about that with the precious institutions of representative government Britain gave to the world also the pernicious principle of parliamentary sovereignty[10] according to which the representative assembly is not only the highest but also an unlimited authority. The latter is sometimes thought to be a necessary consequence of the former, but this is not so. Its power may be limited, not by another superior 'will' but by the consent of the people on which all power and the coherence of the state rest. If that consent approves only of the laying down and enforcement of general rules of just conduct, and nobody is given power to coerce except for the

3

MAJORITY OPINION AND CONTEMPORARY DEMOCRACY

enforcement of these rules (or temporarily during a violent disruption of order by some cataclysm), even the highest constituted power may be limited. Indeed, the claim of Parliament to sovereignty at first meant only that it recognized no other will above it; it only gradually came to mean that it could do whatever it liked—which does not necessarily follow from the first, because the consent on which the unity of the state and therefore the power of any of its organs are founded may only restrain power but not confer positive power to act. It is allegiance which creates power and the power thus created extends only so far as it has been extended by the consent of the people. It was because this was forgotten that the sovereignty of law became the same thing as the sovereignty of Parliament. And while the conception of the rule (reign, sovereignty or supremacy) of law presupposes a concept of law defined by the attributes of the rules, not by their source, *today legislatures are no longer so called because they make the laws, but laws are so called because they emanate from legislatures,* whatever the form or content of their resolutions.[11]

If it could be justly contended that the existing institutions produce results which have been willed or approved by a majority, the believer in the basic principle of democracy would of course have to accept them. But there are strong reasons to think that what those institutions in fact produce is in a great measure an unintended outcome of the particular kind of machinery we have set up to ascertain what we believe to be the will of the majority, rather than a deliberate decision of the majority or anybody else. It would seem that wherever democratic institutions ceased to be restrained by the tradition of the Rule of Law, they led not only to 'totalitarian democracy' but in due time even to a 'plebiscitary dictatorship'.[12] This should certainly make us understand that what is a precious possession is not a particular set of institutions that are easily enough copied, but some less tangible traditions; and that the degeneration of these institutions may even be a necessary result wherever the inherent logic of the machinery is not checked by the predominance of the prevailing general conceptions of justice. May it not be true, as has been well said, that 'the belief in democracy presupposes belief in things higher than democracy'?[13] And is there really no other way for people to maintain a democratic government than by handing over unlimited power to a group of elected representatives whose decisions must be guided by the exigencies of a bargaining process in which they bribe a sufficient number of

4

voters to support an organized group of themselves numerous enough to outvote the rest?

The true content of the democratic ideal

Though a great deal of nonsense has been and still is being talked about democracy and the benefits its further extension will secure, I am profoundly disturbed by the rapid decline of faith in it. This sharp decrease of the esteem in which democracy is held by critical minds ought to alarm even those who never shared the unmeasured and uncritical enthusiasm it used to inspire until recently, and which made the term describe almost anything that was good in politics. As seems to be the fate of most terms expressing a political ideal, 'democracy' has been used to describe various kinds of things which have little to do with the original meaning of the term, and now is even often used where what is really meant is 'equality'. Strictly speaking it refers to a method or procedure for determining governmental decisions and neither refers to some substantial good or aim of government (such as a sort of material equality), nor is it a method that can be meaningfully applied to non-governmental organizations (such as educational, medical, military or commercial establishments). Both of these abuses deprive the word 'democracy' of any clear meaning.[14]

But even a wholly sober and unsentimental consideration which regards democracy as a mere convention making possible a peaceful change of the holders of power[15] should make us understand that it is an ideal worth fighting for to the utmost, because it is our only protection (even if in its present form not a certain one) against tyranny. Though democracy itself is not freedom (except for that indefinite collective, the majority of 'the people') it is one of the most important safeguards of freedom. As the only method of peaceful change of government yet discovered, it is one of those paramount though negative values, comparable to sanitary precautions against the plague, of which we are hardly aware while they are effective, but the absence of which may be deadly.

The principle that coercion should be allowed only for the purpose of ensuring obedience to rules of just conduct approved by most, or at least by a majority, seems to be the essential condition for the absence of arbitrary power and therefore of freedom. It is this principle which has made possible the peaceful co-existence of men in a Great Society and the peaceful change of the directors of

5

MAJORITY OPINION AND CONTEMPORARY DEMOCRACY

organized power. But that whenever common action is necessary it should be guided by the opinion of the majority, and that no power of coercion is legitimate unless the principle guiding it is approved by at least a majority, does not imply that the power of the majority must be unlimited—or even that there must be a possible way of ascertaining what it called the will of the majority on every conceivable subject. It appears that we have unwittingly created a machinery which makes it possible to claim the sanction of an alleged majority for measures which are in fact not desired by a majority, and which may even be disapproved by a majority of the people; and that this machinery produces an aggregate of measures that not only is not wanted by anybody, but that could not as a whole be approved by any rational mind because it is inherently contradictory.

If all coercive power is to rest on the opinion of the majority, then it should also not extend further than the majority can genuinely agree. This does not mean that there must exist specific approval by the majority of any particular action of the government. Such a demand would clearly be impossible to fulfil in a complex modern society so far as the current direction of the detail of the government machinery is concerned, that is for all the day-to-day decisions about how the resources placed at the disposal of government are to be used. But it does mean that the individual should be bound to obey only such commands as necessarily follow from the general principles approved by the majority, and that the power of the representatives of the majority should be unrestricted only in the administration of the particular means placed at their disposal.

The ultimate justification of the conferment of a power to coerce is that such a power is required if a viable order is to be maintained, and that all have therefore an interest in the existence of such a power. But this justification does not extend further than the need. There is clearly no need that anybody, not even the majority, should have power over all the particular actions or things occurring in society. The step from the belief that only what is approved by the majority should be binding for all, to the belief that all that the majority approves shall have that force, may seem small. Yet it is the transition from one conception of government to an altogether different one: from the conception by which government has definite limited tasks required to bring about the formation of a spontaneous order, to the conception that its powers

6

MAJORITY OPINION AND CONTEMPORARY DEMOCRACY

are unlimited; or a transition from a system in which through recognized procedures we decide how certain common affairs are to be arranged, to a system in which one group of people may declare anything they like as a matter of common concern and on this ground subject it to those procedures. While the first conception refers to necessary common decisions requisite for the maintenance of peace and order, the second allows some organized sections of the people to control everything, and easily becomes the pretext of oppression.

There is, however, no more reason to believe in the case of the majority that because they want a particular thing this desire is an expression of their sense of justice, than there is ground for such a belief in the case of individuals. In the latter we know only too well that their sense of justice will often be swayed by their desire for particular objects. But as individuals we have generally been taught to curb illegitimate desires, though we sometimes have to be restrained by authority. Civilization largely rests on the fact that the individuals have learnt to restrain their desires for particular objects and to submit to generally recognized rules of just conduct. Majorities, however, have not yet been civilized in this manner because they do not have to obey rules. What would we not all do if we were genuinely convinced that our desire for a particular action proves that it is just? The result is not different if people are persuaded that the agreement of the majority on the advantage of a particular measure proves that it is just. When people are taught to believe that what they agree is necessarily just, they will indeed soon cease to ask whether it is so. Yet the belief that all on which a majority can agree is by definition just has for several generations been impressed upon popular opinion. Need we be surprised that in the conviction that what they resolve is necessarily just, the existing representative assemblies have ceased even to consider in the concrete instances whether this is really so?[16]

While the agreement among many people on the justice of a particular *rule* may indeed be a good though not an infallible test of its justice, it makes nonsense of the conception of justice if we define as just whatever particular measure the majority approves— justifiable only by the positivist doctrine that there are no objective tests of justice (or rather injustice—see chapter 8 above). There exists a great difference between what a majority may decide on any particular question and the general principle relevant to the issue which it might be willing to approve if it were

7

MAJORITY OPINION AND CONTEMPORARY DEMOCRACY

put to it, as there will exist among individuals. There is, therefore, also great need that a majority be required to prove its conviction that what it decides is just by *committing* itself to the universal application of the rules on which it acts in the particular case; and its power to coerce should be confined to the enforcement of rules to which it is prepared to commit itself.

The belief that the will of the majority on particular matters determines what is just leads to the view, now widely regarded as self-evident, that the majority cannot be arbitrary. This appears to be a necessary conclusion only if, according to the prevalent interpretation of democracy (and the positivistic jurisprudence as its foundation), the source from which a decision emanates rather than its conformity with a rule on which the people agree, is regarded as the criterion of justice, and 'arbitrary' is arbitrarily defined as not determined by democratic procedure. 'Arbitrary' means, however, action determined by a particular will unrestrained by a general rule—irrespective of whether this will is the will of one or a majority. It is, therefore, not the agreement of a majority on a particular action, nor even its conformity with a constitution, but only the willingness of a representative body to commit itself to the universal application of a rule which requires the particular action, that can be regarded as evidence that its members regard as just what they decide. Today, however, the majority is not even asked whether it regards a particular decision as just; nor could its individual members assure themselves that the principle that is applied in the particular decision will also be applied in all similar instances. Since no resolution of a representative body binds it in its future decisions, it is in its several measures not bound by any general rules.

The weakness of an elective assembly with unlimited powers

The crucial point is that votes on rules applicable to all, and votes on measures which directly affect only some, have a wholly different character. Votes on matters that concern all, such as general rules of just conduct, are based on a lasting strong opinion and thus something quite different from votes on particular measures for the benefit (and often also at the expense) of unknown people— generally in the knowledge that such benefits will be distributed from the common purse in any case, and that all the individual can do is to guide this expenditure in the direction he prefers. Such a

8

MAJORITY OPINION AND CONTEMPORARY DEMOCRACY

system is bound to produce the most paradoxical results in a Great Society, however expedient it may be for arranging local affairs where all are fairly familiar with the problems, because the number and complexity of the tasks of the administration of a Great Society far exceed the range where the ignorance of the individual could be remedied by better information at the disposal of the voters or representatives.[17]

The classical theory of representative government assumed that the deputies

> when they make no laws but what they themselves and their posterity must be subject to; when they can give no money, but what they must pay their share of; when they can do no mischief, but what must fall upon their own heads in common with their countrymen; their principals may expect then good laws, little mischief, and much frugality.[18]

But the electors of a 'legislature' whose members are mainly concerned to secure and retain the votes of particular groups by procuring special benefits for them will care little about what others will get and be concerned only with what they gain in the haggling. They will normally merely agree to something being given to others about whom they know little, and usually at the expense of third groups, as the price for having their own wishes met, without any thought whether these various demands are just. Each group will be prepared to consent even to iniquitous benefits for other groups out of the common purse if this is the condition for the consent of the others to what this group has learnt to regard as its right. The result of this process will correspond to nobody's opinion of what is right, and to no principles; it will not be based on a judgment of merit but on political expediency. Its main object is bound to become the sharing out of funds extorted from a minority. That this is the inevitable outcome of the actions of an unrestrained 'interventionist' legislature was clearly foreseen by the early theorists of representative democracy.[19] Who indeed would pretend that in modern times the democratic legislatures have granted all the special subsidies, privileges and other benefits which so many special interests enjoy because they regard these demands as just? That A be protected against the competition of cheap imports and B against being undercut by a less highly trained operator, C against a reduction in his wages, and D against the loss of his job is not in the general interest, however much the advocates of such a measure pretend

9

MAJORITY OPINION AND CONTEMPORARY DEMOCRACY

that this is so. And it is not chiefly because the voters are convinced that it is in the general interest but because they want the support of those who make these demands that they are in turn prepared to support *their* demands. The creation of the myth of 'social justice' which we have examined in the last volume is indeed largely the product of this particular democratic machinery, which makes it necessary for the representatives to invent a moral justification for the benefits they grant to particular interests.

Indeed people often come genuinely to believe that it must in some sense be just if the majority regularly concedes special benefits to particular groups—as if it had anything to do with justice (or any moral consideration) if every party that wants majority support must promise special benefits to some particular groups (such as the farmers or peasants, or legal privileges to the trade unions) whose votes may shift the balance of power. Under the existing system thus every small interest group can enforce its demands, not by persuading a majority that the demands are just or equitable, but by threatening to withhold that support which the nucleus of agreed individuals will need to become a majority. The pretence that the democratic legislatures have granted all the special subsidies, privileges and other benefits which so many particular interests today enjoy because they thought these to be just would of course be simply ridiculous. Though skilful propaganda may occasionally have moved a few soft-hearted individuals on behalf of special groups, and though it is of course useful to the legislators to claim that they have been moved by considerations of justice, the artefacts of the voting machinery which we call the will of the majority do certainly not correspond to any opinion of the majority about what is right or wrong.

An assembly with power to vote on benefits to particular groups must become one in which bargains or deals among the majority rather than substantive agreement on the merits of the different claims will decide.[20] The fictitious 'will of the majority' emerging from this bargaining process is no more than an agreement to assist its supporters at the expense of the rest. It is to the awareness of this fact that policy is largely determined by a series of deals with special interests that 'politics' owes its bad reputation among ordinary men.

Indeed, to the high-minded who feel that the politician should concern himself exclusively with the common good the reality of constant assuaging of particular groups by throwing them titbits or more substantial gifts must appear as outright corruption. And the

10

MAJORITY OPINION AND CONTEMPORARY DEMOCRACY

fact that majority government does not produce what the majority wants but what each of the groups making up the majority must concede to the others to get their support for what it wants itself amounts to that. That this is so is today accepted as one of the commonplaces of everyday life and that the experienced politician will merely pity the idealist who is naive enough to condemn this and to believe it could be avoided if only people were more honest, is therefore perfectly true so far as the existing institutions are concerned, and wrong only in taking it as an inevitable attribute of all representative or democratic government, an inherent corruption which the most virtuous and decent man cannot escape. It is however not a necessary attribute of all representative or democratic government, but a necessary product only of all unlimited or omnipotent government dependent on the support of numerous groups. Only limited government can be decent government, because there does not exist (and cannot exist) general moral rules for the assignments of particular benefits (as Kant put it, because 'welfare has no principle but depends on the material content of the will and therefore is incapable of a general principle'.[21] It is not democracy or representative government as such, but the particular institution, chosen by us, of a single omnipotent 'legislature' that make it necessarily corrupt.

Corrupt at the same time weak: unable to resist pressure from the component groups the governing majority *must do what it can do* to gratify the wishes of the groups from which it needs support, however harmful to the rest such measures may be—at least so long as this is not too easily seen or the groups who have to suffer are not too popular. While immensely and oppressively powerful and able to overwhelm all resistance from a minority, it is wholly incapable of pursuing a consistent course of action, lurching like a steam roller driven by one who is drunk. If no superior judiciary authority can prevent the legislature from granting privileges to particular groups there is no limit to the blackmail to which government will be subject. If government has the power to grant their demands it becomes their slave—as in Britain where they make impossible any policy that might pull the country out of its economic decline. If government is going to be strong enough to maintain order and justice we must deprive the politicians of that cornucopia the possession of which makes them believe that they can and ought 'to remove all sources of discontent.'[22] Unfortunately, every necessary adaptation to changed circumstances is bound to cause widespread

MAJORITY OPINION AND CONTEMPORARY DEMOCRACY

discontent, and what will be mainly demanded from politicians is to make these unwelcome changes unnecessary for the individuals.

One curious effect of this condition in which the granting of special benefits is guided not by a general belief of what is just but by 'political necessity' is that it is apt to create erroneous beliefs of the following kind: if a certain group is regularly favoured because it may swing the balance of the votes the myth will arise that it is generally agreed that it deserves this. But it would of course be absurd to conclude if the farmers, the small business men, or the municipal workers got their demands regularly satisfied that they must have a just claim, if in reality this merely happens because without the support of a substantial part of these groups no government would have a majority. Yet there seems to be a paradoxical reversal of what democratic theory assumes to happen: that the majority is not guided by what is generally believed to be right, but what it thinks it is necessary to do in order to maintain its coherence is being regarded as just. It is still believed that consent of the majority is proof of the justice of a measure, although most members of the majority will often consent only as payment of the price for the fulfilment of their own sectional demands. Things come to be regarded as 'socially just' merely because they are regularly done, not because anyone except the beneficiaries regards them as just on their own merits. But the necessity of constantly wooing splinter groups produces in the end purely fortuitous moral standards and often leads people to believe that the favoured social groups are really specially deserving because they are regularly singled out for special benefits. Sometimes we do encounter the argument that 'all modern democracies have found it necessary to do this or that', used as if it were proof of the desirability of a measure rather than merely the blind result of a particular mechanism.

Thus the existing machinery of unlimited democratic government produces a new set of 'democratic' pseudo-morals, an artifact of the machinery which makes people regard as socially just what is regularly done by democracies, or can by clever use of this machinery be extorted from democratic governments. The spreading awareness that more and more incomes are determined by government action will lead to ever new demands by groups whose position is still left to be determined by market forces for similar assurance of what they believe they deserve. Every time the income of some group is increased by government action a legitimate claim for similar treatment is provided for other groups. It is merely the expectations of

12

MAJORITY OPINION AND CONTEMPORARY DEMOCRACY

many which legislatures have created by the boons they have already conferred on certain groups that they will be treated in the same manner that underlies most of the demands for 'social justice'.

Coalitions of organized interests and the apparatus of para-government

So far we have considered the tendency of the prevailing demo-cratic institutions only in so far as it is determined by the necessity to bribe the individual voter with promises of special benefits for his group, without taking into account a factor which greatly accen-tuates the influence of some particular interests, their ability to organize and to operate as organized pressure groups.[23] This leads to the particular political parties being united not by any principles but merely as coalitions or organized interests in which the concerns of those pressure groups that are capable of effective organization greatly preponderate over those that for one reason or another cannot form effective organizations.[24] This greatly enhanced in-fluence of the organizable groups further distorts the distribution of benefits and makes it increasingly unrelated to the requirements of efficiency or any conceivable principle of equity. The result is a distribution of incomes chiefly determined by political power. The 'incomes policy' nowadays advocated as a supposed means to com-bat inflation is in fact largely inspired by the monstrous idea that all material benefits should be determined by the holders of such power.[25]

It is part of this tendency that in the course of this century an enormous and exceedingly wasteful apparatus of para-government has grown up, consisting of trade associations, trades unions and professional organizations, designed primarily to divert as much as possible of the stream of governmental favour to their members. It has come to be regarded as obviously necessary and unavoidable, yet has arisen only in response to (or partly as defence against being disadvantaged in) the increasing necessity of an all-mighty maj-ority government maintaining its majority by buying the support of particular small groups.

Political parties in these conditions become in fact little more than coalitions of organized interests whose actions are determined by the inherent logic of their mechanics rather than by any general principles or ideals on which they are agreed. Except for some ideological parties in the West who disapprove of the system now

13

MAJORITY OPINION AND CONTEMPORARY DEMOCRACY

prevailing in their countries and aim at wholly replacing these by some imaginary utopia, it would indeed be difficult to discern in the programmes, and even more in the actions, of any major party a consistent conception of the sort of social order on which its followers agree. They are all driven, even if that is not their agreed aim, to use their power to impose some particular structure upon society i.e. some form of socialism, rather than create the conditions in which society can gradually evolve improved formations.[26]

The inevitability of such developments in a system where the legislature is omnipotent is cleary seen if we ask how a majority united on common action and capable of directing current policy can be formed. The original democratic ideal was based on the conception of a common opinion on what is right being held by most of the people. But community of opinion on basic values is not sufficient to determine a programme for current governmental action. The specific programme that is required to unite a body of supporters of a government, or to hold together such a party, must be based on some aggregation of different interests which can only be achieved by a process of bargaining. It will not be an expression of common desire for the particular results to be achieved; and, as it will be concerned with the use of the concrete resources at the disposal of government for particular purposes, it will generally rest on the consent of the several groups to particular services rendered to some of them in return for other services offered to each of the consenting groups.

It would be mere pretence to describe a programme of action thus decided upon in a bargaining democracy as in any sense an expression of the common opinion of the majority. Indeed, there may exist nobody who desires or even approves of all the things contained in such a programme; for it will often contain elements of such contradictory character that no thinking person could ever desire them all for their own sake. Considering the process by which such programmes for common action are agreed upon, it would indeed be a miracle if the outcome were anything but a conglomerate of the separate and incoherent wishes of many different individuals and groups. On many of the items included in the programme most members of the electorate (or many of the representative assembly) will have no opinion at all because they know nothing of the circumstances involved. Towards many more they will be indifferent or even adversely disposed, but prepared to consent as payment for the realization of their own wishes. For most individuals the choice

14

MAJORITY OPINION AND CONTEMPORARY DEMOCRACY

between party programmes will therefore be mainly a choice between evils, namely between different benefits to be provided for others at their expense.

The purely additive character of such a programme for governmental action stands out most clearly if we consider the problem that will face the leader of the party. He may or he may not have some chief objective for which he deeply cares. But whatever his ultimate objective, what he needs to achieve it is power. For this he needs the support of a majority which he can get only by enlisting people who are little interested in the objectives which guide him. To build up support for his programme he will therefore have to offer effective enticements to a sufficient number of special interests to bring together a majority for the support of his programme as a whole.

The agreement on which such a programme for governmental action is based is something very different from that common opinion of a majority which it was hoped would be the determining force in a democracy. Nor can this kind of bargaining be regarded as the kind of compromise that is inevitable whenever people differ and must be brought to agree on some middle line which does not wholly satisfy anybody. A series of deals by which the wishes of one group are satisfied in return for the satisfaction of the wishes of another (and frequently at the expense of a third who is not consulted) may determine aims for common action of a coalition, but does not signify popular approval of the overall results. The outcome may indeed be wholly contrary to any principles which the several members of the majority would approve if they ever had an opportunity to vote on them.

This domination of government by coalitions of organized interests (when they were first observed they were generally described as 'sinister interests') is usually regarded by the outsider as an abuse, or even a kind of corruption. It is, however, the inescapable result of a system in which government has unlimited powers to take whatever measures are required to satisfy the wishes of those on whose support it relies. A government with such powers cannot refuse to exercise them and still retain the support of a majority. We have no right to blame the politicians for doing what they must do in the position in which we have placed them. We have created conditions in which it is known that the majority has power to give any particular section of the population whatever it demands. But a government that possesses such unlimited powers can stay in office

15

MAJORITY OPINION AND CONTEMPORARY DEMOCRACY

only by satisfying a sufficiently large number of pressure groups to assure itself of the support of a majority.

Government, in the narrow sense of the administration of the special resources set aside for the satisfaction of common needs, will to some extent always have that character. Its task is to hand out particular benefits to different groups, which is altogether distinct from that of legislation proper. But while this weakness is comparatively innocuous as long as government is confined to determining the use of an amount of resources placed at its disposal according to rules it cannot alter (and particularly when, as in local government, people can escape exploitation by voting with their feet), it assumes alarming proportions when government and rule-making come to be confused and the persons who administer the resources of government also determine how much of the total resources it ought to control. To place those who ought to define what is right in a position in which they can maintain themselves only by giving their supporters what they want, is to place at their disposal all the resources of society for whatever purpose they think necessary to keep them in power.

If the elected administrators of a certain share of the resources of a society were under a law which they could not alter, though they would have to use them so as to satisfy their supporters, they could not be driven beyond what can be done without interfering with the freedom of the individual. But if they are at the same time also the makers of those rules of conduct, they will be driven to use their power to organize not only the resources belonging to government, but all the resources of society, including the individual's, to serve the particular wishes of their constituents.

We can prevent government from serving special interests only by depriving it of the power to use coercion in doing so, which means that we can limit the powers of organized interests only by limiting the powers of government. A system in which the politicians believe that it is their duty, and in their power, to remove all dissatisfaction,[27] must lead to a complete manipulation of the people's affairs by the politicians. If that power is unlimited, it will and must be used in the service of particular interests, and it will induce all the organizable interests to combine in order to bring pressure upon government. The only defence that a politician has against such pressure is to point to an established principle which prevents him from complying and which he cannot alter. No system in which those who direct the use of the resources of government are not

16

bound by unalterable rules can escape becoming an instrument of the organized interests.

Agreement on general rules and on particular measures

We have repeatedly stressed that in a Great Society nobody can possess knowledge of, or have any views about, all the particular facts which might become the object of decisions by government. Any member of such a society can know no more than some small part of the comprehensive structure of relationships which makes up the society; but his wishes concerning the shaping of the sector of the overall pattern to which he belongs will inevitably conflict with the wishes of the others.

Thus, while nobody knows all, the separate desires will often clash in their effects and must be reconciled if agreement is to be reached. Democratic *government* (as distinguished from democratic legislation) requires that the consent of the individuals extend much beyond the particular facts of which they can be aware; and they will submit to a disregard of their own wishes only if they have come to accept some general rules which guide all particular measures and by which even the majority will abide. That in such situations conflict can be avoided only by agreement on general rules while, if agreement on the several particulars were required, conflicts would be irreconcilable, seems to be largely forgotten today.

True general agreement, or even true agreement among a majority, will in a Great Society rarely extend beyond some general principles, and can be maintained only on such particular measures as can be known to most of its members.[28] Even more important, such a society will achieve a coherent and self-consistent overall order only if it submits to general rules in its particular decisions, and does not permit even the majority to break these rules unless this majority is prepared to commit itself to a new rule which it undertakes henceforth to apply without exception.

We have seen earlier that commitment to rules is in some degree necessary even to a single individual who endeavours to bring order into a complex of actions he cannot know in detail in advance. It is even more necessary where the successive decisions will be made by different groups of people with reference to different parts of the whole. Successive votes on particular issues

17

MAJORITY OPINION AND CONTEMPORARY DEMOCRACY

would in such conditions not be likely to produce an aggregate result of which anyone would approve, unless they were all guided by the same general rules.

It has in a great measure been an awareness of the unsatisfactory results of the established procedures of democratic decision-making that has led to the demand for an overall plan whereby all government action will be decided upon for a long period ahead. Yet such a plan would not really provide a solution for the crucial difficulty. At least, as it is usually conceived, it would still be the result of a series of particular decision on concrete issues and its determination would therefore raise the same problems. The effect of the adoption of such a plan is usually that it becomes a substitute for real criteria of whether the measures for which it provides are desirable.

The decisive facts are that not only will a true majority view in a Great Society exist only on general principles, but also that a majority can exercise some control over the outcome of the market process only if it confines itself to the laying down of general principles and refrains from interfering with the particulars even if the concrete results are in conflict with its wishes. It is inevitable that, when for the achievement of some of our purposes we avail ourselves of a mechanism that responds in part to circumstances unknown to us, its effects on some particular results should be contrary to our wishes, and that there will therefore often arise a conflict between the general rules we wish to see obeyed and the particular results that we desire.

In collective action this conflict will manifest itself most conspicuously because, while as individuals we have in general learned to abide by rules and are able to do so consistently, as members of a body that decides by majority votes we have no assurance that future majorities will abide by those rules which might forbid us to vote for particulars which we like but which are obtainable only by infringing an established rule. Though as individuals we have learnt to accept that in pursuing our aims we are limited by established rules of just conduct, when we vote as members of a body that has power to alter these rules, we often do not feel similarly restrained. In the latter situation most people will indeed regard it as reasonable to claim for themselves benefits of a kind which they know are being granted to others, but which they also know cannot be granted universally and which they would therefore perhaps prefer not to see granted to anybody at all. In the course of

18

MAJORITY OPINION AND CONTEMPORARY DEMOCRACY

the particular decisions on specific issues the voters or their representatives will therefore often be led to support measures in conflict with principles which they would prefer to see generally observed. So long as there exist no rules that are binding on those who decide on the particular measures, it is thus inevitable that majorities will approve measures of a kind which, if they were asked to vote on the principle, they would probably prohibit once and for all.

The contention that in any society there will usually exist more agreement on general principles than on particular issues will at first perhaps appear contrary to ordinary experience. Daily practice seems to show that it is usually easier to obtain agreement on a particular issue than on a general principle. This, however, is a consequence merely of the fact that we usually do not explicitly know, and have never put into words, those common principles on which we know well how to act and which normally lead different persons to agree in their judgments. The articulation or verbal formulation of these principles will often be very difficult. This lack of conscious awareness of the principles on which we act does not disprove, however, that in fact we usually agree on particular moral issues only because we agree on the rules applicable to them. But we will often learn to express these common rules only by the examination of the various particular instances in which we have agreed, and by a systematic analysis of the points on which we agree.

If people who learn for the first time about the circumstances of a dispute will generally arrive at similar judgements on its merits, this means precisely that, whether they know it or not, they are in fact guided by the same principles, while, when they are unable to agree, this would seem to show that they lack such common principles. This is confirmed when we examine the nature of the arguments likely to produce agreement among parties who first disagreed on the merits of a particular case. Such arguments will always consist of appeals to general principles, or at least to facts which are relevant only in the light of some general principle. It will never be the concrete instance as such, but always its character as one of a class of instances, or as one that falls under a particular rule, that will be regarded as relevant. The discovery of such a rule on which we can agree will be the basis for arriving at an agreement on the particular issue.

19

[12]

Excerpt from *Law, Legislation and Liberty*, 20–40

THIRTEEN

THE DIVISION OF DEMOCRATIC POWERS

> The most urgent problem of our age for those who give most urgency to the preservation of democratic institutions is that of restraining the vote-buying process.
>
> W. H. Hutt*

The loss of the original conception of the functions of a legislature

It cannot be our task here to trace the process by which the original conception of the nature of democratic constitutions gradually was lost and replaced by that of the unlimited power of the democratically elected assembly. That has been done recently in an important book by M. J. C. Vile in which it is shown how during the English Civil War the abuse of its powers by Parliament 'had shown to men who had previously seen only the royal power as a danger, that parliament could be as tyrannical as a king' and how this led to 'the realisation that legislatures must also be subjected to restriction if individual freedom was not to be invaded'.[1] This remained the doctrine of the old Whigs until far into the eighteenth century. It found its most famous expression in John Locke who argued in effect that 'the legislative authority is the authority *to act in a particular way*'. Furthermore, Locke argued, those who wield this authority should make only general rules. 'They are to govern by promulgated established Laws, not to be varied in particular cases.'[2] One of the most influential statements is met with in *Cato's Letters* by John Trenchard and Thomas Gordon in which, in a passage already quoted in part, the former could maintain in 1721 that

> when the deputies thus act for their own interest, by acting for the interest of their principals; when they can make no laws but what they themselves, and their posterity must be subject to; when

20

THE DIVISION OF DEMOCRATIC POWERS

they can give no money, but what they must pay their share of; when they can do no mischief but what fall upon their own heads in common with their countrymen; their principals may then expect good laws, little mischief, and much frugality.[3]

Even towards the end of the century, moral philosophers could still regard this as the basic principle of the British constitution and argue, as William Paley did in 1785, that when the legislative and the judicial character

> are united in the same person or assembly, particular laws are made for particlar cases, springing oftentimes from partial motives, and directed to private ends: whilst they are kept separate, general laws are made by one body of men, without foreseeing whom they may affect; and when made must be applied by the other, let them affect whom they will . . . .
>
> When the parties and the interests to be affected by the law were known, the inclinations of the law-makers would inevitably attach on one side or the other . . . .
>
> Which dangers, by the division of the legislative and judicial functions, are effectually provided against. Parliament knows not the individuals upon whom its acts will operate; it has no cases or parties before it, no private designs to serve; consequently its resolutions will be suggested by the consideration of universal effects and tendencies, which always produces impartial and commonly advantageous regulations.[4]

No doubt this theory was an idealization even then and in fact the arrogation of arbitrary powers by Parliament was regarded by the spokesmen of the American colonies as the ultimate cause of the break with the mother country. This was most clearly expressed by one of the profoundest of their political philosophers, James Wilson, who

> rejected Blackstone's doctrine of parliamentary sovereignty as outmoded. The British do not understand the idea of a constitution which limits and superintends the operations of the legislature. This was an improvement in the science of government reserved to the Americans.[5]

We shall not further consider here the American attempts to limit in their Constitution the powers of the legislature, and its limited success. It in fact did no more to prevent Congress from becoming primarily a governmental rather than a truly legislative institution

21

THE DIVISION OF DEMOCRATIC POWERS

and from developing in consequence all the characteristics which
this chief preoccupation is apt to impress on an assembly and which
must be the chief topic of this chapter.

Existing representative institutions have been shaped by the needs of
government, not of legislation

The present structure of democratic governments has been decisively determined by the fact that we have charged the representative assemblies with two altogether different tasks. We call
them 'legislatures' but by far the greater part of their work consists
not in the articulation and approval of general rules of conduct but
in the direction of the measures of government concerning particular matters.[6] We want, and I believe rightly, that both the laying
down of general rules of conduct binding upon all and the administration of the resources and machinery placed at the disposal of
government be guided by the wishes of the majority of the citizens.
This need not mean, however, that these two tasks should be placed
into the hands of the same body, nor that every resolution of such a
democratically elected body must have the validity and dignity that
we attach to the appropriately sanctioned general rules of conduct.
Yet by calling 'law' every decision of that assembly, whether it lays
down a rule or authorizes particular measures, the very awareness
that these are different things has been lost.[7] Because most of the
time and energy of the representative assemblies is taken up by the
task of organizing and directing government, we have not only
forgotten that government is different from legislation but have
come to think that an instruction to government to take particular
actions is the normal content of an act of law-giving. Probably the
most far-reaching effect of this is that the very structure and organization of the representative assemblies has been determined by
the needs of their governmental tasks but is unfavourable to wise
rule-making.

   It is important to remember in this connection that the founders
of modern representative government were almost all apprehensive
of political parties (or 'factions', as they usually called them), and
to understand the reasons for their apprehension. The political
theorists were still concerned chiefly with what they conceived to be
the main task of a legislature, that is, the laying down of rules of just
conduct for the private citizen, and did not attach much importance
to its other task, the directing or controlling of government or

22

THE DIVISION OF DEMOCRATIC POWERS

administration. For the former task clearly a body widely representative of the various shades of opinion but not committed to a particular programme of action would seem desirable.

But, as government rather than legislation became the chief task of the representative assemblies, their effectiveness for this task demanded the existence within them of a majority of members agreed on a programme of action. The character of modern parliamentary institutions has in fact been wholly shaped by these needs of democratic *government* rather than by those of democratic *legislation* in the strict sense of the latter term. The effective direction of the whole apparatus of government, or the control of the use of all the personal and material resources placed under its supervision, demands the continuous support of the executive authority by an organized majority committed to a coherent plan of action. Government proper will have to decide constantly what particular demands of interests it can satisfy; and even when it is limited to the use of those particular resources which are entrusted to its administration, it must continually choose between the requirements of different groups.

All experience has shown that if democratic government is to discharge these tasks effectively it must be organized on party lines. If the electorate is to be able to judge its performance, there must exist an organized group among the representatives that is regarded as responsible for the conduct of government, and an organized opposition that watches and criticizes and offers an alternative government if the people become dissatisfied with the one in power.

It is, however, by no means true that a body organized chiefly for the purpose of directing government is also suited for the task of legislation in the strict sense, i.e. to determine the permanent framework of rules of law under which it has to move its daily tasks.

Let us recall once more how different the task of government proper is from that of laying down the universally applicable rules of just conduct. Government is to act on concrete matters, the allocation of particular means to particular purposes. Even so far as its aim is merely to enforce a set of rules of just conduct given to it, this requires the maintenance of an apparatus of courts, police, penal institutions, etc., and the application of particular means to particular purposes. But in the wider sphere of government, that of rendering to the citizens other services of various kinds, the employment of the resources at its command will require constant choosing of the particular ends to be served, and such decisions

23

THE DIVISION OF DEMOCRATIC POWERS

must be largely a matter of expediency. Whether to build a road
along one route or another one, whether to give a building one
design or a different one, how to organize the police or the removal
of rubbish, and so on, are all not questions of justice which can be
decided by the application of a general rule, but questions of effective organization for satisfying the needs of various groups of people, which can be decided only in the light of the relative importance
attached to the competing purposes. If such questions are to be
decided democratically, the decisions will be about whose interests
are to prevail over those of others.

Administration of common means for public purposes thus
requires more than agreement on rules of just conduct. It requires
agreement on the relative importance of particular ends. So far as
the administration of those resources of society that are set aside for
the use of government is concerned, somebody must have power to
decide for which ends they are to be used. Yet the difference
between a society of free men and a totalitarian one lies in the fact
that in the former this applies only to that limited amount of
resources that is specifically destined for governmental purposes,
while in the latter it applies to all the resources of society including
the citizens themselves. The limitation of the powers of government
that a free society presupposes requires thus that even the majority
should have unrestricted power only over the use of those resources
which have been dedicated to common use, and that the private
citizen and his property are not subject to specific commands (even
of the legislature), but only to such rules of conduct as apply
equally to all.

Since the representative assemblies which we call legislatures are
predominantly concerned with governmental tasks, these tasks
have shaped not only their organization but also the entire manner
of thinking of their members. It is today often said that the principle
of the separation of powers is threatened by the increasing assumption of legislative function by the administration. It was in fact
largely destroyed much earlier, namely when the bodies called
legislatures assumed the direction of government (or, perhaps more
correctly, legislation was entrusted to existing bodies mainly concerned with government). The separation of powers has been
supposed to mean that every coercive act of government required
authorization by a universal rule of just conduct approved by a body
not concerned with the particularly momentary ends of government. If we now call 'law' also the authorization of particular acts of

24

THE DIVISION OF DEMOCRATIC POWERS

government by a resolution of the representative assembly, such 'legislation' is not legislation in the sense in which the concept is used in the theory of the separation of powers; it means that the democratic assembly exercises executive powers without being bound by laws in the sense of general rules of conduct it cannot alter.

Bodies with powers of specific direction are unsuited for law-making

Though, if we want democratic government, there is evidently need for a representative body in which the people can express their wishes on all the issues which concern the actions of government, a body concerned chiefly with these problems is little suited for the task of legislation proper. To expect it to do both means asking it to deprive itself of some of the means by which it can most conveniently and expeditiously achieve the immediate goals of government. In its performance of governmental functions it will in fact not be bound by any general rules, for it can at any moment make the rules which enable it to do what the momentary task seems to require. Indeed, any particular decision it would make on a specific issue will automatically abrogate any previously existing rule it infringes. Such a combination of governmental and rule-making power in the hands of one representative body is evidently irreconcilable, not only with the principle of the separation of powers, but also with the ideals of government under the law and the rule of law.

If those who decide on particular issues can make for any purpose whatever law they like, they are clearly not under the rule of law; and it certainly does not correspond to the ideal of the rule of law if, whatever particular group of people, even if they be a majority, decide on such an issue is called a law. We can have a rule of law or a rule of majority, we can even have a rule of laws made by a majority which also governs[8] but only so long as the majority itself, when it decided particular matters, is bound by rules that it cannot change *ad hoc,* will the rule of law be preserved. Government subject to the control of a parliamentary assembly will assure a government under the law only if that assembly merely restrains the powers of the government by general rules but does not itself direct the actions of government, and by doing so make legal anything it orders government to do. The existing situation is such that even the awareness has been lost of the distinction between law in the sense

25

THE DIVISION OF DEMOCRATIC POWERS

of rules of just conduct and law in the sense of the expression of the
majority's will on some particular matter. The conception that law
is whatever the so-called legislature decides in the manner prescribed by the constitution is a result of the peculiar institutions of
European democracy, because these are based on the erroneous
belief that the recognized representatives of the majority of the
people must have of necessity unlimited powers. American
attempts to meet this difficulty have provided only a limited protection.

An assembly whose chief task is to decide what particular things
should be done, and which in a parliamentary democracy supervises
its executive committee (called government) in the carrying out of
a programme of action approved by it, has no inducement or interest to tie itself by general rules. It can adapt the particular rules it
lays down to the needs of the moment, and these rules will in
general tend to serve the needs of the organization of government
rather than the needs of the self-generating order of the market.
Where it concerns itself with rules of just conduct, this will mostly
be by-products of government and subservient to the needs of
government. Such legislation will tend progressively to increase the
discretionary powers of the government machinery and, instead of
imposing limitations on government, become a tool to assist in the
achievement of its particular ends.

The ideal of a democratic control of government and that of the
limitation of government by law are thus different ideals that certainly cannot be both achieved by placing into the hands of the same
representative body both rule-making and governmental powers.
Though it would be possible to assure the realization of both these
ideals, no nation has yet succeeded in doing this effectively by
constitutional provisions; peoples have approached this state only
temporarily thanks to the prevailing of certain strong political
traditions. In recent times the effect of the existing institutional
set up has been progressively to destroy what had remained of
the tradition of the rule of law.

During the early periods of the representative government members of parliament could still be regarded as representatives of the
general and not of the particular interests.[9] Though governments
needed the confidence of the majority of parliament, this did not yet
mean that an organized majority had to be maintained for the
carrying out of a programme of policy. In peace-time at least most
of the current activities of government were chiefly of a routine
character for which little parliamentary authorization was needed

26

THE DIVISION OF DEMOCRATIC POWERS

beyond the approval of the annual budget; and this became the chief instrument through which the British House of Commons directly guided the activities of government.

The character of existing 'legislatures' determined by their governmental tasks

Although anyone even remotely familiar with modern politics has long come to take the present character of parliamentary proceedings for granted, when we come to think of it it is really astounding how far the reality of the concerns and practices of modern legislature differs from the image that most reasonable persons would form of an assembly which has to decide on the grave and difficult questions of the improvement of the legal order, or of the framework of rules within which the struggle of divergent interests ought to be conducted. An observer who was not used to the existent arrangements would probably soon come to the conclusion that politics as we know it is a necessary result of the fact that it is in the same arena that those limits are laid down and the struggle is conducted which they ought to restrain, and that the same persons who compete, for votes by offering the special favours are also supposed to lay down the limits of governmental power. There exists clearly an antagonism between these two tasks and it is illusory to expect the delegates to deprive themselves of those powers of bribing their mandatories by which they preserve their position.

It is hardly an exaggeration to say that the character of existing representative bodies has in the course of time been shaped almost entirely by their governmental tasks. From the methods of election of the members, the periods for which they are elected, the division of the assembly into organized parties, its order of business and rules of procedure, and above all the mental attitudes of the members, everything is determined by the concern with governmental measures, not with legislation. At least in the lower houses the budget, which is of course as far from legislation proper as anything can be, is the main event of the year.

All this tends to make the members agents of the interests of their constituents rather than representatives of public opinion. The election of an individual becomes a reward for having delivered the goods rather than an expression of confidence that the good sense, honesty and impartiality which he has shown in his private dealings

27

THE DIVISION OF DEMOCRATIC POWERS

will still guide him in his service to the public. People who hope to be
re-elected on the basis of what their party during the preceding
three or four years has conferred in conspicuous special benefits on
their voters are not in the sort of position which will make them pass
the kind of general laws which would really be most in the public
interest.

It is a well-known fact that as a result of his double task the typical
representative has neither time nor interest nor the desire or competence to preserve, and still less to improve, those limits to the
coercive powers of government which is one of the chief purposes of
law (the other being the protection against violence or coercion of
people by their fellows)—and therefore, one may hope, of legislation. The governmental task of the popular assemblies, however,
not only interferes with but often is in outright conflict with the
aims of the law-maker.

We have earlier quoted the comments of one of the closest
observers of British Parliament (a former Parliamentary Counsel of
the Treasury) that 'For lawyer's law, parliament has neither time
nor taste'.[10] It is worth while now to quote Sir Courtenay Ilbert's
fuller account of the position in the British Parliament at the
beginning of the century:

> The bulk of the members are not really interested in technical
> questions of law, and would always prefer to let the lawyers
> develop their rules and procedures in their own way. The sub-
> stantial business of Parliament as a legislature [!] is to keep the
> machinery of State in working order. And the laws which are
> required for this purpose belong to the domain, not of private or
> of criminal law, but what is called on the Continent administra-
> tive law. . . . The bulk of the Statute book of each year will usually
> consist of administrative regulations, relating to matters which lie
> outside the ordinary reading and practice of the barrister.[11]

While this was already true of the British Parliament at the beginning of the century, I know of no contemporary democratic
legislature of which it is not now equally true. The fact is that the
legislators are in general largely ignorant of law proper, the lawyer's
law which constitutes the rules of just conduct, and they concern
themselves mostly with certain aspects of administrative law which
progressively created for them a separate law even in England,
where it was once understood that the private law limited the

28

THE DIVISION OF DEMOCRATIC POWERS

powers of governmental agents as much as those of the ordinary citizens. The result is that the British (who at one time flattered themselves that such a thing as administrative law was unknown in their country) are now subject to hundreds of administrative agencies capable of issuing binding orders.

The almost exclusive concern of the representatives with government rather than legislation is a consequence of the fact that they know that their re-election depends chiefly on the record of their party in government and not on legislation. It is the voters' satisfaction with the immediate effects of governmental measures, not their judgement of the effect of alterations in the law, noticeable only in the long run, which they will express at the polls. Since the individual representative knows that his re-election will depend chiefly on the popularity of his party and the support he will receive from his party, it will be the short run effects of the measures taken by it that will be his chief concern. Considerations about the principles involved may affect his initial choice of party, but since, once he has been elected for one party, a change of party may end his political career, he will in general leave such worries to the leaders of his party and immerse himself in the daily work arising out of the grievances of his constituents, dealing in its course with much routine administration.

His whole bias will thus be towards saying 'yes' to particular demands while the chief task of a true legislator ought to be to say 'no' to all claims for special privileges and to insist that certain kinds of things simply are not done. Whatever may have been the ideal described by Edmund Burke, a party today in general is not agreed on values but united for particular purposes. I do not wish to deny that even present day parties often form around a nucleus united by common principles or ideals. But since they must attract a following by promising other things, they can rarely if ever remain true to their principles and achieve a majority. It certainly is helpful to a party if it has principles by which it can justify the granting of special advantages to a sufficient number of groups to obtain a majority support.

The socialists have in this respect an advantage and, until they have accomplished their first aim and, having achieved control of the means of production, they have to face the task of assigning particular shares of the product to the different groups, are tied together by their belief in a common principle—or at least a form of words like 'social justice', the emptiness of which they have not yet

29

THE DIVISION OF DEMOCRATIC POWERS

discovered. They can concentrate on creating a new machinery rather than its use, and direct all their hopes to what the new machinery will achieve when completed. But they also are of course from the outset, as we have seen, agreed on the destruction of law in the sense of general rules of just conduct and its replacement by administrative orders. A socialist legislature would therefore be a purely governmental body—probably confined to rubber stamping the work of the planning bureaucracy.

For the task of laying down the limits of what government may do clearly a type of person is wanted wholly different from those whose main interest is to secure their re-election by getting special benefits for their supporters. One would have to entrust this not to men who have made party politics their life's concern and whose thinking is shaped by their preoccupation with their prospects of re-election, but to persons who have gained respect and authority in the ordinary business of life and who are elected because they are trusted to be more experienced, wise and fair, and who are then enabled to devote all their time to the long run problems of improving the legal framework of all actions, including those of government. They would have ample time to learn their jobs as legislators and not be helpless before (and the object of contempt of) that bureaucracy which makes in fact today the laws because the representative assemblies have not the time to do so.

Nothing indeed is more conspicuous in those assemblies than that what is supposed to be the chief business of a legislature is constantly crowded out, and that more and more of the tasks which the man in the street imagines to be the main occupation of the legislators are in fact performed by civil servants. It is largely because the legislatures are preoccupied by what in effect is discretionary administration that the true work of legislation is increasingly left in the hands of the bureaucracy, which of course has little power of restraining the governmental decision of the 'legislatures' which are too busy to legislate.

No less significant is it that when parliaments have to deal with true legislation concerning problems on which strong moral convictions exist and which many representatives regard as matters of conscience, such as the death penalty, abortion, divorce, euthanasia, the use of drugs (including alcohol and tobacco), pornography and the like, parties find it necessary to relax control over the voting of their members—in effect in all cases where we really want to find out what is dominant *opinion* on major issues rather

THE DIVISION OF DEMOCRATIC POWERS

than the views on particular measures. It shows that there exist in fact no simple lines dividing the citizens into distinct groups of people who agree among themselves on a variety of principles as the party organization suggests. Agreement to obey certain principles is a different thing from agreeing to the manner of distributing various benefits.

An arrangement by which the interest of the highest authority is directed chiefly to government and not to law can only lead to a steady growth of the preponderance of government over law—and the progressive growth of the activities of government is largely a result of this arrangement. It is an illusion to expect from those who owe their positions to their power to hand out gifts that they will tie their own hands by inflexible rules prohibiting all special privileges. To leave the law in the hands of elective governors is like leaving the cat in charge of the cream jug—there soon won't be any, at least no law in the sense in which it limits the discretionary powers of government. Because of this defect in the construction of our sup-posedly constitutional democracies we have in fact again got that unlimited power which the eighteenth-century Whigs represented as 'so wild and monstrous a thing that however natural it be to desire it, it is as natural to oppose it'.[12]

Party legislation leads to the decay of democratic society

A system which may place any small group in the position to hold a society to ransom if it happens to be the balance between opposing groups, and can extort special privileges for its support of a party, has little to do with democracy or 'social justice'. But it is the unavoidable product of the unlimited power of a single elective assembly not precluded from discrimination by a restriction of its powers either to true legislation or to government under a law which it cannot alter.

Not only will such a system produce a government driven by blackmail and corruption, but it will also produce laws which are disapproved by the majority and in their long-run effects may lead to the decline of the society. Who would seriously maintain that the most fateful law in Britain's modern history, the Trade Disputes Act of 1906, was an expression of the will of the majority?[13] With the Conservative opposition wholly opposed, it is more than ques-tionable whether even the majority of the members of the govern-ing Liberal party approved of a bill 'drawn up by the first generation

31

THE DIVISION OF DEMOCRATIC POWERS

of Labour MPs'.[14] Yet the majority of the Liberal party depended on Labour support, and although the bill shocked the leading representatives of the British constitutional tradition probably more than any other act of modern legislative history,[15] the spectacular legal privileges granted in it to the trades unions has since become the chief cause of the progressive decline of the British economy.

Nor is there, with the present character of the existing Parliament, much hope that they will prove more capable of dealing intelligently with such crucial future tasks of legislation as the limits to the powers of all corporate bodies or the prohibition of restraints on competition. It is to be feared that they will be decided mainly by the popularity or unpopularity of the particular groups that are directly affected rather than by an understanding of the requirements of a functioning market order.

A further peculiar sort of bias of government created by the necessity to gain votes by benefiting particular groups or activities operates indirectly through the need to gain the support of those second-hand dealers of ideas, mainly in what are now called the 'media', who largely determine public opinion. This expresses itself among other manifestations in a support of modern art which the majority of the people certainly does not care for in the least, and certainly also in some of the governmental support to technological advance (the flight to the moon!) for which such support is certainly very questionable but by which a party can secure the sympathy and the support of those intellectuals who run the 'media'.

Democracy, so far as the term is not used simply as a synonym for egalitarianism, is increasingly becoming the name for the very process of vote-buying, for placating and remunerating those special interests which in more naive times were described as the 'sinister interests'. What we are concerned with now is, however, to show that what is responsible for this is not democracy as such but the particular form of democracy which we are practising today. I believe in fact that we should get a more representative sample of the true opinion of the people at large if we picked out by drawing lots some five hundred mature adults and let them for twenty years devote themselves to the task of improving the law, guided only by their conscience and the desire to be respected, than by the present system of auction by which every few years we entrust the power of legislation to those who promise their supporters the greatest special benefits. But, as we shall show later, there are better alternative systems of democracy than that of a single omnipotent assembly

32

THE DIVISION OF DEMOCRATIC POWERS

with unlimited powers which has produced the blackmail and corruption system of politics.

The constructivistic superstition of sovereignty

The conception that the majority of the people (or their elected
representatives) ought to be free to decree whatever they can
agree upon, and that in this sense they must be regarded as omnipotent, is closely connected with the conception of popular sovereignty. Its error lies not in the belief that whatever power there is
should be in the hands of the people, and that their wishes will have
to be expressed by majority decisions, but in the belief that this
ultimate source of power must be unlimited, that is, the idea of
sovereignty itself. The pretended logical necessity of such an unlimited source of power simply does not exist. As we have already
seen, the belief in such a necessity is a product of the false constructivistic interpretation of the formation of human institution
which attempts to trace them all to an original designer or some
other deliberate act of will. The basic source of social order, however, is not a deliberate decision to adopt certain common rules, but
the existence among the people of certain opinions of what is right
and wrong. What made the Great Society possible was not a deliberate imposition of rules of conduct, but the growth of such rules
among men who had little idea of what would be the consequence of
their general observance.

Since all power rests on pre-existing opinions, and will last only so
long as those opinions prevail, there is no real personal source of
this power and no deliberate will which has created it. The conception of sovereignty rests on a misleading logical construction
which starts from the initial assumption that the existing rules and
institutions derive from a uniform will aiming at their creation. Yet,
far from arising from such a pre-existing will capable of imposing
upon the people whatever rules it likes, a society of free men
presupposes that all power is limited by the common beliefs which
made them join, and that where no agreement is present no power
exists.[16]

Except where the political unit is created by conquest, people
submit to authority not to enable it to do what it likes, but because
they trust somebody to act in conformity with certain common
conceptions of what is just. There is not first a society which then
gives itself rules, but it is common rules which weld dispersed bands

33

THE DIVISION OF DEMOCRATIC POWERS

into a society. The terms of submission to the recognized authority become a permanent limit of its powers because they are the condition of the coherence and even existence of the state—and these terms of submission were understood in the liberal age to be that coercion could be used only for the enforcement of recognized general rules of just conduct. The conception that there must be an unlimited will which is the source of all power is the result of a constructivistic hypostasation, a fiction made necessary by the false factual assumptions of legal positivism but unrelated to the actual sources of allegiance.

The first question we should always ask in contemplating the structure of governmental powers is not who possesses such and such a power, but whether the exercise of such a power by any agency is justified by the implicit terms of submission to that agency. The ultimate limit of power is therefore not somebody's will on particular matters, but something quite different: the concurrence of opinions among members of a particular territorial group on rules of just conduct. The famous statement by Francis Bacon which is the ultimate source of legal positivism, that 'a supreme and absolute power cannot conclude itself, neither can that which is in its true nature revocable be fixed'[17] thus wrongly presupposes a derivation of all power from some act of purposive will. But the resolve that 'we will let us by governed by a good man, but if he is unjust we will throw him out' does not mean that we confer on him unlimited powers or powers which we already have! Power does not derive from some single seat but rests on the support by common opinion of certain principles and does not extend further than this support. Though the highest source of deliberate decisions cannot effectively limit its own powers, it is itself limited by the source from which its power derives which is not another act of will but a prevailing state of opinion. There is no reason why allegiance, and therefore the authority of the state, should survive the arrogation of arbitrary powers which has neither the support of the public nor can be effectively enforced by the usurping government.

In the Western world unlimited sovereignty was scarcely ever claimed by anyone since antiquity until the arrival of absolutism in the sixteenth century. It was certainly not conceded to medieval princes and hardly ever claimed by them. And although it was successfully claimed by the absolute monarchs of the European Continent, it was not really accepted as legitimate until after the advent of modern democracy which in this respect has inherited the

34

THE DIVISION OF DEMOCRATIC POWERS

tradition of absolutism. Till then the conception was still kept alive that legitimacy rested in the last resort on the approval by the people at large of certain fundamental principles underlying and limiting all government, and not on their consent to particular measures. But when this explicit consent that was devised as a check upon power came to be regarded as the sole source of power, the conception of unlimited power was for the first time invested with the aura of legitimacy.

The idea of the omnipotence of some authority as a result of the source of its power is thus essentially a degeneration that, under the influence of the constructivistic approach of legal positivism, appeared wherever democracy had existed for any length of time. It is, however, by no means a necessary consequence of democracy, but a consequence only of the deceptive belief that, once democratic procedures have been adopted, all the results of the machinery of ascertaining the will of the majority in fact correspond to the *opinion* of a majority, and that there is no limit to the range of question on which agreement of the majority can be ascertained by this procedure. It was helped by the naive belief that in this way the people were 'acting together'; and a sort of fairy tale spread that 'the people' are doing things and that this is morally preferable to the separate actions by individuals. In the end this fantasy led to the curious theory that the democratic decision-making process always is directed towards the common good—the common good being defined as the conclusions which the democratic procedures produces. The absurdity of this is shown by the fact that different but equally justifiable procedures for arriving at a democratic decision may produce very different results.

The requisite division of the powers of representative assemblies

The classical theory of representative government assumed that its aim could be achieved by allowing the division between the legislature and the administration to coincide with the division between an elected representative assembly and an executive body appointed by it. It failed to do so because there was of course as strong a case for democratic government as for democratic legislation and the sole democratically elected assembly inevitably claimed the right to direct government as well as the power to legislate. It thus came to combine the powers of legislation with those of government. The result was the revival of the monstrous establishment of an absolute

35

THE DIVISION OF DEMOCRATIC POWERS

power not restricted by any rules. I trust there will come a time when people will look with the same horror at the idea of a body of men, even one authorized by the majority of the citizens, who possesses power to order whatever it likes, as we feel today about most other forms of authoritarian government. It creates a barbarism, not because we have given barbarians power, but because we have released power from the restraint of rules, producing effects that are inevitable, whoever the people to whom such power is entrusted. It may well be that common people often have a stronger sense of justice than any intellectual élite guided by the lust for new deliberate construction; yet when unrestricted by any rules they are likely to act more arbitrarily than any élite or even a single monarch who is so bound. This is so, not because the faith in the common man is misplaced, but because he is thereby given a task which exceeds human capacities.

Though government proper in the performance of its characteristic tasks cannot be strictly tied to rules, its powers for this very reason ought always to be limited in extent and scope, namely confined to the administration of a sharply circumscribed range of means entrusted to its care. All power, however, that is not thus confined to a particular mass of material things but is unlimited in extent should be confined to the enforcement of general rules; while those who have the rule-making power should be confined to providing for the enforcement of such general rules and have no power of deciding on particular measures. All ultimate power should, in other words, be subject to the test of justice, and be free to do what it desires only in so far as it is prepared to commit itself to a principle that is to be applied in all similar instances.

The aim of constitutions has been to prevent all arbitrary action. But no constitution has yet succeeded in achieving this aim. The belief that they have succeeded in this has however led people to regard the terms 'arbitrary' and 'unconstitutional' as equivalent. Yet the prevention of arbitrariness, though one of the aims, is by no means a necessary effect of obeying a constitution. The confusion on this point is a result of the mistaken conception of legal positivism. The test of whether a constitution achieves what constitutions are meant to do is indeed the effective prevention of arbitrariness; but this does not mean that every constitution provides an adequate test of what is arbitrary, or that something that is permitted by a constitution may not still be arbitrary.

36

THE DIVISION OF DEMOCRATIC POWERS

If the supreme power must always prove the justice of its intentions by committing itself to general rules, this requires institutional arrangements which will secure that general rules will always prevail over the particular wishes of the holders of authority— including even the case where a very large majority favours a particular action but another, much smaller majority would be prepared to commit itself to a rule which would preclude that action. (This is not incompatible with the former, since it would be entirely rational to prefer that actions of the kind in question be prohibited altogether, yet so long as they are permitted to favour a particular one.) Or, to put this differently, even the largest majority should in its coercive acts be able to break a previously established rule *only* if it is prepared explicitly to abrogate it and to commit itself to a new one. Legislation in the true sense ought always to be a commitment to act on stated principles rather than a decision how to act in a particular instance. It must, therefore, essentially aim at effects in the long run, and be directed towards a future the particular circumstances of which are not yet known; and the resulting laws must aim at helping unknown people for their equally unknown purposes. This task demands for its successful accomplishment persons not concerned with particular situations or committed to the support of particular interests, but men free to look at their tasks from the point of view of the long run desirability of the rules laid down for the community as a whole.

Though true legislation is thus essentially a task requiring the long view, even more so than that of the designing of a constitution, it differs from the latter in that it must be a continuous task, a persistent effort to improve the law gradually and to adapt it to new conditions—essentially helping where jurisdiction cannot keep pace with a rapid development of facts and opinions. Though it may require formal decisions only at long intervals, it demands constant application and study of the kind for which politicians busy wooing their supporters and fully occupied with pressing matters demanding rapid solution will not really have time.

The task of legislation proper differs from the task of constitution-making also in that it will be concerned with rules of greater generality than those contained in a constitution. A constitution is chiefly concerned with the organization of government and the allocation of the different powers to the various parts of this organization. Though it will often be desirable to include in the formal

37

THE DIVISION OF DEMOCRATIC POWERS

documents 'constituting' the organization of the state some principles of substantive justice in order to confer upon these special
protection, it is still true that a constitution is essentially a superstructure erected to serve the enforcement of existing conceptions
of justice but not to articulate them: it presupposes the existence of
a system of rules of just conduct and merely provides a machinery
for their regular enforcement.

We need not pursue this point further at this stage since all that we
want to point out here is that the task of true legislation is as
different from that of constitution-making as it is from that of
governing, and that it ought to be as little confused with the former
as with the latter. It follows from this that, if such confusion is to be
avoided, a three-tiered system of representative bodies is needed,
of which one would be concerned with the semi-permanent
framework of the constitution and need act only at long intervals
when changes in that framework are considered necessary, another
with the continuous task of gradual improvement of the general
rules of just conduct, and a third with the current conduct of
government, that is, the administration of the resources entrusted
to it.

Democracy or demarchy?

We cannot consider here further the changes which the meaning of
the concept of democracy has undergone by its increasingly common transfer from the political sphere in which it is appropriate to
other spheres in which it is very doubtful whether it can be meaningfully applied:[18] and whether its persistent and deliberate abuse
by the communists as in such terms as 'people's democracies', which
of course lack even the most basic characteristics of a democracy,
does not make it unsuitable to describe the ideal it was originally
meant to express. These tendencies are mentioned here merely
because they are contributing further to deprive the term 'democracy' of clear meaning and turn it into a word-fetish used to clothe
with an aura of legitimacy any demands of a group that wishes to
shape some feature of society to its special wishes.

The legitimacy of the demands for more democracy becomes
particularly questionable when they are directed to the manner in
which organizations of various kinds are conducted. The problems
which arise here show themselves at once when it is asked who are
to be regarded as the 'members' of such organizations for whom a

THE DIVISION OF DEMOCRATIC POWERS

share in their direction is claimed. It is by no means obvious that a person who finds it in his interest to sell his services should thereby also acquire a voice in its conduct or in determining the purposes towards which this organization is to be directed. We all know that the conduct of the campaign of an army could not be directed democratically. It is the same with such simple operations as the building of a house or the conduct of an enterprise of the bureaucratic machinery of government.

And who are the 'members' of a hospital, or an hotel, or a club, a teaching institution or a department store? Those who serve these institutions, those whom these institutions serve, or those who provide the material means required to render the services? I ask these questions here simply to make clear that the term democracy, though we all still use it and feel we ought to defend the ideal it describes, has ceased to express a definite conception to which one can commit oneself without much explanation, and which in some of the senses in which it is now frequently used has become a serious threat to the ideals it was once meant to depict. Though I firmly believe that government ought to be conducted according to principles approved by a majority of the people, and must be so run if we are to preserve peace and freedom, I must frankly admit that *if* democracy is taken to mean government by the unrestricted will of the majority I am not a democrat, and even regard such government as pernicious and in the long run unworkable.

A question which has arisen here is whether those who believe in the original ideal of democracy can still usefully avail themselves of that old name to express their ideal. I have come seriously to doubt whether this is still expedient and feel more and more convinced that, if we are to preserve the original ideal, we may have to invent a new name for it. What we need is a word which expresses the fact that the *will* of the greater number is authoritative and binding upon the rest only if the former prove their intention of acting justly by committing themselves to a general rule. This demands a name indicating a system in which what gives a majority legitimate power is not bare might but the proven conviction that it regards as right what it decrees.

It so happens that the Greek word 'democracy' was formed by combining the word for the people (*demos*) with that of the two available terms for power, namely *kratos* (or the verb *kratein*) which had not already been used in such a combination for other purposes. *Kratein*, however, unlike the alternative verb *archein*

39

THE DIVISION OF DEMOCRATIC POWERS

(used in such compounds as monarchy, oligarchy, anarchy, etc.) seems to stress brute force rather than government by rule. The reason why in ancient Greece the latter root could not be used to form the term *demarchy* to express a rule by the people was that the term *demarch* had (at least in Athens) been preempted by an earlier use for the office of the head of a local group or district (the *deme*), and thus was no longer available as a description of government by the people at large. This need not prevent us today from adopting the term *demarchy* for the ideal for which *democracy* was originally adopted when it gradually supplanted the older expression *isonomy*, describing the ideal of an equal law for all.[19] This would give us the new name we need if we are to preserve the basic ideal in a time when, because of the growing abuse of the term democracy for systems that lead to the creation of new privileges by coalitions or organized interests, more and more people will turn against that prevailing system. If such a justified reaction against abuse of the term is not to discredit the ideal itself, and lead people in their disillusionment to accept much less desirable forms of government, it would seem necessary that we have a new name like demarchy to describe the old ideal by a name that is not tainted by long abuse.

[13]

Excerpt from *The Limits of Liberty: Between Anarchy and Leviathan*, 147–65

9 THE THREAT OF LEVIATHAN

Dictionaries define Leviathan as "a sea monster embodying evil." In 1651, Thomas Hobbes applied this term to the sovereign state. Three and one-quarter centuries later, we use the term only when we discuss government and political processes pejoratively, and then only when our purpose is to call attention to the dangers inherent in an expanding public sector of society. I have discussed the paradox of being governed in Chapter 6. In democracy, man considers himself simultaneously to be a participant in government (a citizen) and a subject who is forced to abide by standards of behavior that he may not have selected, including overt acquiescence in the confiscation through taxation of goods that he treats as "his own."

For late twentieth-century man, this bifurcation in his attitude toward the state is "natural" in the sense that it emerges directly from his post-Enlightenment, postsocialist cultural heritage. From our vantage point in the 1970s it is difficult to appreciate the importance of the initial change of vision which first enabled man to see himself as an independent will. I do not pose as an exegetical expert on ancient texts, but can there be much question that the conception of independent man, universalized over all persons, was largely foreign to Greek and Roman philosophy? Medieval Christianity introduces an ambivalence, in that individual salvation was stressed but almost always for the greater glory of God.[1] Only in the full emergence from the Middle Ages, only with Hobbes, Spinoza, and their contemporaries does man become possible independently of other men, of God, of state and city. In the Hobbesian jungle, the life of independent man was indeed described as poor, nasty, bruitish, and short. But in Hobbes's ability to visualize, to conceptualize, such an existence at all lies the critical difference with earlier philosophers. Can we conceive of pre-Hobbesian anarchists?

Once independent man was set against the state, even in an argument that suggested rational bases for obedience, the potential for continuing revolution was guaranteed. The genie could not be put back into the bottle, no matter how logical the arguments of a Malmesbury philosopher. Man could now think himself into a role as king; in his mind's eye, man could now leap out of his estate or order, and some man or men would surely act out these dreams. Althusius, Spinoza, Locke, and, even more emphatically, Rousseau, commenced and continued to talk about a social contract among independent men, not a

147

Hobbesian slave contract between men and a sovereign master. From contract among free men, all things might emerge, including basic law itself. For the first time, man seemed to be offered a prospect for jumping out of his evolutionary history. Man, in concert with his fellows, might change the very structure of social order.

The conception was as revolutionary as its consequences, the age of democratic revolution.[2] Repressed revolt, successful revolution, revolutionary terror, repressive reform, counterrevolution—these various stages in our spatially divergent modern history need not be discussed in detail here. We know that man failed to live up to the promise of his Enlightenment dreams. Hardly had some of the tyrants been overthrown and some elites vanquished, when others emerged. And once the political and social order was put up for grabs and was seen to be so, how could the economic basis of this order withstand assault? Locke's valiant efforts to erect a contractual superstructure over existing property rights were foredoomed to failure. If men, in concerted contract, are not bounded, need any limits be placed on collective action? Why need the economic order stand immune from fundamental structural rearrangements, especially when effective challenges were issued by Karl Marx? Socialism, in its varied guises, came to inform the consciousness of early twentieth-century man. The circle seemed almost complete; independent man once again seemed to have become submerged in an all-embracing collective will.

Once loosed, however, independent man could not be so readily destroyed. The Soviet Union was not the future, as the Webbs had proclaimed in ignorant joy. Even in Russia, where man had scarcely attained individualized independence before communist revolution, his innate stubbornness made efficient control impossible. In the West, where men have experienced freedom, where freedom itself has a history, democratic socialism was foredoomed. Collectivized governmental attempts to do more and more have been demonstrably revealed to accomplish less and less. Man finds himself locked into an impersonal bureaucratic network that he acknowledges to be of his own making. He begins to use the term "Leviathan" in its modern connotation, yet he feels personally unable to offer effective alternatives.

This difference between prerevolutionary and modern man must be understood if the latter's predicament is to be appreciated. Modern man cannot place himself in opposition to a government that is staffed and directed by an exterior elite, by members of a wholly different order or estate. To an American patriot, there was George III. To a member of the French bourgeoisie, there was the ancien régime. To the followers of Lenin, there was the Russian aristocracy. To modern man tangled in the web of bureaucracy, there is only himself, or others of his same breed.

This is not, of course, to suggest that imperfections in democratic process are absent or that all persons possess equal power of influencing governmental policy in the modern world, and in America in particular. I am suggesting that, even if all imperfections could be removed, even if all persons were placed in positions of equal political power, the central issues facing modern man would remain. When we speak of controlling Leviathan we should be referring to controlling self-government, not some instrument manipulated by the decisions of others than ourselves. Widespread acknowledgment of this simple truth might work wonders. If men should cease and desist from their talk about and their search for evil men and commence to look instead at the institutions manned by ordinary people, wide avenues for genuine social reform might appear.

WICKSELLIAN UNANIMITY

Why need there be constitutional limits or controls over the scope and range of governmental activity? In order to understand this, we may first look at the idealized model which gives to the individual full power over his destiny. Consider a community that makes all collective decisions in accordance with a Wicksellian rule of unanimous consent. Let us further assume, this time quite unrealistically, that this rule is operative without major costs of reaching agreement. In such a model, each person is party to all collective decisions, no one of which can be taken without his express consent. How could the dynamics of such a decision model generate results that could be judged undesirable or inefficient by any one or by all of the persons in the community?

Because each person must agree positively to every decision taken, the flaw, if indeed one exists, must lie in the individual precepts for rational choice, not in the amalgamation of individual choices in producing collective outcomes. Analysis should, therefore, be concentrated on individual decision-making. Why would an individual agree to each one of a sequence of collective decisions, separately taken, only to find that the sequence generates an undesired ultimate outcome? Once the question is put in this way, numerous analogies from personal experience are suggested. Perhaps the one that is most pervasive is eating. In modern affluence, individual choice behavior in eating, on a meal-by-meal basis, often leads to obesity, a result that is judged to be undesirable. The individual arrives at this result, however, through a time sequence in which each and every eating decision seems privately rational. No overt gluttony need be involved, and no error need be present. At the moment of each specific choice of food consumption, the expected benefits exceed the expected costs.

The problem is not fully described as one of myopia in individual choice behavior, as a simple failure to take into account the future consequences of present action. Such myopia is, without doubt, one of the important bases for disappointment or regret when undesirable situations are recognized to be the result of a series of earlier choices. In this sense, all temporally related choices can be made to appear to be characterized by myopia. Consider saving and capital formation. From the vantage point of "now," a person may always wish that he had saved more and consumed less in earlier periods, and, in this vision, he may look on past behavior as having been myopic. More reasonable judgment might suggest, however, that each decision, when made, was based on some appropriately weighted calculation of costs and benefits in the "then" time setting. The decision to eat more than is dictated by the maintenance of some long-term weight standard is equivalent to a failure to save an amount sufficient to attain some long-term wealth objective. When this temporal interdependence among separate-period decisions is recognized, rational choice behavior at the "rule-making" level may internalize the interdependence through the explicit adoption of constraints on separate-period freedom of action. When he adopts a rule and insures its enforcement, the individual is exercising his freedom, at a more comprehensive planning stage of choice, only through restricting his own freedom in subsequent potential choice situations.

The person who recognizes his tendency to overeat may adopt a stringent diet. He deliberately imposes self-generated constraints on his own choice options. He locks himself into an eating pattern that he predicts to reduce the utility gains from separate-period behavior in exchange for predicted utility gains over an extended choice domain. The diet becomes the "eating constitution," the person's set of internally chosen rules that act to prevent overindulgence. It seems clear that individuals may want to impose comparable constraints on their separate-period and separate-choice behavior in undertaking joint or collective actions, even in the idealized setting of Wicksellian unanimity. That is to say, individuals might rationally choose to operate under a set of constitutional rules for taking collective actions even if each person knows that he is empowered, personally, to veto any specific proposal that might be presented. In this setting, however, we should note that such a set of rules might be made operative by the choice behavior of a single member of the group. The determination of a single person in the community to abide by some internal constraint on the range of collective action would be effective for the whole group. Collective action would be constrained in this strictly Wicksellian setting by the mere presence of one person who chooses to adopt internal rules for his own participation in collective choices.

MAJORITY VOTING UNDER
BENEFIT-COST CONSTRAINTS

We move somewhat closer to reality when we drop the assumption that collective action requires unanimous consent of all participants. As suggested, under a genuine unanimity rule, individual decisions can keep government under effective controls. Things become quite different, however, once any departure from unanimity is introduced. When the costs of securing agreement are acknowledged, departures from true government by consent become necessary if the political community is to function as a collectivity. In the conceptual constitutional compact establishing this community, some set of rules for making collective or governmental decisions is selected, and these rules, once made operative, are enforceable on all members, whether or not they belong to the decisive coalition which effectively makes particular choices under the rules.

The most familiar decision rule, both in the analytical models of political process and in existing historical structures that are appropriately classified as "democratic," is that of majority voting. We may assume that some constitutional structure exists, a structure that defines individual property rights and enforces contracts among persons and, further, requires that all collective or governmental decisions secure the majority of the representatives of citizens in some legislative assembly. Even in this formulation we have, by assumption, already by-passed a significant part of the issue being discussed. At the stage of constitutional contract, when individual rights are initially defined, few persons would conceptually agree to wholly unconstrained departures from a unanimity rule for collective decision-making. The reason is, of course, that once an individual's consent is not required for a decision that will be enforced upon him, the individual holds no protection of his own nominal assignment of claims, no guarantees that his rights will not be exploited on behalf of others in the name of governmental objectives. At the same time that a collective decision rule, say that of majority voting, is adopted, procedural limits on the exercise of this rule may be incorporated into the constitutional document or understanding. Experience indicates, however, that the procedural limits incorporated in constitutional structures historically have not been very effective in curbing the appetites of majority coalitions.

Nonetheless, it will be useful for analysis to develop the argument in two stages. In the first, we assume that an economically meaningful constraint on majority decision exists. Assume that a constitutional provision requires that all proposals for public or governmental outlay satisfy a benefit-cost criterion; gross benefits must exceed gross project costs, regardless of the array of votes in the legislative assembly.

We want to look at public-goods proposals that do not benefit all members of the group sufficiently to offset fully tax costs, but which do, nonetheless, meet the benefit-cost criterion imposed. If, for example, in a three-person group there should be only two beneficiaries of a project costing $100, and if each of these beneficiaries expects to secure a value of $51, the proposal would meet the benefit-cost criterion no matter how costs are distributed. If the costs are equally distributed among all members, say, by a general tax, the proposal would secure majority approval. The effect would be to impose net losses on the minority. The benefit-cost constraint guarantees, however, that if compensation should be required, the majority could arrange to secure minority acquiescence with appropriate side payments. Another way of saying this is to state that the benefit-cost criterion insures that all spending projects are "efficient" in the strict economic meaning of this term. Still another version, and related to the preceding section, is to say that all projects could conceptually secure unanimous approval if the costs of making side payments are ignored.

If each and every proposal for spending funds governmentally is required to meet the efficiency criterion, how could the aggregate budgetary level fail to do so? How could the overall budget be too large or too small? Since each project, considered independently, meets the efficiency test, it would seem that the test could also be met by the aggregate of all projects. As the discussion of the preceding section may suggest, however, this result need not follow when there exists interdependence among the separate decisions.

Consider, as an example, two interdependent proposals for budgetary spending, Projects I and II. In the absence of, and independently of, the other project, each of these proposals is estimated to cost $100, of which $90 is for outlay on the purchase of resource inputs, and $10 is for outlay on collection and enforcement. For each project, similarily, estimated benefits are $103. Hence, regardless of the way benefits are distributed, each proposal is economically efficient. Suppose now that Project I is approved initially under these conditions and that it is included in budgetary plans. Project II is now considered independently, but subsequent to majority approval for Project I. Direct outlay on resource inputs is again $90, as with Project I. But, because more revenues are now required in total, collection-enforcement costs are now estimated to be $12, for a total project cost of $102. Benefits are estimated to be $103; hence, the project remains apparently efficient, and we assume that Project II is also approved by a majority. In adding Project II to the budget, however, collection-enforcement costs for Project

I may also have been increased, from the $10 initially estimated to the $12 estimated for Project II. The external or spillover cost that the addition of Project II generates for Project I is $2, but this was wholly left out of account in the choice-making sequence that we have outlined.

Note that, in the numerical example, aggregate benefits of the two projects ($206) exceed aggregate costs ($204). Note, however, that gross fiscal surplus is reduced below that which is attainable on the approval of only one of the two projects; the surplus falls from $3 to $2 in the process of adding Project II, which, treated independently, is equivalent to Project I. The numerical example is, of course, illustrative only, and the totals need not be taken as at all descriptive. In terms that are familiar to economists, we can say that there exists a divergence between the direct or separable costs of a single project and the genuine social costs, which must include all external or spillover effects on other projects or components in the budgetary set. When stated in these terms, economists might suggest "internalization" through simultaneous consideration of all the interrelated budgetary items. Care must be taken, however, to insure that the appropriate maximand is selected. Taken as a two-part budgetary package, both projects in the numerical example would secure approval, even if they were jointly selected. Joint benefits exceed joint costs.

The more general phenomenon that the example represents has considerable real-world relevance in terms of widely acknowledged economic effects and of observed political institutions.[3] Collection and enforcement costs are always present, and these costs increase as budget size grows, possibly disproportionately beyond certain ranges. More important, taxation necessarily modifies incentives toward the earning of taxable incomes and accumulating taxable wealth in the private economy. These effects are directly related to budgetary size, and these are genuine social costs that incremental budget-making can scarcely incorporate.

Politically, budgets are made piecemeal.[4] Different legislative committees consider budgetary components independently, and possibly divergent majority coalitions are organized in support of each component. So long as benefits exceed costs, why should members of the effective supporting coalitions be concerned about spillover costs on components, past, present, or future? Political realism suggests the implausibility of achieving reforms at the level of incremental decision-making. Comprehensive budgeting, at either the executive or the legislative level or both, need not eliminate the inefficiency, as we have noted. Consider the position of a budget director or chairman of a legislative committee. By our restrictive assumption, any component must meet the overall benefit-cost constraint. But since this criterion is also satisfied for the budget in the aggregate, or may be, what incentive does this official have for reducing or eliminating particular components or line items so as to increase net fiscal surplus? Even if the official is ideally responsive to the demands of the citizenry, he will be led to incorporate too many components in the budgetary package. Consider again our two-project example. A budget director has overall coordinative responsibility; he must approve a project before it is submitted for a vote. If he eliminates one of the two projects, he incurs the displeasure of all direct beneficiaries. He pleases general taxpayers, but as we have assumed and as the real-world patterns suggest, taxes are more widely shared than the benefits. The indirect net costs that will be reduced by budgetary constraints are not likely to be sensed by the citizenry, and especially not in connection with specific budgetary choices.[5]

The inefficiencies that emerge when there exists interdependence among the separate components of a budget can be reduced only if these are predicted at some planning stage of deliberation. Because of the tendency of budget-makers and of legislative majorities to approve budgets that aggregate to sizes beyond those which maximize fiscal surplus, explicit size limits or other constraints on revenues and/or outlays may be incorporated in the fiscal constitution with the expectation that such limits will be legally enforced.[6]

MAJORITY VOTING WITHOUT
BENEFIT-COST CONSTRAINTS

If we drop the arbitrary requirement that all proposals for spending publicly collected revenues meet criteria of economic efficiency, it is evident that majority voting rules for reaching collective or group decisions will produce at least some budgetary components that are inefficient in net. Some projects that will secure majority approval will yield less in total benefits than they cost. The minority will suffer net losses from these projects, and these losses will exceed the benefits secured for members of the majority. In a regime with costless side payments, the minority could bribe the majority so as to prevent the approval of all such projects. But when the absence of effective side payments is acknowledged, the existence of inefficient spending projects can hardly be questioned.

Consider again a very simple example, a three-person group that has organized itself collectively. Taxes are equal per head, and all spending decisions are made by majority voting. Suppose that there are three potential projects to be considered, each of which costs $99, financed by a tax of $33 on each person. We assume that these projects are wholly independent and that the externality effects analyzed in the preceding section do not arise. The benefits from each project are concentrated as indicated in the following:

Person	Project I Benefits	Project II Benefits	Project III Benefits
A	$35	$35	$ 0
B	35	0	35
C	0	35	35

Under the rules that we have postulated, each of these three projects would be adopted, so long as each project is considered separately. In the process, however, each person will have paid out a total of $99 in taxes and will have received only $70 in benefits. Each person will be worse off with the three-project budget than he would be with no budget at all. It is clear from this example that budgets will tend to be over-expanded under simple majority voting rules if budgetary components are considered separately in the legislative deliberations, and if benefits are more concentrated than taxes.

There is, however, a difference between this and the earlier model where we assumed projects to be interdependent. In this model, which we might call one of simple majority exploitation of the minority, "internalization" in the form of comprehensive or package considera- tion of the whole budget may eliminate some of the inefficiency. If the three-man group in this example should be forced, by institutional- constitutional requirement, to treat projects in a bundle rather than in isolation, and if members of the group accurately measure costs and benefits, projects that are demonstrably damaging in the net for all persons will not secure approval. Alternatively, constitutional restric- tions might be imposed which dictate that only spending proposals that promise *general* benefits to the whole membership of the com- munity can be considered.[7] Historically, procedural requirements have been interpreted to dictate tax uniformity or generality, at least over broad groupings. For the benefits side, however, no fully comparable requirements have been applied. As a result, there are relatively few effective limits on the fiscal exploitation of minorities through orderly democratic procedures in the United States.[8]

Logrolling and Minority Benefits. The majority voting model discussed above suggests that inefficient budgetary projects may secure approval if considered separately, but that, at a minimum, the estimated value of benefits from any proposal to the members of an effective majority coalition must exceed the tax costs borne by those members. Even this minimal constraint on budgetary inefficiency is not operative, however, when logrolling can take place among divergent minorities to produce effective majority coalitions on a subgroup of budgetary items. This procedure is familiarly known as "pork barrel" legislation in the American setting.[9]

POLITICAL INCOME, BUREAUCRATIC RENTS, AND FRANCHISE

To this point, the models of collective decision-making examined have not allowed for the influence of politicians, governmental employees, or bureaucrats on budgetary outcomes. Implicitly, the models have contained the assumption that voters demand publicly supplied goods and services which, once approved, are made available to final beneficiaries or consumers directly. There is no intermediation by legislative representatives and no administration by bureaucratic agencies. Such models are useful for general purposes, and especially so when budgets are relatively small. In modern democracies, however, more than one-third of the national product is organized through the governmental sector. In these settings, neglect of the influence of politicians and bureaucrats on budgetary results may severely weaken the relevance of any analysis.

Politicians' Preferences and Budgetary Bias. Collective decisions are rarely made directly by voters, by those persons who pay the taxes and who are supposed to benefit from the provision of governmental goods and services. Effective political organization requires that the roles of voters be limited largely if not entirely to the selection of representatives, persons from their own ranks, who will then participate in legislative and executive decision-making. These politicians are the men who make the direct and final choices on the quantities of public goods and services and on the size of the total budget along with its composition and financing.

It is unrealistic to assume that elected officials who occupy executive and legislative positions of responsibility have no personal preferences about the overall size of the public sector, its sources of revenue, and, most important, about the particular components for public outlays. A person who is genuinely indifferent in all these respects would not be attracted to politics, either as a profession or as an avocation. Politicians are likely to be those persons who do have personal preferences about such matters and who are attracted to politics precisely because they think that, through politics, they can exercise some influence over collective outcomes. Once this basic, if simple, point is recognized, it is easy to see that budgetary results will not fully reflect voters' preferences, even of those who are members of the effective coalition that achieves victory for its own candidate or party.

Once elected, a politician has considerable freedom for choosing his own preferred position on spending or tax issues. He is constrained by voters indirectly through prospects for reelection, for long-term party support, for generalized public acclaim. But even for the politician who is highly sensitive to these indirect constraints, there remains freedom of choice over substantial ranges of the political spectrum. Within what he treats as his feasible set, the politician will choose that alternative or option which maximizes his own, not his constituents', utility. This opportunity offers one of the primary motivations to politicians. In a meaningful sense, this is "political income," and it must be reckoned as a part of the total rewards of office.[10]

The existence of opportunities for politicians to maximize personal preferences within constraints need not be of relevance to the subject matter of this chapter if the effects on budget-making could be predicted to be symmetrical or unbiased. If the "slippage" between the preferences of voters and the results emerging from the actual budgetary process should involve roughly offsetting differences on the up and down sides, no net influence on aggregate budgetary size would be exercised. Unfortunately, a unidirectional bias toward expansion in the fiscal accounts seems to be present. This direction of the political leader's preference bias involves several distinguishable elements. In the first place, those persons who place relatively high values on the ability to influence collective outcomes, and who do so in the genuinely incorruptible sense of desiring to "do good" for the whole community, are quite likely to be those who seek to accomplish their own preferred social objectives through collective or governmental means. By contrast, those persons who, ideologically, desire that the governmental role in society should be reduced to minimal levels are unlikely to be attracted to politics. Few natural anarchists or libertarians frequent capital cloakrooms.

Ideologues aside, persons may be attracted to politics because they intrinsically place high values on the power to make decisions affecting the lives of others. This characteristic is different from the first, where power to influence collective decision is instrumentally desired for the purpose of furthering social objectives. Some politicians may have very ill-defined objectives for social policy and those that they do have may seem relatively unimportant. They may seek political and/or elected office, however, because they enjoy positions of leadership and authority, positions that make it necessary for other persons actively to seek them out and solicit their assistance. This sort of politician secures utility more directly than his ideologue counterpart; his utility is increased by the emoluments of office that necessarily arise from public knowledge about the location of decision-making authority. If the list or menu for choice should be fixed in advance, the behavior of politicians of such nonideological stripe might produce results that are closer to the true preferences of voters. This correspondence would emerge from the desires to meet the demands of the largest possible number of constituents. In such case, no directional budgetary bias would be introduced by the necessary departures from pure democracy. When the list or menu for political choice is not predetermined, however, the directional bias toward expanded budgets again arises. The politician who secures his utility only because he chooses for and thereby pleases the largest number of constituents will find that favorable action on differentially beneficial spending projects offers more reward than favorable action reducing general tax costs. The politician's bias, in this respect, is an additional institutional aspect of the asymmetry between the spending and taxing sides of the fiscal account. Because taxes cannot readily be lowered in a differential manner, there is a public-goods barrier which inhibits independent politician initiative toward tax reduction. By contrast, because the benefits from government spending may be differentially directed toward particular subgroups in the community, politicians are motivated to initiate the formation of coalitions that will exploit these latent demand opportunities. Given his degree of freedom to influence outcomes, the nonideological politician's behavior will tend to generate an exaggerated version of the nonpolitician model analyzed earlier. Because of the asymmetry in the effective fiscal constitution, aggregate spending will tend to be inefficiently large even if the ultimate demands of voters-taxpayers-beneficiaries could be accurately reflected in final outcomes. The introduction of politicians as the direct decision-makers will extend the results even beyond such limits.

To this point, we have assumed implicitly that both the ideological and the nonideological politicians are incorruptible and seek no pecuniary gain from political office over and beyond formal compensation. To these two types of officials it is now necessary to add a third, that of the politician who does seek pecuniary gains from his office. The direction of budgetary bias is the same as before. The prospect for profitable bribes, kickbacks, or by-product deals is directly related to the size and complexity of total government budgets, and, more generally, of the total governmental operation in the economy. With minimal governmental intrusion into the economy, with minimal and quasi-permanent spending components, the grasping politician may have little or no opportunities for graft. However, with a complex public sector, and one that involves new and expanding spending programs, there may be numerous opportunities. In a newly enacted program, one without established guidelines and procedures, politicians may find ample sources for direct and indirect kickbacks from the producers and producing firms whose rents are enhanced by the program. Such officials will, therefore, seek continually to enlarge budgets and, especially, to introduce new and different programs. On the other hand, the potentially corrupt politician would rarely press for general budgetary reduction. The direction of bias seems apparent, again under the institutional proviso that taxes are distributed more generally than the benefits of public spending.[11]

Elected politicians may fall into either one of the three categories discussed, or a single politician may himself represent some mixture of two or all three of the types. The directional bias on budgetary size is the same for all types. Although their reasons may differ, the ideologue, the seeker after public acclaim, and the profiteer each will be motivated to expand the size and scope of the governmental sector of the economy.

Bureaucratic Rents and Franchise. Even after elected politicians make taxing and spending decisions, public goods and services do not flow automatically and directly from competitively organized suppliers outside the economy to final consumers within the economy. Governments, when authorized to do so, may purchase inputs from independent private suppliers (individuals and firms) and combine these to produce outputs. Or, alternatively, governments may purchase final outputs after these have been produced by private suppliers and distribute these to beneficiaries. In either case, and much more extensively in the former than in the latter, employees must be hired to implement the complex fiscal transaction between the ultimate taxpayer-purchaser on the one hand and the ultimate beneficiary-consumer on the other, even if, in some net accounting, these may be the same persons. Once elected officials, as representatives of the voters, decide on a quantity and a distribution of taxes, other officials (agents) must be employed to collect the revenues. Accountants must be hired to keep the books; auditors must be added to check the agents and the accountants. Inspectors must be available to search out recalcitrant taxpayers. On the spending side, budget specialists are required to maintain and present details of complex programs and to make comparative evaluations. Purchasing agents must carry out buying tasks in the framework of procedures worked out by still another layer of bureaucratic personnel. And personnel specialists are necessary to get personnel.

All of these would be needed even if no direct production of goods and services takes place within the governmental sector itself. Once direct production is attempted, massive numbers of additional employees are needed. If government produces postal services, mail clerks, postmen, and postmasters must be hired. If government produces education, administrators, teachers, supervisors, and custodians become government employees along with others who must evaluate the credentials of those who produce the services. The list can be extended almost without limit.

If taxpayers-voters, acting through their elected politicians, should be able to secure government employees externally at competitively determined wage and salary scales, the necessary existence of a bureaucratic superstructure need not itself introduce major distortion in the budgetary process. As with the enforcement problem discussed in earlier chapters, however, difficulties arise from the necessity of staffing government with persons drawn from within the political community. The sequence of budgetary outcomes tends to be biased toward overexpansion because of the potential for earning producer rents which government employment offers and because employees hold voting rights in the polity. If bureaucrats could not vote, the existence of producer rents from government employment would increase the costs of public-supplied goods and services, but this alone would not bias the results significantly. On the other hand, even if bureaucrats hold the voting franchise, no problem might arise if governmental wage and salary scales, along with tenure and promotion policies, were competitively determined. In the real world, however, governmental employees have full voting rights, *and* governmental salaries and working conditions are not settled in competitive markets.

Regardless of his interest as a demander-taxpayer or final beneficiary of a publicly provided good, a person who expects to be or is already employed by the governmental agency that provides this good will tend to favor increases and to oppose reductions in budgeted outlay. (How many medical researchers at NIH would support reductions in federal government outlays on medical research?) If he holds a voting franchise, the prospective or actual employee becomes a built-in supporter of budgetary expansion and a built-in opponent of budgetary reduction, not only for the particular component within his immediate concern but for other components as well. As students of political economy have long recognized, producer interests tend to dominate consumer interests, and the producer interests of government employees are no different from those of any other group in society. Two additional elements accentuate the effects of bureaucratic franchise on budget size. As with elected politicians, those who are attracted to governmental employment are likely to exhibit personal preferences for collective action, at least by comparison with those who are employed in the private sector. More important, because of specific producer interest that a working bureaucrat recognizes, the exercise of ultimate voting privileges is more likely to occur. Empirical evidence supports this inference; the proportion of governmental employees who vote is significantly higher than the proportion of nongovernmental employees. The result is that members of the bureaucracy can exert a disproportionate influence on electoral outcomes.

The franchising of bureaucrats need not involve serious budgetary bias when total government employment remains small. As the public sector continues to grow, however, the voting power, and hence the political power, of franchised bureaucrats cannot be neglected. In modern America, where roughly one in each five employees works for government, bureaucrats have become a major fiscal constituency, and one that politicians seeking elective office recognize and respect.[12]

This influence would be present even in an ideally working bureaucracy so long as net rents were earned in government employment. As we must recognize, however, no structure can approach the old-fashioned textbook ideal in which bureaucrats merely carry out or execute policy directives chosen for them by legislative authorities.[13] Bureaucrats, like elected politicians, possess varying degrees of freedom to select among alternatives. A collective decision, as made by a legislative assembly, is never sufficiently definitive to leave no scope for exercise of authority on the part of administrators of the program. Within limits, the nonelected government employee makes final decisions about government actions. Stated in a somewhat converse way, the legislature or elected executive can never exercise full control over the behavior of bureaucrats in the structural hierarchy, and any attempts to gain full control would involve prohibitive costs.[14] Within the constraints that he faces, the bureaucrat tries to maximize his own utility. He is no different from anyone else in this respect. He can hardly be expected to further some vaguely defined "public interest" unless this is consistent with his own, as he defines the latter.

Once this point, again a very simple one, is acknowledged, the influence of the bureaucracy on budgetary results can be predicted to be unidirectional. The individual who finds himself in a bureaucratic hierarchy, who knows that he earns net rents when he compares his situation with his private-sector opportunities, looks directly at the reward and penalty structure within the hierarchy. He knows that his career prospects, his chances for promotion and tenure in employment, are enhanced if the size of the distinct budgetary component with which he is associated increases. He will, therefore, exercise his own choices, whenever possible, to increase rather than to decrease project and agency budgets. There is little or no potential reward to the governmental employee who proposes to reduce or limit his own agency or bureau. Institutionally, the individual bureaucrat is motivated toward aggrandizement of his own agency.[15] And, since the effective alternatives for most governmental employees are other agencies and projects, this motivation for expansion will extend to government generally.

DEMOCRACY UNCHAINED

The purpose of the several preceding sections was to demonstrate that even under the most favorable conditions the operation of democratic process may generate budgetary excesses. Democracy may become its own Leviathan unless constitutional limits are imposed and enforced. Historically, government has grown at rates that cannot possibly be long

162   *Chapter Nine*

sustained. In this sense alone, modern America confronts a crisis of major proportions in the last decades of the twentieth century. In the seven decades from 1900 to 1970, total government spending in real terms increased forty times over, attaining a share of one-third in national product. These basic facts are familiar and available for all to see. The point of emphasis is that this growth has occurred, almost exclusively, within the predictable workings of orderly democratic procedures.[16]

The authors of the United States Constitution, the Founding Fathers, did not foresee the necessity or need of controlling the growth of self-government, at least specifically, nor have these aspects been treated in traditional political discourse. The limits or constraints on governmental arms and agencies have been primarily discussed in terms of maintaining democratic procedures. Rulers have been subjected to laws because of a predicted proclivity to extend their own powers beyond procedural limits, at the presumed expense of the citizenry. But implicit in much of the discussion has been the notion that, to the extent that democratic process works, there is no need for limits. The system of checks and balances, ultimately derivative from Montesquieu, has rarely been interpreted to have as one of its objectives the limiting of the growth of the government. The excesses of the 1960s created widespread public disillusionment about the ability of government, as a process, to accomplish specific social objectives. But, before the 1960s, the checks and balances that were present in the United States constitutional structure were far more likely to be criticized for inhibiting the extent of governmental action than for their inability to accomplish an effective limitation on this action. In this respect, the 1970s and beyond present a new and different challenge. Can modern man, in Western democratic society, invent or capture sufficient control over his own destiny so as to impose constraints on his own government, constraints that will prevent the transformation into the genuine Hobbesian sovereign?

BEYOND CONSTITUTIONAL BOUNDARIES

In earlier chapters, we found it useful to make a sharp conceptual distinction between the productive state and the protective state, and the dual functioning of government in these two conceptually different roles was noted. The productive state is, ideally, the embodiment of postconstitutional contract among citizens having as its objective the provision of jointly shared goods and services, as demanded by the citizens. The discussion of Leviathan in this chapter has been wholly concerned with this part or side of government, measured appropriately by the size of the governmental budget. The analysis has shown that budgetary excess will emerge from democratic process, even if overt exploitation is avoided. To the extent that majoritarian democracy uses governmental process to modify the basic structure of individual rights, which are presumably defined in the legal structure, there is an encroachment on the domain of the protective state. Dominant coalitions in legislative bodies may take it on themselves to change "the law," the basic constitutional structure, defined in a real and not a nominal sense. To the extent that the protective state acquiesces in this constitutional excess, the social structure moves toward "constitutional anarchy" in which individual rights are subject to the whims of politicians.

There is, however, an equally if not more significant overstepping of constitutional boundaries when the agencies of government that properly belong to the protective state, and to this state only, begin to act in putative contractual capacities, at both constitutional and postconstitutional stages. A modern treatment of Leviathan would be seriously incomplete if these possible excesses were not discussed. The protective state has as its essential and only role the enforcement of individual rights as defined in constitutional contract. This state is law embodied, and its role is one of enforcing rights to property, to exchanges of property, and of policing the simple and complex exchange processes among contracting free men. In the game analogy that we have used several times before, the protective state is the umpire or referee, and, as such, its task is conceptually limited to enforcing agreed-on rules.

Few who observe the far-flung operation of the executive arm of the United States government along with the ubiquitousness of the federal judiciary could interpret the activities of either of these institutions as falling within meaningful restrictions of the enforcer. Ideally, these institutions may be umpires in the social game; actually, these institutions modify and change the basic structure of rights without consent of citizens. They assume the authority to rewrite the basic constitutional contract, to change "the law" at their own will. At yet other interfaces, these institutions take on legislative roles and effectively displace representative assemblies in making decisions on "public good"—decisions which can in no way be derived from individual evaluations in some quasi-contractual setting. Democracy can generate quite enough of its own excesses even if decision-makers adhere strictly to constitutional norms for behavior. When these norms are themselves subjected to arbitrary and unpredictable change, by decision-makers who are not representative of the citizenry, the omnivorousness of the state becomes much more threatening.

It is more difficult to measure the growth of Leviathan in these dimensions than in the quantifiable budgetary dimensions of the productive state. There is a complementary relationship here, but the two are conceptually independent. An interfering federal judiciary, along with an irresponsible executive, could exist even when budget sizes remain relatively small. Conversely, as noted, relatively large budgets might be

administered responsibly with a judicial system that embodies nonarbi-
trary decision-making. Historically, we observe a conjunction—relatively
large and growing budgets along with increasingly irresponsible interpretations of law. Essentially the same philosophical orientation informs
both extensions of governmental powers. Burgeoning budgets are an
outgrowth of the American liberal tradition which assigns to government
the instrumental role in creating the "good society." The arrogance of
the administrative and, particularly, the judicial elite in changing basic
law by fiat arises from the same source. If the "good society" can first
be defined, and, second, produced by governmental action, then men
finding themselves in positions of discretionary power, whether in legislative, executive, or judicial roles, are placed under some moral obligation to move society toward the defined ideal.

There is a fundamental philosophical confusion here, one that must
be removed if Leviathan is to be contained. A "good society" defined
independently of the choices of its members, *all* members, is contradictory with a social order derived from individual values. In the postconstitutional stage of contract, those outcomes are "good" that emerge
from the choices of men, in both the private and the public sector. The
"goodness" of an outcome is evaluated on procedural criteria applied
to the means of its attainment and not on substantive criteria intrinsic
to such outcome. The politician, who represents the citizenry, however
crudely and imperfectly, seeks to attain consensus, to find acceptable
compromises among conflicting individual and group demands. He is
not engaged in a search for some one "true" judgment, and he is not
properly behaving if he seeks to further some well-defined ideal drawn
from the brains of his academic mentors. The judge is in a distinctly
different position. He does seek "truth," not compromise. But he seeks
truth only in the limits of constitutional structure. He looks for, and
finds, "the law." He does not make new rules. To the extent that he
tries deliberately to modify the basic constitutional contract so as to
make it conform to his independently defined ideals, he errs in his
whole understanding of his social function, even more than the elected
politician who seeks the liberal grail.

False philosophical precepts that are so pervasively held cannot be
readily overthrown. If our Leviathan is to be controlled, politicians and
judges must come to have respect for limits. Their continued efforts
to use assigned authority to impose naively formulated constructs of
social order must produce a decline in their own standing. If leaders
have no sense of limits, what must be expected of those who are limited
by their ukases? If judges lose respect for law, why must citizens respect
judges? If personal rights are subjected to arbitrary confiscation at the
hands of the state, why must individuals refrain from questioning the
legitimacy of government?

Leviathan may maintain itself by force; the Hobbesian sovereign may be the only future. But alternative futures may be described and dreamed, and government may not yet be wholly out of hand. From current disillusionment can come constructive consensus on a new structure of checks and balances.

[14]

Excerpt from *The Limits of Liberty: Between Anarchy and Leviathan*, 166–80

10 BEYOND PRAGMATISM: PROSPECTS FOR CONSTITUTIONAL REVOLUTION

The ethical problem of social change seems to me to have been seriously if not fatally misconceived in the age of liberalism. It must be viewed in terms of *social*-ethical self-legislation, which involves a creative process at a still "higher" (and intellectually more elusive) level than that of individual self-legislation. It is a matter of social choice, and must rest on the conception of society as a real unit, a moral community in the literal sense. It is intellectually impossible to believe that the individual can have any influence to speak of, or especially any predictable influence, on the course of history. But it seems to me that to regard this as an ethical difficulty involves a complete misconception of the social-moral problem or that of the individual as a member of a society striving for moral progress as a society. I find it impossible to give meaning to an ethical obligation on the part of the individual to improve society.

The disposition of an individual, under liberalism, to take upon himself such a responsibility seems to be an exhibition of intellectual and *moral* conceit. It is sheer love of power and self-aggrandizement; it is *un*-ethical. Ethical-social change must come about through a genuine moral consensus among individuals meeting on a level of genuine equality and mutuality and not with any one in the role of cause and the rest in that of effect, of one as the "potter" and others as "clay."

> Frank H. Knight,
> "Intellectual Confusion
> on Morals and Economics"

The analysis of this book is intended to be relevant for America's third century, for the emerging issues that challenge the viability of traditional institutions of social order. Despite disclaimers to the contrary, the American constitutional structure is in disarray. It is time for the social scientist or social philosopher to go beyond the manipulation of elegant but ultimately irrelevant models. He must ask the question: What sort of social order can man create for himself at this stage in his history?

There are two distinct approaches that may be taken in answering this question. The first involves basic structural diagnosis, which is perhaps the best descriptive appellation for my own efforts in this book. The existing as well as the possible institutions for human choice must be analyzed in terms of criteria for promoting "improvement," defined largely by potential agreement and independently of advance descrip-

Beyond Pragmatism: Prospects for Constitutional Revolution 167

tion. The second approach involves description of the "good society" independently either of that which exists or of the means through which attainment might be secured.

Despite the urging of several critics, I have not gone beyond the restrictions imposed by the first approach. I have not tried to present in detail my own private proposals for constitutional reform; I do not offer a description of the "good society," even on my own terms. In part my reluctance is based on comparative advantage. As I noted earlier, many social philosophers seem willing to essay the second of the two tasks suggested, with neither recognition of nor interest in the first. This concentration, in its turn, often promotes intellectual and moral arrogance. An attempt to describe the social good in detail seems to carry with it an implied willingness to impose this good, independently of observed or prospective agreement among persons. By contrast, my natural proclivity as an economist is to place ultimate value on process or procedure, and by implication to define as "good" that which emerges from agreement among free men, independently of intrinsic evaluation of the outcome itself.

The social philosopher who takes either of these two roles must reject the pragmatism that has characterized the American mind-set on social policy reforms. The time has come to move beyond this, to think about and to make an attempt at reconstruction of the basic constitutional order itself. My analysis suggests that there are structural flaws in the sociopolitical system which can scarcely be remedied by superficial tampering. Acceptance of this, as diagnosis, becomes a necessary starting point in the search for alternatives. I am convinced that the social interrelationships that emerge from continued pragmatic and incremental situational response, informed by no philosophical precepts, is neither sustainable nor worthy of man's best efforts. History need not be a random walk in sociopolitical space, and I have no faith in the efficacy of social evolutionary process. The institutions that survive and prosper need not be those that maximize man's potential. Evolution may produce social dilemma as readily as social paradise.[1]

"Dilemma" is explicitly used here in order to draw attention to an interaction that has been exhaustively analyzed in modern game theory. In its most familiar setting, the "prisoners' dilemma," the independent utility-maximizing behavior on the part of each party generates results that are desired by neither party, results that can, with behavioral coordination, be changed to the benefit of all parties within the interaction. In the terminology of economic theory, the results of independent behavior are nonoptimal or inefficient in the Pareto sense; changes can be made which will improve the lot of some without harming anyone.

The generality and ubiquitousness of the social dilemma force concentration on a dual decision process. As we have noted, even an isolated

Crusoe may find it helpful to adopt and abide by rules that constrain his choice behavior. In a social setting, the duality is essential. Men must choose mutually agreeable rules for behavior, while retaining for themselves alternatives for choice within these rules. Recognition of the distinction between what I have called constitutional and postconstitutional contract is an elementary but necessary first step toward escape from the social dilemma that confronts man in the Hobbesian jungle, whether this be in its pristine form or in its more sophisticated modern variants.

The costs of rules, when the alternative is their absence, are measured in the losses that are anticipated to occur because of the defined inability to respond to situations in a strictly short-term utility-maximizing manner.[2] These costs may be dominated by the promised benefits of stability which will allow for planning at the moment when rules are chosen. Once adopted, however, adherence to the rules involves a different choice and a different cost. Because utility is maximized through unilateral violation of existing rules, adherence or obedience to the terms of contract cannot be secured costlessly. This applies to all members of the social group, not just to those who are observed to be the most likely violators. This suggests the necessity of some enforcement structure.[3]

Almost inadvertently, the discussion points toward the derivation of a logical basis for constitutional contract, a basis which involves the demonstration that all members of a community secure gains when rights are defined, when rules imposing behavioral limits are settled, and when enforcement institutions are established. On this, however, no quarrel should arise; even the ardent romantic revolutionary would prefer almost any order when the alternative is pristine Hobbesian jungle. The problem worthy of attention is quite different. Given an existing constitutional-legal order, as it is actually enforced and respected, how can changes be made so as to improve the positions of all or substantially all members of the social group? History produces an evolving status quo, and predictions can be made about alternative futures. If we do not like the particular set of alternatives that seem promised by nonrevolutionary situational response, we are obliged to examine basic structural improvements.

This is the definitional basis for the term "constitutional revolution," which may appear to be internally contradictory. I refer to basic, nonincremental changes in the structural order of the community, changes in the complex set of rules that enable men to live with one another, changes that are sufficiently dramatic to warrant the label "revolutionary." At the same time, however, it is useful to restrict discussion to "constitutional" limits, by which I mean that structural changes should be those upon which all members in the community might conceptually agree. Little, if any, improvement in the lot of modern man is promised by imposition of new rules by some men on other men. Nonconstitutional revolution invites counterrevolution in a continuing zero- or negative-sum power sequence.

If there exist potential structural changes in legal order which might command acceptance by all members of the society, the status quo represents a social dilemma in the strict game-theoretic terminology. Even if we consider ourselves far removed from the genuine Hobbesian jungle, where life is brutish and short, the status quo contains within it elements or features that are in principle equivalent. Life in the here and now may be more brutish than need be, and certainly more nasty. If after examination and analysis, no such potential for change exists, the legal-constitutional order that we observe must be judged to be Pareto optimal, despite the possible presence of discontent among specific members in the body politic.

A central hypothesis of this book is that basic constitutional reform, even revolution, may be needed. The existing legal order may have lost its claim to efficiency, or, in a somewhat different sense, to legitimacy. At the very least, it seems to be time that genuine constitutional change be considered seriously.

INSTITUTIONAL-CONSTITUTIONAL CHANGE AND PRAGMATIC POLICY RESPONSE

The distinction between institutional-constitutional reform and the enactment or adoption of specific policy correctives for blatantly unsatisfactory situations as they emerge must be understood first by working scholars, then by politicians and by the citizenry. Pragmatism has been hailed with approbation as the American behavioral characteristic. When something has gone wrong, our response is to fix it up with baling wire and to go on about our business. This baling-wire syndrome presumes, however, that the underlying structure or mechanism is sound and itself not in need of repair or replacement. But, eventually, baling-wire repairs fail, and more fundamental change becomes necessary. When such a stage is reached, continuation of the established response pattern may create more problems than it resolves.

"Politics," by which I mean governmental action, notably federal governmental action, has been the social analogue to baling wire. The identification of a "social need," whether this be real or manufactured, has come to suggest, almost simultaneously, a federal program. Social progress has been measured by the quantity of legislation, and our assemblies are deemed to be political failures when new programs are lacking. Properly interpreted, the succession of New Deal, Fair Deal,

New Frontier, Great Society, and New Federalism formats represents the pragmatic and essentially nonideological working of American democratic process. Little or no attention has been paid to the possible interlinkage of program with program, to the ability of the underlying structural system to sustain the growing pressures put upon it, to the questions of aggregate size and scope for political activity.

There have been ideological supports for the pragmatist policy directions, but these have not really informed the attitudes of practicing politicians or their constituents. Even without John Dewey, and perhaps even without either Marxian or non-Marxian socialism, the American policy history might have been much the same. The faith in politics exhibited by twentieth-century man, at least until the 1960s, stems ultimately from his loss of faith in God, accompanied by an ignorance about the effective working of organizational alternatives. Eighteenth- and early nineteenth-century men seem to have possessed greater wisdom, but skepticism is suggested even here. Perhaps their judgments were based on a closer observation of governments, and their negative attitudes may have reflected not so much a faith in the nongovernmental alternative as their rejection of statist attempts at "solution."

There is, nonetheless, a fundamental difference between the approach taken by the philosophers of the eighteenth century and that which I have referred to as the pragmatic or incremental political response to issues that emerge. The difference is methodological, in that the earlier emphasis was on structural or institutional change, not on the particulars of programs. Adam Smith sought to free the economy from the fetters of mercantilist controls; he did not propose that the specific goals of policy be laid down in advance. He did not attack the failures of governmental instruments in piecemeal, pragmatic fashion; he attacked in a far more comprehensive and constitutional sense. He tried to demonstrate that, by removing effective governmental restrictions on trade, results would emerge that would be judged better by all concerned. Precisely because of this comprehensiveness, this concentration on structural-institutional change, Adam Smith deservedly won acclaim as the father of political economy. He and his compatriots proposed genuine "constitutional revolution," and their proposals were, in large part, adopted over the course of a half-century.

The triumph of laissez-faire was achieved because intellectual and political leaders came to accept a new *principle* for social order, a principle that enabled them to rise above the narrow and short-sighted pragmatic vision that must accompany analytical ignorance. The principle was that of ordered anarchy: a regime described by well-defined individual rights and by freedom of and enforcement of voluntary contracts. An understanding of this principle enabled man to conceptualize a social process that was orderly and efficient *without* the detailed direction of a centralized decision-maker, *without* a necessary major role for governmental action beyond that of the strictly protective state. The importance of conversion to a new organizing principle cannot be overemphasized. It was this conversion that facilitated what can only be judged as a genuine constitutional revolution in Britain. Adam Smith and his colleagues could not have been successful had they chosen to attack the previously existing order on a pragmatic, policy-by-policy basis. The shift in vision was essential, the shift that established new benchmarks against which departures might be measured.

Socialist critics were successful in identifying particular flaws in the conceptually ideal order of laissez-faire, as well as in its practicable counterparts. These critics did not, however, offer an alternative organizing principle that was even remotely comparable in intellectual appeal. Marxian doctrine is characterized by an absence of analytical description of society "after the revolution." Later attempts to model the working of socialist order amounted to a translation of laissez-faire precepts, almost in a literal sense. In practice, regimes organized under socialist rubrics are acknowledged to be bureaucratic monstrosities.

Because of the negative impact on the laissez-faire principle exercised by socialist ideas, however, the pragmatically generated erosion of the minimal government principle achieved intellectual-ideological respectability. The central organizing principle that dominated early nineteenth-century thinking, one that embodied a vision of viable society with minimal government direction, was gradually undermined in particularistic stages. Failures were first identified and acknowledged by intellectually honest men. Following this, corrections were proposed, corrections that almost always took the institutional form of governmental action. Intellectual controversy and political debate shifted away from concentration on alternative principles for social organization and toward specific policy choices in a situational context. Social scientists and/or social philosophers abandoned attempts to examine large-scale institutional differences, and they came to look upon their own functional roles as particularistic critics of the existing structure. Welfare economics, in its twentieth-century gloss, became a theory of *market* failure.

It should not have been at all surprising that this setting proved to be highly conducive to very rapid growth in the size and scope of the public or governmental sector. Governmental correctives to presumed particular flaws in the operation of markets were considered piecemeal and independently one from the other. More important, these correctives were presumed to work ideally once they were introduced. Because there existed no principle or vision of the process of governmental operation, the naive presumption was made that intention was equivalent to result. Program was piled on top of program, with little or no attention being paid to the effects of such aggregation on the supporting structure, on the principle of constitutional-legal order itself.[4]

By the middle of the twentieth century, American pragmatism seemed to reign supreme, and there was almost no talk about fundamental revolutionary change, either in the academy or in the streets.

CONFUSION AND CHALLENGE

This pattern changed dramatically and unpredictably in the 1960s. There were several causal factors. Scholars in the academic groves commenced, as early as the late 1940s and early 1950s, to advance simplified theories or models of democratic process, models that must have given pause to those who thought seriously of implementing socialist ideals. Governmental action which emerged from majoritarian institutions, held to be the essence of democracy, need not produce "public good." And perhaps even more damaging was the intellectually formidable proof that such action need not itself be internally consistent.[5] Furthermore, it came to be recognized that governmental programs, once enacted, were necessarily administered by bureaucratic personnel, and theories of behavior were developed on the elementary presumption that bureaucrats are ordinary men.[6] Conceptually, the base was laid for the emergence of theories of *government* failure that are on all fours with the more familiar theories of market failure.

These essentially intellectual developments were accompanied and overshadowed in public consciousness by accumulating evidence that governmental nostrums do not effect miracles. By a sequence of events, collective decision-makers were led to enact programs which found their origins, not in the demands of citizens, but in the brains of academicians and the slogans of politicians. Unfortunately, many citizens, and some politicians, expected more results than the institutional structure could possibly deliver. "New Frontier" slogans were too hurriedly translated into "Great Society" realities, precisely at a time when the public began to lose its tolerance for governmental wastage. Citizen reaction was acerbated by an activist judiciary, whose behavior indicated widespread departures from any protective-state limits, departures that were seen as such by the public at large. These legislative and judicial excesses were more than matched by the independence exerted by the executive branch of the United States government in foreign affairs, notably in the Viet Nam involvement. The observed failures, at all levels of the federal government, combined to foster an antigovernmental attitude that was perhaps unique in American history.

The implications for policy were, however, clouded by the accompanying behavioral revolution of the 1960s, itself motivated in part by the same forces. As governmental failures came to be more widely acknowledged, personal respect for "law" deteriorated. Politics and politicians became more blatantly profit-seeking, and pressures for governmental handouts accelerated. As the federal courts were seen to "make" law in their own idealized image, by natural extension individuals came to think of their own private criteria for discriminating between "good" and "bad" law. Initially motivated by wholly admirable precepts for achieving racial justice, unlawful demonstrations were mounted against the operation of "bad laws" generally, demonstrations that were condoned ex post by judicial failure to enforce existing legal norms. The limited manpower needs for a limited war guaranteed that conscription could be and would be judged to be unjust and highly discriminatory. Protest came to be the order of the day in the late years of the decade. Venerable institutions that had long survived by adherence to unwritten behavioral rules, workable ordered anarchies such as universities, proved to be exceedingly vulnerable to disruption once voluntary respect for the rules broke down. An inability and an unwillingness to defend established "rights" could mean only that there was a genuine shift in the basic structure of control.

These confusions of the 1960s were compounded as the nonprotesting citizenry called for "law and order," overlooking the governmental origins of the turmoil. The law-abiding citizen failed to understand his own plight. He observed apparent erosion in public capital; he read about and sometimes suffered from rising crime rates; he saw behavioral changes that he considered to represent losses of personal respect and tolerance. He demanded "law and order," which meant increased rather than decreased collectivization of society. He was, in this stance, trying to evoke response on the part of the protective state, the external enforcer, and he was asking that this state reestablish the apparent claims embodied in constitutional contract.

The state cannot, however, wave some magic wand and produce instant improvements. If individual rights are in some disarray, better and more effective enforcement requires more investigation and more severe punishment for offenders. But here the punishment dilemma emerges. The selfsame citizen who demands enforcement may be quite unwilling to allow for the increased severity or certainty of punishment that efficient enforcement may require. The state responds by moving along those dimensions of adjustment which generate minimal feedbacks. It hires more policemen, and keeps punishment levels stationary or declining. It responds to prison riots by rewarding the inmates with better facilities. The costs are borne by the general taxpayer and the size of government grows.

The citizen responds to George Wallace's attacks on the bureaucratic superstructure. He rejects claims of legitimacy on the part of agents of the state, and he senses increasing insecurity against governmental domination. At the same time, however, he is quite unwilling to yield up his own share in the special benefits that he thinks only government can provide. The American suburbanite who is most vehement in his opposition to cross-city bussing of his children to publicly financed schools is unwilling even to question the right of the collectivity to levy taxes, coercively, on all families in order to finance the schooling of children for some families (and, in the process, to subsidize the production of more children in an overcrowded world).

INTELLECTUAL BANKRUPTCY

In sociopolitical matters, the 1970s can be described as an era of intellectual bankruptcy. Theoretical welfare economists continue to develop sophisticated demonstrations of market failures; public choice theorists, who have been charged with dabbling in "welfare politics," match the welfare economists with their own demonstrations of governmental failures. The theorems of the economists are put to alleged practical usage in the discussion of pollution-environmental issues that occupies policy debates. The "solutions" that are proposed, however, involve widening the sphere of bureaucratic control rather than shrinking it. The libertarians are scarcely preferred over their liberal counterparts. They score effectively when they point to the analytically demonstrable and empirically verified flaws in the collectivist alternatives. Positively, however, they can suggest little other than a shift of organizational structure toward the marketplace. Both liberals and libertarians alike presume implicitly that their task is to offer advice to some nonexistent but benevolent wisdom that will accept rational argument.

The facts are different. Both markets and governments fail, and there is no such benevolent wisdom. The man of the 1970s is trapped in his own dilemma. He recognizes that the "grand alternatives," laissez-faire and socialism, are moribund, and that revival is not to be predicted.[7] What modern man does not recognize, in either an intellectual or an intuitive sense, is that the pragmatic alternative is equally suspect, and that viable social order may be seriously threatened by long-continued failure to consider his situation systematically and nonincrementally. In this as in other aspects of his life, modern man seems to be in need of sociopolitical "conversion" to a new conception of society. Without such a conversion, the constitutional revolution that may be necessary for survival cannot take place.

In this respect at least, the modern radical revolutionaries may be correct; improvement may well require changes in the system, not in the personnel that man it and not through peripheral adjustments. But if both markets and governments fail, what is the organizational alternative? Throughout the ages men have dreamed of character ideals descriptive of the person who acts out of love for others or duty toward his fellow men. There is a role for ethics in social order. It is, however, extremely dangerous to generalize ideally personal behavior into the basis for social organization, taking the route of William Godwin and other of the romantic anarchists. Regardless of the organizing principle, the larger the proportion of "good" men in the community, the "better" should be the community, provided the terms are defined in accordance with individualistic precepts. But it is folly to expect *all* men to be behaviorally transformed. Yet this becomes the minimal requirement for an acceptably orderly society without organization.

Social order may be imposed by a despotic regime, through either an individual ruler or through an elite ruling group. Despotism may be the only organizational alternative to the political structure that we observe. In which case, those who claim no special rights to rule had best judge existing institutions in a different light. This would amount to a counsel of despair, however, and there may be alternatives worthy of consideration.

THE CONTRACTARIAN REVIVAL

It is in this respect that the modern contractarian revival, stimulated largely by the publication of John Rawls's book, *A Theory of Justice* (1971), is highly encouraging. In this work, Rawls made no attempt to lay down precepts or principles of justice on the basis of any externally derived ethical norms, utilitarian or otherwise. Instead, he advanced the individualistic conception of "justice as fairness." Those principles are just which emerge from the unanimous agreement of men participating in a setting where each places himself behind a veil of ignorance concerning his own position in postcontractual sequence. No man counts for more than any other, and no precepts for justice are defined independently of this conceptualized contractual setting. Unfortunately, in my view, Rawls went further than this and attempted to identify those precepts that might be predicted to emerge. In this extension, Rawls was, perhaps, responding to the pressures of critics who demand specific reform proposals. And, predictably, it is this aspect of his work that is drawing attention away from his more basic contribution, which is the relationship of justice to the outcome of the contractual *process* itself.

My efforts in this book are simultaneously more and less ambitious than those of Rawls, or some of my own earlier works.[8] Rawls is content to discuss the emergence of potential agreement on principles of justice from an idealized contractual setting within which men are led to behave as moral equals. He does not discuss the critically important bridge between such an idealized setting and that within which any discussion of basic structural rearrangement might, in fact, take place. In this respect, my approach is more ambitious. I have tried to examine the prospects for genuine contractual renegotiation among persons who are not equals at the stage of deliberation and who are not artificially made to behave as if they are, either through general adherence to internal ethical norms or through the introduction of uncertainty about post-contract positions. It is for this reason that the return to the conceptual emergence of contract from Hobbesian anarchy has been necessary to develop my argument.

In another respect that has been noted, however, my efforts are much less ambitious than those of Rawls. He identifies the principles of justice that he predicts to emerge from his idealized contractual setting. Although perhaps this was not Rawls's specific intent, these principles may become the basis of proposals for specific institutional changes, which may then be debated in the pragmatically oriented arena of day-to-day politics. I take no such step. I do not try to identify either the "limits of liberty" or the set of principles that might be used to define such limits.

The "principles" that might be said to be implied in this book are that the multidimensional tradeoff between liberty and law should be recognized, that the interdependence among different laws as they constrain individual liberties should be reckoned with, that continued misunderstanding and confusion above the separate constitutional and postconstitutional stages of collective action leads to disaster. The reform that I seek lies first of all in attitudes, in ways of thinking about social interaction, about political institutions, about law and liberty. If men will only commence to think in contractarian terms, if they will think of the state in the roles as defined, and if they will recognize individual rights as existent in the status quo, I should not at all be insistent on particulars. It is as if a less ambitious John Rawls might have limited his concern to ways that men think about justice.

POLITICAL AND PUBLIC PHILOSOPHY

The contractarian revival suggests that there may be widespread agreement among scholars that a renewed discussion of basic problems of social order is desirable. To the extent that this revival continues, the groundwork may be laid for a rebirth of political and legal philosophy in our institutions of higher learning. To the extent that contractarian precepts emerge victorious in this discourse, the ways of thinking that I have called for here may come into being. The tradeoffs between law and liberty may be recognized, and the dual role played by the state more fully understood, along with some appreciation for the problem of keeping collective action within limits. General acceptance by working scholars is perhaps a necessary prelude to acceptance of such ideas by a frustrated public.

The emergence of a modified public philosophy in this respect should not be beyond the bounds of hope. Both the ideas and the events of the preceding decades have created a potentially receptive attitude in the ordinary man. He has lost his faith in government as it operates, but he remains unwilling to jettison the governmental crutch. He searches silently for a philosophy that might offer him some reconciliation and that might partially restore his social faith.

If this were all there is to it, reform of basic constitutional structure might be, relatively speaking, an easy task. Judges would cease legislating and stick to adjudicating conflicts, enforcing laws, and imposing punishments. Legislators would cease using the political mechanism to make uncompensated transfers of rights among individuals and groups. Citizens would not seek private profits, individually or in groups, from resort to the governmental sector, and they would refrain from supporting political entrepreneurs who promise to deliver such profits. Those who observe and discuss governmental processes, be they journalists or professors, would cease measuring social progress by the amount of legislation enacted, by the sheer size of the budget account. Individual liberty, as an independent value, is inversely correlated with these familiar scalars, and this would be given its proper place among other social values in the attitudinal revolution which I am suggesting here. Individuals would recognize that government, the state, is ultimately subject to their own control. They would no longer accept, implicitly, the positivist view that the state, and only the state, can define and redefine individual rights, and, by inference, its own. Democracy remains conceptually possible only if individuals view government in the consent paradigm.

INDIVIDUAL RIGHTS IN DEMOCRACY

On cursory examination, the attitudinal shift that I have outlined seems to be in accord with straightforward laissez-faire precepts. The orthodox libertarian would find no apparent difficulty in associating himself with the position suggested. When the level of discussion is brought back one stage, however, a new set of issues emerge which have been glossed over in the traditional conceptions. Too often, the libertarian, like his socialist counterpart, discusses reforms under the "as if" assumption that he is simply advising some benevolent despot who will lay down the proposed changes, with little or no reference to the consent of participating parties. With this political presupposition, it becomes relatively easy for the market-oriented libertarian to neglect any analysis of the existing distribution of rights and claims among persons. But unless these rights and claims are first identified and agreed on, what do the terms used above mean? What is an uncompensated transfer? What qualifies as profit-seeking through the use of the political mechanism?

Once such questions as these are raised, elements of the social dilemma come to light that are too readily ignored when we remain at the level of philosophy. Practical operational significance can be placed on the precepts only when a major condition is fulfilled: the agreement of all members of the social group on the assignment of individual rights that exists in the status quo. So long as there is continuing disagreement on just who has the right to do what with what and to do what to whom, the attitudinal shift suggested above may remain operationally empty.

A necessary step in the process of genuine constitutional revolution is a *consensual redefinition* of individual rights and claims. Many of the interventions of government have emerged precisely because of ambiguities in the definition of individual rights. The central issue here concerns the reconciliation of nominally expressed claims by individuals to private property, to human as well as nonhuman capital, and the equalitarian distribution of the "public property rights" through the voting franchise. Whether treated as value or as fact, modern democracy incorporates universal adult suffrage. From this elementary base, several questions arise. How can the poor man (with "poor" defined in terms of private-property claims) exert his putative claims to the wealth nominally held by the rich man except through exercise of his voting franchise? Acknowledging this, how can the rich man (or the libertarian philosopher) expect the poor man to accept any new constitutional order that severely restricts the scope for fiscal transfers among groups? Consensual support for such restriction could scarcely be predicted to be forthcoming. This need not, however, suggest that all attempts at renegotiation of the basic constitutional structure should be abandoned before they commence. There may well exist potential gains-from-trade for all participants, but the existing as well as the prospective distribution of rights and claims must inform the bargaining process. The rich man, who may sense the vulnerability of his nominal claims in the existing state of affairs and who may, at the same time, desire that the range of collective or state action be restricted, can potentially agree on a once-and-for-all or quasi-permanent transfer of wealth to the poor man, a transfer made in exchange for the latter's agreement to a genuinely new constitution that will overtly limit governmentally directed fiscal transfers.

Consider a highly simplified two-person example. A rich man, A, nominally owns an asset that yields $100,000 in annual income, which is taxed at 50 percent, leaving a posttax income of $50,000. A poor man, B, owns no assets, and earns $5,000 annually from his labor services. The "government" (here treated as exogenous) collects taxes exclusively from the rich man, for a total revenue of $50,000, which it uses for a variety of projects, with varying degrees of efficiency. The benefits accrue in such a manner as to provide the rich man with a benefit value of $10,000, and the poor man with a benefit value of $20,000. Can the "social contract" be renegotiated with gains to both parties? Suppose that the rich man offers to transfer to the poor man one-third of his asset, with a gross income of $33,333, in exchange for the latter's agreement to reduce the size of the governmental budget to zero. The rich man, under this arrangement, retains a new real income of $66,667, higher than he retained under the previous arrangement ($60,000). The poor man, B, secures a real income of $38,333 (own earnings plus governmental benefits) higher than he secured under the other arrangement ($25,000). Both parties are made better off under the postulated terms of the new contract.[9]

Potential agreement might be secured even if the present value of claims is not increased in a strictly measurable sense. If the rich man, A, anticipates onerous tax burdens in the future, even if these do not currently exist, he may agree to the sort of rearrangement suggested. Or, more dramatically, if either or both parties fear nonconstitutional revolution, during which all claims are abrogated, agreement may well be forthcoming on terms that do not seem mutually beneficial under direct measurements. There seems little doubt that, at least conceptually, distributional aspects of the renegotiation can be settled.[10]

THE CREATION OF RIGHTS

Assume that the problems of income and wealth distribution among persons could be satisfactorily settled in a renegotiated constitutional contract, one that would redefine individual rights and reduce the scope for collectively determined coercive activity. Would this basic step be sufficient to allow for the implementation of laissez-faire principles? If property rights should be redefined so that distributional results are acceptable to all participants, would the operations of private markets, with minimal collective enforcement of contracts, be sufficient to insure efficient outcomes, to remove the social dilemma? A negative answer is immediately suggested with reference to the many problems summarized under the rubrics: congestion, pollution, environmental quality. Here the issues are specifically not distributional, or at least not exclusively or predominantly so. The alleged failures of existing social arrangements in many of these situations cannot legitimately be attributed to markets or to government, if we think of these as alternative processes of postconstitutional contracting. The social dilemma reflected in apparent results here stems from incomplete constitutional agreement, from first-stage failure to define and to limit individual rights. Resolution of this dilemma lies not in any explicit redistribution of rights among persons, not in some reshuffling of claims, but in the *creation* of newly defined rights in areas where none now exist, at least none that can offer a basis for predictability and exchange. In essence, congestion and pollution describe settings analogous to that generalized in Hobbes's model of anarchy. Individuals find themselves in conflict over the use of scarce resources, with results that are desired by no one because there is no agreed-on and enforced set of rights. The constitutional revolution suggested involves mutual agreement on those restrictions on behavior that are required to achieve tolerably efficient outcomes.

To the extent that there is mutuality of gain in prospect, agreement should be conceptually attainable. The status quo provides a reasonable base from which limitations can be measured. "Congestion on the common" can be eliminated by guaranteeing to each participant a level of well-being at least as high as that which he secures in the dilemma of commonality. Improvement is precisely analogous to that which is achieved through the mutual disarmament contract which first enables man to leap from the brutish dilemma of Hobbes.

Idealized constitutional revolution here would require that limits be placed on behavior with respect to *all* scarce resources, whether this be in the form of assigning individual ownership titles or of imposing restrictive behavioral limits under common titles. Much of the dilemma summarized under the pollution rubric finds its origins in the presumption made by the founders of our constitutional-legal order that certain resources were in permanent abundance. Growth and technological advance have converted once-free resources into scarce resources, but existing property assignments have failed to keep pace. The resulting dilemma was predictable. This alone suggests that genuine constitutional change must take place as population grows, as technology develops, and as demand shifts through time.

CONCLUSION

The alternative that falls between anarchy on the one hand and Leviathan on the other must be articulated, analyzed, and, finally, made into models amenable to public comprehension. As an organizing principle, laissez-faire is too closely associated with the rights of property in the historically determined status quo, defined in nominal independence of the contingency claims represented in modern democracy. Socialism is the throughway to Leviathan. The failure of these two grand alternatives need not, however, dispel all of the Enlightenment dreams. The vision of the eighteenth-century philosophers which enabled them to describe a social order that did not require the centralized direction of man over man may yet stir excitement. *Free relations among free men*—this precept of ordered anarchy can emerge as principle when successfully renegotiated social contract puts "mine and thine" in a newly defined structural arrangement and when the Leviathan that threatens is placed within new limits.

[15]

KYKLOS, Vol. 35 – 1982 – Fasc. 4, 575–602

RENT SEEKING: A SURVEY

ROBERT D. TOLLISON*

I. INTRODUCTION

The purpose of this essay is to survey the emerging theory of the rent-seeking society. The initial problem is to clarify terminology. Rent is a venerable concept in economics. Defined as a return in excess of a resource owner's opportunity cost, economic rent has played a prominent role in the history of economic analysis ('corn is not high because rent is paid, rent is paid because corn is high'). In this sense it is a fair guess that most economists would consider 'rent seeking' to be equivalent to 'profit seeking', whereby it is meant that the expectation of excess returns motivates value-increasing activities in the economy. Such excess returns (positive *and* negative) are typically viewed as short-lived (quasi-rents) because competition will drive them to normal levels.

The competitive dissipation of rents, however, is not what is meant by 'rent seeking'. Rents emanate from two sources. They arise *naturally* in the price system by, for example, shifts in demand and supply curves. The pursuit of rents under these circumstances is the sense in which rent seeking is equivalent to profit seeking. Rents can also be contrived *artificially* through, for example, government action. The fact that rents are contrived, however, does not mean that they are exempt from competition, and this is where rent seeking comes into play.

* Federal Trade Commission and Clemson University, Washington D.C. – Thanks go to JAMES BUCHANAN, ROBERT MCCORMICK and DENNIS MUELLER for helpful comments. The usual caveat applies.

ROBERT D. TOLLISON

Consider the example of monopoly rents. The typical discussion depicts such returns as a transfer from consumers to a monopolist. Treated as such, monopoly rents embody no social costs. Yet if the process by which monopoly rents are contrived is subject to competition (*e.g.*, lobbying), the analytical fiction of these rents as a pure transfer vanishes because resources spent in the pursuit of a transfer are *wasted* from society's point of view. These expenditures add nothing to social product (they are zero-sum at best), and their opportunity cost constitutes lost production to society.

The theory of rent seeking involves the study of how people compete for artifically contrived transfers. Like the rest of economic theory, rent seeking has normative and positive elements. Normative rent-seeking theory refers to the specification and estimation of the costs of rent-seeking activities to the economy. Are contrived rents dissipated by competition to capture them? Are they exactly dissipated by competitive rent seeking, or are there imperfections in rent-seeking processes such that expenditures to capture monopoly positions either exceed or fall short of the rents that inhere in them? What role does the consumer play in the theory of the rent-seeking society? What is the domain of rent-seeking behavior, that is, is government required for rent-seeking theory to be applicable or can rents be contrived and dissipated in private settings?

The positive side of rent-seeking theory is directed to the question of what explains the sources of contrived rents in a society. For example, in normal textbook presentations monopoly is introduced by drawing a downward sloping demand curve and its associated marginal revenue curve. The effects of monopoly are explained, but the issue of why some industries consist of price-takers and others consist of price-searchers is largely begged. Positive rent-seeking theory goes behind the facade of microeconomic theory and attempts to explain why some sectors of the economy are sheltered and some not.

This essay will survey the economic theory of rent seeking. In Section II, a more detailed discussion of the differences between rent seeking and profit seeking is given. In Section III, normative rent-seeking theory and empirical measures are discussed. In Section IV, positive rent-seeking theory is covered. Some concluding remarks are offered in Section V.

576

RENT SEEKING: A SURVEY

II. RENT SEEKING VERSUS PROFIT SEEKING

In economic analysis the definition of economic rent is a payment to a resource owner above the amount his resources could command in their next best alternative use. An economic rent is a receipt in excess of the opportunity cost of a resource. It has been observed that it is not necessary to pay economic rents in order to procure an efficient allocation of resources. This argument, however, is based on a faulty perception of the dynamics of the competitive market process. Over time, the presence of economic rents provides the incentive for resource owners to seek out more profitable allocations of their resources. When competition is viewed as a dynamic, value-creating, evolutionary process, the role of economic rents in stimulating entrepreneurial decisions and in prompting an efficient allocation of resources is crucial [KIRZNER 1973]. 'Rent seeking' or 'profit seeking' in a competitive market order is a normal feature of economic life. The returns of resource owners will be driven to normal levels (on both the intensive and extensive margins) by competitive profit seeking as some resource owners earn positive rents which promote entry and others earn negative rents which cause exit. Profit seeking and economic rents are inherently related to the efficiency of the competitive market process. Such activities drive the competitive price system and create value (*e.g.*, new products) in the economy.

The task at hand is to distinguish what is meant by rent seeking from profit seeking. Consider a simple example in which the king wishes to grant a monopoly right in the production of playing cards. In this case artificial scarcity is created by the state, and as a consequence, monopoly rents are present to be captured by monopolists who seek the king's favor. Normally, these rents are thought of as transfers from playing card consumers to the card monopolist. Yet in the example, this can only be the case if the aspiring monopolists employ no real resources to compete for the monopoly rents. To the extent that real resources are spent to capture monopoly rents in such ways as lobbying, these expenditures create no value from a social point of view. It is this activity of wasting resources in competing for artificially contrived transfers that is called rent seeking.

577

ROBERT D. TOLLISON

If an incipient monopolist hires a lawyer to lobby the king for the monopoly right, the opportunity cost of this lawyer (*e.g.*, the contracts that he does not write while engaged in lobbying) is a social cost of the monopolization process. Moreover, the deflection of lawyers from productive to transfer-seeking pursuits will generate a disequilibrium in the market for lawyers, with the implication that there will be excessive entry into the legal profession. As will be presented in more detail in Section III, such rent-seeking costs must be added to the standard welfare-triangle loss associated with monopoly to obtain an estimate of the total social costs of monopoly and regulation.

'Real' rents are different from 'government' or 'fake' rents because rent seeking has productive implications in the first case but not in the second. Just to drive the point home, consider the following example. The return to professional baseball players includes some (inframarginal) rents which leads young children to play baseball rather than practice the piano. This increases the supply of baseball players tomorrow (because young children practiced today), and the amount and quality of baseball is altered (improved?). In the case of monopoly rents lobbying is the analogy to practicing, and lobbying does not increase output because output is fixed by definition. It is the restricting of output artificially that creates the rents.

Rent seeking is the expenditure of scarce resources to capture an artificially created transfer. The implications of the economic wastefulness of rent-seeking activity are difficult to escape once an artificial scarcity has been created [BUCHANAN 1980a]. At one level the king can allow individuals to compete for the playing card monopoly and waste resources through such activities as bribery. Such outright venality is perhaps the simplest and most readily understood level of rent seeking. At a second level the state could sell the monopoly right to the highest bidder and put the proceeds at the disposal of government officials. In this case the monopoly rents will most likely show up in the wages of state officials, and to capture rents at this level individuals will compete to become civil servants. This competition might be thought of in terms of excess returns to bureaucratic agents where these returns are competed away by excessive expenditures on education to prepare for civil service exami-

RENT SEEKING: A SURVEY

nations [TULLOCK 1980b]. At still another level should the monopoly right be sold to the highest bidder and the resources dispersed through the state budget in terms of expenditure increases and/or tax reductions, rent-seeking costs will be incurred as individuals seek to become members of the groups favored by the tax-expenditure program. Rent-seeking costs are incurred in each case, and only the form that such costs take is influenced by how the government transacts its business in artificially contrived scarcity values.

III. THE WELFARE ANALYSIS OF RENT SEEKING

The welfare analysis of rent seeking concerns the issue of how costly such activities are to the economy. It was, in fact, through an effort to assess the nature of these costs that TULLOCK [1967] first analyzed the concept of rent seeking. Subsequent research has concentrated on expanding TULLOCK's theoretical insight and on developing empirical measures of rent-seeking costs.

1. Competitive Rent Seeking

In *Figure 1* a simple monopoly diagram is drawn ($Q_m = \frac{1}{2}Q_c$). This model is sufficient to yield all of the insights generated by competitive rent-seeking theory.

In the standard analysis of monopoly a competitive industry is *costlessly* transformed into a simple monopoly. This analysis is developed as if a snapshot of equilibrium conditions were taken at two instants of time. One photograph reveals P_cQ_c as the market equilibrium and the other P_mQ_m. In this conceptual experiment the welfare cost is the lost consumer surplus given by *ABC*. In its modern form this partial equilibrium analysis was pioneered by HARBERGER [1954], who developed a reduced-form equation for *ABC* and used it to measure the extent of such losses in the U.S. manufacturing sector *circa* 1929. His empirical results showed the welfare loss from monopoly to be a negligible proportion (less than 1 percent) of GNP. By modifying the assumptions underlying the reduced-form for *ABC* (*e.g.*, the elasticity of demand), a variety of subsequent estimates of welfare losses from monopoly have been published.

ROBERT D. TOLLISON

Figure 1

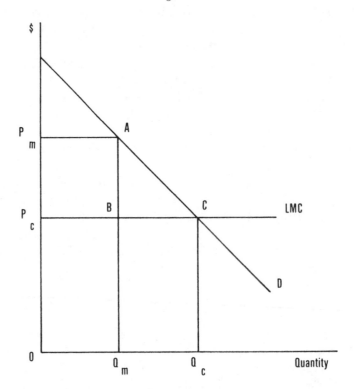

These estimates generally follow the HARBERGER result in not constituting monopoly as an overwhelming social problem[1].

Commenting upon the relatively low estimates of the welfare costs of monopolies and tariffs, MUNDELL [1962, p. 622] observed that 'unless there is a thorough re-examination of the validity of the tools upon which these studies are founded ... someone will in-

1. Since this paper is concerned with rent seeking and not with the conventional welfare loss from monopoly, a review of the efforts to improve upon HARBERGER's original formulation of the latter problem is not pursued here. The interested reader may consult SCHERER [1980, Ch. 17] and the references cited there.

RENT SEEKING: A SURVEY

evitably draw the conclusion that economics has ceased to be important'. TULLOCK rose to this challenge in a 1967 paper in the *Western Economic Journal* (now *Economic Inquiry*)[2]. TULLOCK's insight was simple and straightforward. He argued that any resources spent to capture P_mP_cAB were *also* a social cost of monopoly and that the conventional model of the welfare loss from monopoly, in which monopoly profits are treated as a lump-sum transfer from consumers to the monopolist, was incomplete if potential monopolists spent resources to capture the monopoly right. Since economists typically believe that competition is ever present, the relevance of TULLOCK's argument is apparent – monopoly rights will not generally be exempt from competition and expenditures to capture such contrived transfers are a social cost. The earlier application of this discussion to the employment of lawyer-lobbyist resources by monopoly-seekers need not be repeated here[3].

What can be termed competitive rent seeking implies that the monopoly rents in *Figure 1* (P_cP_mAB) are exactly dissipated. TULLOCK's original formulation of the problem was in these terms, as were the subsequent contributions by KRUEGER [1974] and POSNER [1975]. Consider POSNER's example of how competitive rent seeking might work in practice. A monopoly right is worth $100,000. There are ten risk-neutral bidders among whom there is no collusion. Each will bid $10,000 for the right, an expenditure which cannot be returned if theirs is not the winning bid. The result is that the monopoly returns are dissipated at a social level – $100,000 is spent to capture a transfer of $100,000.

Empirical work with the competitive rent-seeking model is relatively easy to implement. In effect the analyst must estimate the area of a trapezoid rather than just a triangle. Both KRUEGER [1974] and POSNER [1975] have applied variations of such a model to derive estimates of rent-seeking costs. KRUEGER estimated that the value of rents in various parts of the Indian public sector constituted 7.3

2. Also see TULLOCK [1971, 1974] and BROWNING [1974].
3. One immediate implication of TULLOCK's insight, noted by POSNER [1974], is that studies of the distributional effects of monopoly are misleading (*e.g.*, COMANOR and SMILEY [1975]). Monopoly rents are *dissipated* (provided that lawyer-lobbyist earn normal returns) not *transferred*.

ROBERT D. TOLLISON

percent of national income. She also estimated the rents in Turkish import licenses in 1968 to be approximately 15 percent of GNP. POSNER has presented measures of rent-seeking costs in the U.S. economy. He asserts that such costs constitute roughly 3 percent of GNP, an amount which would have to be added to HARBERGER-type losses in the economy to obtain an estimate of the total social costs of monopoly and regulation. Rent-seeking analysis tends to magnify the problem of monopoly over and beyond the traditional measurements made by HARBERGER, rising to the challenge laid down by MUNDELL.

2. Rent Seeking and Consumers

In the usual presentation of the welfare costs of monopoly, whether of the HARBERGER- or the TULLOCK-POSNER-type, the role of the consumer is entirely passive. No account is made of potential consumer activities to counter monopolization efforts by producers. This assumption of economic impotence is typically made on the basis of stylized facts which portray consumers as an unorganized, widely dispersed group without incentive to try to restrain the political monopolization process.

Two things can be said about this non-treatment of consumers. First, as an empirical issue, it is surely wrong. Since the 1960's there has been a rapid growth in the number and size of organized consumer groups; EVANS [1980, p. 5] lists twenty-one major consumer organizations active in the U.S., including such familiar groups as Common Cause, the American Farm Bureau Federation, and the network of NADER organizations. The major groups concentrate on lobbying Congress and state legislatures, but there are also many smaller local groups which regularly appear in such mundane places as rate hearings to lobby for lower prices. Second, to the extent that welfare analysis does not include a role for consumer lobbying, it is lagging behind developments in the positive economic theory of rent seeking. PELTZMAN [1976], for example, offers a model in which a vote-maximizing regulator trades-off industry price and profits between consumer and producer forces. This formulation is squarely based on the idea that consumers impinge on political prices. As a corollary to PELTZMAN's contribution, it seems useful to expand the

RENT SEEKING: A SURVEY

normative theory of rent-seeking to include a role for consumers. Consider briefly how such an extension might be made[4].

A regulated producer is pricing his output at $LMC = LAC$ and wishes to obtain a variance in his license so that he can charge a higher price. He prefers any price above average cost in order to capture some portion of consumer surplus in the form of rent. It is assumed that direct bargaining between producers and consumers is not feasible and that consumers are effectively organized and informed of attempts by the producer to obtain licensing variances[5]. Finally, obtaining a monopoly right or preventing a monopoly price are not certain prospects for producers or consumers. Assume that the regulator decides cases by granting a price (in *Figure 1*) at or near P_m if the producer's arguments are convincing, at or near P_c if consumers' arguments hold sway, and between P_m and P_c if each sides' arguments have some element of merit.

In the determination of (total) social costs the expectations of both producer and consumers groups will play a key role. Given rational expectations on the part of both producers and consumers, social costs will be dependent upon the actual price chosen by the regulator. To the allocative losses resulting from various price-output solutions (between P_cQ_c and P_mQ_m) must be added the cost of monopolization – the cost of rent-seeking by producers *as well as* any blocking investment made by consumers.

The decision by producers to allocate resources to rent-seeking activities will be affected by their expectations regarding the behavior of the regulator. If producers expected that price would always be set at P_c, their investment in rent-seeking activities would be zero. But if they expected a price above P_c, some level of rent-seeking investment would be undertaken, up to the expected value of the prospective rent. Similarly, if consumers expected that P_m would always prevail, then rational consumer expenditures on efforts to lower the regulated price would be zero. When the expected value of the proceeding for consumers is negative, the magnitude is minimized by accepting the POSNER trapezoid loss and avoiding the loss

4. See BAYSINGER and TOLLISON [1980] for a more complete discussion of the following points.
5. See BUCHANAN and TULLOCK [1968] for a neglected analysis of monopoly where consumers and producers bargain directly over market outcomes.

ROBERT D. TOLLISON

of legal resources in futile litigation. When consumers assign a positive probability to the prospect of a favorable regulatory decision,
they will rationally invest resources in blocking efforts, up to the
amount of the expected value of such efforts.

The social cost of monopoly and regulation in this formulation
is a variable which is related to the behavior of regulators who set
political prices. Past behavior of the regulatory agency is important
since it influences the formation of expectations by those affected
by the regulatory process. These expectations determine the optimal
level of resources that the parties will devote to the 'monopolization-
demonopolization' process. It stands to reason that attempts to extract rents will be fought by affected parties unless such a contest
is deemed futile. Thus, while the conventional result that rent-
seeking expenditures are socially wasteful stands, the extent of such
welfare losses is related to the nature of the institutional environment in which rent seeking takes place.

Moreover, as should be readily apparent, even the expanded
analysis argued for here only scratches the surface of a complicated
problem. The competition for rents in any particular case is not
likely to be so simply characterized as a struggle between consumers
and (constant-cost) producers. Where, for example, consumers face
an upward sloping supply curve, their interest will lie in forming
a buyers' cartel in order to monopsonize against producers. In this
case producers seek monopoly rents, and consumers seek monopsony
rents in an analogous fashion. And this model is based on an assumption that when price is above its competitive equilibrium value,
it is constrained by demand (buyers cannot be forced to buy), and
when it is below its equilibrium value, it is constrained by supply
(sellers cannot be forced to sell). There is clearly much work to be
done in this virtually untouched area.

3. Non-Competitive Rent Seeking

The use of the competitive rent-seeking model (without the complications of introducing consumers into the underlying theory) results in a tractable estimation procedure. Rents are *exactly* dissipated
in this model, a result that avoids the messy problem of formulating
an alternative specification in which rents are not exactly dissipated.

RENT SEEKING: A SURVEY

Nonetheless, the competitive rent-seeking model began to come un-
raveled as the result of a loosely organized experimental game.

BRENNAN proposed the following type of game which can easily
(and perhaps profitably) be played with one's students. A fixed
money prize is offered, for example, ten dollars. Participants are
asked to make a sealed bid for the prize under the conditions that:
(a) there is no collusion among bidders, (b) bids are not refunded,
and (c) the highest bidder wins. The lottery pockets any profit or
funds any loss associated with the game. The general analogy of
the game to rent seeking is clear.

Although the game has not been run on a carefully controlled
basis, the results have been all over the board. Both cases of overbidding and underbidding have been observed, and there appears
to be no general tendency toward either type of result, most certainly not toward exact dissipation. Such evidence suggests that
competitive rent seeking may not be a viable general theory with
which to model cases of rent-seeking behavior.

Work to construct a useful model of imperfectly competitive rent
seeking is in its infancy, and TULLOCK [1980a] has done the major
seed work along these lines. In contrast to the BRENNAN game, where
marginal adjustments in bids are *not* allowed, TULLOCK investigates
the outcome of rent seeking where marginal changes in the bids for
a specified reward are allowed. The conditions of his experiment
are essentially the same as those for the BRENNAN game (*e.g.*, ticket
revenues are kept by the lottery), except that he introduces the additional assumption that if there is a correct strategy in the game, all
participants will discover it. Under these conditions TULLOCK considers the case of two individuals bidding for a $100 prize. In the
BRENNAN game each party would invest $50 as bidders compare
total cost with *total return*. Yet if marginal adjustments in bids are
allowed and players can compare *marginal cost* and *marginal return*,
each party will invest only $25 in the lottery, for only at that level
is the cost of an additional ticket equated to the marginal expected
value of winning. By postulating a game that is not a linear function of contributions, TULLOCK is able to produce an *underbidding*
result in the theory of rent seeking[6].

6. A problem with TULLOCK's game is that it does not yield a NASH equilibrium.

ROBERT D. TOLLISON

TULLOCK goes on in this paper to investigate the impact of the number of players (more rent seeking), the shape of the marginal cost function with respect to rent seeking (a flatter marginal cost function means less rent seeking) and the role of precommitment bids (a game within itself) on the extent of rent-seeking activities. Perhaps more importantly, however, he investigates some of the properties of strategy games in which virtually anything can happen. For example, there are rent-seeking games in which individual players will make contributions larger than the specified prize or in which the sum of players' bids exceeds the value of the prize. While these *overbidding* results seem irrational on the face of it (a player could increase his wealth by not playing), as TULLOCK points out, the general rule of not playing may be vitiated by the fact that if all players followed this rule except one, he could make large profits by playing. As in cartel or oligopoly theory, formal theory is little help in analyzing strategy games. In small-number situations such features as personality, bargaining skills, facial expressions, and, most importantly, the ability to interpret what others will do will be the basic determinants of outcomes.

The importance of TULLOCK's work on efficient rent seeking is to show the potential complexity of rent-seeking games. While the competitive rent-seeking model will continue to be useful in applied, empirical studies, it surely cannot be taken as *the* general rent-seeking model. As TULLOCK's work makes clear, many results are plausible, and institutional parameters will affect observed rent-seeking results.

4. Second-Best Considerations

BHAGWATI and SRINIVASAN [1980] and BHAGWATI [1980] apply the theory of second-best to rent seeking. They draw on earlier contributions to the theory of immiserizing growth where it is shown that additional resources can lead to negative growth in a tariff-distorted economy. With tariff distortions resources withdrawn from a project can have a negative shadow price 'such that even a zero-output "project" ... may be socially desirable' [BHAGWATI and SRINIVASAN 1980, p. 1077]. They produce a similar proof for lobbying expenditures in which the diversion of resources into lobbying

RENT SEEKING: A SURVEY

can be welfare-improving if the shadow price of the resources used for lobbying is negative.

The curious aspect of their proof is that it depends on an assumption that part of the revenues potentially available for rent seeking are ruled to be a lump-sum transfer and hence are *not* subject to rent seeking. This virtually guarantees the welfare-improving result in that it rules out the prospect that resources are simply reallocated from one wasteful activity to another, with welfare on net unchanged. Such an assumption poses problems. As argued above, once the state contrives a scarcity value, rent seeking will ensue on the relevant margin, either directly in lobbying activities or indirectly in some other manner. Lump-sum transfers or taxes are hard fictions to sustain in the rent-seeking society, a fact which detracts from the relevance of the type of analysis presented by BHAGWATI and SRINIVASAN.

5. *The Domain of Rent Seeking*

Before turning to the literature on positive rent-seeking theory, a transitional point, which applies to both normative and positive theory, is worth noting. The applicability of rent-seeking theory does not depend on a government-propped up monopoly right. The domain of rent seeking also includes institutional processes in the private sector. A well known example concerns non-price competition among imperfectly competitive firms (CHAMBERLIN [1933]; BUCHANAN [1942]). Many variations of this analysis have appeared in the literature of industrial organization. The basic structure of these models is that non-colluding firms face a prisoners' dilemma with respect to non-price competition. All could increase their net worth by resisting additional advertising expenditures, but unilateral defections from such an 'agreement' appear worthwhile to the individual firm. Yet if all firms defect, 'excessive advertising' and lower average profitability appear in the industry. Moreover, multilateral disarmament is ruled out by antitrust considerations.

There will be no attempt here to take a detailed look at the extensive literature embodying this type of analysis. The point is to draw the implication that rent seeking can readily inhere in a pri-

587

vate setting. In fact, Cowling and Mueller [1978] include such
assumptions about non-price expenditures in their calculations of
the social costs of monopoly in the U.S. and the U.K. Naturally,
the problem of monopoly becomes much more significant in such
an estimation procedure, and the Cowling and Mueller paper is
a radical but suggestive approach about how the empirical implications of private rent-seeking processes can be handled in terms of
their implications for welfare analytics[7].

IV. THE POSITIVE ECONOMIC THEORY OF RENT SEEKING

Rent-seeking theory generalizes in positive economic terms to the
interest-group theory of government and legislation. This follows
in the sense that the basis for evaluating the welfare costs of rent
seeking was primarily related to the nature of the competition
among various individuals and groups for government-protected
rents. Positive rent-seeking theory seeks to enlarge upon this analysis
by proposing *testable* explanations of the behavior of interest groups[8].

1. Self-Interest and Political Behavior

The interest-group approach to understanding government is based
on the observation that there is a sizeable gap between standard
economic rationalizations for state intervention in the economy and
the actual properties of specific instances of state intervention. This
theory seeks refutable propositions and predictions about how
government agents function in order to explain the divergencies
between the prescriptions of economists and governmental practice.
The interest-group model implies that the behavior of political actors within given political institutions can be usefully analyzed by

7. A final point about the domain of rent seeking is that the industrial organization literature on non-price competition analyzes rent seeking *across* firms in
an industry. A companion problem relates to the potential for rent-seeking behavior and costs *within* firms. See Williamson [1975], Marris and Mueller
[1980], and Faith, Higgins and Tollison [1982] for analyses of this problem.
8. This section draws heavily on McCormick and Tollison [1981, especially
Chs. 1 and 2].

RENT SEEKING: A SURVEY

following the guideline that individual economic agents obey the postulates of self-interest.

A paramount difference between politics and the market consists of the different constraints that confront self-interested actors in the two cases. The market is a proprietary setting where individuals bear the consequences of their actions in the form of changes in their net wealth. The political setting is a non-proprietary setting where individual agents do not always feel the full benefit and cost of their decisions. Behavior will differ in the two cases, not because the objectives of behavior are different, but because constraints on behavior are different.

The problem can be discussed in agent-principal terms. An agent agrees to perform a service for a principal. Because the agent and principal are both wealth-maximizers and because it is costly to monitor and control the behavior of the agent, it is not likely that the behavior of the agent will always comport with the interest of the principal. The point is that political agents face different constraints than private agents because their principals (*e.g.*, voters and stockholders) face different incentives to control the behavior of their agents. Managers of private firms have increased incentives to control costs because increased costs come at the expense of firm profitability. Managers of political firms do not have similar incentive to control costs because they cannot receive personally any savings that they effect for their agencies and since it is costly for voters to delimit shirking by political managers (*e.g.*, recall).

2. The Basis of a Transfer Society

Wealth transfers in a representative government must be predicated on the existence of certain types of costs. Without the existence of such costs wealth would never be willingly given up by an individual voter unless a proposed transfer were PARETO-superior in nature. In a world of zero transaction and information costs only welfare-enhancing transfers will be passed by political representatives. When information and transaction costs are possible, some groups will be able to organize and acquire information more cheaply than others, and these differences among groups will give rise to a demand and supply of wealth transfers.

589

ROBERT D. TOLLISON

Voting rules are also crucial. A unanimity rule and costless voting would yield no PARETO-inferior transfers. Majority rule will increase the amount of transfers because it lowers the costs of influencing collective decisions. A key to understanding transfers resides in the costly voting side of the problem.

The individual faces two types of information costs with respect to engaging in transfer-seeking. He must spend resources to discover the effects of a policy on his personal wealth and to identify other individuals who will join him on the issue. Several possibilities arise in this regard. (1) Winners and losers are well identified and can easily find out who each other are. (2) Winners and losers are not easily identified. (3) Winners can be easily identified while losers cannot. (4) Losers can be easily identified while winners cannot. The major implication that follows from this taxonomy is the well known result that more transfers are expected in a category such as (3). Politicians will have incentives to search for the issues on which well organized groups gain transfers at the expense of the diffuse general polity.

Another point about organization costs is that these costs are like start-up costs. Once they are borne, they do not affect marginal costs. Groups that have already incurred start-up costs, for reasons unrelated to lobbying, will have a comparative advantage in seeking transfers. This is a point about jointness in production. Some groups will be able to produce lobbying as a by-product of performing some other function, thereby avoiding start-up costs for lobbying. There are many examples of this phenomenon in the economy, among which are labor unions, trade associations, and corporations.

In addition to organization and information costs there are costs which are due to the potential for individuals to 'free ride' on the lobbying efforts of others. Lobbying groups will find it useful to devise institutions which cut down on free riding by members. For example, organized labor relies upon institutions such as union halls, labor bosses and national federations to overcome the paradox of voting and to bring forth a supply of votes from its members. Labor union members will vote because they know that other members will vote and their votes will thus 'count' in an expected value sense[9].

9. For the general analysis underlying this discussion, see STIGLER [1974] and McCORMICK and TOLLISON [1980].

RENT SEEKING: A SURVEY

3. The Interest-Group Theory of Government and Legislation

Building on these widely recognized points, the interest-group theory of government has evolved in two dimensions. The first is the theory of economic regulation which seeks to explain *prevailing* government regulation in interest-group terms. The second is the economic theory of legislation which seeks to explain the *origin* of government regulation and other wealth-transfer schemes.

In its simple form the interest-group theory of economic regulation has a long history, primarily in the literature of political science and public choice [POSNER 1974]. The most elementary form of the theory is a 'capture theory' of regulation. In this form of the model there are a small number of producers who are able to overcome free riding costs and organize to wield *complete* (wealth-maximizing) influence over regulators. Despite the losses in real income which they suffer from monopoly-enhancing legislation, consumer interests are left out of account in the pure capture theory because they have no rational incentive to organize to resist regulations in favor of producers (it costs more than it is worth).

This simple version of the capture theory is easy to confuse with Marxism. It seems to suggest that Capital uses the state to capture income from Labor. The confusion with Marxist theory is more apparent than real. STIGLER [1971] presented the interest-group theory in terms of the costs and benefits to various groups of using the state to increase their wealth. He showed that under certain configurations of costs and benefits some large producer groups (*e.g.*, farmers and union members) will find it feasible to seek wealth transfers from the state, while some small producer groups (*e.g.*, automobile firms) will organize mainly to resist negative regulation. Moreover, any group of sellers or buyers potentially qualifies as an interest group in this theory. Labor and capital can form potent interest groups in STIGLER's theory and will sometimes (often?) find themselves allied in the pursuit of a wealth transfer for a particular industry[10].

The most important subsequent contribution to the theory of economic regulation was made by PELTZMAN [1976]. PELTZMAN

10. Another important contemporaneous contribution to this theory is POSNER [1971].

591

ROBERT D. TOLLISON

presents a generalization of STIGLER's theory by introducing the role of opposition groups in determining regulatory behavior. He presents a model of equilibrium political prices in which a vote-maximizing regulator trade-offs the rents he gives to producers relative to the costs imposed on consumers in the process of setting regulated prices. PELTZMAN's contribution removes the interest-group theory a step further from the simple capture theory because it demonstrates the validity of STIGLER's conjecture that political price-setting does not always take place in a way that is pure profit-maximizing to the regulated industry. PELTZMAN's vote-maximizing regulator, however, remains a mystery actor in the theory since a voting process is not specifically addressed in the analysis[11].

The second general line of attack in the interest-group theory concerns the role of legislators in promoting wealth-transfer programs. A number of works have appeared dealing with what might be called the interest-group theory of legislation. A basic paper here is again by STIGLER [1976]. The approach taken by STIGLER is to consider political processes as analogous to economic processes and therefore subject to the same analysis as other economic organizations. As stressed above, participants in politics are viewed as utility-maximizers operating under different institutional constraints.

STIGLER models the sizes of legislatures as responsive to desires of group interests. He perceives that representatives are chosen by these groups on the basis of the values that the groups assign to particular policies. These values are found by summing and discounting the net benefits of any particular action over the potentially affected people. There will normally be quite a few issues which affect the welfare of individual voters in a trivial way. Some of the issues will be important, however, and these issues will be responsible for the selection of representatives.

The valuations that interest groups place on issues are perceived as a demand for legislation. This does not automatically mean that every interest group will have its own representatives. As STIGLER stresses, many groups have similar interests and can use the same

11. For other and more recent contributions to the theory of economic regulation, see BROCK and MAGEE [1978], CRAIN and McCORMICK [1981] and MALONEY, McCORMICK and TOLLISON [1981].

RENT SEEKING: A SURVEY

representatives. Furthermore, some groups will not find it efficient to seek representation (their organizational costs exceed the expected benefits from legislation).

Having taken the view that the political process can be analyzed in a positive economics framework, STIGLER presents a model of the sizes of legislatures. He hypothesizes legislative size (for both U.S. state senates and houses) as a function of population, the rate of change in population, population density and a dummy variable for New England which has unusually large legislatures. His predictions are that larger populations represent more demand for legislators while larger rates of change in population and higher population densities imply smaller legislatures. The model is statistically robust with the exception of the population density variable[12].

STIGLER [1976, p. 31] concludes with the following observation: 'The foregoing discussion of the sizes of legislatures is long on problems and short on solutions. The problems are commended to economists, not only because of their obvious political importance, but also because these problems in general have counterparts in the organization of economic activity.' He offers a powerful brief for this point of view in an earlier paper [STIGLER 1972]. He suggests that the tendency of economists to view politics and the market as fundamentally different institutional processes is misplaced and that the typical *all-or-nothing* characterization of political competition needs to be revised. STIGLER offers a theory of political competition in which, like the market, the output of a political process is construed as ranging *continuously* from failure to success. An implication of his approach is that it is incorrect to label the winning of 51 percent of legislative seats as a victory and 49 percent a defeat. Alternatively, he models political process in marginal and not all-or-none terms[13].

STIGLER, of course, is talking in positive economic terms here. He fully recognizes that one must use care in drawing normative

12. There is a remarkably small variation in legislative sizes across U.S. states. This follows from the fact that transactions costs increase at an increasing rate as size increases in any collective decision making arrangement.

13. For some evidence on STIGLER's characterization of political competition, see CRAIN and TOLLISON [1976] and McCORMICK and TOLLISON [1980].

ROBERT D. TOLLISON

analogies between market and political processes. When economists talk about competition in a private setting, certain efficiency implications follow. These same implications do not necessarily follow from competition in political markets.

In a representative democracy voter-taxpayers can be seen as owners (principals) and politicians as managers (agents). Elections are a means to choose political managers to monitor and control the governmental enterprise until the next election. In this light consider three points about elections. First, the right to run the government is not sold to the highest bidder; it is granted in a voting process. As is well known, not only will the size of bids from aspiring politicians be important, but their distribution among voters will be crucial in determining outcomes under majority voting. A major difference, then, between politics and the market is that the highest bidder will not necessarily secure control of the 'political firm'. Second, voter-taxpayers have no way to liquidate their ownership rights in government. Unlike owners of private firms, voters cannot sell their ownership rights to politicians in exchange for a payment before productive activity begins. Contract owners in politics get paid after production has taken place. Third, politicians are elected for their positions on many issues. This is in contrast to market decision making where consumers can unbundle and make marginal decisions.

The point of this discussion is that political competition under one man-one vote conditions does not lead to efficient outcomes in the same sense that such outcomes are produced by competition in private markets. One cannot therefore rely on supply-side forces in politics to generate efficient outcomes. This does not mean that economic efficiency will never impinge on political choices; it means that rent seeking poses costs (lost votes because of welfare reduction) and benefits (rent capture) which the politician will try to equate at the margin.

There have been a number of other useful developments in the interest-group theory of legislation. Perhaps the most important effort is the theory of the independent judiciary proposed by LANDES and POSNER [1975]. They view the independent judiciary as a long-term contracting institution in the interest-group theory. They contend that since judicial decision makers typically resolve legal dis-

RENT SEEKING: A SURVEY

putes by enforcing the desires of the legislature which originally enacted the legislation (an empirical observation), granting the judiciary independence (life tenure) and thereby breaking its bond with the current legislature increases the present value of the 'contracts' that legislators make with special interests. Moreover, in a similar vein LANDES and POSNER examine how the rules of the legislature can impart durability to legislation by making its repeal more costly[14].

The interest-group theory has evolved beyond these basic papers in a series of works which essentially treat politicians as an interest group in their own right. CRAIN [1977] models the turnover of politicians with a model which stresses the cartel-like aspects of representative government (*e.g.*, one representative per district). McCORMICK and TOLLISON [1978] investigate the pay of legislators and find that legislator pay is a function of whether legislators are allowed to set their own pay versus having it set by voters in the constitution. They also offer a theory of the occupational composition of legislatures in which lawyers dominate low-pay legislatures because they are comparatively proficient at procuring outside earnings as legislators. Beyond and inclusive of these papers, McCORMICK and TOLLISON [1981] present a theory of legislative activity based on the principle that legislation is equivalent to wealth transfers and that a useful way to model legislative activity is in terms of the role of politicians as brokers of transfers.

4. Applications

Several recent applications of rent-seeking theory have appeared in the area of economic history. LANE [1979], in fact, is a neglected precursor of rent-seeking theory, and his discussion of the role of 'protection rents' in the development of the colonial policies of the early nation-states is fascinating, and as DAVIS [1980] stresses, very relevant to modern scholarship in economic history. Also writing in this tradition, EKELUND and TOLLISON [1980; 1982] present a positive economic theory of mercantilism which uses rent-seeking

14. For two tests of the LANDES-POSNER theory, with results favorable to their basic hypotheses, see CRAIN and TOLLISON [1979a, 1979b].

595

ROBERT D. TOLLISON

analysis to explain the extensive economic regulation of the mercantile economies. For related and complementary approaches to
developing explanations of economic history the reader should also
see NORTH [1979] and NORTH and THOMAS [1973].

Also in economic history note should be taken of a recent application of interest-group theory by MARVEL [1977] to explain the
origin of the English Factory Acts. The conventional analysis explains the restrictions placed on child and women laborers as inspired by humanitarian motives. MARVEL pierces this rhetoric by
examining the intra-industry effects of the output restrictions en-
gendered by the acts. His evidence points to the interests of steam-
powered relative to water-powered owners and underscores the important point that an industry is not a monolithic demander of rents
from government. Legislation can impact on the intra-industry distribution of rents across firms with differing marginal cost functions,
and a struggle for these differential rents will inform the legislation
affecting an industry in many cases. Other examinations of intra-
industry competition for rents include GUTTMAN [1978], BRENNAN
and TOLLISON [1980], LANDES [1980], and MALONEY and McCOR-
MICK [1982].

International trade is another area in which positive applications
of the interest-group model have appeared. PINCUS [1975] presents
and tests an interest-group model to explain the U.S. Tariff Act of
1824. Using 1820 structural data, he offers an explanation of 1824
duty levels with his model. CAVES [1976] sets out to explain the
variation in tariff protection accorded Canadian industries. To do
so he posits three basic political models, one of which is an interest-
group model. Empirically, the interest-group model works best in
explaining 1963 Canadian tariff rates.

There have been several recent applications of rent-seeking theory
in the area of public economics. GOETZ [1978] analyzes tax preferences and the concept of horizontal equity using the principle of
rent capitalization as earlier outlined by TULLOCK [1975]. BUCHANAN
[1980b] examines traditional prescriptions to internalize external
economies in the context of rent-seeking behavior. He argues that
the prevalence of direct regulation versus an auction approach to
externality problems results from the desire of rent seekers to avoid
the dissipation of the potential rents inherent in the solution of

RENT SEEKING: A SURVEY

common-property problems. FOSTER [1981] examines the impact of rent seeking on traditional conclusions in cost-benefit analysis. Conventional theory says that when demand- and supply-price diverge and rents exist in the private sector, the reallocation of resources from such activities into public investments should reflect a shadow price *inclusive* of the value of these rents. In other words, a dollar of public investment has an opportunity cost of more than a dollar. FOSTER argues, however, that if private rents are dissipated by rent seeking, all private resources are earning normal returns, both those involved in production and those involved in rent seeking, and hence a dollar of public investment involves an opportunity cost of a dollar of private investment.

Finally, there are a number of recent applications of the interest-group theory in the area of public choice. SILBERMAN and DURDEN [1976] and KAU and RUBIN [1978] examine the impact of economic interests on the pattern of voting on minimum-wage legislation. ABRAMS and SETTLE [1978] apply the economic theory of regulation to explain the recent change to public financing of presidential elections in the U.S. ECKERT [1973] develops an insightful discussion of the incentives of regulators as a function of whether they are full-time civil servants or part-time elected commissioners[15].

V. CONCLUDING REMARKS

Economic rent is not new to economists. Yet as this essay hopefully demonstrates, the full implications of the role of rents in the economy are just starting to emerge. In this sense rent seeking is an interesting intellectual innovation. As a rereading of TULLOCK's 1967 paper would convince virtually anyone, the insight that brought about the idea of rent seeking was exceedingly simple. Rents are competed for, and where rents are contrived, this competition has important normative and positive implications for economic analysis. The moral is perhaps that important advances in economics do not naturally have to flow from a highly mathematical or statistical approach

---

15. This review of applications could undoubtedly be easily expanded, but the point is not to be copious. It is only to suggest the direction of applied scholarship in this area. Apologies are tendered for any glaring omissions.

597

ROBERT D. TOLLISON

to the subject. In this regard TULLOCK's original paper on rent seeking calls to mind COASE's [1960] seminal work on social cost.

REFERENCES

ABRAMS, BURTON A. and SETTLE, RUSSELL F.: 'The Economic Theory of Regulation and the Public Financing of Presidential Elections', *Journal of Political Economy*, Vol. 86 (April 1978), pp. 245–258.

BAYSINGER, BARRY, EKELUND, ROBERT B. Jr. and TOLLISON, ROBERT D.: 'Mercantilism as a Rent-Seeking Society', in: BUCHANAN, TOLLISON and TULLOCK (Eds.): *Toward a Theory of the Rent-Seeking Society*, Texas A&M University Press, College Station, 1980, pp. 235–268.

BAYSINGER, BARRY and TOLLISON, ROBERT D.: 'Evaluating the Social Costs of Monopoly and Regulation', *Atlantic Economic Journal*, Vol. 8 (December 1980), pp. 22–26.

BHAGWATI, JAGDISH N.: 'Lobbying and Welfare', *Journal of Public Economics*, Vol. 14 (1980), pp. 355–363.

BHAGWATI, JAGDISH N. and SRINIVASAN, T. N.: 'Revenue Seeking: A Generalization of the Theory of Tariffs', *Journal of Political Economy*, Vol. 88 (December 1980), pp. 1069–1087.

BRENNAN, H. GOEFFRY and TOLLISON, ROBERT D.: 'Rent Seeking in Academia', in: BUCHANAN, TOLLISON and TULLOCK (Eds.): *Toward a Theory of the Rent-Seeking Society*, Texas A&M University Press, College Station, 1980, pp. 344–356.

BROCK, WILLIAM A. and MAGEE, STEPHEN P.: 'The Economics of Special Interest Politics: The Case of the Tariff', *American Economic Review*, Vol. 68 (May 1978), pp. 246–250.

BROWNING, EDGAR K.: 'On the Welfare Cost of Transfers', *Kyklos*, Vol. 26 (April 1974), pp. 374–377.

BUCHANAN, JAMES M.: 'Rent Seeking and Profit Seeking', in: BUCHANAN, TOLLISON and TULLOCK (Eds.): *Toward a Theory of the Rent-Seeking Society*, Texas A&M University Press, College Station, 1980a, pp. 3–15.

BUCHANAN, JAMES M.: 'Rent Seeking Under External Diseconomies', in: BUCHANAN, TOLLISON and TULLOCK (Eds.): *Toward a Theory of the Rent-Seeking Society*, Texas A&M University Press, College Station, 1980b, pp. 183–194.

BUCHANAN, JAMES M. and TULLOCK, GORDON: 'The "Dead" Hand of Monopoly', *Antitrust Law and Economics Review*, Vol. 1 (Summer 1968), pp. 85–96.

BUCHANAN, JAMES M., TOLLISON, ROBERT D. and TULLOCK, GORDON (Eds.): *Toward a Theory of the Rent-Seeking Society*, Texas A&M University Press, College Station, 1980.

BUCHANAN, NORMAN S.: 'Advertising Expenditures: A Suggested Treatment', *Journal of Political Economy*, Vol. 50 (August 1942) pp. 537–557.

RENT SEEKING: A SURVEY

CAVES, RICHARD E.: 'Economic Models of Political Choice: Canada's Tariff Structure', *Canadian Journal of Economics*, Vol. 9 (May 1976), pp. 278–300.

CHAMBERLIN, EDWARD H.: *The Theory of Monopolistic Competition*, Harvard University Press, Cambridge, Massachusetts, 1933.

COASE, RONALD H.: 'The Problem of Social Cost', *Journal of Law and Economics*, Vol. 3 (October 1960), pp. 1–44.

COMANOR, WILLIAM S. and SMILEY, ROBERT H.: 'Monopoly and the Distribution of Wealth', *Quarterly Journal of Economics*, Vol. 89 (May 1975), pp. 177–194.

COWLING, KEITH and MUELLER, DENNIS C.: 'The Social Costs of Monopoly Power', *Economic Journal*, Vol. 88 (December 1978), pp. 727–748.

CRAIN, W. MARK: 'On the Structure and Stability of Political Markets', *Journal of Political Economy*, Vol. 85 (August 1977), pp. 829–842.

CRAIN, W. MARK and McCORMICK, ROBERT E.: 'Regulators as an Interest Group', unpublished manuscript, 1981.

CRAIN, W. MARK and TOLLISON, ROBERT D.: 'Campaign Expenditures and Political Competition', *Journal of Law and Economics*, Vol. 19 (April 1976), pp. 177–188.

CRAIN, W. MARK and TOLLISON, ROBERT D.: 'Constitutional Change in an Interest-Group Perspective', *Journal of Legal Studies*, Vol. 8 (January 1979a), pp. 165–175.

CRAIN, W. MARK and TOLLISON, ROBERT D.: 'The Executive Branch in the Interest-Group Theory of Government', *Journal of Legal Studies*, Vol. 8 (June 1979b), pp. 555–567.

DAVIS, LANCE E.: 'It's a Long Road to Tipperary, or Reflections on Organized Violence, Protection Rents, and Related Topics: The New Political History', *Journal of Economic History*, Vol. 40 (March 1980), pp. 1–16.

ECKERT, ROSS D.: 'On the Incentives of Regulators: The Case of Taxicabs', *Public Choice*, Vol. 14 (Spring 1973), pp. 83–100.

EKELUND, ROBERT B., Jr. and TOLLISON, ROBERT D.: 'Economic Regulation in Mercantile England: Heckscher Revisited', *Economic Inquiry*, Vol. 18 (October 1980), pp. 567–599.

EKELUND, ROBERT B., Jr. and TOLLISON, ROBERT D.: *Mercantilism as a Rent-Seeking Society: Economic Regulation in Historical Perspective*, Texas A&M University Press, College Station, 1982.

EVANS, JOEL R. (Ed.): *Consumerism in the United States*, Praeger, New York 1980.

FAITH, ROGER L., HIGGINS, RICHARD and TOLLISON, ROBERT D.: 'Managerial Rents and Outside Recruitment in the Coasian Firm', unpublished manuscript, 1982.

FOSTER, EDWARD: 'The Treatment of Rents in Cost-Benefit Analysis', *American Economic Review*, Vol. 71 (March 1981), pp. 171–178.

GOETZ, MICHAEL L.: 'Tax Avoidance, Horizontal Equity, and Tax Reform: A Proposed Synthesis', *Southern Economic Journal*, Vol. 44 (April 1978), pp. 798–812.

GUTTMAN, JOEL M.: 'Interest Groups and the Demand for Agricultural Research', *Journal of Political Economy*, Vol. 86 (June 1978), pp. 467–484.

ROBERT D. TOLLISON

HARBERGER, ARNOLD C.: 'Monopoly and Resource Allocation', *American Economic Review*, Vol. 44 (May 1954), pp. 77-87.

KAU, JAMES B. and RUBIN, PAUL H.: 'Voting on Minimum Wages: A Time-Series Analysis', *Journal of Political Economy*, Vol. 86 (April 1978), pp. 337-342.

KIRZNER, ISRAEL: *Competition and Entrepreneurship*, University of Chicago Press, Chicago, 1973.

KRUEGER, ANNE O.: 'The Political Economy of the Rent-Seeking Society', *American Economic Review*, Vol. 64 (June 1974), pp. 291-303.

LANDES, ELISABETH M.: 'The Effect of State Maximum-Hours Laws on the Employment of Women in 1920', *Journal of Political Economy*, Vol. 88 (June 1980), pp. 476-494.

LANDES, WILLIAM M. and POSNER, RICHARD A.: 'The Independent Judiciary in an Interest-Group Perspective', *Journal of Law and Economics*, Vol. 18 (December 1975), pp. 875-901.

LANE, FREDERIC C.: *Profits From Power: Readings in Protection Rent and Violence Controlling Enterprises*, State University of New York Press, Albany, 1979.

MALONEY, MICHAEL T. and McCORMICK, ROBERT E.: 'Environmental Quality Regulation', *Journal of Law and Economics*, Vol. 25 (April 1982), pp. 99-123.

MALONEY, MICHAEL T., McCORMICK, ROBERT E. and TOLLISON, ROBERT D.: 'Exporting Economic Regulation', unpublished manuscript, 1981.

MARRIS, ROBIN and MUELLER, DENNIS C.: 'The Corporation, Competition, and the Invisible Hand', *Journal of Economic Literature*, Vol. 18 (March 1980), pp. 32-63.

MARVEL, HOWARD P.: 'Factory Regulation: A Reinterpretation of Early English Experience', *Journal of Law and Economics*, Vol. 20 (October 1977), pp. 379-402.

McCORMICK, ROBERT E. and TOLLISON, ROBERT D.: 'Legislatures as Unions', *Journal of Political Economy*, Vol. 86 (February 1978), pp. 63-78.

McCORMICK, ROBERT E. and TOLLISON, ROBERT D.: 'Wealth Transfers in a Representative Democracy', in: BUCHANAN, TOLLISON and TULLOCK (Eds.): *Toward a Theory of the Rent-Seeking Society*, Texas A&M University Press, College Station, 1980, pp. 293-313.

McCORMICK, ROBERT E. and TOLLISON, ROBERT D.: *Politicians, Legislation, and the Economy: An Inquiry into the Interest-Group Theory of Government*, Martinus-Nijhoff, Boston 1981.

MUNDELL, ROBERT A.: 'Review of Jansenn's *Free Trade, Protection and Customs Union*', *American Economic Review*, Vol. 52 (June 1962), pp. 621-622.

NORTH, DOUGLASS C.: 'A Framework for Analyzing the State in Economic History', *Explorations in Economic History*, Vol. 16 (1979), pp. 249-259.

NORTH, DOUGLAS C. and THOMAS, ROBERT P.: *The Rise of the Western World*, Cambridge University Press, Cambridge, 1973.

PELTZMAN, SAM: 'Toward a More General Theory of Regulation', *Journal of Law and Economics*, Vol. 19 (August 1976), pp. 211-240.

PINCUS, JONATHAN J.: 'Pressure Groups and the Pattern of Tariffs', *Journal of Political Economy*, Vol. 83 (August 1975), pp. 757-778.

RENT SEEKING: A SURVEY

POSNER, RICHARD A.: 'Taxation by Regulation', *Bell Journal of Economics and Management Science*, Vol. 2 (Spring 1971), pp. 22–50.

POSNER, RICHARD A.: 'Theories of Economic Regulation', *Bell Journal of Economics and Management Science*, Vol. 5 (Autumn 1974), pp. 335–358.

POSNER, RICHARD A.: 'The Social Costs of Monopoly and Regulation', *Journal of Political Economy*, Vol. 83 (August 1975), pp. 807–827.

SCHERER, F.M.: *Industrial Market Structure and Economic Performance*, Rand McNally, Chicago, 1980.

SILBERMAN, JONATHAN I. and DURDEN, GAREY C.: 'Determining Legislative Preferences on the Minimum Wage: An Economic Approach', *Journal of Political Economy*, Vol. 84 (April 1976), pp. 317–329.

STIGLER, GEORGE J.: 'The Theory of Economic Regulation', *Bell Journal of Economics and Management Science*, Vol. 2 (Spring 1971), pp. 3–21.

STIGLER, GEORGE J.: 'Economic Competition and Political Competition', *Public Choice*, Vol. 13 (Fall 1972), pp. 91–106.

STIGLER, GEORGE J.: 'Free Riders and Collective Action: An Appendix to Theories of Economic Regulation', *Bell Journal of Economics and Management Science*, Vol. 5 (Autumn 1974), pp. 359–365.

STIGLER, GEORGE J.: 'The Sizes of Legislatures', *Journal of Legal Studies*, Vol. 5 (January 1976), pp. 17–34.

TULLOCK, GORDON: 'The Welfare Costs of Tariffs, Monopolies, and Theft', *Western Economic Journal*, Vol. 5 (June 1967), pp. 224–232.

TULLOCK, GORDON: 'The Cost of Transfers', *Kyklos*, Vol. 24 (December 1971), pp. 629–643.

TULLOCK, GORDON: 'More on the Cost of Transfers', *Kyklos*, Vol. 27 (April 1974), pp. 378–381.

TULLOCK, GORDON: 'The Transitional Gains Trap', *Bell Journal of Economics*, Vol. 6 (Autumn 1975), pp. 671–678.

TULLOCK, GORDON: 'Efficient Rent Seeking', in: BUCHANAN, TOLLISON and TULLOCK (Eds.): *Toward a Theory of the Rent-Seeking Society*, Texas A&M University Press, College Station, 1980a, pp. 3–15.

TULLOCK, GORDON: 'Rent Seeking as a Negative-Sum Game', in: BUCHANAN, TOLLISON and TULLOCK (Eds.): *Toward a Theory of the Rent-Seeking Society*, Texas A&M University Press, College Station, 1980b, pp. 16–36.

WILLIAMSON, OLIVER E.: *Markets and Hierarchies: Analysis and Antitrust Implications*, The Free Press, New York, 1975.

SUMMARY

This paper offers a survey of the theory of the rent-seeking society. Rent seeking is defined as the study of how individuals compete for artificially contrived transfers. Both the normative and positive implications of rent seeking are covered. The former refers to the estimation of the social costs of rent-seeking behavior to the economy. The latter are attempts to explain the source and form of contrived rents in the political-economic system. Possible extensions of rent-seeking theory are also presented.

ROBERT D. TOLLISON

ZUSAMMENFASSUNG

Der Aufsatz gibt einen Überblick über die Theorie der *rent-seeking society*. Diese Theorie beschäftigt sich mit der Frage, wie sich Individuen um künstlich geschaffene Transfers bewerben. Sowohl auf die normativen als auch auf die positiven Aspekte wird eingegangen. Bei den ersten geht es um die Schätzung der sozialen Kosten des *rent-seeking*-Verhaltens; bei den letzten um die Erklärung der Quelle und Form der gebildeten Renten im politisch-ökonomischen System. Ausserdem werden mögliche Erweiterungen der Theorie erläutert.

RÉSUMÉ

Cet article présente un résumé de la théorie de la *rent-seeking society*. *Rent-seeking* se définit comme l'étude de la manière dont les individus rivalisent pour les transfers artificiellement imaginés. L'auteur examine les implications normatives et positives du *rent-seeking*. Ces dernières font référence à l'estimation des couts sociaux du comportement de *rent-seeking* dans l'économie. Les premières cherchent à expliquer la source et la forme des rentes dans le système politico-économique. L'auteur présente également des extensions possibles de la théorie.

[16]

Bureaucrats, Legislators, and the Size of Government

GARY J. MILLER
Michigan State University

TERRY M. MOE
Stanford University

Some recent theories have blamed the growth of government on budget-maximizing bureaucrats who are assumedly capable of imposing their most preferred budget-output combination on legislatures, subject to cost and demand constraints. However, theoretical examination of the range of bargaining outcomes that might occur between bureau and legislature shows that budget-maximizing behavior does not necessarily lead to super-optimal levels of production, nor do the suggested reforms of competition and privatization necessarily improve the situation. In this bargaining model, the central determinants of governmental growth are not budget-maximizing bureaucrats, but the legislature's decisions regarding mode of oversight and form of internal organization.

Public bureaucracy has never been especially popular, but in recent years its image has gone from bad to worse. Citizens frustrated by big government and excessive taxation have focused much of the blame on the entrenchment and inefficiency of administrative institutions. Elected politicians—responsible for creating, funding, and overseeing these institutions all along—have reaped political gains by echoing (and sometimes leading) such popular sentiments. And the media have contributed regular exposes on bureaucratic behavior, with emphasis on mindless inefficiency, unresponsiveness, and unchecked growth.

Within the social sciences, all of this has been paralleled by enhanced interest in the study of bureaucracy, and by a growing conviction among scholars that bureaucracy is indeed a root cause of overextended government. The most influential work in support of this position is Niskanen's *Bureaucracy and Representative Government* (1971). In a pioneering departure from traditional, essentially sociological approaches to administration, Niskanen offers an economic theory in explaining the link between public bureaucracy and governmental growth.

Niskanen's view is that bureaus can be modelled in much the same way that economists model business firms, but with a few differences, such as: bureaucrats seek to maximize budgets rather than profits; their resources typically derive from lump-sum legislative appropriations rather than from selling goods in the marketplace; and,

in dealing with the legislature, they have an effective monopoly over information about the true costs of supply. Incorporating these properties into a model of bureaucratic behavior, he demonstrates that budget-maximizing bureaucrats will put their monopoly powers to use in securing budget and output levels that are higher than socially optimal.

During the last decade, Niskanen's novel perspective has shaped scholarly thinking about bureaucracy.[1] Above all, it has provided theoretical justification for the view that bureaucracy is a basic cause of excessive governmental growth, and it has riveted attention on the expansionary incentives and monopoly advantages of public bureaucrats. In the process it has become the cornerstone of a scientific movement of sorts, led by the public choice school of economists and political scientists, against the bureaucratic supply of public services and in favor of two fundamental dimensions of reform: privatization and competition. Privatization involves the provision of public services through contracting arrangements with private firms. Competition, whether among bureaus or firms, involves provision via multiple sources of supply. Both proposals, usually offered in combination, are natural extensions of conventional economic principles to the problem of governmental organization.[2]

Criticism of Niskanen's model has centered most often around the assumption of budget-

The authors are indebted to a number of readers for their helpful comments, including Randy Calvert, Morris Fiorina, Tom Hammond, James Laing, Douglas Rivers, David Weimer, Barry Weingast, an anonymous reviewer, and especially Harrison Wagner, whose comments motivated the last half of this article.

[1] Its influence has been bolstered by empirical research demonstrating the relative inefficiency of bureaucratic supply. See, for instance, Ahlbrandt (1973), Davies (1971), DeAllesi (1974), Savas (1976).

[2] See for example, Borcherding (1977), Savas (1977), Savas (1982), Ostrom and Ostrom (1971), Tullock (1965), and Mackay and Weaver (1978).

maximization, with the suggestion that bureaucrats may in fact pursue other goals—e.g., slack resources—in addition to or instead of large budgets.[3] These sorts of motivational issues are clearly important, since different assumptions can give rise to quite different conclusions about the behavior of bureaucrats, and, in a later article, Niskanen (1975) has recognized as much by incorporating a more complex bureaucratic value structure into a revised model.

The most instructive and far-reaching criticism of Niskanen's work, however, is that it fails to integrate the legislature into its formal framework. Budgets and service levels, after all, are not really bureaucratic decisions—they are *joint* decisional outcomes that arise from bureau-legislature interaction. and they should be modelled as such. Niskanen has implicitly recognized this all along, yet, at least in part to minimize the analytical complexities that interaction often entails, his model of bureaucratic behavior essentially focuses on the bureau alone. In his book, the legislature is introduced in a less formal, less systematic way late in the analysis, and, in his subsequent article, he carries out a more sustained and formal analysis of legislative decision making without developing an overarching model in which legislative and bureaucratic decision making are truly interdependent. This general approach, however much it helps to simplify his analysis, cannot produce a coherent perspective on bureau-legislature interaction and, as a result, threatens to generate inappropriate conclusions about the nature and determinants of decisional outcomes.

In this article we move toward a broader perspective on bureaucracy which recognizes the integral role of the legislature.[4] To enhance comparability and highlight the implications of bureau-legislature interaction, we retain the basic components of Niskanen's original budget-maximization model.[5] With this as a foundation, we go on to incorporate the legislature and allow

<hr>

[3] See Migue and Belanger (1974), which applies the literature on "managerial discretionary profit" to Niskanen.

[4] For other efforts to model bureau-legislature interaction, but along different lines, see Miller (1977), Spencer (1980), and Breton and Wintrobe (1975). For a general equilibrium approach, see Fiorina and Noll (1978).

[5] In particular, we maintain the quadratic forms of the cost and valuation functions used by Niskanen. A generalization of this form is desirable, but we maintain the quadratic form for consistency with Niskanen and because we later show, in the section entitled "Rules of Thumb," that assumptions of linearity in marginal cost and demand functions (which are equivalent to the quadratic for valuation and total cost) may be stra-

for important aspects of legislative organization: its modes of oversight, the representativeness of its committees, and its decisional rules of thumb. When these legislative considerations are integrated into the analysis, bureaucratic behavior is placed in larger, more meaningful context. Viewed from this standpoint, the dimensions of the "bureaucracy problem" begin to look very different from those stressed by Niskanen and other critics. In particular, the model implies that their negative assessments of bureaucracy are overdrawn, that their proposals for privatization and competition are often ill-advised, and that the legislature, not the bureaucracy, is primarily to blame for problems of big government.

Needless to say, we offer this model in the spirit of cumulative science and not as the final word. The point we wish to emphasize at this stage is simply that the familiar economic logic Niskanen and others have relied upon in justifying their anti-bureaucratic position does not necessarily lead in this direction at all. A more comprehensive —and, we think, more reasonable—version of their own model, guided by the same line of economic reasoning, leads in fact to far more positive views of public bureaucracy. At the least, this should raise some doubts about a perspective that is fast becoming conventional wisdom.

The Niskanen Model

The strength of Niskanen's model derives from its simplicity. Like other economic models of producer behavior, it is built around the notions of supply and demand. The demand for a bureau's services is assumed to come from the legislature, which places a value upon levels of output, Q, and offers a schedule of budgets, B, equal to this total evaluation. Specifically, the legislature's budget-total evaluation curve is assumed to be $B = aQ - bQ^2$ (a, $b > 0$). On the supply side, output is produced by a monopolistic bureau headed by a budget-maximizing bureaucrat. The cost of producing each level of output, $C = cQ + dQ^2$ (c, $d > 0$), is known only by the bureaucrat, not by the legislature. His task is to secure the largest budget he can for his bureau, subject to the constraint that he must be able to deliver the level of Q he promises—that his budget must cover his costs.

How do legislatures and bureaucrats interact to arrive at a decision? Niskanen recognizes that the bureau is typically a monopoly supplier of Q and the legislature a monopoly buyer (a monopsonist), and thus that their relationship constitutes a bilateral monopoly. But he does not incorporate this feature into his model. He assumes instead a rather peculiar process of decision making: the legislature reveals the maximum amount it is willing to pay for each level of Q (its total evaluation curve), and the bureaucrat then picks any budget-output combination he likes consistent with this legislative budget function. This seems odd for two reasons. First, the legislature behaves irrationally. It does not even try to maximize its net benefits on the exchange, but instead simply turns its utility function over to the bureaucrat. Second, the final budgetary choices are made by the bureaucrat, when, in the real-world budgetary process, final choices are obviously made by the legislature.

Niskanen does not treat this model as the curiosity it is. In the latter part of this book, however, after the basic conclusions about bureaucratic supply have already been derived, he introduces what amounts to an explanation. Legislators, he notes, make decisions in committees, and decisions about particular bureaus tend to be made by committees whose demand for bureau services is much higher than that of the legislature as a whole. The high-demand committee *is* a rational decision maker that seeks to maximize its own utility in overseeing the bureau, but it is on the bureau's side in preferring high budget-output combinations. Moreover, it is in an excellent position for getting its way, because its decisional role is to present the legislature with a take-it-or-leave-it budgetary choice. The legislature does not choose a budget from a whole range of possible alternatives, but simply votes yes or no on the single alternative produced by the committee. And, although the legislature might prefer a low level of Q, the committee can force it to accept a much higher level, since the legislature will vote for any budget-output combination that it prefers even slightly to the alternative of nothing at all. Thus the committee can choose (as Niskanen's bureaucrat does) budget-output combinations infinitely close to the legislature's total evaluation curve, achieving the largest feasible outcome.[4]

Following this logic, then, Niskanen justifies

his simple model as a reflection of empirical features of the budgetary process, and he suggests (but does not prove) that it leads to the same conclusions as would a more complex model explicitly incorporating these elements. He does not "really" assume that the legislature is irrational, nor that the bureaucrat makes the final budgetary decision; it only appears that way in the simplified structure of the model.

We can now turn to the conclusions entailed by the model itself, since these are the claims for which Niskanen's analysis is best known. Most fundamentally, they derive from the bureaucrat's constrained optimization problem, which is to maximize his budget (equaling the legislature's total evaluation curve), subject to the constraint that the budget must cover the costs of production:

$$\text{maximize } B = aQ - bQ^2$$
$$\text{subject to } aQ - bQ^2 \geqslant cQ + dQ^2$$

The maximum budget corresponds to $Q = a/2b$, but this output level is not always attainable. In particular, if the budget and cost curves intersect at some $Q < a/2b$, as they do for C_2 in Figure 1, then the maximum budget cannot be reached; the costs of supplying $Q = a/2b$ will outweigh the legislative budget, and the bureaucrat will be unable to follow through on any promise to provide this level of output. Under these "cost-constrained" conditions, the largest budget the bureaucrat can secure corresponds to $Q = (a-c)/(b+d)$, the level of output for which the budget is just large enough to cover costs. If, on the other hand, the budget and cost curves do not intersect at some $Q < a/2b$, as is true for C_1 in Figure 1, then the legislative budget forthcoming at $Q = a/2b$ will be at least enough to cover the costs of supply. Under these conditions (which Niskanen calls "demand-constrained"), the rational bureaucrat will simply make the unconstrained choice of $Q = a/2b$ and secure the maximum budget.

Thus, there are two solutions to the budget-output decision, depending on the prevailing supply and demand conditions. And these two solutions, it turns out, have different implications for the internal efficiency and social optimality of bureaucratic performance.[7] Consider the question

---

tegically useful assumptions for some of the participants in the bargaining process.

[4]Note that it is the legislative committee, not the bureau, that exercises agenda control by presenting the legislature with a take-it-or-leave-it choice. (See our discussion under "Rules of Thumb.") Perhaps the clearest case of agenda control in a take-it-or-leave-it form is that by the local school board in placing tax millage proposals before the electorate. Here the school board, as legislature, is the agenda monopolist and the population is the relatively passive "sponsor." Romer and Rosenthal (1979) develop this case in a seminal article which is probably the most realistic application of the Niskanen model because of the relative passivity of large electorates and because of the control of the agenda by the school board.

[7]We should perhaps clarify the difference between internal efficiency and social optimality, as we use the terms here. Internal efficiency occurs when the supplier produces any possible level of Q at the least possible cost, given the current state of technology. Social optimality occurs at the particular level of output that maximizes the difference between the sponsor's evalua-

300 The American Political Science Review Vol. 77

Figure 1. Sponsor's Total Evaluation Function and Alternative Total Cost Functions.

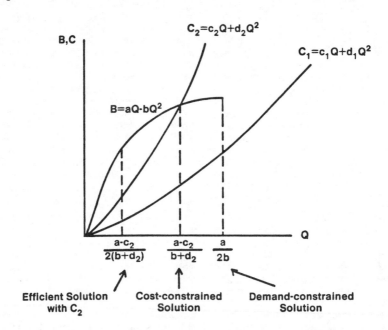

of efficiency. Under demand-constrained conditions, some portion of the legislature's appropriated budget will be wasted in the supply of Q; the budget generally exceeds the true costs of supply and, because the legislature is not privy to this information, the bureaucrat is able to use his discretion in allocating the slack resources in uneconomical ways—e.g., by hiring unnecessary staff. If budget and cost curves force the cost-constrained solution, however, the entire budget will be allocated toward the production of Q at minimum cost. In this sense, the cost-constrained bureau will operate efficiently.

The social optimality question prompts Niskanen to make two additional assumptions: that the legislature's total evaluation curve is an accurate reflection of the underlying social evaluation of Q, and that the bureau's cost curve represents the minimum social costs of supplying Q. Given these assumptions, it follows that the social optimum occurs at $Q = (a-c)/2(b+d)$, the output

level that equates marginal social benefits with marginal social costs. The cost-constrained solution, although internally efficient, therefore involves larger budgets and outputs than are socially optimal. It generates no social surplus whatever, and neither the legislature nor social consumers realize any net benefit on the exchange. The demand-constrained solution involves still larger levels of budget and output. Some social surplus is generated, but the bureau captures it all and puts it to socially inefficient use. Once again, the legislature and social consumers gain nothing.

All of this provides the foundation for Niskanen's central critique of bureaucracy: when governmental services are supplied by monopolistic bureaus, both the level of services and the amount spent on them will be higher than socially optimal. Government will be too large. Outcomes are more efficient under the cost-constrained than the demand-constrained bureaucratic solution, and Niskanen encourages a search for mechanisms that would promote the former result, e.g., committee restructuring to lower committee demand. But his major emphasis is on moving away from reliance upon monopoly bureaus and toward alternative arrangements that, particularly to an economist, have a capacity for improving social efficiency: privatization and competition.

---

tion curve and the minimum cost function: this difference is the social surplus. Niskanen's critique of bureaucracy is primarily a social optimality critique—bureaus produce too much.

A Broader Framework for Analysis

A basic problem here is that the connection between Niskanen's simple model and his general line of reasoning is ambiguous. In the first place, it is unclear whether the actions of legislative committees do indeed allow bureaucrats to act as if they are choosing from the legislature's total evaluation curve—a crucial foundation for his conclusions. This is unclear on logical grounds, for he never demonstrates the linkage by fully incorporating committees into his model. But it is also unclear for empirical reasons, because the literature on budgeting, which highlights the frugality of appropriations committees, suggests that high-demand committees may not be the norm at all.[8] Second, it remains a question whether the culprit in this tale is really the bureaucracy. After all, it could be the legislature that deserves most of the blame, owing to the way in which it organizes itself for budgetary decision making.[9] Niskanen's model, by implicitly combining the roles of bureaus and legislative committees, confounds their effects and makes the assignment of blame virtually impossible.

In this and subsequent sections, we develop a somewhat more elaborate model that addresses these ambiguities and, in so doing, allows for a more comprehensive analysis. To facilitate comparison with Niskanen's original model, however, the basic assumptions structuring his analysis are retained. We continue to focus on the same set of actors, to adopt the same functional forms for cost and benefit curves, and to assume that the latter accurately reflect social costs and benefits.[10] We depart from Niskanen in offering an explicit model of bureau-committee interaction. In its simplest form, this model is structured by four general assumptions:

1) The relationship between the actors is one of bilateral monopoly: the bureau is a monopoly supplier, the committee a monopoly buyer, and each tries to maximize its own utility in shaping budget-outcome decisions.

2) The relationship is hierarchic. a) Final budget-output decisions are taken by the committee, subject to approval by the full legislature. The role of the bureau is to supply cost information—not necessarily accurate—on the basis of which the committee makes its determinations. b) The sequence of steps in the decision process is implied by the committee's characteristic "mode of oversight," where the latter largely reflects the committee's (and the full legislature's) imposition of structure on budgetary interactions. This imposition may be the result of conscious choice or it may simply be the result of habit or tradition.

3) There are two polar modes of legislative oversight. a) *Demand revealing,* in which the legislature reveals a demand function for Q, then solicits cost information from the bureau, then makes its final decision. b) *Demand concealing,* in which the committee reveals nothing, requires the bureau to "go first" in transmitting a supply schedule, then makes its final decision.

4) The committee, knowing that its only information about costs comes from the bureau, does not try to arrive at a comprehensive estimate of the bureau's cost function. Instead, it adopts the simplest possible rule of thumb by announcing its intention to pay a flat amount, p, for each unit of Q. Its cost-estimation problem, then, reduces to the much easier task of settling upon a value for p.

Assumptions 1 and 2a are clearly consistent with Niskanen's general line of reasoning. Assumption 2b is added because it serves a necessary function: in order for there to be deterministic solutions in a bilateral monopoly game, some structure must be imposed on the interactions. Empirically, it is reasonable to posit that this structure is implicit in the modes of oversight employed by legislative committees. Assumption 3 is a useful way of entering the oversight factor into the analysis. As we will see, each model depicts an extreme case: in one the bureaucrat is able to extract maximum monopoly gains, and in the other the committee is able to extract maximum monopsony gains. Analysis of these polar cases, along with references to the continuum of cases in between, offers useful insights into the determinants of budget-output decisions and leads to reference solutions against which the Niskanen results can be evaluated. Assumption 4 is useful because it provides a common cost parameter, p, that structures the calculations of both participants—and because, as we will show, it makes possible an inquiry into the roles of legislative rules of thumb. But the assumption also

---

[8] For a discussion of the "watchdog" attitudes and central role of the appropriations committees, see Fenno (1966) and Wildavsky (1964). There is some evidence, however, that during the last decade or so, high-demand individuals have been more successful at landing the seats they want on the appropriations subcommittees. Whether this is significant for budgeting outcomes remains to be determined. For an overview of the literature, see Dodd and Schott (1979) and also Cowart (1981).

[9] The centrality of the legislature in the growth of the federal government is argued by Fiorina (1977), Hardin, Shepsle, and Weingast (1982), and Weingast (1979).

[10] Also, for simplicity and purposes of comparison, we follow Niskanen in assuming that the reversion level is zero (i.e., that the alternative to the committee's proposed budget is a budget of zero). An analysis allowing nonzero reversion levels is developed in Romer and Rosenthal (1979).

seems reasonable enough in itself. In some policy areas—defense, for instance—committees clearly do use per-unit prices as decision guides, and this practice may in fact be widespread.[11] More generally, the use of a per-unit price is consistent with an underlying legislative assumption that bureaucratic costs are linear functions of Q; since the committee cannot know whether costs are increasing or decreasing over the relevant range, and since either is feasible, it is reasonable to suggest that legislators often "muddle through" by assuming costs are approximately linear—and thus that budgetary cost can be represented as the quantity pQ.

This model does not require a high-demand committee. The relationship between the committee's demand for Q and the full legislature's demand for Q is a variable whose value remains to be filled in. We will do so by developing the analysis in two stages. In the first, we will derive a full range of conclusions based on the assumption that the committee is perfectly representative of the legislature as a whole. In the second, we will show how these conclusions change as the committee becomes increasingly unrepresentative. This two-stage treatment of committee demand, combined with attention to legislative oversight, allows us to distinguish the independent effects of these important components of legislative organization, and thus to explore the extent to which the legislature—rather than simply the budget-maximizing bureaucrat—can be responsible for problems of over-extended government.

Oversight by Representative Committee

A committee's benefit and cost functions are not the same as the legislature's. The committee receives some fraction of the total benefits deriving from Q, and it must pay some fraction of the total cost burden. When these fractions are equal, however, the committee's own cost-benefit calculations lead it to choose the same budget-output combination that the legislature itself would have chosen in seeking to maximize its net benefits. The representative committee, in other words, calculates as though it were acting on the

basis of the legislature's total-benefit and total-cost curves. And when its decision is presented in take-it-or-leave-it form to the whole body, of course, approval is always forthcoming. By focusing our analysis in this section on representative committees, then, we simplify matters substantially. Niskanen's benefit curves can be employed as though they are the committee's, and the constraint of legislative approval need not be entertained, since it is unbinding.

Bureaucratic Supply

Assume first that oversight is demand revealing. The committee is interested in maximizing its net benefits on the exchange, and thus (in effect) in maximizing $N = aQ - bQ^2 - pQ$, the difference between total benefits and budgetary costs. Treating p as a bureaucratically determined parameter, the committee maximizes with respect to Q, yielding

$$N' = a - 2bQ - p = 0$$
$$p = a - 2bQ$$

This is the demand curve the committee reveals to the bureaucrat, who must now respond by providing the committee with cost information. In general, he will want to supply information that maximizes his agency's budget. In making his decision, however, he can take advantage of his knowledge of legislative demand, which tells him how the committee will react to whatever choices he makes. Taking this committee reaction function into account, his constrained optimization problem becomes:

maximize $B = pQ$
subject to $pQ \geqslant cQ + dQ^2$
and $p = a - 2bQ$.

As in Niskanen's model, the bureaucrat is led to two solutions (Figure 2). Under demand-constrained conditions, he simply acts to maximize total revenue (the budget) by setting marginal revenue equal to zero and reading off the optimal price, $p = a/2$, from the committee demand curve. Given the committee's reaction curve, however, the bureaucrat knows full well that it will respond to $p = a/2$ by picking the companion output level he desires, $Q = a/4b$. Under cost-constrained conditions, illustrated in Figure 2, this price-output combination is unattainable because it calls for a price that does not cover the average cost of production. Here, the bureaucrat obtains his largest budget under the circumstances by setting average cost equal to

---

[11]For example, in the controversy surrounding close air support, there was a fixed per-unit "price" or procurement cost for each of the potential aircraft. The per-unit cost for the Harrier was $4.6 million. There was no expectation that the Department of Defense or other bureaucratic agency had offered a take-it-or-leave-it budget; on the contrary, the committee seemed perfectly capable of ordering any number of each type of aircraft at the per-unit price given for each. See Liske and Rundquist (1974).

Figure 2. Demand Revealing Solutions with Budget-Maximizing Bureaucrat.

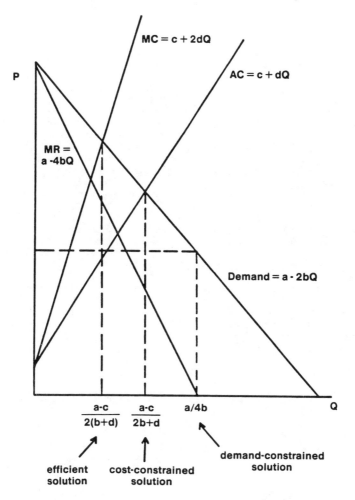

committee demand, yielding a price of $p = (2bc + ad)/(2b + d)$. This is the information the bureaucrat transmits about costs. He knows that the committee will react to this information by choosing $Q = (a-c)/(2b+d)$, his preferred output level.

The final step in the decision process is now pro forma. The committee acts to maximize its net benefits based on bureaucratically supplied cost information, and, in so doing, chooses the budget-output combination preferred by the bureaucrat. The committee makes the "final decision," but the bureaucrat's prior knowledge of its

reaction function has allowed him to engineer the whole process and predetermine the results.

These results are not immediately comparable to Niskanen's, because the parameter restrictions defining the demand-constrained and cost-constrained regions are different across models. In particular, for $d < b - 2bc/a$, both models are demand-constrained; for $d > 2(b - 2bc/a)$, both models are cost-constrained; and for parameter values in between, Niskanen's model is cost-constrained, whereas ours is demand-constrained. Comparisons are properly drawn within these sets, and when this is carried out, a sometimes messy process, the following conclusions emerge.

If we think of social welfare in terms of total social surplus, which is standard, then these levels of output generally correspond to higher levels of welfare that are closer to optimal than Niskanen's. They imply, in other words, better governmental outcomes for society. The only exception, ironically, is that demand-constrained output may be so far *below* the optimal level that Niskanen's own demand constrained result—which itself represents a government grown far too large—is actually a preferable outcome for society. The latter possibility can be illustrated with reference to Figure 2. Were the cost curves in the figure to shift downward, the socially optimal level of Q (given by the intersection of marginal costs and demand), would shift to the right, and there is clearly a whole range of cost conditions for which the optimum would be greater than $a/4b$, the demand-constrained solution. In general, the lower the true costs of production, the more likely the demand-constrained solution will obtain—and the more likely that it will actually imply a government that is too small, relative to the social optimum.

We may also want to think of social welfare in terms of legislative net benefit, for there is something rather perverse about measuring social welfare purely in terms of social surplus when all or most of it may be soaked up by the bureau. Looking at welfare in this way, comparison across models is unambiguous. Given our representative-committee model, the legislature and social consumers always realize net benefits on the budgetary exchange· under cost-constrained conditions they capture the entire surplus, whereas under demand-constrained conditions they divide the surplus with the bureau. By contrast, Niskanen's model implies that they never realize net benefits on the exchange, regardless of the underlying conditions. By this criterion, then, the representative-committee model associates uniformly higher levels of social welfare with the bureaucratic production of services than Niskanen's does.

Now assume that legislative oversight is demand concealing. Here, the decision process consists of two steps. First, the committee requires the bureaucrat to transmit a supply function indicating, for each possible price, how much Q he can promise to produce. The committee then takes this information into account in making the final budget-output decisions.

The bureaucrat must begin the process, then, by determining what supply function is best suited to the maximization of his own budget—with the committee providing him with no prior information about its demand. Treating p as a parameter, he calculates his optimal response by

maximizing $B = pQ$
subject to $pQ \geqslant cQ + dQ^2$

Figure 3. Demand-Concealing Oversight with Budget-Maximizing Bureaucrat.

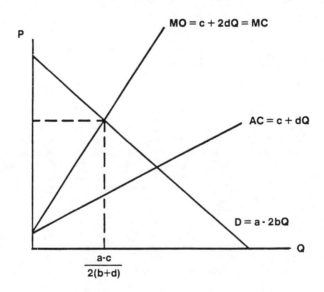

This leads to one solution. For any fixed p, the maximum budget the bureaucrat can achieve (i.e., the highest point along the line p_iQ), given the constraint, corresponds to the output at which $pQ = cQ + dQ^2$. Thus, the optimal budget-output combinations always lie along the bureaucrat's own cost curve—which means that, for any and all levels of Q, the supply schedule he or she reports to the committee is his or her true average cost curve. This is the bureaucrat's best budget-maximizing response, even though he is free to transmit any supply information he likes.

The committee takes this information, which describes the bureaucrat's reaction curve, and puts it to use in maximizing its net benefits on the exchange. As illustrated in Figure 3, its constrained optimization problem,

maximize $N = aQ - bQ^2 - pQ$
subject to $p = c + dQ$,

then leads it to calculate just as a classic monopsonist would: namely, by choosing the price-output combination that equates its marginal evaluation with its marginal outlay. The latter, however, is identical in this case to the bureaucrat's (and society's) marginal cost. Thus, the committee, in maximizing its own net benefits, is automatically led to choose the socially optimal level of output, $Q = (a-c)/2(b+d)$, at a price just covering the average cost of bureaucratic supply. The size of government, then, is "just right" under demand-concealing oversight. Social surplus is at a maximum, the legislature and social consumers capture it all (legislative net benefit is equal to social surplus), and the bureau produces efficiently.

There is no guarantee, of course, that either of these polar modes of oversight, demand concealing or demand revealing, will obtain empirically. And it is unlikely that any given legislative committee will be perfectly representative of the legislature as a whole. As a first step, however, this simplified analysis has been useful as a means of investigating basic relationships, and several of its implications stand out as particularly important.

1) Social welfare varies directly with the mode of legislative oversight. Society is better off when the committee hides its demand and requires the bureaucrat to go first in supplying cost information. To the extent that the committee reveals its demand for services beforehand, the bureaucracy will take advantage of the situation and impose less favorable outcomes.

2) The relationship between size of government and legislative oversight is contingent. Demand-concealing oversight leads to a government of optimal size, but a shift to demand-revealing oversight produces outcomes that may be larger or smaller than this.

3) Regardless of the mode of oversight, a representative committee system always produces smaller government and (except when outputs are far below optimal) higher levels of social welfare than Niskanen's model implies. Since he implicitly assumes high-demand committees, this is a preliminary indication that, if his logic is roughly correct, a good portion of the problem of oversized government is not the result of bureaucracy, but rather of the legislative committee system.

4) There are social conditions—demand-concealing oversight, representative committee system—under which monopolistic supply by budget-maximizing bureaus is socially optimal. Although these conditions are unrealistic, they are no less realistic than those underlying standard economic models of perfect competition, and it is unclear why this model of bureaucratic supply, as an ideal model of governmental service provision, should be any less useful or attractive than perfect competition itself.

Reform: Privatization

The fact is that perfect competition and its underlying logic have had major influences on scholarly thinking about government organization. In view of all the benefits associated with competition among profit-maximizing firms and all the costs associated with monopoly, it is a short step to the conclusion that governmental supply by monopoly bureaus produces serious social inefficiencies—and another short step to the conclusion that government can reduce social inefficiency through greater reliance upon private firms and competitive supply. For years, these points went without formal demonstration, and it was simply assumed they were consistent with the tenets of economic theory. When Niskanen's "demonstration" came along, his innovative analysis was widely acclaimed, but its effect was to justify general conclusions about bureaucracy that many economists (and, increasingly, political scientists) had already embraced.

It is certainly reasonable to argue that privatization and competition each have something important to offer. Privatization substitutes a profit-maximizing firm (e.g., through contracting arrangements) for a budget-maximizing bureau. Even in the absence of competition, the firm seeks to maximize the *difference* between revenues (budgets) and costs rather than to seek the greatest possible revenue. The result should be a smaller and presumably more optimal budget-output combination for society. Similarly, competition, even if it is only among public bureaus, should also lead to greater social efficiency, for it undermines the monopoly power of suppliers and loosens their exclusive control over cost information. Thus, granting that political realities may not allow for an ideal merging of privatization and competition, reform along either dimension would seem to promise socially beneficial results.

In this section we will evaluate the privatization argument by applying the two modes of legislative oversight to a new mode of supply: supply by a monopoly contractor. The method of analysis will be the same as before, except that the supplier now calculates with reference to a profit function, $Y = pQ - cQ - dQ^2$, rather than the bureaucrat's budget function, $B = pQ$.[12] Competition among suppliers, whether public or private, will be evaluated at a later point.

Suppose that oversight is demand revealing. Here, the committee begins the process by revealing the same demand schedule it would provide to the bureaucrat, $p = a - 2bQ$. The contractor takes advantage of this information in

maximizing $Y = pQ - cQ - dQ^2$
subject to $p = a - 2bQ$,

which leads to the standard monopolist solution: he chooses (implicitly) the output level at which marginal revenues and marginal costs are equal, and reads off the corresponding price from the revealed demand curve (Figure 4). The contractor then transmits this optimal price, $p = (ab + ad + bc)/(2b + d)$, to the committee, knowing that, given the committee's reaction curve, it will respond by picking the final output level he desires, $Q = (a-c)/(2b+d)$. As a comparison of Figures 2 and 4 illustrates, this output level is always smaller than the one yielded by bureaucratic supply under the same mode of oversight, and it is also smaller than the social optimum.

Now suppose oversight is demand concealing. The committee requires the contractor to begin

the process by submitting a supply schedule that indicates how much he will produce for different levels of price. Calculating without information on committee demand, the contractor seeks to

maximize $Y = pQ - cQ - dQ^2$

under the assumption that p is an unknown parameter whose value is ultimately chosen by the committee. His solution is to transmit the supply curve $p = c + 2dQ$, which is in fact his true marginal cost curve. The committee then takes this supply information into account in maximizing its own net benefits. This does *not*, however, lead the committee to choose the social optimum by setting marginal costs equal to its marginal evaluation. Instead, as shown in Figure 4, the committee behaves as any monopsonist would: it sets marginal *outlay* equal to its marginal evaluation, and thus chooses a level of output smaller than the social optimum. This level is also smaller, of course, than the one supplied by the bureau under demand-concealing oversight, since bureaucratic output equals the social optimum.

Some useful summary comparisons can now be made with the help of Tables 1, 2, and 3, which present figures on output, legislative net benefit, and social surplus, for both the bureaucratic and private modes of supply. Algebraic manipulation of these data leads to the following conclusions:

1) The relationship between legislative oversight and the level of private output is contingent. For $b > d$, demand-concealing oversight leads to larger outcomes than demand-revealing oversight, and, for $b < d$, the reverse is true.[13] This contingency reflects the actors' use of market power. When the committee acts as a monopsonist, constructing a marginal outlay curve from the supply schedule, its utility is more sensitive to the rate of increase in costs (d) than the rate of decrease in benefits (b). As Table 1 indicates, an increase in d therefore causes a greater reduction in its preferred output than does an identical change in b. Just the opposite occurs for the supplier, who, acting as a monopolist, finds that his profits are more sensitive to the rate of change in revenues (b) than the rate of change in costs (d). Because the committee and the supplier respond to the b and d terms differently, then, the demand-revealing (monopoly) solution will increase relative to the demand-concealing (monopsony) solu-

---

[12]Note that an analysis of "profit" (or slack or managerial discretionary profit) maximizing bureaucrats would follow precisely these lines, and that the results we obtain for the private monopolist could be employed (although we will not pursue it in this article) to investigate the implications of motivational diversity among bureaucrats. That is, the more a public bureaucrat values the *difference* between costs and budget, instead of the total budget, the more he will approximate the behavior of the profit-maximizing private entrepreneur. Conversely, private managers who maximize total sales revenue will behave exactly like public budget maximizers if they are facing the same kind of market. The only difference between private revenue maximizers and public budget maximizers is that private sales maximizers are normally thought of as facing a large number of buyers, whereas the public budget maximizer faces a monopsonistic legislature.

[13]Note that Figure 4 shows the demand-concealing solution larger than the demand-revealing solution, because of the relative steepness of the demand curves. For $b < d$, the reverse would have been true.

**Figure 4. Demand-Revealing and Demand-Concealing Oversight
with Profit-Maximizing Supplier.**

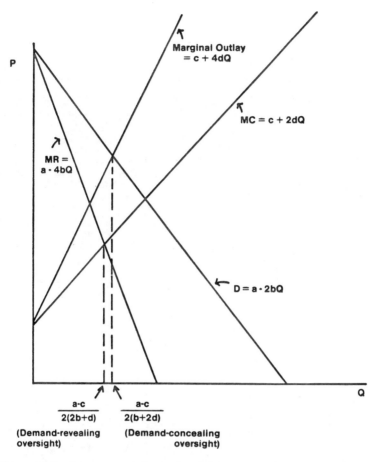

tion to the extent that b increases relative to d, and vice-versa.

2) By the social surplus criterion of welfare, bureaucracy is usually the preferable mode of supply. Specifically, bureaucracy can always be counted upon to yield higher levels of social welfare than private supply, except when oversight is demand revealing and $b > d$.

3) Given the social surplus criterion, society is usually better off when the committee adopts demand-concealing oversight. Specifically, this mode of oversight always gives rise to higher levels of social welfare than demand-revealing oversight does, except when $b < d$ and the mode of supply is private.

4) For either mode of oversight, the committee and the legislature are uniformly better off with bureaucratic supply. If we measure social welfare in terms of legislative net benefit, the same conclusion follows for society as a whole.

5) For either mode of supply, the committee and the legislature are uniformly better off with demand-concealing oversight. If social welfare is measured by legislative net benefit, then the same conclusion follows for society as a whole.

6) Whether social welfare is measured in terms of social surplus or legislative net benefit, society's best combination of modes is always bureaucratic supply/demand-concealing oversight.

7) Generally speaking, then, the emphasis of reformers on the beneficial consequences of privatization is not justified—not, at any rate, when the legislative committee system is representative.

308				The American Political Science Review				Vol. 77

Table 1. Output

	Demand-concealing oversight		Demand-revealing oversight
bureau			$\dfrac{(a-c)}{2b+d}$, $d \geqslant 2b - \dfrac{4bc}{a}$
			(greater than efficient)
	$\dfrac{a-c}{2(b+d)}$	(efficient output)	-------------------------------------
			$\dfrac{a}{4b}$, $d < 2b - \dfrac{4bc}{a}$ (indeterminate)
firm	$\dfrac{a-c}{2(b+2d)}$	(less than efficient)	$\dfrac{a-c}{2(2b+d)}$ (less than efficient)

Table 2. Legislative Net Benefit

	Demand-concealing oversight	Demand-revealing oversight
bureau		$\dfrac{b(a-c)^2}{(2b+d)^2}$, $d \geqslant 2b - 4bc/a$
	$\dfrac{(a-c)^2}{4(b+d)}$	-------------------------------
		$a^2/16b$, $d < 2b - 4bc/a$
firm	$\dfrac{(a-c)^2}{4(b+2d)}$	$\dfrac{b(a-c)^2}{4(2b+d)^2}$

Table 3. Social Surplus

	Demand-concealing oversight	Demand-revealing oversight
bureau		$\dfrac{b(a-c)^2}{(2b+d)^2}$, $d \geqslant 2b - 4bc/a$
	$\dfrac{(a-c)^2}{4(b+d)}$	--------------------------------
		$\dfrac{3a^2b - 4abc - a^2d}{16b^2}$, $d < 2b - 4bc/a$
firm	$\dfrac{(a-c)^2(b+3d)}{4(b+2d)^2}$	$\dfrac{(a-c)^2(3b+d)}{4(2b+d)^2}$

Although a shift to private supply does indeed lead to smaller government, government is "too small"; and, except under special conditions, social welfare is lower than it would be under bureaucratic supply.

Strategic Interaction

In the real world of politics, sophisticated maneuvering and anticipated reactions are everyday facts of life that influence budgetary decision making. To this point, our analysis has been built around polar categories that, taken singly, do not allow for such complex interactions on the part of participants. Considered together, however, these

same categories can be shown to constitute a very useful framework for thinking systematically about a full range of behavioral patterns—including not only strategic interaction between suppliers and committees, but also competition among suppliers.

A bilateral monopoly game, pitting monopolist against monopsonist, is strictly indeterminate. Depending upon their relative skills and resources, rational behavior may lead to outcomes falling anywhere between (or including) two extremes: one at which the monopolist gains maximum advantage by acting with full knowledge of the monopsonist's reaction curve, and one at which such advantages accrue only to the monopsonist.[14] Although these end-points are not necessarily the outcomes to be expected, they function to place important limits on the range of behavioral expectations. And when we recognize the kinds of resources and skills that tend to produce these extremes, we also gain broader insight into questions of why various interactions should lead to outcomes falling at different points in between.

In our framework, demand-revealing oversight guarantees maximum monopoly gains for the supplier, and demand-concealing oversight guarantees maximum monopsony gains for the committee. They therefore represent polar cases of the bilateral monopoly game, anchoring the ends of the continuum of possible outcomes. Note that this continuum *does not contain the Niskanen result.* Strategic interaction between bureaucrats and representative committees may lead to various levels of governmental output, but all of these are smaller than Niskanen predicts and, except under special conditions, social welfare is uniformly higher. This is true even if the committee *loses* the bargaining game entirely and passively allows the bureaucrat to exploit his monopoly position to the fullest.

Exactly where along the continuum will actual outcomes fall? This answer turns largely on each participant's success in learning the other's reaction curve. At the demand-concealing extreme, for example, the supplier is assumed to have no information about the committee's demand function; thus, he cannot strategically misrepresent his cost function with any assurance whatever that this misrepresentation will raise rather than lower his final budget or profit. On the other hand, once the supplier begins to gather clues about committee demand, he will have a foundation for misrepresenting the cost information he transmits. What holds for the supplier, however, also holds for the committee. The committee is best off if the supplier has no information about its evaluation of Q. Once it learns that the supplier is using available information to shape his cost transmissions, the committee will have an incentive to misrepresent the demand information on which the supplier bases his decisions, as well as to collect data on accurate supplier "prices."

The relative success of the players depends upon their relative resources and skills. The supplier, for instance, has a major informational advantage: he is the only one who knows the actual costs of supply, and the cost information he transmits need not reflect these actual costs in any respect. The committee, by contrast, must make the final decision, and thus, assuming that each final decision is taken to maximize its net gains, its budget-output choice ultimately demonstrates something about its true demand. Over time, therefore, the budgetary process tends to reveal more reliable information to the supplier than to the committee, other things being equal.

The supplier's informational advantage is offset, however, by several factors working in favor of the committee. First, committee demand is prone to change over time with such factors as changes in membership, constituency demands, and issue salience; to the extent that this is true, past decisions are less useful as indicators of present committee demand, and the supplier is forced to rely more heavily upon current information, which is more susceptible to manipulation by the committee. Second, although the supplier can only try to estimate the legislature's changing evaluation of Q, the supplier's own value function does not change at all and is likely to be transparent: if a bureaucrat, he is trying to maximize his budget, and, if a contractor, he is trying to maximize profit. Thus, it is much easier for the committee to know what the supplier is maximizing than for the supplier to know what the committee is maximizing, and this gives the committee a strategic advantage. Third, the committee can use its authority to impose any structure it wants on the budgetary process. Thus, it can require that the supplier go first in submitting cost information, while simply refusing to guarantee any prior information about demand. It can also specify what types of information are to be transmitted by the supplier, in what forms, and other requirements. The supplier will of course adjust to these requirements in his strategies of misrepresentation, but he cannot change the fundamental asymmetry in their relationship: he is subordinate to the committee in the hierarchy of governmental authority, and he must play the budgetary game within a structural framework set by the legislature.

In view of these considerations, there is no reason to think that the bargaining game is inherently stacked against the legislature, nor that budgetary outcomes should tend to approximate the demand-revealing end of the continuum. Legislators have important resources at their disposal, and, to the degree that they put these resources to use wisely, the budgetary process will yield smaller budget-output levels that are more nearly optimal for society as a whole. Better budgetary decisions are thus within the legislature's scope of action. Problems of seriously over-

---

[14]"Economists view the monopoly and monopsony solutions as the bargaining limits of the bilateral monopoly situation; the buyer can do no worse than the monopoly solution, and . . . the seller can do no worse than the monopsony solution." Henderson and Quandt (1980, p. 226).

310   The American Political Science Review   Vol. 77

sized government, should they occur, are not in-evitable—they are indications that the legislature is not taking advantage of its resources and is con-sistently losing a bargaining game that it could well win.

The bargaining game may, however, tend to favor bureaucratic suppliers over private sup-pliers. Bureaucrats are governmental insiders and may be in a better position than contractors to gain special insight into legislative demand, to understand the politics of budgeting, and to ob-tain sympathetic treatment from legislators. If bureaucrats do indeed have these resource advan-tages, then outcomes under bureaucratic supply may tend to be closer to the demand-revealing end of the continuum than would be true under pri-vate supply, and this will tend to lower (but not eliminate) the comparative benefits we associated with bureaucratic supply in the previous section. Although this possibility is worth noting, its im-portance should not be exaggerated. Most private contractors are *not* really outsiders; they have in-centives to seek the same kinds of information and special treatment that bureaucrats do, and their efforts along these lines often lead to estab-lished, regular roles in the political process. In many respects, they are just as much a part of politics as bureaucrats are. Thus, although it is reasonable to think that bureaucrats may have some advantages in the budgetary bargaining game, these advantages are unlikely to be very dramatic.

Reform: Competition

In conventional economic analysis, a compari-son of monopoly and competition is simplified by assuming that the costs of production are the same for both. Prices and outputs are understood to differ across the two modes of supply, then, not because of their cost characteristics, but because the monopolist exercises market power that competitive suppliers cannot. The monopo-list is able to pick both his optimal price and his optimal level of output, based on his knowledge of downward sloping market demand, whereas the competitive supplier must accept the going market price and is constrained to pick an output relative to that price. It is this greater degree of decisional control that allows the monopolist to produce less, receive a higher price, and make more profit than a set of competitive suppliers operating under precisely the same cost conditions.

This is the way competition and monopoly in the private sector are normally compared. Our own analytical framework, based upon polar modes of legislative oversight, easily allows an ex-tension of this logic in comparing competition and

monopoly in the provision of governmental ser-vices.[15] Demand-revealing oversight maximizes the monopoly power of the supplier, whether bureaucratic or private; the committee provides a demand schedule, and the supplier picks both his optimal price and his optimal output based on this information about demand. Demand-concealing oversight eliminates the supplier's monopoly power entirely; he transmits a supply schedule to the committee and then must accept whatever price-output decisions the latter makes. Thus, even though the prior analysis was developed in terms of a single supplier, the continuum of out-comes between the two poles in fact reflects an underlying movement from maximum to zero monopoly power—that is, from monopoly to competition. Holding cost conditions constant, then, the effect of introducing a degree of com-petition into the provision of governmental ser-vices is to shift social outcomes toward the demand-concealing end of the continuum. The more competitive the supply, the more closely the polar outcome will be approximated.

This does not mean that competition leads to a demand-concealing mode of oversight—just to the social outcomes associated with it. To illus-trate, suppose that oversight is demand revealing, supply is initially monopolistic, and additional suppliers are then introduced. A major effect of this new competition is to bring about—e.g., through supplier bidding or other market-like mechanisms—revelations of information about the actual costs of supply, putting the committee in a better decisional position for dealing with suppliers. At the same time, suppliers are *less* able to put the committee's revealed demand schedule to profitable use, owing to the uncertainties created by their own competition and inter-dependence. The net effect, then, when competi-tion is taken to its extreme, is to maximize the relative power of the committee over suppliers. Social outcomes will therefore be those associated with the demand-concealing pole of the con-tinuum—even if, in political practice, the commit-tee continues with a demand-revealing style of oversight.

A second point also needs to be stressed here we are only talking about competition on the sup-

---

[15]Niskanen's own analysis of competition among bureaus is inappropriate. He focuses on the (presumed) cost advantages associated with dividing supply among multiple suppliers, rather than holding (industry) costs constant and focusing solely on the implications of market power. Neither empirically nor theoretically is there a solid basis for concluding that small, competitive firms must supply goods at a lower cost than large, monopolistic firms. The question is a controversial one that remains unsettled.

ply side. On the demand side, there remains one buyer—the committee. Because of this, competitive supply does not produce anything like a competitive market for governmental services; it produces, rather, a one-sided competition that enhances the monopsony power of the committee. Under some conditions, however, we may observe competition on the demand side as well: for example, a large number of private buyers, plus the legislative committee, demanding services from a private monopoly supplier. In this case, competitive demand maximizes the monopoly power of the supplier vis-à-vis buyers, and shifts social outcomes toward the demand-revealing end of the continuum (whatever the prevailing mode of oversight may be). Thus, movement along the continuum can take place in either direction, depending upon how competition affects the monopoly power of sellers and the monopsony power of buyers. The market can only be "truly competitive" if both kinds of power are eliminated.

Given this background, it is now a straightforward matter to evaluate the reformist position on competitive supply. The question is: does the movement from monopoly to competition, whether among public bureaus or private firms, promise higher levels of social welfare? A comparison of polar social outcomes (presented in Tables 1, 2, and 3) leads to the following summary conclusions.

1) If governmental services are bureaucratically supplied, then the effects of competition are uniformly beneficial. The level of output moves toward (which usually means: declines toward) the social optimum, and both social surplus and legislative net benefit increase. Thus, the committee and the full legislature are better off with competition, as is society as a whole.

2) If governmental services are privately supplied, competition is *not* necessarily beneficial. When $b > d$, competition leads to higher, more nearly optimal levels of output, as well as to higher levels of social surplus and legislative net benefit. When $b < d$, on the other hand, competition leads to lower output than monopoly and to lower levels of social surplus—although legislative net benefit increases. By the usual social surplus measure of welfare, then, competition is socially beneficial when $b > d$ and socially harmful when $b < d$. From the standpoint of the committee and the full legislature, however, competition is always beneficial because it uniformly increases legislative net benefit.

There is a bit of irony in these results. Reformers' arguments on behalf of competition are invariably derived from an underlying belief in the benefits of competition among firms in the private sector. Yet, by their own measure of social welfare, competition in the supply of governmental services is only uniformly beneficial when the mode of provision is bureaucratic. When the private sector is relied upon, competition may actually be harmful. Thus, privatization and competition do not necessarily go hand-in-hand. Indeed, when these results are added to those in the preceding section, we find that the best combination for society—under a representative committee system—is bureaucratization and competition.

Oversight by High-Demand Committee

To this point, the analysis suggests that budget-maximizing bureaucracy has shouldered more than its share of the blame for problems of big government. If government is in fact too large, it appears to be because the legislature has made unwise decisions (or simply drifted into suboptimal patterns of behavior) regarding modes of oversight and service delivery. But this is only part of the story, for there is an entire dimension of legislative impact that remains to be investigated: the legislature also makes decisions about its own internal organization, decisions that determine the extent to which its committee system will be representative. To round out the analysis, we need to know what happens when the legislature undergoes an organizational shift from representative to unrepresentative committees—particularly when this leads to oversight by high-demand committees of the sort envisioned by Niskanen. What does such a change imply for the size of government and levels of social welfare?

Following Niskanen, we can assume the legislature is divided into three groups of equal size, each with its own evaluation function, V_i, and each assigned a tax share (a share of the total costs), t_i, of $1/3$.

$$V_1 = a_1aQ - (b/3)Q^2$$
$$V_2 = a_2aQ - (b/3)Q^2$$
$$V_3 = a_3aQ - (b/3)Q^2$$

For simplicity, the evaluation functions are assumed to differ only as a result of the a_i, where $a_1 \geqslant a_2 \geqslant a_3$ and $a_1 + a_2 + a_3 = 1$. Thus, group 1 is the high-demand group, group 2 is the middle-demand group, and group 3 is the low-demand group. Legislative oversight responsibilities are given over to the high-demand group, which makes budget-output decisions subject to final approval by the legislature as a whole. This approval is not automatically forthcoming, however, as it was for the representative committee. The high-demand committee's final budget-outcome decisions must guarantee net benefits to (or at least not impose net costs upon) the middle-demand group—which holds the balance of power in a majority voting scheme, and which places a lower value on Q than the committee does. The committee's task, then, is to maximize its own net benefits in dealing with the suppliers of governmental services, subject to the following constraint:

$$a_2aQ - (b/3)Q^2 \geqslant t_2pQ \text{ or, since } t_2 = 1/3,$$
$$p \leqslant 3a_2a - bQ.$$

Two issues need to be addressed before the analysis can be carried out. First, the evaluation function of the middle-demand group is now relevant to the behavior of both the committee and suppliers, and it makes a difference who (if anyone) knows what this function is. We will assume that the committee, as part of the legislature, always has information on this dimension, whereas the supplier may or may not: under demand-revealing oversight the middle-demand constraint is revealed to the supplier, and under demand-concealing oversight, it is not. This is a reasonable assumption empirically. It also maintains the market-power implications of the polar cases, while simplifying informational complexities in a way that is analytically workable, for if the committee did not possess the requisite information, it would be unable to express a meaningful demand and thus unable to follow through on its promises. Second, since budgetary outcomes will often reflect the middle-demand constraint, an evaluation of social consequences depends upon the representativeness of this middle-demand group. Niskanen seems to assume that this group is representative of the legislature as a whole (and thus of society), which implies $a_2 = 1/3$. To enhance comparability, we will go along with this assumption initially. In subsequent analysis, however, we will allow for the possibility that the middle-demand group, too, may be unrepresentative. In conjunction with the foregoing work, then, this will yield three perspectives on budgetary outcomes: one in which the oversight committee is representative, one in which the oversight committee is not (necessarily) representative, but the middle-demand group is, and one in which neither is (necessarily) representative.

High-Demand Committee, Representative Middle-Demand Group

Suppose first that oversight is demand revealing and supply is bureaucratic. Here the committee can reveal its own demand function only when it offers p-Q combinations acceptable to the middle-demand group, and thus only when its demand function lies below the middle-group con-

straint, as it does for $Q > Q_x$ in Figure 5. Should its demand be too high over some range of output, as it is for $Q < Q_x$, the best the committee can do is to reveal the middle-group constraint as its own demand. The net result is committee revelation of a kinked demand curve, dd', to the bureaucrat.

To simplify matters, we can concern ourselves with the extreme—and, given Niskanen's argument, most interesting—case in which the disproportion between the high-demand and middle-demand groups is at its greatest. This case occurs when $a_1 = 2/3$, $a_2 = 1/3$, and $a_3 = 0$. Under these conditions of maximum skewness, the committee's demand is sufficiently high that it lies above the constraint for all values of Q. The kink therefore disappears, and the committee's revealed demand is simply the middle-group constraint.

The bureaucrat calculates in the same way as in our earlier analysis, except that he now seeks to maximize his budget subject to this new revealed demand curve. His solutions, displayed in Figure 6, prove to be *identical to Niskanen's*. Under cost-constrained conditions, he chooses $Q = (a-c)/(b + d)$ and, under demand-constrained conditions, he chooses $Q = a/2b$. For the former solution, output is far too large and social surplus and legislative net benefit are both zero. For the latter, output remains too large and, although social surplus is positive, it accrues entirely to the bureaucrat, leaving the legislature with zero net benefits. Both solutions offer net benefits to the high-demand committee—which pays the same costs as the other groups, but values the provision of Q far more. Net costs are imposed on the low-demand group.

Now suppose that oversight is demand concealing. The bureaucrat, as before, begins the process by revealing a supply schedule equal to his actual average costs. The committee, acting as a monopsonist, then uses this supply information to construct a marginal outlay curve, and it solves for Q by setting marginal outlay equal to its own marginal evaluation (Figure 6). Under the high-demand conditions represented by $a_1 = 2/3$, however, the resulting price-output combination is outside the feasible region defined by the middle-demand constraint. The best it can do under the circumstances is to choose $Q = (a-c)/(b+d)$, which, again, *is the Niskanen result*.

Niskanen's model can therefore be viewed as a special case of the more general model developed here: it describes bureaucratic behavior when the disproportion between the high-demand committee and the middle-demand group is at a maximum, and it applies *regardless* of the mode of oversight. The differences between our model and Niskanen's, as outlined in earlier sections of the

Figure 5. Kinked demand curve resulting from high-demand committee subject to majority rule constraint

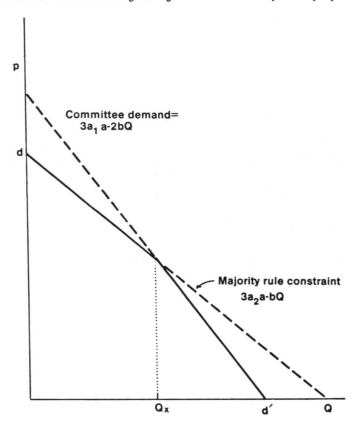

analysis, can thus be explained by the decisional impact of the committee system. For, when representative committees give way to very high-demand committees, the two models turn out to have identical implications for bureaucratic supply.

They are identical, however, when committee demand is very high. When the disproportion is less severe, our model continues to imply smaller levels of government and higher levels of social welfare than Niskanen's, as is illustrated in Figure 7, which outlines the relevant solutions. (For simplicity, only the cost-constrained result is presented for demand-revealing oversight.) The familiar ordering is preserved: the Niskanen output is the largest, followed by the demand-revealing output and then the demand-concealing output. A quick comparison with Figure 2, however, suggests an important difference: both the demand-revealing and the demand-concealing outputs are now larger than they were under a

representative committee system. Thus, the effect of the high-demand committee is to shift the whole continuum of outcomes to the right. The higher the committee's demand, the farther to the right the continuum shifts, and the shorter the distance between the demand-revealing and demand-concealing outputs. In the limit, the continuum collapses on the extreme right point: the Niskanen result.

Now suppose the supplier is a private contractor. Under demand-revealing oversight, the very-high-demand committee reveals the middle-group constraint as its own demand. The profit-maximizing contractor then uses this information to calcullate his (her) marginal revenue, which he equates to marginal cost in arriving at an output choice, as shown in Figure 8. Because of its anchoring in the representative group's total evaluation, however, his marginal revenue is in fact identical in this case to marginal social benefit— and his decisional calculus, as a result, leads him to choose *the social optimum.*

Under very-high-demand conditions, then, the combination of demand-revealing oversight and private supply maximizes social surplus and produces a government whose size is "just right." The benefits of social efficiency, however, are not immediately felt by the legislature or consumers, for their net benefit is zero. The only legislative group to benefit from this arrangement is the high-demand group—which shares the social surplus with the monopoly contractor. It is worth noting, moreover, that the high-demand group benefits *less* from this social optimum than it would from nonoptimal bureaucratic supply. As a comparison of Figures 6 and 8 suggests: under demand-revealing oversight, the committee is better off choosing bureaucratic over private supply

because the former, in overproducing, generates greater net benefits for the committee at the same time that it generates less surplus for society as a whole. If the committee has its way, then, the social optimum is not likely to be chosen.

Now consider demand-concealing oversight. As in the earlier analysis, the private contractor begins the process by revealing a supply schedule equal to his marginal costs. The committee then responds by constructing a marginal outlay curve, which it equates to its own marginal evaluation in arriving at its desired level of output, as shown in Figure 9. When $a_1 = 2/3$, however, this output is outside the feasible region defined by the constraint. The best the committee can do is to opt for $Q = (a-c)/(b+2d)$, the boundary point at which marginal cost (supply) and the demand

Figure 6. Oversight by very high demand committee with bureaucratic supplier

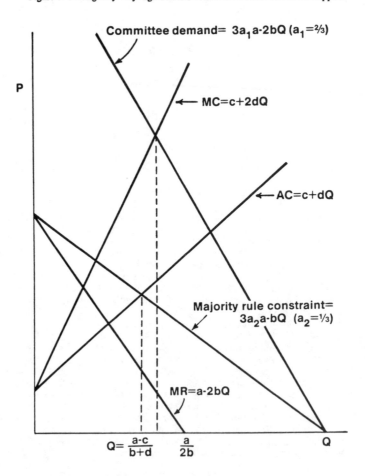

Figure 7. Demand-revealing oversight by moderately high demand committee with bureaucratic supplier

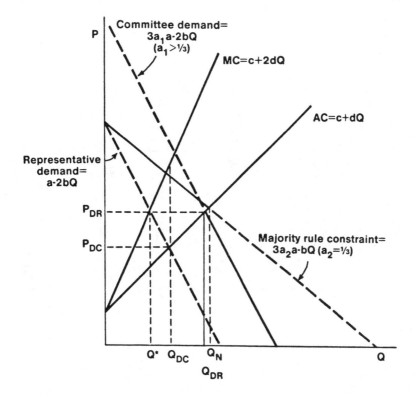

constraint are equal. This level of output is larger than the social optimum (although smaller than the Niskanen result) and yields a correspondingly lower level of social surplus. Legislative net benefit remains zero. The high-demand committee is actually better off as a result of these developments—which is not surprising, since this mode of oversight maximizes its power—but these benefits still do not make privatization an attractive mode of supply. As Figures 6 and 9 indicate, the committee continues to prefer bureaucracy. Under demand-concealing oversight as under demand-revealing oversight, bureaucratic supply guarantees greater output and greater net benefits for the committee despite its relative inefficiency for society.

Comparison of these results to those of the representative-committee model helps to suggest what happens under demand conditions that are less extreme. When the committee and the middle group have roughly equal evaluation functions, the combination of private supply and demand-revealing oversight leads to a suboptimal level of output; as the disproportionality between the two

groups increases, this suboptimal solution moves toward and finally equals the social optimum, $Q = (a-c)/2(b+d)$. The combination of private supply and demand-concealing oversight also produces a suboptimal solution under conditions of roughly equal demand; but here, as the disproportionality increases, output surpasses the social optimum and reaches its superoptimal boundary value, $Q = (a-c)/(b+2d)$.

In short, as demand increases, the whole continuum of results shifts to the right—to the point where private supply is no longer associated with levels of government that are too small. Moreover, although roughly equal demand conditions lead to ambiguity about which mode of oversight implies better social outcomes, high demand leads to the dominance of the demand-revealing solution. This only makes sense, because in minimizing the relative power of the high-demand committee, the demand-revealing mode of oversight allows the contractor to choose the smaller, more nearly optimal levels of government he actually prefers.

Given the foregoing analysis, a comparison of

bureaucratic and private supply is now a straight-forward matter. Under high-demand conditions, private supply yields uniformly smaller levels of output. Ranking the combinations from smallest to largest output, we have: private/demand-revealing, private/demand-concealing, bureaucratic/demand-concealing, bureaucratic/demand-revealing. (In the limit, the latter two are equal.) Similarly, private supply also yields uniformly higher levels of social surplus, with supply/oversight combinations ranked precisely as above in order of social preferability. The dominance of private supply must be qualified, however, by two factors. First, legislative and consumer net benefit are zero for *both* private and bureaucratic supply under very high demand; thus, whereas the former is "better" in generating a social surplus, the surplus is captured entirely by the contractor and the committee. Second, the committee always prefers bureaucratic to private supply, and thus, to the extent the committee is able to make legislative choices about the mode of supply,

bureaucracy will be the winner despite its greater social inefficiency.

A final conclusion is that competition has different effects across these alternative modes of supply. Competition among public bureaus is beneficial under conditions of roughly equal demand, but as demand increases, the benefits from competition decline until, with a very-high-demand committee, competition makes no difference at all. Competition among private suppliers, by contrast, is actually *harmful*. Under very-high-demand conditions, the demand-revealing solution yields the social optimum at the same time that it maximizes the monopoly power of the contractor; competition operates to increase the relative power of the committee, allowing the latter to impose a larger, less optimal level of output than a monopoly contractor would choose on his own.

The general thrust of this section's analysis, then, suggests that the critics of bureaucracy are largely but not entirely correct, if we assume the

Figure 8. Demand-revealing oversight by very high demand committee with private supplier

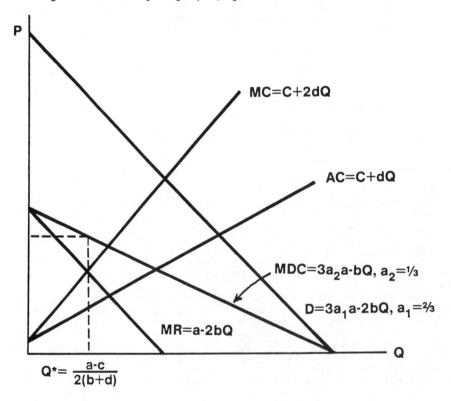

Figure 9. Demand-concealing oversight by very high demand committee with private supplier

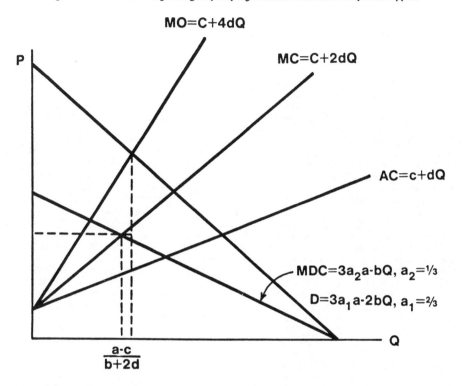

$$MO=C+4dQ$$

$$MC=C+2dQ$$

$$AC=c+dQ$$

$$MDC=3a_2a\text{-}bQ, a_2=\tfrac{1}{3}$$

$$D=3a_1a\text{-}2bQ, a_1=\tfrac{2}{3}$$

$$\frac{a\text{-}c}{b+2d}$$

legislature is organized into high-demand committees, and if we assume the middle-demand group is representative of the legislature as a whole. Under these conditions, bureaucracy does lead to the Niskanen results, government is far too large, and a shift to private supply does imply smaller government and higher levels of social welfare. They are wrong, however, in stressing the value of competition; under these assumed conditions, competition does not work for public bureaus, and it makes matters worse when supply is private. The best combination for society, given these conditions, is private supply, demand-revealing oversight, and no competition.

High-Demand Committee, Unrepresentative Middle Group

All of this assumes the middle-demand group is representative of the legislature as a whole. Empirically, however, there is no reason to think that this assumption is generally or even usually tenable. Most interestingly, demand for some services—agricultural subsidies, urban renewal, and others—could easily be skewed to the point that virtually all legislative demand is concentrated in one group, with the rest of the legislature fairly indifferent. If so, this high-demand group's a_1 could clearly be greater than 2/3 and perhaps close to 1. Since we must have $a_1 + a_2 + a_3 = 1$, the middle-demand group's a_2 would correspondingly be less than 1/3 and perhaps near 0. With tax shares equally allocated across groups at 1/3, it follows that the middle group is no longer representative of the legislature as a whole. In particular, its evaluation of these governmental services is now lower, possibly by a great deal, than representativeness would require.

Suppose that social demand happens to be concentrated in the group with oversight responsibilities, and that its decisions are constrained by a middle-demand group of the sort described here. What are the implications for the size of government and social welfare? The committee now demands more than before, owing to its upward shift in a_1, but its greater demand is irrelevant. The only relevant change is the downward shift in the middle-demand constraint, reflecting the smaller value of a_2. For both modes of oversight the final output choice is $Q = (3a_2a-c)/(b+d)$, given by the intersection of average cost and the constraint. Under a representative middle-group constraint, when $a_2 = 1/3$, this is simply the Niskanen result. But as the constraint shifts downward, implying a more and more unrepresentative middle-demand group, the decline in a_2 signals a corresponding decline in final output, until a point is reached at which the middle-demand group refuses to approve *any* feasible appropriation for Q. The tendency, then, is toward *undersupply in the extreme.*

When we drop the restrictive assumption of representativeness, therefore, an increasingly high-demand committee does not imply larger government. Ironically, it implies just the opposite. The key decisional role is played not by the committee, but by the middle demand group. As the committee's demand increases as a proportion of the total legislative demand, the middle group's proportion automatically decreases and imposes a constraint more and more unrepresentative of the entire body. Under these conditions, Niskanen's emphasis is quite misplaced: bureaucracy overseen by an increasingly high-demand committee threatens society with a problem of undersupply, not oversupply, and the decision maker most responsible for the suboptimality is the middle-demand group, which refuses to approve higher output levels more beneficial for society.

A shift from bureaucratic to private supply cannot remedy the problem. Whatever the mode of oversight, a monopoly contractor will produce even less than a monopoly bureau, thus exaggerating the undersupply. Nor can competition be of much help. It has no effect on bureaucratic supply, and although it does serve to increase private supply, the output still remains lower than with a monopoly bureau. Thus, when the middle-demand constraint is severe, neither of these familiar reforms represents even a partial solution to the problem of undersupply.

This problem seems to have gone unrecognized by Niskanen and other critics of bureaucracy. But, particularly for policy areas in which benefits have a skewed distribution, there is good reason to think that it will often arise. Under such distributions, and in the absence of generalized logrolling, the vast power critics have attributed to budget-maximizing bureaus and high-demand committees simply does not exist. They may well be "in bed with each other," as Niskanen claims, owing to their common interest in securing high levels of output, but they also share a true powerlessness to do anything about the binding constraint from the legislature as a whole. Both would like a larger level of production, but neither can get it, even if it is socially preferable for them

to do so.

Empirically, this may or may not prove to be a serious problem, for they may be able to get out of the bind by entering into logrolling relationships with elements of the middle-demand group. All legislators serve both as committee members and as voters on each others' proposals, so there is clearly an incentive for horsetrading in which some members of the middle-demand group agree (in effect) to loosen the constraint in return for reciprocal action when their own committee proposals come up for a vote. In practice, then, legislative politics may tend to correct somewhat for the undersupply problem, and in some cases even convert it into an oversupply.[16]

The important theoretical point, however, remains: once we get beyond the restrictive assumption of a representative middle-demand group, the "problem of bureaucracy" can cut both ways. Government may be too large, but it may also be too small. The direction of the problem (if there is one) depends on the characteristics and decisional roles of all three participants—the supplier, the oversight committee, and the middle-demand group. To focus on budget-maximizing bureaucracy and high-demand committees, as critics tend to do, overlooks a whole dimension of the budgetary decision: a dimension which, as we have seen, can generate social outcomes precisely the opposite of what the critics would have us expect.

Rules of Thumb

Throughout this analysis, we have assumed that the legislative committee does not even try to estimate the supplier's cost function, but adopts instead a simplifying rule of thumb. It proceeds as though budgetary costs rise linearly with output, and it concerns itself with deciding upon final values for both Q and the parameter of linearity (which we have called "price"). Niskanen does not allow the relevance of rules of thumb, nor does he explore the theoretical roles of the implicit, nonmarket "prices" that might be inherent in them. Instead, he stresses that there are generally no market prices for the services of bureaus and argues that this is the key to bureaucratic power. In part, his explanation turns on the monopoly control over cost information that this affords the bureaucrat. But it also turns on the strategic advantages entailed by the use of total rather than

[16]Note that the conditions obtaining in this section are essentially those of distributional politics, and that our conclusions about potential undersupply and incentives for logrolling (or universalistic norms) are consistent with recent theoretical work in the area. See Weingast (1979), Shepsle and Weingast (1981), Ferejohn (1974), and Arnold (1979).

per-unit budgetary figures. As he models it, the bureau (or private supplier, in the absence of market prices) presents a total budget level as a take-it-or-leave-it item for the legislature's decision, which allows the bureau to control the legislature's agenda and engineer the final outcome. Orzechowski (1975, p. 231) describes the model approvingly as follows:

> (Niskanen) assumes that bureaus possess a unique monopoly advantage and asserts that bureaus can exercise monopoly power to the degree of perfect price discrimination. Bureaus are able to extract almost the full amount of consumer surplus generated by government output. The highest degree of monopoly power is afforded bureaus because of the institutional features of the budgetary process. Bureaus bargain with appropriations committees on the basis of a total budget. Bargaining does not proceed on a per unit basis. The fiscal purchaser, in effect, is constrained to buy the output of a monopoly bureau in one large package. That is, he is constrained to buy at all-or-nothing prices.

Before contrasting these approaches, a basic ambiguity must be cleared away: legislatures are indeed confronted with take-it-or-leave-it choices, as Niskanen contends, but this agenda control is actually exercised by legislative committees, not by bureaus. Bureaus and committees interact in the stage before legislative ratification. At this stage, appropriations committees may well focus on total budgets, but they are hardly limited to the evaluation of just one budget level submitted by the bureau. They clearly consider a range of budgetary options in the process of arriving at a final choice to be submitted to the full body. Thus bureaus can only exercise a degree of agenda control in the larger legislative arena by working through legislative committees, and, in attempting to do so, must come to grips with the fact that legislative committees need not allow their *own* agendas to be controlled. Even if budgets are considered entirely in terms of total expenditures rather than per-unit prices, it does not follow that bureaus are able to achieve agenda control or the favorable budgetary outcomes such control entails. These results are determined by the strategic relationship between the bureau and the committee, and it is here that theoretical interest properly centers.

In the preceding sections, we analyzed this relationship by assuming the committee adopts a linearity rule of thumb. But now suppose it does not, and that instead both the committee and the bureau are free to consider or propose any functional form linking budgets to outputs. Does this removal of the rule-of-thumb constraint on budgetary interactions lead to the kinds of results Niskanen says we should expect?

The answer is mixed. Under demand-concealing oversight, behavior is the same as before; the bureaucrat, acting in complete ignorance of committee demand, continues to reveal his true costs. Under demand-revealing oversight, however, things are now quite different indeed. Whereas the bureaucrat was previously constrained to report a supply schedule that takes account of the committee's linearity assumption, he now has the flexibility to *fit* his reported supply schedule precisely to the committee's total evaluation curve— i.e., to report that the cost of supplying any Q is (virtually) identical to the maximum amount the committee would under any conditions be willing to pay. Knowledge of the committee's total evaluation curve and complete flexibility in reporting a supply schedule therefore combine to extend the bureaucrat strict control over the committee's agenda. He then uses this power to capture the committee's entire consumer surplus. This may or may not involve larger levels of Q, however, depending on the representativeness factor. As formal analysis could show, output increases to what we have called the Niskanen level when the committee is representative of the full legislature, or when the committee expresses a high demand but the middle legislative group remains representative. When the latter is unrepresentative, on the other hand, output remains the same and is likely to be severely suboptimal.

In sum, elimination of the committee's linearity rule of thumb does give the bureau real strategic advantages, and these advantages translate into budget-output combinations that, relative to those derived in the foregoing sections of this article, are more consistent with Niskanen's original conclusions, although they remain, given the mitigating effects of representativeness and modes of oversight, less pessimistic than Niskanen's about the "bureaucracy problem."

Knowing this, we can now learn a far more important lesson by turning the comparison around and asking: what can we say about the role of legislative rules of thumb? Above all, we can now see that these rules of thumb are *rational* in these kinds of budgetary games, regarding their consequences for both the committee and society as a whole. Legislative rules of thumb, whatever their precise content, *prevent* the bureaucrat from reporting a supply schedule that mirrors the committee's total evaluation. They constrain his flexibility and thus undercut a crucial prerequisite for agenda control. The result is that the bureaucrat must package his supply information within a framework imposed by the committee, and, as we saw in the case of the linearity rule of thumb, this requirement will tend to block him from achieving budgets and outputs as large as he would like. Perhaps surprisingly, then, a legislative rule of thumb adopted entirely in ignorance and *not* designed to discover true bureaucratic costs is in fact well suited to the pursuit of legislative and social ends.

The rationality of legislative rules of thumb takes on special importance in light of three additional considerations. The first is that the adoption of rules of thumb is within the committee's power; it is a step the committee can take *on its own* to improve its strategic position. It is a tool for gaining leverage in the budgetary game, and it is even more powerful in this respect than the mode of oversight (another dimension of committee choice), because the latter can be undermined by forces beyond the committee's control. A high-demand individual on a representative committee, for example, may secretly leak information on the committee's total evaluation function, thus defeating the purpose of demand-concealing oversight, whereas a rule of thumb, once adopted, structures decisional outcomes without need of secrecy or universal cooperation.

The second point is that rules of thumb need not be consciously adopted to be effective. They may be the product of habit, tradition, or accident, or they may be uncalculated adjustments to reduce uncertainty. Whatever the explanation, once rules of thumb emerge and become ingrained as components of the process, they can structure decision making and place constraints on bureaucrats just as effectively as if they had been chosen for that purpose. The very fact that they should tend to work to the committee's advantage in practice, moreover, can only promote their continued use and deeper entrenchment. Thus, just as informational monopoly works to the bureaucrat's advantage, so rules of thumb work to the committee's advantage, but they can work unobtrusively, even if no one plans it that way.

Finally, if anything at all is clear from the empirical literature on budgeting, it is that legislative committees *do* rely upon rules of thumb as guides in decision making and that these rules *do* in fact play important roles in structuring political interactions and outcomes. For real-world budgetary contexts, therefore, it is only reasonable to suggest that bureaucrats ordinarily find their flexibility constrained by legislative rules of thumb. The extent to which these rules are strategically chosen rather than nonrationally embraced remains to be determined, but this is not, at any rate, of real consequence. The important point is that the context is in fact structured by decision rules, however implicit, and that bureaucrats indeed must operate within a decisional framework not entirely of their own making.

In short, legislative committees should, can, and in fact do adopt rules of thumb, which in turn serve to structure bureaucratic as well as committee decision making in significant ways. It seems apparent that an adequate model of bureaucratic behavior must recognize this in some fashion. As a first step, we have tried to do this by means of the linearity rule, but there are obviously various ways in which it might be approached. A model that assumes no constraints on bureaucratic strategies, as Niskanen's implicitly does, can only exaggerate the bureaucrat's ability to exercise agenda control and win large budgets and outputs.

Conclusion

By integrating bureaucratic and legislative behavior, this model places the "bureaucracy problem" in broader perspective and discourages simple evaluations and solutions. Will government be too large? Does bureaucracy inevitably overproduce? Do privatization and competition yield smaller government and higher social welfare? Given our model, the answers to these and other questions depend upon conditions reflecting the way the legislature organizes itself for decision making. In particular, through the design of its committee system, the operation of rules of thumb, and the adoption of characteristic modes of oversight, the legislature sets the parameters of governmental supply. It is this structure imposed by the legislature that most fundamentally shapes the size of government, the performance of bureaucracy, and the impact of reforms.

In effect, the critics' position on the "bureaucracy problem" assumes a specific legislative structure: oversight by very-high-demand committees, total bureaucratic flexibility in framing decisional alternatives, and final choice by a representative middle-demand group. Under these conditions, regardless of the mode of oversight, it does indeed follow that bureaucracy generates big government. But when committee demand is less extreme, bureaucrats are constrained by legislative rules of thumb, or the middle-demand group is to some degree unrepresentative, very different substantive conclusions may be entailed.

Given the linearity rule of thumb, for instance, a dramatic contrast emerges when both the committee and the middle-demand group are representative. Within this structure bureaucracy is generally superior to private supply, government is smaller than the critics expect, and, when the committee adopts a demand-concealing mode of oversight, bureaucracy actually produces at the social optimum. Another striking departure from the critics' position emerges when a high-demand committee is combined with an unrepresentative middle-demand group; under these conditions, government tends not only to be smaller than they expect, but may be far below the social optimum, perhaps justifying fears of a "small government problem," and bureaucracy is again associated with higher levels of welfare than private supply.

In general, different legislative conditions give rise to different conclusions about bureaucracy and the size of government, and the conclusions of Niskanen and other critics, implicitly pegged to a specific set of conditions, portray the "bureaucracy problem" in its extreme, most negative form. Virtually *any* other set of conditions implies a more moderate and positive perspective, and, not surprisingly, a less enthusiastic evaluation of their proposed reforms.

A broader theory of this sort does more than simply challenge the general conclusions of bureaucracy's critics. Precisely because it does generate implications of a contingent rather than universal nature, it also underlines the need for certain kinds of empirical research. This involves, of course, the testing of hypotheses, but it also involves inquiry into what is perhaps the most fundamental question at this point: what legislative conditions do in fact prevail? We need to know, in particular, what modes of oversight legislative committees adopt, how representative these committees are, how representative the middle-demand group is, and which rules of thumb obtain. Research on Congress and other legislatures has yet to provide the kind of empirical foundation necessary for confident evaluation. It is only reasonable to suggest, however, that modes of oversight, degrees of representativeness, and (perhaps to a lesser extent) rules of thumb will vary across committees as well as with types of policies, and thus that the incidence, severity, and effective reforms of the "bureaucracy problem" will vary, too, in a corresponding way. Some parts of the government are likely to be overgrown and proper targets of structural reform, whereas others are systematically underfunded and quite undeserving of criticism. The interesting question, then, is not whether we have a "bureaucracy problem," but where and to what extent the problem surfaces. The key to an answer rests with the underlying patterns of legislative organization and with empirical research to discover what those patterns are.

The theory can also be put to prescriptive use, particularly in linking legislative reforms to bureaucratic behavior. Most important, it implies that the legislature can take positive steps to minimize the problems commonly associated with bureaucratic supply. As Hardin, Shepsle, and Weingast claim (1982, p. 22), "Bureaucracies are 'runaways,' and spending programs are 'uncontrollable,' because Congress made them that way." Specifically, by purposely moving toward representative oversight and decision structures, demand-concealing modes of oversight, and appropriate rules of thumb, legislatures may do a great deal to get runaway bureaucracies under control. This may involve, for instance, applying different criteria for assigning individuals to committees, adopting different rules governing committee jurisdiction, requiring different oversight procedures, embracing simplified decisional assumptions, or even taking some kinds of final decisions out of the hands of the full legislature.

It also implies that certain kinds of legislative reforms should *not* be adopted. As we have seen, this is often true of privatization and competition, particularly when proposed in combination, but it is also true of other popular reforms. PPBS, ZBB, and other proposals for rationalizing the budgetary process, for example, are likely to aggravate rather than relieve problems of bureaucratic supply, and they should be avoided. In requiring policymakers to articulate mechanisms and costs, they effectively impose a demand-revealing mode of oversight that encourages overproduction.[17] When supply is bureaucratic, both the legislative committee and society as a whole tend to be better off if the committee conceals its policy preferences, and in effect refuses to become part of a nonstrategic, analytical process of choice. Better programmatic information, rather than producing better decisions, simply enhances the power of the bureaucracy to extract larger budgets. Here again, "muddling through," because it does not require a clear and accurate statement of legislative consensus regarding demand, serves a strategic and useful purpose.

In sum, there is a simple theme running throughout this discussion of our model and its implications: that bureaucratic behavior must be understood in its legislative context. This theme is hardly controversial; students of public administration have been making the same point for decades, and substantive analyses of bureaucratic politics have long emphasized the importance of the legislature's role. Formal models of bureaucracy, however, have not done an adequate job of reflecting this substantive tradition. Taking the bureau as their theoretical focus, they have given undue emphasis to its independence, flexibility, and decisional control—and, in the process, either ignored or downplayed the capacity of the legislature, specifically its committees, to act just as purposely and forcefully in achieving ends which may be quite at variance with those of the bureau. In this article we offer an alternative model that integrates bureaucratic and legislative behavior

---

[17]See, for example, Schick (1966), Pyhrr (1973), and more generally, Hammond and Knott (1980).

within the same framework, and we argue its merits. More generally, though, we are making an argument for balance in the formal analysis of bureaucracy. The legislature must be extended a theoretical role that squares with its substantive importance, and it must be resurrected from a secondary status that hides not only important dimensions of legislative behavior, but the fundamental constraints on bureaucracy as well.

References

Ahlbrandt, R. S., Jr. Efficiency in the provision of fire services. *Public Choice*, 1973, *19*, 1-42.

Arnold, D. *Congress and the bureaucracy*. New Haven, Conn.: Yale University Press, 1979.

Borcherding, T. E. (Ed.). *Budgets and bureaucrats: the sources for government growth*. Durham, N.C.: Duke University Press, 1977.

Breton, A., & Wintrobe, R. The equilibrium size of a budget-maximizing bureau: a note on Niskanen's theory of bureaucracy. *Journal of Political Economy*, 1975, *82*, 195-207.

Cowart, S. C. Representation of high-demand constituencies on review committees. *Public Choice*, 1981, *37*, 337-342.

Davies, D. G. The efficiency of public versus private firms: the case of Australia's two airlines. *Journal of Law and Economics*, 1971, *14*, 149-165.

DeAllesi, L. An economic analysis of government ownership and regulation: theory and the evidence from the electric power industry. *Public Choice*, 1974, *19*, 1-42.

Dodd, L. C., & Schott, R. L. *Congress and the administrative state*. New York: Wiley, 1979.

Fenno, R. F., Jr. *The power of the purse: appropriations politics in Congress*. Boston: Little, Brown, 1966.

Ferejohn, J. A. *Pork barrel politics*. Stanford, Calif.: Stanford University Press, 1974.

Fiorina, M. *Congress: keystone of the Washington establishment*. New Haven, Conn.: Yale University Press, 1977.

Fiorina, M., & Noll, R. G. Voters, bureaucrats, and legislators: a rational choice perspective on the growth of bureaucracy. *Journal of Public Economics*, 1978, *9*, 239-253.

Hardin, C. M., Shepsle, K., & Weingast, B. R. *Public policy excesses: government by congressional subcommittee*. St. Louis: Washington University Center for the Study of American Business, Formal Publication No. 50, 1982.

Hammond, T., & Knott, J. *A zero-based look at zero-based budgeting*. New Brunswick, N.J.: Transaction Books, 1980.

Henderson, J. M., & Quandt, R. E. *Micro-economic theory: a mathematical approach* (3rd ed.). New York: McGraw-Hill, 1980.

Liske, C., & Rundquist, B. *The politics of weapons procurement: the role of Congress*. Denver: University of Denver Press, 1974.

Mackay, R. J., & Weaver, C. L. Monopoly bureaus and fiscal outcomes: deductive models and implications for reform. In G. Tullock & R. Wagner (Eds.), *Deductive reasoning in the analysis of public policy*. Lexington, Mass.: D.C. Heath, 1978, pp. 141-165.

Migue, J. L., & Belanger, G. Towards a general theory of managerial discretion. *Public Choice*, 1974, *17*, 27-43.

Miller, G. J. Bureaucratic compliance as a game on the unit square. *Public Choice*, 1977, *29*, 37-52.

Niskanen, W. *Bureaucracy and representative government*. Chicago: Aldine-Atherton, 1971.

Orzechowski, W. Economic models of bureaucracy: survey, extensions, and evidence. In T. Borcherding (Ed.), *Budgets and bureaucrats*. Durham, N.C.: Duke University Press, 1975, 229-259.

Ostrom, E., & Ostrom, V. Public choice: a different approach to the study of public administration. *Public Administration Review*, 1971, *31*, 302-316.

Pyhrr, P. A. *Zero-based budgeting: a practical tool for evaluating expenses*. New York: John Wiley, 1973.

Romer, R., & Rosenthal, H. Political resource allocation, controlled agendas, and the status quo. *Public Choice*, 1979, *33*, 27-43.

Savas, E. S. Solid waste collection in metropolitan areas. In E. Ostrom (Ed.), *The delivery of urban services*. Beverly Hills, Calif.: Sage Publications, 1976, pp. 201-229.

Savas, E. S. (Ed.). *Alternatives for delivering public services: toward improved performance*. Boulder, Colo.: Westview Press, 1977.

Savas, E. S. *Privatizing the public sector: how to shrink government*. Chatham, N.J.: Chatham House Publishing, 1982.

Schick, A. The road to PPB: the stages of budget reform. *Public Administration Review*, 1966, *26*, 243-258.

Shepsle, K. A., & Weingast, B. R. Political preferences for the pork barrel: a generalization. *American Journal of Political Science*, 1981, *25*, 96-111.

Spencer, B. Outside information and the degree of monopoly power of a public bureau. *Southern Economic Journal*, 1980, *47*, 229-233.

Tullock, G. *The politics of bureaucracy*. Washington, D.C.: Public Affairs Press, 1965.

Weingast, B. A rational choice perspective on congressional norms. *American Journal of Political Science*, 1979, *23*, 243-262.

Wildavsky, A. *The politics of the budgetary process*. Boston: Little, Brown, 1964.

[17]

Political Solutions to Market Problems

KENNETH A. SHEPSLE
BARRY R. WEINGAST
Washington University

For some, market failures serve as a rationale for public intervention. However, the fact that self-interested market behavior does not always produce felicitous social consequences is not sufficient reason to draw this conclusion. It is necessary to assess public performance under comparable conditions, and hence to analyze self-interested political behavior in the institutional structures of the public sector. Our approach emphasizes this institutional structure—warts and all—and thereby provides specific cautionary warnings about optimistic reliance on political institutions to improve upon market performance.

We may tell the society to jump out of the market frying pan, but we have no basis for predicting whether it will land in the fire or a luxurious bed.

George Stigler, *Citizen and the State*

For Bator (1958), Baumol (1965), Head (1962), and others, the presence of externalities, the undersupply of public goods, and, generally, the existence of market failures serve as now-standard justifications for (if not explanations of) a positive governmental role in the private economy. Governmental coercion, it is maintained, can resolve the free rider problem, mitigate third-party effects, regulate natural monopolies, and otherwise restore market competition or substitute for it. In short, political governance of the marketplace enhances efficient performance.

The idea of political solutions to market problems became something of a political-economic orthodoxy in the post-New Deal period. In recent years, however, this orthodoxy has spawned a revisionist literature that identifies some of the warts on the body politic. Models of bureaucratic, regulatory, and legislative institutions;[1] of self-

interested pressure groups, elected politicians, and bureaucrats;[2] and of fiscal illusion and incrementalism[3] all underscore potential biases that may neutralize the anticipated efficiency gains associated with political solutions. Political solutions may entail efficiency gains or they may exacerbate market failures. The common theme in these models is that political actors do not reserve a privileged place for efficiency in their solutions to market problems. In fact, politicians, either in reaction to or in anticipation of constituency clamoring, often have no incentive to discriminate between market failures and market successes.[4]

According to the market failure orthodoxy, inefficiency in the marketplace provides a prima facie case for public intervention. To the public failure school, on the other hand, efficiency distortions associated with political choice constitute a basis for strongly qualifying, if not rejecting, this case. The lesson of these contending arguments is that alternative institutional arrange-

Received: November 22, 1982
Revision Received: July 30, 1983
Accepted for publication: November 7, 1983

We acknowledge the support of the National Science Foundation (SES-8112016). We appreciate the comments and suggestions of Thomas Borcherding, James Buchanan, Arthur Denzau, and Charles Wolf.

[1] See Niskanen (1971), Stigler (1971), and Buchanan (1967). More generally, for the "public failure" school, see Mitchell (1978), Buchanan (1979), and Wolf (1979).

[2] See Aranson (1980) and Wolf (1979).

[3] See Aranson and Ordeshook (1977a, b, 1978) and Wagner (1976).

[4] In our view the mechanism that enables a political agent to detect the concerns of his principal (the constituency) is much like a decibel-meter. Noise from the folks back home grabs his attention. The problem with this kind of mechanism is that it does not identify the reasons for all the noise. In some cases it may derive from complaints about negative externalities, monopolistic practices, or undersupplied public goods. On other occasions, it may derive from the fact that in efficiently operating markets, changes in relative prices adversely affect individuals, eroding their capitalized wealth position ("prices push people around"). Both those bearing externality burdens and those "victimized" by price changes scream loudly; politicians hear undifferentiated noise.

417

418   The American Political Science Review   Vol. 78

ments are imperfect, implying that the ultimate choice of institutions must depend upon comparative performance (Buchanan, 1967; Buchanan & Brennan, 1980). This conclusion requires a theory of comparative institutional performance—a theory that currently does not exist.

The tension between the public failure and market failure schools remains alive today. The issues over which they quarrel, as indicated by Musgrave's (1981) recent article, "The Leviathan Cometh—or Does He?," remain unresolved. In our opinion, insights on these controversies will not be forthcoming unless grounded in a theory of comparative performance. The analyses of both the market failure and the public failure schools entail comparisons of an institution's performance against an *ideal*. We believe it is more fruitful (and scientifically appropriate) to compare the performance of one institutional arrangement with that of another. This practical perspective is especially appropriate for students of public policy. Much of the discussion of public policy has assumed that political solutions can improve on market failures. The model we offer shows that this assumption is not justified. Consequently, students of public policy must pose for themselves questions of *comparative* institutional performance rather than those that compare markets against an unattainable ideal.

This article points the way toward the development of the missing theory. We develop models of legislatures in a manner that allows direct comparison of political performance with market performance. The models are simple and hardly definitive, but they do focus the debate squarely on the issue of comparative institutional performance and on endogenous political institutions that are the counterpart to market mechanisms. It is important to emphasize that the simple models we develop initially are barren of complex institutional detail; their purpose is to sharpen intuitions about how a stripped-down institutional arrangement works. These intuitions, in turn, serve to focus analysis in richer institutional settings, which we then develop. Finally, we explore, even in the richer setting, the effects of relaxing some still restrictive features of our analysis.

The article proceeds as follows. After developing a model of political preference in the next section, we investigate the performance of a majority-rule legislature in the context of some familiar market failures. In each case, we compare the political solution, the market failure outcome, and the efficient outcome in order to gain some purchase on the question of comparative institutional performance. The techniques that are more clearly developed in a simple context are then applied to more complex and realistic institutional arrangements like those found in existing legislatures.

A Model of Political Preferences

The simple model of political choice we develop is one in which legislative institutions and processes of representation induce net benefit functions for legislative agents. These benefit functions differ from their normative economic counterparts because politicians pursue private purposes that need not be consonant with broader public ideals. Specifically, the geographic basis of representation encourages a truncated form of cost-benefit calculation in which the geographic impact of policy looms large in the politician's calculus.

Consider a public policy or project $\pi(x)$ where x is initially assumed to be a scalar measure of project size, scope, or scale. This is a restrictive assumption that is relaxed below under "Political Solutions in Richer Institutional Settings." Let $\beta(x)$ and $x(x)$ represent the present values, respectively, of the social benefits and costs flowing from $\pi(x)$. The benefit and cost functions may be "unpacked" into politically relevant components by examining them from the point of view of the agents of the n legislative districts into which the polity is partitioned. Since $\beta(x)$ and $x(x)$ have distributional characteristics, and since the relevant distributional characteristic for legislators is geographic (because that is the basis on which their constituencies are determined), we decompose the benefits and costs according to their incidence on the jth legislative district. Consider benefits first. Letting $\hat{b}_j(x) = \underset{i \neq j}{\Sigma} b_i(x)$, we characterize total benefits as

$$\beta(x) = b_j(x) + \hat{b}_j(x). \qquad (1)$$

Equation (1) distinguishes economic benefits according to their incidence. For the constituency-oriented representative of the jth district, $b_j(x)$, not $\beta(x)$, is the politically relevant benefit function when the policy $\pi(x)$ is evaluated. Benefits flowing to other districts, $\hat{b}_j(x)$, do not figure in j's calculations. We assume that the various $b_k(x)$ functions, and consequently $\beta(x)$, are concave and increasing in x:

Assumption 1. $b_k'(x) > 0$, $b_k''(x) < 0$, $k = 1, \ldots, n$.

Similarly, costs may be represented in terms of their respective incidences. Two kinds of costs are distinguished. First, there are public expenditures that are authorized and appropriated by the legislature to purchase inputs for the policy or project. By $c_{1k}(x)$ we designate the amount earmarked to be spent in the kth district; by $\hat{c}_{1k}(x) = \underset{i \neq k}{\Sigma} c_{1i}(x)$ we designate the amount earmarked for all districts but the kth. The amount $c_1(x) = \sum_{i=1}^{n} c_{1i}(x)$ represents total *expenditure cost* for $\pi(x)$. Second, there are *nonexpenditure costs* borne by each of the n districts, e.g., project externalities. By $c_{2k}(x)$, we denote externalities borne by the kth district and, by $\hat{c}_{2k}(x)$, those borne by all other districts. Total cost for the project $\pi(x)$ is the sum of expenditure and nonexpenditure costs:

$$x(x) = [c_{1j}(x) + c_{2j}(x)]$$
$$+ [\hat{c}_{1j}(x) + \hat{c}_{2j}(x)]. \quad (2)$$

Regarding expenditure and nonexpenditure costs, we assume

Assumption 2. $c_{ik}'(x) > 0$, $c_{ik}''(x) > 0$, $i=1,2$, $k=1,\ldots,n$.

That is, both expenditures and externalities increase with project scale x at an increasing rate; so, too, does $x(x)$.

Taxes are raised to cover all expenditures, with district j's share exogenously given as t_j. Regarding taxes, we assume

Assumption 3. There is a vector of tax shares, $t = (t_1,\ldots,t_n)$, with $t_k \geq 0$ and $\sum_{k=1}^{n} t_k = 1$. For project $\pi(x)$, the tax bill, $T(x)$, satisfies

$$T(x) = \sum_{k=1}^{n} c_{1k}(x),$$

with district k's share given by

$$T_k(x) = t_k T(x), k=1,\ldots,n.$$

That is, taxes just cover expenditures, with the tax bill apportioned among districts according to a fixed sharing rule, t. Some policies do not entail expenditures and thus do not require taxes (see below).

As in his evaluation of benefits, legislator j is concerned with (and only with) district-specific components of cost: geographically earmarked expenditures, $c_{1j}(x)$; nonexpenditure costs borne by the district, $c_{2j}(x)$; and the district's tax bill, $T_j(x)$. By virtue of our specification in equations (1) and (2) and Assumptions 1-3, then, the project $\pi(x)$ has (present-value-adjusted) benefit and cost flows that have an associated geographic incidence. Notice that we place great weight on geography as the basis of representation and hence as the politically relevant feature of policy incidence. This is a narrow construction of the "electoral connection." Indeed, our legislators are mere

shadows of their real-world counterparts. In our concluding section we show that the form of our conclusions is not fundamentally altered by richer conceptualizations of representation. Further discussion of this point is best left until after our simple models are presented.

Having described the incidence of benefits, expenditures, external costs, and tax shares in terms of political districting, we now complete the initial characterization of our model with a discussion of political accounting. The geographical basis for representation determines, in a natural way, a political objective function for legislative agents. The political objective functions, in turn, induce preferences over various values of x for these agents, and hence over various projects $\pi(x)$. Political institutions aggregate these preferences, usually through some voting rule or bureaucratic process, into political choices.

Consider the *objective function* of the jth legislative agent:

$$N_j(x) = b_j(x) + f[(c_{1j}(x)] - c_{2j}(x) - t_j T(x) \quad (3)$$
$$j=1,\ldots,n.$$

The n equations of formulation (3) represent the evaluative criteria by which each of the n legislative agents assesses the project $\pi(x)$ in terms of impact on his district. $N_j(x)$ is the *legislator's* objective function since his political support is enhanced by consumption benefits and public spending targeted for his district and, conversely, his support erodes with increasing externality and tax burdens for his district. Notice first that, in contrast to equation (1), j includes only his district's benefits in the calculation; he ignores $\hat{b}_j(x)$. Second, in contrast to equation (2), the taxation mechanism induces j to focus only on his district's tax bill, thereby ignoring $(1-t_j)T(x)$. Third, and again in contrast to equation (2), j internalizes in his calculation only those externality costs his district bears, paying no attention to $\hat{c}_{2j}(x)$. Finally, j attributes indirect benefits, $f[c_{1j}(x)]$, to project expenditures targeted for his district to purchase project inputs.[5] In $c_{1j}(x)$, the constituents of district j see employment, business contracts, local tax revenues, and generally increased economic activity in the district.

In equation (3), the $b_j(x)$, $-c_{2j}(x)$, and $-t_j T(x)$ terms need no further elaboration except to re-

---

[5] In equation (3) we represent the political benefits derived from district-earmarked expenditures by $f[c_{1j}(x)]$. We assume throughout that f is concave and increasing in x—that political benefits from expenditures increase in project scale at a decreasing rate—and that $f(0) = 0$.

emphasize that, in the political arena, geographic incidence matters profoundly. However, the transformation of expenditures earmarked for the jth district, $c_{1j}(x)$, into a kind of political benefit requires a few additional comments (a more detailed discussion is found in Weingast, Shepsle, & Johnsen, 1981). First, and perhaps most transparent, legislators and their constituents regard $c_{1j}(x)$ as a source of rent for the district. Citizens (at least those that own inputs) support public expenditures in the local economy because, by increasing the demand for the project's inputs, these expenditures produce windfall gains for input owners. These gains, in turn, filter through the local economy. In response to constituent desire for local public expenditures, the district representative, moreover, seeks to attract local expenditures because they are "credit-claimable" (Mayhew, 1974). Although a single legislator cannot credibly claim responsibility for broad public policies like national defense, for example, he can claim credit for the weapons contract given the local defense contractor, the uniform order for the textile plant in the district, or the increased personnel expenditures at the local military base. Because expenditures made in a given legislator's district redound to his credit, legislators go after c_{1j}-type expenditures, thus making it appropriate for us to treat this peculiar form of cost accounting as in equation (3).[6]

Equation (3) and Assumptions 1-3 provide the basis for deriving the preferences of legislative agents. Once political institutions are specified, public choices on policies may be deduced from the preferences given by the $N_j(x)$ functions and the institutional rules of preference aggregation.

As a baseline against which to compare political choices given the political objective functions of equation (3), consider the objective function that embodies the criterion of economic efficiency:

$$E(x) = \beta(x) - x(x). \tag{4}$$

[6]Our notion of political cost accounting displayed in equation (3) formalizes some ideas originally presented in a somewhat different context by Aranson and Ordeshook (1977a, b, 1978) and discussed by Shepsle (1980). They seek to learn why interest groups lobby for public goods in view of the fact that the same logic that implies market failure in the private supply of public goods also applies to the phenomenon of private lobbying for public provision. They note, however, that *goods public in consumption are typically private in production,* that is, contracts for inputs are appropriable and excludable. A private interest group lobbies in anticipation of private pecuniary gain (the public good is a by-product of that enterprise). Our model complements their analysis by allowing the politician to target these private pecuniary gains to his constituency.

Economic efficiency requires the selection of a project scale that maximizes net benefits (with $x = 0$ if $E(x) < 0$ for all positive project scales), irrespective of the incidence of those net benefits. It is this last feature that distinguishes the economic norm from political objectives and, as we show below, is the basis for efficiency distortions caused by political intervention. With the efficiency model as a normative benchmark, we may begin the task of comparative institutional performance.

Market Failure

Since our concern here is with political performance in the context of market failures, we now turn to a definition of the latter. We shall say that a market has failed whenever the market equilibrium is inefficient. As this outcome constitutes the status quo ante for potential political intervention, we label it x^0. Thus, *a market failure is an inefficient status quo.* Specifically, letting equation (4) serve as our criterion or objective function, an efficient outcome is a point $x = x^E$ satisfying

$$E'(x^E) = \beta'(x^E) - x'(x^E) = 0 \tag{5}$$

and

$$E''(x^E) = \beta''(x^E) - x''(x^E) < 0. \tag{6}$$

From Assumption 1 and 2, there is a unique global maximum of $E(x)$; thus, x^E is the unambiguous normative solution to the problem of policy choice according to equation (4).

Definition. The political status quo, x^0, is said to constitute a *market failure* if and only if $x^0 \neq x^E$.

That is, x^0 is a case of market failure if and only if $E'(x^0) \neq 0$. If $E'(x^0) > 0$, then Assumptions 1 and 2 imply x^0 is "too small," whereas the converse is implied if $E'(x^0) < 0$. Of course, market failures may manifest themselves in distinct ways —externalities, public goods, and other market imperfections. For now it is the existence of a market failure rather than its particular form that is important.

Political Choice: A Simple Legislature

As noted above, comparing political solutions to market failures requires specific, clear notions of each. We already have a precise definition of market failure. We now require a model of political institutions and an identification of their equilibrium outcomes.[7] We begin with an examination of majority rule in a one-dimensional special case where the market has failed ($x^0 \neq x^E$). The results derived in this case are then extended in the next section to choices by structured legislatures in multidimensional settings.

A political equilibrium in the one-dimensional case is the familiar Condorcet winner, where the preferences of individual legislators are induced by the $N_j(x)$ functions given in equation (3). That is, a majority rule equilibrium is a policy alternative x^* having the property that no other policy alternative can command a majority against it. Technically, we have

Definition. A political outcome x^* is said to be a *majority rule equilibrium* (MRE) if and only if it is strictly preferred by more than $n/2$ legislators in paired comparison with each other feasible outcome. Specifically, if $S(x^*, x) = \{j|N_j(x^*) > N_j(x)\}$, where N_j is given in equation (3), then x^* is a MRE if and only if $|S(x^*, x)| > n/2$ for all feasible $x \neq x^*$.[8]

Thus, in our terminology, a "political solution to a market failure" is an outcome x^* which is a MRE given a status quo, $x^0 \neq x^E$.

Public policies differ in their characteristics, and it will be useful to distinguish between two classes, regulatory and expenditure.

---

[7] A troublesome feature with political institutions is that they often lack equilibrium outcomes. Rarely, in Riker's (1980) terms, is there an "equilibrium of tastes," since political choices typically entail preference cycles. For our purposes, the lack of equilibrium implies that there is no basis for unambiguously claiming that a political solution will improve or fail to improve upon the market failure it sought to correct. However, even though there is normally no equilibrium of tastes owing to preference cycles, there may nevertheless be equilibrium outcomes induced by structural arrangements. For example, rules governing the comparison of alternatives, various forms of agenda control, requirements on the order of voting like considering the status quo last, all serve to prevent endless cycling. Consequently, we believe the pure majority rule/unstructured legislature, that has been the object of analysis for most political equilibrium theorists, is a very special case. Some insight on the question of political solutions to market failures can be obtained by studying legislatures, not as atomistic collections of legislative agents, but rather as structured institutions (see Shepsle, 1979a, and Shepsle and Weingast, 1981b).

[8] This definition characterizes *strong Condorcet winners.* If the requirement is relaxed to $|S(x^*, x)| > |S(x, x^*)|$ for all feasible $x \neq x^*$, we have *strong plurality winners.* And if the requirement is further relaxed to $|S(x, x^*)| < n/2$ for all $x \neq x^*$, we have characterized the *strong majority core.* Each reflects slightly different treatments accorded indifferent voters.

Definition. A policy, $\pi(x)$, is said to be a *regulatory policy,* whenever $c_{1j}(x) = 0$ for every j; otherwise it is said to be an *expenditure policy.*

A regulatory policy entails no public expenditure, and, since taxes are collected only to cover expenditures, it thus entails no taxes. The costs of a regulatory policy are borne by the private sector directly; the government plays no role as fiscal intermediary in this class of policies. An expenditure policy, as in selective subsidies to the private sector or in the public provision of a public good, entails governmental spending and taxing with their geographic incidences as noted earlier. Whenever $\pi(x)$ is a regulatory policy, political objective functions given in equation (3) specialize to

$$N_j(x) = b_j(x) - c_{2j}(x) \tag{7}$$

For regulatory policy, the standard median voter theorem affords the following result.

Proposition. For any regulatory policy $\pi(x)$ decided by a majority rule, a MRE exists. In particular, $\pi(x^M)$ is the MRE, where $x^M = $ median $\{x_j^*|x_j^* = \underset{x}{\mathrm{argmax}}\ N_j(x)\}$.
$\quad\quad j \in N$

From Assumptions 1 and 2, $N_j(x)$ as given in equation (7) is strictly concave in x. It may be established that a function concave in x is single peaked in x. Consequently, the proposition follows from Black's Median Dominance Theorem (Black, 1958). Thus, the majority rule equilibrium in this context is the most-preferred point of the median legislator, x^M.

The main effect of a regulatory policy is through the benefits and costs that are distributed as a consequence of compliance (Weidenbaum, 1978). In contrast to expenditure policies, government expenditures and tax burdens in the regulatory realm figure much less prominently (indeed, we have stipulated here that they are zero). The Proposition establishes that the process of regulatory policymaking in a majority-rule legislature is both decisive and stable. To be sure, the MRE Policy might be $\pi(0)$ if the incidence of costs and benefits for a majority of legislators is such that $c_{2j}(x) > b_j(x)$ for every $x > 0$. Alternatively, for other distributions and costs, $x^M > 0$, as is illustrated for a five-person legislature in Figure 1. Under these conditions there exists a positive policy scale that defeats all contenders in a majority rule contest.

In order to explore the application of this well-known result to the question of market failure, we state an obvious

422					The American Political Science Review					Vol. 78

Figure 1. Majority Rule Equilibrium for Regulatory Policy

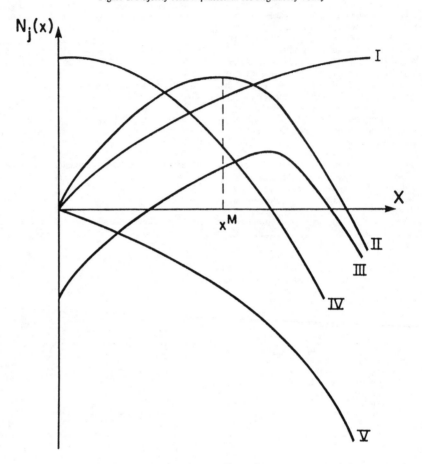

Corollary 1. A regulatory policy, $\pi(x)$, is a MRE if and only if $b_M{}'(x) - c_{2M}{}'(x) = 0$ (or $x=0$ if the median ideal point is a corner solution of equation (7)).

That is, for legislative decision making in the regulatory realm, the political solution that emerges in a simple majority-rule context is one for which the first-order condition is satisfied *for the median legislator*. Contrast this fact with the efficient scale $x = x^E$ satisfying:

$$\sum_{j=1}^{n} b_j{}'(x) - \sum_{j=1}^{n} c_{2j}{}'(x) = 0. \qquad (8)$$

This follows from substituting equations (1) and (2) into equation (5) with the stipulation that $c_{1j}(x) = 0$ for all j and all x.

Letting x^E be the efficient solution, x^0 the market solution (which constitutes the political status quo), and x^L the regulatory solution of a simple legislature, we know, in the case of market failure, only that $x^E \neq x^0$ and $x^L = x^M$. If $x^L \neq x^0$— that is, if the regulatory solution differs from the market (failure) solution—then we know only that a majority of legislators prefers x^L to x^0, viz. $N_j(x^L(> N_j(x^0)$ for more than $n/2$ legislators. What we do not know is the relationship of x^L to x^E, and only a very benign view of political institutions allows the belief that x^L "improves" upon x^0.

Combining the first-order conditions of Corollary 1 and equation (8), we may specify the rather stringent requirement for efficient regulatory solutions.

Corollary 2. $x^L = x^E$ if and only if

$$\sum_{j\neq M} b_j{}'(x^M) - \sum_{j\neq M} c_{2j}{}'(x^M) = 0.$$

That is, for the legislative equilibrium to be efficient, the distribution of marginal net benefits at the policy scale preferred by the median legislator must sum precisely to zero. This knife-edge condition is very stringent and unlikely to be observed in practice.

An additional implication follows from this analysis. Since x^L is the ideal point of the median legislator, i.e., $x^L = x^M$, and since it is highly unlikely that $x^L = x^E$, it follows from the definition of an MRE that x^L beats x^E. That is, a majority actually prefers the chosen outcome to the efficient point. As noted, political agents worry about benefit and cost incidences, not efficiency.

This treatment has paralleled the traditional market-failure analysis, comparing expected institutional performance against an ideal. Like its counterpart in market-failure analysis, however, it fails to take the next step. That is, it neglects to compare expected performance under one institutional regime with performance under alternative institutional arrangements. This we now proceed to do. Therefore, of more interest, and at bottom of greatest importance to an accurate assessment of political solutions in market-failure situations, are the six possible orderings of x^E, x^0, and x^L (notice that *strict* inequalities are sometimes used to be consistent with an assumed market failure):

1. $x^0 \leqslant x^L \leqslant x^E$
2. $x^0 < x^E \leqslant x^L$
3. $x^E \leqslant x^L \leqslant x^0$ (*)
4. $x^L \leqslant x^E < x^0$
5. $x^L \leqslant x^0 < x^E$
6. $x^E < x^0 \leqslant x^L$.

Here we inquire not whether $x^L = x^E$—the unlikely circumstances for this are given in Corollary 2 —but rather whether x^L improves upon x^0. Cases 1 and 2 are traditional market-failure situations in which the market operates at suboptimal scale. In each of these cases, the regulatory solution is a scale exceeding x^0. In case 1 the political solution is an unambiguous improvement upon the market failure/political status quo. Case 2, on the other hand, has the scale of the regulatory solution exceeding both x^0 and x^E; whereas the market fails to produce enough of, say, a positive externality,

the public solution may entail too much public provision. At any rate, the signals are ambiguous and there is no prima facie case for either tolerating market failures or permitting public intervention. Cases 3 and 4, respectively, are mirror images of cases 1 and 2. Here the market operates at an undesirably high level, producing too much of, say, pollution or some other public bad. Case 3 is, and case 4 is not, an unambiguous public improvement over the market-produced status quo. Cases 5 and 6 are interesting because they describe instances of perverse public intervention in which x^L represents a deterioration of the market-produced status quo. These are unanticipated consequences *in extremum!*

Cases 1, 2, and 5—market failures representing "undersupply"—may be examined more systematically in the following simple example (cases 3, 4, and 6—instances of "oversupply"—are simply mirror images). Cases 1 and 5 are instances of improvement and deterioration in x^0, respectively, from political intervention. Case 2 is more ambiguous. We set $x^0 = 0$, and choose a very simple representation for political preferences:

$$N_j(x) = k_j - (a_j - x)^2 \text{ for } j = 1, \ldots, n.$$

Legislator j's ideal point is a_j. At that level, $N_j(x)$ is maximized with $N_j(a_j) = k_j$. Defining $E(x) = \sum_{j=1}^{n} N_j(x)$, the first-order condition for a maximum, $E'(x) = 0$, implies that the efficient point is simply the *mean* ideal point:[9] $x^E = 1/n \sum_{j=1}^{n} a_j = \bar{a}$. The political choice, on the other hand, is $x^L = \text{med } \{a_j\} = a_m$. Thus, cases 1, 2, and 5 become (see Figure 2):

1. $0 \leqslant a_m \leqslant \bar{a}$.
2. $0 < \bar{a} \leqslant a_m$.
5. $a_m \leqslant 0 < \bar{a}$.

From Figure 2, we observe that there is an unambiguous improvement from political intervention (case 1) when the mean ideal point exceeds the median (both positive), a circumstance reflecting a distribution of ideal points skewed toward $x^0 = 0$. If, on the other hand, both mean and

$$E'(n) = \sum_{j=1}^{n} N_j{}'(x)$$
$$= \sum_{j=1}^{n} 2(a_j - x).$$
$E'(x) = 0$ implies $\sum_{j=1}^{n} (a_j - x) = 0$, or $\sum_{j=1}^{n} a_j = nx$, and the result follows.

424   The American Political Science Review   Vol. 78

Figure 2. Comparison of Market "Problem" with Political "Solution"

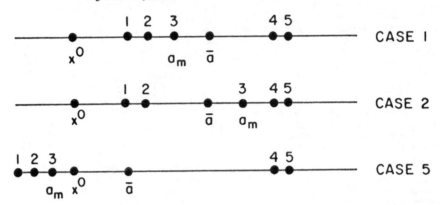

median are positive but the distribution is skewed away from zero (case 2), the improvement from political intervention is ambiguous. The more extreme the skew, the less warranted is the political intervention. That is, the more extreme the skew (i.e., move 1 and 2 closer to x^0, with $\bar{a}$ moving toward x^0 as well), the more likely the costs imposed on constituencies from political intervention will exceed total benefits (even though a majority of districts will, on net, experience an improvement). Finally, if more than half of the legislators prefer a level of x below x^0, i.e., $a_j < 0$ for $n/2$ or more legislators, but a minority of districts prefer positive levels that, on average, more than compensate for the majority wishes (case 5), then politicizing this market failure will actually lead to a reduction in social welfare.[10]

This example illustrates the results that can be derived under specific assumptions about preferences. Before turning to our more general analysis, we identify some circumstances in which public policies outperform market institutions, and vice versa. These results are of a more substantive nature.

1. Assume there is a market failure but that the potential net beneficiaries of a political solution

do not involve a majority of districts. Then x^0 is an MRE. In short, absent additional ingenuity, the political solution exactly duplicates the market failure. Market failures that do not impose burdens on a majority of districts will not be improved upon by political intervention.

2. Assume there is a market failure that affects a large number of districts. Some legislators will prefer high values of x, some low values. As long as the median legislator prefers a level x^M greater than x^0 but less than x^E, then Pareto improvements follow from public intervention. This is the most sanguine conclusion of our model, and shows that public sector performance is not, in principle, strictly inferior to market performance.

3. Suppose that markets are working perfectly, i.e., $x^0 = x^E$. Here, too, x^M need not equal x^E. It may well be that large numbers of districts, possibly including a majority, benefit from some type of market intervention. Intervention in efficient markets occurs whenever a majority of districts can benefit from it. Nothing in the model constrains current, temporary majorities from advantaging themselves at the expense of others, and in the process destroying efficient markets.

4. Consider, finally, a very troubling result that underscores how fundamentally arbitrary political choice is in relation to the underlying configuration of districts. Assume a market failure exists so $x^0 \neq x^E$ and let x^M be the legislative solution based upon some set of districts. Now, fix the economic interests of every citizen (so that the underlying economic problem remains unchanged), but redraw the boundaries of political districts. Regrouping citizens in different districts changes the preferences of political representatives, since the politically relevant incidences now differ. In particular, redistricting may alter the

[10]This last case is reminiscent of the classic democratic paradox of the intense minority opposed by a (relatively) indifferent majority. Perhaps it should not be surprising that, in general, political solutions improve upon market failures when (with appropriate qualifications) means and median preferences do not differ by much. Indeed, when equal, we have efficient political intervention. However, if mean and median diverge, and especially when the mean and median are on opposite sides of the status quo, then opening the gates to political intervention produces "public failure."

preferences (indeed, change the identity) of the median legislator, thereby altering the location of x^M. This implies that the political solution to a given market problem is not invariant with respect to arbitrary political divisions associated with geographic representation. This underscores our main point, namely that there is no determinate relationship between x^M and x^E.

What, on balance, does this simple but suggestive analysis say about the ameliorative impact of political solutions on market failures? We have some positive results (result 2), some null results (result 1), and some negative results (results 3 and 4). In some specific circumstances, however, we can provide realistic expectations. In economies suffering pervasive, geographically dispersed, and wide-ranging, market failures, result (2) may well provide the inspiration and justification for market intervention. However, in economies with competitive markets prevalent and market failures minor and few in number, most political interventions will themselves fail to correct these failures. Indeed, they will more likely have a destructive effect on reasonably well-functioning markets.

We have developed our model of political incidence in some detail for the one-dimensional world of regulatory policymaking in an unstructured legislature. We have conducted this analysis, not because we believe it to model real legislative choice adequately, but rather because it reveals cleanly and in an unencumbered fashion the *potential* divergence between social choice and social welfare. We underscore "potential" to emphasize that public failure proponents are quite wrong to maintain their viewpoint everywhere and in all circumstances. But so, too, are the market failure advocates.[11]

---

[11]We mention for completeness that the results just obtained are not substantially changed when we switch from regulatory to expenditure policy. Technically, adding $f[c_{1j}(x)] - t_jT(x)$ to equation (7) preserves concavity and hence single peakedness. Thus, although the details differ somewhat, we still obtain a majority rule equilibrium. Similarly, an efficient expenditure policy, like an efficient regulatory policy, depends upon the satisfaction of a knife-edge condition that parallels the one given in Corollary 2 above. So, as in the case of regulatory policy, efficiency is unlikely in expenditure policies, and "public success" is a chancy business. The only detail worth stressing is that social choices and their welfare consequences, in the expenditure realm, depend on a public production process, and hence on where inputs are purchased and taxes extracted. These incidences are a complicating factor that likely cause distortions in productive efficiency. A more complete analysis of expenditure policy is contained in an earlier draft of this article, issued as Working Paper No. 74 of the Center for Study of American Business, Washington University, and available from the authors.

Political Solutions in Richer Institutional Settings

In the simple, one-dimensional context of an unstructured legislature, we have argued that there is no basis for presuming political interventions improve upon market failures. Our principal aim now is to enrich our simple legislative model in ways that are relatively general, but which nevertheless possess features characteristic of real legislatures. Although our strictly geographic representation of benefit and cost incidences remains simple and mechanical, we define our task now as that of moving beyond the abstract world of Duncan Black and public choice theory to the more substantive world of David Mayhew and Richard Fenno. Our modest objective is to trace the consequences of our simple "incidence analysis" for policy formation in a political institution more structured than the pure majority rule legislature.

Three elements are described: committees with agenda power, a status quo that prevails if committees fail to make proposals or if the parent legislature rejects such proposals, and a policy space, multidimensional in nature, partitioned into committee jurisdictions. Our purpose here is not so much to provide a finely fashioned model of a legislature; rather we intend to demonstrate the robustness of our earlier claims for political solutions in circumstances that possess the prominent features of legislatures like the U.S. Congress.

Observers since the time of Woodrow Wilson (1885) have been struck by the importance of legislative committees in shaping policies within the jurisdictions entrusted to their care by the entire legislature. In developing a legislative committee model, we assume that a subset of the legislature, called a committee, is delegated agenda power or jurisdiction over a particular set of policy issues. We model this jurisdiction as a subspace, X, of a multidimensional policy space. For the present, we rule out the possibility of amendments to committee proposals so that committees have exclusive agenda control. Further, we abstract from the question of committee composition and assume that the committee can be characterized by a transitive utility function, U^C.[12]

---

[12]Since committees are legislatures writ small, unless the committee assignment mechanism selects out only special subsets of preferences, majority committee cycles are normally expected. However, precisely the same argument we are about to present for committees (with agenda control) in legislatures can be made for a chairman (with agenda control) in committees. That is, ultimately we can claim to be dealing with a "well-

426   The American Political Science Review   Vol. 78

Figure 3. Voter *j*'s Preferred-to and Indifferent-to Sets

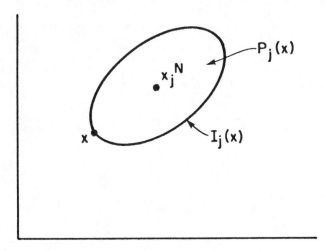

Finally, we impose the restriction, common in most Anglo-American legislatures including the U.S. Congress, that the status quo is voted upon last. Legislator preferences, as before, are induced by the policy incidence of an alternative, $x \epsilon X$, on his district (where X is multidimensional and x is a vector). Legislator j's most preferred policy alternative is x_j^N, the point in X that maximizes $N_j(x)$. Notice that the dimensions of X are not restricted to a single level of some public intervention; x is no longer a scalar, so that we no longer retain the restrictive interpretation required in the one-dimensional setting.

The process of legislative choice in this model differs systematically from the simple legislature described in the previous sections. First, in a multidimensional policy space, majority rule is not well-behaved. Specifically, following from the theorems of Cohen (1979), Matthews (1979), McKelvey (1976, 1979), Plott (1967), Schofield (1978), and Slutsky (1979), for any alternative in the policy space, there exists a set of points that command a majority of votes against it. In terms of our earlier development, this may be seen as follows. From each legislator's incidence-induced preference function $N_j(x)$, given in equation (3), we may define his preferred-to set:

$$P_j(x) = \{x' \epsilon X | N_j(x') > N_j(x)\}.$$

___
behaved" utility function. For further details, see Shepsle and Weingast, 1981c.

$P_j(x)$ is the set of points j prefers to x. Our assumptions about $N_j(x)$ imply that $P_j(x)$ is a strictly convex set, a two-dimensional illustration of which is found in Figure 3. There, the ellipse passing through x, labeled $I_j(x)$, is an iso-preference contour of $N_j(x)$, and its interior, a convex set, is j's preferred-to set. From the individual $P_j(x)$ sets, the *majority win set*, $W(x)$, is constructed. $W(x)$ is the set of points contained in the $P_j(x)$ sets of at least a simple majority of legislators:

$$W(x) = \{x' \epsilon X | x' \epsilon P_j(x) \text{ for more than } n/2$$
$$\text{legislators}\}.$$

Thus, $W(x)$ is the set of points preferred by legislative majorities to x. The theorems cited above show that generally $W(x) \neq \phi$ for all $x \epsilon X$ (a fact illustrated shortly).

Second, the legislative committee model differs from the pure majority rule model of the last two sections in that agenda control is delegated to the committee with jurisdiction. The results of McKelvey (1976) and Plott and Levine (1979) show that agenda power, within limits, allows those controlling the agenda to manipulate the outcome. Even though our assumptions require the committee in its agenda formation role to allow the status quo to be voted last—a requirement that imposes significant restrictions upon the committee's ability to manipulate the outcome (Shepsle & Weingast, 1984)—committee members

Figure 4. Structure-Induced Equilibrium for Three Voters

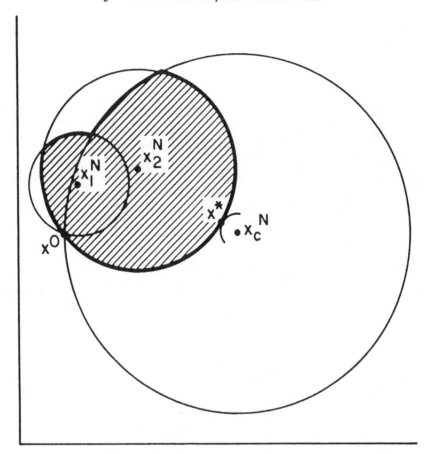

have greater influence over outcomes than other legislative agents.

Consider the set of policy alternatives that command a majority against the status quo, $W(x^0)$. The committee will only propose alternatives from $W(x^0)$ since any other would be rejected by the full legislature when paired against x^0 in the final vote. Knowing this, the committee treats $W(x^0)$ as a constraint—a feasible set—over which it maximizes. Let x^* be the point in this set that the committee prefers most, i.e.,

$$x^* = \underset{x \in W(x^0)}{\text{argmax}} \; U^C(x).^{13}$$

[13]Since $W(x^0)$ is defined as an open set, a limit argument is required for x^* to be well defined.

Complete agenda power allows the committee to propose this point for a vote against x^0 (which then replaces x^0 since $x^* \epsilon W(x^0)$).

Alternative x^* is the policy outcome of this legislative committee game in the following sense. Even though $W(x^*) \neq \phi$, so that points exist that command a majority of votes against x^*, the committee in its gatekeeping, agenda-setting role assures that only its proposals are moved for a vote. Those individuals who prefer some alternative $y \epsilon W(x^*)$ are prohibited by the legislative rules from proposing y. Given this structural arrangement imposed by the legislative rules, x^* is a *structure induced equilibrium* (Shepsle, 1979).

Figure 4 illustrates this discussion for three ideal points. The (one-man) committee's ideal point is located at x_c^N. Also depicted are the

428   The American Political Science Review   Vol. 78

status quo, x^0, and two other ideal points, x_1^N and x_2^N. The interiors of the ellipses passing through x^0 are the preferred-to sets of the three legislators, and the shaded petals—points common to the preferred-to sets of at least a majority of legislators—constitute $W(x^0)$. The point x^* is simply the best one the committee can secure, given that its proposal must satisfy the constraint of being an element of $W(x^0)$, i.e., must command a majority against x^0.

So far we have not considered x^E in our discussion. It should be apparent, however, that x^E plays no necessary role in legislative choice. The legislative outcome, x^*, is determined by an optimization process over $W(x^0)$ by a particular committee. Both the constraint set, $W(x^0)$, and the function constituting the committee maximand are determined by the legislator objective functions, $N_j(x)$. These functions tell us the set of policies that legislator j prefers to x^0, and hence the set of policies preferred by a majority to x^0.

Similarly, the objective functions of the committee members determine x^* from among the alternatives in $W(x^0)$. Since these functions and their respective optima, x_j^N, stand in no particular relationship to x^E, neither do $W(x^0)$ and x^*.

Our model of choice in a structured, majority-rule legislature implies that the status quo (which constitutes a market failure, i.e., $x^0 \neq x^E$) is replaced by an extreme point of the constraint set $W(x^0)$.[14] Even if $x^E \epsilon W(x^0)$, it would be sheer accident for it to be an extreme point, and even more unlikely for it to be the constrained maximum of $U^c(x)$. It is clear, then, that a highly implausible knife-edge condition must once again hold to insure efficient legislative choice.

We may also show the change in policy that accompanies a change in committee membership

[14]With one exception to be noted in the next two paragraphs.

Figure 5. Policy Change Following Committee Turnover

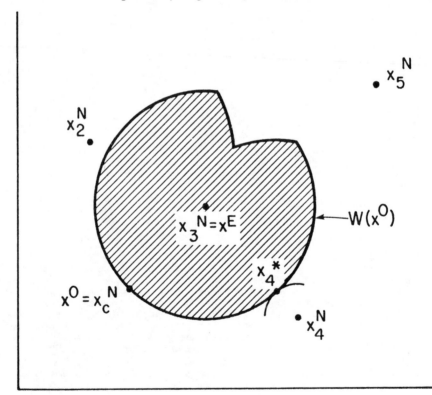

(Weingast & Moran, 1983). Suppose that the status quo is preferred by the current committee to all other points that beat this policy alternative. Then the committee qua agenda setter "keeps the gates closed," and the legislature is in equilibrium even though $W(x^0) \neq \phi$ (Denzau & Mackay, 1983). The legislative rules yield x^0 as a structure-induced equilibrium which cannot be upset as long as committee preferences remain unchanged. This holds regardless of the relation of x^0 to x^E. Thus, even if $W(x^0)$ is large relative to the convex hull of ideal points, and even if x^E is contained in $W(x^0)$, x^0 remains an equilibrium. The case of two-dimensional choice with five legislators is illustrated in Figure 5, where $x^0 = x_c^N$ is both the status quo and the ideal point of the committee, and x^E is the efficient point, a centrally located alternative that also is the ideal point of legislator 3.

If the committee changes hands, it is apparent that no matter which legislator takes over the committee, x^0 is no longer an equilibrium. For all other legislators, alternatives exist in $W(x^0)$ that are preferred to x^0. Notice, moreover, that all prefer x^E to x^0. The new equilibrium depends upon which member takes over the committee. Unless the new committee ideal is located at x^3 (the exception referred to in note 14), the new equilibrium is not x^E, but rather is defined by maximizing the new committee's objective function over $W(x^0)$. If, for example, legislator 4 takes over, then the new equilibrium is x^{*4}. This new equilibrium need bear no necessary relation to x^E. In particular, this equilibrium is determined by the preferences of a small subset of legislators—the committee. It could be closer to or further away from x^E than is x^0. The rule or practice according to which members are assigned to committees will tell us the nature and extent of this bias.

The rules for assigning members to the committee attenuate any relationship between x^* and x^E. In order for x^* to bear some direct relation to x^E, the committee assignment process must select particular committee members on the basis of the relationship of their ideal points to x^E. Other assignment mechanisms may be biased away from x^E. In practice, assignment rules in the U.S. Congress typically select for qualities that are at best unrelated to x^E, and may in fact be negatively related. For example, in both the House and Senate the mechanism used assigns members to committees on the basis of their demand for committee positions. Those with the highest stake in a given jurisdiction generally gain membership on the relevant committees (Shepsle, 1978). Thus, this mechanism is disposed toward members from districts that bear either mostly costs or mostly benefits. The empirical evidence in the congressional literature lends strong support to the conclusion that committees typically consist of "preference outliers." The predictions of our models are consistent with these empirical regularities.

To see this, return to the situation illustrated in Figure 5. Suppose we are considering a multidimensional policy like environmental protection. The status quo is x^0 and represents a market failure. Initially, it is an equilibrium since the committee's ideal is located there. These individuals might represent the Southern Democrats in the early 1960s who see little benefits but significant costs in changing the policy on environmental matters from the status quo. Environmentalists, who appear in the mid-1960s, are "high demanders" (that is, they prefer very high levels of environmental protection, see benefits everywhere, and do not bear much of the costs). Their ideal might be placed at x_5^N. As well, we have other legislators who bear different mixes of benefits and costs, including one centrally located representative whose ideal is precisely the efficient point. Now, what happens as the Southern Democrats, through attrition, begin turning power in the committee over to the environmentalist legislators—in particular, what happens if the high demanders at x_5^N are able to take over the committee? The new equilibrium is determined by maximizing the new committee objective function, $N_5(x)$, over the set $W(x^0)$. Since this maximand includes a disproportionate amount of benefits over costs, it selects a much higher level of environmental protection than x^E. In fact, this choice does not even guarantee an improvement over x^0, and may involve "too much" environmental protection. Since the committee system selects outliers from the distribution of preferences, it ensures that the political solution, x^*, to market problems, x^0, is biased away from x^E. Indeed, this conclusion holds even if many legislators prefer outcomes close to x^E—the latter a case of market failure that would seem to be the most amenable to a democratic resolution. Although there are only a few outliers, the committee system nevertheless advantages them.

This basic message about political solutions holds, a fortiori, in the case of no market failure. If $x^0 = x^E$, the earlier theorems cited on majority rule imply that $W(x^E) \neq \phi$. Thus, if the committee with jurisdiction prefers points in $W(x^E)$ to x^E, the political intervention has the counterproductive effect of destroying an efficiently operating sector of the political economy. In short, once the political machinery is established, political "solutions" will be imposed everywhere, even in markets that have not failed.

There is one additional point we wish to emphasize, and it is best developed in a comparative statics framework. Nonempty win sets provide opportunities for agenda setters. Agenda setters,

430   The American Political Science Review   Vol. 78

Figure 6. Preference Outliers and the Comparative Statics of Win-Sets

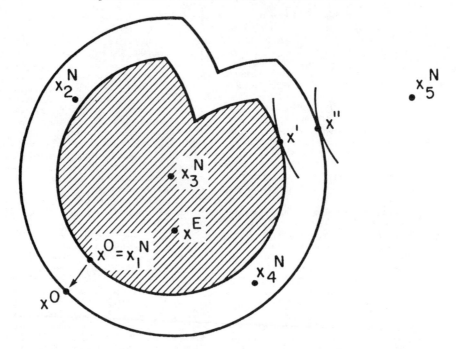

by virtue of the committee assignment mechanism, are outliers of the legislature's preference distribution. Agenda setters, therefore, pick extreme points of $W(x^0)$. Replacing one set of agenda setters with another effects a switch from one extreme point of $W(x^0)$ to another. Such changes bear no relationship to efficiency as, for example, when agenda setters preferring too little market intervention (in relation to x^E) are replaced by those wanting too much. A counterintuitive comparative statics result follows in this setting (and generalizes ideas of Romer & Rosenthal, 1978). Fix x^E, and consider the effect of moving x^0 away from x^E (thus worsening the market failure). The ironic consequence is that outlier agenda setters are now in a position to select an outcome even further away from x^E as a result of $W(x^0)$ growing larger. In Figure 6, with x_5^N the ideal of the high-demand agenda setter, as x^0 moves toward the southwest, $W(x^0)$ grows so that the choice of Mr. 5 changes from x' to x'' (the latter even farther away from x^E than the former). Put simply, the worse the problem, the worse the solution!

Discussion and Extension

Having conceded at various points in this article the simplicity and restrictiveness of our model, it is appropriate to conclude our analysis with an attempt to address these complexities. We have little more than suggestions to offer at this point, although others (Cox, McCubbins & Sullivan, 1983; Fiorina, 1982, 1983) are already taking our model and enriching it in useful ways. We turn now to some of our sins of omission to determine whether and how they affect our conclusion.

Alternative Evaluations of Incidence by Legislators

In the development of our model, the geographic incidence of benefits and costs, and only these incidences, induce legislator preferences. This observation suggests an almost religious attachment to Mayhew's "electoral connection," and perhaps a naive version of it at that. Yet one might ponder, even after having granted considerable weight to geographic incidence, the extent to which other sources attenuate the tugs of geography. In most Anglo-American legislatures, for example, there is a tension between party and constituency. In a similar spirit, we may explore the effects of subgeographic constituencies (like Fenno's (1978) reelection, primary, and personal constituencies) and extrageographic constituencies (like organized groups, outside the district, which possess election-relevant resources). For each of the substantive extensions developed below, we show how our framework can handle the broader perspective. We emphasize that these modifications entail changes in the $N_j(x)$ preference functions, but do not alter the form of our conclusions about policy choice.

Sub-geographic constituencies. Our incidence analysis takes the legally defined geographic constituency as the source of all electoral rewards. Although this view properly emphasizes the efficiency distortions of political solutions entailed by the less-than-national district perspective of legislators, it may not have gone far enough. There are two ways to think about the effects of subgeographic constituencies on the legislator's calculus, each of which reinforces our earlier conclusions.

The first, popularized by economists (Olson, 1965; Peltzman, 1976; Stigler, 1971), emphasizes the role of organization, transactions costs, and rational ignorance. According to this view, the transactions costs involved in organizing for political action give small groups, who may already be organized for other purposes, a distinct political advantage over unorganized groups. Because such groups are more easily mobilized, more skilled at raising resources to make their views and preferences known, and more capable of using their resources to reward or punish politicians, the induced political preferences of a given representative may give disproportionate weight to incidence on these privileged groups. Unorganized voter-citizens, on the other hand, may be victimized by policies tilted toward privileged groups.

The second view, articulated by Fenno (1978), suggests that politicians partition their geographic districts in politically relevant ways. The legislator is especially attentive to policy incidence on his political allies—his reelection, primary, and personal constituencies inside the geographic district —a perspective given some analytical force by Fiorina (1974).

Each of these views suggests that politicians, whom we had modeled as provincially oriented toward their geographic constituencies, may be more provincial still. Not only are the benefits and costs falling on citizens in other districts ignored, but the same may also hold for the powerless and unorganized, according to the first view, or the opposition, according to the second, *within* the geographic constituency. Benefits, therefore, are targeted by politicians toward subgeographic constituencies, whereas costs are permitted to fall not only on those outside the district, but also on those inside the district who either will not notice, cannot mobilize, or would not support the legislator in any event.

Both of these considerations can be handled by a simple modification of our model. This involves disaggregating each district into a politically relevant set of groups (a la Fiorina, 1974, or Cox, McCubbins, & Sullivan, 1983). For example, $N_j(x)$ may become

$$N_j(x) = \sum_i (b_{ij}(x) - c_{ij}(x)) \, a_{ij}$$

where i is an index over politically relevant groups and $b_{ij}(x)$ and $c_{ij}(x)$ are the benefits and costs, respectively, received from policy x by the members of the ith group located in district j. The term a_{ij} is a weighting factor which depends on group responsiveness and whether the group is in legislator j's electoral support coalition (see Cox, McCubbins, & Sullivan, 1983, for an explicit model of this process).

This modification of our model gives greater play to subgeographic constituencies, and it implies an even less sanguine appraisal of political solutions to market problems than we had initially given. Legislator attention to specific groups within the district implies political preferences for policies beneficial to narrow strata of the constituency, with the pool of citizens available to absorb costs including nonconstituents and (some) constituents alike. It is clientele politics with a vengeance!

Extra-Geographic Constituencies. Unlike the effects of subgeographic constituencies on the geographic calculus of legislators, which tend to exacerbate politically induced inefficiencies, extrageographic constituency effects are more ambiguous. On the negative side, an interest group, like the National Association of Car Dealers or the American Medical Association, is prepared to bribe legislators with campaign resources in exchange for a policy geared to its interests. A legislator would willingly accept his share of such bribes if the expected constituency votes that these payments could ultimately secure exceeded the votes the legislator expected to lose by virtue of his support for the policy (Denzau & Munger, 1983).

The paucity of empirical knowledge of the relative magnitudes of these various effects leaves us in the unhappy position of not being able to draw firm conclusions. Since little is known about how contributions drawn from outside the district can be turned into votes within the district, the trade-off between district and extradistrict welfare remains unknown.

Nevertheless, two hypotheses seem reasonable to assert. First, since the biggest source of extra-district funds is interest groups, this process seems to build a bias into the legislative system away from efficient solutions in favor of those benefiting groups that can readily mobilize funds. Second, unless extradistrict resources completely dominate local elections, geographic incidence, in some form, survives.

Party. There is some reason to believe that partisan pressures attenuate legislator ties to geography and push political preferences toward less provincial policies. At the extreme, where a party regards the nation as a single constituency, the optimal party policy is driven toward x^E as external effects, ignored by individual legislators, are internalized (see Weingast, Shepsle, & Johnsen, 1981).[15] To the extent, then, that a party position is responsive to these forces, it is one that pushes toward efficient resolution of market failures.

The model studied above can be modified in several different ways to include a party system. Again, we focus on how party impact at the district level alters the induced preference functions for legislators. Let the new induced preference functions be $M_j(x, \alpha)$ where

$$M_j(x,\alpha) = \alpha N_j(x) + (1-\alpha) \, Q_j(x).$$

$Q_j(x)$ is legislator j's party evaluation function on policy x, $N_j(x)$ is defined as above, and α $(0 \leqslant \alpha \leqslant 1)$ is a shift parameter that varies with the strength of the party system. This formulation allows for a direct trade-off between a legislator's parochial, district defined evaluation of a given policy, i.e., $N_j(x)$, and that of his party, i.e., $Q_j(x)$. α represents the strength of the party system. As it declines, for example, the weight a legislator gives party evaluations increases relative to that of district incidence.

A perfect party system is one in which $\alpha = 0$, i.e., legislator preferences are induced solely by

[15] A closely related argument is made by Olson (1982, p. 53): "Encompassing organizations have some incentive to make the society in which they operate more prosperous, and an incentive to redistribute income to their members with as little excess burden as possible, and to cease such redistribution unless the amount redistributed is substantial in relation to the social cost of the redistribution." A party or president that treats the entire nation as a single constituency, and whose political success depends on producing policies that improve constituency well-being, is precisely an "encompassing organization" of which Olson speaks.

the position taken by his party, regardless of the incidence of the policy on his district. Although our model is capable of handling this substantive change, it is unclear what conclusions if any can be derived; this follows because there is virtually no theoretical understanding of party dynamics, i.e., from whence the $Q_j(x)$ functions derive. Once some dynamics are assumed, however, conclusions from this perspective can be given.

This view of a strong party system is incomplete, however, since party "ideals" are not self-enforcing. If partisan pressure is to attenuate individual legislator ties to constituency, then there must be some mechanism of leverage on individual legislators by which the party enforces its positions. Control over party nominations and committee assignments in the United States, for example, are the tools with which party leaders could impose greater observance of party positions. Neither would appear to be of much significance in the contemporary American context. Local interests control nominations, and neither the national parties nor the president intrude on these local prerogatives. During most of the post-World War II period, committee assignments have essentially been by self-selection (Shepsle, 1978), although the last decade has witnessed a somewhat more active role by party leaders in the process. In neither the case of nominations nor that of committee assignments has the force of partisanship successfully competed with geography as a basis for legislator preferences.

Essentially the same conclusion is reached if we examine other possible sources of party leverage over individual legislators. Parties figure in only a minor way in the raising and allocating of campaign resources, so that the possibility of denying them to some legislator too attached to local interests is likely only to earn that party the enmity of one of its members. The same may be said of internal institutional resources, such as staff and office space, which tend to be distributed relatively evenly within parties.

In short, the absence of strong parties in the United States, exogenous to the legislature, means that the parties are legislative parties, composed of precisely the legislators for whom district-related incidences are paramount. It should come as no surprise that, if anything, parties facilitate the ties to constituency by giving legislators district-relevant committee assignments, by not intruding in local nominating processes, and by distributing campaign and institutional resources in a relatively evenhanded fashion.[16] Thus,

[16] The key appears to be whether or not a party has strength, resources, and leverage derived from sources outside the legislature itself. Polities with strong parties

although it would be useful to enrich our model with a partisan component to preferences, it would also be something of a surprise if such a component counted for much in the modern American context.

Conclusions

Market failures derive from structural defects in which self-interested market behavior does not produce the felicitous social consequences found in the externality-free world of perfect competition. In order to assess public performance in a comparable context, it would appear necessary to analyze self-interested political behavior in institutional structures of the public sector. One of the major advantages of our approach, therefore, is its emphasis on this institutional structure. The division-of-labor in a legislature represented by its committee system is not merely an economical way of doing business. Based on its gatekeeping and other agenda control power, a legislative committee may block changes in the status quo of which it disapproves and may strongly influence the menu of alternatives from which the parent legislature chooses. Given the propensity in the U.S. Congress for "preference outliers" to gravitate to appropriate committees, public interventions are distorted toward the extremes of the preference distribution represented in the legislature.

Our purpose in this article has been that of modeling public sector institutions which are the counterparts to market institutions in the private sector. Although it is well known that markets fail owing to various imperfections in production, consumption, and, more generally, in the system of property rights, it is presumed, according to one orthodoxy, that public interventions ameliorate such failure. This presumption involves a comparison of market institutions, richly detailed in terms of their divergence from the perfectly competitive model, with a smoothly operating, detail-free, public sector. There is no basis for this presumption. Our results provide specific cautionary warnings about optimistic reliance on political institutions to improve upon market performance.

Students of public policy need especially to take heed of this possibility—the cure may be worse than the disease. This conclusion is all the more important when it is noted that once the political machinery for market intervention is created, no market is immune, even those that are tolerably efficient. Since majority preferences in a legislature diverge from those of social welfare maximization, even an efficient outcome, x^E, is vulnerable to democratic tinkering. The majority win set of x^E, $W(x^E)$, is nonempty, so there are points which provide net improvements for a majority of districts at an expense to the minority that more than wipes out those gains. Thus, our analysis suggests not only that political interventions are no panacea for market failures; as well, they may be positively destructive of well-functioning markets.

References

Aranson, P. H. *The uncertain search for regulatory reform,* unpublished, 1980.
Aranson, P. H., & Ordeshook, P. C. A prolegomenon to a theory of the failure of representative democracy. In R. Auster & B. Sears (Eds.). *American re-evolution papers and proceedings,* Tucson: University of Arizona Press, 1977, 23-47. (a)
Aranson, P. H., & Ordeshook, P. C. Incrementalism, the fiscal illusion and the growth of government in representative democracies. Delivered at the Fourth Interlaken Seminar on Analysis and Ideology, Interlaken, Switzerland, 1977. (b)
Aranson, P. H., & Ordeshook, P. C. The political bases of public sector growth in a representative democracy. Delivered at the Conference on the Causes and Consequences of Public Sector Growth, Dorado Beach, Puerto Rico, 1978.
Aranson, P. H., Bruff, H. H., & Gellhorn, E. The legislative creation of legislators. Delivered at Annual Meeting of the American Political Science Association, Denver, 1982.
Bator, F. M. The anatomy of market failure. *Quarterly Journal of Economics,* 1958, *72,* 351-379.
Baumol, W. J. *Welfare economics and the theory of the state* (2nd rev. ed.). Cambridge, Mass.: Harvard University Press, 1965.
Black, D. *The theory of committees and elections.* Cambridge: Cambridge University Press, 1958.
Buchanan, J. M. *Public finance in democratic process.* Chapel Hill: University of North Carolina Press, 1967.
Buchanan, J. M. *What should economists do?* Indianapolis: Liberty Press, 1979.
Buchanan, J. M., & Brennan, G. *The power to tax.* Cambridge: Cambridge University Press, 1980.
Cain, B. E., Ferejohn, J. A., & Fiorina, M. P. The house is not a home: British MPs in their constituencies. *Legislative Studies Quarterly,* 1979, *4,* 501-524.
Cohen, L. Cyclic sets in multidimensional voting models. *Journal of Economic Theory,* 1979, *20,* 1-12.
Cox, G., McCubbins, M., & Sullivan, T. Policy and constituency: Reelection incentives and the choice of policy intervention. Unpublished, University of Texas, Austin, 1983.

in this sense, like Great Britain, do produce legislators with less than all-consuming ties to geography (although even here the tugs of constituency are felt—see Cain, Ferejohn, & Fiorina, 1979).

434   The American Political Science Review   Vol. 78

Denzau, A. T., & Mackay, R. J. The gate keeping and monopoly power of committees: An analysis of sincere and sophisticated behavior. *American Journal of Political Science*, 1983, *27*, 740-762.

Denzau, A. T., & Munger, M. C. Legislators and interest groups: How unorganized interests get represented. Working Paper No. 81, Center for the Study of American Business, Washington University, St. Louis, 1983.

Fenno, R. F. *Home style*. Boston: Little, Brown, 1978.

Fiorina, M. P. *Representatives, roll calls, and constituencies*. Boston: Lexington Books, 1974.

Fiorina, M. P. Legislative facilitation of government growth: Universalism and reciprocity practices in majority rule institutions. Presented at the Conference on the Causes and Consequences of Public Sector Growth, Dorado Beach, Puerto Rico, 1978.

Fiorina, M. P. Legislative choice of regulatory forms: Legal process or administrative process? *Public Choice*, 1982, *39*, 33-66.

Fiorina, M. P. Some observations on policy-relevant models of legislative decision making. Presented at Annual Meeting of the Midwest Political Science Association, Chicago, 1983.

Head, J. G. Public goods and public policy. *Public Finance*, 1962, *17*, 197-219.

Lowi, T. *The end of liberalism* (2nd ed.). New York: Norton, 1969.

Matthews, S. A simple directional model of electoral competition. *Public Choice*, 1979, *34*, 141-156.

Mayhew, D. *Congress: The electoral connection*. New Haven, Conn.: Yale University Press, 1974.

McKelvey, R. D. General conditions for global intransivities in formal voting models. *Econometrica*, 1979, *47*, 1085-1111.

McKelvey, R. D. Intransitivities in multidimensional voting models. *Journal of Economic Theory*, 1976, *12*, 472-482.

Miller, G. J., & Moe, T. M. Bureaucrats, legislators, and the size of government. *American Political Science Review*, 1983, *77*, 297-323.

Mitchell, W. C. The anatomy of public failure: A public choice perspective. Original Paper 13. Los Angeles: International Institute for Economic Research, 1978.

Musgrave, R. A. The Leviathan cometh, or does he? In H. F. Ladd & T. N. Tideman (Eds.). *Tax and expenditure limitations*. Washington, D.C.: Urban Institute, 1981, pp. 77-121.

Niskanen, W. A. *Bureaucracy and representative government*. Chicago: Aldine-Atherton, 1971.

Olson, M. *The logic of collective action*. Cambridge, Mass.: Harvard University Press, 1965.

Olson, M. *The rise and decline of nations*. New Haven, Conn.: Yale University Press, 1982.

Peltzman, S. Toward a more general theory of regulation. *Journal of Law and Economics*, 1976, *19*, 211-240.

Plott, C. R. The notion of equilibrium and its possibility under majority rule. *American Economic Review*, 1967, *57*, 787-806.

Plott, C. R., & Levine, M. E. A model of agenda influence on committee decisions. *American Economic Review*, 1979, *68*, 146-160.

Riker, W. H. Implications from the disequilibrium of majority rule for the study of institutions. *American Political Science Review*, 1980, *74*, 432-447.

Romer, T., & Rosenthal, H. Political resource allocation, controlled agenda, and the status quo. *Public Choice*, 1978, *33*, 27-45.

Samuelson, P. A. The pure theory of public expenditure. *Review of Economics and Statistics*, 1954, *36*, 387-389.

Schofield, N. Instability of simple dynamic games. *Review of Economic Studies*, 1978, *45*, 575-594.

Shepsle, K. A. *The giant jigsaw puzzle: Democratic committee assignments in the modern house*. Chicago: University of Chicago Press, 1978.

Shepsle, K. A. Institutional arrangements and equilibrium in multidimensional voting models. *American Journal of Political Science*, 1979, *23*, 27-59.

Shepsle, K. A. The private use of the public interest (with apologies to Charles L. Schultze). *Society*, 1980, *17*, 35-42.

Shepsle, K. A., & Weingast, B. R. Political preferences for the pork barrel: A generalization. *American Journal of Political Science*, 1981, *25*, 96-112. (a)

Shepsle, K. A., & Weingast, B. R. Structure-induced equilibrium and legislative choice. *Public Choice*, 1981, *36*, 221-237. (b)

Shepsle, K. A., & Weingast, B. R. Structure and strategy: The two faces of agenda power. Delivered at Annual Meeting of the American Political Science Association, New York, 1981. (c)

Shepsle, K. A., & Weingast, B. R. Uncovered sets and sophisticated voting outcomes with implications for agenda institutions. *American Journal of Political Science*, 1984, *28*, 49-75.

Slutsky, S. Equilibrium under α-majority voting. *Econometrica*, 1979, *47*, 1113-1125.

Stigler, G. J. The theory of economic regulation. *Bell Journal of Economics and Management Science*, 1971, *2*, 3-21.

Stigler, G. J. *The citizen and the state*. Chicago: University of Chicago Press, 1975.

Wagner, R. E. Revenue structure, fiscal illusion, and budgetary choice. *Public Choice*, 1976, *25*, 45-61.

Weidenbaum, M. L. The impacts of government regulation. Prepared for the Joint Economic Committee, Subcommittee on Economic Growth and Stabilization, U.S. Congress, 1978. (Issued as Working Paper Number 32, Center for the Study of American Business, Washington University, St. Louis), 1978.

Weingast, B. R. A rational choice perspective on congressional norms. *American Journal of Political Science*, 1979, *24*, 245-263.

Weingast, B. R., Shepsle, K. A., & Johnsen, C. The political economy of benefits and costs: A neoclassical approach to the politics of distribution. *Journal of Political Economy*, 1981, *89*, 642-664.

Weingast, B. R., & Moran, M. J. Bureaucratic discretion or congressional control: Regulatory policymaking by the Federal Trade Commission. *Journal of Political Economy*, 1983, *91*, 765-801.

Wilson, W. *Congressional government*. Boston: Houghton Mifflin, 1885.

Wolf, C., Jr. The theory of nonmarket failure: Framework for implementation analysis. *Journal of Law and Economics*, 1979, 107-139.

[18]

THE GROWTH OF GOVERNMENT*

SAM PELTZMAN
University of Chicago

I. INTRODUCTION

By conventional budget and gross national product (GNP) measures, government's role in the allocation of resources has increased considerably over the last century, and the growth shows no sign of abating. As a result, governments everywhere in the developed world have moved from a sometimes trivial to a now uniformly considerable role in shaping national expenditures. My task will be to try to explain this growth and size. To do so, I am going to equate government's role in economic life with the size of its budget. This is obviously wrong since many government activities (for example, statutes and administrative rules) redirect resources just as surely as taxation and spending, but the available data leave no other choice. My operating assumption has to be that large and growing budgets imply a large and growing substitution of collective for private decision in allocating resources. But the main intellectual problem I want to explore is the sources of this substitution generally.

I first review the facts about the growth of government and some standard explanations. Since none of the explanations seems very satisfactory, I then present my own explanation, which focuses on the incentives to use a political mechanism to redistribute wealth. Finally, I confront my theory with some relevant data. The main result is counterintuitive: greater equality of private incomes increases the demand for political redistribution.

II. TRENDS IN THE SIZE AND GROWTH OF GOVERNMENT

Table 1 presents a few scraps of historical data on the ratio of government budgets relative to GNP in four developed countries. The data are meant only to illustrate the extent and durability of government growth. Since important sectors of government (for example, social security, local governments) are sometimes excluded, these data cannot be used to compare the size of government across countries. The data do show that government

* The author wishes to thank Gerald Dwyer, Bart Taub, and William Pelletier for their valuable assistance. The support of the Walgreen Foundation, the Center for the Study of the Economy and the State, and the National Science Foundation is gratefully acknowledged.

budgets have grown faster than GNPs since at least 1900, and that they may
have grown more slowly before. A more precise date for the transition from
decline to growth of government would center around World War I and its
aftermath. Since then, without any important exception or reversal, the
government/GNP ratio in these data has increased on the order of three- or
four-fold.

More comprehensive data for two decades ending in the mid-1970s are
summarized for the United States and the major developed economies in
Table 2. They show the extent and growth of government spending at all
levels relative to gross domestic product (GDP) according to international
income accounting conventions. While these data are still less comprehen-

TABLE 1
TRENDS OF GOVERNMENT SPENDING/GNP, UNITED STATES AND THREE EUROPEAN
COUNTRIES, 1860-1974

Country and Year		Approximate Ratio × 100	Percentage Change from Previous
United States	1870	12	
	1880	8	−30
	1900	8	0
	1920	13	+60
	1940	18	+40
	1960	27	+50
	1974	32	+20
United Kingdom	1860	10	
	1880	10	0
	1900	10	0
	1922	23	+130
	1938	23	0
	1960	30	+30
	1974	45	+50
Germany	1880	3	
	1900	6	+100
	1925	8	+30
	1935	12	+50
	1960	15	+25
	1974	15	0
Sweden	1880	6	
	1900	6	0
	1920	8	+30
	1940	12	+50
	1960	24	+100
	1974	27	+15

Sources: United States and United Kingdom: See Section V *infra.* Germany and Sweden: Brian R. Mitchell, European
Historical Statistics: 1790-1970, (1975).

Note: All figures are generously rounded. The numerator for the United States and United Kingdom is spending by all levels
of government and for Germany and Sweden *central* government receipts *excluding* social security taxes. For Germany and
Sweden 1960 and 1974 total government/GNP ratios are 35, 41 and 32, 49.

sive than we would like (see note to Table 2), they seem to reveal the following broad patterns.

(1) The relative size of the government sector in the typical developed country expanded by over one-third in the two decades, from just over a quarter to around two-fifths of the GDP.

(2) The growth accelerated markedly in the last decade, which accounts for about three-quarters of the total growth.

(3) This accelerated growth is evident both in direct consumption and in transfers. However, transfers have been growing two or three times faster per year than government consumption throughout the period.

(4) The higher recent growth rates also seem slightly more variable across countries, so that the spread among the sizes of their public sectors has widened. The growing importance of transfers, which vary more than consumption, provides an arithmetic explanation for this widening dispersion.

(5) The U.S. government sector has been a comparative laggard. Essentially, the rest of the world has caught up to the United States in public consumption. And despite doubling the share of its GDP going to transfers, the United States has made only a modest dent in the rest of the world's lead in transfers. More specifically, the locus of the United States's lag is its defense sector. By 1974 only Australia and Japan had smaller public sectors than the United States.

III. Some Explanations for the Trends and Their Deficiencies

The literature on the size of government uses two modes of analysis for explaining the trends just described. The first focuses on specific historical events as the primary cause, whereas the second focuses on a market for "public goods." Both types of analysis demonstrate considerable variety which this brief summary cannot hope to reflect adequately. This is especially true of the first type, which prevails in studies of particular countries and time periods where questions of the generality of the analysis tend to be deemphasized.

One widely known example of the historical mode of analysis is Peacock and Wiseman's study of the growth of British government, which develops what has come to be called the "displacement-concentration" hypothesis.[1] Briefly put, the government/GNP ratio tends to be a constant until it is displaced upward by a national crisis—war, in the specific case at hand. This displacement is not completely offset at war's end, first, because the expanded bureaucracy is now better able to assert its interests and, second,

[1] Alan T. Peacock & Jack Wiseman, The Growth of Public Expenditure in the United Kingdom (Nat'l Bureau Econ. Research, 1961).

TABLE 2
SIZE AND GROWTH OF GOVERNMENT EXPENDITURES/GDP, U.S. AND 16 DEVELOPED COUNTRIES, 1953-1974

Expenditure Category and Country	Year (Ratio × 100)					Percentage Change from Previous Ten Years	
	1953-54 (1)	1958-59 (2)	1963-64 (3)	1968-69 (4)	1973-74 (5)	1963-64 (6)	1973-74 (7)
Total Government							
United States	27.0	27.5	28.0	31.1	32.2	4%	15%
Avg. of 16 countries	28.9	29.9	31.7	35.8	39.4	10	24
SD of 16 countries	4.1	4.3	4.8	5.9	7.2	9	12
CV of 16 countries	14.1	14.2	15.0	16.6	18.3		
Total Government Less Defense							
United States	14.7	17.6	19.6	22.1	26.5	33	35
Avg. of 16 countries	24.4	26.2	28.2	32.6	36.7	17	30
SD of 16 countries	4.7	4.5	4.6	5.9	7.0	13	14
CV of 16 countries	19.1	17.1	16.3	18.2	19.0		
Government Consumption							
United States	21.5	20.8	20.5	22.4	21.2	-4	3
Avg. of 16 countries	17.2	17.2	18.2	19.8	20.9	7	15
SD of 16 countries	2.7	2.4	2.5	3.4	3.6	12	11
CV of 16 countries	15.8	14.2	13.7	17.4	17.1		

TABLE 2 (Continued)

Expenditure Category and Country	Year (Ratio × 100)					Percentage Change from Previous Ten Years	
	1953-54 (1)	1958-59 (2)	1963-64 (3)	1968-69 (4)	1973-74 (5)	1963-64 (6)	1973-74 (7)
Transfers							
United States	5.5	6.7	7.5	8.7	11.0	36	46
Avg. of 16 countries	11.9	12.9	13.8	16.2	18.8	23	38
SD of 16 countries	4.3	4.2	4.3	4.9	5.9	23	23
CV of 16 countries	36.4	32.5	31.0	30.2	31.6		

Sources of Data: Organization for Economic Cooperation & Development, National Accounts of OECD Countries, various years for all countries except United States. United States data from Council of Economic Advisors, Economic Report of the President (1976).

Notes: Numerator for columns (1)–(5) is current revenue of all levels of government plus net borrowing if any (that is, any net lending to other sectors is not deducted). The data are classified according to the United Nations' new System of National Accounts (SNA) in which receipts and expenditures of separately incorporated nationalized industries are excluded from the government sector. However, subsidies and loans made by governments to nationalized industries are included.

Government consumption includes purchases of goods and services, gross capital formation, and wages paid to government employees. Transfers include subsidies, social security benefits, and interest on debt. (This breakdown is unavailable for Switzerland.)

The sample includes: Australia, Austria, Belgium, Canada, Denmark, Finland, France, Germany, Italy, Japan, the Netherlands, Norway, Sweden, Switzerland, the United Kingdom, and the United States. These countries have adopted the new SNA at different times. Where a particular series could not be reconstructed from the previous SNA, it was spliced to the series from the new SNA.

The denominator is gross domestic product at market prices (that is, includes indirect taxes), which is essentially equal to GNP. The ratios in columns (1)–(5) are averages for the two years indicated. "SD of 16 countries" is the standard deviation of the level or percentage change for the 16 (or 15) country sample, and "CV of 16 countries" is the coefficient of variation.

The years 1975-1976, the last for which I have data, show a marked acceleration of government growth. The first two figures under "Total Government" for these years would be 34.8 (U.S.) and 43.0 (16 country averages). The growth from 1973-1974 is on the order of 40 or 50% that of the entire preceding decade. Although none of the qualitative conclusions is thereby affected, I exclude 1975-1976 because they may atypically bear the brunt of the effects of the most pronounced worldwide recession since the 1930s.

because the war concentrates power at the national level. This concentration of power limits the restraint on taxes provided by competition among localities.

A glance at the British and American data underlying Table 1 (see Figures I and II in Section V) indicates some of the attraction of this generalization. The British variable fluctuates around .10 from 1880 to World War I, when it leaps to a high over .5. From 1920 to World War II, the ratio fluctuates around .20 to .25, when it is again displaced upward and then declines only to a range between .3 and .5. The U.S. data also show a ratcheting effect of the two wars, but much less pronounced than for Britain.

This hypothesis has been evaluated critically elsewhere,[2] but a few simple facts can illustrate its problems. Consider the sixteen countries summarized in Table 2. Half were active combatants for most or all of World War II (Australia, Canada, Germany-Austria, Italy, Japan, the United States, and the United Kingdom). The rest did not enter the war or were defeated quickly. The first group ought to have had (*a*) larger public sectors just after the war and/or (*b*) more rapid growth since then. In fact, the 1953 government/GDP ratios are nearly the same (28.2 for the combatants versus 29.7 for the rest), and the noncombatants' ratios have grown significantly *more* rapidly since then (the difference in mean growth rates to 1974 is 22.2 per cent, $t = 2.09$). From today's vantage, participating in a major war seems ultimately to limit the size of government.

The displacement-concentration hypothesis implies that high and increasing centralization of government produces large and growing governments. This notion plays an important role in Niskanen's interesting contributions to the "specific-event" literature.[3] I put Niskanen in this category because, even though he develops a general model of bureaucracy, he ultimately relies on a few specific events exogenous to his model to explain the size and growth of government.

Niskanen's model contemplates a bureaucracy that values larger budgets and always has some power to extract budget dollars from a legislature that values bureaucratic output. An important constraint on the bureaucracy's ability to gain unproductive budget dollars is competition among bureaucrats and among jurisdictions. Thus, institutional developments that weaken competition imply growing budgets. Among these developments, Niskanen cites centralization of governmental functions, the consolidation of governmental functions into fewer bureaus, and enhancement of bureaucratic

---

[2] D. Davies, The Concentration Process and the Growing Importance of Non-Central Governments in Federal States, 18 Public Policy (1970).

[3] William A. Niskanen, Bureaucracy and Representative Government (1971); and his Bureaucrats and Politicians, 18 J. Law & Econ. 617 (1975).

tenure (civil service). He gives these factors greater weight than increases in the "rational ignorance" of legislators, another source of a bureau's monopoly power.

A primary difficulty with this theory, one which Niskanen explicitly recognizes, is its treatment of centralization of bureaucratic power as an exogenous event. An obvious alternative is that the same forces generating growth of government generally produce conditions facilitating that growth. This may help explain the temptation to fall back on discrete events, like wars, to rationalize subsequent growth of government. Another difficulty stems from the model's sketchy outline of the relationship between politicians and bureaucrats. Politicians do not benefit directly from bureaucratic budgets, and Niskanen presents evidence that they lose votes from marginal budget expansions.[4] (This is meant to corroborate the model's implication that bureaucracies are able to "overexpand.") But the estimated size of this loss—the elasticity of votes lost by an incumbent president with respect to federal revenues during his term is about .6—is easily large enough so that modest reductions of expenditures would have changed the results of some recent elections. In that case, one has to wonder how "rational" it is for politicians to "ignore" bureaucratic expansion.

However, there are clear factual problems with the general-concentration hypothesis taken on its own terms. The evidence that high or rising concentration of government function is essential for large or growing government is weak at best. One measure of concentration is the fraction of all government revenues collected nationally. It is, to be sure, imperfect, because national policies can affect incentives to tax locally.[5] For the United States, the broad trend of this measure supports Niskanen, in that centralization is now higher than in 1900 (about .60 versus .35). However, most of the increase took place in World War II, which is fifteen to twenty years after the persistent growth of the government/GNP ratio began. Growth since 1950 has been accompanied by a mild (about .10) decline in the centralization ratio. A comparison of the developed countries' recent experiences also yields weak support for the role of centralization. What seems most impressive about (measured) centralization is its temporal stability in the face of the considerable worldwide expansion of public sectors in the past two decades. Only Canada has experienced a larger change than the United States (also toward decentralization), and nowhere else has the centralization ratio changed by more than .10. Thus, increased centralization can hardly have

---

[4] Niskanen, Bureaucrats and Politicians, *supra* note 3.

[5] Although Thomas E. Borcherding, The Sources of Growth of Public Expenditures in the United States, 1902-1970, in Budgets and Bureaucrats: The Sources of Government Growth 53-54 (T. E. Borcherding ed. 1977), summarizes evidence that this is unimportant, at least for the United States.

TABLE 3
REGRESSIONS OF SIZE AND GROWTH OF GOVERNMENT
ON CENTRALIZATION MEASURES, 1953-1973,
(16 Developed Countries)

| Dependent Variable | Coefficient (t-ratio) | | | R^2 |
	Centralization 1953	Centralization 1973	Growth of Centralization	SE
(1) Government Spending/GDP	.097			.09
1953-1954	(1.161)			4.2
1973-1974		.218		.22
		(1.965)		6.7
(2) Growth of Government/GDP	.121		.275	.05
1953-1954 to 1973-1974	(.343)		(.571)	17.1

Source: Organization for Economic Cooperation and Development, National Accounts of OECD Countries. Variables (all × 100).

Notes: Centralization: Current Revenues of National Government/Current Revenues of All Levels of Government in year indicated or closest year for which data are available. Series spliced to current SNA where appropriate.

Growth of Centralization: log change of centralization over 20-year period (or extrapolated to 20 years, where required). Government Spending/GDP: see Table 2.
Growth of Government/GDP: log change of Government spending/GDP over 20-year period.

played a crucial role in recent growth. The role of centralization is shown a bit more systematically in the regressions of Table 3 which relate the size and growth of the government/GDP ratio to the level and change in centralization. The simple correlation of levels is weakly positive, and in 1973, even significant. However, neither the extent of centralization nor the small changes in centralization seem to explain much of the growth of government. The meager support these results provide for the centralization hypothesis still has to confront the potential endogeneity of both the level and growth of the centralization variable. The "special-event" explanations of centralization may not be adequate; for example, of the eight full-time combatants in World War II, five rank among the *least* centralized half of our sample in 1953 (or 1973). Centralization of political power can clearly occur without a major war.

In its application to the problem at hand, the "public goods" model is more an analytical framework than the expression of a single widely accepted theory of government expenditure. The common strand of the literature is the treatment of expenditures as the implicit or explicit outcome of a market for government services. That is, demand and cost conditions for publicly provided goods determine expenditures. A vast empirical literature, much of it concentrated on cross-sectional analyses of local government finance,[6] fits

---

[6] See Roy Bahl, Studies in the Determinants of Public Expenditures: A Review, in Sharing Federal Funds for State and Local Needs (F. J. Mushkin & J. F. Cotton eds.) (Brookings Inst., 1968).

this mold, even though much of it is so ad hoc that even this very general categorization is risky. The prototypical procedure goes back at least to Brazer.[7] It consists of regressing aggregate or individual service expenditures on a list of variables which shift the constituents' demand for them (for example, personal income, education) and the government's cost of providing them (for example, wage rates, population densities). A somewhat more theoretically sophisticated branch of this literature tries to take account of the political process that mediates this market or the indivisibilities that the traditional normative theory of government implies will characterize publicly provided services. But these factors have little impact on empirical practice. For example, the well-known collective choice model[8] in which politicians cater to the preferences of the "median voter" is sometimes cited.[9] However, there is no overall consensus that, say, median income is a better proxy for this demand than average income.[10] Similarly, discussions of the "publicness" of government services often serve to rationalize inclusion of, say, a population variable and help in the interpretation of its effect.[11]

For present purposes, an adequate summary of this literature would be an equation like

$$E = bY + cP + dN + A',$$

where (all variables are logs)

E = real per capita (N) government spending;

Y = real per capita income;

P = relative price of a unit of public services;

A' = all other factors;

b, c, d = elasticities with $b > 0$ if public goods are normal,
  $d < 0$ if there are "publicness" scale economies, and the sign of
  c is dependent on the price elasticity of the demand for public goods
  ($c < 0$ if this elasticity > 1).

It is sometimes argued that government shares with other service industries

---

[7] Harvey Brazer, City Expenditures in the U.S. (Nat'l Bureau Econ. Research, Occasional Paper No. 66, 1959).

[8] Howard R. Bowen, The Interpretation of Voting in the Allocation of Economic Resources, 58 Q. J. Econ. 27 (1943); Anthony Downs, An Economic Theory of Democracy (1957); Gordon Tullock, Towards a Mathematics of Politics (1967).

[9] See, for example, Theodore C. Bergstrom & Robert P. Goodman, Private Demands for Public Goods, 63 Am. Econ. Rev. 280 (1973); and Thomas E. Borcherding & Robert T. Deacon, The Demand for the Services of Non-federal Governments, 62 Am. Econ. Rev. 891 (1972).

[10] See James L. Barr & O. A. Davis, An Elementary Political and Economic Theory of the Expenditures of Local Governments, 33 S. Econ. J. 149 (1966), for an explicit test of the median voter model.

[11] Again see Bergstrom & Goodman and Borcherding & Deacon, *supra* note 9.

a labor intensive production function,[12] so P will increase with wage rates. Since wage rates increase with Y over time and cross-sectionally, it is adequate to write this as

$$P = F + hY$$
$$h = \text{constant}, \ 0 < h < 1$$
$$F = \text{"other factors."}$$

Then, focusing on the government/income ratio, our equation would be

$$e = E - Y = (b + ch - 1)Y + dN + A$$
$$A = A' + cF.$$

It is clear that secular population growth could hardly explain the secular growth of e since d is supposed to be negative. In fact, it turns out that $d \approx 0$ is the better summary of the empirical results, at least for aggregate expenditures.[13] Thus, we have to focus on the coefficient of Y if this model yields insights about e. The simplest explanation, which goes by "Wagner's Law," is that $b > 1$. However, this law remains to be enacted: Borcherding's survey of the empirical literature finds $b = .75$ a more plausible central tendency.[14] If so, there remain the price effects (ch) as a potential source of secular growth in e. Again, I rely on Borcherding's survey for an estimate of $c \approx +.5$. To get at h, note that real GNP increased at 3.2 per cent annually from 1929 to 1974, the private-goods and services deflator at 2.5 per cent, and the government-goods and services deflator at 3.9 per cent. These percentages imply an h around .4 to .5 $\left(\dfrac{3.9 - 2.5}{3.2}\right)$. Rounding up, we get $ch \approx .25$ and the whole coefficient of $Y \approx 0$. On this admittedly crude summary of conventional income and price effects, e should thus be a constant over time or across space. In fact, simple cross-sectional data are roughly consistent with trivial total income effects. For example, note the following elasticities (t-ratios) from regression estimates of the equation for e for our sixteen-nation sample:

	1953–1954	1973–1974
Income	.035	.059
	(.464)	(.297)
Population	.0003	−.075
	(.0089)	(1.916)

---

[12] See William J. Baumol, The Macroeconomics of Unbalanced Growth: The Anatomy of Urban Crisis, 57 Am. Econ. Rev. 415 (1967).

[13] See the summary in Borcherding, *supra* note 5.

[14] *Id.*

The one result here that is distinguishable from zero (the last population elasticity) makes growing government more rather than less intelligible, given secular population growth.

A cross section of U.S. states yields similar results. In Table 4, per capita budget measures are regressed on per capita income and population for 1942, 1957, and 1972 (lines 1-3). The income elasticities here are a little below unity, but the shortfall seems mainly due to transitory components of income. The temporal transitory components can be reduced by averaging over time. When we do this (lines 4 and 5), the income elasticities move closer to unity. Other income components may be transitory across space: one state may temporarily gain some income lost by another. As a crude correction for this, I aggregated states into census regions. The regressions on the census region data (lines 6 and 7) yield income elasticities of almost precisely unity, just what our crude summary of the literature would lead us to expect and what we found for the cross-nation sample. The state and local data, in whatever form, also yield the negative but numerically trivial population elasticity alluded to above.

The main purpose of this brief summary and extension of the empirical public-goods literature is to establish a foundation for the subsequent empirical work on the size and growth of government relative to income. The main virtue of the "public-goods" framework is precisely its suggestion that the government/GNP ratio is a variable of prime analytic interest. When the framework is given empirical content, it suggests that this ratio ought to be roughly a constant across space and time. This is the happily fortuitous counterpart of the unit income elasticity and near-zero population elasticity. We are then left with the mystery, which we shall try to resolve, of why this ratio has in fact grown over time and varies considerably across space.

A cursory glance at recent history may help explain why "public-goods" models have not resolved that mystery. The public-goods paradigm characteristically is concerned with collective decisions about classically indivisible "community goods." It seems reasonable to expect broad community agreement to expand these provisions with community income. That agreement, however, ought to be less broad for much of what government today in fact does. For example, about half of the typical developed country's public spending today goes for direct transfers, the community-wide benefits of which are dubious. Similar doubts arise about many public-consumption expenditures. For example, the human-capital literature makes clear that there is a large private element in the returns from public provision of education (about one-quarter of government consumption in the United States). And historical evidence indicates that these private returns elicited a considerable private supply which has not clearly been enhanced by subse-

TABLE 4

REGRESSIONS OF STATE AND LOCAL PER CAPITA EXPENDITURES OR RECEIPTS ON INCOME AND POPULATION
(1942, 1957, 1972, U.S. 48 States)

Dependent Variable (Per Capita)	Coefficients/t-ratios of				R^2	SE	N
	Income per Capita	Population	1972	1957			
1. Revenue, includes federal aid	.802[1] 14.87	−.056 −4.49	.927 9.70	.382 6.92	.975	.153	144
2. Revenue, excludes federal aid	.870[1] 16.55	−.035 −2.84	.696 7.48	.297 5.53	.974	.149	144
3. Expenditures	.860[1] 16.40	−.054 −4.41	.980 10.55	.540 10.06	.979	.148	144
4. Revenue, excludes federal aid: average of 3 years' data	946 9.72	−.035 −2.06			.677	.116	48
5. Expenditures: average of 3 years' data	.897 9.25	−.048 −2.83			.659	.116	48
Census Regions							
6. Expenditures	1.029 12.12	−.046[2] 1.90	.877 5.97	.553 6.56	.994	.092	27
7. Expenditures: average of 3 years' data	1.072 5.54	−.022[2] .53			.846	.086	9

Sources: Expenditures and Revenue: U.S. Bureau of the Census, Census of Governments; and *id.*, Governmental Finances, various years. Income and Population: *id.*, Statistical Abstracts of the U.S. (1978).

Notes: All variables are in logs, except: 1957 = +1 for 1957, 0 otherwise; 1972 = +1 for 1972, 0 otherwise.
[1] Significantly different from unity.
[2] Population per state in region.

quent public provision.[15] Whatever the community-good element in public education, a large indirect transfer is clearly involved in the typical public financing arrangements for it.

Such considerations suggest the riskiness of ignoring redistributive elements when analyzing the size or growth of government, and in the remainder of this paper I will focus on these elements. In doing so, I am not denying the importance of the collective-good aspects of public activity. However, my basic working hypothesis is that incentives to redistribute wealth politically are the more important determinants of the *relative* size and growth of the public and private sectors. This hypothesis entails deemphasis of governments' direct cost of collecting and redistributing resources. This does not have the same empirical basis as our deemphasis of public goods, in that evidence on the effect of, for example, modern communications and record keeping on tax-collection costs is lacking. Accordingly, most of the empirical analysis focuses on groups of governments where differences in tax-collection costs are plausibly minor. In the case of less developed countries where such differences may be large, collection costs are given an explicit role in the analysis.

In the next section, I elaborate a model of the incentives to political redistribution of income, which shows how these incentives are related to the distribution of income that would prevail in the absence of political redistribution.

IV. Theory of the Equilibrium Size of Government

I treat government spending and taxing as a pure transfer. This is, of course, only meant to focus issues, and the literal-minded reader can interpret spending as an increment over expenditures of a purely public-goods character. I also assume that the amount of spending is determined entirely by majority-voting considerations. This assumption also should not be interpreted literally, since it is meant only to highlight an important difference between political and private resource allocation. What is essential here is simply that popular support contributes to the viability of public policies, so that more such support is better than less. Part of this support may eventually be traded for other goods—monetary gain, relaxed relationships with the bureaucracy, and so forth—but I eschew development of a multifaceted objective function for simplicity. In particular, there is no need to confine the analysis to democratic systems. As long as suppressing dissent is costly to a dictator, he ought to be sensitive to the popular support for his policies. In

[15] For example, E. G. West, Education and the State: A Study in Political Economy (Inst. of Econ. Affairs, 1965).

the empirical work I touch on the question whether redistributive considerations are more important in democratic governments.

My analysis of the democratic case can best be understood as a two-step process. The first consists of a search for a politically "dominant" redistributive program, which, speaking loosely, yields the greatest benefits for the greatest number. Once that policy is described, I take a large second step by assuming that competition among politicians will lead them to converge on that policy in their platforms and implement it upon election. Hence, I brush past the rather formidable problems connected with the uniqueness and stability of political equilibrium.

What then is meant by a "politically dominant" policy? I am going to assume that political preferences are motivated purely by self-interest. A voter will favor only those policies which promise to benefit him; social altruism plays no role. Any redistributive policy creates gainers and losers, and thus, in my scheme, potential supporters and opponents. But we need to know more than who gains or loses from a policy if we want to find the policy that will attain the widest support; the per capita stakes will also be important. To illustrate, consider a proposal whereby all of J. Paul Getty's wealth would be confiscated and redistributed equally to everyone else. This policy would maximize the number of beneficiaries, but it is unlikely to dominate alternative policies. Getty and those closely linked with him would oppose it, since they would do no worse. Perhaps Rockefeller and a few other wealthy individuals would favor it, more out of gratitude for being spared Getty's fate than for the trivial share of Getty's wealth they receive. However, most of the beneficiaries would oppose this proposal, for they could surely do better by waiting for a politician to come along and propose the expropriation of both Getty and Rockefeller. Indeed, they would continue to withhold support until a candidate came along who proposed a policy that maximized their benefits.

Of course, the identity of "they" is changing in this scenario: Rockefeller is converted from a beneficiary to a loser in the second round of this political competition. The outline of a politically dominant policy should, however, be clear. It is the policy that maximizes the difference between the number of beneficiaries perceiving the policy as the best deal and losers perceiving it as the worst deal. In a world of certainty and homogeneous beneficiaries, those perceptions should be identical among individuals. We assume neither certainty nor homogeneity. In the more general case, beneficiaries, for example, are more likely to perceive a policy as "best" the greater the per capita gains it promises, and the policy which receives most support will be the one that maximizes the *product* of the number of beneficiaries and the fraction of these perceiving it to be the best deal.

My first task will be to formalize this description of the politically dominant policy, so that we can say something about its characteristics and, crucially, about the forces which shape it. Given our twin assumptions that political competition leads actual policy to converge on the dominant policy and that incentives to redistribution drive the size of government, we can then derive predictions about the forces that shape the size of government. Important among these, I will argue, is the distribution of income.

A. *Full Information*

As a convenient starting point, I assume a world of fully informed voters. Each voter understands costlessly the details of a proposed policy and its implications for his well being. He does *not* know with certainty what other proposals may be offered, nor does he necessarily ignore nonredistributive issues (for example, the charisma or ethics of candidates). All that will matter is that, having understood the nature and consequences of a policy, he is more likely to vote for the candidate offering it the more it would materially benefit him. The purpose of assuming full knowledge is both methodological and substantive. It helps to show where the political system is driven when knowledge becomes less costly, and it helps isolate the effects of ignorance, which I consider subsequently.

There are two relevant pools of voters: those whom the policy proposes to tax (let their number be Q) and those who will be paid (P). Let us first focus on the P's, and the political support they will offer for a policy. In line with our previous discussion, this support will be $P \cdot F$, where F is the fraction of the P's who prefer this particular policy to all others that they may possibly face (that is, "pie-in-the-sky" will not be well received). This fraction can, in principle, vary between -1 and $+1$. When F equals -1, every P is sure he can do better by favoring an alternative policy and they all oppose this one, so "support" equals $-P$. When F equals $+1$, every P is sure he can do no better and all support it. One obvious determinant of F is the per capita gain promised by the policy. If the per capita gain is low, as in the Getty expropriation, F will be low also; as the per capita gain increases, so will F.

Thus it appears that F would rise sharply only when a proposed policy moves toward expropriating the wealthiest 49 per cent for the benefit of the poorest 51 per cent. It requires at least 51 per cent support for a policy to dominate, and maximizing the loot with which to buy the favor of beneficiaries requires taxing the rich to pay the poor. While I will immediately consider some forces—the costs of redistribution—that will eliminate this sort of discontinuity, the reader should be forewarned that the Robin Hood feature of this and similar models[16] will be retained. In this stylized demo-

---

[16] For example, Thomas Romer, Individual Welfare, Majority Voting, and the Properties of a Linear Income Tax, 4 J. Pub. Econ. 163 (1975); Robert Aumann & Mordechai Kurz, Power and

cratic process, the rich are taxed to keep down the numerical opposition to redistribution.

The costs of redistribution will limit the appeal of the massive, 49-paying-51, type of redistribution. The costs I focus on are those imposed on private markets by redistribution, rather than, say, the direct costs of running government programs. The P's and Q's deal with each other in goods, labor, and capital markets, so a tax on the Q also decreases the private income of the P. For example, if the Q are major suppliers of capital, a tax on their wealth will discourage saving and so lead to a reduction in the demand for the P's labor services. Thus, any redistribution policy short of pure lump-sum taxes is a mixed blessing for the P; they gain directly but at an indirect cost to their private wealth. This requires two amendments to our story. First, the tax rate levied on the Q to finance any redistributive policy is a political "bad"; the higher it is, *ceteris paribus,* the less attractive the policy is *to the P's*. Thus, extreme Robin Hoodism (tax rate = 1) is not likely to be politically dominant. In fact, it can easily impose net losses on many or most of the P's.

The second amendment to the story is more technical but helps motivate the subsequent formalism. Specifically, I argue for the Marshallian mistrust of discontinuities: F, the fraction of P who view a policy as "best," will not suddenly leap from -1 to $+1$ for some critical change in policy. The P's are never unanimous about a particular policy, because the importance of private-market links to the Q's will vary among P's. To illustrate, consider a proposed redistributive policy consisting of a per P transfer, g, financed by tax rate R, on Q taxpayers. Now compare this to a proposal for more redistribution, and trace out the effects of the change on F. One possible new proposal is to raise both g and R. Given the varying negative effects of R on the P, some will favor the new proposal, others the old one; F may rise or fall, but is unlikely to go to a corner. Or the proposal might be to raise g but not R. The only way to do this without violating the irrelevance-of-pie-in-the-sky rule is to raise Q. But this also adversely affects P's generally, some more than others. So some will prefer the old policy, others the new. About all we can say at this level of analysis is that, if the old policy involved little redistribution, F (new policy) is more likely to be higher than if there is already much redistribution (and hence much deadweight loss).

The different responses among the P to any program play a crucial role in the theory. To elaborate, let us first recapitulate the discussion so far:

1.   A politically dominant redistributive policy maximizes

$$M = P \cdot F - \text{numerical opposition},\qquad(1)$$

Taxes, 45 Econometrica 1137 (1977); and Alan Meltzer & Scott Richard, The Growth of Government (1979) (mimeographed paper at Carnegie-Mellon Univ., Econ. Dep't).

where

> P = number of beneficiaries of the policy
> F = fraction of P who prefer this policy over all others.

2. F depends on at least two parameters of the policy; the payment per $P(g)$ and the tax rate levied to raise the funds (R):

$$F = F(g, R) \tag{2}$$
$$F_g > 0, \; F_R < 0.$$

3. Beyond some point, F_g can be < 0, and in general, $F_{gg} < 0$. The reason, to repeat, is that if g is increased, *given R*, more people are being taxed. This is a "bad" for the P which can more than offset the direct benefit of the increased g for at least some of them. Moreover, pushed far enough, proposals to increase g will become too risky for politicians to support even if the proposals would benefit P's on balance. Since such proposals involve adding hostile taxpayers, the politician advocating them increases his risk of losing an election. He or his constituents may prefer to cast their lot with a more modest proposal.

I have argued that any proposal for a dominant policy will involve taxing the rich to benefit the poor. This is because any g can be raised this way at the smallest cost in terms of numerical opposition and at the smallest R for a given numerical opposition. I now want to argue that the income of beneficiaries is also relevant to the likely success of a proposal. One reason for this may be diminishing marginal utility of income, so that the perceived benefits of any g are smaller the higher the private incomes of beneficiaries. But I focus here on the deadweight losses of redistribution borne by the P. These losses are likely to increase with income, at least in absolute dollar terms. Consider, for example, a general reduction in the demand for labor as a result of an increase in R. Surely the dollar loss will be higher the higher the pretax labor income of a P. If the tax discourages nonhuman capital formation, the relative loss to higher income P's will also be greater. If their high income is partly a return on human capital, the rise in the human/nonhuman capital ratio lowers the rate of return to human capital. Those P with a trivial human-capital investment can escape this cost. Put briefly, a P with trivial private income has little at stake in private dealings with the Q and is therefore less resistant to a large tax than a P with substantial income.

This hypothesis requires two further amendments:

1. Equation (2) needs to be expanded to

$$F = F(g, R, Y), \; F_Y < 0, \tag{3}$$

where Y = per capita income of the P. This says that if Y falls, it has the same effect as if R falls or g rises—it improves the net benefits of any redistributive policy and hence the likelihood of the policy becoming politically dominant.

2. The complement of "tax the richest" is "benefit the poorest." By our logic, if we had to pick 100 individuals from whom to raise any given total tax, they would always be the richest 100. This would minimize R, implying that any proposal to expand the number taxed means adding less wealthy individuals to Q. Similarly, if 100 individuals are to be benefited, they should be the poorest 100. They will bear the lowest indirect cost of the associated tax and so be the least ambivalent about supporting it. The implication is that Y, the per capita income of the P, is endogenous to the policy: if you propose to increase P, you are proposing to increase Y, because the new members will have higher income than the average of the 100 poorest. So

$$Y = Y(P), \ Y_P > 0. \tag{4}$$

To conclude the analysis, we need to elaborate on the opposition to redistribution from those taxed, the Q's. They face a choice complementary to that of the P's, but simpler: all redistributive policies are bad for the Q's, but some are worse than others. Thus, the degree of opposition from the Q's to any proposed policy will depend on how much the policy would hurt them if adopted *and* how much worse or better off they might be under alternative policies. A simple general statement about the numerical opposition (ϕ) to a proposed policy would be

$$\phi = Q(1 - E), \tag{5}$$

where E = the fraction of the Q who tolerate (that is, do not oppose) the policy. In principle, E could range from zero (the policy is so harmful that no alternative is likely to be worse and all Q's oppose it) to $+2$ (the policy is so mild that *any* alternative is likely to be worse, so all the Q's actually favor it). In practice, we ought to be concerned only about policies for which $0 < E < 1$, since no politician is likely to count on the support of those he proposes to tax as his path to victory. Generally, we expect

$$E = E(R), \ E_R < 0. \tag{6}$$

That is, the higher the proposed tax rate, the larger the proportion of Q's who will conclude that an alternative will be no worse and therefore oppose the proposal.

I now summarize the discussion by rewriting (1) in a modified form, which makes subsequent manipulation more tractable by avoiding inessential complexity. First, express (1) in exponential form

$$M = e^{P+F} - e^{Q-E}. \tag{7}$$

All symbols, except M, are now and henceforth to be understood as natural logs. For example, "P" is now ln P, "E" is a transformation of ln $(1 - E)$, and so on. In doing this, we implicitly focus on policies that the P's support and the Q's oppose. That is, the new F is bounded by $[-\infty, 0]$ and the new E by $[0, \infty]$. In the new notation $E = \infty$ means "none of the Q's oppose the policy," so opposition is $e^{-\infty} = 0$; $E = 0$ means "all the Q's oppose the policy." Next, I write

$$F = F(g, R), \tag{8}$$

where $g = G - J$,

   G = (log of) *total* government expenditures and taxes (recall that we
      are assuming all expenditures to be on redistribution),
   J = (log of) total private income of the P's,
   $R = G - I$, the log of the tax rate on Q's total income (I).

In (8), I have simplified (3) to make the critical benefits variable depend on the ratio of the direct transfer to private income rather than on the two separately. This expresses the crucial notion that transfers lose appeal to the P's the higher their private incomes.[17] The discussion leading to (4) implies: $J_P > 1$ (J is determined by P, and the "marginal" P is richer than the average), and $I_Q < 1$ (the "richest-first" tax policy implies that the "marginal" Q is poorer than the average). Finally, with the new notation understood, (6) is left unchanged.

The formal problem emerging from the theory is to find the redistributive policy that maximizes (7) and toward which political platforms will converge, a policy described by specific values of P, Q, and G, and subject to the constraint that benefits equal taxes.[18] The first-order conditions for the solution to this problem ($M_P = M_Q = M_G = 0$) yield the following marginal "revenue-cost" equalities (the gain is on the left-hand side):

$$1 = F_g J_P. \tag{9}$$

This says that the dominant platform pushes P until the direct gain (always a

[17] The simplification costs some detail. The theory implies that a simultaneous increase in G and J can, beyond some point, decrease support. This is because, given R, the increase in G increases Q, which is a "bad" for the P's.

[18] Another possible constraint would be something like total voters = beneficiaries + taxed. The motivation for not introducing the constraint is more descriptive than substantive. The subsequent analytical results would hold under such a constraint. However, tax and spending policy are typically kept separate both in political platforms and practice, resulting in a large group which receives substantial benefits and pays large taxes. In terms of the formal model, one can regard a member of this group as facing two decisions—one in the role of a P another as a Q—to which equations like (8) and (6) apply separately.

1 per cent increase in supporters) is balanced by the added cost, which comes from diluting benefits over a wider and wealthier base of beneficiaries.

$$-I_Q[e^{P+F+E-Q} \cdot F_R + E_R] = 1. \tag{10}$$

In (10) the gain from expanding Q by 1 per cent is indirect; the tax base is expanded and permits a lower R, which is valued by both P's and Q's (F_R, $E_R < 0$). The cost is the 1 per cent expansion of numerical opposition.

$$F_g = - [e^{Q-E-P-F} \cdot F_R + E_R]. \tag{11}$$

Here the gain from expanding G is that a larger proportion of P's will support the policy ($F_g > 0$); the cost is that both P's and Q's do not like the resulting higher taxes.[19]

There are two second-order conditions minimally required for (9)-(11) to describe an interior maximum: diminishing returns to benefits and increasing costs to taxation. I have already discussed the economic rationale behind the former ($F_{gg} < 0$).[20] There is also a mechanical rationale; since F cannot be greater than zero (in logs), beyond some point F_g must diminish. With respect to increasing costs, we have a choice: either $E_{RR} < 0$ or $F_{RR} < 0$. Since E has a finite lower bound, it is more convenient to assume $F_{RR} < 0$. This says that a given tax increase leads the Q's to withdraw more wealth from market exchange with the P's at higher than at lower tax rates. There is no strong economic reason for the deadweight losses to accelerate in this manner. However, if they did not, the model would permit completely confiscatory taxes. To make the subsequent results clear, I do not go beyond these minimal second-derivative conditions.

---

[19] A more general version of (9)-(11) would begin from something like

$$F = (g', L),$$

where $g' = G - P$ (that is, the per capita benefit instead of the benefit-income ratio)
L = loss to P from taxation = $L(Y, R, I)$.

This L-function summarizes the P's private interest in trading with the Q; this would be related to the P's private income (Y) as well as R *and* I (the tax base). Presumably, the same R on a larger base is worse for the P's private welfare. My more tractable specialization already has $F_Y < 0$ implicitly and $F_R < 0$ explicitly, but does not embody a potential offset to the gain in expanding Q (left-hand side of (10)): When Q is expanded it raises I ($I_Q > 0$) as well as reducing R; the former is "bad" for the P, the latter "good." Allowing the ambiguity, (10) would be

$$-I_Q[e^{P+F+E-Q}(F_R - F_I) + E_R] = 1.$$

Note, however, from (9) that $F_g < 1$ ($J_P > 1$) and, consequently, from (11) that $-E_R < 1$. So the term ($F_R - F_I$) must be < 0, to satisfy (10) in spite of $F_I < 0$. In my specialization I assure this by setting $F_I = 0$. All this says is that there has to be some marginal gain for the P from expanding Q to offset the hostility of the Q's. Given this logical necessity, the specialization $F_I = 0$ is only a simplifying detail.

[20] Note that, while this is required for an interior maximum, diminishing returns in logs is not necessarily implied by diminishing returns in natural numbers for this variable.

THE GROWTH OF GOVERNMENT   229

We can now proceed to derive formally the effects of income distribution characteristics on the equilibrium size of government. First I introduce a variable (X) into the two cumulative income functions $(J(P), I(Q))$ which changes them exogenously in some prescribed way. Then I derive the total effect of this shift on G (that is, dG/dX) from the general relationship

$$[di/dX] = -[M_{iX}][M_{ij}]^{-1}, \qquad (12)$$

where $i, j = P, Q, G$,

$[di/dX]$ = vector of total derivatives,
$[M_{iX}]$ = vector of cross-partial derivative with respect to X,
$[M_{ij}]^{-1}$ = inverse of the matrix of cross-partials.

Consider first an exogenous event that increases every member of P's income by 1 per cent while reducing every Q's income by 1 per cent so $J_X = -I_X = +1$, while $J_{PX} = I_{QX} = 0$. This yields the following sign condition:

$$\text{sgn } dG/dX = \text{sgn } F_{gg}[1 + I_Q F_g] < 0. \qquad (13)$$

This is the "Robin Hood" result: as the poor P's get wealthier, the political forces for redistribution weaken. The now wealthier P's have a larger stake in private transactions with the Q's and are therefore less anxious to see the latter's wealth taxed. $J_x > 0$ implies $g_x < 0$; and this lower g reduces support for redistribution, since $F_g > 0$. In effect, the private-market redistribution has substituted for part of the task of the political market.

Now consider what happens when inequality is reduced *within* the beneficiary group, while between-group inequality remains the same. To stylize this event, let the two groups' total incomes remain unchanged $(I_X = J_X = 0)$, but let the marginal (wealthiest) beneficiary's income decline, or, more generally, the slope of the cumulative income function decline $(J_{PX} < 0)$. Application of (12) yields

$$\text{sgn } dG/dX = \text{sgn } \frac{-[F_{RR}I_Q + F_R(1 + E_R I_Q + F_R I_Q)]}{[1 - I_Q F_g]}. \qquad (14)$$

Both numerator and denominator are positive, so the right-hand side of (14) is also positive.[21] The former reflects the political costs of taxation and the latter the gains of spending, so (14) is telling us that both are altered in a way favorable to *more* spending when inequality among beneficiaries is *reduced*.

Since this result is important for the empirical work, it deserves some

---

[21] Both F_{RR} and $F_R < 0$. The parenthetical expression in the numerator > 0 in equilibrium (see equation (10) and note that $e^{P+F-(Q-E)}$ must > 1 for an interior solution). Since $F_g < 1$ by (9) and $I_Q < 1$, the denominator must be > 0.

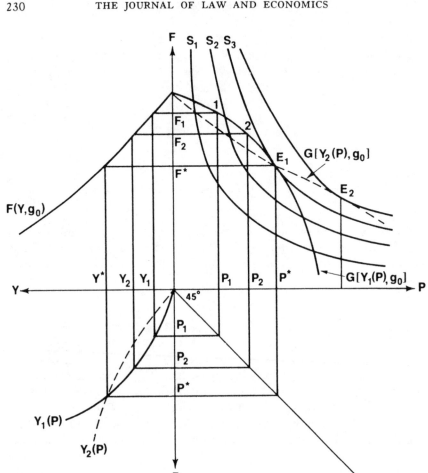

FIGURE I

elaboration. A key element of the result is displayed in Figure I, where I have had to suppress parts of the general solution for the sake of exposition, and where, for a similar reason, I temporarily suspend the log notation. Specifically, suppose the per capita transfer to the P's is fixed (at g_0). The political decision in this restricted version of the general problem is the number of P's who will get g_0, so total transfers will be proportional to this number. Recall our crucial assumption that the higher the per capita income of the P's, the less avid their support for any particular redistributive policy. This is shown as $F[Y, g_0]$ in quadrant II of Figure I: given g_0, a smaller fraction (F) of P's will support a policy that gives each of them g_0 the higher their average income. Recall also that, since high income dulls the appetite

THE GROWTH OF GOVERNMENT   231

for redistribution, any P chosen will be the poorest P in the population. This enables us to express Y as a function of P as displayed by $Y_1(P)$ in quadrant III. If $P = 1$, Y is the income of the poorest person (0); if $P = 2$, $Y = $ the average income of the two poorest, and so on. So $Y_1(P)$ describes the income distribution of P's; as drawn it is meant to describe a relatively [to $Y_2(P)$, which we discuss later] unequal distribution. There are many poor P's, so Y does not increase much if we propose adding P's to a modest set of beneficiaries. However, if we go further and try to add middle class P's, Y starts increasing sharply, for they are much richer than the poor.

These two functions would, except for one difficulty, enable a politician to answer the question: if I proposed giving g_0 to each of P_0, what fraction of them would find this the most preferred policy? The difficulty is that higher levels of P_0 imply higher taxes and/or more people taxed, which, we have argued, are "bads" for P's as well as Q's. One inelegant way around this problem is to imagine that all of the negative effects of taxation are incorporated into the negatively sloped $F(Y, g_0)$ function. That is, the politician says something like: if I widen P, there are more potential votes for redistribution, but I necessarily raise Y *and* increase R and/or Q. *All* of the latter three effects will offset some or all of the potential political gain from widening P. The crucial notion is simply that there is a trade-off between *increasing P* and *reducing* the fraction of the electorate that supports or tolerates redistribution. For expositional purposes, I will ignore parts of this trade-off—the increased opposition and tax effects—and focus on P-income distribution effects.

All of the above understood, the relevant trade-off available in the political market is $G[Y_1(P), g_0]$ in quadrant I, which shows that if a policy proposes a larger set of P a smaller fraction will support it. It is constructed as follows. Suppose benefits are limited to P_1 people. They will have an average income of Y_1, which I find by (i) locating P_1 on the vertical axis of quadrant III by means of a 45-degree line and then (ii) reading off from $Y_1(P)$. For $Y = Y_1$, I can determine F_1 from $F(Y, g_0)$ in quadrant II. The resulting combination (P_1, F_1), labeled (1), is one point on this political "transformation" locus, $G[Y_1(P), g_0]$. In a similar fashion, point (2) is generated, starting with P assumed $= P_2$, and the locus of all such points is $G[Y_1(P), g_0]$.

The political objective to be sought in a choice of P is maximum numerical support (again read "support" as "support net of all opposition"). Support is simply the product PF. In quadrant I of Figure I, this objective is characterized by a series of rectangular hyperbolae (S_i), each of which collect the P, F combinations consistent with a given support (S_i). The dominant policy is characterized by (P^*, F^*), or point E, where S is maximized, given $G[Y_1]$.

Imagine the sort of exogenous event that occurs in (14). The average income of the P^*, $Y(P^*)$ is unchanged, but it is more equally distributed among them as represented by the new income function, $Y_2(P)$, in quadrant III. It crosses $Y_1(P)$ at P^* and is flatter at P^* and steeper near the origin. Poor marginal beneficiaries now add more and rich marginal beneficiaries less to the average income of the group. This, in turn, implies a new $G[\cdot]$ which cuts the old one from below at the old equilibrium E_1. The dominant policy is now E_2 which implies a higher P^* and, given g_0, a higher level of government spending.

To understand what is involved here, recall why P^* was an equilibrium when $Y_1(P)$ prevailed. There was a positive probability that the $P^* + $ 1st beneficiary would himself favor extra redistribution. But this small expected gain was insufficient to overcome the adverse effects of the added taxes on the remaining P^*. The gain was small because $P^* + 1$ is so wealthy that he bears a heavy indirect cost of the added taxes required to pay him g_0. Now $P^* + 1$ is less wealthy and would bear correspondingly smaller losses to his private wealth if taxes are raised. He is thus more likely to return the favor if a politician proposes to include him among the beneficiaries. Rational politicians will respond by proposing to expand the set of beneficiaries.

The principle that more similar interests in redistribution broaden the support for it could be extended to the direct costs of redistribution, which the formal model ignores. If more diverse interests imply a greater variety of programs (transfers for the poor, state opera for the rich) and each has its own "set-up" costs, the benefits perceived per dollar expenditure will be smaller than otherwise. If we permit benefits to be a fraction of total expenditures to reflect these government "brokerage" costs, it is straightforward to show that the equilibrium expenditure rises as the brokerage costs fall. A corollary to this is that governments will not want to completely offset the effects of divergent within-beneficiary-group interests with different per capita transfers. Equalization of benefit/income ratios among beneficiaries, for example, would be too costly, since it would entail complete exclusion of the poorer beneficiaries from access to some programs. Moreover, even if equalization were feasible, our model implies that an optimal policy redistributes wealth *within* as well as *between* groups.[22] This also has a corollary:

---

[22] This is seen most easily in the following restricted problem (log notation again suppressed): A given G is to be distributed among two equal-sized ($\bar{P}$) groups of beneficiaries, who differ only in their incomes (J), to maximize the political support (S) forthcoming from the two groups. Thus, the objective is to maximize

$$S = \bar{P}[F(g_1) + F(g_2)],$$

where F has the same meaning as before and

$$g_i = G_i/J_i, \quad i = 1, 2.$$

the total support produced by any given redistribution is enhanced if the pretransfer income differences among beneficiaries narrow.[23] So while we have, for simplicity, ignored problems connected with the distribution of benefits, their resolution reinforces the previous result that homogeneity among potential beneficiaries increases the demand for redistribution.

In any event, the model suggests a distinction between two types of inequality, that *between* beneficiaries and taxpayers and that *within* the former group. It also suggests that a reduction in within-beneficiary-group inequality stimulates the growth of government, whereas reduced inequality between groups retards it. Thus no straightforward connection is implied between any overall measure of income inequality and the size of government. As we shall see, there are formidable empirical problems in disentangling the two types of inequality from the available data.

B. *Costly Information*

Learning about the effects of a proposed policy or candidate is not, of course, costless, as we have been assuming it to be. There will also be costs of organizing groups to support or oppose adoption of a policy. These costs of access to the political mechanism mean that some voters will be ignorant of the effects of a policy. This section discusses the effects of ignorance on the results just derived.

I will continue to assume that all members of Q are fully informed. This simplification is intended to capture a qualitative difference between them and members of P rather than for descriptive accuracy. Any dominant policy will have to keep Q smaller than P, so Q members will have the larger per capita incentive to become informed about the effects of a policy and organize their interests. Therefore, incomplete knowledge should have the strongest impact on the behavior of group P. To get at this differential impact of ignorance, I confine the analytical burden of ignorance to the P group.

Since $G = G_1 + G_2$, this reduces to selecting the optimum G_1. The solution is to select G_1 such that

$$\frac{F_{g_1}}{F_{g_2}} = \frac{J_1}{J_2}.$$

If group 1 is poorer, this $(J_1/J_2 < 1)$ and diminishing returns imply $g_1 > g_2$—i.e., the poorer receive higher transfers relative to income.
[23] To stylize this, let $J_{1x} = -J_{2x} = +1$, and note that

$$\frac{ds}{dx} = \frac{dg_1}{dx} (F_{g_1} - F_{g_2}).$$

Since group 1 is now richer, the optimal response is to reduce g_1. Since $F_{g_1} < F_{g_2}$ in equilibrium, $ds/dx > 0$. So the narrowing of within-group inequality enhances the political payoff to the total transfer expenditure.

I allow for two effects of ignorance. The *direct* effect is simply that only a fraction of the P who would support a policy if all were informed ($P + F$, in logs) will actually know enough to do so. The ignorant remainder either "stay home" or vote randomly. The *secondary* effect is that politicians will try to exclude some of the ignorant from benefits, so as to concentrate benefits on those most likely to reciprocate. To get both effects, I expand (8) as follows

$$F = H(g, R, Z). \tag{15}$$

The added variable, Z, is an "exclusion" parameter, which varies between $(0, 1)$ in natural numbers or $(-\infty, 0)$ in logs. The variable P is now to be interpreted as the maximum number of beneficiaries, that is, the number who would share G under "free" information. If Z is at its lower bound (no exclusion), the "free-information" case obtains: all the P are informed and share in G. An increase in Z represents more ignorance, which means a smaller fraction of the P support a policy and a smaller fraction are rewarded. If Z ever attained its upper bound (total ignorance), $e^F = 0$ and no redistribution policy would be politically viable.

The indirect (concentrated-benefits) effect of ignorance can be expressed as follows. Retain the definition of $g = G - J$, but redefine J to be the total income of those actually receiving benefits. So

$$\begin{aligned} J &= J(P, Z) \\ J_z &< 0. \end{aligned} \tag{16}$$

That is, the more P excluded, the lower the total income of *actual* beneficiaries. For simplicity, assume that those excluded are a random selection of the P's, $J_z = -1$ (Z in logs); that is, if 1 per cent of the P are randomly excluded, those left have 1 per cent less total income.[24]

If we now combine the indirect with the direct effect of exclusion and examine the overall consequences of increasing the exclusion of P's from benefits, we get for the effects of exclusion

$$F_Z = H_Z + H_g \cdot g_z = H_Z + H_g \quad (\text{since } g_z = -J_z = +1). \tag{17}$$

The second right-hand side term is the indirect effect of exclusion which states that the more concentrated benefits improve support for any given total expenditure. The H_Z term will be the resultant of two opposing forces. On the one hand, there are fewer potential supporters, since a subset of the P

---

[24] More plausibly $-1 < J_z < 0$. This would hold if those excluded tend to be a poorer than average subset of the P's, which is what would be implied by the positive correlation between income and likely indicators of the ability to process political information (education).

A counterforce is that high income implies high time costs of acquiring information. The optimal included beneficiary is poor and well-educated.

receives no benefits. This would imply $H_Z = -1$. On the other hand, the remaining beneficiaries are of higher "quality"—that is, more responsive to any benefits, and this implies $H_Z > 0$. Presumably, a rational selection process of excluding the dumbest first will imply diminishing "quality" effects with exclusion, so $H_{ZZ} < 0$. We also know that beyond some point $H_Z <$ 0 on balance, since total exclusion implies $e^F = 0$.

As it happens, a first-order condition for the expanded policy choice problem (which now requires selecting Z as well as P, Q, G) is

$$H_g = -H_Z. \tag{18}$$

So $H_Z < 0$ in equilibrium. Exclusion is pushed until its direct effects are negative at the margin and counterbalanced by the favorable effects of concentrated benefits. The remaining first-order conditions carry over intact from the free-information case ((9)-(11)). As a result, the effects of income-distribution changes on the growth of government are the same in both models. The added insight we gain into the size of government concerns changes in the "ability" or quality of voters. The effects of some manifestations of such change can be summarized as follows:

1. An exogenous increase in the average "ability" of the P's ($H_X > 0$ at any Z) increases the equilibrium G.

2. There is no ability counterpart to the within-group income equality effect. Specifically, suppose those individuals at the margin of exclusion suddenly become more able, while average ability is the same. Thus, the difference in ability between the most and least able beneficiary narrows ($H_{ZX} < 0$, $H_X = 0$). This generates two conflicting forces which exactly offset each other: (*i*) the degree of exclusion is reduced, but (*ii*) the maximum set of beneficiaries (P) is contracted. This latter occurs to mitigate the otherwise adverse tax and benefit-dilution effects from a net addition of beneficiaries.

3. Simil.rly, an exogenous increase in the ability of P's to translate marginal changes in g into political support ($H_{gX} > 0$, while $H_X = 0$) has no effect on G. The temptation to expand P is countered by the negative consequences of higher taxes, which lead to increased exclusion.

In short, G will vary directly with average ability of beneficiaries, but only its distribution among beneficiaries is altered by changes in the distribution of ability. If income and "ability" are positively related, it would no longer necessarily follow that the poor*est* citizens would be prime beneficiaries of redistribution. But the corollary (2, above) to this version of "Director's Law" is that, if the poorest become *relatively more* able, the middle class will lose some of its benefits.

The main theoretical results whose empirical content is the subject of the next section can now be summarized.

1. If potential beneficiaries' incomes increase relative to those of taxpayers, G will fall.

2. But if there is a similar increased equality of the ability of the two groups to recognize their interests, G will increase.

3. Anything which increases the efficiency of G in "buying" support can be put under the "ability" rubric. Thus lower costs of collecting taxes, or of transforming them into benefits, increases the gross G.

4. More equal income among beneficiaries increases G, but more equal ability has no effect.

V. EMPIRICAL ANALYSIS

The theory shows how some "pregovernment" distribution of income and ability affects the politically optimal level of government spending. Since no such pristine distributions will ever be found in the world, any attempt to relate empirically the size of government to an actual distribution entails a classic "identification" problem; the distribution can both affect the size of government and be affected by it. Moreover, we would not want to abstract entirely from this feedback effect, even if we could. For example, suppose a progressive income tax is levied and the proceeds are shipped abroad or used to pay for public goods that everyone agrees ought to be bought. Now we want to predict the size of redistributive government spending, the main choice variable in our model. My argument that the stake of potential beneficiaries in private dealings affects optimal redistribution implies that *after*-tax income and its distribution are the relevant variables. On the other hand, it could be argued that the progressive tax is the outcome, not a contributing cause, of the optimal policy. Transfer incomes would seem even more clearly an outcome of the process. But that does not imply that, for example, pretransfer income is the appropriate proxy for the "private" income in our model. Someone with only transfer income might have substituted private income absent the transfer. Government affects the distribution of earned income before as well as after taxes. But how? Presumably progressive taxes lead to more pretax inequality, but egalitarian social policies could offset this, by directly or indirectly shifting demand toward lower wage labor. This listing of the potential crosscurrents in government's effect on any empirical distribution of income or ability could be extended.

I deal with the lack of any real-world counterpart to the theoretical "state-of-nature" distributions in two ways. First, I ignore the complications and use what is available, assuming implicitly that the crosscurrents cancel each other. I focus mainly on income concepts (for example, earned income) where some of the direct effects of government (transfers) are absent, but ultimately there is no obvious income concept that is more nearly "right" for our purposes.[25] Second, I focus on the growth as well as the level of govern-

---

[25] Simultaneous equation techniques might appear to offer a way out. But with government

ment spending, assuming a lagged adjustment to any target level of G. In this framework, one can explicitly control for the current actual level of G and implicitly for any effects on other determinants of the target G. To elaborate, consider this version of a familiar lagged adjustment model:

$$\Delta G = a(G^* - G), \tag{19}$$

where $*$ = target value and a = fractional adjustment coefficient; and

$$G^* = bX, \tag{20}$$

where b = vector of constants and X = vector of variables determining G^*. For simplicity, assume only one determinant of G^*, say a summary measure of income inequality. However, the measure ought to be one that would prevail in the absence of at least some effects of the current G, and we cannot observe this directly. Instead, we observe Y, which, for simplicity, can be expressed

$$Y = X + cG, \tag{21}$$

where c = coefficient (we do not know its sign). Substituting (21) into (20) and (20) into (19), we get

$$\Delta G = abY - a(1 + bc)G. \tag{22}$$

Here the coefficient of G amalgamates the usual partial adjustment effect, a, and the influence of G on the observed measure of income inequality, c. Empirical implementation of (22) thus entails all the econometric problems of partial adjustment models plus that of collinearity between Y and G (if $c \neq 0$).

The model and the preceding discussion of the empirical literature imply that the target level of G or of the G/income ratio is affected by at least three characteristics: between- and within-group income inequality and some average level of "ability." The available data do not always permit anything like this level of detail. Frequently, nothing more than a crude proxy for overall income equality is available, and the model makes clear that this variable has ambiguous effects on G^*. The initial empirical work is an attempt to see if any of the conflicting forces embedded in an overall equality measure dominate; the refinements are dealt with subsequently. To compensate partly for the crudity of the data, I will examine a few distinct sets of data to see if they yield a consistent story. These include British, American, Canadian, and Japanese time series and cross sections of developed countries, U.S. state and local governments, and less developed countries. Most

---

spending 40% of GNP and regulating much of the remainder, specifying "exogenous" determinants of, say, the distribution of income involves as much risk as assuming that the distribution is itself exogenous.

238   THE JOURNAL OF LAW AND ECONOMICS

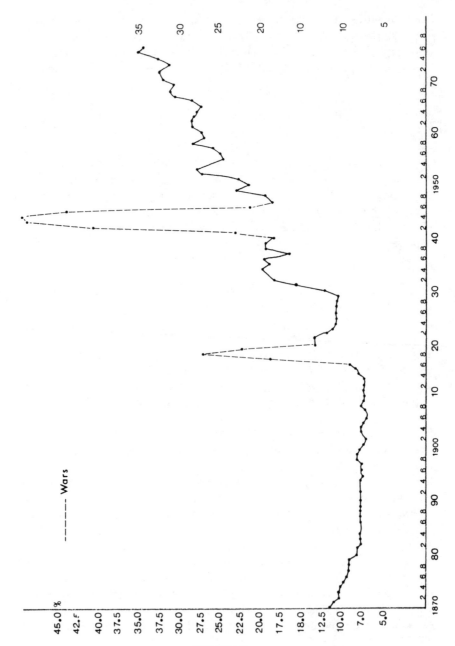

FIGURE II
U.S. GOVERNMENT EXPENDITURES/GNP
Annual, 1870-1976

THE GROWTH OF GOVERNMENT   239

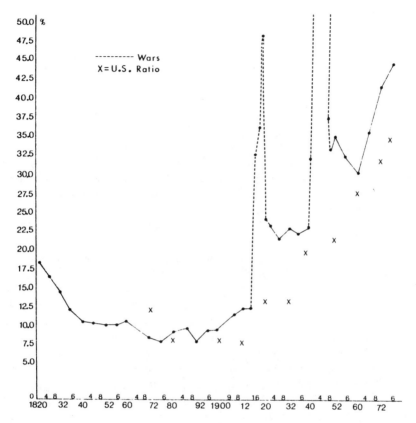

FIGURE III
BRITISH GOVERNMENT SPENDING/GNP
Five-Year Intervals, 1829-1974

of these data imply that income inequality, on balance, retards growth of government. We shall see, however, that this connection is more complex than just stated.

A. *Time Series*

1. *Britain and the United States.* The historical patterns we seek to explain were described broadly in Section I. In light of our review of the empirical public-goods literature, I focus on the government budget share of GNP as shown in detail in Figures II and III for the United States and Britain. The history of government's share of GNP is similar for both countries: decline or stability in the nineteenth century and growth in the twentieth. The most notable differences between the two countries seem to be: (1) the earlier completion of the British nineteenth-century decline, (2) the larger

ratcheting effect of the two world wars for Britain, (3) the substantial U.S. growth in the 1930s versus none for Britain, and (4) the sharper recent growth for Britain.

Is there some plausible connection between this history and income inequality? In asking this, I ignore for now a host of potential complicating factors such as, for example, the extent of the franchise and changes in political structure. This leaves a major empirical problem of devising a proxy for income equality that can be matched to the data. Nothing like the standard size distributions is available for most of the period covered by the data, although Kuznets has conjectured they would show inequality following a path opposite to that in Figures II and III, with inequality first widening then narrowing in consequence of the gradual shift of resources from the low-income agricultural sector.[26]

The only inequality-related data of which I am aware that are useful for a long time series concern intra-industry wage dispersion, specifically skill differentials (the ratio of wage rates of skilled to unskilled labor). In a way, this crude measure is better for our purposes than an overall inequality measure, because it should be more closely connected to inequality within the beneficiary group. More recent data, however, imply that it may be difficult to make the sort of distinctions about inequality required by the model. Figure IV illustrates the scattered data we have on U.S. skill differentials over the past 135 years. For the last 60, we also have a series of the share of national income going to the richest 5 per cent of the population. This is labeled "Kuznets," since the pre-1950 data are his.[27] Since 1915, the Kuznets series and the building industry skill differential (journeymen's wages divided by laborers' in union contracts)[28] have followed the same path

---

[26] Simon Kuznets, Modern Economic Growth: Rate Structure and Spread (1966). His argument in its simplest form is as follows. Suppose that there are no differences in income within either of the two sectors, but that the nonagricultural incomes are higher. Then the variance of logs (VL) of individual incomes (a standard inequality measure) in the community at a moment in time is

$$VL = a(1 - a)(A - N)^2,$$

where a = fraction of population in agriculture and A, N = log of agricultural and nonagricultural incomes, respectively. If A and N do not change, the change in VL over time is

$$d(VL)/dt = (A - N)^2(1 - 2a)da/dt.$$

Thus if a starts out high ($>1/2$) and declines steadily ($da/dt < 0$), inequality at first rises, then falls (when $a < 1/2$). Kuznets's conjecture assumes that this effect dominates any offsetting changes in $(A - N)$ and within-sector income dispersion.

[27] Simon Kuznets, Share of Upper Income Groups in Income and Savings (Nat'l Bureau Econ. Research, 1953). Post-1950 data are for families—the two series are virtually identical where they overlap—from Historical Statistics of the U.S. and Statistical Abstract.

[28] From U.S. Bureau of the Census, Historical Statistics of the U.S. (1975) [hereinafter cited as Historical Statistics]; id., Statistical Abstract of the U.S. (1978); and Harold F. Lydall, The Structure of Earnings (1968).

THE GROWTH OF GOVERNMENT   241

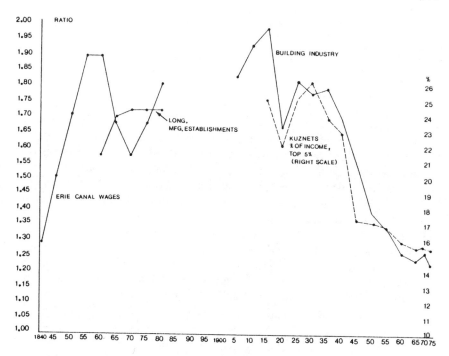

FIGURE IV
SKILL DIFFERENTIALS, UNITED STATES 1840-1975
AND INCOME SHARE, TOP 5 PER CENT, 1915-1975

(their correlation exceeds .8), even though they measure very different aspects of inequality. These data imply that the forces promoting equality have been pervasive.

The skimpy nineteenth-century American data are from Long's study of wages in manufacturing and Smith's study of Erie Canal wages.[29] The pattern emerging from all these data is one of increasing wage disparity over most of the nineteenth and early twentieth centuries and a long decline from World War I to the present. The two world wars, in particular, have coincided with profound movements toward equality, though some of the change of World War I was offset in the 1920s. These historical patterns are roughly the obverse of the secular path of government. They hint that, on balance

[29] Clarence Long, Wages and Earnings in the United States, 1860-1900 (Nat'l Bureau of Econ. Research, 1960); and Walter Smith, Wage Rates on the Erie Canal, 1828-1881, 23 J. Econ. Hist. 298 (1963).

Interpolating over the 1885-1905 gap is likely to be as reasonable a procedure as any. For 1890-1900, we know that the ratio of building trades' wages (where skilled labor is important) to manufacturing wages rose.

and perhaps counter to intuition, income equality stimulates the growth of government. I pursue this hint shortly.

Another kind of inequality deserves mention here, namely, inequality across legislative constituencies. The theoretical discussion abstracts from the legislative mechanism through which conflicting individual interests are actually adjudicated. This is analytically convenient, but risks obscuring some aspects of political choice in a representative system. For one thing, legislators can specialize in collecting and communicating political information and thus a "full-information" model might adequately describe bargaining among legislators. More to the immediate point, bargaining would be more closely focused on the constituencies' average interests than on the interests of income groups who have members everywhere. The legislator will, of course, still have to worry about the disparity of interests within his constituency, but we ought to expect him, all else the same, to more easily ally with a legislator from a district with, for example, a similar average income. Thus, if greater personal income equality facilitates agreement on expanding the size of government, greater interdistrict equality ought to facilitate legislative agreement to implement the expansion.

Given the nature of the American political system at the national level, inequality of average incomes across states can serve as a proxy for the diversity of legislator interests. Figure V shows the relevant history for the available data,[30] which corresponds roughly to the pattern for skill differentials. But the narrowing of disparities began earlier (around 1890 versus 1915), was hardly affected by World War I, and was more profoundly affected by World War II. Also, unlike the relatively small changes in income equality after World War II, a substantial narrowing of interregional disparities continues to this day.

In the empirical work, I investigate whether this narrowing of interregional disparities has contributed to or retarded the growth of government.[31] Any connection between the two ought, strictly speaking, to apply only at

---

[30] Sources of data are as follows: "Taxable Wealth" from U.S. Bureau of the Census, Wealth, Debt, and Taxation (1915). "Easterlin" from estimates by R. Easterlin of per capita personal income by census region relative to U.S. average as reported and updated in Historical Statistics, *supra* note 28. My calculation assigns each state its region's income relative. "Factory Workers' Earnings" from Paul F. Brissenden, Earnings of Factory Workers (U.S. Bureau of the Census, 1929). "Personal Income" from Survey of Current Business (various issues); 1920 figure is from Maurice Leven, Income in the Various States (Nat'l Bureau Econ. Research, 1925).

[31] It is difficult to argue that growth of government is itself responsible for the narrowing, at least directly. For 1970, the coefficient of variation of private income per capita across states is about 18% versus 14.5% for all personal income. This difference is an exaggerated measure of the role of direct government payments, since it assumes that government workers, for example, would earn zero in the private sector. Yet 18% is still half the 1930 figure. Of course, past government activity—World War II—seems to have had a permanent effect on interregional inequality.

THE GROWTH OF GOVERNMENT   243

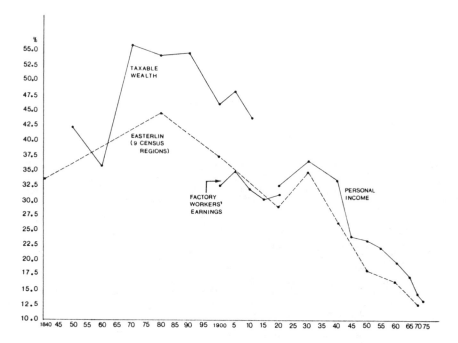

FIGURE V
COEFFICIENTS OF VARIATION PER CAPITA
INCOME OR WEALTH
STATES (UNITED STATES) 1840-1975

the federal level, unless disparities among regions within states have tended to follow the same path as interstate inequality.

Table 5 contains regressions of U.S. government expenditures relative to GNP on the two crude inequality measures just discussed. A trend variable is included as a proxy for "other forces" which may have produced secular growth of government. Clearly any comprehensive investigation would have to spell out these "other forces," and several are suggested by the theoretical model (for example, mean education, "between-group" inequality). However the limitations of the time series preclude anything more refined than Table 5. For example, a glance at Figure II indicates that our 105 annual observations are hardly independent. There are really two or three distinguishable episodes, with a few much less important subcycles. Consequently, I draw observations at five-year intervals, which yield only around twenty degrees of freedom, and even this may overstate the number of independent observations. In addition, the trend variable is itself a proxy for

TABLE 5

REGRESSIONS OF U.S. GOVERNMENT/GNP ON INEQUALITY MEASURES, 1870-1975 (5-Year Intervals, 22 Observations)

| | Coefficients (t-ratios) of | | | | | | |
| | Skill Differential (1) | State Inequality (2) | Trend (3) | Lagged Government/GNP (4) | R^2 | SE | D-W or H |
Regression							
(1)	−21.99	.08	.147		.943	2.28	1.09
	−5.33	.42	3.47				
(2)	−20.90		.132		.942	2.23	1.01
	−6.67		5.82				
(3)	−6.50	.10	1.07	.650	.979	1.48	−2.19
	−1.51	.81	3.24	4.03			
(4)	−5.20		.088	.648	.978	1.46	−1.33
	−1.31		3.74	4.06			
Mean	1.63	30.9		14.85			
SD	.23	9.0		7.92			

Notes: The dependent variable is government spending/GNP × 100. See Figure II and text for sources. The time interval between observations is five years, and each value is a three-year average centered on 1870, 1875, ... To eliminate effects of wars, 1922 replaces 1920 and 1946 replaces 1945 in this sequence.

The skill differential is the series labeled "Long" in Figure IV for 1870-1980, the "Building Industry" series for 1905-1975, and a linear interpolation of the two for 1885-1900.

State inequality is the "personal income" coefficient of variation (see Figure V) for 1920-1975, the series labeled "factory workers' earnings" spliced to later data at 1920 for 1900-1915, and the series labeled "taxable wealth" spliced to later data at 1900-1910 for 1870-1995. Gaps in this series are eliminated by linear interpolation.

D-W and H are "Durbin-Watson" statistic and Durbin's H. The latter is calculated for regressions (3) and (4) where D-W is inappropriate. For (1) and (2) the D-W test implies positive serial correlation with about 5% risk of error. For (3) H implies negative autocorrelation with risk of < 5%.

some aspects of inequality. The agricultural share of the labor force, for example, crossed 50 per cent at about our starting point of 1870. Thus, on Kuznets's argument,[32] the subsequent further industrialization would have contributed to equality. Even the two inequality measures in Table 5 are hardly time independent. The correlations with time are −.75 and −.93 for the skill and state measures, respectively. Table 5 thus addresses a limited question: is there any plausible connection between inequality and the size of government?

The answer seems to be a qualified "yes." There is no perceptible effect from the narrowing of cross-state inequality, but in equations (1) and (2) there is a substantial and significant expansionary effect from the narrowing skill differential. To put this effect in perspective, note that from 1870 to 1975, the government/GNP ratio increased by around 23 percentage points, while the skill differential narrowed by about .5. Equation (2) assigns over

---

[32] See note 26 *supra*.

40 per cent of this growth (.5 × the 20.9 coefficient = 10.45 percentage points) to the skill differential variable.

The link between inequality and government becomes more obscure, but does not disappear, when we allow for lagged adjustment and the possible effect of government on measured inequality. Equations (3) and (4) in the table are slightly modified versions of (22). The point estimates of the skill-differential effect remain substantial: if we assume no feedback effect ($c = 0$) in (22), then the implied derivative of the target government/GNP ratio with respect to the skill differential—which equals (coefficient of skill differential)/(1 − coefficient of lagged government/GNP)—is on the order of −15 to −20. Indeed, the derivative becomes still larger if we go to the other extreme. Suppose the growth of government is responsible for *all* of the .5 decline in the skill differential since 1870. Then, from (21) and (22), we can estimate c ($\approx -.02$), and the implied derivative (b) is about −30. However, given the relevant standard errors, we cannot attach much confidence to these calculations. They simply encourage examination of other data.

Figure VI shows the history of British skill differentials since the Napoleonic Wars, mainly for the same industry that dominates our U.S. data.[33] The major difference between the two countries seems to be the earlier peak in the British data, around 1850. Skill differentials in the United States do not clearly peak until World War I. Given the U.S. time-series results, this earlier reversal of the Industrial Revolution's trend toward inequality may help explain Britain's earlier completion of the nineteenth-century decline in the size of government. The twentieth-century pattern for skill differentials in the two countries is, however, broadly similar—a World War I downward jolt that was incompletely offset in the 1920s and a subsequent downward trend that only recently has flattened. As I point out later, this pattern is characteristic of much of the developed world in the twentieth century.

The British data, summarized in Table 6, show a stronger connection between equality and government than the American data. The effect is numerically larger, completely dominates "trend" effects, and remains significant in the lagged-adjustment formulation. It also holds up in first differences (regression (2)), which is motivated by the autocorrelation of the re-

---

[33] The "building industry" series is composed of the following: 1810-1880: weekly or hourly rates for bricklayers relative to helpers at London (or Manchester, if rates for London are unavailable) British Labour Statistics: Historical Abstract (1971). 1880-1950: K.G.J.C. Knowles & D.J. Robertson, Differences between the Wages of Skilled and Unskilled Workers, Bull. of Oxford Inst. Stat. 109 (1951). 1950-1975: the London series, with 1970-75 from British Labour Statistics, *supra* (various years).

The engineering series is also from Knowles & Robertson *supra* for 1880-1950, then spliced to a series of union pay scales for skilled and unskilled labor in London area engineering industry establishments as reported in British Labour Statistics, annual issues and Historical Abstract.

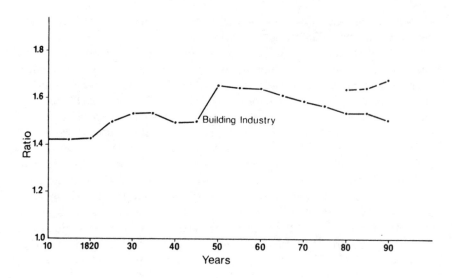

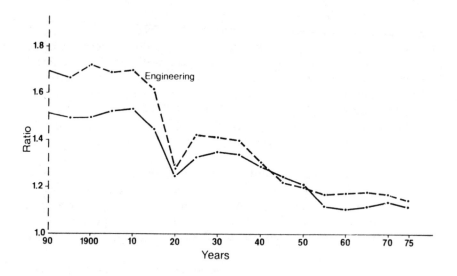

FIGURE VI
BRITISH SKILL DIFFERENTIALS, 1810-1975

siduals from (1)). Finally, as with the American data, the lagged-adjustment regression implies that, unless growth of government has retarded the decline in skill differentials, the coefficients of this variable in (1) and (2) may actually understate the extent of the relevant relationship.

THE GROWTH OF GOVERNMENT

247

TABLE 6
REGRESSIONS OF BRITISH GOVERNMENT/GNP ON SKILL DIFFERENTIAL, 1820-1975
(5-Year Intervals, 32 Observations)

| Regression | Coefficients/t-ratios of | | | R^2 | SE | D-W or H |
	Skill Differential (1)	Trend (2)	Lagged Government/GNP (3)			
(1)	−48.63 −9.05	.001 .52		.898	3.61	.98*
(2) First differences	−22.97 −3.03	.118 1.08		.240	3.02	1.83
(3)	−20.92 −3.03	.002 1.01	.596 5.07	.948	2.68	0.76
Mean SD	1.469 .207		18.27 10.96			

Sources and Notes:

Dependent variable is government spending/GNP × 100 at five-year intervals from 1820-1975. The following replacements are made to eliminate effects of wars: 1898 (instead of 1900), 1913 (1915), 1922 (1920), 1938 (1940), 1947-1948 average (1945); also 1974 (1975) due to data availability.

The numerator is from Organization for Economic Cooperation & Development, National Accounts of OECD Countries for 1955-74. Data for 1820-1950 are from Alan Peacock & Jack Wiseman, The Growth of Public Expenditures in the United Kingdom (1961). They give data at irregular intervals which usually correspond to a year divisible by 5 However, I used their 1822, 1831, and 1841 figures for 1820, 1830, and 1840 respectively. Missing years in the Peacock & Wiseman series were interpolated from percentage changes in British central government expenses (Brian Mitchell & Phyllis Deane, Abstract of British Historical Statistics (1962).

The denominator is GDP at market prices. Data for 1900-1950 are from The British Economy: Key Statistics, 1900-64 (1965), Organization for Economic Cooperation & Development, National Accounts of OECD Countries; for 1820-1900 from estimates of net national product in Mitchell & Deane, *supra*, spliced to GDP at 1900.

The skill differential is an average of the two series in Figure VI for 1880-1975. The building industry series is spliced at 1880. See text for sources.

* = Significant autocorrelation of residuals.

The coefficient of "Trend" in regression (2) is the annualized constant term in this regression.

Putting the data in Tables 5 and 6 together would imply that Britain has a larger government sector than the United States because the movement toward equality has gone farther there and because the British political system seems more sensitive to the resulting pressures (that is, the coefficient of the same skill differential is larger). This may be too sweeping a generalization from very crude data. To see if it is, I ask the following question. Do the historical *differences* in the size of the U.S. and British governments have anything to do with the minor *differences* in their histories of inequality? The answer is hardly obvious from the preceding data. The broad movements in both government and inequality in the two countries are more notable for their similarities than differences, making it more plausible that some common "third" force is pushing on both variables in both countries at any moment. By focusing on relative effects and thereby eliminating this third force, we might easily be left with data reflecting national idiosyncrasies.[34]

[34] To put this more formally, suppose the true relationship is

This does not, however, appear to be the case. In Table 7 the differences between or ratios of the British and U.S. government/GNP are regressed on differences or ratios of their skill differentials. In either form, the results indicate that any other forces propelling the growth of government seem to be enhanced by more equality. Thus a good part of the differences between the development of British and U.S. government seems explainable by different movements in equality. The main qualification comes from regressions (2) and (5) in the table, which allow for lagged adjustment of relative sizes. Collinearity between the two independent variables makes it hard to separate relative inequality and lagged-adjustment effects, but the direction of the inequality effect is consistent with the other results.[35]

To summarize, the British and American data did not allow the separation of the between-group and within-group components of income inequality as our model requires. Instead, we were forced to use skill differentials, which come closer conceptually to the within-group measure but which are also highly correlated, at least in the U.S. data, with a plausible between-group measure (the share of income going to the top 5 per cent). The empirical results all point in one direction: the within-group effects in the model dominate. More equality appears to stimulate expansion of the government sector.

2. *Canada and Japan.* These countries are of interest for divergent rea-

---

$$g_i = \beta Y + \epsilon_i,$$

where g_i = country i's government/GNP ratio; Y = the cosmic force determining both g_i and g_j which we do not observe; and ϵ_i = random error. We do, however, observe X_i, a country-specific variable (skill differentials) which may be related to Y. For example, suppose

$$X_i = Y + u_i.$$

u_i = country-specific random measurement error. When we estimate the regression

$$g_i = bX_i + v_i,$$

b will be biased toward zero but will have the same sign as β, because of the correlation between X_i and Y. However, if we estimate

$$g_i - g_j = b'[X_i - X_j] + v_i - v_j,$$

which is akin to what is done in Table 7, we remove the presumed "cosmic force" (Y) and are left with

$$g_i - g_j = b'[u_i - u_j] + v_i - v_j.$$

Our independent variable would be purely random and $E(b') = 0$ (so long as the country-specific components of X_i really do not matter).

[35] The significant trend term in regressions (1) and (2) is better taken as recommending the ratio model than evidence of any unexplained divergence in government growth. The trend term reflects mainly the post-World War II experience, where both government sectors have grown so large that the absolute gap between the two today (about 12 percentage points) is larger then either government sector 100 years ago.

THE GROWTH OF GOVERNMENT   249

TABLE 7
REGRESSIONS OF RELATIVE SIZE OF BRITISH AND U.S. GOVERNMENT
SECTORS ON SKILL DIFFERENTIALS, 1870-1975
(5-Year Intervals, 22 Observations)

Regression	Coefficients/t-ratios of			R^2 (4)	SE (5)	D-W (6)
	Relative Skill Differential (1)	Trend (2)	Lagged Relative Size (3)			
Differences						
1	−10.76 −2.19	.103 5.05		.645	3.01	1.69
2	−7.59 −1.28	.076 2.21	.226 .94	.608	3.09	*
Ratios						
3	−3.03 −4.04	.001 .86		.531	.235	1.23
4	−3.24 −4.59			.513	.233	1.21
5	−1.27 −1.24		.464 2.15	.573	.210	*
Mean/SD differences	−.23 .13		5.21 4.80			
Ratios	.86 .07		1.33 .33			

* = H statistic cannot be calculated because of large standard error of coefficient in column (3).

sons, Canada for its historical similarities to the United States and Japan for its sharp differences from Canada, the United States, and Great Britain. I review the Canadian history first to see if the preceding findings can be corroborated. The broad pattern of Canadian economic development is so similar to that of the United States, more so than is Britain's, that it provides a strong check on these findings.

The results in Table 8 generally corroborate and in one respect extend those for Britain and the United States. For Canada, unlike the United States, cross-regional income disparities seem important, and they push in the same direction as personal income equality (column (2), regressions (1)-(3)): both are negatively related to the size of government. This result tends to confirm the importance of the "within-group" inequality effect that has so far dominated the results. Were the "between-group" effect important, large regional inequalities would stimulate rather than retard redistribution in a political system with regional representation. Of course, the inconsistency between the U.S. and Canadian results for this variable ought to give us

TABLE 8

CANADIAN GOVERNMENT/GNP REGRESSIONS, 1880-1975

Dependent Variable: Government Spending/GNP	Coefficients/t-ratios						
	Skill Differential (1)	Regional Inequality (2)	Trend (3)	G_{-1} (4)	R^2 (5)	SE	D-W
1. Canada: level	−12.59 5.02	−54.52 3.90	.30 16.76		.96	2.0	1.08
2. Canada: level	−9.06 2.45	−39.89 2.25	.22 3.39	.30 1.30	.97	2.0	—
3. Canada: first differences	−8.71 2.01	−51.24 2.84	.31[1] 3.29		.41	2.1	2.00
4. Canada/U.S.	−1.01 1.24	−.31 1.02	.41 .70		.30	.173	1.26
5. Canada/U.S.	−.47 2.11	−.14 .79			.28	.171	1.24
6. Canada/U.S.	−.63 2.30	−.76[2] .65			.27	.172	1.20

Sources of Canadian Data:

1. *Government spending*

1955-1975. Organization for Economic Cooperation & Development, National Accounts of OECD Countries.

1926-1955. Richard M. Bird, The Growth of the Government Spending in Canada (Canadian Tax Papers No. 51, July 1970).

1870-1926. The annual data are estimates from benchmark data in Bird, *supra*. He gives total government spending for 1870 and decennially from 1890, federal spending annually for 1867-1926, and an "Alternative Series" which includes a part of nonfederal expenditures annually for 1900-26. I use year-to-year percentage changes in these two annual series to estimate annual changes in total expenditures between benchmark years.

2. *GNP*

1926-1975. Same as government expenditures.

1870-1926. Annual estimates from decennial benchmarks for nominal and real GNP, 1870-1910, in Bird, *supra*. I assumed that real GNP grew at a constant rate between benchmarks, and I interpolated annual fluctuations in the GNP deflator from the annual wholesale price index in M.C. Urquhart & K.A.H. Buckley, Historical Statistics of Canada (1965) [hereinafter cited as Historical Statistics]. Nominal GNP in nonbenchmark years is the resulting estimate of real GNP × the estimated GNP deflator. For 1910-1920, the interpolation uses an annual national income series and for 1920-1926 a net domestic product series in Historical Statistics, *supra*.

3. *Skill differentials.* 1920-1975. An average of skilled/unskilled hourly wages in the building and printing industries for five cities (Halifax, Montreal, Toronto, Winnipeg, and Vancouver). The skilled wage for the building industry is an average of wages for carpenters, electricians, and plumbers, and the unskilled wages is for "labourers." The skilled printing occupations are compositors and pressmen and the unskilled "bindery girls." The printing skill differential is set equal to the building industry differential at 1920 and the two are averaged thereafter. Building industry data for 1920-1960 are from Historical Statistics; for 1960-1975, from Canada Year Book (Ministry of Trade & Commerce, various years). Printing industry data are from Wage Rates, Salaries, and Hours of Labour (Dep't of Labour, now Labour Canada, various years).

1901-1920. Building industry differential from data in Historical Statistics (see above).

1880-1900. These are estimates, spliced to and extended backward from the 1901 value, taken from Historical Statistics. For 1890-1900, an Ottawa and Toronto sample of wages for carpenters, masons, painters, and unskilled laborers are used. For 1885-1890, I use immigration agents' reports of carpenters' and laborers' wages at Halifax, Montreal, Toronto, and Winnipeg. For 1880-1885, I use similar 1882-1885 data for Montreal, Ottawa, Hamilton, and Winnipeg.

4. *Regional differentials.* This is a standard deviation of the log of wage rates across cities. The cities, except where noted, are Halifax, Montreal, Toronto, Winnipeg, and Vancouver, each of which represents an important Canadian region. The sources are the same as for the skill differentials. For 1900-1920, the variable is an average of that for the four building occupations. For 1920-1975, an average of the three printing occupations is spliced to the building industry average at 1920. For 1885-1890, we have a subsample of the post 1900 building industry data (see above—Vancouver and plumber and electrician data are missing). I spliced data from this subsample to a similar one drawn from 1901 data and estimate the 1895 value by linear interpolation. The 1880 values are set equal to 1885.

Notes:

All variables are, where the data permit, three-year centered averages at five-year intervals from 1880-1925. To remove effects of the World Wars on government/GNP, the following replacements are made. 1923 for 1920, a linear interpolation of 1910 and 1923 for 1915, 1939 for 1940, and 1947 for 1945. In lines 1-3, Canadian data only are used. In lines 4-6, Canadian data are divided by the U.S. counterpart. Sample size = 20 (19 for line 3).

[1] Annualized constant term.

[2] Canadian variable *not* divided by United States.

THE GROWTH OF GOVERNMENT   251

pause. One possible explanation, elaborated below, is that changes in Canadian regional inequality over the last century have not been nearly as trend-dominated as in the United States, so collinearity problems are less likely to obscure any true effect of regional inequality.

The negative effect of inequality on the size of government persists in the last three regressions, which focus on the relative size of the Canadian and U.S. government sectors. The effect is predictably weaker in these data and seems confined to the personal income-inequality proxy, which again suggests caution in pushing too far the preceding results for regional inequality. But it is more interesting that a negative inequality effect remains in these data, which abstract from the shared history of the two countries.[36]

We gain further insight into these results from Figure VII, which displays the data underlying (4)-(6) in Table 8. Canada has typically had the larger government sector, but the difference tended to be greater up to, say, 1930. Relative skill differentials have moved in the opposite direction; they are higher for Canada in the most recent fifty or so years. These opposing movements are reflected in the negative coefficients of the relative skill differentials in (4)-(6) of Table 8.

Figure VII also raises the possibility of lags in the adjustment of government to equality that the regressions have not captured. The relevant labor market history summarized in Figure VII is that the United States has a ten-to-fifteen year headstart on Canada in the movement toward equality. Up to World War I, skill differentials tend to widen in both countries. They then begin to decline in the United States, but only do so in Canada with the onset of the Great Depression. Notice, however, that, whereas the effects of the U.S. headstart toward equality on relative skill differentials ends around 1930, a major part of the narrowing in the relative sizes of the two government sectors occurs thereafter. Indeed, if the relative skill differentials in equations (4)-(6) of Table 8 are lagged by twenty years, explained variation roughly doubles. The relevant lag may be even longer. Glancing back at the U.S. data in Figure IV, another kind of lag is apparent, that of the skill differential behind the broader ("Kuznets") measure of inequality.[37] Since all of this implies that movements in the size of government tend to lag behind those of inequality, a model in which the latter "causes" the former gains some credibility. While we cannot pursue the lag structure further with the

---

[36] Note that the standard errors for regression (4)-(6) in Table 8 are on the order of a fourth smaller than those of the British-U.S. counterparts in Table 7.

[37] The relevant regression is

$$\text{Skill differential}_t = \text{constant} + 3.3\ \text{Kuznets}_t$$
$$(t = 4.7)$$
$$+\ 2.4\ \text{Kuznets}_{t-1};\ R^2 = .97.$$
$$(t = 3.4)$$

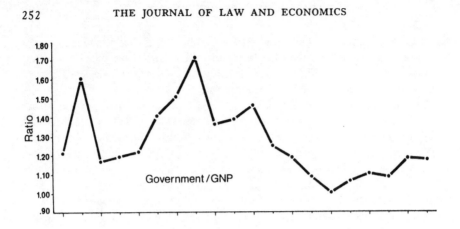

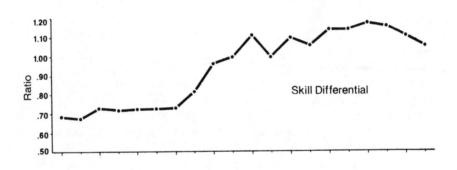

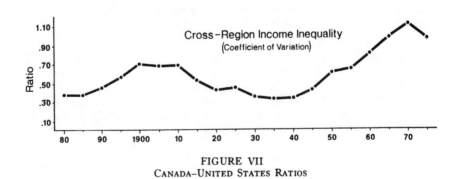

FIGURE VII
CANADA–UNITED STATES RATIOS

crude data and small samples, subsequent data reveal lags to be an important part of the story. In fact, the twenty-or-so year lag that is clear in Figure VII is close to the order of the lag magnitudes that these data will reveal.

The bottom panel of Figure VII reflects a substantial recent divergence between Canadian and U.S. movements in cross-regional equality. From 1900 to World War II, regional disparities narrowed in both countries. Whereas this decline accelerated in the United States, it has actually been reversed in Canada in the postwar period, a fact which may help explain the recent centripetal pressures in that country.[38] However, it is evident from Figure VII (and regressions (4)-(6)) that this reversal has not slowed the growth of Canada's government sector. The negative coefficient of regional inequality in regressions (1)-(3) appears to reflect mainly the earlier history. Unlike the United States, Canadian regional disparities widened up to 1900, while its government sector declined or grew slowly. Regional income disparities then narrowed sharply up to about 1930, and this roughly coincides with a period of relatively rapid growth of government.

A Note on the Role of Voting Behavior in the Three Countries

I have so far ignored the role of political institutions in the growth of government in the three basically Anglo countries. Since the theoretical model suggests that they have a role, it is worth asking if the role is sufficiently important to qualify any of the preceding results. In the theory, political institutions would enter under the rubric of "ability." Anything which makes it easier for beneficiaries to return political support ought to stimulate growth of government. Since all three countries have had democratic structures for the periods studied, we must ask whether differences in the administration of these structures have had perceptible effects. One such difference has been the extent of the franchise. Here, there is a sharp division around 1920 when suffrage was extended to women, and the franchise became virtually universal in all three countries. Although the suffrage of women coincided with the beginning of a continuing expansion in the size of government in all three countries, such a crude correlation should be greeted skeptically. Since women represent a roughly random sample from the income distribution, it is unclear that women's suffrage heralded a shift in the demand for redistribution. More to the point, it is doubtful that, with the possible exception of female-headed households, women lacked influence on voting patterns prior to 1920. So we ought to look to the pre-1920 period for unambiguous political effects.

The considerable variety among the three countries prior to 1920 does not

---

[38] In fact, it is Quebec and the maritime province wages which have lagged the rest of the country, at least up to 1970.

seem to explain the role of government.[39] Here we must distinguish voter
eligibility from participation. In all three countries, participation rates in
national elections have been essentially trendless since at least 1900. They
have ranged around 70 to 80 per cent for Canada and the United Kingdom
and about 15 points less for the United States.[40] So no change in participation seems connected to the dramatic change in the growth of government
experienced by all three countries after World War I. The main differences
among the countries occur in pre-1920 eligibility rates (eligible voters/male
population over twenty-one). The United States had attained near-universal
(90 per cent) male suffrage by 1870. For the United Kingdom, on the other
hand, this figure is only one-third. It required an electoral reform in 1884,
which doubled eligibility, and another in 1918 for the United Kingdom to
close the gap. Canada is the intermediate case. In the immediate aftermath
of the British North America Act, it appears that roughly half of Canadian
adult males had the franchise. Over the next thirty or so years, most provinces gradually removed property qualifications so that eligibility exceeded
three-fourths by 1900. A 1920 federal law made suffrage universal. If the
extent of suffrage promotes growth of government, Britain clearly should
have had the most rapid growth of government in the nineteenth century,
since significant franchise extensions took place in 1832 and 1867 in addition
to 1884. But, as we have seen, British government growth was actually
negative in the wake of the earlier reforms, and after 1870, all three countries are more notable for their similarities—generally stable government/
GNP ratios—than any differences.

These data are too crude to rule out a connection between suffrage and the
size of government. They do, however, suggest, that the major changes in
the size of government have little to do with extension of the franchise;
otherwise the United States would have had by far the largest government
sector in 1870.

Japan. Japan provides perhaps a better test of the role of politics than any
of the three countries we have looked at so far. The basically democratic
institutions that prevailed in these three countries are absent for most of
Japan's history. Japanese economic development was also somewhat isolated from the common forces affecting the three Atlantic countries. Japan's
particularism is mirrored amply in the growth of its government, which is
shown in the upper panel of Figure VIII. Unlike any of the Atlantic triad,
the major growth in Japan occurs before World War I. It shares virtually

[39] The data here are from Historical Statistics, *supra* note 28; Howard A. Scarrow, Canada
Votes (1962), for Canada; and Stein Rokkan & Jean Meyriat, International Guide to Electoral
Statistics (1969), for the United Kingdom.

[40] There was a perceptible, but temporary, decline in all three countries in the decade or so
after women's suffrage.

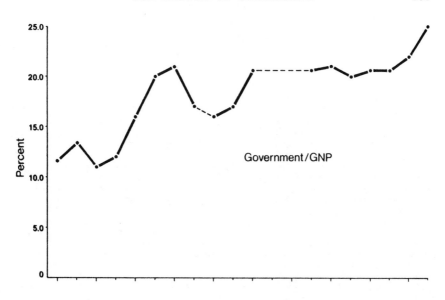

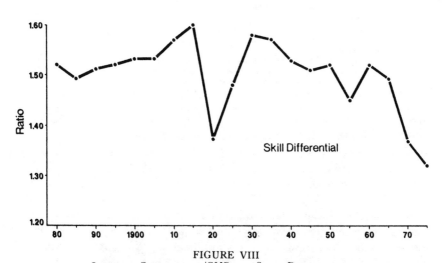

FIGURE VIII
JAPANESE GOVERNMENT/GNP AND SKILL DIFFERENTIAL

none of their subsequent growth and today has the smallest government sector in the developed world.

To what extent can Japan's singular history be reconciled with the previous findings? The first two regressions in Table 9 suggest reconciliation may be difficult. The inequality proxy is positively, rather than negatively, re-

256 THE JOURNAL OF LAW AND ECONOMICS

TABLE 9
JAPANESE GOVERNMENT/GNP REGRESSIONS, 1880-1975

	Coefficients							
	Skill Differential (1)	Regional Inequality (2)	Trend (3)	D (4)	D × SK (5)	R^2	SE	D-W
1.	11.45 1.58	−10.24 −.67	.11 4.75			.77	1.98	1.22
2.	11.50 1.68		.12 6.94			.76	1.95	1.16
3.	17.87 2.05		.14 6.42	41.35 1.89	−29.66 1.98	.82	1.76	1.58

Sources: 1. Data for government spending and GNP 1953-1975, are from Organization for Economic Cooperation & Development, National Accounts of OECD Countries. For 1880-1953, government expenditures are those in the "general account" budgets of national and local governments from Koichi Emi & Yuichi Shinoya, Government Expenditures, 7 Estimates of Long Term Economic Statistics of Japan since 1868 (Kazushi Ohkawa, Miyohei Shinohara, Mataji Umemura eds. 1966). The general account excludes war expenditures which were financed through a "special account" and it excludes operating budgets of, but not subsidies to, nationalized industries. GDP is from Kazushi Ohkawa, Nobukiyo Takamatsu, & Yuzo Yamamoto, National Income, 1 Estimates of Long Term Economic Statistics of Japan since 1968 (Kazushi Ohkawa, Miyohei Shinohara, Mataji Umemura eds. 1965).

2. Skill differential is the ratio of daily wages for skilled workers to day laborers in construction. Data for 1880-1939 are from Ohkawa, et al., *supra;* for 1945-1960 from Koji Taira, Economic Development and the Labor Market in Japan (1970); 1960-1975: Japan Statistical Yearbook (Bureau of Statistics, Office of the Prime Minister, various years).

3. Regional inequality is the coefficient of variation of average wages across 13 cities spliced to series for 46 prefectures at 1940. Data are from Taira, *supra.*

4. $D = +1$ for 1955-1975, 0 otherwise.

5. $D \times SK = D \times$ skill differential.

Note: The dependent variable is government expenditures/GNP, constructed in the same way as for Britain, Canada, and the United States. Since Japan was more frequently involved in wars, there is more extensive adjustment for Japan. Specifically, the following substitutions are made: 1895 (average of 1893 and 1896), 1905 (average of 1902 and 1908), 1915 (1913), 1920 (average of 1921 and 1922), 1935 and 1940 are linear interpolations of 1930 and 1945 (which is set at the 1947-1948 average).

lated to the size of government, though the coefficient is of marginal significance. (And we cannot replicate the significant effect of regional inequality found in the Canadian data.) A slightly different perspective is gained by looking at the two series in Figure VIII. Except for the "blip" around World War I, the Japanese skill differential shows remarkable stability at least up to 1960. It is within 10 points of its mean of about 150 for the entire period, when the Western differentials tended to lie between 100 and 200. This lack of any pronounced move toward greater equality, a move which is almost universal in the Western world, seems confirmed by other data.[41] A negative

[41] See, for example, Akira Ono & Tsunehiko Watanabe, Changes in Income Inequality in the Japanese Economy, in Japanese Industrialization and Its Social Consequences 363 (Hugh Patrick ed. 1973). Also Yasukichi Yasuba, Evolution of the Dualistic Wage Structure, in *id.* at 49, calculated coefficients of variation in average wages across operatives in each manufacturing industry for selected years from 1909 to 1951. There is no tendency for the coefficients to decline over time for comparable industries. While such a measure will reflect, *inter alia,* age, sex, and skill mix changes, this stability does seem to conform to the general pattern of comparatively minor changes in inequality before 1960.

corroboration of the previous results may be that Japanese government did *not* grow in the twentieth century because it lacked the crucial stimulant, a decline in inequality. Of course, this leaves us with the need to explain the rapid growth before World War I. It seems reasonable to raise here the issue of cost of tax collection even if we must postpone explicit analysis of it. The important changes in transportation and communication costs, the size of businesses, the extent of impersonal markets, and so forth, which occurred in the West in the nineteenth century and which presumably reduce tax collection costs ought to have stimulated growth in government's share of national income there. That this did not occur in the West may imply that, once a fairly rudimentary legal and institutional infrastructure is in place, most important tax-collection economies are achieved. But Japan may not have been so endowed immediately following the Meiji restoration. Its per capita income in the late nineteenth century appears to have been on the order of one-fifth or one-tenth that of the United States, and modern local government institutions did not replace the feudal structures of the To-kugawa era until 1878.[42] Thus it seems risky to dismiss tax-collection costs as a factor in the growth of Japan's government in the early Meiji years as easily as we can for the Western countries.

The post-World War II period in Japan is especially interesting for two reasons. The obvious one is the radical change in its political institutions from dictatorship to democracy, a change that permits a sharper test of the role of political institutions than for the three Western democracies. The second reason has to do with changes in income inequality. As in its economic development generally, Japan seems to have lagged behind the Western world by around thirty years. The bottom panel of Figure VIII shows a sustained narrowing of skill differentials starting in 1960. I would be reluctant to draw firm conclusions from this brief period's data except that they seem to comport well with other data. Ono and Watanabe, after examining a variety of inequality measures, also date the start of a perceptible decline in inequality at about 1960.[43]

From Figure VIII it seems clear that neither the political nor income inequality changes has so far produced any dramatic change in the size of Japan's government. But to determine if there are any symptoms of change, line 3 of Table 9 repeats the basic regression with an intercept and slope dummy variable (columns (4) and (5), respectively) for the period from 1955 (the "democratic" era in Japan). The coefficient of the slope dummy $(D \times SK)$ addresses the question: did the process linking inequality to the

----

[42] Koichi Emi, Government Fiscal Activity and Economic Growth in Japan, 1868-1960, (1963).

[43] *Supra* note 41.

size of government change when Japan became a democracy? The answer seems to be "yes" and, more interesting, the change is toward the same process that characterized the three other democracies of more equality being associated with bigger government. This regression is, in effect, telling us that the "Robin Hood" motive to redistribution predominates in the non-democratic era (note the now significantly positive coefficient of the skill differential in column (1), line 3), but that within-beneficiary-group considerations are more important in a democracy.

Moreover, this strengthened importance of within-group equality is predicted by the theory. Refer back to (14), which summarizes the within-group effect. Of the variables in that expression, the one most immediately affected by a shift from dictatorship to democracy would be the variable reflecting the ability of the numerous beneficiaries to give their interests political weight. This is F_g, the marginal political product of the benefit, which should be higher in a democracy. After substitution of some first-order conditions[44] and rearrangement of terms, (14) can be rewritten schematically

$$D = \frac{A + BF_g}{1 - I_Q F_g} > 0, \tag{14'}$$

where A and B are positive expressions not involving F_g, and D is the derivative on the left-hand side of (14). Treating the advent of democracy as an event (X) which raises F_g by a unit. The effect on D is summarized

$$\operatorname{sgn} \frac{dD}{dX} = \operatorname{sgn}(B + AI_Q) > 0. \tag{23}$$

Note that (23) does *not* say that government will grow if F_g increases, but rather that government growth will be *more responsive* to *changes* in inequality within the beneficiary group, whether the changes push for more government or less. This is precisely what the Japanese findings show: no vast expansion of government, but a larger weighting of the within-group equality effect. Moreover, the model implies no correspondingly unambiguous shift in the importance of the between-group effect, which could have obscured the shift we observe in the Japanese data.[45]

---

[44] To eliminate F_R, which may also be affected by the shift to democracy.

[45] The reason for the ambiguity here can be seen most easily by focusing on the marginal political product of numbers of beneficiaries (M_p). This is proportional to $1 - F_g J_p$. An exogenous increase in F_g reduces the marginal product of numbers. When P's become more responsive, the first-order response is to cultivate them more "intensively," with a higher g given to fewer P so that the ambivalence of the highest income P's about redistribution can be economized. (This is analogous to Ricardo's extensive margin shrinking when the marginal product of labor rose.) This is why a rise in F_g, by itself, will not increase the optimal G. However, if the rise in F_g is compensated by a decline in J_p, the ambivalence of the marginal Ps is reduced, and the force shrinking the "extensive" margin is attenuated. Now, when there is an

If this analysis is valid (we will subsequently pursue this interaction between equality and political ability), there are profound implications for Japan's future. It appears that the Japanese government sector is on the verge of substantial growth, if its recent move toward greater income equality is as permanent and far-reaching as that experienced in the West some thirty years before. It now has the democratic political structure in which more equality seems to fuel expanding governments. Thus all the conditions now seem in place for Japan to repeat the vast expansion of government which has characterized the Western world since the depression, including perhaps the replacement of its famed intracorporate welfare system with a national social security system.

B. *Post-World War II Experience in the Developed World*

I now want to see whether the postwar experience among developed countries is consistent with the time-series evidence. While government has grown everywhere, there is enough variety to make the investigation interesting. Table 10 provides some relevant data. The general pattern has been that of rapid growth in Northern Europe, slow growth following high initial levels for France and Germany, and slow growth from low or average levels for the non-European countries. There are, of course, some notable exceptions such as Canada recently, Finland for the whole period, and Britain in the 1950s when it was liquidating its empire. The simple question I try to answer is: can income inequality differences help rationalize this variety?

Comparing inequality across countries poses important problems. The data come from a variety of sources in which income concepts, coverage, and so forth can differ greatly among countries and are susceptible to bias. For example, many income distributions have been compiled from tax returns, which are heavily influenced not only by coverage and income definition differences but by differences in enforcement of the tax laws. I am aware of only two attempts to systematically surmount these comparability problems so that a credible ranking of countries by inequality emerges. The first by Lydall, focuses on pretax wage and salary income.[46] Since it excludes both transfers and property income, this income concept seems like a good proxy for the potential beneficiary-incomes of the theoretical model. Lydall had to rely mainly on tax-based distributions, which he then tried to

---

increase in between-group inequality, J_p is unaffected, so there is no necessary reason for a rise in F_g to induce a larger rise in G than would otherwise occur; the same rise in G could be optimal if concentrated on fewer P's. But a reduction in within-group inequality *does* lower J_p. When F_g rises in *these* circumstances, it calls for both more intensive *and* extensive cultivation of the P's and thus an unambiguously larger rise in G than would otherwise occur.

[46] Lydall, *supra* note 28.

TABLE 10

THE SIZE AND GROWTH OF GOVERNMENT/GDP

16 Developed Countries Selected Years, 1953-1974

	Government Spending/GDP			Percentage Increase		
	1953-54	1963-64	1973-74			
Country	(1)	(2)	(3)	(2)/(1)	(3)/(2)	(3)/(1)
Australia	24.2%	25.4%	30.1%	4.8%	18.5%	24.2%
Austria	31.9	34.8	38.3	9.3	10.0	20.3
Belgium	28.1	31.2	39.5	10.9	26.6	40.4
Canada	26.2	28.0	36.4	6.7	30.1	38.7
Denmark	24.4	30.3	46.6	24.4	53.8	91.4
Finland	31.1	31.3	38.4	0.6	22.7	23.5
France	35.6	37.8	38.5	6.2	1.9	8.1
Germany	35.5	36.6	41.9	3.0	14.5	17.9
Italy	27.6	31.5	39.6	14.1	25.6	43.3
Japan	21.0	20.9	24.0	−0.2	14.6	14.3
Netherlands	31.8	36.9	50.7	16.0	37.3	59.3
Norway	30.5	36.5	48.7	19.5	33.5	59.5
Sweden	28.0	36.3	49.0	29.5	35.2	75.0
Switzerland	27.8	28.9	35.2	4.1	21.8	26.8
United Kingdom	32.7	33.7	42.0	2.9	24.8	28.4
United States	27.0	28.0	32.2	3.9	14.8	19.3
Average	28.9	31.7	39.4	9.7	24.1	36.9

Sources: See notes to Table 2 for sources.

adjust to a common basis (adult male full-time workers). He is sometimes cryptic about how these adjustments are made, particularly where resolving conflicts among different data for the same country. His ranking, however, can be useful here, since it is independent of this problem.

The more recent study by Sawyer for the Organization for Economic Cooperation and Development (OECD) has the advantage of drawing its data from household budget surveys, rather than tax records, supplemented by unpublished data designed to mitigate comparability problems.[47] The major drawback, for our purposes, is the inclusion of transfers in the basic income concept (household pretax money income). Sawyer is able to estimate income distributions, standardized for household size,[48] for ten countries in Lydall's sample. For six countries, the two studies are in broad agreement about inequality rankings. For four there are clear discrepancies since the countries wind up in different halves of the two rankings. Columns (1) and (2) of Table 11 summarize the findings of the two studies.

[47] Malcolm Sawyer, Income Distribution in OECD Countries, in 19 OECD Economic Outlook, Supp. at 3 (Occasional Studies, July 1976).

[48] The standardization is important. Countries with generous pension and unemployment insurance schemes have many one-person households: more retired and young single people find it feasible to set up their own households. These households typically have below average incomes, so their proliferation tends to increase inequality measured over all households.

TABLE 11

COUNTRIES RANKED BY INCOME EQUALITY—TWO COMPARATIVE STUDIES AND RELATED DATA

	Rank Order (1 = Most Equal)		Coefficient of Variation– Factory Workers (3)
Country	Lydall (1)	Sawyer-OECD (2)	
Australia	1	7	—
Austria	10	—	—
Belgium	8	—	13.5
Canada	7	6	15
Denmark	2	—	—
Finland	12	—	—
France	13	10	19
Germany	5.5	9	15
Japan	14	5	—
Netherlands	11	1	4
Norway	5.5	3	10
Sweden	4	2	11
United Kingdom	3	4	8
United States	9	8	18.5

Notes: See text for income concepts used, years covered, and so on. A dash indicates the country is not in the sample. Norway is here assigned equal rank with Germany in the Lydall sample, partly on the basis of the OECD data. Lydall is unable to reconcile two sources of data, one of which would place it "near Germany (1968, p. 161)—that is, relatively high in degree of equality—and another which would place it much lower. Given the OECD findings, the "tie" with Germany may still leave Norway's ranking too low.

Column (3) is the coefficient of variation × 100 of average wage rates for production workers across manufacturing industries *ca.* 1960 from Organization for Economic Cooperation and Development, Wages and Labour Mobility (1965). Industries are approximately two-digit SIC level. Wages are hourly for males, except: United States and Germany (both sexes), France (yearly), and Belgium (daily).

The four discrepancies are divided equally in direction. They occur with Australia and Germany (lower OECD ranks), on the one hand, and Japan and the Netherlands, on the other. The following two obvious possible sources of these discrepancies cannot explain them.

1. *Time period.* Lydall's ranking is for the late 1950s, and Sawyer's is for the late 1960s. However, Sawyer provides data for three of the countries in question (Germany, Japan, the Netherlands) which go back to the Lydall period. In no case is there any change in inequality remotely close to explaining the discrepancy. More generally, Sawyer's retrospective data imply that any 1960 ranking would essentially duplicate that for 1970.

2. *Income definition.* The inclusion of transfers in Sawyer's data raises forcefully the issue of the endogeneity of equality. While transfers may affect cardinal measures of inequality, they do not appear to explain the discrepancies in rank. Sawyer provides decile income shares. If the bottom two deciles—where transfers are heavily concentrated—are deleted and the countries re-ranked, the discrepancies remain. Notice that each discrepant couplet contains one country with extensive transfers (Germany, the Nether-

lands) and one with unusually low transfers (Australia, Japan). Similarly, each couplet has one "big government" and one "small government" country. So government-induced effects on inequality do not appear to resolve the specific discrepancies, though they still may affect the general pattern of the ranks.

The third column of Table 11 shows coefficients of variation in average hourly wages across manufacturing industries from another OECD study. While such a measure will be affected by, for example, differences in skill mix across industries and in national industry definitions, it shares with Lydall the advantage of focusing on income least directly affected by the tax-transfer system. Nevertheless, it would resolve two of the disputed cases (Germany and the Netherlands) in favor of Sawyer. For the remaining seven countries, column (3) basically corroborates both the Sawyer and Lydall rankings.

Since it is beyond the scope of this paper to resolve these differences, I will assume that a "true" ranking of late 1950s earnings inequality is given by: $L + kD$, where L = Lydall rank, k = constant, and $D = -1$ for Japan and the Netherlands and $+1$ for Australia and Germany. Presumably, $k > 0$. The essential question is whether any such ranking scheme can rationalize either the size or growth of government.

The size-growth distinction is especially important in this cross section in light of Lydall's discussion of the recent history of inequality. He finds that the broad outlines of the British, American, and Canadian twentieth-century experience hold almost everywhere in the developed world. Some time around World War I, wage and salary inequality began to decline and some time around 1950, the decline flattened or stopped. Kuznets's data give much the same impression about upper-tail money incomes.[49] He simply reports what is available in the literature, so comparability across countries is risky. But a clear pattern emerges. Around World War I the top 5 per cent of income recipients in the typical developed country account for around 30 per cent of national income and the fragmentary nineteenth-century data show no clear trend from 1870 to World War I. However, by about 1950 this share falls to just under 20 per cent. Crude interpolation of Sawyer's data for the upper two declines implies that the *circa*-1970 figure is around 17 per cent. In broad outline, the growth of government follows a similar path, in that the aftermath of World War I coincides with a permanent enlargement and sustained growth of government. An important detail, however, is that for many countries a major part of the growth of government has occurred in the last twenty-five years, or after the main force of the trend toward equality had been spent. If equality is indeed a major determinant of the

---

[49] Kuznets, *supra* note 26.

equilibrium size of government, a lagged-adjustment process has been dominating recent experience. Thus recent *growth* of government would be more closely related to the level of inequality than absolute size.

This conjecture is confirmed by the data in Table 12, where the size of government at the time of Lydall's ranking and its subsequent growth are regressed on his ranking and the correction factor from Sawyer's study. Size of government and inequality were essentially uncorrelated in the late 1950s. But there is a very strong negative correlation between inequality then and subsequent growth. Some combination of the Lydall and Sawyer data can explain most of the recent growth no matter how the growth is measured, whether we include or exclude defense spending, or focus on transfers or on consumption.

A major puzzle in the table, however, is lack of evidence of convergence toward equilibrium. None of the coefficients of the government-size variable have the expected negative sign and two (in 6 and 9) suggest an explosive system. The puzzle did not disappear, though the explosive tendency did, when I replicated the relevant regressions for growth in the last ten years instead of the last fifteen. It seems scarcely credible that the governments of, for example, the Scandinavian countries and Holland will continue to grow substantially faster than the rest of the world, yet that is what Table 12 implies.[50]

One way to rescue stability from these data is hinted at by the scheme in (19)-(22). Let X in (17) increase with equality, so $b > 0$. From (22) the whole coefficient of the size of government $[-a(1 + bc)]$ can be zero or even positive while $-a < 0$ if $c < 0$. This would mean that increased government spending *reduces* measured equality. Since our basic equality measure is of pretax earnings, less equality may not be so far-fetched. And the simultaneous slowing of the decline of inequality and growth of government is at least crudely consistent with this sort of process. However, crude extrapolation of prewar-inequality trends hardly provides sufficient evidence.

The broad outlines of the results from the international cross section strongly confirm the time-series evidence. At least for developed democracies, reduced inequality of income stimulates the growth of government. The results also imply, much more strongly than do the Canadian and U.S. time series, a considerable lag in response of the size of government to greater equality.

[50] The essential results in Table 12 are reproduced if the arguably atypical years, 1975-76, are substituted for 1973-74. Also, if the OECD dummy is replaced by a synthetic OECD ranking of the fourteen countries which uses the Lydall rank to interpolate the missing data, the counterpart to regression (10) gives about twice as much weight to this variable as to the Lydall ranking, though both are significant. If, as column (3) of Table 11 suggests, the Sawyer data more accurately measure inequality, we would expect those data to get the larger weight if there is a negative correlation between growth of government and "true" inequality.

TABLE 12

REGRESSIONS OF SIZE AND GROWTH OF GOVERNMENT/GDP ON INCOME EQUALITY
MEASURES, 14 COUNTRIES, 1958-1959 TO 1973-1974

Dependent Variable	Coefficients/t-ratios			R^2	SE
	Lydall Rank (L)	OECD Dummy (D)	1958-1959 Government/ GDP		
Size 1958-1959					
1. Rank (1 = largest)	$-.22$ $-.77$			.048	4.24
2. Rank	$-.47$ -1.32	-3.03 -1.14		.145	4.19
3. Log (Government/GDP)	.27 .67	2.26 .74		.054	4.80
Growth, 1958-1959 to 1973-1974					
4. Rank (1 = most % growth)	.56 2.35			.315	3.60
5. Rank	.56 2.17		.028 .11	.316	3.76
6. Rank	1.20 6.80	7.26 5.55	.226 1.61	.832	1.95
7. Rank	1.10 6.24	6.58 4.97		.789	2.09
8. Log Δ (Government/GDP) × 100	-1.77 2.41		.306 .16	.346	11.04
9. Log Δ	-3.43 -6.55	-20.17 -5.06	.151 1.41	.816	6.14
10. Log Δ	-3.31 -6.14	-18.92 -4.66		.780	6.41
11. Δ Government/GDP × 100	-1.28 -4.64	-7.65 -3.67		.673	3.29
Subcategories of Government/GDP, Log Δ × 100					
12. Nondefense	-3.49 -3.36	-5.90 $-.76$		.561	12.34
13. Government consumption	-2.88 -3.88	-3.09 $-.55$		.646	8.80
14. Government transfers	-4.35 -4.16	-39.64 -5.02		.711	12.47

Notes: The 14 countries are listed in Table 11. L = "Lydall" variable in Table 11. D = +1 for Australia and Germany, -1 for Japan and the Netherlands, 0 for all other countries.

Transfers in the 14 include interest on public debt.

The 1958-1959 Government/GDP independent variable is a rank for 5 and 6, and a log for 8 and 9.

The international data seem to say something even stronger. Nothing much besides income inequality is needed to explain the growth of government. We are able to pretty much write the history of government growth in the next fifteen years from what we know about income inequality in 1960. In the next section, we show that the relationship is more complex. Moreover, the complexity is hinted at in the international data. Consider the cases of Finland, France, and Germany which appear not to have been nearly as affected by this century's egalitarian tendencies as, say, Holland or Sweden.[51] Yet, by the early 1950s, their government sectors were all larger than average. To be sure, they have now been surpassed by the more egalitarian countries, but their experience hints that Japan may not be alone in the recent emergence of the stimulative effect of equality on government.

C. *State and Local Governments in the United States*

An examination of state and local government budgets promises to extend as well as corroborate the previous results. We can employ a fairly extensive sample of comparable data on both government budgets and a diverse set of population characteristics to test parts of the theory that were inaccessible with the preceding data. For example, we can at least hope to exploit cross-sectionally comparable data on income distribution to distinguish "between-" from "within-" group inequality effects

These virtues are, however, bought at a considerable potential cost. The exigencies of statistical analysis force us to treat the nonfederal jurisdictions as essentially independent observations. Yet they are neither independent of what goes on at the federal level nor of each other. To cite just one problem raised by interdependence, the ability of a local government to serve redistributionist motives is going to be constrained by interjurisdictional competition, both for the tax base and potential supporters. Whereas that possibility did not seem important in the cross-country comparison—small open economies, for example, Denmark, did not appear constrained to have small government sectors—the possibility seems substantially more important across states and localities. Our fears may be partly allayed by data on the actual redistributive impact of governmental tax-spending programs. Reynolds and Smolensky's results indicate that both federal and nonfederal budgets entail substantial rich-to-poor redistribution, and that the nonfederal redistribution is actually the more extensive.[52]

Even if there is considerable redistribution at the local level, a cursory

---

[51] For France, this is confirmed by fragmentary skill differential data in Organization for Economic Cooperation and Development, Wages and Labour Mobility (1965). Unlike Britain, the United States, and Canada, these show no narrowing at all since 1930.

[52] Morgan Reynolds & Eugene Smolensky, Public Expenditures, Taxes, and the Distribution of Income: The U.S., 1950, 1961, 1970, (1977).

266   THE JOURNAL OF LAW AND ECONOMICS

TABLE 13

REGRESSIONS OF STATE AND LOCAL GOVERNMENT EXPENDITURES/STATE PERSONAL INCOME
(48 States, 1942-1972)

Form of Dependent Variable	1942, 1957, 1972 Average		1972	(1972)- 1/2(1942)	1972-1942	
Model	Complete Adjustment after 15 Years		Complete Adjustment, 30 Years	50% Adjustment 30 Years	Indefinite Adjustment	
Independent Variables	(1)	(2)	(3)	(4)	(5)	(6)
POP	−.73	−.82	−.41	−.35	−.29	−.14
	2.65	3.21	.31	.29	.25	.12
ED	.35	.47	.35	.35	.34	.13
	.60	.80	.37	.41	.41	.16
SD2095	2.05	2.06	−6.50	−6.56	−6.61	−6.98
	.33	.33	.68	.76	.79	.84
SH5	−8.02		−7.45	1.36	10.18	
	.82		.53	.11	.82	
R^2	.26	.25	.12	.10	.10	.08
SE	1.71	1.71	2.67	2.39	2.32	2.31

Notes: The dependent variables are constructed from the ratio of general expenditures by state and local governments in a state to that state's disposable personal income ($\times$ 100). Government expenditures are from the U.S. Bureau of the Census, Census of Governments (various years), while personal income is from U.S. Bureau of the Census, Survey of Current Business (various years). Columns (1) to (5) are variants of the partial adjustment model:

$$g_{72} - g_{42} = k(g^* - g_{42}),$$

where g_t is this ratio for year t, g^* is its target, and k is a fractional adjustment coefficient. This can be expressed

$$g_{72} - jg_{42} = kg^*, j = (1 - k)$$

and the variables in (2) and (5) are constructed accordingly. In column (1), g_{57}, represented by an average centered on 1957 to reduce error, replaces g_{72} and k is set $= 1$.

Independent Variables

ED: Mean years of schooling attained by population over 27 in 1940 from U.S. Bureau of the Census, Census of Population. State Volumes. For college graduates, I assume 90% complete 16 years and 10% 17 years.

SD2095: Average of 1950 value and *ca.* 1920-1930 estimate of the standard deviation of log of income of male heads of households in the 20th to 95th percentile of the income distribution. 1950 data are from Census of Population. State Volumes, *supra,* which gives a distribution by dollar intervals. For each state, a continuous function was fit to these data by method of cubic splices up to the open-ended upper income interval; this latter was approximated by a Pareto distribution. From this, we were able to estimate income $= f(R)$ where R is an individual's ranking in the distribution. For this purpose, each state's population was set $= 1000$, and we computed SD2095 from $f(200), f(201), \ldots f(950)$.

The 1920 value is estimated from

$$SD2095_{20} = A + \Sigma b_i X_{i,1920},$$

where the X_i are

1. log of per capita income.
2. $\sqrt{w(1 - w)}$, $w =$ proportion of population white.

TABLE 13 (Continued)

3. $|\sqrt{f(1-f)}|I_f - I_0||$, f = proportion farmers. I_f, I_0 is log of per capita income of farmers and other respectively. (The motivation for the square root constructs is that, if the only source of dispersion in the population is, for example, $I_f \neq I_0$, this formula gives the standard deviation of log income in the population.)

4. SH5 (see below).

With the exception of w, which is from U.S. Bureau of the Census, Historical Statistics of the U.S. (various years), all these variables are from Leven, Income in the Various States (1925). The b_i are coefficients from a regression of the 1950 SD2095 on the 1950 counterparts to X_i (R^2 = .9 and all coefficients were significant).
(The coefficient of $\sqrt{w(1-w)}$ was multiplied by 1.5. In principle, this variable should include an income difference term like that in 3. I had to exclude such a term because the 1920 counterpart does not exist. The 1950 coefficient therefore includes the average racial income difference. For the mid-1930s, when the first racial income data are available, that difference is around 1.5 × that of 1950). A is set so that the mean of the 1920 estimate = .53, which is the value for the first comparable U.S. income distribution (1929)).

SH5: share of state income of wealthiest 5%, average of 1950 and 1920. The 1950 value is from $f(R)$, described above, and the 1920 value is from Leven, *supra*. (It is restricted to nonfarm incomes.)

POP: log of state population in 1942, or (columns (3)-(6)) change between 1942 and 1972. From U.S. Bureau of the Census, Statistical Abstract (various years). The means (standard deviations) of the variables are: Average of $g_{72,42,57}$ = 14.7 (1.9); g_{72} – g_{42} = 11.8 (2.3); ED = 8.40 (.89); SD2095 = .451 (.083); SH5 = .246 (.031). t-ratios are below coefficients.

glance at the data suggests another problem. Clearly broad historical forces producing ubiquitous growth of government dominate any local variety. For the period 1942-1972, the average ratio of state and local spending to personal income across forty-eight states was .15 with a standard deviation of only .02. The average change (standard deviation) between these years is .12 (.02). Variation across states is thus much smaller than across countries (see Tables 2 and 10). This small variation left to be "explained" by local factors poses a substantial constraint on the added insight these data may provide.

In Table 13, I attempt to implement the three main implications of the theory, which are that the size of government responds (*a*) positively to income inequality between prospective beneficiaries and taxpayers, (*b*) negatively to inequality among beneficiaries, and (*c*) positively to the "ability" of beneficiaries to process information. The empirical counterparts to these three notions are:

1. Between-group equality: the share of a state's income accounted for by the richest 5 per cent of the population (SH5).

2. Within-group equality: the standard deviation of the log of income of the group in the twentieth to ninety-fifth percentile of the income distribution in each state (SD2095).

3. Ability: average years of schooling (ED). The choice of the ninety-fifth percentile as a lower bound for the SH variable was forced by the data. When this bound is lowered, the correlation between the SH and any corresponding SD variable rises dramatically; for example, it is on the order of .8 to .9 if the lower bound of SH is the eightieth percentile and the upper bound of SD is anything up to eighty, compared to .4 when ninety-five is the lower bound. This intercorrelation makes it difficult to distinguish "between-" from "within-" group effects. The motive for excluding the poorest 20 per cent of the population was the model's suggestion of "Director's Law": the

very poorest may not have sufficient ability to be included as beneficiaries. The results, however, were basically the same when the lower bound for SD was zero and the upper bound was the sixtieth or eightieth percentile.[53] In light of the results in Table 4, state population is included as an independent variable.

The dependent variable is the ratio of state and local government expenditures to personal income, or its change, for each of forty-eight states. The data are for 1942, 1957, and 1972. The motive for this lengthy time span was to gain insight into the lag process, which the international cross section and some of the time series suggested was an important part of the story. An initial attempt at implementing a conventional partial adjustment model like (19) failed.[54] Therefore, Table 13 shows a range of results. Specifically, the income distribution and ability variables are defined as of *circa* 1940, that is, the start of the thirty-year period.[55] These initial conditions are assumed to determine a target level of the ratio of government spending to personal income. Then a range of adjustment rates to this target is imposed on the data via suitable definition of the dependent variable.[56] The last column of the table departs from the partial adjustment framework in favor of a less specific form: the initial conditions *circa* 1940 simply determine the rate of change over the indefinite future.

The results are uniformly disappointing. None of the coefficients of interest are distinguishable from zero. Some hint of the source of this sharp contrast with previous results is, however, given by the underlying data. The simple correlations between the ability (ED) and within-group inequal-

---

[53] Similarly, cutting out either the lower or upper tail of the education distribution made no substantial difference.

[54] Entering the lagged dependent variable as an independent variable always yielded absurdly low adjustment coefficients—on the order of .2 for 30 years. The reason appears to be that "state-specific" effects not captured by the model persist over time—for example, New York had unusually large governments in 1942 as well as 1972. Thus, when a 1972 expenditure variable is regressed on its 1942 counterpart, the coefficient of the latter (1 − adjustment coefficient) tends to have a positive bias.

[55] Usable data on income distributions begin with the 1950 census. (There are some in 1940, but always with a frighteningly large group reporting no or trivial income.) But these data are an implausible proxy for initial conditions around 1940. We have seen that there was a sharp narrowing of income dispersions generally beginning around 1930 and ending around 1940, so the 1950 distribution is more likely to typify the end rather than the beginning of our 30-year period.

The way I took out of this difficulty is as follows. For the early 1920s data are available on several important correlates of SD2095 in 1950. The 1920 counterparts are then weighted and summed to generate an estimate of SD2095 for 1920 (see note to Table 13). This is then averaged with the 1950 value to generate the variable used in the regression. In substance, we are assuming that policy decisions made in 1940 respond to about half of the profound change in inequality that occurred during the depression and World War II.

[56] This procedure confines any state-specific effect to the residual of the regression, thereby avoiding any obvious bias of the coefficients.

ity (SD2095) variables, on the one hand, and the dependent variable, on the other, always have the "correct" signs (positive and negative, respectively). These correlation coefficients range between .2 and .4 in absolute value, depending on the definition of the dependent variable. While these values are not spectacularly high, they are often significant with only moderate risk of error. (The simple correlation on between-group inequality (SH5) is, however, typically negative, sometimes significant. Yet, when that variable is deleted from the regression, as in column (2) or (6) there is no improvement in the performance of the remaining variables.) There is, however, a substantial negative correlation (around $-.9$) between ED and SD2095, which may be helping to obscure their independent effects.

The negative correlation between education and inequality may be a systematic outcome of the human-capital accumulation process.[57] If this is so, it raises not only statistical problems but important interpretive problems for our previous results of a fairly consistent negative correlation between inequality and government/GNP. But if inequality and education are also negatively related, could not part of the negative correlation reflect the effects of increased education (political "ability")? To be sure, increased education may have been partially reflected in the typically positive "trend" components of the time-series regression. Our cross-sectional data, however, raise the possibility that inequaltiy is a better proxy for ability than simple trend. A still more subtle possibility, encountered both in the Japanese data and the theory, is summarized by (14') and (23). Perhaps there is no simple relationship between the size of government, on the one hand, and inequality and ability, on the other. Rather, the latter two interact. Explicitly the general scheme estimated in Table 13 is

$$g = a \cdot \text{ABILITY} + b \cdot \text{INEQUALITY} + X, \qquad (24)$$

where X = other factors influencing the size of government (g)

   $a, b,$ = constants, $a > 0, b$?

---

[57] In what Gary S. Becker, Human Capital (1975), terms the "egalitarian approach" to human capital accumulation, interpersonal differences in the costs of funds are the major determinants of differences in education. So those with a lower cost of funds buy more education and, at least on the margin, earn lower rates of return. *Ceteris paribus,* the income distribution is more equal, the lower the rate of return. Becker cites scattered evidence of a decline over time in rates of return, which, given the simultaneous spread of education, would seem consistent with the "egalitarian approach." Barry R. Chiswick, Income Inequality: Regional Analyses within a Human Capital Framework (Nat'l Bureau Econ. Research, 1974), shows a strong negative correlation between rates of return and mean education across states, which is also consistent with the egalitarian approach. In his work, this rate of return × standard deviation of education is the crucial systematic determinant of income inequality. Since schooling inequality and mean schooling are uncorrelated, the clear implication is that the negative schooling–income inequality relationship which we observe is driven by the tendency for more schooling to lower rates of return.

In spite of our attempt to decompose INEQUALITY, measures like SD2095 tend to be highly correlated with any summary measure of the whole income distribution, like SD0100. So, if SD2095 is our proxy for "INEQUALITY," b will absorb both within- and between-group effects. But if increased ability—whether due to a shift to democracy, as in Japan, or to more education—raises the marginal political impact of g, then (14′) and (23) tell us that the weight on the within-group effect is increased. Since this effect is negative, (23) would imply the approximation

$$b = b_0 + b_1 \cdot \text{ABILITY}; \ b_1 < 0, \ b_0? \tag{25}$$

The second term here approximates the derivative in (23); it says that an increase in ability enhances the stimulative effect of equality on the size of government. (Since b_0 still contains both within- and between-group effects, its sign remains uncertain.) Substitution of (25) into (24) yields

$$g = a \cdot \text{ABILITY} + b_0 \cdot \text{INEQUALITY}$$
$$+ b_1 \cdot (\text{ABILITY} \cdot \text{INEQUALITY}) + X. \tag{26}$$

The scheme in (26) is estimated in Table 14, and many of the uncertainties evident in Table 13 appear to be clarified. The explanatory power of the regressions in Table 14 (R^2, SE) increases substantially over their counterparts in Table 13, which lends credibility to the interactive scheme in (26). The precision of the coefficients is correspondingly improved, allowing some conclusions:

1. The coefficient of ED is now always significantly positive, as the theory implies, if ED is a proxy for "ability."

2. There is some evidence for a positive between-group inequality effect. Most of this evidence derives from the significantly positive coefficient of SD2095, which is the counterpart to b_0 in (25). This says that, at low levels of ability, more inequality *increases* the size of government. An effort to further isolate this between-group effect in the coefficient of SH5 yields mixed results. The coefficient varies from insignificantly negative to "suggestively" positive, depending on the form of the dependent variable. If SH5 is deleted, none of the other coefficients changes very much.

3. Most important, the significant negative coefficient of the interaction term corroborates what we found in the Japanese data: The within-group effect gets stronger (and eventually outweighs the between-group effect) the more "able" the populace.

4. We are unable to pin down the relevant lag structure. The various lag structures explain the data about equally well,[58] and the pattern of the

[58] Regressions (3)-(5) of Table 14 purport to explain g_{1972}. When we generate predicted values of this variable and compare them to the actual g_{1972}, we get roughly the same standard errors (2.52, 2.38, and 2.41, respectively). Regression (1) explains a different variable, $\bar{g}_{1942,57,72}$.

TABLE 14
STATE AND LOCAL GOVERNMENT EXPENDITURES/PERSONAL INCOME REGRESSIONS

Form of Dependent Variable	1942, 1957, 1972 Average		1972	(1972)-1/2(1942)	1972-1942	
Model	Complete Adjustment after 15 Years		Complete Adjustment, 30 Years	50% Adjustment, 30 Years	Indefinite Adjustment	
Independent Variables	(1)	(2)	(3)	(4)	(5)	(6)
POP	−.71	−.75	−.67	−.60	−.53	−.27
	2.69	3.10	.53	.54	0.49	0.24
ED	4.51	4.71	7.27	7.10	6.92	5.81
	2.39	2.59	2.48	2.74	2.75	2.39
SD2095	72.11	74.50	109.88	107.02	104.17	90.65
	2.33	2.47	2.29	2.53	2.54	2.23
ED × SD2095	−9.01	−9.32	−14.98	−14.62	−14.26	−12.60
	2.30	2.45	2.47	2.74	2.75	2.45
SH5	−4.07		−.01	8.62	17.26	
	0.43		0.00	.71	1.46	
R^2	.34	.34	.23	.24	.23	.19
SE	1.63	1.62	2.52	2.22	2.16	2.19

Note: See Table 13 and text for definitions and sources of variables.

coefficients provides no further illumination.[59] Some experimentation with different lags than those assumed in Table 14 did, however, suggest that very short lags in response were inappropriate.[60]

Table 14 shows that the concept of "ability" is important both in its own right and on account of its interaction with equality. I therefore try to improve the simple proxy used in Table 14 (education). The theoretical

---

However, if one (a) assumes that standard deviations of g are proportional to means and then (b) synthesizes a $\bar{g}$ with the same mean and variance as g_{1972}, the standard error of that synthetic variable from regression (1) would also be about the same (2.33) as the others.

[59] In the lagged-adjustment model, the implied coefficient of the target g = regression coefficient/adjustment coefficient. Thus, if the regression coefficients increased roughly in proportion to the assumed adjustment coefficient, we would at least know something about the target g, even if we could not specify how quickly the adjustment proceeded. However, the regression coefficients are largely invariant to the assumed adjustment coefficient.

[60] For example, when the dependent and independent variables were made contemporaneous, the precision of the regression coefficients and the overall fit of the regression tended to deteriorate, though the overall pattern of the results was the same as in Table 14.

TABLE 15
STATE AND LOCAL GOVERNMENT EXPENDITURES REGRESSIONS
WITH ADDED POLITICAL ABILITY VARIABLES

Dependent Variables	1942, 1957, 1972 Average		1972-1942 Change	
Independent Variables (Coefficient Symbol, Equation (28))	(1)	Weights for Ability Index (2)	(3)	Weights for Ability Index (4)
POP	−.69 2.41 [3.05]		−1.23 1.10	
Ability Index: (a)	.86 3.95 [4.58]		1.09 3.78 [4.41]	
VPAR (c_1)		−.77 3.05		−.97 3.60
FARM (c_2)		.73 2.03		−.11 .37
LABOR (c_3)		.16 .60		.21 .98
SD2095 (b_0)	186.95 2.24 [4.37]		15.50 0.15 [2.21]	
SD2095 × Ability (b_1)	−1.78 2.24 [4.38]		−2.23 3.51 [4.05]	
SH5	12.00 1.24 [1.30]		24.67 1.93 [2.41]	
R^2	.51		.40	
SE	1.46		1.53	

Note: See text and Table 13 for sources and definitions of variables.
   The numbers in brackets are *t*-ratios calculated on the assumption that the index weights are known beforehand. They are obtained by computing the ability index for each state and substituting the index for ED in ordinary least squares regressions like those in Table 14.

concept can, after all, comprehend any factor facilitating the political re-payment of benefits. In Table 15, I consider two additional factors that might have such potential: voter participation and the size of organized interest groups (specifically labor unions and farmer cooperatives). The historical evidence did not imply an important role for voter turnout, but the cross-section data permit a more refined test. There is also a historical motivation for the interest-group variables. The early twentieth-century expansion of government coincides with the emergence of broad-based interest groups, like labor and farm organizations, which successfully exerted influence on the political process. By 1940, the start of our period of analysis for the states, these groups had attained roughly their present size. I want to see if the influence they subsequently exerted at the local level led to a net expansion of local governments. Also, since these groups did not organize primarily for local political action, we can distinguish the impact of organized interests on the growth of government from any stimulus to such organization provided by that growth. (For similar reasons, I use voter participation in presidential, rather than purely local, elections.)

The empirical implementation follows (26) except that an index is the proxy for "ability" instead of a single variable. Specifically,

$$\text{ABILITY} = \text{ED} + c_1 \text{ VPAR} + c_2 \text{ FARM} + c_3 \text{ LABOR}, \qquad (27)$$

where the c_i are weights, measured as fractions of the weight on ED, and VPAR = ratio of votes cast in the 1940, 1944, and 1948 presidential elections to the population over twenty-one in each state.

FARM and LABOR equal the ratio of membership in farm cooperatives and labor unions respectively to the population of the state.[61] When (27) is substituted back into (26), we get

$$g = [a \cdot \text{ED} + \Sigma a \cdot c_i A_i] + b_0 \cdot \text{INEQUALITY}$$

$$+ [b_1 \text{ ED} \cdot \text{INEQUALITY} + \Sigma b_1 c_i A_i \cdot \text{INEQUALITY}] + X, \qquad (28)$$

where A_i are the three additional components of the ability index. The resulting overidentified scheme is then estimated by nonlinear least squares, where the restrictions in (28) (that the c_i in the two bracketed expressions be the same) are imposed. To facilitate comparisons, ED and the A_i are each entered as standardized variables with the mean equal to 100 and standard deviation equal to 10. Thus $c_1 = .5$ would mean that if VPAR is one standard deviation above the mean, ability is enhanced by half as much as if ED is a standard deviation above the mean.

The results, for two forms of the dependent variable, the 1942–1972 average level and 1942–1972 change, are summarized in Table 15. There is another substantial improvement in explanatory power and in the precision of the ability and inequality coefficients. Our confidence in the crucial result of Table 14—that ability and within-group inequality interact negatively—is clearly strengthened by Table 15. In addition, the role of the wealthiest citizens as tempting targets for taxation seems better defined here than in

[61] To avoid distortion by one-party dominance in the South in the 1940s, I calculate VPAR for the 1968 election for the southern states. I then multiply the ratio of VPAR in a state to the national average in 1968 by the national average for the 1940 elections to get estimates of the "true" VPAR in the South for those years.

Data on membership in labor unions and farm cooperatives are unavailable for the early 1940s, so I use the earliest available dates (1960 for cooperatives and 1964 for unions). All data are from Statistical Abstract.

Table 14; the coefficient on SH5 is consistently positive. All this is compatible with the notion that changes in the political process, as well as in personal capabilities of voters, play a role in the growth of government. But the nature of this role seems peculiar. The role of organized interest seems generally weak, statistically and numerically. The one exception of the large and significant impact of farm cooperatives on the level of government (column (2)) does not carry over to the change (column (4)). The unexpected result of a consistent and strong *negative* effect of voter participation on expenditures deserves more study that I can give it here. It is broadly consistent with certain nineteenth-century historical facts. Recall that Britain had a rapidly expanding franchise in the nineteenth century, while the United States did not, and apparently experienced a sharper contraction in the size of government. The result is also consistent with the spirit of bureaucratic-monopoly models, such as Niskanen's or Peacock and Wiseman's,[62] which have at their core the notion of government expansion being antithetical to the interest of the broad mass of citizens. Our result implies that when the masses indicate they have sufficiently overcome their "rational ignorance" to come to the polls, the political process pays more heed to their interest.

There would then remain the question of just whose interest the political process is serving. It could not plausibly be just the bureaucracy's, given the empirical importance of broad measures of education and income equality. But our theory does not require that everyone in a specific income-education range be a beneficiary either. In fact, the technology of government, in which benefits are conferred through specific programs, rather than per capita grants, pretty much rules this out. One plausible interpretation of Table 15 is that government expands when specific programs attract a sufficiently broad constituency, but this constituency is always smaller than a majority of voters. However, a bigger potential coalition is better than a smaller one, and the chances for forming a successful coalition would be greater the larger the pool of voters who are prime potential beneficiaries. In our analysis, the size of this pool is larger the more educated voters with similar economic interests there are.

I now address the issue of the quantitative, as opposed to the statistical, significance of the ability-inequality nexus uncovered in Tables 14 and 15. Specifically, do the results explain any substantial part of the recent growth of government, or are the ability-inequality effects merely a sideshow on how spending is distributed among locales? This question is relevant for two reasons. First, even if ability, inequality, and their interaction help explain variation in the size and growth of local government, we have already noted there is not much variation to explain. Since the similarity among states is

---

[62] Niskanen, *supra* note 3; and Peacock & Wiseman, *supra* note 1.

THE GROWTH OF GOVERNMENT   275

more notable than their differences, our regression can be measuring empirically trivial deviations from an all-important average. Second, the results imply that changes in inequality or ability, standing alone, have no clear-cut empirical implications for the size or growth of local government. This is most clear in Table 13 and confirmed by measuring the partial effects of either inequality or ability in Table 14 or 15 at the sample means (they are essentially nil). The issue of empirical significance thus rests on the importance of the interaction effect when there are substantial changes in *both* inequality and ability. Even at this level, the issue has no clear *a priori* answer. The differential form of (26) is

$$\Delta g = \Delta \text{ABILITY} \, [a + b_1 \cdot \text{INEQUALITY}] + \qquad (26')$$
$$\Delta \text{INEQUALITY} \, [b_0 + b_1 (\text{ABILITY} + \Delta \text{ABILITY})].$$

Since we find a, $b_0 > 0$ and $b_1 < 0$, there is no obvious prediction even for the direction of Δg.

To get at the empirical import of the results, I use the coefficients in Tables 14 and 15 to estimate the effects of the sorts of changes that have characterized the relevant history, namely an increase in education or ability coupled with a decrease in income inequality. Specifically, for Table 14 I ask: what is the predicted effect on the level (column (1) is the relevant regression) or the change (column (6)) in the size of government if education increases two standard deviations while inequality (SD2095 and SH5) decreases two standard deviations from the sample mean: The effect on the level is +4.28 percentage points and on the change +6.57 percentage points. For Table 15, we can perform a similar exercise in which the ability index, is also increased by two standard deviations. The results are +8.05 for level and +7.36 for change.

There are three points to note about these results.

1. The effects are substantial by any measure, running between 2.6 and 5.5 times the relevant regression standard errors. The effects on the level are between 30 and 60 per cent of the sample mean, and on the change about 60 or 70 per cent of the mean. Put differently, the level regressions purport to describe the change over the fifteen years from 1942 to 1957, while the change regressions pertain to 1942–1972. The 1942–1957 actual change is around +6.0 and the 1942–1972 change around +12.0. If our simulated ability-inequality changes accurately describe what went on in the interwar period, the regression parameters account for over half of the subsequent growth of government.

2. Our simulation roughly corresponds to the relevant historical change. For example, the simulated change in education is a little less than +2 years. Whereas we do not have pre-1940 data on ED, we know that mean schooling has been rising at over one year per decade subsequently (from 8 ½ years

in 1940 to over 12 in 1970). We also know that prior to World War I no more than 5 per cent of seventeen-year olds were graduating from high school and that secondary school enrollment was also only 5 per cent of elementary school enrollment. So extrapolating the post-1940 experience back to around 1920, as done in the simulations, could not be far off the mark. Our assumed changes in inequality and the ability index are also reasonably accurate caricatures of the relevant history.[63]

3. The driving force behind our results is the negative effect of the interaction between education-ability and inequality. The combination of increasing education-ability and decreasing inequality decreases their product and thereby accounts for the bulk of the historical growth in government that the cross-section results can rationalize. Consequently, considerable weight must be given to the confluence of these two forces, rather than to either separately, in any explanation of the growth of government.[64]

D. *The Less Developed Countries (LDCs)*

The less developed countries (LDCs) pose a severe test of our model, perhaps too severe. Quite apart from the data problems, which are discussed subsequently, one can be skeptical whether the same processes that affect the size of government in the developed countries (DCs) carry over more or less intact to societies with markedly different economic and political structures. Yet the severity of the test is also an attraction, one that is enhanced by the diversity of the LDCs. While they differ on average from the DCs in most measures of political and economic development, they also span a much wider range—from countries with living standards only moderately below the DCs to those with virtually all the population in subsistence

---

[63] For SD2095 and SH5 our simulations entail decreases of .16 and .06, respectively. The former roughly corresponds to the actual change between 1930 and 1950, so we may be overstating the pre-1940 change. The latter figure describes roughly what occurs between 1930 and 1942; this series is shown in Figure IV. We have almost surely understated the historical change in the ability index. The relevant history is a change of around +2 SD for ED and unionization, +1 for farm cooperatives, and 0 for VPAR. If we sum these changes with the weights in columns (2) or (4) of Table 15, we would get changes in the index of around +30 or +20, respectively. The simulations entail only changes two-thirds as large.

[64] I attempted unsuccessfully to replicate the results in Tables 14 and 15 for the developed country cross section. I first constructed an inequality index $= L + 6 \cdot \emptyset$ which seems to be roughly the weighting scheme implied by the regressions in Table 12. Then I constructed an ability index: a simple average of standardized indices of newspaper circulation per person over 25 and school attendance per person under 15. When these two variables and their interaction were entered in a regression like 10 in Table 12, none of the coefficients was significant. However, when the interaction term was dropped, both of the remaining variables had significant *negative* coefficients and the R^2 increased from .8 in Table 12 to about .9. This implies that the "ability" index may be improving our inequality measure: as in our state and local data, "ability" and inequality are negatively ($-.5$) correlated in this sample. If our ability measure is partly a proxy for inequality, detection of the interaction effect would be difficult, since inequality would interact with itself rather than with "ability."

THE GROWTH OF GOVERNMENT 277

agriculture, from democracies to dictatorships, from income distributions more equal than those in the DCs to inequality far exceeding any recorded in the DCs over the last century. This enormous diversity creates a special opportunity to clarify the relative impact of political institutions and personal "abilities" on the growth of government. So far we have been able to treat this issue only in the context of isolated events (for example, the advent of Japanese democracy) or fairly homogeneous populations (for example, education differences across American states).

The basic facts about the size of government in the LDCs can be summarized succinctly. They are neither as large nor growing as rapidly relative to GDP as those in the DCs.

1. In the sample we will analyze (42 LDCs in the decade 1960–1970), the average government/GDP ratio is 17.6 per cent, or about half that of our DC sample (see Table 2).

2. There is substantially more diversity among the LDCs, at least relative to the lower mean. The standard deviation of government/GDP for the LDCs is 5.1 per cent, which is comparable to that for the DCs, so the coefficient of variation is about double that of the DCs.

3. The average 1960–1970 growth in government/GDP in the LDCs tends to be smaller than for the DCs; the mean change (standard deviation) is +3.4 (2.2) percentage points.

This combination of small and slowly growing governments is somewhat reminiscent of the pre-1920 history of the Western DCs (and of Japan for most of the twentieth century). And the crude data on LDC income distributions seem compatible with the explanation offered for DC history. A within-group measure of inequality which we subsequently exploit is the ratio of eighth to third decile incomes. This exceeds 3, on average, for the LDCs versus 2+ for the DCs. (The same sort of difference holds for the upper tail: the average share of income for the tenth decile is 39 per cent for the LDCs and 25 per cent for the DCs.) But there is considerable overlap in the two samples, and, of course, much more than differences in income inequality distinguish them. So the crude consistency ought to be greeted cautiously. We are on even slipperier ground with the changes in inequality in the LDCs. The earlier history of the DCs, the more recent experience of Japan and Kuznets's elaboration of the conflicting implications of development for inequality are all we have to create a presumption that nothing like the pervasive shrinking of inequality in the DCs has gone on in the LDCs.

My strategy in analyzing the LDC data is to replicate the analysis of the U.S. state and local government data, thereby forcing a comparison between the most and least homogeneous samples. Analogues to the variables in (26) (namely, ABILITY, INEQUALITY) are required, thus entailing considerable compromise with the poor quality of LDC data. For example, while

TABLE 16
GOVERNMENT EXPENDITURES/GDP REGRESSIONS
42 LESS DEVELOPED COUNTRIES, 1960-1970

Form of Dependent Variable	1960-70 Average	1970	1970-½(1960)	1970-1960
Model	Complete Adjustment, 5 Years	Complete Adjustment, 10 Years	50% Adjustment, 10 Years	Indefinite Adjustment
Independent Variables	(1)	(2)	(3)	(4)
POP	−.28	−.30	−.17	−.05
	.69	.67	.58	.20
MODERN	.18	.18	.10	.01
	2.61	2.40	1.88	.21
MODERN 2	−.10	−.10	−.05	−.01
	.93	.86	.69	.10
ABILITY	−.06	−.04	.01	.05
	.56	.30	.07	.78
INEQUALITY	−.26	−.32	−.22	−.13
	2.90	3.23	3.37	2.47
R^2	.54	.55	.54	.30
SE	3.66	4.08	2.72	2.08

Notes:
Definitions and Sources of Variables

Independent variables are derived from the 1960 and 1970 ratios × 100 of current government revenue from domestic sources to GDP, from United Nations Yearbook of National Account Statistics (various years). Revenue rather than expenditures is used, because data on capital expenditures are sketchy and, where available, they imply that capital expenditures are financed mainly from current revenues. In the rare case where current expenditures exceeded current revenues, the former is used.

For some countries, either 1960 or 1970 government revenue data are unavailable. If data over an interval of at least 5 years are unavailable, the country is excluded. Otherwise, I computed the ratio of government revenue to government consumption in the first or last available year and multiplied government consumption in the terminal year by this ratio. In two cases (Israel and South Vietnam), I extrapolated the 1960-1966 growth in government/GDP to 1970 to eliminate the effects of post-1966 wars.

Independent Variables

POP: Log of 1960 population. Statistical Yearbook, *supra.*

ABILITY: Average of four indexes, each normalized to mean = 100, standard deviation = 10. The components are:

1) *Democracy:* An index of the "strength of democratic institutions" which ranges 0-100 from I. Adelman & C. T. Morris, Society, Politics, and Economic Development: A Quantitative Approach (1971) (hereinafter cited as AM). Their sample covers about three-fourths of mine. For the remainder (non-AM countries) I first regressed the AM index on a set of dummy variables which were based on my reading of each country's political history in Political Handbook of the World: 1975, (Arthur S. Banks ed. 1975).

(a) Degree of party competition: +1 if, *ca.* the early 1960s, a democratically elected parliament wielded effective political power; −1 if power was held by one person or party and rivals were outlawed; 0 for intermediate cases.

(b) Post-World War II history of party competition: +1 if a multiparty democracy had prevailed for the whole period; −1 if the country had always been a dictatorship; 0 if some party rivalry had occurred for some of the period.

(c) Press freedom: +1 if, up to the early 1960s, the press was largely free of government control; −1 if the press was government controlled; 0 for intermediate cases.

(d) Military coups: −1 if a military coup had been attempted since World War II; +1 if a military coup had never been attempted up to 1965; 0 for doubtful cases (for example, civilian disturbances with military participation).

(e) Coups in one-party states: −1 if a coup had *not* been attempted in a one-party state, 0 otherwise. The notion here is that military opposition to a dictator means more "democracy" than a totally unopposed dictatorship.

THE GROWTH OF GOVERNMENT 279

(f) Log of GDP per capita in 1963 in U.S. dollars, to capture any positive income elasticity of democracy. The regression (R^2 = .7) coefficients were then used to generate an estimate of the "demoracy index" for non-AM countries.

2) *Freedom of Political Opposition and of Press:* Index from AM with estimates for non-AM sample from regression technique described above. The independent variables for the estimating regression are the same as above (R^2 = .5).

3) *Extent of Mass Communication:* Index from AM, for non-AM countries a regression estimate of the AM index is used. The independent variables in the estimating regression (R^2 = .95) were the logs of per capita newspaper circulation and radio ownership (from UNESCO, Statistical Yearbook, various years)—that is, the AM index is essentially a weighted average of newspaper and radio use.

4) *Literacy:* Percentage of population literate ca. 1960 (UNESCO, Statistical Yearbook, various years).

MODERN: Weighted average of two AM indexes: The level of modernization of techniques in (1) agriculture and (2) industry. The weights are the percentage of population in agricultural and nonagricultural sectors. For non-AM countries, a regression estimate of the AM index (on log per capita GDP, R^2 = .6) is used.

MODERN 2: MODERN-$\overline{\text{MODERN}}$ if this difference > 0; 0 otherwise.

INEQUALITY: This is an average of two standardized (Mean = 100, S.D. = 10) indexes based on:

1) $R83$, the ratio of the share of income in the 8th to the share in the 3rd decile of the income distribution. The main data source is Shail Jain, Size Distribution of Income: A Compilation of Data (World Bank, 1975), which gives decile share estimates for most published income distribution. Where possible, I use a national household distribution ca. 1960. (Alternatives in order of preference are national population, urban households, national income recipients. For the latter 0.3% is added to the 3rd decile share, because this was the average (significant) difference between income recipient and household 3rd decile shares where both are available for the same countries. No other similar difference among distributions was found.) For some countries data are from a similar, partly overlapping, compendium in Irma Adelman & Cynthia T. Morris, Economic Growth and Social Equity in Developing Countries (1973) (hereinafter cited as AM2). They provide five points on the cumulative income distribution, rather than decile shares. To estimate the relevant decile shares, I first regressed the logs of the shares in Jain on the logs of the five values in AM2 for the 16 cases where both summarize the same distribution (R^2 > .9, SE < .05 for both decile shares), then I used the regression coefficients as weights to estimate 3rd and 8th decile shares from the AM2 data for other countries. The Jain and AM2 data cover about three-fourths of our sample. For the remainder, I averaged available estimates of R for countries in the same region at roughly the same level of per capita GDP.

2) $\sqrt{t(1 - t)}$, where t = percentage of population in traditional agriculture, as estimated by AM. For non-AM countries, estimates are based on weights from a regression of the AM estimate (on the percentage of the population in agriculture and log per capita GDP, R^2 = .8). The sample comprises the following 42 countries:

Argentina	Nigeria
Barbados	Panama
Bolivia	Paraguay
Burma	Peru
Chile	Philippines
Colombia	Portugal
Costa Rica	Sierra Leone
Dominican Republic	Singapore
Ecuador	South Africa
Greece	South Vietnam
Guatemala	Southern Rhodesia
Guyana	Spain
Honduras	China (Taiwan)
India	Tanzania
Israel	Thailand
Jamaica	Togo
Jordan	Trinidad
Korea (Republic of)	Tunisia
Malaysia	Turkey
Malta	Uruguay
Nicaragua	Venezuela

there are published income distributions for most LDCs, there is none of the refinement of their conceptual differences as in the Lydall-Sawyer data for the DCs.[65] Nevertheless, I take from these raw data the ratio of income in the 70-80 percentile of the distribution to income in the 20-30 percentile (R83) as a proxy for "within-group" inequality. (See notes to Table 16 for

[65] Sawyer, *supra* note 47; Lydall, *supra* note 28.

details on this and the other variables discussed below.) In preliminary work, I also used the tenth decile share as a proxy for between-group inequality. Since this variable proved even less helpful than its analogue in the state and local data (SH5), none of the results reported here use it.

I supplemented R83 with the same sort of nonmonotonic transform ($\sqrt{x(1-x)}$) of the agricultural share of the population that proved useful in estimating U.S. income distributions and is suggested by Kuznets's work.[66] Here some facts about LDCs are useful. Most have substantial agricultural population shares (about 50 per cent on average), but they span virtually all of the relevant range. In addition, a large share of the typical LDC's farmers are in a "traditional" or subsistence sector where income differences with the rest of the economy are especially great. Accordingly, I use for "x" above the share of the population in this traditional sector as estimated by Adelman and Morris.[67] I then simply average indexes of this variable and R83 to construct an index of INEQUALITY (see below for refinements).

An ABILITY proxy for the LDCs should make use of the considerable variety of their political institutions as well as of relevant population characteristics. Therefore, I constructed an ABILITY measure which weights the two kinds of ability equally. "Political ability" is an average of two indexes constructed by Adelman and Morris of the "strength of democratic institutions" and of the "degree of freedom of political opposition and press."[68] These indexes contain large subjective elements but are at least independent of this study and may shed light on a major unresolved question: does more active representation of broad groups of potential beneficiaries ("democracy") stimulate the growth of government? Data on educational attainment, the personal-ability proxy used in Table 14, are too fragmentary to permit a direct analogue. Accordingly, I used an average of two proxies for personal ability, the fraction of the literate population and an Adelman-Morris index of the "effect of mass communication" (essentially a weighted average of newspaper circulation and radio ownership per capita).[69] The ABILITY measure is the average of the "political" and "personal" ability indexes.

My only substantive departure from the analysis of U.S. local governments is to add variables reflecting the level of economic development and, implicitly, tax collection costs. The motive is to use this diverse sample to elaborate on two aspects of the earlier data: Japan's atypical pre-World War I growth of government and the general absence among DCs and U.S. states

[66] See text at note 26 *supra*.

[67] Irma Adelman & Cynthia Taft Morris, Society, Politics, and Economic Development: A Quantitative Approach (1971). Data on income differences between sectors are unavailable.

[68] See *id*.

[69] In the subsample of countries where median schooling attainment is available, the simple correlation with either proxy is about .9.

of any correlation between per capita income and the relative size of governments. Taken together, these two factors seemed to imply that major income-related reductions in revenue-raising costs occur only fairly early in the development process. To verify the implication, I use two variables. One is an index of the extent to which the economy has adopted "modern" techniques,[70] which presumably entail monetary exchange, modern record keeping, and so forth and hence serve as a proxy for tax collection costs. The second is simply this variable less its sample mean for countries with above average modernization. If tax-collection-cost economies diminish with development, the first variable should have a positive partial correlation and the second a negative partial correlation with the size of government.

All of these variables are defined *circa* 1960 and are used to explain the size and growth of government in the subsequent decade, which is about as long a period as the data permit.[71] Our sample consists of forty-two LDCs for which government budget data are available and which were substantively independent political entities around 1960.[72] The analogues to the regressions in Table 13, which implement equation (24), are in Table 16. One notable difference from Table 13, where essentially nothing but population worked,[73] is the consistently negative correlation between inequality and either the size or growth of government. We also find a pattern of coefficients for the tax-collection-cost proxies (MODERN, MODERN 2) consistent with the hints in the Japanese, DC, and state data. That is, lower collection costs stimulate the growth of government (the coefficient of MODERN is positive), but at what appears to be a diminishing rate (the negative coefficient of MODERN 2 is insignificant). Table 16 duplicates the insignificant ABILITY effect of Table 13.

We learned from Table 14, however, to mistrust the too easy inference that effects of ability play no role in determining the size or growth of government. Accordingly, Table 17 implements the interaction model of

[70] This is a weighted average of two Adelman-Morris indexes, *supra* note 67: the "level of modernization of industry" and of agriculture, with urban-rural population shares as weights.

[71] Pre-1960 budget data are unavailable for most LDCs, and the gaps and reporting lags get more serious the closer we approach the present. In addition, the sharp rise in oil prices post 1973 leads to major departures from trend for revenues of some of the governments in our sample.

[72] That is, if the country was *de jure* a colony for a substantial part of the period, it had to have been granted at least local autonomy by around 1960 to be included in the sample. The *de facto ca.*-1960 status was determined from the country narratives in Political Handbook of the World: 1975 (Arthur S. Banks ed. 1975).

[73] The role of population here is less clear-cut than for U.S. states. In the public goods framework, there are both "set-up-cost" and density economies, and among U.S. states population and density are positively correlated. However, in this sample the smallest entities include some of the most densely populated (Barbados, Malta, Singapore). I include the population variable here only for the sake of completeness.

TABLE 17
LDC GOVERNMENT/GDP REGRESSIONS, WITH
ABILITY-INEQUALITY INTERACTION

Form of Dependent Variable	Average, 1960-70	1970	1970–½ (1960)	1970–1960
Model	Complete Adjustment, 5 Years	Complete Adjustment, 10 Years	50% Adjustment, 10 Years	Indefinite Adjustment
Independent Variables	(1)	(2)	(3)	(4)
POP	.06	.04	−.00	−.05
	.16	.09	.01	.19
MODERN	.18	.19	.10	.01
	3.06	2.72	2.03	.21
MODERN 2	−.13	−.14	−.07	−.01
	1.40	1.25	.93	.10
ABILITY	3.29	3.31	1.68	.05
	3.29	2.89	2.09	.08
INEQUALITY	3.16	3.10	1.48	−.12
	3.10	2.65	1.82	−.18
ABILITY × INEQUALITY	−.034	−.034	−.017	−.001
	3.37	2.93	2.09	.01
R^2	.65	.64	.59	.30
SE	3.23	3.71	2.60	2.11

Note: See notes to Table 16 for definitions and sources of variables.

equation (26) on the LDC data, yielding a remarkable consistency with the results for U.S. states in Table 14: (1) The ABILITY and INEQUALITY variables both tend to have significantly positive coefficients as in Table 14. (2) The interaction effect (coefficient of ABILITY × INEQUALITY) tends to be significantly negative as in Table 14. (3) There is a substantial improvement in the fit of the Table 17 regressions over their Table 16 counterparts, again duplicating the pattern for U.S. states.

The only exception to these conclusions is in column (4) of Table 17, where the interaction model clearly fails to work. However, the indefinitely long adjustment process implied by column (4) seems to be an inappropriate characterization of the growth of LDC governments.[74] And this, too, appears

[74] We can use the same test as for the state data (see note 58 *supra*). Note that columns (2)-(4) of Table 17 purport to explain Government/GDP for 1970. When we compute the standard error of the value of this variable predicted by each of these regressions we get 3.70 for (2), 3.87 for (3), and 4.82 for (4). So (2) and (3) do about equally well in explaining the data, but (4) is clearly inferior. Column (1) describes a different dependent variable (1960-70 average). To compare that regression with the others, we compute the standard error of this regression after

reasonable. The rationale for a long drawn-out adjustment process is strongest when the determinants of the size of government have changed profoundly over a relatively short interval. This was true of the developed world, especially with respect to inequality, up to about 1950, but it is not obviously true of the LDCs. Although Table 17 does not permit pinning down the adjustment lag for the LDCs to anything closer than a five- to twenty-year range, it does rule out much longer lags. The LDCs thus appear to have adjusted faster to their smaller gap between actual and "desired" size of government than the DCs.

Finally, note that Table 17 is slightly more emphatic about the diminishing effect of tax collection costs. If we take the results for the MODERN variables at face value, they imply the marginal impact of "modernization" is only about one-fourth as great for the more developed LDCs as for the least developed. The implication for the historical experience is that Japanese government grew rapidly prior to World War I while Western governments did not, because Japan was then developing the sort of revenue-raising infrastructure that the others had achieved much earlier.

The results in Table 17 raise two questions:

(1)   What is the relative importance of political ability (democracy, and so on) and personal ability (literacy, and so on)? An attempt to use the technique of Table 15 failed for the LDC data.[75] However, experimentation with different weights on the "political" and "personal" components of the ABILITY index revealed that both are important and that it is tolerably accurate to give them equal weight.[76] So these LDC results are consistent with both the Japanese results, which isolated a political ability effect (the shift to democracy), and the U.S. state results, which isolate personal ability effects (education).

---

adjusting the dependent variable to the same mean and variance as the 1970 variable. This turns out to be 3.93, or about the same as for (2) and (3).

[75] In an attempt to estimate the weights of the components of ABILITY and INEQUALITY, the nonlinear-least-squares regression failed to converge.

[76] For example, consider the following weighting schemes for the political (average of "democracy" and "freedom" indexes) and personal (average of "literacy" and "mass communications") components and the resulting R^2s for regressions otherwise identical to (2), Table 17.

ABILITY = j POLITICAL + k PERSONAL	R^2
$j = 0, k = 1$	.607
$j = \frac{1}{4}, k = \frac{3}{4}$	.628
$j = \frac{1}{2}, k = \frac{1}{2}$ (as in Table 17)	.644
$j = \frac{3}{4}, k = \frac{1}{4}$	.648
$j = 1, k = 0$	.641

They suggest only that very low weights on the political variables are inappropriate. I conducted a similar exercise for the components of INEQUALITY (see note to Table 16). Here, too, nothing much improved on the equal weighting in Table 17, and only low weights on the $R83$ component could be ruled out.

284   THE JOURNAL OF LAW AND ECONOMICS

(2)   Is the ability-inequality nexus important empirically? The LDC data suggest an even more positive answer than the state data. One useful formulation of the problem is to see if the results in Table 17 can rationalize any of the substantial difference in size of government between LDCs and DCs. Recall that the average DC government sector spends fully twice as large a fraction of GDP as the average LDC government. Therefore, I plugged values of the independent variables appropriate to the DCs into Table 17 regressions to obtain estimates of what the size of the average LDC government sector would be if these countries had the characteristics of DCs.[77]

For regression (1) Table 17, the results of this exercise were:

1)	Average government/GDP, 1960-70, for LDCs	17.62%
2)	Predicted change, if LDC industry became as modernized as DCs (MODERN = 100, MODERN 2 = 42)	+3.55
3)	Predicted change, if LDC ABILITY and INEQUALITY = DC average	+12.49
4)	Predicted government/GDP for LDC with DC characteristics (1 + 2 + 3)	33.7%
5)	Actual average for 16 DCs, 1960-70	33.4

For regression (2), which describes 1970 data, the counterparts to lines (1), (4), (5) above were:

1)	Average government/GDP, LDCs, 1970	19.2%
4)	Predicted 1970, DC characteristics	36.9
5)	Actual average, 1970, DCs	36.7

(The relative magnitudes of the counterparts to lines (2) and (3) were roughly the same as above.)

The essential result is that we are able to rationalize *all* of the differences between DCs and LDCs, virtually to the decimal point. These remarkable[78] results suggest that the large behavioral differences between these two groups are really the outcomes of precisely the same process, one which is dominated by the ability-inequality nexus (compare lines (2) and (3) above).

[77] Specifically, the characteristics assumed for a *DC* are: (1) A fully modernized industrial structure. MODERN = 100. (2) A democratic society with no restraints on opposition or the press, that is, "democracy" and "freedom" indexes = 100. (3) A fully literate society. (4) A "mass communications" index as implied by the AM index and the average values of radio ownership and newspaper circulation for the DC sample of Table 12 (see note to Table 16). This index = 106. (5) A nominal .01 share of the population in subsistence agriculture. (6) The average value of $R83$ for the DCs in Sawyer's data (*supra* note 47).

[78] There is one catch. The predicted values, line (4), are for an *equilibrium* size of government. But our analysis of DCs suggested that the *actual* values around 1970 or 1965 were subequilibrium.

If that is so, there are some strong implications for the future growth of government in the LDCs. As (if) the LDCs' overall level of economic development, their degree of income inequality, and the "personal" characteristics of their populations approach those of contemporary DCs, the recent slow growth of LDCs' government sectors will accelerate. Whether the gap between them and contemporary DC governments closes completely depends on political developments that are difficult to predict. If there is no corresponding move toward more democratic political institutions at all, a nontrivial gap will remain.[79]

VI. Concluding Remarks

The broad conclusion to which our diverse data point is that governments grow where groups which share a common interest in that growth *and* can perceive and articulate that interest become more numerous. The view that sharp differences are (should be?) an important source of government sponsored redistribution seems to carry less weight. Our results do detect a stimulative role of inequality but only where the population is least capable of articulating support for more government spending.[80] As this capability increases, homogeneous interests become a more important source of government growth. Our results imply that the *leveling* of income differences across a large part of the population—the growth of the "middle class"—has in fact been a major source of the growth of government in the developed world over the last fifty years. On our interpretation, this leveling process, which has characterized almost every economically developed society in the latter stages of industrialization, created the necessary conditions for growth of government: a broadening of the political base that stood to gain from redistribution generally and thus provided a fertile source of political support for expansion of specific programs. At the same time, these groups became more able to perceive and articulate that interest (as measured by, for example, educational attainment). On our interpretation, this simultaneous growth of "ability" served to catalyze politically the spreading economic interest in redistribution.

The counterintuitive result that, on balance, more equality breeds a political demand for still more income equalization runs through virtually all our data and proves capable of rationalizing a wide variety of experience—for example, why Britain's government declined in the early nineteenth century

---

[79] If one carries out the extrapolation above keeping the levels of "democracy" and "freedom" at the LDC sample mean, the predicted size of government is on the order of 5 percentage points less than on line (4).

[80] In both the U.S. state and LDC data, the net effect of more inequality on the size of government is positive only at below average levels of ability.

and grew in the twentieth, why Sweden's government has grown faster than ours, why the developed world has larger and more rapidly growing government sectors than the underdeveloped. The role we assert for "ability" as a catalyst for equality-induced growth also has a broad base of support, and the concept appears to comprehend attributes of both the political system and its constituency. We were able to see the catalyzing process at work in Japan, when it became a democracy, in the U.S. states with above average levels of education, and in less developed countries that were both more democratic and had better educated populations than is typical of that group. It is, in fact, the enormous diversity of experience that the ability-equality nexus proves capable of rationalizing, rather than any single result, that provides the main empirical message of this paper. This common process seems capable of rationalizing a substantial part of the differences among and between constituencies as diverse as local school boards, European welfare states, and traditional agricultural societies.

A caveat is in order, lest my conclusion be read as implying that all or even most members of groups which contribute support to growth of government have benefited from that growth. The "bourgeoisification" of Western societies widened the political base from which support for expansion of government could be drawn. But the particular programs that expand will, at least in each instance, benefit a subgroup. It is at least arguable, and compatible with "rational ignorance" in politics, that the net result is for a minority of the population to receive large per capita net benefits at the expense of the majority. Our one result relevant to this issue—that large voter turnout retards the growth of government—tends to support this view.

If the foregoing analysis is correct, it points to a future somewhat different from the recent past. In developed countries, the leveling process in the labor market has been far more gradual in the last quarter century than the preceding. At the same time, the scope for increased educational attainment of their population, at least in the United States (and Canada, Australia, and—to some extent—Britain) has narrowed. A high school education has become the norm, and the waves of the unschooled immigrants who produced the high school and college graduates of a subsequent generation have long since crested. If the twin forces of increased equality and increased education are indeed petering out, our analysis implies that the pressure for further growth of government is likely to abate in the developed world. It would be imprudent to try to be precise about this prediction, especially in light of our evidence that these forces can take considerable time to work themselves out and of our lack of success in pinning down just how long it is before they are spent. Nevertheless, it would be fair to infer from the evidence here that the next quarter century will witness a perceptible, perhaps substantial, deceleration of the relative growth of government in the developed world. If anything, this ought to be more profound in the United States than in Continental Europe, where there still may be some scope for the spread of education. The one exception is Japan, where the emergence of a broad middle class as a concomitant of a mature industrial economy seems to be a comparatively recent phenomenon, and where, in consequence, we are led to predict a narrowing in the gap between the size of its government sector and that of the Western democracies. With less confidence, we can also predict a narrowing of differences between the developed and less developed worlds.

The larger message of this paper is that there is nothing inevitable or inexorable about the growth of government, nor is there some arbitrarily limiting ratio of government to GNP.[81] Instead, our argument is that the size of government responds to the articulated interests of those who stand to gain or lose from politicization of the allocation of resources. The balance of those interests can make for declining governments, as they appear to have done in the last century, as well as for the growth we have experienced more recently.

[81] Not even 100 per cent. Government transfers, for example, can be taxed, retransferred, retaxed, and so on, so that the annual government budget can be a multiple of GNP. In fact, this ratio exceeds 1 in Israel currently.

[19]

A THEORY OF NONMARKET FAILURE: FRAMEWORK FOR IMPLEMENTATION ANALYSIS*

CHARLES WOLF, JR.
The Rand Corporation

I. THE INADEQUACIES OF MARKETS

THE principal rationale for public policy intervention lies in the inadequacies of market outcomes. Yet this rationale is really only a necessary, not a sufficient, condition for policy formulation.[1] Policy formulation properly requires that the realized inadequacies of market outcomes be compared with the potential inadequacies of nonmarket efforts to ameliorate them. The "anatomy" of market failure provides only limited help in prescribing therapies for government success.[2]

That markets may fail to produce either economically optimal or socially desirable outcomes has been elaborated in a well-known and voluminous literature.[3] Although the last word has not been written, the essential points

* Many of the central ideas of this paper have developed from discussions I have had with Graham Allison over the past six years. Indeed, the question of whether the paper we agreed should be written would be written jointly or separately, and if the latter then by whom, was almost as frequent a topic of these discussions as the content of the paper. Fortunately, a six-month stay at Oxford in 1976, for whose support I am indebted to The Rand Corporation and the Ford Foundation, provided the answer to this question. I am also indebted to Pat Crecine, George Eads, Gene Fisher, John Flemming, Robert Klitgaard, Nathan Leites, John Martin, Joseph Newhouse, Robert Roll, and Harry Rowen for comments on an earlier draft.

[1] The point is the same as Sidgwick's familiar comment: "It does not follow that whenever *laissez faire* falls short government interference is expedient; since the inevitable drawbacks of the latter may, in any particular case, be worse than the shortcomings of private enterprise." Henry Sidgwick, Principles of Political Economy 414 (1887). See also Alexander Cairncross, The Market and the State, in Essays in Honour of Adam Smith (Thomas Wilson & Andrew S. Skinner eds. 1976).

[2] For some cogent observations closely similar to this line of argument, see Roland N. McKean, Divergence between Individual and Total Costs within Government, 54 Am. Econ. Rev. 243 (Papers & Proceedings, May 1964).

[3] See, for example, Melvin W. Reder, Studies in the Theory of Welfare Economics (1947); I. M. D. Little, A Critique of Welfare Economics (1950); Paul A. Samuelson, The Pure Theory of Public Expenditure, 36 Rev. Econ. & Stat. 387 (1954); Richard G. Lipsey & Kelvin Lancaster, The General Theory of Second Best, 24 Rev. Econ. Stud. 11 (1956); Francis M. Bator, The Anatomy of Market Failure, 72 Q. J. Econ. 351 (1958); E. J. Mishan, The Relationship between Joint Products, Collective Goods, and External Effects, 77 J. Pol. Econ. 329 (1969); and Kenneth J. Arrow, Political and Economic Evaluation of Social Effects and Externalities in Frontiers of Quantitative Economics 3 (Michael D. Intriligator ed. 1971).

THE JOURNAL OF LAW AND ECONOMICS

in the accepted theory are worth summarizing as background for the subsequent discussion of *non*market failures.[4]

There are four sources or types of market inadequacies:[5]

A. *Externalities and Public Goods*

Where economic activities create "spillovers," whether benefits or costs, that are not, respectively, appropriable by or collectible from the producer, then market outcomes will not be (Pareto) efficient. Since these external benefits or costs do not enter the calculations upon which production decisions are based, too little output will tend to be produced where the externalities are (net) benefits, and too much where they are (net) costs, compared with socially efficient output levels. Education is an example of putatively positive externalities (benefits), which provide a rationale for government intervention—through subsidy or direct public sector production—to compensate for the market's tendency toward insufficient output. Chemical and noise emissions from aircraft or other industrial activities are examples of negative externalities (costs), which provide a rationale for government intervention—through taxing or direct regulation—to compensate for the market's tendency toward excessive output.

A distinction can be made between private goods with externalities and public goods: the former applies where *most* of the benefits or costs associated with output are, respectively, collected or paid by the producer, although *some* are not; and the latter applies where most of an activity's consequences comprise nonappropriable benefits (for example, national security) or noncollectible costs (for example, crime, an archetypical public "bad").[6] Externalities and public goods are thus one condition—though neither necessary nor sufficient—for government intervention.

---

[4] As Arrow observes: "The clarification of these concepts [relating to market failure] is a long historical process, not yet concluded." Kenneth J. Arrow, *supra* note 3, at 13.

[5] I use the term "market inadequacies" and "market failures" interchangeably, although strictly speaking the former is more inclusive. Most economists would confine "market failure" to departures from Pareto-efficient outcomes, thereby excluding distributional issues except to the extent that distribution affects efficiency (see pp. 110–11 *infra*). By way of contrast, some noneconomists argue that distribution has, or should have, priority over efficiency (for example, Rawls's second principle of a just society), and they fault the market precisely because of its failure to accord this priority. See John Rawls, A Theory of Justice (1971). As will be clear in the text, I am including distributional considerations within market "inadequacies."

[6] Externalities are thus a more general concept than public goods. Stated another way, a public good is the limiting case of a "private" good with externalities: "private" benefits approach zero, and the external benefits remain. More precisely, if $v_{ij}{}^s$ is the valuation placed, or price paid, by the ith person for the jth unit of a good s, and $mc_j{}^s$ is its marginal cost of production, then the condition for an optimum (efficient) level of output for a private good with externalities is:

$$mc_j{}^s = v_{ij}{}^s + \sum_{m=i+1}^{k} v_{mj}{}^s,$$

B. *Increasing Returns*

Where economic activities are subject to increasing returns and declining marginal costs, the market mechanism will also fail to generate an efficient outcome. Under conditions of decreasing costs, the lowest cost mode of production is by a single producer. In a free market, the result will therefore be monopoly, and, assuming single-part pricing, the outcome will be inefficient in both static and dynamic terms: statically, because output will be less than is efficient; dynamically, although more arguably (*vide* Schumpeter), because incentives for innovation will be weaker than would likely prevail under a more competitive regime.

Where increasing returns exist, various types of government intervention may be justified to correct the market outcome: (1) by directly regulating a "natural" monopoly (for example, public utilities) or by setting prices or allowable rates of return on capital; (2) by legal protection to prevent a single-firm takeover and to encourage competition (for example, through antitrust legislation). The various types of intervention admittedly depart from a theoretically efficient outcome, although they seek to approach it.[7]

---

where v_{ij} is the price paid by i, and the $\Sigma v_{mj}{}^s$ are externalities (experienced by all other k individuals as a result of i's consumption of the jth unit of s), positive if the externalities are benefits and negative if costs.

For a pure public good, $v_{ij}{}^s = 0$. Consumption is collective and no single unit is purchased by anybody. The optimum condition then is

$$mc_j{}^s = \sum_{m=1}^{k} v_{mj}{}^s.$$

Compare E. J. Mishan, *supra* note 3.

Total demand for public goods is determined by *vertical* summation of individual demand curves, rather than horizontal summation as in the case of private goods. (The point is sometimes misstated as equivalent to a zero marginal cost of production. For example, the marginal cost of national defense in, say, the United States or NATO is *not* zero, although non-taxpayers, as well as citizens of other countries, receive the benefits of such defense.)

The generalized explanation for the existence of externalities and public goods is that markets do not exist for capturing some benefits or levying some costs. Nonexistence of markets in these cases is explained by (1) the high costs or inability of excluding beneficiaries (for example, from benefits of national defense or police expenditures), or of establishing property rights as a basis for claiming liability when they are infringed (for example, noise emissions in airport vicinities); and (2) the lack of information required for market transactions to be concluded (for example, ascertaining what the "true" v_{ij} are in the previous discussion), in part at least because of the free-rider problem associated with (1).

[7] Some discussions of market failure include increasing returns (for example, Francis M. Bator, *supra* note 3), while others exclude it. Arrow, for example, contrasts increasing returns ("essentially a technological phenomenon") with market failure (which relates to "the mode of economic organization"). Kenneth J. Arrow, *supra* note 3. I think this causation does not always hold. Improvements in technology can eliminate or at least reduce externalities by resolving the exclusion problem; for example, electronic warning and protection devices may be an efficient means of lowering the risk of theft for households purchasing them. One can imagine acoustical and air-filtration devices that would reduce the injury inflicted by the emissions or identify their source as a basis for imposing and collecting costs. Conversely, the "technological" phenomenon

C. *Market Imperfections*

Where the price, information, and mobility characteristics of "perfect" markets depart significantly from the realities, market outcomes will not be efficient, again providing a rationale for government intervention. Where prices and interest rates, for one reason or another, do not indicate relative scarcities and opportunity costs, where consumers do not have equal access to information about products and markets, where information about market opportunities and production technology is not equally available to all producers, or where factors of production are restricted in their ability to move in response to such information, market forces will not allocate efficiently and the economy will produce below its capacity. In such cases, which apply to some extent in all markets and to a greater extent in some, the implication for public policy is to reduce, if not remove, these imperfections: to facilitate availability of information, to lower barriers to entry and mobility, and so on.

However, where many of the conditions required for efficient functioning of markets do not exist, improving some of these conditions will not necessarily improve the efficiency of the market as a whole. Consequently, the policy implications of market imperfections may be ambiguous.[8] And in some cases, public intervention may be justified even where it seems to *add* to these imperfections. For example, patent regulations, which are intended to restrict access to technological information, reduce the efficiency of resource use in the short run in the interest of long-run efficiency.

D. *Distributional Inequity*

Most economists exclude distributional effects from market failure strictly defined. That the distributional results of well-functioning markets may not accord with society's preferences is acknowledged, as is the plausible trade-

---

of increasing returns can be reconciled with efficient pricing and output by suitable modes of economic organization, for example, through multipart pricing. For a discussion of various pricing and market devices to reconcile increasing returns with efficient operation, see Charles Wolf, Jr., William R. Harris, Robert E. Klitgaard, J. Richard Nelson, John P. Stein, & Mario Baeza, Pricing and Recoupment Policies for Commercially Useful Technology Resulting from NASA Programs (Rand Corp. No. R-1671-NASA, Jan. 1975). For increasing returns are a source of market inefficiency only as long as markets do not exist for *separate* units of the same good. Allowing for enough subscripting, in the Arrow-Debreu sense, and hence separability of commodities, increasing returns are theoretically as compatible with competitive equilibrium as are externalities.

[8] This is, of course, the essential message of second-best theory (Richard G. Lipsey & Kelvin Lancaster, *supra* note 3). For example, changing a tariff that has applied equally to imports from all countries, so that it applies instead only to a few countries, may reduce efficiency. Trade will be diverted as well as created, and the loss from the former may exceed the gains from the latter. See Jacob Viner, The Customs Union Issue (Carnegie Endowment for International Peace, 1950).

A THEORY OF NONMARKET FAILURE   111

off between efficiency and equity.[9] In welfare economics the trade-off is usually dealt with by considering the relative efficiencies of various redistributive measures (for example, income taxes, excises, subsidies, unemployment relief, and income transfers), for achieving a specified redistribution (that is, minimizing the allocative distortions resulting from the income and substitution effects of redistribution). The term "market failure" is usually confined to departures from competitive equilibrium and Pareto-efficient outcomes, and excludes departures from distributional equity.

Nevertheless, from one perspective, it is theoretically correct to consider distributional *in*equity as an example of market failure. From this perspective, income distribution is a particular type of public good.[10] An "equitable" redistribution does not result from freely functioning markets because philanthropy and charity yield benefits that are not appropriable by donors. Left to its own devices, the market outcome will entail no redistribution or too little, because of the usual free-rider problem associated with public goods and incomplete markets.[11]

There is also a different perspective for viewing distributional equity, quite unrelated to market failure in the strict sense. From this perspective, the equilibrium redistribution previously described may be inequitable in terms of one or another ethical norm. Even if the market could surmount the "failure" discussed above, its distributional outcome might still be socially and ethically *inadequate*.[12]

On these grounds, many people criticize the distributional outcomes of even perfectly functioning markets.[13] Furthermore, most public policy deci-

[9] I. M. D. Little, *supra* note 3; Tibor Scitovsky, The State of Welfare Economics, 41 Am. Econ. Rev. 303 (1951); Arthur Okun, Equality and Efficiency: The Big Trade-Off (Brookings Institution, 1975).

[10] Compare Walter Nicholson, Microeconomic Theory (1972).

[11] The point can be formulated more precisely. Individual demand functions for redistribution can be defined in the same notional sense they can be defined for defense or for law and order. For example, the demand for redistribution can be expressed as the desired *change* in current distribution (as measured, say, by the Gini coefficient) with demand declining as the required amount of voluntary individual philanthropy per dollar of earned income rises. Presumably, individual willingness to pay for redistribution declines as its price rises. A cost function for redistribution can also be defined in terms of the same two variables. In principle, individual demands would be summed (vertically), and the social equilibrium level of redistribution would be that for which the marginal optimization condition is satisfied (see note 6 *supra*). This equilibrium redistribution is not achieved because there is either no market or an incomplete market for philanthropy, just as there is an incomplete market for defense. In both cases, voluntary donations (if unmotivated by special tax incentives) would be lacking for the usual nonappropriability, nonexcludability reasons.

[12] In this sense, distributional inequity is a market "inadequacy" rather than "failure."

[13] John Rawls, *supra* note 5, is probably the most cogent recent effort to distinguish equity from efficiency and, accordingly, to fault market outcomes and the Pareto-efficient criterion of competitive equilibrium. Sometimes Rawls's points about equity or fairness, in contrast to efficiency, seem to me to have peculiar implications. For example, one of his central ideas, the

sions are usually at least as concerned with distributional issues (namely, *who* gets the benefits and who pays the costs) as with efficiency issues (namely, how *large* are the benefits and costs). Since my principal aim is to compare mareket inadequacies with the inadequacies of nonmarket remedies, I include distributional inequity among the offenders.

II. A THEORY OF NONMARKET FAILURE
Demand and Supply Characteristics

Market failure provides the rationale for attempted nonmarket (that is, government) remedies. Yet the remedies may themselves fail, for reasons similar to those accounting for market failure. In both cases, incentives influencing individual organizations ("firms," in the one case, and entities acting for or constituting "government," in the other) may lead to outcomes that diverge substantially from what is socially preferable.[14] The basis for the market/nonmarket distinction is that market organizations derive their revenues from prices charged for output sold in markets where buyers can choose what to buy as well as whether to buy, while nonmarket organizations receive their revenues from taxes, donations, or other nonprice sources.[15] Just as the absence of particular markets accounts for market failure, so nonmarket failures are due to the absence of nonmarket mechanisms for reconciling calculations by decision makers of their private and organizational costs and benefits with total costs and benefits. Nor, for reasons we will suggest, are prospects for invention of suitably compensatory nonmarket mechanisms to avoid nonmarket failure notably brighter than for creating suitable markets where their absence leads to market failures.

"difference principle," is intended to provide a tightly constrained basis for permissible differences in income and status, where the constraints derive from initial premises relating to justice or equity in contrast to efficiency. In elaborating the principle, Rawls argues that extra benefits received by the advantaged are just (fair) if and only if directly linked with *some* benefits realized by the least advantaged. According to the difference principle, a distribution is "just" even if benefits are *forgone* that have this property, as long as the original distribution retains it.

Some curious consequences follow from this position. Suppose a particular program (say, subsidized loans to new entrepreneurs from disadvantaged minority groups) provides tangible benefits to the disadvantaged, and even more substantial gains as a by-product to already advantaged groups. As I understand him, Rawls would term the distribution resulting from this program "just" or fair ("but not the *best* just arrangement"), even though it forgoes an *alternative* program that might entail small extra benefits for the already advantaged, as well as huge extra benefits for disadvantaged groups. "Dog-in-the-manger" behavior and spite become "just" in this curious formulation.

[14] Although government is the principal nonmarket organization, there are also others: foundations, state-supported universities, churches, PTAs, and the Boy Scouts. The theory and types of nonmarket failure to be developed here apply to the performance shortfalls of these other nonmarket organizations, as well as governments.

[15] This is essentially the same criterion used by Robert Bacon & Walter Eltis, Britain's Economic Problem: Too Few Producers (1976).

A THEORY OF NONMARKET FAILURE   113

Where the market's "hidden hand" does not turn "private vices into public virtues," it may be hard to construct visible hands that effectively turn nonmarket vices into public virtues.

Public policies intended to compensate for market inadequacies generally take the form of legislative or administrative assignment of certain functions to a government agency in order thereby to produce certain outputs, which are expected to redress the shortcomings of the market. These outputs are of four types: (1) regulatory services (environmental regulation, radio and television licensing, interstate commerce regulation, pure food and drug control); (2) "pure" public goods (national defense, space research and development; (3) quasi-public goods (education, postal services, health research); or (4) administering transfer payments (federal, state, and local welfare programs, social security, and so on). The "value" of these outputs is expressed in national accounts as exactly equal to the cost of inputs used in producing them. But this accounting convenience does not tell us anything about the efficiency or social value of the outputs. Nor does it tell us why producing these outputs is likely to result in specific types of nonmarket failure. To explain this prospect, we need to examine the distinctive supply and demand characteristics that differentiate nonmarket outputs from market outputs.

On the supply side, there are several such characteristics:

(a) Nonmarket outputs are usually hard to define in principle, ill-defined in practice, and extremely difficult to measure independently of the inputs which produce them. They are generally intermediate products which are, at best, only remote proxies for the "real" or final intended output: for example, environmental impact precautions enforced by the Environmental Protection Agency; licenses issued or rejected by the Federal Commerce Commission; forces and equipment developed and deployed by the military services; students taught at different levels by the public school system; research projects funded by the National Institutes of Health; cases processed and payments disbursed by social welfare agencies. Units for measuring final product are usually nonexistent, and it is often hard even to distinguish "more" from "less." Consider, for example, the difficulty of measuring military "worth," specifying "quantities" of national defense, or education, or even regulatory services, in terms that are *separate* from the inputs used in producing them. Measuring outputs by their inputs becomes accepted because measuring outputs directly is so difficult.

(b) Evidence of output quality is also elusive, in part because the information that would in the market be transmitted by consumer behavior is missing. Consider, for example, the difficulty of determining whether the "quality" of education or welfare programs or environmental regulation is "better" or "worse" now than two or three years ago. Moreover, such signaling as may be provided concerning "consumer" (that is, citizen) reactions tends to be too little and possibly nonrepresentative (for example, letter writers may be cranks, but the nonwriters are not thereby implying approval), or too gross and too late (for example, through congressional hearings or the ballot box) to be an effective means of monitoring output quality. To monitor output quality requires precise, representative, and regularized feedback which is hard to realize for nonmarket output.[16] Congressional committees, the Congressional Budget Office, ombudsmen, consumer groups, voter and consumer surveys, and other "watchdog" devices help, but their separate and collective effectiveness in monitoring output quality inspires only limited confidence.

(c) Nonmarket outputs are usually produced by a single agency whose exclusive cognizance in a particular field is legislatively mandated, administratively accepted, or both (for example, the regulatory agencies, the public school system, NASA's role in space). It is rare that this exclusivity is contested. Where it is (for example, between the Air Force and the Army in providing battlefield air support), resolution is frequently on grounds unrelated to output quality. In sum, the absence of sustained competition is another factor contributing to the difficulty of evaluating output quality.

(d) Finally, nonmarket output is generally not connected with any "bottom line," comparable to the profit-and-loss statement of market output, for evaluating performance. Nor is there a reliable mechanism for terminating nonmarket activities if they are unsuccessful. Perhaps the closest analogy to a market "test" in the case of nonmarket output is military performance in war. Because it faces competition in war, the military does have special incentives to produce quality output. Yet even in this case, the effectiveness of these incentives is diminished by a paradox. The more successful potential military performance is, the more likely is military conflict to be deterred; and the more effective deterrence is, the less seriously is the risk of war likely to be taken and, hence, the weaker it becomes as an incentive to motivate high performance.

There are also distinctive characteristics that apply to the demand for nonmarket activities and to the process by which these demands become effective.

(a) As a result of the activity, perhaps hyperactivity, of information media, environmental groups, and consumer organizations, there has in the past few decades been an enormous expansion in public awareness of the

---

[16] Hirschman's notions of "exit" and "voice" satisfy some of these criteria, but their effectiveness as monitoring and signaling devices is limited because they apply only to "insiders," not to consumers. Albert O. Hirschman, Exit, Voice, and Loyalty: Responses to Decline in Firms, Organizations, and States (1970).

A THEORY OF NONMARKET FAILURE   115

shortcomings of market outcomes. Increased awareness of monopolies, oligopolies, imperfect markets, negative externalities (for example, pollution), and distributional inequities, has resulted in intensified and politically effective demands for remedial action by government.

(b) In the political process, which mediates these demands, rewards often accrue to legislators or executives from articulating and publicizing problems, and legislating proposed solutions rather than assuming responsibility for implementing them.[17]

(c) In part as a consequence of this reward structure, the rate of time discount of political actors tends to be higher than that of "society." Furthermore, there is often an appreciable disjuncture between the time horizons of political actors and the time required to analyze, experiment, and understand a particular problem (namely, a market inadequacy) in order to see whether a practical remedy exists at all.

The result of these demand characteristics is often a premature, but politically effective, demand to establish public programs for producing some nonmarketed output, as a symbolic response to the originally perceived market inadequacy. The equal opportunity and model cities programs of the 1960s and the decision in the early 1970s to emphasize "targeted" cancer research are examples. In these cases, as in others, the political effectiveness of public demands can lead to nonmarket activities with infeasible objectives and redundant costs.[18]

The supply and demand characteristics of the nonmarket sector are fundamental to the theory of nonmarket failure. They provide a basis for formulating a typology of nonmarket failure analogous to that which already exists for market failure. In both cases, the "failures"—whether market or nonmarket—are evaluated against the same criteria of success: allocative Pareto efficiency[19] and distributional equity judged according to some explicit social or ethical norm. Nonmarket remedies "fail" to the extent they, too, result in outcomes that depart from the efficiency or distributional goals by which market outcomes are judged to fail. Although the touchstones of success are similar, the ways in which nonmarket solutions fail differ from those in which market outcomes fail.

---

[17] Anthony Downs, Inside Bureaucracy (1967).

[18] See pp. 124–26 *infra.*

[19] Hence, in both cases other efficiency criteria are neglected, namely, dynamic efficiency, x-efficiency, and technological efficiency. Except for the later treatment of one type of nonmarket failure (namely, redundant and rising costs, pp. 124–26 *infra*), these other sources of efficiency are omitted from the discussion. This omission does not gainsay the argument that the additional types of efficiencies may be larger in their collective impact on economic performance (productivity) than is allocative efficiency. See Charles Wolf, Jr., Efficient Performance with Inefficient Pricing: A Puzzle for Economists Who Believe in the Free Market (Rand Corp. No. P-5915-1, July 1978).

Types and Sources of Nonmarket Failure

There are four types of nonmarket failure resulting from one or more of the distinctive demand and supply characteristics of nonmarket output.

A. *Internalities and Private Goals*

All operating agencies require, to conduct their activities, certain explicit standards. The requirement does not principally arise from an agency's need to justify its activities externally but rather from the practical problems associated with internal, day-to-day management and operations: evaluating personnel; determining salaries, promotions, and perquisites; comparing subunits within the agency in order to help in allocating budgets, offices, parking space, and so on.[20] Lacking the direct-performance indicators available to market organizations from consumer behavior and the profit-and-loss bottom line, public agencies must develop their own standards. These standards are what I will call "internalities": *The goals that apply within nonmarket organizations to guide, regulate, and evaluate agency performance and the performance of agency personnel.* I refer to these internalities synonymously as "private" goals because they, rather than, or at least in addition to, the "public" purposes stipulated in the agency's assigned responsibilities, provide the motivation behind individual and collective behavior within the agency. This structure of rewards and penalties constitutes what Arrow refers to as "an internal version of the price system."[21]

It is, of course, true that market organizations also must develop their own internal standards in order to regulate the same quotidian functions required for the management of any organization. But there is an important difference. The internal standards of market organizations are generally related, even if indirectly, to meeting a market test, to responding to or anticipating consumer behavior, to contributing to the firm's bottom line. Sales, revenues, and costs materially affect the internal standards of market organizations. For market organizations, the internal version of the price system must be connected to the external price system. If the two are disconnected, the survival of a market organization will be jeopardized by the response of consumers, competitors, or stockholders, even in imperfect markets.

[20] Much of the organizational behavior literature of the past two decades advances similar points of view. See, for example, James G. March & Herbert A. Simon, Organizations (1958); Herbert A. Simon, The New Science of Management Decision (1960); Richard M. Cyert & James G. March, A Behavioral Theory of the Firm (1963); Anthony Downs, *supra* note 17; Graham T. Allison, Essence of Decision: Explaining the Cuban Missile Crisis (1971). See also Charles L. Schultze, The Role of Incentives, Penalties, and Rewards in Attaining Effective Policy, in Public Expenditures and Policy Analysis 145 (Robert H. Haveman & Julius Margolis eds. 1970).

[21] Kenneth J. Arrow, The Limits of Organization (1974).

The situation of nonmarket organizations is different because the supply and demand characteristics associated with their output are different. Because measures of output are often so hard to define, because feedback and signaling from "consumers" are lacking or are unreliable, internal standards for nonmarket organizations cannot be derived from these sources. Furthermore, because there are usually no competing producers, the incentive to devise internal standards that will control costs is weakened. Under these circumstances, nonmarket agencies often develop internalities that do not bear a very clear or reliable connection with the ostensible public purpose which the agencies were intended to serve.

In formal terms, internalities or private goals become arguments in the utility functions that agency personnel seek to maximize. Hence, internalities affect the results of nonmarket activities, as predictably and appreciably as externalities affect the results of market activities, in both cases causing divergences between actual outcomes and socially preferable ones. The existence of externalities means that some *social* costs and benefits are not included in the calculus of *private* decision makers. The existence of internalities means that "private" or *organizational* costs and benefits *are* included in the calculus of *social* decision makers. Whereas externalities are central to the theory of market failure, what goes on within public bureaucracies—the "internalities" that motivate their action and performance—are central to the theory of nonmarket failure.

In the market context, externalities result in social demand curves higher or lower than market demand curves, depending on whether the externalities are, respectively, positive or negative. And the levels of market output that result will be, respectively, below or above the socially efficient ones; hence, there is market failure.[22] In the nonmarket context, "internalities" boost agency *supply* curves above technically feasible ones, resulting in redundant total costs, higher unit costs, and lower levels of real nonmarket output than the socially efficient ones; hence there is nonmarket failure.[23]

Whether the nonmarket failure associated with internalities is greater or less than the market failure associated with externalities is an analytically interesting, and operationally crucial, question. Unfortunately, the answer is, in general, indeterminate. The nonmarket sector in principle allows for

---

[22] Recalling the optimum condition noted earlier (note 6 *supra*), if the Σv_{mj} are positive, the j units produced under market conditions will be less than is socially optimal; where the Σv_{mj} are negative, the j units produced will exceed the social optimum.

[23] If the optimal condition were complied with, producing j units of output would be less than is socially optimal absent internalities, because mc_j is inflated by the internalities of the nonmarket producers. See note 41 *infra*.

externalities in determining social demand,[24] and hence comes closer on this count to an efficient level of output. But it does so at a likely cost in terms of internalities arising on the supply side. These are reflected in inflated total costs, which push the nonmarket sector away from a socially efficient level, as well as mode, of output. Which failure is the greater, nonmarket or market, depends on whether the supply distortions created by internalities in nonmarket output are larger or smaller than the demand distortions created by externalities in market output.

What determines the specific internalities developed by particular nonmarket organizations? Three different hypotheses suggest possible answers.

One hypothesis is that internal standards are based on norms that, when an organization was started, appeared to be reasonable proxies for the elusive final output it was intended to produce.[25] Thereafter, they may become formalized as organizational routines or standard operating procedures which are accepted as a principal measure of the organization's performance. While market organizations also establish standard operating procedures, these must generally meet a market test. If the costs of adhering to them exceed those connected with changing them, they will be altered. The standard operating procedures of nonmarket organizations must stand up to a different test. Generally, a congressional hearing or scandal of some sort is required for change; and these may or may not be related to agency performance.

A second hypothesis is that those internalities are selected which maximize the income (and nonincome perquisites) of agency members.[26]

The third hypothesis is that specific internalities arise because they tend to

---

[24] The $\Sigma v_{mj}{}^s$ are, in principle, included in determining output decisions.

[25] For example, a budget-maximizing internality (see *infra*) may arise at the time nonmarket organizations are first established because new organizations have to hire staff and acquire facilities to handle their assigned responsibilities. Through a simple, inertial process, the proxy variable (increased staff and budget), which was essential for a particular nonmarket agency to get started, becomes accepted and retained as a convenient indicator of agency performance. McFadden's attempt to infer what an agency (namely, California State Highway Division) is trying to maximize by observing its prior behavior (for example, with respect to project and route selection compared to optimal choices) is in the spirit of this hypothesis. See Daniel McFadden, The Revealed Preferences of a Government Bureaucracy: Theory, 6 Bell J. Econ. 401 (1975).

[26] For example, larger budgets generally mean larger numbers of supergrade jobs, and the anti-new-technology internality of primary schools (see p. 122 *infra*) protects skills, positions, and income of senior members. This hypothesis is close to the view taken in Roland N. McKean, *supra* note 2; William A. Niskanen Jr., Bureaucracy and Representative Government (1971); and Jack A. Stockfish, Analysis of Bureaucratic Behavior: The Ill-Defined Production Process (Rand Corp. No. P-5591, Jan. 1976). In some cases, the first and second hypotheses lead to similar predictions, for example, the budget maximand. In others, the predictions probably differ; for example, the information-acquisition maximand (see pp. 122–23 *infra*) is hard to reconcile with the first hypothesis.

A THEORY OF NONMARKET FAILURE   119

increase the benefits received by a constituency group which has succeeded in co-opting a particular nonmarket organization. Often, the co-optation is by a constituency that the nonmarket agency has been set up to regulate.[27]

What are some of the specific internalities that often accompany nonmarket activities, and lead to nonmarket failures?

1. *Budget growth ("more is better")*. Lacking profit as a standard for motivating and evaluating performance, a nonmarket agency may adopt the agency's budget as its maximand, or at least as an important argument, in the agency's utility function. Performance of the agency's personnel and subunits is then evaluated in terms of their contribution to expanding its budget or protecting it from cuts. Incentives within the agency will develop to reward participants for "justifying costs rather than reducing them,"[28] a characterization that has been applied to the Defense Department and the military services, but surely is not confined to them.

The following instruction from a former Chief of Naval Operations to subordinate commands shows how government budgetary procedures may be translated into internal agency pressures to spend rather than save resources:

Fiscal Year 1972 outlay targets promulgated . . . as part of the President's budget for FY 1973 are over $400 million above targets in the earlier FY 1972 budget . . . Difficulty of achieving these targets during remaining months of 1972 fully appreciated, but importance of avoiding shortfall in meeting newly established FY72 targets to avoid resultant adverse effects on anticipated FY73 outlay ceiling *dictates need for top management attention. Anticipate any shortfall in FY72 outlay target could be translated into program loss under FY 1973 outlay ceiling.*[29]

Stripped of bureaucratic jargon, the commander is advising his subordinates to find ways to spend funds quickly and plainly implying his intention to evaluate their performance in terms of how well they succeed! As one observer, commenting on the motivations behind actions of the military services, notes: "The welfare of a service is measured by its budget."[30] The result of a budget internality is likely to be a distortion in the level of agency activity; in other words, a nonmarket failure to produce a socially optimal outcome.[31]

[27] This hypothesis is favored in George J. Stigler, The Theory of Economic Regulation, 2 Bell J. Econ. & Management Sci. 3 (1971), and applied empirically to transportation and professional licensing. The list in note 51 *infra* of regulatory agencies, and of the constituencies they affect most directly, suggests other examples of this hypothesis.

[28] Defense Science Board quoted in Nancy Nimitz, Organization Motivations in Weapon Acquisition: Some Hypotheses 1 (1975) (unpublished paper).

[29] Quoted in Arthur E. Fitzgerald, The High Priests of Waste 385-86 (1972).

[30] Nancy Nimitz, *supra* note 28, at 1.

[31] Using plausible demand and cost functions, William A. Niskanen, Jr., *supra* note 26, shows how the budget internality will lead to an output level above the socially efficient one.

Variants of the budget maximand can lead to similar nonmarket failures. For example, managers of the West German public television and telephone system reportedly have asserted that their primary objective is to raise rates and sales so as to maximize *gross* revenues. This, they explained, was necessary to "finance their further growth."[32] If revenue maximization is the internal performance standard, output will rise as long as marginal revenue is positive, again resulting in nonmarket failure to produce a socially efficient outcome.

When an American businessman was asked in 1972 to assume management responsibility for the postal service, he found that its serious financial predicament was due, in part, to its system of determining pay scales for postmasters: "Postmasters were actually paid [based] on how many employees they had, how many branch offices they had, or how many trucks . . . Can you imagine a greater disincentive?"[33]

A variant of the budget internality is the agency's employment level. A public agency, eschewing or precluded from profit maximization as its objective, may attempt to maximize the size of its staff. For example, British Rail, a nationalized industry and one of the half-dozen largest employers in Britain, operates under acute pressure from trade unions and government to maintain high employment levels and avoid "redundancies." Operating under such incentives, featherbedding by managers and foremen becomes a rewarded practice. High employment per unit of service, the reciprocal of high labor productivity, is aspired to, resulting once again in nonmarket failure.

2. *Technological advance ("new and complex is better")*. Often compatible with the budget internality is one relating to "advanced," "modern," "sophisticated," or "high" technology.[34] Nonmarket agencies, whose activities may be justified in the first instance by one or more of the acknowledged sources of market failure, may establish technical "quality" as a goal to be sought in agency operations. In medicine, a bias toward "Cadillac"-quality health care may result, and in the military a sometimes compulsive tendency toward development of the "next generation" of more sophisticated equipment. Explicit consideration of whether these advances are worth their extra costs is regarded as inappropriate because the operating agencies either are not intended to maximize net revenues (in the case of hospitals) or earn no

---

[32] I am indebted to James Rosse for this example.

[33] The Los Angeles Times, Dec. 3, 1972.

[34] This is not the place to attempt to define precisely what is meant by "high technology," a subject richly clothed in confusion in both popular and professional discussion. To consider whether the term does, or should, refer to products or processes, novelty or efficiency, costs and/or effectiveness would take us too far afield. For present purposes, I will conveniently assume that high technology, like a camel, is easy to recognize if difficult to describe.

A THEORY OF NONMARKET FAILURE   121

revenue since they are producing a public good (in the case of military services).[35]

An example is provided by the purchase of disposable syringes by the British national health service in the late 1960s when these gadgets were invented. Their novelty suggested merit. Only later was it demonstrated that repeated use of durable syringes had, in fact, been accompanied by equal or lower rates of attributable infection, and at lower cost.[36]

Perhaps especially in the military services is the development of systems embodying the latest technology taken to be an organizational imperative. As one practitioner has observed: "In the Air Force, advancing technology has become a part of the professional ethic."[37] The technological ethic is not confined to the Air Force. Organizational pressures toward sophistication, complexity, and technological novelty play a powerful role in the acquisition process of other services as well.[38] Nuclear-powered supercarriers are no less an illustration than the FB-111 or the F-15 aircraft.

The American space program is pervaded by a similar, indeed legislatively encouraged, imperative. From NASA's legislative mandate for "the

---

[35] Newhouse has shown formally how the addition of a "quality" argument in the maximands of nonprofit hospitals tends toward misallocation of resources in the health care industry. A nonmarket failure results because managers trade off quality against quantity, producing a different product from that which consumers would choose if they were spending the resources that nonprofit hospitals receive from public or philanthropic sources. Joseph P. Newhouse, Toward a Theory of Nonprofit Institutions: An Economic Model of a Hospital, 60 Am. Econ. Rev. 64 (1970). In the Newhouse model misallocation is reduced because a nonprofit hospital's choice of high quality is assumed to shift consumer demand upward, thereby adding to the market value of outputs. However, this may not occur. As long as the nonprofit hospital draws a subsidy (from government or philanthropy) based on the presumed market failure (for example, externality) which the subsidy is intended to correct, the hospital can price its output below cost, while indulging its practitioners' taste for quality. The original source of market failure is not thereby redressed.

[36] Martin S. Feldstein, Economic Analysis for Health Services Efficiency: Econometric Studies of the British National Health Service (1968).

[37] Richard G. Head & Ervin J. Rokke, American Defense Policy (3rd ed. 1973). The particular attraction in the U.S. Air Force of technological advance as an organizational internality is well known. The process of its adoption is probably an example of the hypothesis concerning initially valid proxies whose validity may have diminished after the proxy had already become accepted and engraved in agency operating routines. For example, when the Air Force was established as a separate service in 1947, two circumstances impelled it toward emphasizing technological advance as an organizational internality: (a) the two decades of struggle with the U.S. Army to win acceptance of the new aviation technology, independent of artillery and infantry; and (b) the major technological advances achieved during World War II (for example, in radar and nuclear weapons) and the resulting belief that the outcome of a future war "would be determined solely by the technological power of weapons that adversaries could bring to bear in its first moments." Harvey Sapolsky, The Polaris System Development: Bureaucratic and Programmatic Success in Government 77 (1972).

[38] Arthur J. Alexander, Armor Development in the Soviet Union and United States (Rand Corp. No. R-1860-NA, April 1976); U.S. Dep't of Defense, Report to the President and the Secretary of Defense on the Department of Defense by the Blue Ribbon Defense Panel (1970).

preservation of the role of the United States as a leader in aeronautical and space science and technology,"[39] it has been a short step to formalize the development of novel and complex technology as an internal agency norm, whether or not it seems likely to be efficient.

The technological internality can have perverse consequences, not only in excessive zeal for what is complex and novel, but in mindless opposition to what is simple and familiar. In the Vietnam War, use of a modified propeller-driven cargo aircraft, with long loiter time and a slow stalling speed as a platform for delivering guided munitions as well as airborne artillery, was by far the most efficacious source of American firepower. Yet turning this "gunship" idea into an operating system was delayed five years, largely because of service opposition to what was viewed as a technologically retrograde step!

A bias *against* new technology can, of course, equally lead to nonmarket failure. Parts of the American educational system, for example, resist even the experimental use of such new technology as videotaping for presentations to large classes, computer-aided instruction, and performance contracting, all of which might reduce the demand for teachers. Indeed, the education industry's behavior often suggests the opposite of the maxim that "new and complex is better." While a maxim that "familiar and simple is better" may be *generally* preferable, rigid application of it can have equally perverse effects on performance. Resistance by the education sector to technological advance is similar in quality, although opposite in direction, to the military's frequently uncritical enthusiasm for technology. In both cases, a private organizational goal, an "internality," contributes to nonmarket failure.

3. *Information acquisition and control ("knowing what others don't know is better")*. Another element in the utility functions of some nonmarket organizations is information. Frequently in nonmarket, as well as in market, organizations, information is readily translated into influence and power.[40] Consequently, information becomes valued in its own right—an internality for guiding and evaluating the performance of agency members.

Acquisition and control of information may be particularly important as a goal for agencies involved in foreign policy, because existing constraints already limit such other possible internalities as budget growth or technological advance. An example is Kissinger's use of the National Security Council framework and the Committee of 40 as means of acquiring exclusive information and, hence, of increasing influence for the National Security Council in the 1968-73 period. The careers of council staff members came to depend

[39] National Aeronautics and Space Act of 1958, Public Law 85-568, Section 102(c)(5).

[40] For a more general treatment of the importance of informational access and control in "post-industrial" society" see Daniel Bell, The Coming of Post-Industrial Society (1973).

on their ability to understand and adjust to the incentives created by this particular internality. Staff members succeeded by demonstrating their ability to collect and protect new information, which Kissinger's organizational and procedural rearrangements made possible, for the "private" use of the council. Information available only to the National Security Council seemed to become an end in itself, an internal standard motivating staff behavior. The effect of this internality on the conduct of foreign policy, and more particularly on the effectiveness of the State Department, in contrast with the council, is surely debatable. That the informational internality will lead to nonmarket miscarriages is likely, since it connects in no obvious way with the final and elusive outcome sought, the successful conduct of foreign policy.

In associating these specific types of internalities with nonmarket activity, I do not imply their absence from market activity. For the usual reasons pertaining to more or less imperfectly competitive markets—which, of course, are the only markets that exist—these characteristics also apply, to some extent, to market activity. But this extent is likely to be more limited. Price competition among firms and products, as well as competition within firms among managers seeking promotions, generally limits the extent of cost-inflating internalities in market activities, as compared with nonmarket activities.

What can be said to summarize the difference between internalities associated with nonmarket output and externalities associated with market output? Whereas externalities in the market sector are costs and benefits realized by the public but not collectible from or by producers, the internalities associated with nonmarket output are usually *benefits* perceived as such by producers and paid for by the public as part of the costs of producing the nonmarket output. Consequently, internalities tend to raise costs and supply functions. These shifts, moreover, are likely to increase over time as nonmarket agencies succeed in building special constituencies within the Congress and the public that are more immediately concerned than is the broader taxpaying public over whom the costs are spread.

Internalities are thus elements of the private goals of producers: private in the sense that their role is primarily that of satisfying interests of nonmarket producers rather than contributing to the public sector's intended final output. Such internalities and private goals, often quite remote from an elusive final product, are as frequent and important in nonmarket activities as externalities are in market activities.[41]

---

[41] The existence of internalities in organizations producing nonmarket outputs can be related to the condition for determining an optimal (efficient) level of output. Recalling the notation used earlier (note 6 *supra*) the condition is:

B. *Redundant and Rising Costs*

Whether policy takes the form of regulation, administering transfer payments, or direct production of public goods, there is a tendency for these nonmarket activities to exhibit redundant costs ("*x*-inefficiency")—that is, for production to take place *within* production possibility frontiers—and for cost functions to rise over time. If technological possibilities exist for lowering cost functions, raising productivity, or realizing economies of scale, these opportunities are likely to be ignored or exploited less fully by nonmarket than by market activities. Nonmarket failure, in the form of technically inefficient production and redundant costs, is the result. Moreover, these redundancies may well rise over time.[42]

The sources of these nonmarket failures lie in the demand and supply characteristics associated with nonmarket output. As public awareness of the inadequacies of market outcomes grows, demands for remedial action intensify. Dissatisfaction with existing circumstances may result in misperceiving the cause as a market failure, rather than something more intractable like genetics, physical laws, or resistant sociology. With rewards frequently accruing in the political arena to publicizing the problems and initiating action labeled as a remedy, nonmarket activities may be authorized which have quite infeasible objectives. Objectives may be internally inconsistent: for example, bringing all students' reading scores up to the mean; or minimizing the time individuals are unemployed while maximizing their earnings; or providing foreign aid to accord with "need" but also to encourage better development. Or objectives may be specified for which no known technology exists; for example, providing "dignified" work for people with low IQs, or training people with IQs of 70 to be draftsmen, or achieving a

$$mc_j^s + \sum_{p=1}^{q} mc_{pj}^s = \sum_{m=1}^{k} v_{mj}^s,$$

where mc_{pj}^s is the marginal cost of the pth internality associated with production of the jth unit of the sth public good.

This specification is closely related to Stigler's "positive" theory of regulation: a benefit of some outside constituency becomes an agency goal and an argument in the agency maximand. I think Stigler errs, however, in denying what seems to me a generally valid proposition about public policy intervention: even though co-optation of a regulatory agency frequently occurs *after* it gets underway, nonmarket activity is rarely undertaken without a case being first made on normative grounds, based on market failure or distributional equity. George J. Stigler, *supra* note 27; see also Richard A. Posner, Theories of Economic Regulation, 5 Bell J. Econ. & Management Sci. 335 (1974).

[42] The term "redundancies" has a different meaning here from that referred to at pp. 119–20 *supra*. Clearly, maintaining low productivity to avoid *employment* redundancies, as in the case of British Rail cited earlier, is one source of *cost* redundancies.

A THEORY OF NONMARKET FAILURE   125

cure for cancer by 1980.[43] Redundant costs may result at *any* positive level of nonmarket output.[44]

Redundant costs may also result from the difficulty of measuring output, and the resulting need, as well as latitude, to establish agency goals—the internalities that become accepted as proxies for nonmarket output. The cost-inflating effect of internalities may endure because nonmarket activity is conducted without competition. Or redundant costs may rise over time because of the absence of a reliable termination mechanism for nonmarket output, thereby allowing agency managers to move toward higher levels of internal goals.

Those responsible for market activities usually have an incentive to expand production and to lower costs over time, because of actual or potential competition or because of opportunities for additional profits. By contrast, those responsible for nonmarket production may be spurred to increase costs (for example, staff), or to increase output even if its incremental value is less than incremental costs (for example, the German TV case cited earlier), resulting in redundant costs that rise over time.[45] These tendencies toward

---

[43] In the words of one observer, whose comment is all the more insightful because it preceded his own not inconsiderable role in providing evidence in its support: "[N]ew agencies, from which better things might be hoped, are put under unremitting pressure to produce glamorous new programs—before the necessary analysis has been performed." James R. Schlesinger, Systems Analysis and the Politicial Process, 11 J. Law & Econ. 281, 293 (1968).

[44] In effect, demand and supply functions may not intersect, yet the demand for nonmarket activity may still be politically "effective." Nonmarket output of at least q^* will be politically

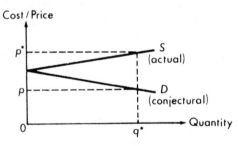

supportable if those receiving the benefits, $\int_0^{q^*} D(q)dq$, are politically more effective (even though they pay nothing or at least pay less than the benefits) than those who pay the full costs, $\int_0^{q^*} S(Q)dq$, or at least pay the difference between the full costs and the amount paid by the first group. To avoid tautology requires that the ingredients of "political effectiveness" (for example, organizational skill, media pressure) for the gainers and the losers can be evaluated independently of the nonmarket undertaking.

[45] Hence, cost functions for nonmarket activity are likely to drift upward because of private goals (internalities). This upward drift is what I mean by "rising costs." By "redundant costs," I

redundant and rising costs were described by a departing director of the United Nation's Food and Agriculture Organization with reference to his own organization:

> Eighty percent of its budget is destined to pay for a gigantic centralized bureaucracy in Rome, 11 percent to put out publications that no one reads, and the remaining 9 percent to holding meetings and for travel expenses that are largely unnecessary.[46]

The details of this example may be extreme, but the general picture probably has wide applicability to nonmarket agencies and activities.

C. *Derived Externalities*

Government intervention to correct market failure may generate unanticipated side effects, often in areas remote from that in which the public policy was intended to operate. Indeed, there is a high likelihood of such derived externalities, because government tends to operate through large organizations using blunt instruments whose consequences are both far-reaching and difficult to forecast. In the Russian proverb, "When elephants run, other animals tremble."

The likelihood of externalities is further enhanced by both demand and supply characteristics associated with nonmarket output. Strong political pressure for nonmarket intervention may create an effective demand for action before there is adequate knowledge or time to consider potential side effects. Furthermore, derived externalities are generally more likely to occur later than sooner. Hence, the short time horizon and high time discounts of political actors predispose them to overlook potential externalities. And, finally, the frequently ill-defined nature of both quantity and quality of nonmarket outputs limits the motivation, as well as the means, for thinking seriously about their potential unintended side effects.

---

mean the tendency of nonmarket activities to be carried on inside, rather than on, the production possibility frontier at any given time. The two tendencies thus relate to dynamic efficiency and *x*-efficiency, respectively.

It should be possible to test the hypothesis advanced here that (a) rising costs and (b) redundant costs tend to be associated with nonmarket activities compared with market activities. One might use for this purpose cost data in sectors where production has been carried on in both a market and a nonmarket mode (for example, education, fire protection, housing) within a given country or in comparisons between market and nonmarket modes in different countries (for example, health care in the United Kingdom and in the United States). The few empirical studies already done of production by market and nonmarket organizations (for example, private versus governmental production in fire protection and in refuse collection) suggest that the former tends to be more efficient and that redundant costs tend to be associated with nonmarket organizations. See Roger S. Ahlbrandt, Municipal Fire Protection Services: Comparison of Alternative Organizational Forms (1973); and Robert M. Spann, Public versus Private Provision of Government Services in Budgets and Bureaucrats: The Sources of Governmental Growth 71 (Thomas E. Borcherding ed. 1977).

[46] International Herald Tribune, April 26, 1976.

A THEORY OF NONMARKET FAILURE   127

Of course, cost-benefit analysis tries to internalize such externalities, for example, by calculating the benefits of hydroelectric projects to include flood control, irrigation, and "feeder industries," as well as electric power. But the limitations of such analyses are numerous and well known, resulting in part from the unanticipated nature of some of the side effects.[47]

Derived externalities are hard to anticipate because the consequences of public policies may be far removed from the target. For example, when standards for noise emissions were established by the Environmental Protection Agency to compensate for the market's failure to allow for these externalities, it was unanticipated that one result would be strains (that is, costs) in American foreign policy relations with the French and British over the Concorde. That an embargo in soybean exports to Japan in 1973 would affect U.S. military-base negotiations in that country was also not anticipated (although perhaps it should have been). That long-standing "Buy America" and other trade restrictions—once again, presumably based on a need for public-policy intervention to compensate for market inadequacies—would make more difficult a move toward standardization and rationalization of weapons systems and forces in NATO was also difficult to forecast.

Another instance of derived externalities is provided by public regulation of utilities. Permissible profits are typically calculated on the basis of return on capital, with the intention of holding prices closer to marginal cost, thereby overcoming one source of market failure. But a derived externality often results as an unintended consequence. The regulated utilities may respond by inefficient substitution of capital for labor to raise the allowable profit base.[48] The resulting nonmarket failure may equal or exceed the market failure that regulation was intended to remedy.

Of course, derived externalities may be positive rather than negative. Construction of a North Sea barrier in the Veere inlet, for the safety of the Zeeland population in the Netherlands, meant the loss of mussel and oyster beds but also the start of trout raising, the end of ocean-going boating but the beginning of a recreational industry based on smaller vessels in the new Veere Lake, none of which was anticipated when the Veere barrier was originally decided upon.

---

[47] A detailed attempt to internalize such externalities, as well as a candid acknowledgment of the limitations of cost-benefit analysis which tries to do so, is contained in Jack Hirshleifer, James C. DeHaven, & Jerome W. Milliman, Water Supply: Economics, Technology, and Policy (1960). Hirschman, in his notion of the "hiding hand," emphasizes the benefits, rather than the costs, of unanticipated consequences from *selected* development projects undertaken by governments. Of course, whether the hand principally hides benefits or costs depends on which development projects are selected for retrospective examination. Albert O. Hirschman, Development Projects Observed (1967).

[48] Harvey Averch & Leland L. Johnson, Behavior of the Firm under Regulatory Constraint, 52 Am. Econ. Rev. 1052 (1962).

All of these examples represent a type of nonmarket failure: externalities, whether negative or positive, deriving from a public policy intended to compensate for an existing market failure. They have in common, also, the characteristic of not having been foreseen at the time the policy was initiated. Clearly, policy choice would be improved if such derived externalities, could be taken into account when policy analysis and choice are under way.[49]

D. *Distributional Inequity*

Nonmarket activities, whether intended to overcome the distributional inequities of market outcomes or to remedy other inadequacies in the market's performance, may themselves generate distributional inequities. The resulting inequities are often indexed on power rather than income or wealth.

Public policy measures—whether intended to correct distributional inequities, or to regulate industry (because of externalities or increasing returns), or to produce public goods, or to redress market imperfections—place authority in the hands of some to be exercised over others. Whether the authority is exercised by the social worker, the welfare-case administrator, the tariff commissioner, the utilities regulator, the securities examiner, or the bank investigator, power is intentionally and inescapably lodged with some and denied to others. The power may be exercised with scruple, compassion, and competence. It may be subject to checks and balances, depending on the law, on administrative procedures, on the information media, and on other political and social institutions. Nevertheless, such redistribution of power provides opportunities for inequity and abuse. Corrupt practices are one type of abuse; for example, government contracts obtained through bribery, perhaps illustrated by the case of Lockheed's F-104 sales abroad; import licenses or preferential exchange rates conferred on the relatives, friends, or associates of officials and politicians who exercise discretionary authority. Less conspicuous inequities can result from the decisions of welfare authorities in classifying cases and conferring or withholding aid to fatherless families with dependent children, or to potential recipients of aid for the aged. Anecdotes reflecting the vagaries, perversities, and inequities associated with welfare programs are too numerous to recount, as well as too inexact to yield precise conclusions.

---

[49] To the extent that better analysis can anticipate and calibrate the derived externalities associated with nonmarket output, they become analytically identical to the externalities associated with market output. Hence, the optimum condition for nonmarket output with derived externalities is the same as that specified above for market output with externalities. See note 6 *supra*. However, determining the Σv_{mj}^s ex ante may be even harder for nonmarket "derived" externalities because of the bluntness of nonmarket instruments and the frequent remoteness of their effects both in time and place.

A THEORY OF NONMARKET FAILURE   129

In the specific case of public policies intended to redistribute income, a frictionless, impersonal, and automated redistributive mechanism might avoid the inequitable distribution of power that can result from discretionary authority. But even a sharply progressive tax system—which is intended to serve this purpose—reserves considerable room for auditors to exercise judgment and hence power. The same applies to the redistributive expenditure programs mentioned above. One need not ascribe to those who administer public programs less humane motives than the average to contend that some distributional inequities may result from efforts to rectify other inequities, as well as from efforts intended to remedy still other market inadequacies. And, of course, there is still a presumption that the distributional inequities created by progressive taxes or by redistributive expenditure programs are smaller than the original inequities which such measures relieve.

Nonmarket activities may also result in distributional inequities indexed on income rather than power. It is truistic that any public policy will benefit some and take from others. Indeed, this will ensue *whether or not* the particular market inadequacy, which gave rise to a nonmarket intervention in the first place, was explicitly distributional in character. Public policy measures will increase the demand for some factors, skills, services, and products, and levy costs on others. Those who are specialized in the former will benefit at the expense of those in the latter, by comparison with the previously prevailing situation. If public expenditures are increased for defense or education, because these are instances of public goods in the one case or private goods with large externalities in the other, organizations and individuals specialized in producing one or the other output will realize increases in their real income.[50]

Consequently, groups that are potentially benefited by a public policy measure intended to compensate for market failure can be expected to urge, and very likely believe, that more compensation is needed to bring about a socially optimal outcome than would otherwise be estimated. Educators, accepting the argument that some government subsidy is necessary to take account of positive externalities ignored by the market, are likely to argue that these externalities are greater than was originally allowed for and hence warrant a larger subsidy. A similar point applies to the professional and business community concerned with aerospace technology and research and development.[51] The result is likely to be nonmarket failure in the form of a

[50] Imposition of nondistorting lump-sum taxation to capture these economic rents is arguable in theory and unrealistic in practice.

[51] A recent paper by an executive of the General Electric Company displays the following suggestive matching between certain government organizations and policy areas, on the one hand, and their business and professional "constituencies," on the other:

130   THE JOURNAL OF LAW AND ECONOMICS

larger public subsidy or a more protective regulatory policy for the benefit of "constituencies" that are well organized. Hence, a distributional inequity from the standpoint of nonbenefiting groups occurs, even though they may have acknowledged the existence of a market failure and the legitimacy of nonmarket intervention in the first place.[52]

The role of nonmarket activities in producing distributional inequities, whether these are reflected in maldistribution of power or of income, derives from specific demand and supply characteristics associated with nonmarket output.

On the demand side, the principal causal characteristic is heightened public awareness of the inequities generated by the market and the resulting clamor for redistributive programs, often without prior consideration of the inequities that may be generated by these programs themselves.

On the supply side, distributional inequities result from the typical monopoly of nonmarket output in a particular field and the related absence of a reliable feedback process to monitor agency performance. In the absence of competing producers, those who feel adversely affected, whether as victims of arbitrary administrative authority or as general taxpayers, have notably less direct and less effective means of expressing their dissatisfaction than is available to consumers of marketed output who can withhold purchases or shift them to other producers. By contrast, those who realize special distributive benefits from particular nonmarket activities are likely to have, or to create more direct and more effective means for expressing their support, through organized lobbying and advocacy, than is available to consumers in the marketplace.

This does not imply that the inequities of the market are less than those of

---

Government Organizations	*Related Business Organizations*
Department of Defense, NASA	Defense-space contractors
Department of Agriculture	Farmers; dairy, meat processors
Environmental Protection Agency	Auto manufacturers; electric utilities
Securities and Exchange Commission	Brokers; underwriters; issuers
Interstate Commerce Commission	Railroads; truckers
Federal Communications Commission	Radio & TV stations & networks; cable and pay TV
Tariff Commission	Trade unions; business subject to import competition
Food and Drug Administration	Drug industry; food & beverage industry
Federal Power Commission	Electric utilities; natural gas producers
Nuclear Regulatory Commission	Atomic energy equipment builders

See L. Earle Birdzell, Business and Government: The Walls Between, in The Business-Government Relationship: A Reassessment (Neil H. Jacoby ed. 1975) (U.C.L.A.).

[52] The distributional type of nonmarket failure is the core of Stigler's theory of economic regulation. Stigler finds empirical evidence to support this hypothesis in interstate variations in trucking regulation and in occupational licensing. George J. Stigler, *supra* note 27.

the nonmarket, but it does suggest there is an identifiable process by which inequities can result from nonmarket activities, as they result from market activities.

*   *   *   *

In summary, nonmarket inadequacies can be tabulated in comparison with the inadequacies of the market.

MARKET AND NONMARKET FAILURES

Market	*Nonmarket*
1. Externalities and public goods	1. Internalities and private goals
2. Increasing returns	2. Redundant and rising costs
3. Market imperfections	3. Derived externalities
4. Distributional inequity (income and wealth)	4. Distributional inequity (influence and power)

These parallel categories should not be misunderstood. Nonmarket inadequacies are not the "duals" of those associated with market activities. The externalities on the market side are qualitatively related to the internalities on the nonmarket side only in the sense that each is a major source of failure in the market and nonmarket contexts, respectively. (Indeed, externalities in the market sector are conceptually closer to derived externalities in the nonmarket sector than either is to its horizontal neighbor in the two lists.)

However, two points apply to both lists.

(1) For the several types of market and nonmarket failures, it is much easier to estimate signs than magnitudes. Estimating magnitudes requires detailed empirical work in specific cases and contexts. Moreover, it is no easier to determine the magnitude of, say, the (negative) national security externalities associated with U.S. reliance on Middle Eastern oil than to determine, say, the magnitude of internalities that affect the behavior of the U.S. Air Force. Or, to take a more tractable example, it is probably no more difficult to estimate the derived externalities (negative as well as positive) resulting from environmental regulation than it is to estimate the (negative) externalities resulting from unregulated strip mining, or from noise emissions near metropolitan airports.

(2) The types and sources of market failure indicate the circumstances in which government intervention is worth contemplating, and in which alternative policies are worth analyzing as possible remedies. Similarly, the types and sources of nonmarket failure indicate the circumstances in which government intervention may itself misfire, and in which potential correctives are worth analyzing as possible remedies for likely shortcomings of government intervention.

The existing theory of market failure provides a useful corrective to the theory of perfectly functioning markets. In a similar sense, the theory of nonmarket failure outlined in the preceding pages is intended as a corrective for the implicit theory of perfectly functioning governments. Just as market failures or inadequacies have provided the theoretical underpinning for applied *policy analysis,* so nonmarket failures may provide the theoretical underpinning for *implementation analysis.* The analysis of how specific nonmarket activities (public policies) can be expected to operate and to depart in predictable ways from their costs and consequences as originally estimated.

III. IMPLEMENTATION ANALYSIS

Even the most sophisticated policy analysis usually neglects implementation issues. Policy studies rarely raise, and almost never answer such questions as *who* would have to do *what,* and *when,* and with what foreseeable resistance, modifications, and compromises if alternative A were chosen, or B, or C? As far as implementation is concerned, the Napoleonic dictum, *"On s'engage et puis on voit,"* is tacitly accepted. Analysts implicitly assume that the costs and benefits, as modeled in the analysis, will not be altered by implementation.

One numerical estimate suggests how badly policy studies turn out when prior estimates are compared with later results. Cost-estimating relationships, based on several dozen weapons systems developed in the United States, showed that on average costs for these systems (holding constant system differences in technology, performance, size, and so on) rose by a factor of three between the time development was begun and delivery was completed.[53]

The question is whether policy studies can better deal with implementation matters so that the implementation chapter of policy studies will not remain "missing."[54] In recent years, interest in the question of implementation has increased substantially, as reflected in the new public policy journals (*Policy Analysis, Policy Sciences*), several recent books and case stud-

[53] Robert Summers, Cost Estimates as Predictors of Actual Weapon Costs: A Study of Major Hardware Articles (Rand Corp. RM-3061-PR abridged, March 1965); Alvin J. Harman, Acquisition Cost Experience and Predictability (Rand Corp. P-4505, Jan. 1971).

[54] For a survey of this literature, see Erwin C. Hargrove, The Missing Link: The Study of Implementation of Social Policy (Urban Inst. 1975); Jeffrey L. Pressman & Aaron Wildarsky, Implementation: How Great Expectations in Washington Are Dashed in Oakland, or, Why It's Amazing That Federal Programs Work At All (1973); Graham T. Allison, Implementation Analysis: The Missing Chapter in Conventional Analysis—A Teaching Exercise, in 1974 Benefit-Cost and Policy Analysis 369; and Paul Berman, The Study of Macro- and Micro-Implementation, Public Policy, Spring 1978, at 157.

ies, and the curricula of graduate schools of policy analysis.[55] Most discussion has emphasized the typically large gaps between programs as designed and as executed, the lack of appropriate methods for anticipating these gaps and taking them into account, and consequently the failure of virtually all policy analysis to address implementation issues systematically.

To move from these justifiable criticisms to the systematic analysis of implementation issues requires an acceptable paradigm. In the following discussion, I will suggest that the preceding treatment of nonmarket failures provides this paradigm: a method of analyzing how public policy (that is, nonmarket) efforts to compensate for market failures may themselves fail in predictable ways. Anticipating nonmarket failures can be invaluable for trying to avoid them, or for developing mixed market and nonmarket alternatives that will diminish the more undesirable consequences of each.

Policy analysis can deal more effectively with implementation issues by linking the theory of nonmarket failure with explicit consideration of the "who-what-when" questions mentioned above. The reasons for implementation shortfalls—for costs to rise and effectiveness to fall ex post—in public policies intended to correct inadequacies of the market lie in the predictable inadequacies of nonmarket activities themselves. Hence, implementation analysis, as a regular segment of policy analysis, should proceed by applying the theory of nonmarket failures outlined above.

The principal connections among these stages and processes are summarized in Figure I. Emphasis in the preceding and following discussion is on the connections marked with solid lines. The roman numerals refer to the sections of this paper where the indicated connections have been discussed. Section I has focused on the connection between market output and market failures, Section II on those between market failures, nonmarket output and nonmarket failures; and Section III emphasizes the connections between nonmarket failures, implementation analysis, and policy analysis. The connections shown with dotted lines are alluded to, but not treated in detail.

The aim of this section is thus to incorporate implementation analysis systematically into policy studies. As a first step it is useful to distinguish two parts: (A) descriptive and (B) normative-inventive.

(A) The descriptive part of implementation analysis should use the structure of nonmarket failure outlined above as a check list for comparing each policy alternative under consideration. More specifically, the following implementation questions would be addressed as part of the analysis of policy alternatives and prior to choosing among them:

---

[55] The term "missing chapter" was first used in print by Graham T. Allison, *supra* note 56, although it was originated by Andrew Marshall and me five years earlier, to describe the usual neglect of implementation analysis in policy studies.

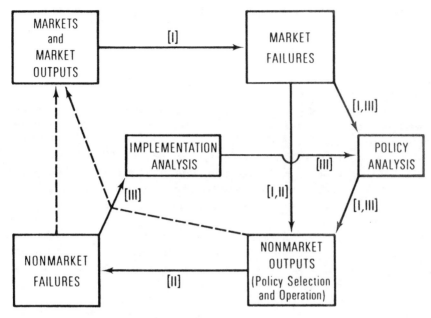

FIGURE I

1. If policy A (or B, or C) were to be adopted, what government departments, agencies, or bureaus would have to be assigned what precise responsibilities?

2. To the extent these designated agencies are already in existence, rather
than new agencies to be created, what are the *internalities and private goals*
that now motivate them, and how is behavior affected as a result? (If one
looks at how these agencies really operate, especially at their criteria for
recruiting, evaluating, and promoting personnel, how is output actually
measured, and how are success and effectiveness in producing it assessed?
Are staff members rewarded for adding to or justifying costs, or for reducing
them; for generating new technology, or opposing it, or objectively evaluating different types; for connecting the agency with new information sources
and restricting access to them, or for facilitating informational flows to and
from other agencies?)

If the policies under consideration call for creating new administering
agencies, can the corresponding internalities, and the way in which they will
influence agency behavior, be anticipated (for example, by the evident connection between particular policies and the interest groups advocating
them)? Can these prospective agency internalities be modified by program
redesign, and with what expected effects on agency behavior?

A THEORY OF NONMARKET FAILURE   135

3. What *externalities* may result from the alternative policies—over what time period and with what prior probabilities attached to them—in consideration of the content, scale, and impact, perhaps in policy areas remote from the target area of the programs under consideration? From the analyst's point of view, allowing for unforeseen externalities is thus an exercise in trying hard to remember what he would otherwise overlook.

4. Based on the track records of the agencies involved, on scrutiny of the alternative policies for the possible existence of inconsistent or otherwise infeasible program objectives, and on considerations covered in (2) above, can estimates be made of the prospective occurrence of *redundant and rising costs* associated with the agency responsibilities identified in (1) above? Can cost-estimating relationships be calculated (as in the system acquisition example referred to earlier) expressing the upward drift in cost functions to be expected over time?

5. Finally, in accord with the way in which each of the policies or programs would be expected to operate, how much discretionary authority is allowed, and to whom? What changes would ensue in *distribution,* not only income distribution but also in the distribution of *power* that may be wielded by some over others?

It is evident that many, indeed most, of the foregoing questions are not answerable in precise terms. Answers are likely to be judgments and opinions, hence subject to some disagreement by reasonable people even after substantial empirical work to attain "objective" information. Nevertheless, even "soft" answers, which display divergent opinions, should be valuable for the normative dimensions of implementation analysis.

(B) There are three normative purposes to be served by the previous descriptive treatment of alternative policies and programs. One purpose is simply to facilitate evaluation of the specified alternatives with respect to the ease or difficulty of implementing them: of translating "what is good to be done" into an estimate of what actually would get done.[56] In effect, this would amount to an ex post adjustment in the costs and benefits as modeled before implementation considerations were brought into the analysis.

A second purpose is to facilitate comparison between the actual inadequacies associated with the market and the potential inadequacies associated with implementing the nonmarket remedies under consideration. Juxtaposing the market failures to be remedied, and the nonmarket failures to be anticipated from the intended remedies, would permit an assessment that has

---

[56] "If to do were as easy as to know what were good to do, chapels had been churches, and poor men's cottages princes' palaces . . . I can easier teach twenty what were good to be done, than be one of the twenty to follow mine own teaching." William Shakespeare, The Merchant of Venice 224 (Classics Club Library ed. 1937).

been rare in previous policy studies and should become difficult to avoid in future ones.[57]

The third purpose of applying the paradigm of nonmarket failure is to stimulate invention: new ideas for policies and programs, or combinations among those under consideration, or of parts of them, or of entirely different approaches to the problem. A systematic comparison between market failures and nonmarket failures in a particular problem area (the second purpose mentioned above), and among the potential nonmarket failures associated with various alternative policies (the first purpose), should contribute to a result Dr. Johnson associated with the prospect of being hanged: namely, "to concentrate the mind wonderfully." Invention of new options, or discovery of ways to improve existing options, may result. If nonmarket solutions have been needed as countermeasures against market failures, we now need to develop countermeasures against nonmarket failures (hence, "counter-countermeasures" against market failures).

Besides evaluation of the existing set of options, the normative-inventive part of implementation analysis should focus on the following set of questions, which are as important, and as formidable, as the previous set:

1. Are there relatively simple and easily administered "fixes" in the operation of markets which would sufficiently alleviate the acknowledged market failure to provide an acceptable solution?[58]

2. Can policies be invented that, while recognizing the need for nonmarket interventions because the market's inadequacies are so great (for example, in the case of public goods or of private goods with major externalities), nevertheless try to retain certain valuable characteristics of market solutions (for example, competition by several producers, tangible and public performance measures, a bottom-line incentive structure in operating agencies)? In particular, can mechanisms be devised for the "reprivatization" of certain public services, for example, using publicly funded vouchers for the "purchase" of education or open bidding on private contracts for waste disposal or postal services.[59]

---

[57] This comparison is similar to what has been referred to as "zero-based budgeting" in discussions of planning, programming, and budgeting systems (PPBS). Arthur Smithies, The Budgetary Process in the United States (1955). The inadequacies of a particular market outcome, with little or no public intervention (a "zero" budget), may be preferable to the inadequacies of the nonmarket remedy.

[58] Some possible examples are: (a) estimating the separate effect of noise emissions on property values in airport vicinities and obliging airlines to compensate property owners accordingly, while leaving to the airlines the choice of aircraft power plant, acoustical damping, or other measures to reduce noise; (b) using foreign trade policy as an adjunct or alternative to antitrust policy in maintaining competitive pressures in monopolistic industries; (c) reducing market imperfections (for example, by removing or lowering barriers to entry or providing adjustment assistance to facilitate factor mobility).

[59] Peter F. Drucker, The Age of Discontinuity: Guidelines to Our Changing Society (1969);

3. Can improved measures for nonmarket output be devised, so that those nonmarket failures resulting from the lack of a suitable metric can be reduced? Can tests be made of the connections, or lack thereof, between the intermediate outputs that are often reflected in agency internalities and the final outputs that are intended?

4. Can the internalities (standards, goals) that provide the incentives for individual and agency behavior be revised so as to be more closely connected with the final intended output?[60]

5. Can improved information, feedback, and evaluation systems be built into new policies and programs in order to reduce the risks of co-optation by a "client" group and to publicize it if it occurs?

The normative questions of implementation analysis are no less formidable than those relating to the descriptive aspects discussed earlier. At best, attempts to respond systematically to the implementation questions raised by the nonmarket failure paradigm are likely to result in uncertain answers. Yet even without firm or complete answers, or indeed even without answers at all, there is considerable merit in the exercise. Addressing the questions in specific policy contexts requires that they be reformulated with precise reference to those contexts. For each policy alternative, the cardinal implementation issues ("who has to do what, when, how?") cannot be avoided. What has been omitted from virtually all policy studies, and what has significantly contributed to the failure of many implemented policies, must then be given explicit attention.

Another type of criticism can also be advanced. If, in fact, these formidable implementation questions *can* be answered in some fashion, why can't the answers simply be fed back into conventional policy analyses in accord with the standard methodology described earlier? Why can't the descriptive aspects of implementation analysis be made part of the analytical models and included in the usual cost-effectiveness calculations? And why can't the normative-inventive aspects simply be added to the policy alternatives to be run through the analytical models? These questions imply a direction of development that policy analysis should take: incorporation of implementation considerations *within* the existing "chapters" of the standard analyses, rather than as a separate chapter. However, we just don't know enough yet

---

Anthony H. Pascal, Clients, Consumers, and Citizens, Using Market Mechanisms for the Delivery of Public Services (Rand Corp. No. P-4803, March 1972); Donald B. Rice, The Potentialities of Public Policy Research in The Business-Government Relationship, *supra* note 51. The use of market analogues, incentives, and mechanisms to improve government performance is forcefully argued in Charles L. Schultze, Public Use of Private Interest, Harper's, May 1977, at 43-50, 55-62.

[60] Such revisions are apt to involve consideration of agency personnel practices, and in this respect would move implementation analysis in a direction taken by management consulting.

138   THE JOURNAL OF LAW AND ECONOMICS

to be able to do this. Raising the implementation questions as issues for consideration can perhaps elicit enough of a response to fill an important gap in existing policy studies. But the response is unlikely to be sufficiently rigorous for formal inclusion in analytical models at this stage. We need first to consider in a rough and qualitative way what has been largely ignored in policy research as a step toward more systematic inclusion in analytic methodology in the future.

IV. CONCLUSIONS

The foregoing argument can be summarized in several propositions:

1. The essential rationale for public policy measures lies in specific failures of the market of itself to produce efficient or otherwise socially preferred outcomes.

2. However, this rationale provides only a necessary, not a sufficient, justification for public policy interventions. Sufficiency requires that specifically identified market failures be compared with potential nonmarket failures associated with the implementation of public policies. Such a comparison is needed to arrive at a balanced assessment of whether, as well as what kind of, policy intervention will come closer to a socially preferred outcome.

3. There are four sources of the market's failure to produce socially preferred outcomes: externalities and public goods, increasing returns, market imperfections, and distributional inequity. The most general explanation for these failures is that markets don't exist, and perhaps can't be created, that will suitably capture the full social benefits or levy the full social costs of market activity. (This general explanation can be extended to include in part, though not completely, the last of the four market failures, distributional inequity.)

4. Similarly, as a result of distinctive demand and supply characteristics associated with nonmarket output, there are four sources and types of nonmarket failure: "internalities" and private goals (relating, for example, to agency budgets, technology, and information acquisition and control); redundant and rising costs; derived externalities; and distributional inequity (indexed on power, as well as on income or wealth). The distinctive demand and supply characteristics that give rise to these nonmarket failures include the following: premature but politically effective demands for government action; difficulties of defining and measuring output; lack of a "bottom line" for evaluating performance; absence of competition; and lack of an effective termination mechanism. Where there is nonmarket failure, there is an absence of nonmarket incentives that reconcile the calculations of costs and benefits by government decision makers with *total* costs and benefits.

5. In order to make more reliable comparisons among alternative public policies, as well as between them and market outcomes, policy analysis should explicitly consider how particular policy alternatives will be implemented. Implementation analysis, as a regular component of policy analysis, should link the formal modeling and cost-effectiveness comparisons among alternative policies with consideration of how policies are likely to be altered if implemented. It is intended to explain and anticipate the frequent tendency of implemented policies to result in higher costs and lower benefits, as well as different consequences, from those calculated in conventional policy studies.

6. There are two parts to implementation analysis: (a) a descriptive part, in which the previously mentioned sources of nonmarket failure are systematically traced for each policy alternative, and (b) a normative-inventive part, in which the costs and consequences of each alternative—as modified by the description of implementation realities—are compared with one another, as well as with the market outcome and its attendant shortcomings. This part of implementation analysis should explicitly consider changes and inventions in the policy options under consideration—changes that can be expected to reduce either the failures of nonmarket activities (for example, by devising improved measures of final output and translating them into agency internalities, or by reprivatizing public services) or the failures of market solutions (for example, by measures that reduce market imperfections).

[20]

Journal of Public Economics 28 (1985) 287-308. North-Holland

EXCESS BIAS AND THE NATURE OF BUDGET GROWTH

Richard A. MUSGRAVE

University of California at Santa Cruz, CA 95064, USA and Harvard University

To examine the hypothesis that budget growth has been excessive, the concept of 'correct' budget size must first be defined. This proves a difficult task for the level of public services, but especially so regarding redistribution and transfer payments. Next, potential sources of bias are explored, including distortions in voting, bureaucracy and political leadership. Analysis shows that bias may be in either direction, making for deficient as well as excess budgets. Institutional reform, therefore, should not prejudge the outcome by imposing limitations. The goal should be to improve the budget process, however this may affect budget size.

1. Introduction

The traditional concern of fiscal theory [Pigou (1928), Musgrave (1958)] has been to prescribe remedial action for market failure, mainly in situations where externalities arise. Beyond this, the assumption was that government, once advised of proper action, will proceed to carry it out. Recent literature, emerging from the theory of public choice, has addressed the way on which fiscal decisions are made. Initially, the fiscal process was viewed in terms of an economic model of democracy [Black (1958), Downs (1957)]. Interacting in the political market, voters (qua consumers) and politicians (qua entrepreneurs) combine to provide public goods so as to approximate an efficient outcome. More recently, emphasis has been placed on the defects in that process [Buchanan and Tullock (1962), Niskanen (1971)]. The traditional concern with market failure came to be replaced by a preoccupation with public sector failure. Indeed, such failure has come to be viewed as a major, if not the major, source of budget growth. Thus, a new theory of fiscal crisis has emerged [Musgrave (1980)]. The hypothesis is that the political and administrative process carries an innate bias towards adoption of programs which do not reflect the preferences of the public and which, under a more efficient procedure, would not pass. Based on this diagnosis, the remedy is seen in institutional changes which restrict expansion. The popularity of this thesis, especially in the United States, has paralleled a rising budget share and swing in political attitudes from their liberal stance of the mid-century to a more critical view. In fact, fiscal writings have made a major contribution to that swing. The vision of a Leviathan (an oppressive monster, unlike Hobbes' fatherly monarch) has replaced that of the benevolent welfare state [Musgrave (1981)].

My purpose here is not to applaud or decry this shift, or to argue that by my personal tastes the budget is too large or too small. Rather, my purpose is to examine the hypothesis that budget growth is explained in substantial part by an inherent bias towards excess budgets. Much of the modelling of budgetary behavior, as I see it, is based on just that hypothesis. But there can be no judgment that excess bias is the underlying cause without first determining the criteria for an optimal level or, if you wish, an optimal rate of growth. Closer consideration shows this to be difficult for the budgetary provision of goods and services, and even more difficult for the optimal level of redistributional activities. On both counts, the appropriate budget share will change over time. Demographic and technological changes, changes in relative costs, and the growth of per capita income will have major bearing on the correct level of budgetary provision for goods and services [Musgrave (1969)]. The optimal level of redistributive policies, in turn, may change with changes in the distribution and level of income. It will also respond to changes in social attitudes, i.e. reigning views of distributive justice. Since there are many reasons why the optimal share for budgetary activity may change, an observed increase in that share is no proof of excess. It may also reflect adjustment to an increase in the optimal level, or compensation for earlier deficiency. In brief, a complex set of factors need be considered to establish a norm of optimal budget size. Without such a norm, there can be no determination of whether actual growth has been 'excessive'. And without such determination, there can be no sound prescription for budgetary reform.

2. Budgetary provision of goods and services: (1) Voting bias

Even though the growth of transfers has been the major factor in the more recent growth of the public sector, theories of excess bias have related largely to the budgetary provision of goods and services.

2.1. Provision of public goods

Optimal provision for public goods, as defined in Samuelson's decisive contribution, must meet his familiar efficiency conditions as well as the distributional requirements of a social welfare function [Samuelson (1954, 1955)]. The division of output between public and private goods and the distribution of private goods among individuals are thus made simultaneously. This solution could be implemented by an omniscient referee to whom all preferences are known. Taxation would not enter the picture. But in reality there is no such referee. A voting process must be applied to induce preference revelation. This process, in turn, must be based on a given distribution of income, with taxes imposed to finance expenditures. Given this more realistic setting, what criteria can be chosen which, given the prevailing distribution of income, will signal an efficient outcome?[1]

2.1.1. Single issue voting

Suppose first that there is only one public service, so that budget size is the only issue. As one optimality criteria, consider the size of the budget which would be reached under Lindahl pricing [Lindahl (1919)]. We examine a situation where three voters, H, M and L, vote upon the size of the budget. Their demand or marginal evaluation schedules are shown by D_h, D_m, and D_l, with total demand, added vertically, of D_t. If the unit cost of the services equals OS, the Lindahl solution calls for output OV, with our three demanders contributing V_h, V_m, and V_l respectively (fig. 1). But the demand curves are not known (they are pseudo demand curves, as Samuelson put it)

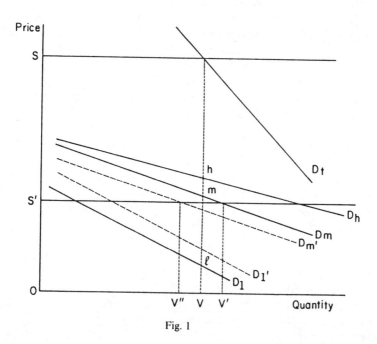

Fig. 1

---

[1]This approach, which views public goods provision against the background of a given distribution of income, has been variously critiqued as involving circular reasoning, but it does not. Indeed, it is essential for a formulation of fiscal theory which permits a bridge to efficient conduct of policy. For further discussion, see Musgrave (1969) and Musgrave and Musgrave (1984, p. 67).

and the solution has to be determined by vote. Suppose first that the division of costs or tax shares are determined prior to the budget vote. To take the simplest case, let there be a head tax, dividing the cost equally between the three. Each voter is thus confronted with a unit price $OS' = 1/3 \ OS$. The largest budget which can command a majority then equals OV', i.e. the amount at which the median voter equates cost and price. Since $OV' > OV$, the budget is excessive. This is one possible outcome, but to construct the opposite result we need only consider an alternative pattern where the demand schedules for M and L are given by D'_m and D'_l, leaving D_h and D_t unchanged. The largest output which demands a majority now falls to OV'' and give $OV'' < OV$, the budget is deficient. Whether the budget is excessive or deficient simply depends on whether D_m intersects $S'S'$ to the right or left of V. Majority rule will only accidentally lead to the Lindahl output OV, but may err in either direction. Thus, so far, there is no presumption as to which direction.

Comparison with the budget under Lindahl pricing is, however, a questionable standard. Introduction of the budget based on majority rule involves redistribution from the minority to the majority, whereas under the Lindahl solution all gain. As an alternative, the optimal budget might be defined as that for which the net gain (majority gains minus minority losses) is maximized. To simplify, we assume that the social value of a dollar of consumer surplus is the same, whoever receives it. We may then picture the problem in terms of fig. 2, where HH, MM, and LL show the marginal gains (positive and negative) which the voters derive from successive additions to the budget, given again a predetermined setting of tax shares. The aggregate marginal valuation is given by TT. The efficient outcome (given the predetermined tax shares) is OV, but majority rule decides on OV', the largest budget which can still gain a majority. Since $OV' > OV$, the budget is excessive. But suppose that MM drops to $M'M'$ while LL rises to $L'L'$, leaving HH and TT unchanged. The voter now chooses OV'' and since $OV'' < OV$, the budget is deficient. Once more we find that the departure from the optimum may be in either direction. The widely held presumption that an excess budget will result, simply because the majority dumps part of the burden on an unwilling minority — is thus incorrect.[2] It may also be that the majority disallows outlays from which larger minority gains could be obtained. Once more, further evidence is needed to establish an excess hypothesis.

2.1.2. Tax–expenditure linkage

We have assumed so far that budget size is voted upon after tax shares are

---

[2]See, for instance, Tullock (1959), Buchanan and Tullock (1962, p. 139) and Buchanan (1975, p. 155).

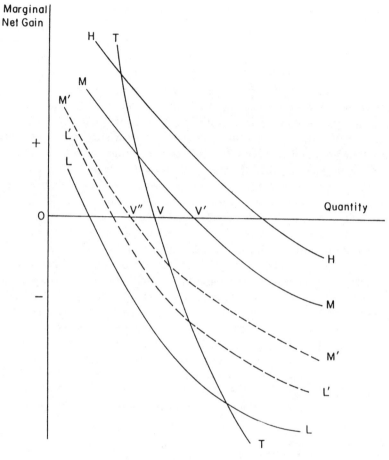

Fig. 2

set. The outcome thus depends on how the tax shares are distributed. Returning to fig. 1 and the demand curves as given by D_h, D_m, and D_l, the optimal supply equals OV. Assuming an equal cost distribution, such as results under a head tax, each must pay a price OS' and the voting rule leads to acceptance of OV', and excess budget. But suppose now that M's cost share is raised while that of L is reduced, so as to have M's cost exceed V_m. The budget is reduced and now falls short of OV. The outcome depends on whether the cost schedule for the median voter intersects D_m to the right or left of V. Indeed, the identity of the median voter depends on the share distribution.

As noted above, the simultaneous tax-expenditure solution suggested by the Lindahl model cannot be realized in practice where there is no referee to whom true preferences are known. But linkage may be introduced into the voting process. For any budget size, M and H may agree to lower their own cost shares, while raising that of L; and similar agreements may be reached between M and L or H and L. In the first two cases, the share of M is reduced, which leads him to choose a larger budget. This may be a reason for claiming that the system tends to redistribute towards the middle, a factor to which we return below. But this is too simple a view. Bargaining for tax shares will be associated with bargaining for budget size. Thus, M in bargaining with L may agree not to expand budget size as his cost share is reduced; or he may agree with H to expand the budget size by more than he would prefer. The outcome thus depends on the potential gains or losses in consumer surplus which the three parties would experience under various agreements, and there is no ready conclusion whether a larger or smaller budget will emerge than under the Lindahl solution.

Nevertheless, we may expect joint determination of tax shares and budget size to lead to more efficient results. This is in line with the Wicksellian prescription for successive voting on various combinations of tax shares and budget size, in search for that which will command unanimous approval or, to be realistic, will command 'qualified unanimity' [Wicksell (1896)]. While expenditure bills are typically voted upon against the background of given tax shares and vice versa, it does not follow that the two sides of the budget are unrelated. In the long run, at least, voters will require a more or less satisfactory match of tax and expenditure mixes, or they will vote to revise the system, be it on the tax or expenditure side of the budget. The error range may be reduced, however, and the system be improved by institutional arrangements which move the two parts of the budget more closely together.

2.1.3. Multiple issue voting

So far we have considered voting on only one issue, i.e. the size of a budget of given composition. We now turn to a situation where more than one issue is to be decided upon, the provision of two public goods, X and Y. This opens the possibility of vote trading and the formation of coalitions. With it the specter of 'log rolling' rears its ugly head, suggesting once more a presumption for excess budgets.

Consider table 1, where the numbers show the values which voters attach to two budget propositions, providing for X and Y, respectively. Since the propositions reflect the net gain (once more we assume that tax shares are given), the values may well be negative. Beginning with case I, single issue voting on X and Y rejects both propositions. But both will pass if B promises C to support Y, in turn for C's promise to support X. B and C each gain 3, while A loses 2. The budget has been increased and (assuming additivity) has resulted in a net gain to the group. B and C could compensate A, thus

Table 1

Voters	Case I Proposition X	Y	Case II Proposition X	Y	Case III Proposition X	Y	Case IV Proposition X	Y
A	−1	−1	−2	−2	+1	+1	+5	+5
B	+5	−2	+3	−2	+1	−10	+1	−2
C	−2	+5	−2	+3	−10	+1	−2	+1

leaving all better off. Turning to case II, single issue voting again rejects both propositions, while a coalition of B and C again leads to acceptance of both. B and C each have a net gain of 1 while A suffers a loss of 4. The budget has been increased, but now with a loss to the group. Cases III and IV are such that single issue voting leads to the acceptance of both propositions, while a coalition of B and C now rejects both. In both cases vote trading shrinks the budget, leaving an aggregate gain in case III and loss in case IV.

Once more we conclude that the formation of coalitions and vote trading may either raise or lower the budget, thereby improving or worsening the efficiency of the outcome. If the term 'log-rolling' is applied to outcomes which leave the budget with a loss, the negative flavor of the term is appropriate. But the argument should not be expanded to imply that the formation of coalitions is necessarily harmful or tends to excess budgets. On the contrary, coalitions are at the heart of a working democratic process, as they serve to find acceptable program packages. Parties may strive to maximize a social welfare function [Wittman (1974)], thereby overcoming the divisiveness of single issue voting.

2.2. Provision of private goods

While there is no ready presumption for the excess provision of public goods, the excess hypothesis fares better for budgetary provision of private goods.

To test for excessive provision of such goods, we must again set a standard of comparison. For this, we may compare the levels of public and of private provision. Such a situation is depicted in fig. 3, where D_l, D_m, and D_h are the demand schedules of L, M, and H, with D_t the horizontally added market demand schedule and SS the supply schedule. Privately purchased output equals OA. Now budgetary provision is introduced.[3] Let us define this to require (1) that the budget is balanced and (2) that output and cost

---

[3] We assume that public and private provision of the same good occurs at the same cost. The issue considered here thus differs from a situation where different techniques permit a need to be satisfied via either the private or the public good route, e.g. private door locks vs. police patrols.

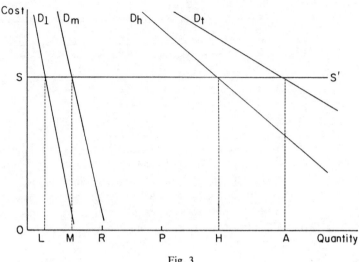

Fig. 3

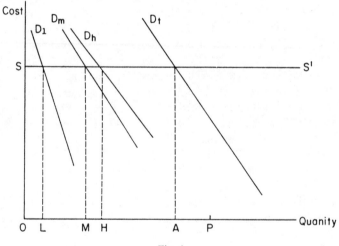

Fig. 4

are divided equally between L, M, and H. It follows that all three voters are charged at unit cost OS. The majority rule decides on $OP = 3OM$. Since $OP < OA$, public provision has reduced supply. The opposite result is shown in fig. 4, where $OP > OA$, so that public provision raises total supply. The outcome depends on whether $3OM \lesseqgtr OA$. Once again it appears that substitution of public for private provision may either raise or lower the total supplied.

But this is not the entire story. If supplementary private transactions are allowed for, further adjustments will result. If, as in fig. 3, OP falls short of

OA, H will want to purchase an additional amount MH. With L willing to sell $LM = MR$, H will purchase the remainder or RH in the market. Total supply thus equals $OP + RH = OA$.[4] The outcome, with regard to total supply and its distribution among H, M, and L, is the same as under private provision. Consider now fig. 4, where public provision OP exceeds OA, the level of private provision. H again wishes to purchase an additional amount MH. Since this falls short of LM, his need is met by purchase from L and no additional market purchases are required. Thus, total supply remains at OP. However, additional market purchases will be needed and total supply will increase above OP if $MH > LM$.

Two conclusions follow. If no private transactions are allowed, public provision may either exceed or fall short of the private case. If supplementary private transactions are permitted, a shortfall of public supply may be made up (or an excess of public supply may be increased) in the process. However, in most cases public provision will be less efficient. In the case of public goods, provision through the budget results in a gain to the group, as the goods in question could not be had otherwise. Budgetary provision, even though the voting solution only approximates the optimal outcome, still tends to generate a net gain. But not so for budgetary provision of private goods. Whether total supply is increased or reduced, substitution of public provision is inherently a negative sum game. Absent distributional weights, L's loss outweights the gains of M and H. A cash transfer imposing the same burden on L would have resulted in a larger gain to M and H. The same holds if distributional weights are applied. The optimal budget for the provision of purely private goods is thus zero.

The question remains whether increased provision of private goods has played a major role in budget expansion, thus sustaining the excess hypothesis. This view is supported by pointing to the growth of programs such as housing, health care, selective welfare services, regional development, and so forth. It remains to be seen, however, whether these programs reflect purely private goods. The mere fact that certain public services are desired by only part of the group, or that their benefits are tied to certain characteristics (e.g. age or location), need not render them private goods. People differ in their preferences for public as well as for private goods; and coalitions may contain bundles of programs favored by particular groups. Such may be the case even though the goods are public in nature and, given the free-rider problem, not provided efficiently through private purchase.

Moreover, allowance need be made for the role of merit goods. That is to

---

[4]To show that total provision will be the same under both cases, we set

$$OL + OM + OH = 3\ OM + MH - LM,$$

where the left-hand term equals private provision and the right-hand term equals public provision with private adjustment. By substitution this equality may be shown to hold.

say, public policy may wish to encourage the consumption of certain goods (public or private) beyond that called for by the play of private preferences alone.[5] This may take the form of subsidies, leaving it to the individual to determine his/her own consumption, or provision may be limited to assuring a set minimum level of consumption. Finally, certain private goods may be provided because society views the problem of distribution in categorical terms: inequality may be viewed as less acceptable with regard to the availability of certain 'basic' needs such as food and shelter than with regard to the acquisition of 'frills'. Thus, equality is viewed in terms of basic consumption items, rather than in terms of minimum levels of income, independent of use. As noted below, this approach may apply particularly in the context of voluntary redistribution.

What may at first sight appear as an inappropriately public provision of private goods may thus emerge in a different light after these and related factors are allowed for. In the United States, major components of budget growth such as defense, welfare and in some respects even social security, do not fit the private good concept. Education, housing, and some highways may, but even here externality features and merit aspects enter. In short, although the public provision of purely private goods is the one case which justifies a clear presumption towards excess, it does not appear to have played a decisive role in budget growth, at least not as seen from the perspective of the United States, where the excess hypothesis has been pressed most strongly. For the remainder, including the provision of public and of mixed goods, more specific evidence is needed to support the hypothesis that budget growth has in large part reflected illegitimate (inefficient) expansion due to voting bias. To such evidence we now turn, including the role of promotion costs and, once more, of pressure groups.

2.3. Promotion costs and pressure groups

In an imperfect political market, the success of expenditure propositions depends greatly on their promotion, be it to activate and persuade voters, to organize coalitions, or to support legislators who will vote favorably. All these involve costs. To establish a presumption towards excess, it must be shown, however, that promotion can be undertaken more readily (transaction or promotion costs are lower) by proponents than by opponents of expenditure proposals. It must be shown that gainers stand to gain more than losers stand to lose, or that they have a lower organization cost.

---

[5]The concept of merit goods, as introduced in my earlier work (Musgrave (1958)], has been interpreted variously. To bring out its peculiar nature, I think it best to view the concept not as relating to externalities, or even to situations where educational objectives (to improve the individual's ability to choose) are pursued, but to situations where society wishes to overrule minority preferences.

The majority, to be sure, is in a better position to enjoy economies of scale, e.g. to share advertising contributions but this holds whether the majority is pro or con. Proponents, however, may stand to gain more because they value the particular service, whereas opponents only lose a general tax dollar. Gainers may also stand in a neighborhood relation or share characteristics which makes it easier to identify them, while opponents are diffused. Thus, proponents may find it easier to organize. However, considerations such as these [Olson (1965)] are more valid for a simple setting in which itinerant politicians wander from village to village to make their case, than in modern society where political promotion works through the media which is generally accessible but costly. Availability of funds for media and campaign finance become all-important factors.

Hypotheses about excess or deficiency thus depend on the relative amounts of funds available to promote or oppose expenditure propositions. With contributions from few large gainers more readily available than many small contributions from small losers, proponents will tend to have an advantage. However, it must not be overlooked that along with promotion of particular expenditure proposals there goes promotion of anti-tax legislation. Given limited availability of deficit finance (see below) anti-tax promotion thus equals promotion against public expenditures in general. It would be interesting to compare the relative levels of pro-expenditure and anti-tax finance, and how they have changed over time. In the current U.S. setting, in particular, there is surely no presumption that pro-expenditure finance dominates. The reverse may well be the case.

Nor is it evident that voter myopia generates an excess bias. While voters may be unaware of tax burdens, especially with regard to non-direct taxes, anti-tax promotion may also lead to an exaggerated view of tax burdens. Moreover, the indirect and remote nature of benefits from certain expenditure programs may lead to an under-evaluation [Downs (1960)]. Once again the net effect is not easily assessed.

While voting models have typically focused on the behavior of individual voters, a more realistic interpretation of the political fiscal process runs in terms of interest groups. Voters with similar concerns band together to express common interests, thereby to establish voting blocs, and to spread the cost of promoting common concerns. Individuals, moreover, will view their membership in such groups from various perspectives. On the one hand, they will associate with others who have similar interests as consumers; and on the other, they will join those who share their interest as producers. Thus, defense expenditures are supported by those who wish stronger defenses as well as by those who derive earnings from the defense industry. Highway construction is supported by drivers as well as by the construction industry. Eduction is promoted in support of learning, but also of teacher employment. Common interests from the production side will combine capital and labor, thus running counter to a one-dimensional interpretation of group conflict along lines of class or income groups. Since the control of producer interests tends to be concentrated in a smaller number of decision-makers (corporations and unions), their impact may well dominate that of user groups. Yet, while consumer promotion may contribute to efficient budget choice, producer pressure tends to distort budget composition (within the restraint of a given total) or to make for excess budget size.

But once more, the impact of pressure groups on budget size does not come from the expenditure side only. Interest groups to promote expenditure programs are matched by others working against taxation, be it lower taxes in general or in support of preferential treatment for specific uses or sources of income. If a mechanism for counter-veiling power [Galbraith (1952)] could be relied upon to establish a balanced power structure, distorting influences might wash out, but such will hardly be the case. Nor does it seem realistic to expect that a neat equilibrium comes to be established as incremental gains fall and efficiency costs rise with continuing program expansion [Becker (1983)]. The efficiency cost of isolated bargains need not be borne by the parties of the particular bargain but may be translated into a social cost. The interplay of pressure groups cannot be relied upon, therefore, to produce optimal results. But once both sides (i.e. pro-expenditure and anti-tax) or pressure group activity are allowed for, it is not at all evident that distorting net effects on the size of the budget have to be towards over-expansion, of that such net effects have been an increasing force, thus explaining budget growth. Here, as in other aspects of the social process, the problem is more complex than can be allowed for by a simple theorem. Modelling the fiscal bargain, it appears, will be more successful if related to particular situations, e.g. the growth of highway outlays in the U.S. budgets of the 1950s, that of education outlays in the 1960s, welfare and social security expansion in the 1970s, or defense in the 1980s.

3. Budgetary provision of goods and services: (2) Bureaucratic imposition

In addition to voting bias, a further source of excessive budget growth is said to follow from the behavior of public officials or 'bureaucrats'. Government is viewed as an essentially coercive force of increasing power, independent of and opposed to the interest of the people. In the fiscal context, the assumption is that officials wish to maximize their budgets and also have the power to impose their wishes.

3.1. Monopoly bureaus

Bureau heads, so it is argued, wish to maximize the size of their budgets [Niskanen (1971)]. They present the legislature with the largest possible budget for which total cost can still be shown to exceed total benefits, and the legislature will accept this. As this exceeds the efficient budget where marginal cost and benefits are equated, an excess budget results. Moreover, increasing bureaucratic power adds to the explanation of budget growth. The underlying hypothesis of bureaucratic behavior has some merit, but is far from conclusive.

First, it is unrealistic to assume that the legislature will be conscientious enough to compare benefits and costs (rather than to go easy on costs) and at the same time be so naive as to consider totals only while disregarding marginal conditions. Legislatures have been increasingly equipped with technical staffs which do not lack sophistication, so that this should be a decreasing, not increasing, source of bias.

Second, we question whether the overriding objective of bureau heads is indeed to maximize their budgets. This assumption follows from the proposition that budget expansion involves personal gains, and that self-interest is 'the only game in town'. This extreme proposition, if correct, would imply that only market-type organizations can function efficiently, while public sector operations are inherently doomed to inefficiency. But so extreme a proposition misreads human nature. Bureau heads may also be guided by what they conceive to be the public interest [Colm (1955)], by a desire to transmit expertise, or, as Weberian civil servants, by a commitment to implement policies which have been assigned to them. Acting in these capacities, their objective will be an optimizing rather than a maximizing budget. While the bureau head may tend to over-estimate the importance of his/her particular programs, this need not rule out allowance for overall budget composition. Moreover, even with self-interest as the guiding motivation, bureau heads may find budgetary prudence to be rewarded by their superiors. The semantics of the current discussion itself is telling. In one decade, the virtues of civil servants are compared with the vices of capitalists, while in the next the vices of bureaucrats are compared to the virtues of entrepreneurs.

Finally, it must not be overlooked that a bureau head typically operates in the context of a general budget process. In this adversary setting, each bureau head presents the claims of his/her bureau. These claims are then weighed against those of others, and final selection is constrained by an overall budget size. This overall size is set by considerations of tax policy or an acceptable deficit margin, and in the end is subject to voter control. Elected officials, therefore, are subject to constraints and this works back to the options available to bureau heads. The quality of the budgetary process and the technical expertise of the personnel involved has been improved over time rather than worsened. While reality does not match the picture of an idealized civil servant, neither is it reflected by the now popular caricature of heavy-handed bureaucrats imposing their interest on the public.

3.2. Agenda-setting

A second devise by which officials are viewed as expanding the budget is through agenda-setting. Operating in the context of direct democracy, officials are assumed to have the power to choose on what proposition voters are to be allowed to vote. They will then submit the largest proposition for which a majority can still be obtained, whereas given free choice, voters would have preferred a lesser budget. Once more questions of power, motivation, and voter naiveté arise, i.e. whether administrators do in fact have the power to set agenda, whether they consistently wish to maximize budgets, and whether voters are indeed helpless pawns of bureaucratic agenda setters. The 'tax revolt' movement and increased use of referenda to limit fiscal activity does not give much credence to this proposition.

4. Redistribution policies

Budgetary provision for goods and services, as noted above, generates distributional side-effects, effects which are not the intent of policy but arise because the voting process yields an imperfect solution. As distinct from these side-effects, we now turn to policies the very purpose of which is to redistribute income in a systematic fashion, say from high to low income groups, or as between generations or regions. These two types – incidental vs. planned – need be distinguished [Tullock (1983)], and our concern now is with the latter. As noted above, such programs have contributed greatly to budgetary growth; and in analyzing the nature of this growth, we must consider once more whether these programs reflected legitimate choices or a bias of the political system towards excess budgets. As before, this cannot be done without first establishing a standard for the optimal level. The setting of an operational standard proved difficult with regard to the provision of public goods, but this difficulty is vastly increased with regard to distribution.

4.1. Voluntary redistribution

We begin with the simple case of voluntary redistribution. Here the prevailing distribution of income (or wealth) is not questioned as a point of departure, so that only voluntary redistribution is allowed. Two situations may be distinguished: (1) where high income recipient *H* receives satisfaction from his own giving to low income recipient *L*, and (2) where *H* derives satisfaction from seeing *L*'s income increase, independent of whether the grant is made by himself or by someone else.

In the first case, redistribution is a private good. No externalities and hence no need for budgetary action arises.[6] H gives to L until his/her marginal utility of giving equals that of other uses of income. Thus, an equilibrium of Pareto-optimal giving is achieved [Hochman and Rogers (1969)].

In the second case, redistribution is a public good. Donors, acting independently, now encounter a free-rider problem. The benefits of A's giving to Z are shared by B and C. The free-rider problem again requires budgetary action and the situation is analogous to that of fig. 1. The size of the redistribution budget may now be measured on the horizontal axis, while $OS = \$1$ on the vertical axis shows the aggregate cost of \$1 of redistribution. The D_h, D_m, and D_l schedules now show the marginal evaluations which H, M, and L place on successive dollars of transfers to Z. Z benefits, but his preferences (or demand for transfers) do not enter or do so only indirectly, by affecting the donors' gains. Since we deal with the case of voluntary redistribution, Z does not vote. The optimal redistribution budget calls for OV, the Lindahl solution, where H contributes V_h, M contributes V_m, and L contributes V_l. But preferences are not known and voting is needed. The voting outcome once more may result in a smaller or larger budget, depending on the previously noted conditions. As before, it may be preferable to define the optimal outcome in terms of aggregate welfare gains by $H + M + L$, as shown in fig. 2, but there is still no presumption whether the outcome will be excessive or deficient.

4.2. Standards of primary distribution

However this may be, note that these processes of voluntary redistribution – be they for redistribution as a private good or as a social good – deal with a secondary aspect only. Their outcome reflects the initially prevailing distribution of income and the preferences of its recipients [Musgrave (1970)]. The more fundamental problem of primary distribution (and with it the base for potential voluntary redistribution) remains to be considered. Although discussed through the ages, this issue once more became a lively topic of discussion in recent years. Three distinct models (entitlement, utilitarian, and fairness) may be distinguished.

On one end of the scale stands the entitlement model. Growing out of the Lockean tradition, based upon divine or natural law, this model holds that earnings in the market place constitute a legitimate entitlement. To this is added a concept of just transfer by exchange or gift, and the resulting state of distribution (whatever its pattern) is considered just [Nozick (1974)]. While the concept of just transfer is not a simple one (for instance: are

---

[6]We here disregard that a perverse externality effect may arise even in this case as giving by H, by raising L's income, may reduce the satisfaction available to H by similar giving.

competitive markets required, and how about external costs?), the basic premise is clear. Only voluntary redistribution, as dealt with in the preceding section, is permissible. Primary redistribution, based on majority vote or some other specified voting rule, is excluded. Measured by these criteria, much of the growth of transfers which has occurred in recent decades may be viewed as illegitimate.

According to the alternative models, the distribution of talent is considered arbitrary, so that earnings capacity does not constitute a basis for desert. An independent norm of distributive justice is required. At an earlier stage of the discussion, from Bentham over Mill and Edgeworth to Pigou, that norm was set by maximizing total utility for the group. With the advent of the 'new welfare economics' in the 1930s, the underlying assumption of utility comparison was dropped, and the concept of a social welfare function appeared. This function, first viewed as reflecting the social values of a particular counsellor [Bergson (1938)] was then translated into a collective group preference via voting and the feasibility of arriving at a consistent function was questioned [Arrow (1951)]. Nevertheless, social welfare functions are now widely postulated, using mathematically convenient shapes such as constant elasticity, and serve to introduce distributional weights into policy evaluation.

The philosphopher's view of social justice, however, has to go behind mathematical convenience in formulating the social welfare function, and inquire into the standard which *should* be met. Going back to the golden rule of scriptures or a Kantian principle of universality, the principle of fairness, as formulated by Rawls [Rawls (1971)], called for individuals, engaged in the formation of a social contract, to view distributive justice from an impartial perspective. Deprived of the knowledge of what a person's place in the distribution will be, his or her choice of the desired state of distribution (say, level of Gini coefficient) then becomes an exercise in utility maximization under uncertainty. It is not surprising, therefore, that early contributions to this approach were made by economists [Harsanyi (1953) and Vickrey (1960)]. Given a fixed amount of income that is to be distributed, the presence of risk aversion calls for an equal distribution. But after allowing for the efficiency costs of redistribution, infinite risk aversion leads to maximin, while a lesser degree of risk aversion calls for varying degrees if inequality. The concept of fairness underlying this approach is appealing, but analysis of distributive justice in terms of risk aversion seems questionable. I find it troublesome, at the initial stage, to combine the assumption of disinterestedness under the veil with choice based upon own risk aversion. Also, I find it inconsistent first to choose in a disinterested fashion but then, after the 'constitutional stage' has passed, to revert to self-interest and to block redistributive measures by adverse responses in labor supply [Musgrave (1974)]. Yet, it is precisely this response which (given extreme risk aversion) leads to the conclusion of maximin. Nor need the assumption of extreme risk aversion be accepted [Arrow (1973)]. While utility maximization under uncertainty is a fine instrument to explain gambling behavior, it may not be equal to generating a theory of justice.

Where, then, does this leave us in the search for a valid norm? While I find the fairness approach to my liking, I see no objective basis on which to conclude that a particular fairness pattern is 'correct', or that Lockean entitlement is 'wrong'. While Nozick has been criticized for postulating Lockean entitlement without proving its validity [Nagel (1974)], I wonder whether such a proof (be it for entitlement or for fairness) can be given. By the same token, Hayek [Hayek (1976)] is mistaken in his assertion that only a concept of just process has meaning, while distributive justice as an end state is only a mirage. If, as Hayek holds, a just end state cannot be conceived of, how can a just point of departure be defined, and what merit is there in a just process which takes off from an unjust base? Nozick is aware of this, but his escape via a baseline concept hardly overcomes the problem [Musgrave (1983)]. In conclusion, there is more than one defensible position, and which one one chooses (e.g. Lockean entitlement or fairness) not only depends on workability in the social process but also on personal value judgment, on how one views the good society, and the individual's role therein.

While such views will differ among members of the society, it does not follow that whatever policies are undertaken are by necessity legitimate reflections of these views. In judging whether the level of redistribution policy is too high or too low, reference must thus be to what might be called the considered intent of society, as derived from the views of its members. This in fact calls for a combination of entitlement and fairness considerations (e.g. tax rates not to exceed x percent or income floors not to fall below y dollars). Moreover, distributional concerns may be in categorical as well as in general terms [Tobin (1970)], a somewhat special case of merit goods. As noted above, use of justice in primary distribution also may relate to levels of availability of certain goods, rather than to overall levels of income.

Setting the standard is complicated further by the fact that perceptions of distributive justice change over time. Social values are cultural phenomena and not just matters of isolated individual perception. What seemed desirable to a majority from the 1930s to the 1970s – that era of the rising welfare state – may not seem so in the changing climate of the 1980s and thereafter. Kontradieffs may operate in the cultural as well as in the economic sphere.

4.3. Bargaining over distribution

Consider now a setting in which society accepts the entitlement to earnings as the valid criteria, but subject to adjustment (redistribution) by majority rule. Let there be three people, H, M, and L, engaged in bargaining over income redistribution. To simplify and to avoid total indeterminateness, we suppose further that transfers are subject to the constraint that rank order cannot be reversed, thus limiting adjustments to changes within the initial income spreads. There may then be three combinations, L and M vs. H, M and H vs. L, and H vs. M and L. Which coalition prevails depends on a number of factors, including feasibility of implementation, the spread between income levels, and voting participation.

Coalitions among L and M, syphoning income from H, may be implemented by a negative income tax or a combination of progressive taxation with regressive (pro-poor) transfers. A coalition of M and H would call for regressive taxes and progressive transfers, while one among L and H would require a U-shaped pattern of transfers and a humped schedule of effective tax rates. The development of modern fiscal institutions, especially the rise of progressive income tax, has facilitated implementation of the H, M coalition [Stigler (1970)]; but it may also be argued, and perhaps more validly so, that these institutions have developed to accommodate the goals of that coalition.

Next, the choice of coalition depends on the income spreads between H and M and between M and L. To simplify, let us assume further that coalitions divide the gain equally between the partners. It may then be shown under what conditions one or the other coalition will result. Coalition M, L will prevail if $\frac{1}{3}(H-M)$ exceeds both $\frac{1}{2}L$ and $\frac{1}{2}(M-L)$. Coalition M, H will prevail if $\frac{1}{2}L$ exceeds both $\frac{1}{3}(H-M)$ and $\frac{1}{2}(M-L)$. Coalition H, L finally prevails if $\frac{1}{2}(M-L)$ exceeds both $\frac{1}{3}(H-M)$ and $\frac{1}{2}L$. Given that the distribution of income typically shows $H-M$ to exceed $M-L$, so that average income exceeds the median, the M, L coalition is most likely to prevail [Meltzer and Richard (1981)]. With H standing to gain from both the more likely coalitions, it has been suggested by 'Director's Law' [Stigler (1970)] that redistribution will be towards the middle. But this need not follow. The major role of the M, L coalition (rather than dividing gains equally) may well have been to transfer from H to L. Our estimates of the distribution of net benefits for the United States, though necessarily crude, suggest that upper incomes lose while lower incomes gain, with a break-even point at about the median income [Musgrave, Case and Leonard (1974)].

The choice of coalition further depends on voting participation. With participation related positively to incomes, as has been the case in the United States, L's weight as coalition partner is reduced. By the same token, the rising participation of low income voters (actual or potential) raises L's weight. This may be a major factor in explaining the expansion of social programs in the United States following the civil rights legislation of the 1960s. Nevertheless, the actual level of redistribution has been less than the bargaining model would suggest. A substantial spread (after adjustment) between both H and M, and M and L, remains. There are various reasons for this. Individuals may oppose redistribution in the hope of reaching a higher level in the income scale. Also, their self-interest may be constrained by what they consider a just state of distribution along Lockean lines. Or, they may fear detrimental effects of redistribution on the total level of income and with it on their own position.

4.4. Churning

Viewed from a somewhat different perspective, it is argued that although distributive programs have grown rapidly in scope, their combined net effect on distribution has been slight. The argument is that such programs have been ineffective, resulting in a mere 'churning' of funds, without much systematic redistribution towards the bottom. In large part, this reflects the combination of programs such as welfare and the growth of social security systems, the two items which have been major factors in the expansion of transfers. But allowing for the distinct purposes of the two programs, their combination is inappropriate. Welfare programs are designed to redistribute downward, but old-age security, properly understood, is to provide old-age security in a fashion which avoids inequity among generations [Musgrave (1981)], and not to redistribute between high and low income groups. Once again, the causes of budget growth have to be explained, and its merits have to be assessed in relation to particular programs. What appears as churning in the aggregate may reflect a more meaningul pattern if the particulars are examined.

4.5. Efficiency costs

It remains to note that budgetary activity – be it in the provision of public goods or in the implementation of transfer payments – involves an efficiency cost which exceeds the budgetary amount. Public programs thus involve deadweight losses which add to their social cost. This of course does not make an a priori case against such programs, but the additional cost should be allowed for in weighing the benefits. To the extent that such costs are overlooked, a bias towards excess budget occurs; and an increasing tendency to do so may have been a source of excessive budget growth. Since the efficiency cost per dollar of revenue tends to rise with rising levels of taxation, the potential for inefficient decision-making is increased. At the same time, the efficiency cost, growing larger, also comes to be detected more readily and allowance for it or even over-allowance, becomes more likely.

Viewed more broadly, extension of the budgetary sector may at some point become incompatible with the function of a market economy. But it may also be that institutional adjustments come to be required to accommodate public sector goals. While the problem of work incentives is unavoidable under any form of organization, the role of saving and investment incentives is a function of economic organization. The relation, therefore, works in both directions. 'Public sector goals may be limited by economic organization, but the latter may also be adapted to serve public sector goals.

Placed into a still broader context, distribution policies bear on the general framework of rules in which individuals operate, and thus on the scope and quality of liberty. But that quality is not unrelated to distributive justice (freedom to suffer want is not a highly valued freedom), and both must be judged in conjunction. Thus, the circle closes as the argument returns to how a 'good society' is viewed, and how divergent views can be reconciled in the democratic process.

The growth of redistributive programs – be they in cash or of the in-kind (categorical) variety – has been a major factor in budgetary expansion. But it is by no means evident to what extent this growth has been the outcome of a 'legitimate process' reflecting changing voter preferences in distributive matters, or the product of a malfunctioning of the political system by which budgetary decisions are reached.

5. Conclusion

Earlier in this paper we concluded that there is no ready presumption of excess bias in the provision of public goods; and the difficulty of deriving an 'objective' standard against which to measure the 'correct' scope of redistribution is even more severe. As I see it, a realistic appraisal does not sustain the hypothesis that distortions in the fiscal process have been the primary cause of budget growth; nor does it sustain the proposition that bias must necessarily be towards excess. Quite possibly the public, by and large and subject to correction over time, gets what it wants. One's own preferences may applaud or deplore budget growth, but this differs from a finding of excess as measured against the standards which we have examined.

If this interpretation is correct, fiscal reform should not be derived from a premise of excess, thus calling for limitation only, as is now the fashion [Brennan and Buchanan (1980), McKenzie (1984)]. Rather, it should be designed to improve information and to facilitate the translation of voter preferences into policy action, thereby improving budget composition and scope, whether the result be to raise or lower budget size.

References

Arrow, Kenneth, 1951, Social choice and individual value (Wiley, New York).
Arrow, Kenneth, Some ordinalist-utilitarian notes on Rawl's theory of justice, Journal of Philosophy 70, 245–280.
Becker, Gary S., A theory of competition among pressure groups for political influence, The Quarterly Journal of Economics XCVIII, 3, 371–406.

Black, R.D., 1958, The theory of committees and elections (University Press, Cambridge).

Bergson, Abram, 1938, A reformulation of certain aspects of welfare economics, Quarterly Journal of Economics 52, 310–334.

Brennan, Geoffrey and Buchanan, James, 1980, The power to tax (University Press, Cambridge).

Buchanan, James and Tullock, Gordon, 1962, The calculus of consent (University of Michigan Press, Ann Arbor).

Buchanan, James, 1975, The limits of liberty (University of Chicago Press, Chicago).

Colm, Gerhardt, 1955, Essays in public finance and fiscal policy (Irwin, Homewood).

Downs, Anthony, 1957, An economic theory of democracy (Harper and Row, New York).

Downs, A., 1960, Why the government budget is too small in a democracy, World Politics.

Friedman, Milton, 1948, A monetary and fiscal framework for economic stability, American Economic Review XXXVIII, 3, 245–265.

Galbraith, Kenneth, 1952, American capitalism; The concept of countervailing power (Houghton, Mifflin, Boston).

Hayek, Friedrich, 1976, Law, legislation and liberty, vol. II: The mirage of social justice (University of Chicago Press, Chicago).

Harsanyi, J. 1953, Conditional utility in welfare and in the theory of risk-taking, Journal of Public Economy 61, 434–435.

Hochman, H. and Rogers, J., 1969, Pareto-optimal redistribution, American Economic Review 59, 542–557.

Lindahl, E., 1919, Die Gerechtigkeit in der Besteuerung (Lund, Sweden). See also excerpts in Musgrave and Peacock, eds., 1967, Classics in the theory of public finance (St. Martin's Press, New York).

McKenzie, R., ed., 1984, Constitutional economics (Heath & Company, Lexington).

Meltzer, A.H., and S.F. Richards, 1981, Tests of a rational theory of the size of government, Journal of Political Economy, October.

Musgrave, R., 1958, The theory of public finance (McGraw Hill, New York).

Musgrave, R., 1969, Provision for social goods, in J. Margolis and T. Guitton, eds., Public economics (Macmillan, London).

Musgrave, R., 1970, Pareto optimal redistribution: Comments, American Economic Review 60, no. 5.

Musgrave, R., 1974, Maximin, uncertainty, and the leisure trade-off, Quarterly Journal of Economics.

Musgrave, R., K. Case and H. Leonard, 1974, The distribution of fiscal burdens and benefits, Public Finance Quarterly.

Musgrave, R., 1981, Financing social security, in Skidmore, eds., Social security financing (MIT Press, Cambridge).

Musgrave, R., 1981, Leviathan cometh, or does he?, in: H. Ladd and H. Tideman, eds., Taxable expenditure limitations (Urban Institute Press, Washington, DC).

Musgrave, R., 1980, Theories of fiscal crisis, in: H. Aaron and M. Boskin, eds., The economics of taxation (Brookings Institution, Washington, DC).

Musgrave, R., 1983, Private labor and common land, in: C. Break, ed., State and local finance (University of Wisconsin Press, Madison).

Musgrave, R. and A. Peacock, 1984, Public finance in theory and practice, 4th edn. (McGraw Hill, New York).

Nagel, T., 1975, Libertarianism without foundation, The Yale Law Journal.

Niskanen, W., 1971, Bureaucracy and representative government (Aldine, Chicago).

Nozick, R., 1974, Anarchy, state, and utopia (Basic Books, New York).

Olson, Mansor, 1965, The logic of collective action (Harvard University Press, Cambridge).

Pigou, A., 1928, A study in public finance (Macmillan, London).

Rawls, John, 1971, A theory of justice (Harvard University Press, Cambridge).

Samuelson, Paul, 1954, The pure theory of public expenditures, Review of Economics and Statistics 36, 350–356.

Samuelson, Paul, 1955, Diagrammatic exposition of a theory of public expenditures, Review of Economics and Statistics, 35, 387–389.

Stigler, George, 1970, Director's law of public income redistribution, Journal of Law and Economics 13, 1–4.

Tobin, James, 1970, On limiting the domain of inequality, Journal of Law and Economics 13, 263–279.

Tullock, Gordon, 1959, Some problems of majority voting, Journal of Political Economy 67, 571–579.

Tullock, Gordon, 1983, Economics of income redistribution (Boston, Klumer).

Vickrey, William, 1960, Utility, strategy and social decision rules, Quarterly Journal of Economics 74, 507–535.

Wicksell, Knut, 1968, Finanztheoretische untersuchungen (Fischer, Jena). For excerpts, see Musgrave and Peacock, eds., (1896, Classics in the Theory of Public Finance) (St. Martin's Press, New York).

Wittman, Donald, 1974, Parties as utility maximizes, American Political Review 9.

Name Index

Thoden van Velzen, H.V.W. 76
Thomas 326
Tilly, C. 61
Tobin, J. 505, 510
Tocqueville, A. de 31
Tollison, R.D. 305–31
Tolstoy, A. 19
Trenchard, J. 250
Tucker, B. 163
Tullock, G. 16, 309, 311, 312, 313, 315, 316,
    326, 327, 328, 331, 333, 358, 385, 489, 492,
    502, 509, 510
Turner, V.W. 83
Tylor, E.B. 73, 74

Vickrey, W. 504, 510
Vile, M.J.C. 250
Viner, J. 459

Wagner, H. 333
Wagner, R.E. 359, 376
Wallace, G. 297
Watanabe, G. 424, 425
Weaver, C.L. 333, 358
Webb 272
Weber, M. 175
Weidenbaum, M.L. 363, 376
Weimer, D. 333
Weingast, B.R. 333, 337, 354, 357, 358, 359–
    76

Weiss, T.G. 37
West, E.G. 389
Wetering, W. van 76
Wicksell, K. 494, 510
Wildarsky, A. 337, 358, 481
Williamson, O.E. 318, 331
Wilson, J. 251
Wilson, M. 75
Wilson, T. 456
Wilson, V. 367, 376
Wintrobe, R. 334, 358
Wiseman, J. 379, 415, 442
Wittman, D. 495, 510
Wohlstetter, R. 173
Wolf, C. 359, 376, 456–88
Woodstock, G. 26, 39

Xenophon 231

Yasuba, Y. 424
Yeats, W.B. 17
Young, M.W. 88, 89

Zagoria, D. 40
Zinn, H. 23, 33, 38, 39, 41

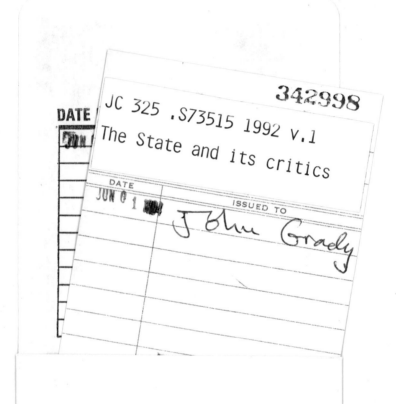